PEARSON

ALWAYS LEARNING

Ronald J. Ebert • Ricky W. Griffin

Business Essentials

Custom Edition for Chemeketa Community College

Taken from:
Business Essentials, Eighth Edition
by Ronald J. Ebert and Ricky W. Griffin

Pearson Learning Solutions, 501 Boylston Street, Suite 900, Boston, MA 02116
A Pearson Education Company
www.pearsoned.com

Printed in the United States of America

1 2 3 4 5 6 7 8 9 10 v092 16 15 14 13 12 11

000200010270758641

MT

ISBN 10: 1-256-09277-0
ISBN 13: 978-1-256-09277-3

Dedicated to my loving companion Riley. Earning her trust showed me how simple kindness overcomes fear and begets unconditional friendship. —R. J. E.

For Pap, who influenced my life in more ways than he ever knew. —R. W. G.

BRIEF CONTENTS

CONTENTS

Part III: People in Organizations

Chapter 8: Employee Behavior and Motivation 118

Chapter 9: Leadership and Decision Making 132

What's New in This Edition

■ Recent events in domestic and global economies are presenting unprecedented challenges, excitement, and disappointments for business. This eighth edition of *Business Essentials* captures the widespread significance of these developments and presents their implications for business today. For example, the new chapter opener in Chapter 15 looks at today's top economic issue—the shaken U.S. financial system, including bank closures, bad loans, cash shortages, bailouts by governments, TARP, and frozen credit markets.

■ Although business conditions are continually changing, we emphasize the basics of business. Updates throughout the eighth edition reinforce the foundations of business, including its vocabulary, practices, and concepts. In Chapter 7, the section on "Operations Processes" is rewritten to reduce and simplify jargon and clarify terminology. Instead of abstract terms, it is now defined in a few straightforward words and in context of brief real examples, such as a bill payments process.

■ An abundance of the latest real-world business developments provides clear illustrations of business concepts and current dilemmas, and we show in every chapter how basic practices apply not only in business upswings but also during not-so-good times. Chapter 1, page 4, for instance, includes an example of how 2009 business closings at Circuit City and Linens 'n Things provided new business opportunities for businesses specializing in inventory liquidations.

■ A new feature—"Managing in Turbulent Times"—that appears in every chapter shows how the economic downturn relates to one or two of that chapter's key business practices, decisions, or concepts. It uses current, real experiences to illustrate why that practice, decision, or concept is so important for business success. With tighter credit and a scarcity of cash, for example, the box in Chapter 13 shows how many businesses (and consumers) have turned to Internet bartering as a means to navigating through the current economy.

■ Businesses everywhere, both small and large, are dealing increasingly with external influences that give rise to new opportunities, place new demands on them, and impose ethical dilemmas. The eighth edition presents examples of these influences arising from changing technologies, political forces and government regulation, environmental movements, consumerism, economic conditions, and competition. Chapter 3, page 43, illustrates this point by noting the impact of the 2009 recession on the availability of credit to small businesses.

■ All chapters have been updated using the latest available data, reference sources, and current events. In Chapter 16, the coverage on stock exchanges is updated to include the merger of NYSE and Euronext, bringing together marketplaces across Europe and the U.S. It also discusses the new partnership of NYSE Euronext and Qatar Exchange, which brings a stronger presence of the Middle East into international markets.

What's in It for You?

If you're like many other students, you may be starting this semester with some questions about why you're here. Whether you're taking this course at a two-year college, at a four-year university, or at a technical school, in a traditional classroom setting or online, you may be wondering just what you're supposed to get from this course and how it will benefit you. In short, you may be wondering, "What's in it for me?"

Regardless of what it may be called at your school, this is a survey course designed to introduce you to the many exciting and challenging facets of business, both in the United States and elsewhere. The course fits the needs of a wide variety of students. You may be taking this course as the first step toward earning a degree in business, you may be thinking about business and want to know more about it, or you may know you want to study business but are unsure of the area you want to pursue. Maybe you plan to major in another field but want some basic business background and are taking this course as an elective. Or you may be here because, frankly, this course is required or is a prerequisite to another course.

For those of you with little work experience, you may be uncertain as to what the business world is all about. If you have a lot of work experience, you may even be a bit skeptical about what you can actually learn about business from an introductory course. One of our biggest challenges as authors is to write a book that meets the needs of such a diverse student population, especially when we acknowledge the legitimacy of your right to ask "What's in it for me?" We also want to do our best to ensure that you find the course challenging, interesting, and useful.

The world today is populated with a breathtaking array of businesses and business opportunities. Big and small businesses, established and new businesses, broad-based and niche businesses, successful and unsuccessful businesses, global and domestic businesses—throughout this book we'll discuss how they get started and how they work, why they grow and why some fail, and how they affect you. Regardless of where your future takes you, we hope that you look back on this course as one of your first steps.

Going forward, we also urge you to consider that what you get out of this course—what's in it for you—is shaped by at least three factors. One factor is this book and the various learning aids that accompany it. Another factor is your instructor. He or she is a dedicated professional who wants to help you grow and develop intellectually and academically.

The third factor? You. Learning is an active process that requires you to be a major participant. Simply memorizing the key terms and concepts in this book may help you achieve an acceptable course grade. But true learning requires that you read, study, discuss, question, review, experience, and evaluate as you go along. While tests and homework may be a "necessary evil," we believe we will have done our part if you finish this course with new knowledge and increased enthusiasm for the world of business. We know your instructor will do his or her best to facilitate your learning. The rest, then, is up to you. We wish you success.

New!

Look and Feel

For those of you who are visual learners, the book's new design and improved art will help you better process and understand chapter content.

New!

"Managing in Turbulent Times" Features

Whether you are planning to work for a large corporation or start your own business, you need to see the challenges firms encounter during economic downturns. The new "Managing in Turbulent Times" boxed features tie into each chapter's topics. Experiences from real companies reveal both disappointments and unexpected new opportunities arising from the 2008–2009 recession.

Glindex

In addition to the marginal key terms from previous editions, the eighth edition also features a combined glossary and index—a glindex—to make it even easier to find the definitions of key terms and where they are referenced in the text.

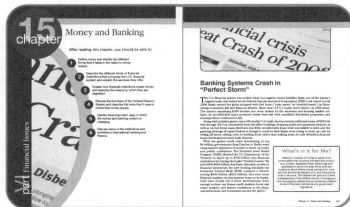

Updated!

"Managing Finances" Content

You asked for more finance content, and we've responded with a chapter and an appendix on managing finances, both business and personal. From basic principles, we push forward to explore debt and equity financing, risk, and capital-growth maximization. We also delve into securities markets and the opportunities they present to businesses and individuals.

Updated!

Chapter Case Vignettes

We've updated or completely replaced the chapter-opening cases to keep them fresh, relevant, and up-to-date. Covering companies from Facebook to eBay to Apple, these chapter case vignettes will pique your interest at the beginning of the chapter and reinforce concepts you've learned throughout your reading at the chapter's end.

Updated!

"Entrepreneurship and New Ventures" Features

If your plan is to work for a large corporation, start your own business, or anything in between, you need to be both entrepreneurial and intrapreneurial. These updated popular boxed features cover entrepreneurs who have really made a difference.

Entrepreneurship and New Ventures

Doing Good in a Bad Economy: wowOwow!

The five founders of a new social networking service in 2008 had no idea that wowOwow.com would reinvigorate the talents of midlife professionals into new, more promising careers in the economic downturn. The site's business concept is simple: (a) Women over 40 enjoy social networking but with different interests than the younger crowd. (b) The fame and sophistication of its founders' personal lives, interests, and experiences is an attraction for the target audience. Plus, a contributing cast, including Whoopi Goldberg, Candice Bergen, and Lily Tomlin, provides added punch. (c) The $1 million start-up investment is shared equally among its media-savvy founders; all are pace-setting veteran businesswomen: Lesley Stahl (broadcast journalist), Mary Wells (advertising executive), Joni Evans (publishing executive), Peggy Noonan (political commentator), and Liz Smith (gossip columnist). (d) Branding—the distinctive wowOwow.com (for Women on the Web)—signifies the site's mature audience and its goal of sharing professional and personal experiences to encourage one another and to make the world better. (e) The price is right for social networkers: Sign-up is free. Revenues from advertisers will be firmed up later, after wowOwow demonstrates that it can attract a massive audience: Grow the audience, and advertisers will come. (f) Publicity gives wowOwow's message a powerful boost, including interviews on National Public Radio, prominent articles in *The New York Times* and *The Los Angeles Times*, and television features on NBC's *Today Show*.

The surprising career-change twist came with wowOwow.com's Executive Intern Program, begun in late 2008. It's not for newcomer youth interns but, rather, for experienced businesswomen with marketable skills, who, in the business downturn, especially in media industries, need new skills leading to another job. With more and more newspapers and magazines moving online, newer print-Web skills are required, while traditional print media personnel are being displaced. That was the situation for the first intern (unpaid), who at age 55 started listening, watching, and learning by doing and asking for help from much younger tech-savvy Web writers at WOW's offices. She learned new skills in writing URLs, tags, headlines, subheads, and links in story development for wowOwow.com content. Positive buzz created by the internship program confirms that wowOwow's social network endorses the site's goal of sharing professional and personal experiences to encourage others and to make the world better.[6]

Commenting on potential contributions by mature women, co-founder Liz Smith says, "A long time ago, Margaret Mead, the great anthropologist, said that there was nothing to equal the power of the menopausal woman. And I think she is right."

Acknowledgments

Although two names appear on the cover of the book, we could never have completed the eighth edition without the assistance of many fine individuals. First, we would like to thank all the professionals who took time from their busy schedules to review materials for *Business Essentials*:

Andrea Bailey, Moraine Valley Community College

Carlton Raines, Lehigh Carbon Community College

Leatha Ware, Waubonsee Community College

Janet Seggern, Lehigh Carbon Community College

Wendi Achey, Northampton Community College

Joy Clark, Auburn Montgomery

We'd also like to thank the reviewers of all our previous editions.

A number of other professionals also made substantive contributions to the text. We are most indebted to two people. Jodi McPherson, our executive editor, has instilled a continuing commitment to elevate the quality and profile of this book and to help us maintain and enhance our leadership position in this highly competitive market. Judy Leale, our senior managing editor, ensured that all activities came together to produce a coherent, timely product. In addition, Melissa Arlio joined us as our project manager in what was truly a team effort. Melissa competently coordinated the activities of our many contributors and consistently challenged us in working together for quality and timeliness. We'd also like to acknowledge the professional contributions of Heidi Allgair and GGS Higher Education Resources, a Division of PreMedia Global, Inc., a partnering company whose creative resources have added much to the development of the eighth edition's design and content.

Of course, this edition builds on past successes. Hence, we would be remiss not to acknowledge Kristen Kaiser, Shannon LeMay-Finn, and Ron Librach, the development editors on our previous editions. The unique ideas and contributions by Professor Barbara Van Syckle carry over from past editions and continue to influence the tone of *Business Essentials*. We'd also like to thank the reviewers of the previous edition, whose contributions have strengthened this eighth edition.

Our colleagues at the University of Missouri–Columbia and Texas A&M University also deserve recognition. Each of us has the good fortune to be a part of a community of scholars who enrich our lives and challenge our ideas. Finally, we want to acknowledge the people who are the foundation of our lives. We take pride in the accomplishments of our wives, Mary and Glenda, and draw strength from the knowledge that they are there for us to lean on. And we take joy from our children, Matt, Kristen, and Brayer and Ashley, Dustin, and Matt. Thanks to all of you for making us what we are.

Ronald J. Ebert
Ricky W. Griffin

Eighth Edition

Business Essentials

chapter 1

The U.S. Business Environment

After reading this chapter, you should be able to:

1 Define the nature of U.S. business and identify its main goals and functions.

2 Describe the external environments of business and discuss how these environments affect the success or failure of any organization.

3 Describe the different types of global economic systems according to the means by which they control the factors of production.

4 Show how markets, demand, and supply affect resource distribution in the United States.

5 Identify the elements of private enterprise and explain the various degrees of competition in the U.S. economic system.

6 Explain the importance of the economic environment to business and identify the factors used to evaluate the performance of an economic system.

What Goes Up . . . Can Go Even Higher!

The sign in front of a Texas Mobil gasoline station summed it up nicely: The "prices" for the three grades of gasoline sold at the station were listed as "an arm," "a leg," and "your first born." While the sign no doubt led to a few smiles from motorists, its sentiments were far from a laughing matter. The stark reality is that gas prices have fluctuated dramatically in recent years, reaching an all-time high of over $4.00 per gallon in early 2008 before dropping back to less than $2.00 per gallon in early 2009. The dramatic price fluctuations that began in mid-2004 have left consumers, government officials, and business leaders struggling to cope with uncertainty about future prices.

What makes this gas crisis unusual is that it began with an unusual mix of supply, demand, and global forces. In the past, gas prices generally increased only when the supply was reduced. But the circumstances underlying the increases that started in 2004 and continued through 2009 were much more complex. First, global supplies of gasoline have been increasing at a rate that has more than offset the steady decline in U.S. domestic production of gasoline since 1972. As a result, the United States has been relying more on foreign producers and is, therefore, subject to whatever prices those producers want to charge. Second, demand for gasoline in the United States has continued to rise as a result of a growing population, the continued popularity of large gas-guzzling vehicles, and a strong demand for other petroleum-based products.

Another major piece of the puzzle has been a surging global economy that until recently caused a higher demand for oil and gasoline. China, in particular, has become a major consumer of petroleum, passing Japan in 2005 to trail only the United States in total consumption. The global recession that started in 2008, however, reduced demand in most industrialized countries.

The price fluctuations have led to a wide array of consequences. Automobile manufacturers stepped up their commitment to making more fuel-efficient cars even as automobile sales plummeted. Refiners posted record profits (indeed, some critics charged that the energy companies were guilty of price gouging). And even local police officers were kept busy combating a surge in gasoline theft, yet another indication that gas was becoming an increasingly valuable commodity![1]

What's in It for Me?

Gasoline price swings are an example of how external environments, a global economy, and supply and demand affect business and distribution in the United States. In addition to these factors, this chapter will discuss the nature and purpose of a business and the elements of private enterprise and competition. It will also prepare you to analyze how different factors affect a business's success or failure and to evaluate the performance of an economic system in the context of business.

The Concept of Business and the Concept of Profit

What do you think of when you hear the word business? Does it conjure up images of successful corporations, such as General Electric? Or are you reminded of smaller firms, such as your local supermarket, or family-owned operations, such as your neighborhood pizzeria?

All these organizations are **businesses**—organizations that provide goods or services that are then sold to earn profits. Indeed, the prospect of earning **profits**—the difference between a business's revenues and its expenses—is what encourages people to open and expand businesses. After all, profits are the rewards owners get for risking their money and time. The right to pursue profits distinguishes a business from those organizations—such as most universities, hospitals, and government agencies—that run in much the same way but that generally don't seek profits.[2]

Consumer Choice and Demand   In a capitalistic system, such as that in the United States, businesses exist to earn profits for owners; an owner is free to set up a new business, grow that business, sell it, or even shut it down. But consumers also have freedom of choice. In choosing how to pursue profits, businesses must take into account what consumers want and/or need. No matter how efficient, a business won't survive without a demand for its goods or services. Neither a snowblower shop in Florida nor a beach-umbrella store in Alaska is likely to do well.

Opportunity and Enterprise   If enterprising businesspeople can spot a promising opportunity and then develop a good plan for capitalizing on it, they can succeed. For example, as large retailers like Circuit City and Linens-N-Things closed their doors in 2009, other firms profited by handling the inventory liquidations of those failed retailers. The opportunity always involves goods or services that consumers need and/or want—especially if no one else is supplying them or if existing businesses are doing so inefficiently or incompletely.

The Benefits of Business   Businesses produce most of the goods and services we consume, and they employ most working people. They create most new innovations and provide a vast range of opportunities for new businesses, which serve as their suppliers. A healthy business climate also contributes to the quality of life and standard of living of people in a society. Business profits enhance the personal incomes of millions of owners and stockholders, and business taxes help to support governments at all levels. Many businesses support charities and provide community leadership. However, some businesses also harm the environment, and their decision makers sometimes resort to unacceptable practices for their own personal benefit.

The External Environments of Business

All businesses, regardless of their size, location, or mission, operate within a larger external environment. This **external environment** consists of everything outside an organization's boundaries that might affect it. (Businesses also have an *internal environment*, more commonly called *corporate culture*, which is discussed in Chapter 5.) Managers must have a complete and accurate understanding of the external environment and strive to operate and compete within it or their organizations will not survive. Table 1.1 describes the external environment for the clothing retailer Urban Outfitters.

Domestic Business Environment
The **domestic business environment** refers to the environment in which a firm conducts its operations and derives its revenues. In general, businesses seek to be close to their customers, to establish strong relationships with their suppliers, and to distinguish themselves from their competitors.

Global Business Environment
The **global business environment** refers to the international forces that affect a business. Factors affecting the global environment at a general level include international trade agreements, international economic conditions, political unrest, and so forth. At a more immediate level, any given business is likely to be affected by international market opportunities, suppliers, cultures, competitors, and currency values.

Technological Environment
The **technological environment** generally includes all the ways by which firms create value for their constituents. Technology includes human knowledge, work

methods, physical equipment, electronics and telecommunications, and various processing systems that are used to perform business activities.

Political-Legal Environment

The **political-legal environment**, which reflects the relationship between business and government, is important for several reasons. The legal system defines and regulates many aspects of what an organization can and can't do, including advertising practices, safety and health considerations, and acceptable standards of business conduct. Pro- or anti-business sentiment in government and political stability are also important considerations, especially for international firms. For instance, shortly after President Obama took office in 2009, a number of new regulations were imposed on businesses. And the president himself forced the resignation of General Motors' CEO in exchange for infusing new capital into the struggling automaker.

Sociocultural Environment

The **sociocultural environment** includes the customs, mores, values, and demographic characteristics of the society in which an organization functions. Sociocultural processes also determine the goods and services, as well as the standards of business conduct, that a society is likely to value and accept.

Economic Environment

The **economic environment** refers to relevant conditions that exist in the economic system in which a company operates. For example, if an economy is doing well enough that most people have jobs, a growing company may find it necessary to pay higher wages and offer more

benefits in order to attract workers from other companies. But if many people in an economy are looking for jobs, as was the case in 2009, a firm may be able to pay less and offer fewer benefits.

Economic Systems

The economic system of a firm's *home country*—the nation in which it does most of its business—is a key factor is determining how a firm operates. An **economic system** is a nation's system for allocating its resources among its citizens, both individuals and organizations.

Factors of Production

A basic difference between economic systems is the way in which a system manages its **factors of production**—the resources that a country's businesses use to produce goods and services. Economists focus on five factors of production. Note that the concept of factors of production can also be applied to the resources that an individual organization *manages* to produce goods and services.

POLITICAL-LEGAL ENVIRONMENT relationship between business and government

SOCIOCULTURAL ENVIRONMENT customs, mores, values, and demographic characteristics of the society in which an organization functions

ECONOMIC ENVIRONMENT relevant conditions that exist in the economic system in which a company operates

ECONOMIC SYSTEM nation's system for allocating its resources among its citizens

FACTORS OF PRODUCTION resources used in the production of goods and services—labor, capital, entrepreneurs, physical resources, and information resources

Table 1.1   The External Environments of Business: Urban Outfitters

Domestic Business Environment	Global Business Environment	Technological Environment	Political-Legal Environment	Sociocultural Environment	Economic Environment
• Initially located stores near urban college campuses; now has locations in more upscale neighborhoods as well • Strong network of suppliers • Wholesale supplier to other retailers through its Free People division • Competing with Gap and Abercrombie & Fitch for customers and market share	• Global presence with stores in Belgium, Canada, Denmark, Ireland, Sweden, and United Kingdom as well as an online presence in Japan • Many suppliers are foreign companies	• Sophisticated information system that tracks sales and inventory levels, allowing for quick response to customers • Successful e-commerce Web sites	• Subject to a variety of political and legal forces, including product identification and local zoning requirements • Actively protects assets by monitoring copyright infringement by competition	• Pulled items after unfavorable publicity in 2003 for Monopoly-like game called Ghettopoly that was criticized for making light of poverty and social problems • Discontinued sale of Jesus Dress Up magnets in 2004 after pressure from family activist groups	• Employee opportunities are desirable, with competitive salaries and a strong benefits package

LABOR (HUMAN RESOURCES) physical and mental capabilities of people as they contribute to economic production

CAPITAL funds needed to create and operate a business enterprise

ENTREPRENEUR individual who accepts the risks and opportunities involved in creating and operating a new business venture

PHYSICAL RESOURCES tangible items that organizations use in the conduct of their businesses

INFORMATION RESOURCES data and other information that businesses use

Labor Sometimes called **human resources**, **labor** includes the physical and intellectual contributions people make to a business while engaged in economic production. Starbucks, for example, employs more than 194,000 people,[3] including baristas who prepare coffees for customers, store managers, regional managers, coffee tasters, quality-control experts, coffee buyers, marketing experts, financial specialists, and other specialized workers and managers.

Capital Obtaining and using labor and other resources requires **capital**—the financial resources needed to start a business, operate it, and keep it growing. For example, Howard Schultz used personal savings and a loan to finance his acquisition of the fledgling Starbucks coffee outfit back in 1987. As Starbucks grew, he came to rely more on its profits and eventually sold stock to other investors to raise even more money. Starbucks continues to rely on a blend of current earnings and both short- and long-term debt to finance its operations and fuel its growth. Moreover, even when the firm decided to close several hundred coffee shops in 2008 and early 2009, it employed capital to pay off leases and provide severance pay to employees who lost their jobs.

Entrepreneurs An **entrepreneur** is a person who accepts the risks and opportunities entailed in creating and operating a new business. Howard Schultz was willing to accept the risks associated with retail growth and, after buying Starbucks, he capitalized on the market opportunities for rapid growth. Had his original venture failed, Schultz would have lost most of his savings. Most economic systems encourage entrepreneurs, both to start new businesses and to make the decisions that allow them to create new jobs and make more profits for their owners.

Physical Resources **Physical resources** are the tangible things that organizations use to conduct their business. They include natural resources and raw materials, offices, storage and production facilities, parts and supplies, computers and peripherals, and a variety of other equipment. For example, Starbucks relies on coffee beans and other food products, the equipment it uses to make its coffee drinks, paper products for packaging, and other retail equipment, as well as office equipment and storage facilities for running its business at the corporate level.

Information Resources The production of tangible goods once dominated most economic systems. Today, **information resources**—data and other information used by businesses—play a major role. Information resources that businesses rely on include market forecasts, the specialized knowledge of people, and economic data. In turn, much of what they do results either in the creation of new information or the repackaging of existing information for new users. For example, Starbucks uses various economic statistics to decide where to open new outlets and to identify current outlets that are not profitable and thus can be closed. It also uses sophisticated forecasting models to predict the future prices of coffee beans. And consumer taste tests help the firm decide when to introduce new products.

Types of Economic Systems

The various types of economic systems differ in how they manage these factors of production and make decisions about production and allocation. In some systems, all ownership is

Starbucks uses various factors of production, including labor such as these baristas.

What Goes Around . . .

It seems like just yesterday. In 2005 the global economy was booming. In the United States, for example, business profits were soaring, jobs were plentiful, and home ownership was at any all-time high. The stock market reached unprecedented highs, pension plans were burgeoning, and new business opportunities were plentiful.

Fast-forward just four short years to 2009, and things looked a lot different. Business profits were down, hundreds of thousands of jobs were lost and unemployment claims soared, and mortgage foreclosures were the order of the day. The stock market plummeted, pension plans went broke, and it seemed like no one wanted to start a new business.

What happened in this short period of time? Economists call it the business cycle. Historically, our economy has followed long periods of growth and prosperity, with periods of cutbacks and retreats. And that's where we were in 2009. During extended periods of prosperity, people sometimes think the good times will last forever. They continue to bid up stock prices, for instance, far beyond rational value. They also take on too much debt, save too little money, and spend beyond their means. But things have a way of correcting themselves, and that's what happened beginning in 2008.

So what does the future hold? Well, while no one has a real crystal ball, most experts agree that the bad times will

run their course, and then things will start looking up again. It may take another year, or it may take five. But one day soon, profits will again start to surge, businesses will embark on ambitious hiring plans, the stock market will surpass all previous highs, and business opportunities will again be plentiful. Until then, though, managers have to focus on following core business principles and do their best to steer their organizations through today's turbulence.

---

private; in others, all factors of production are owned or controlled by the government. Most systems, however, fall between these extremes.

Planned Economies A **planned economy** relies on a centralized government to control all or most factors of production and to make all or most production and allocation decisions. There are two basic forms of planned economies: *communism* (discussed here) and *socialism* (discussed as a mixed market economy).

As envisioned by nineteenth-century German economist Karl Marx, **communism** is a system in which the government owns and operates all factors of production. Under such a system, the government would assign people to jobs, own all business, and control all business decisions—what to make, how much to charge, and so forth. Marx proposed that individuals would contribute according to their abilities and receive benefits according to their needs. He also expected government ownership

of production factors to be temporary: Once society had matured, government would wither away, and workers would take direct ownership of the factors of production.

The former Soviet Union and many Eastern European countries embraced communism until the end of the

PLANNED ECONOMY economy that relies on a centralized government to control all or most factors of production and to make all or most production and allocation decisions

COMMUNISM political system in which the government owns and operates all factors of production

Free Enterprise in China?

Once strictly synonymous with the Maoist communist regime, China is slowly demonstrating internal change. Fundamental events, such as the 2008 Olympics in Beijing, gradually alter the way domestic commerce is conducted as the demand for goods and services drastically increases. The changes will still not affect much of the population, but free enterprise is fragmentarily affecting certain businesses. Although not always the rule, as a country becomes richer, its economy is likely to become less rigid.

twentieth century. In the early 1990s, one country after another renounced communism as both an economic and a political system. Today, North Korea, Vietnam, and the People's Republic of China are among the few nations with openly communist systems. Even in these countries, however, planned economic

MARKET ECONOMY economy in which individuals control production and allocation decisions through supply and demand

MARKET mechanism for exchange between buyers and sellers of a particular good or service

CAPITALISM system that sanctions the private ownership of the factors of production and encourages entrepreneurship by offering profits as an incentive

MIXED MARKET ECONOMY economic system featuring characteristics of both planned and market economies

PRIVATIZATION process of converting government enterprises into privately owned companies

Despite becoming a territory of the communist People's Republic of China in 1997, Hong Kong remains one of the world's freest economies. In Hong Kong's Lan Kwai Fong district, for example, traditional Chinese businesses operate next door to standard U.S. chains.

systems are making room for features of the free enterprise system.

Market Economies In a **market economy**, individual producers and consumers control production and allocation by creating combinations of supply and demand. A **market** is a mechanism for exchange between the buyers and sellers of a particular good or service. (Like *capital*, the term *market* can have multiple meanings.) Market economies rely on capitalism and free enterprise to create an environment in which producers and consumers are free to sell and buy what they choose (within certain limits). As a result, items produced and prices paid are largely determined by supply and demand.

To understand how a market economy works, consider what happens when you go to a fruit market to buy apples. While one vendor is selling apples for $1 per pound, another is charging $1.50. Both vendors are free to charge what they want, and you are free to buy what you choose. If both vendors' apples are of the same quality, you will buy the cheaper ones. If the $1.50 apples are fresher, you may buy them instead. In short, both buyers and sellers enjoy freedom of choice.

Individuals in a market system are free to not only buy what they want but also to work where they want and to invest, save, or spend their money in whatever manner they choose. Likewise, businesses are free to decide what products to make, where to sell them, and what prices to charge. This process contrasts markedly with that of a planned economy, in which individuals may be told where they can and cannot work, companies may be told what they can and cannot make, and consumers may have little or no choice in what they purchase or how much they pay. The political basis of market processes is called **capitalism**, which allows the private ownership of the factors of production and encourages entrepreneurship by offering profits as an incentive.

Mixed Market Economies In reality, there are no "pure" planned or "pure" market economies. Most countries rely on some form of **mixed market economy** that features characteristics of both planned and market economies. Even a market economy that strives to be as free and open as possible, such as the U.S. economy, restricts certain activities. Some products can't be sold legally, others can be sold only to people of a certain age, advertising must be truthful, and so forth. And the People's Republic of China, the world's most important planned economy, is increasingly allowing and overseeing certain forms of private ownership and entrepreneurship.

When a government is making a change from a planned economy to a market economy, it usually begins to adopt market mechanisms through **privatization**—the process of converting government enterprises into privately owned companies. The Netherlands, for example, has privatized its TNT Post Group N.V., transforming it into one of the world's most efficient post-office operations. Generally speaking, privatizing enterprises can reduce payroll expenses and boost efficiency, productivity, and profits.

In the partially planned system called **socialism**, the government owns and operates selected major industries. In such mixed market economies, the government may control banking, transportation, or industries producing such basic goods as oil and steel. Smaller businesses, such as clothing stores and restaurants, are privately owned. Many Western European countries, including England and France, allow free market operations in most economic areas but keep government control of others, such as health care.

As part of the bail-out of large U.S. banks and other financial enterprises in 2009, the government took an ownership stake in those businesses. In large part this was done to make it easier for government officials to keep tabs on how the firms were using the resources that tax dollars were providing. Critics of these measures, though, were quick to label them as a move toward socialism.

The Economics of Market Systems

Understanding the complex nature of the U.S. economic system is essential to understanding the environment in which U.S. businesses operate.

Demand and Supply in a Market Economy

A market economy consists of many different markets that function within that economy. As a consumer, for instance, the choices you have and the prices you pay for goods and services are all governed by different sets of market forces. Businesses also have many different choices about buying and selling their products. Managers make decisions about inventory levels, prices, and distribution. Literally billions of exchanges take place every day between businesses and individuals; between businesses; and among individuals, businesses, and governments. Moreover, exchanges conducted in one area often affect exchanges elsewhere. For instance, the high cost of gas may also lead to prices going up for other items, ranging from food to clothing to delivery services, because of the reliance on gas for transportation.

The Laws of Demand and Supply On all economic levels, decisions about what to buy and what to sell are determined primarily by the forces of demand and supply.[4] **Demand** is the willingness and ability of buyers to purchase a product (a good or a service). **Supply** is the willingness and ability of producers to offer a good or service for sale.

Generally speaking, demand and supply follow basic laws:

- The **law of demand**: Buyers will purchase (demand) *more* of a product as its price *drops* and *less* of a product as its price *increases*.

- The **law of supply**: Producers will offer (supply) *more* of a product for sale as its price *rises* and *less* of a product as its price *drops*.

The Demand and Supply Schedule To appreciate these laws in action, consider the market for pizza in your town. If everyone is willing to pay $25 for a pizza (a relatively high price), the town's only pizzeria will produce a large supply. But if everyone is willing to pay only $5 (a relatively low price), it will make fewer pizzas. Through careful analysis, we can determine how many pizzas will be sold at different prices. These results, called a **demand and supply schedule**, are obtained from marketing research, historical data, and other studies of the market. Properly applied, they reveal the relationships among different levels of demand and supply at different price levels.

Demand and Supply Curves
The demand and supply schedule can be used to construct demand and supply curves for pizza in your town. A **demand curve** shows how many products—in this case, pizzas—will be demanded (bought) at different prices. A **supply curve** shows how many pizzas will be supplied (baked or offered for sale) at different prices.

Figure 1.1 shows demand and supply curves for pizzas. As you can see, demand increases as price decreases; supply increases as price increases. When demand and supply curves are plotted on the same graph, the point at which they intersect is the **market price** (also called the **equilibrium price**)—the price at which the quantity of goods demandedand the quantity of goods supplied are equal. In Figure 1.1, the equilibrium price for pizzas in our example is $10. At this point, the quantity of pizzas demanded and the quantity of pizzas supplied are the same: 1,000 pizzas per week.

Surpluses and Shortages

What if the pizzeria decides to make some other number of pizzas—if the owner tried to increase profits by making *more* pizzas to sell or if the owner *reduced* the number of pizzas offered for sale to lower overhead and cut back on store hours? In either case, the result would be an inefficient use of resources and lower profits. For instance, if the pizzeria supplies 1,200 pizzas and tries to sell them for $10 each, 200 pizzas will not be bought. Our demand schedule shows that only 1,000 pizzas will be demanded at this price. The pizzeria will therefore have a **surplus**—a situation in which the quantity supplied exceeds the quantity demanded. It will lose the money that it spent making those extra 200 pizzas.

Conversely, if the pizzeria supplies only 800 pizzas, a **shortage** will result. The quantity demanded will be greater than the quantity supplied. The pizzeria will "lose" the extra profit that it could have made by producing 200 more pizzas. Even though consumers may pay more for pizzas because of the shortage, the pizzeria will still earn lower total profits than if it had made 1,000 pizzas. It will also risk angering customers who cannot buy pizzas and encourage other entrepreneurs to set up competing pizzerias to satisfy unmet demand.

Figure 1.1
Demand and Supply[5]

DEMAND AND SUPPLY SCHEDULES

Price	Quantity of Pizzas Demanded	Quantity of Pizzas Supplied
$2	2000	100
$4	1900	400
$6	1600	600
$8	1200	800
$10	1000	1000
$12	800	1200
$14	600	1300
$16	400	1600
$18	200	1800
$20	100	2000

When the price of pizza is high, fewer people are willing to pay for it. But when the price goes down, more people are willing to buy pizza. **At the lower price, in other words, more people "demand" the product.**

When the price of pizza is low, more people are willing to buy pizza. Pizza makers, however, do not have the money to invest in making pizzas and so they make fewer. Supply, therefore, is limited, and **only when the price goes up will pizza makers be willing and able to increase supply**.

When the pizza makers increase supply in order to satisfy demand, there will be **a point at which the price that suppliers can charge is the same as the price that a maximum number of customers is willing to pay.** That point is the market price, or **equilibrium** price.

Businesses should seek the ideal combination of price charged and quantity supplied so as to maximize profits, maintain goodwill among customers, and discourage competition. This ideal combination is found at the equilibrium point.

Our example involves only one company, one product, and a few buyers. The U.S. economy—indeed, any market economy—is far more complex. Thousands of companies sell hundreds of thousands of products to millions of buyers every day. In the end, however, the result is much the same: Companies try to supply the quantity and selection of goods that will earn them the largest profits.

Private Enterprise and Competition in a Market Economy

Market economies rely on a **private enterprise** system—one that allows individuals to pursue their own interests with minimal government restriction. In turn, private enterprise requires the presence of four elements:

1 *Private property rights.* Ownership of the resources used to create wealth is in the hands of individuals.

2 *Freedom of choice.* Individuals can choose which employers to sell their labor to and which products to buy, and producers can choose whom to hire and what to produce.

3 *Profits.* The lure of profits (and freedom) leads some people to abandon the security of working for someone else and to assume the risks of entrepreneurship. Anticipated profits also influence individuals' choices of which goods or services to produce.

4 *Competition.* If profits motivate individuals to start businesses, competition motivates them to operate those businesses efficiently. **Competition** occurs when two or more businesses vie for the same resources or customers. To gain an advantage over competitors, a business must produce its goods or services efficiently and be able to sell at a reasonable profit by convincing customers that its products are either better or less expensive than those of its competitors. Competition, therefore, forces all businesses to make products better or cheaper. A company that produces inferior, expensive products is likely to fail. Of course, it's also important to recognize that the nature of competition varies widely. For instance, Ford and GM compete for customers interested in buying an automobile. But they also compete with bicycle and motorcycle manufacturers and public transit systems for customers who are more broadly looking for transportation. Likewise, movie theaters, bowling alleys, skating rinks, and video game stores compete for customers looking for leisure pursuits.

Degrees of Competition

Even in a free enterprise system, not all industries are equally competitive. Economists have identified four degrees of competition in a private enterprise system: *perfect competition*, *monopolistic competition*, *oligopoly*, and *monopoly*. Note that these are not always truly distinct categories but actually tend to fall along a continuum; perfect competition and monopoly anchor the ends of the continuum, with monopolistic competition and oligopoly falling in between. Table 1.2 summarizes the features of these four degrees of competition.

Perfect Competition For **perfect competition** to exist, two conditions must prevail: (1) all firms in an industry must be small, and (2) the number of firms in the industry must be large. Under these conditions, no single firm is powerful enough to influence the price of its product. Prices are, therefore, determined by such market forces as supply and demand.

In addition, these two conditions also reflect four principles:

1 The products of each firm are so similar that buyers view them as identical to those of other firms.

2 Both buyers and sellers know the prices that others are paying and receiving in the marketplace.

3 Because each firm is small, firms can easily enter or leave the market.

4 Going prices are set exclusively by supply and demand and accepted by both sellers and buyers.

PRIVATE ENTERPRISE economic system that allows individuals to pursue their own interests without undue governmental restriction

COMPETITION vying among businesses for the same resources or customers

PERFECT COMPETITION market or industry characterized by numerous small firms producing an identical product

U.S. agriculture is a good example of perfect competition. The wheat produced on one farm is the same as that from another. Both producers and buyers are aware of prevailing market prices. It is relatively easy for a farmer to start producing wheat and relatively easy to stop when it's no longer profitable.

Table 1.2   Degrees of Competition

Characteristic	Perfect Competition	Monopolistic Competition	Oligopoly	Monopoly
Example	Local Farmer	Stationery Store	Steel Industry	Public Utility
Number of Competitors	Many	Many, but fewer than in perfect competition	Few	None
Ease of Entry into the Industry	Relatively easy	Fairly easy	Difficult	Regulated by government
Similarity of Goods/Services Offered by Competing Firms	Identical	Similar	Can be similar or different	No directly competing goods or services
Level of Control over Price by Individual Firms	None	Some	Some	Considerable

Monopolistic Competition

In **monopolistic competition**, numerous sellers try to make their products at least seem to be different from those of competitors. While there are many sellers involved in monopolistic competition, there tend to be fewer than in pure competition. ifferentiating strategies include brand names, design or styling, and advertising.

Product differentiation also gives sellers some control over prices. For instance, even though Target shirts may have similar styling and other features, Ralph Lauren polo shirts can be priced with little regard for lower Target prices. But the large number of buyers relative to sellers applies potential limits to prices: Although Ralph Lauren might be able to sell shirts for $20 more than a comparable Target shirt, it could not sell as many shirts if they were priced at $200 more. Monopolistically competitive businesses may be large or small, but they can still enter or leave the market easily. For example, many small clothing stores compete successfully with larger apparel retailers, such as Abercrombie & Fitch and Banana Republic. A good case in point is bebe stores. The small clothing chain controls its own manufacturing facilities and can respond just as quickly as firms like the Gap to changes in fashion tastes.

Oligopoly

When an industry has only a handful of sellers, an **oligopoly** exists. As a general rule, these sellers are quite large. The entry of new competitors is hard because large capital investment is needed. Thus, oligopolistic industries tend to stay that way—for example, only Boeing and Airbus make large commercial aircraft. Furthermore, as the trend toward globalization continues, most experts believe that oligopolies will become increasingly prevalent.

Oligopolists have more control over their strategies than monopolistically competitive firms, but the actions of one firm can significantly affect the sales of every other firm in the industry. When an airline announces new fare

Entrepreneurship and New Ventures

Business... and Pleasure

Americans are multitaskers. We sip lattes while driving, we walk the dog while checking stock quotes, and we pay our bills online while watching TV; it is no surprise that this trend has taken on bigger dimensions. Business and entertainment are no longer considered two separate entities. Entertainment used to be defined as amusement parks, miniature golf, baseball games, and movies. Business was business: work, dine, shop, etc. But now, in a recessionary market economy, industries feel even more pressure to mix business with entertainment. The brightly colored play structures in McDonald's and the first mall roller coaster paved the way for this upsurge of integration that is now almost impossible to avoid.

In September of 2007, Apple and Starbucks announced a partnership that allows customers to preview millions of Apple iTunes while waiting in line. The customers also have the option to buy or download music onto their iPod touch, iPhone, PC, or Mac. JetBlue partnered with XM Radio to offer passengers a sample of the new wave of satellite radio. Select Wal-Mart stores host live broadcasts of concerts enticing shoppers to linger just a little longer. This growing trend is not likely to change anytime soon. But businesses should be wary of new business cycles created in the entertainment realm. Entertainment-driven corporations are always at a high risk of deflation when the economy falters. Those businesses that rely on partnerships with these high-risk firms may not be as grounded as they seem.

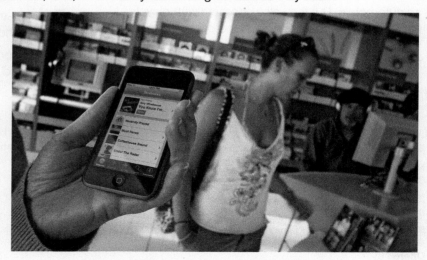

discounts, others adopt the same strategy almost immediately. Just as quickly, when discounts end for one airline, they usually end for everyone else. Therefore, the prices of comparable products are usually similar.

Monopoly A **monopoly** exists when an industry or market has only one producer (or else is so dominated by one producer that other firms cannot compete with it). A sole supplier enjoys nearly complete control over the prices of its products. Its only constraint is a decrease in consumer demand due to increased prices or government regulation. In the United States, laws, such as the Sherman Antitrust Act (1890) and the Clayton Act (1914), forbid many monopolies and regulate prices charged by **natural monopolies**—industries in which one company can most efficiently supply all needed goods or services.[6] Many electric companies are natural monopolies because they can supply all the power needed in a local area. Duplicate facilities—such as two power plants and two sets of powerlines—would be inefficient.

Economic Indicators

Because economic forces are so volatile and can be affected by so many things, the performance of a country's economic system varies over time. Sometimes it gains strength and brings new prosperity to its members; other times it weakens and damages their fortunes. But knowing how an economy is performing is useful for both business owners and investors alike. Most experts look to various **economic indicators**—statistics that show whether an economic system is strengthening, weakening, or remaining stable—to help assess the performance of an economy.

Economic Growth, Aggregate Output, and Standard of Living

At one time, about half the U.S. population was involved in producing the food that we needed. Today, less than 2.5 percent of the U.S. population works in agriculture, and this number is expected to decrease slightly over the next decade.[7] But agricultural efficiency has improved because better ways of producing products have been devised, and better technology has been invented for getting the job done. We can say that agricultural productivity has increased because we have been able to increase total output in the agricultural sector.

We can apply the same concepts to a nation's economic system, although the computations are more complex. Fundamentally, how do we know whether an economic system is growing or not? Experts call the pattern of short-term ups and downs (or, better, expansions and contractions) in an economy the **business cycle**. The primary measure of growth in the business cycle is **aggregate output**—the total quantity of goods and services produced by an economic system during a given period.[9]

To put it simply, an increase in aggregate output is growth (or economic growth). When output grows more quickly than the population, two things usually follow:

- Output per capita—the quantity of goods and services per person—goes up.

- The system provides more of the goods and services that people want.

When these two things occur, people living in an economic system benefit from a higher **standard of living**, which refers to the total quantity and quality of goods and services that they can purchase with the currency used in their economic system. To know how much your standard of living is improving, you need to know how much your nation's economic system is growing (see Table 1.3).

MONOPOLY market or industry in which there is only one producer that can therefore set the prices of its products

NATURAL MONOPOLY industry in which one company can most efficiently supply all needed goods or services

ECONOMIC INDICATOR statistic that helps assess the performance of an economy

BUSINESS CYCLE short-term pattern of economic expansions and contractions

AGGREGATE OUTPUT total quantity of goods and services produced by an economic system during a given period

STANDARD OF LIVING total quantity and quality of goods and services people can purchase with the currency used in their economic system

Table 1.3 **U.S. GDP and GDP per Capita[8]**

2008 Gross Domestic Product (GDP) ($ Trillion)	2008 GDP: Real Growth Rate (%)	2008 GDP per Capita: Purchasing Power Parity
$14.58	1.40	$48,000

GROSS DOMESTIC PRODUCT (GDP) total value of all goods and services produced within a given period by a national economy through domestic factors of production

GROSS NATIONAL PRODUCT (GNP) total value of all goods and services produced by a national economy within a given period regardless of where the factors of production are located

Gross Domestic Product

Gross domestic product (GDP) refers to the total value of all goods and services produced within a given period by a national economy through domestic factors of production. GDP is a measure of aggregate output. Generally speaking, if GDP is going up, aggregate output is going up; if aggregate output is going up, the nation is experiencing *economic growth*.

Sometimes, economists also use the term **gross national product (GNP)**, which refers to the total value of all goods and services produced by a national economy within a given period regardless of where the factors of production are located. What, precisely, is the difference between GDP and GNP? Consider a General Motors automobile plant in Brazil. The profits earned by the factory are included in U.S. GNP—but not in GDP—because its output is not produced domestically (that is, in the United States). Conversely, those profits are included in Brazil's GDP—but not GNP—because they are produced domestically (that is, in Brazil). Calculations quickly become complex because of different factors of production. The labor, for example, will be mostly Brazilian but the capital mostly American. Thus, wages paid to Brazilian workers are part of Brazil's GNP even though profits are not.

Real Growth Rate GDP and GNP usually differ by less than 1 percent, but economists argue that GDP is a more accurate indicator of domestic economic performance because it focuses only on domestic factors of production. With that in mind, let's look at the middle column in Table 1.3. Here we find that the real growth rate of U.S. GDP—the growth rate of GDP *adjusted for inflation and changes in the value of the country's currency*—is 1.40 percent. How good is

that rate? Remember that *growth depends on output increasing at a faster rate than population*. The U.S. population is growing at a rate of 0.90 percent per year.[10] The *real growth rate* of the U.S. economic system, therefore, seems only modest at present. Indeed, the 1.40 percent rate in 2008 reflected a drop from 2007, when growth was 2.20 percent. This decline was a result of the recession that began in 2008.

GDP per Capita The number in the third column of Table 1.3 is a reflection of the standard of living: *GDP per capita* means GDP per person. We get this figure by dividing total GDP ($14.58 trillion) by total population, which happens to be about 301 million.[11] In a given period (usually calculated on an annual basis), the United States produces goods and services equal in value to $48,000 for every person in the country. Figure 1.2 shows both GDP and GDP per capita in the United States between 1950 and 2008. GDP per capita is a better measure than GDP itself of the economic well-being of the average person.

Real GDP **Real GDP** means that GDP has been adjusted to account for changes in currency values and price changes. To understand why adjustments are necessary, assume that pizza is the only product

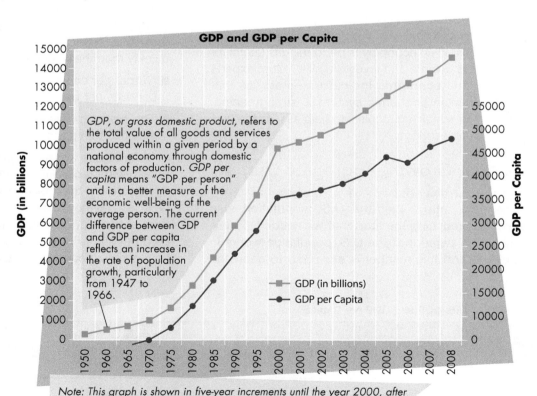

GDP and GDP per Capita

GDP, or gross domestic product, refers to the total value of all goods and services produced within a given period by a national economy through domestic factors of production. GDP per capita means "GDP per person" and is a better measure of the economic well-being of the average person. The current difference between GDP and GDP per capita reflects an increase in the rate of population growth, particularly from 1947 to 1966.

● GDP (in billions)
● GDP per Capita

Note: This graph is shown in five-year increments until the year 2000, after which it is shown in one-year increments so as to provide more detail for recent periods. Hence, the curve artificially "flattens" after 2000.

Figure 1.2
GDP and GDP per Capita[12]

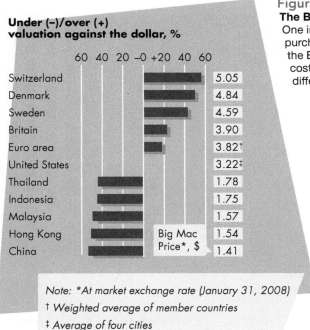

Under (−)/over (+) valuation against the dollar, %

60 40 20 −0 +20 40 60

	Big Mac Price*, $
Switzerland	5.05
Denmark	4.84
Sweden	4.59
Britain	3.90
Euro area	3.82†
United States	3.22‡
Thailand	1.78
Indonesia	1.75
Malaysia	1.57
Hong Kong	1.54
China	1.41

*Note: *At market exchange rate (January 31, 2008)*

† Weighted average of member countries

‡ Average of four cities

Figure 1.3
The Big Mac Index[14]
One interesting method for comparing purchasing power in different countries is the Big Mac Index—a comparison of the costs of a McDonald's hamburger in different countries.

REAL GDP gross domestic product (GDP) adjusted to account for changes in currency values and price changes

NOMINAL GDP gross domestic product (GDP) measured in current dollars or with all components valued at current prices

PURCHASING POWER PARITY principle that exchange rates are set so that the prices of similar products in different countries are about the same

PRODUCTIVITY measure of economic growth that compares how much a system produces with the resources needed to produce it

in a hypothetical economy. In 2008, a pizza cost $10; in 2009, a pizza cost $11. In both years, exactly 1,000 pizzas were produced. In 2008, the local GDP was $10,000 ($10 × 1,000); in 2009, the local GDP was $11,000 ($11 × 1,000). Has the economy grown? No. Because 1,000 pizzas were produced in both years, *aggregate output* remained the same. The point is to not be misled into believing that an economy is doing better than it is. If it is not adjusted, local GDP for 2009 is **nominal GDP**—GDP measured in current dollars or with all components valued at current prices.[13]

Purchasing Power Parity In the example, *current prices* would be 2009 prices. On the other hand, we calculate real GDP when we adjust GDP to account for changes in *currency values and price changes*. When we make this adjustment, we account for both GDP and **purchasing power parity**—the principle that exchange rates are set so that the prices of similar products in different countries are about the same. Purchasing power parity gives us a much better idea of *what people can actually buy with the financial resources allocated to them by their respective economic systems*. In other words, it gives us a better sense of standards of living across the globe. Figure 1.3 illustrates a popular approach to see how purchasing power parity works in relation to a Big Mac. For instance, the figure pegs the price of a Big Mac in the United States at $3.22. Based on currency exchange rates, a Big Mac would cost $3.90 in Britain and $5.05 in Switzerland. But the same burger would cost only $1.54 in Hong Kong and $1.78 in Thailand.

Productivity A major factor in the growth of an economic system is **productivity**, which is a measure of economic growth that compares how much a system produces with the resources needed to produce it. Let's say that it takes 1 U.S. worker and 1 U.S. dollar to make 10 soccer balls in an 8-hour workday. Let's also say that it takes 1.2 Saudi workers and the equivalent of 1.2 riyals, the currency of Saudi Arabia, to make 10 soccer balls in the same 8-hour workday. We can say that the U.S. soccer-ball industry is more productive than the Saudi soccer-ball industry. The two factors of production in this extremely simple case are labor and capital.

If more products are being produced with fewer factors of production, the prices of these products go down. As a consumer, therefore, you would need less of your currency to purchase the same quantity of these products. In short, your standard of living—at least with regard to these products—has improved. If your entire economic system increases its productivity, then your overall standard of living improves. In fact, *standard of living improves only through increases in productivity*.[15] Real growth in GDP reflects growth in productivity.

Productivity in the United States is increasing, and as a result, so are GDP and GDP per capita. Ultimately, increases in these measures of growth

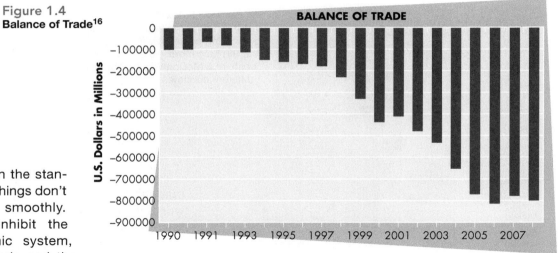

Figure 1.4
Balance of Trade[16]

mean an improvement in the standard of living. However, things don't
always proceed so smoothly.
Several factors can inhibit the
growth of an economic system,
including *balance of trade* and the
national debt.

Balance of Trade A country's **balance of trade** is
the economic value of all the products that it exports
minus the economic value of its imported products.
The principle here is quite simple:

- A *positive* balance of trade results when a country
  exports (sells to other countries) more than it
  imports (buys from other countries).

- A *negative* balance of trade results when a country
  imports more than
  it exports.

A negative balance of trade is commonly called a
trade deficit. In 2008, the U.S. trade deficit was almost
$800 billion. The United States is a *debtor nation* rather
than a *creditor nation*. Recent trends in the U.S. balance of trade are shown in Figure 1.4.

Trade deficit affects economic growth because the
amount of money spent on foreign products has not
been paid in full. Therefore, it is, in effect, borrowed
money, and borrowed money costs more in the form
of interest. The money that flows out of the country to
pay off the deficit can't be used to invest in productive enterprises, either at home or overseas.

National Debt Its **national debt** is the amount of
money that the government owes its creditors. As of this
writing, the U.S. national debt is over $10 trillion. You
can find out the national debt on any given day by going

to any one of several Internet sources, including the
U.S. National Debt Clock at **www.brillig.com/
debt_clock**.

How does
the national
debt affect eco-
nomic growth?
While taxes are
the most obvi-
ous way the
government
raises money, it
also sells *bonds*
—securities
through which
it promises to

The U.S. government uses the Federal Reserve
System to implement its monetary policies. The
chairman of "the Fed" is Ben Bernanke. He is
shown here listening to opening remarks before
the U.S. Senate Banking Committee in
Washington, D.C.

pay buyers certain amounts of money by specified
future dates. (In a sense, a bond is an IOU with interest.)[17] These bonds are attractive investments
because they are extremely safe: The U.S. government

Rising unemployment and gas prices, combined with slumping housing prices and sluggish GDP growth, led many analysts to conclude that the economy was in recession.

is not going to default on them (that is, fail to make payments when due). Even so, they must also offer a decent return on the buyer's investment, and they do this by paying interest at a competitive rate. By selling bonds, therefore, the U.S. government competes with every other potential borrower for the available supply of loanable money. The more money the government borrows, the less money is available for the private borrowing and investment that increase productivity.

Economic Stability

Stability is a condition in which the amount of money available in an economic system and the quantity of goods and services produced in it are growing at about the same rate. A chief goal of an economic system, stability can be threatened by certain factors.

Inflation **Inflation** occurs when an economic system experiences widespread price increases. Instability results when the amount of money injected into an economy exceeds the increase in actual output, so people have more money to spend but the same quantity of products available to buy. As supply and demand principles tell us, as people compete with one another to buy available products, prices go up. These high prices will eventually bring the amount of money in the economy back down. However, these processes are imperfect—the additional money will not be distributed proportionately to all people, and price increases often continue beyond what is really necessary. As a result, purchasing power for many people declines.

Keeping in mind that our definition of inflation is the occurrence of widespread price increases throughout an economic system, it stands to reason that we can measure inflation by measuring price increases. Price indexes such as the **consumer price index (CPI)** measure the prices of typical products purchased by consumers living in urban areas.[18]

Unemployment Finally, we need to consider the effect of unemployment on economic stability. **Unemployment** is the level of joblessness among people actively seeking work in an economic system. When unemployment is low, there is a shortage of labor available for businesses to hire. As businesses compete with one another for the available supply of labor, they raise the wages they are willing to pay. Then, because higher labor costs eat into profit margins, they raise the prices of their products. Although consumers have more money to inject into the economy, this increase is soon undone by higher prices, so purchasing power declines.

There are at least two related problems:

■ If wage rates get too high, businesses will respond by hiring fewer workers and unemployment will go up.

RECESSION period during which aggregate output, as measured by GDP, declines

DEPRESSION prolonged and deep recession

FISCAL POLICIES policies that a government uses to direct how it collects and spends revenue

MONETARY POLICIES policies that a government uses to control the size of its money supply

STABILIZATION POLICY government economic policy intended to smooth out fluctuations in output and unemployment and to stabilize prices

■ Businesses could raise prices to counter increased labor costs, but they won't be able to sell as many of their products at higher prices. Because of reduced sales, they will cut back on hiring and, once again, unemployment will go up.

What if the government tries to correct this situation by injecting more money into the economic system—say by cutting taxes or spending more money? Prices in general may go up because of increased consumer demand. Again, purchasing power declines and inflation may set in.[19] During the recession of 2008–09 millions of workers lost their jobs as businesses like Circuit City closed their doors and others, such as General Motors and Kodak, cut thousands of jobs in an effort to stem losses. Indeed, in early 2009 unemployment in the United States reached a 25-year high of 8.5%.

Recessions and Depressions   Unemployment is sometimes a symptom of a system-wide disorder in the economy. During a downturn in the business cycle, people in different sectors may lose their jobs at the same time. As a result, overall income and spending may drop. Feeling the pinch of reduced revenues, businesses may cut spending on the factors of production—including labor. Yet more people will be put out of work, and unemployment will only increase further. Unemployment that results from this vicious cycle is called *cyclical unemployment.*

If we look at the relationship between unemployment and economic stability, we are reminded that when prices get high enough, consumer demand for goods and services goes down. We are also reminded that when demand for products goes down, producers cut back on hiring and, not surprisingly, eventually start producing less. Consequently, aggregate output decreases. When we go through a period during which aggregate output declines, we have a recession. During a *recession*, producers need fewer employees—less labor—to produce products. Unemployment, therefore, goes up.

To determine whether an economy is going through a recession, we start by measuring aggregate output. Recall that this is the function of real GDP, which we find by making necessary adjustments to the total value of all goods and services produced within a given period by a national economy through domestic factors of production. A **recession** is more precisely defined as a period during which aggregate output, as measured by real GDP, declines. As noted earlier, most economists agree that the U.S. economy went into recession in 2008; most also predicted that we would not begin to emerge from recession until 2010 at the earliest. A prolonged and deep recession is a **depression**. The last major depression in the United States started in 1929 and lasted over 10 years. Most economists believe that the 2008–2009 recession would not become a depression.

Managing the U.S. Economy

The government acts to manage the U.S. economic system through two sets of policies: fiscal and monetary. It manages the collection and spending of its revenues through **fiscal policies**. Tax rates, for example, can play an important role in fiscal policies helping to manage the economy. One key element of President Barrack Obama's presidential platform was an overhaul of the U.S. tax system. Among other things, he proposed cutting taxes for the middle class while simultaneously raising taxes for both higher-income people and businesses.

Monetary policies focus on controlling the size of the nation's money supply. Working primarily through the Federal Reserve System (the nation's central bank, often referred to simply as "the Fed"), the government can influence the ability and willingness of banks throughout the country to lend money.[20] For example, to help offset the 2008–2009 recession, the government injected more money into the economy through various stimulus packages. On the one hand, officials hoped that these funds would stimulate business growth and the creation of new jobs. On the other hand, though, some experts feared that increasing the money supply might also lead to inflation.

Taken together, fiscal policy and monetary policy make up **stabilization policy**—government economic policy whose goal is to smooth out fluctuations in output and unemployment and to stabilize prices. In effect, the economic recession that started in 2008 was a significant departure from stabilization as business valuations dropped and jobs were eliminated. The various government interventions, such as financial bailouts, represented strategies to restore economic stability.

Questions for Review

1. What are the factors of production? Is one factor more important than the others? If so, which one? Why?

2. What is a demand curve? A supply curve? What is the term for the point at which they intersect?

3. What is GDP? Real GDP? What does each measure?

4. Why is inflation both good and bad? How does the government try to control it?

Questions for Analysis

5. In recent years, many countries that previously used planned economies have moved to market economies. Why do you think this has occurred? Can you envision a situation that would cause a resurgence of planned economies?

6. Cite an instance in which a surplus of a product led to decreased prices. Cite an instance in which a shortage led to increased prices. What eventually happened in each case? Why?

7. Explain how current economic indicators, such as inflation and unemployment, affect you personally. Explain how they may affect you as a manager.

8. At first glance, it might seem as though the goals of economic growth and stability are inconsistent with one another. How can you reconcile this apparent inconsistency?

Application Exercises

9. Visit a local shopping mall or shopping area. List each store that you see and determine what degree of competition it faces in its immediate environment. For example, if there is only one store in the mall that sells shoes, that store represents a monopoly. Note those businesses with direct competitors (two jewelry stores) and show how they compete with one another.

10. Interview a business owner or senior manager. Ask this individual to describe for you the following: (1) how demand and supply affect the business, (2) what essential factors of production are most central to the firm's operations, and (3) how fluctuations in economic indicators affect his or her business.

chapter 2

Business Ethics and Social Responsibility

After reading this chapter, you should be able to:

1 Explain how individuals develop their personal codes of ethics and why ethics are important in the workplace.

2 Distinguish social responsibility from ethics, identify organizational stakeholders, and characterize social consciousness today.

3 Show how the concept of social responsibility applies both to environmental issues and to a firm's relationships with customers, employees, and investors.

4 Identify four general approaches to social responsibility, and describe the four steps that a firm must take to implement a social responsibility program.

5 Explain how issues of social responsibility and ethics affect small business.

BP
Products
North Ameri

bp

2005
F
T
A
IA

USD

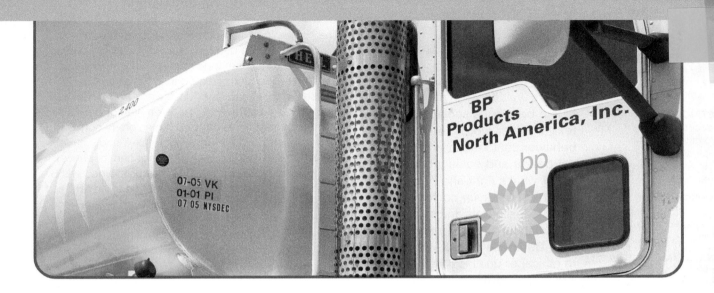

Under the Guise of Green

Oil companies aren't usually known for their environmentally responsible reputations. Global energy giant BP, however, has made an effort to market an environmentally friendly image. For the most part, this strategy has worked—leading many to overlook the facts suggesting that BP is not entirely the environmentally responsible exception it claims to be.

For the past several years, BP has committed environmental offenses almost annually. In 2000, the company was convicted of an environmental felony for failing to report that its subcontractor was dumping hazardous waste in Alaska. In 2005, BP allegedly ignored knowledge that its Texas City refinery was unsafe in a cost-cutting effort that led to an explosion, 15 deaths, and even more injuries. The following year, BP's negligence at its Prudhoe Bay oil field caused a 200,000-gallon oil spill and misdemeanor violation of the Clean Water Act. Then, in 2007, BP lobbied Indiana regulators for an exemption allowing it to increase its daily release of ammonia and sludge into Lake Michigan.

Despite these misdeeds, BP maintains its image as a "green" company. The Natural Resource Defense Council has even praised it for being a leader in the industry's move toward renewable energy. Indeed, true to the tag line, "Beyond Petroleum," that accompanies its green logo, BP's 2007 Sustainability Report projects spending $8 billion over the next ten years on renewable energy products. Its Web site even offers a carbon footprint calculator that lets visitors see how their own choices affect the environment.

BP risks compromising its green image by engaging in what Greenpeace calls the "greatest climate crime" in history—extracting oil from the tar sands of Alberta, Canada. The project is energy- and water-intensive, produces excessive amounts of greenhouse gases, destroys acres of forest, and harms indigenous communities, but it comes at a time when oil prices are high and western consumers are dependent on Middle Eastern oil. It remains to be seen whether BP's seemingly socially responsible ends can justify their environmentally damaging means.[1]

What's in It for Me?

To make an informed assessment about a company's social responsibility, it's important to understand how individual codes of ethics develop and play a role in the workplace, to distinguish between ethics and social responsibility, and to understand social consciousness. In addition to these elements, this chapter will explore the ethical and social responsibility issues that businesses face in terms of their customers, employees, investors, and immediate and global communities. In addition, it will look at general approaches to social responsibility, the steps businesses must take to implement social responsibility programs, and issues of social responsibility and ethics in small businesses.

Ethics in the Workplace

Ethics are beliefs about what's right or wrong and good or bad based on an individual's values and morals, plus a behavior's social context. In other words, **ethical behavior** conforms to individual beliefs and social norms about what's right and good. **Unethical behavior** conforms to individual beliefs and social norms about what's wrong or bad. **Business ethics** refers to ethical or unethical behaviors by employees in the context of their jobs.

Individual Ethics

Because ethics are based on both individual beliefs and social concepts, they vary among individuals, situations, and cultures. People may develop personal codes of ethics reflecting a wide range of attitudes and beliefs without violating general standards. Thus, some ethical

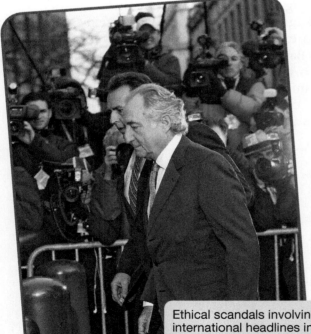

Ethical scandals involving business leaders have made international headlines in recent years. Events ranging from the fall of Enron to the investment scam headed by Bernard Madoff (shown here) have undermined public confidence in business and its leaders. Madoff, for example, cost hundreds of major investment clients their entire life savings.

Tax Revenues Disappear into Bermuda Triangle

The epidemic of scandals that dominated business news over the past decade shows how willing people can be to take advantage of potentially ambiguous situations—indeed, to create them. For example, Tyco sold itself to the smaller ADT Ltd. Because its new parent company was based in the tax haven of Bermuda, Tyco no longer had to pay U.S. taxes on its non-U.S. income. Tyco's subsidiaries in such tax-friendly nations soon doubled, and the company slashed its annual U.S. tax bill by $600 million. "Tyco," complained a U.S. congressman, "has raised tax avoidance to an art," but one tax expert replies that Tyco's schemes "are very consistent with the [U.S.] tax code."[2] Even in the face of blistering criticism and the indictment of its former CEO, Tyco retains its offshore ownership structure.[3]

---

and unethical behaviors are widely agreed upon, while others fall into gray areas.

Ambiguity, the Law, and the Real World Societies generally adopt formal laws that reflect prevailing ethical standards or social norms. We try to make unambiguous laws, but interpreting and applying them can still lead to ethical ambiguities. It isn't always easy to apply statutory standards to real-life behavior. For instance, during the aftermath of Hurricane Katrina in 2005, desperate survivors in New Orleans looted grocery stores for food and other essentials. While few people criticized this behavior, such actions were technically illegal.

Individual Values and Codes The ethics of business start with the ethics of individuals—managers, employees, and other legal representatives. Each person's personal code of ethics is determined by a combination of factors that are formed and refined throughout our lives.

Business and Managerial Ethics

Managerial ethics are the standards of behavior that guide individual managers in their work.[4] Although managerial ethics can affect business in any number of ways, it's helpful to classify them into three broad categories.

Behavior Toward Employees This category covers such matters as hiring and firing, wages and working conditions, and privacy and respect. Ethical and legal guidelines suggest that hiring and firing decisions should be based solely on the ability to perform a job.

Managing in Turbulent Times

Just When They Need It Most

In many ways, it's a pretty bitter irony. Volunteer organizations and charitable enterprises like the American Red Cross, the Salvation Army, and the United Way do much good in our society. When emergency strikes, the Red Cross is usually first on the scene. The Salvation Army provides much-needed relief for people without means. And the United Way supports a wide array of charities and social programs.

All three of these organizations depend on contributions from people and businesses to provide the services people often need. Salvation Army volunteers, for example, ring holiday bells outside retailers and collect spare change in red kettles. The United Way helps organize giving campaigns within business and government organizations. And the Red Cross calls on the assistance of more than a million volunteers each year.

But when the economy takes a downturn, as it did in 2008 and 2009, charitable giving almost always goes down. Most individuals and businesses, for example, find that they have less discretionary income and so have to reduce their spending. And giving to help others is one area that gets cut back. Indeed, the Red Cross, Salvation Army, and United Way all reported a drop in income during 2008 and forecast even bigger drops in 2009.

Ironically, it's in these very times that more people than ever need just the kind of assistance these organizations provide. When people lose their jobs, when their savings disappear, when they can't make their mortgage payment

or when second jobs during holiday periods are reduced, people need to be able to turn to the Salvation Army, for example, to help feed their children.

Fortunately, the leadership at these organizations anticipates difficult times and has plans in place that allow them to dip into reserves and cut back on their own expenses as necessary. As a result, at least for the time being, they have been able to provide the same basic levels of support as in past years. Hopefully, economic conditions will begin to improve soon, and they can begin to once again think about expanding services and providing more support to those who need it most.

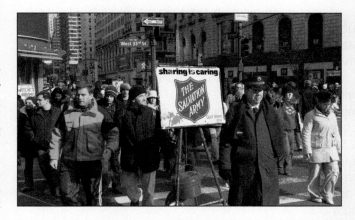

Wages and working conditions, while regulated by law, are also controversial. Consider a manager who pays a worker less than he deserves because the manager knows that the employee can't afford to quit or risk his job by complaining. While some see the behavior as unethical, others see it as a smart business move.

Behavior Toward the Organization   Employee behavior toward employers involves ethical issues in such areas as conflict of interest, confidentiality, and honesty. A *conflict of interest* occurs when an activity may benefit the individual to the detriment of his or her employer. For example, suppose the shoe buyer for a large department store chain accepts a free vacation from a major shoe manufacturer. If the manufacturer then asks the buyer to increase the size of an order, the buyer may feel both an obligation to do so (because of the vacation) and assume that more large orders could result in another vacation next year.

To avoid even the appearance of bribery or favoritism, most companies have policies that forbid buyers from accepting gifts from suppliers. Businesses in highly

"From a purely business viewpoint, taking what doesn't belong to you is usually the cheapest way to go."

competitive industries—software and fashion apparel, for example—have safeguards, such as nondisclosure agreements, against designers selling company secrets to competitors. Relatively common problems in the general area of honesty include stealing supplies and padding expense accounts.

Behavior Toward Other Economic Agents advertising, bargaining and negotiation, financial disclosure, ordering and purchasing—ethical ambiguity is possible in just about every activity businesses conduct with *primary agents of interest*—mainly customers, competitors, stockholders, suppliers, dealers, and unions. Bernard Madoff's investment scams cost hundreds of his clients their life savings. He led them to believe their money was safe and that they were earning large returns when in fact their money was being hidden and used to support his own extravagant life style. He used funds from new clients to pay returns to older clients. Madoff's scheme showed a blatant disregard for his investors.

Global variations can complicate ethical business practices. For example, while U.S. law forbids bribes, many countries incorporate them into normal business practices. A U.S. power-generating company recently lost a $320 million contract in the Middle East because it refused to pay bribes that a Japanese firm was willing to pay to get the job. Chapter 4 discusses more ways that social, cultural, and legal differences affect international business.

Assessing Ethical Behavior

The following steps set a simplified course for making ethical decisions about ethically subjective and ambiguous business situations:

1 Gather the relevant factual information.

2 Analyze the facts to determine the most appropriate moral values.

3 Make an ethical decision based on the rightness or wrongness of the proposed activity or policy.

The process may not work this smoothly, though; facts may not be clear-cut, and moral values may not be agreed upon. Nevertheless, a judgment and a decision must be made in order to maintain trust, an indispensable element in any business transaction.

Consider a common dilemma faced by managers with expense accounts to cover work-related expenses when they're traveling for business or entertaining clients for business purposes. If a manager takes a client to a $150 dinner, submitting a $150 reimburse-

ment receipt for that dinner is accurate and appropriate. But suppose that this manager has a $150 dinner the next night with a friend for purely social purposes. Submitting that receipt for reimbursement would be unethical. But some employees would disagree, rationalizing that they're underpaid, so submitting this receipt as well is just a means of "recovering" income due to them.

Consider the following ethical *norms*, which Figure 2.1 incorporates into a model of ethical decision making that can be applied in cases like this:[5]

1 *Utility*. Does a particular act optimize the benefits to those who are affected by it? (That is, do all relevant parties receive equally useful benefits?)

2 *Rights*. Does it respect the rights of all individuals involved?

3 *Justice*. Is it fair?

4 *Caring*. Is it consistent with people's responsibilities to one another?

While the utility norm acknowledges that the manager benefits from a padded account, others, such as coworkers and owners, don't. Most would also agree that the act doesn't respect the rights of others (such as investors, who have to foot the bill). Moreover, it's clearly unfair and compromises the manager's responsibilities to others. This particular act, then, appears to be clearly unethical.

Figure 2.1, however, also provides mechanisms for dealing with unique circumstances that make ethical issues more or less clear-cut. Suppose, for example, that our manager loses the receipt for the legitimate dinner but retains the receipt for the social dinner. Some might argue that it's okay to submit the illegitimate receipt because the manager is only doing so to get proper reimbursement. Others, however, will reply that

---

Do No Evil

Although strategies, practices, and objectives can change, an organization's core principles and values should remain steadfast. For example, Google must be flexible enough to adapt its strategies and practices to meet the challenges posed by the rapidly evolving technology industry. Google's core principle is simple: "Don't be evil." Google's code of conduct is built around this idea; ethical responsibility is central to Google's identity, which is especially important for a company that has access to vast amounts of private and sensitive information.

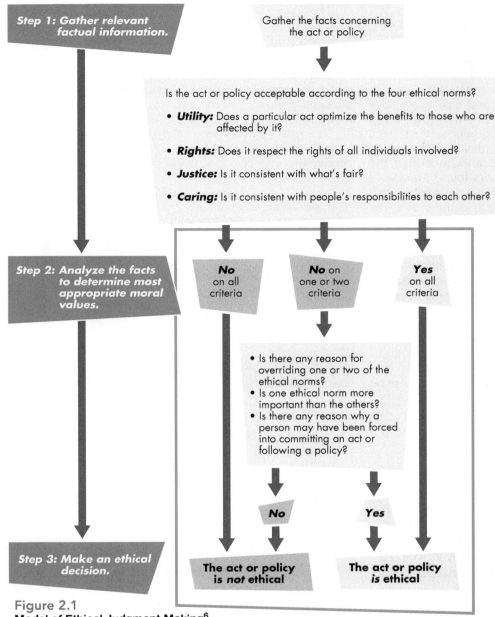

Step 1: Gather relevant factual information.

Gather the facts concerning the act or policy

Is the act or policy acceptable according to the four ethical norms?

- **Utility:** Does a particular act optimize the benefits to those who are affected by it?

- **Rights:** Does it respect the rights of all individuals involved?

- **Justice:** Is it consistent with what's fair?

- **Caring:** Is it consistent with people's responsibilities to each other?

Step 2: Analyze the facts to determine most appropriate moral values.

No on all criteria

No on one or two criteria

Yes on all criteria

- Is there any reason for overriding one or two of the ethical norms?
- Is one ethical norm more important than the others?
- Is there any reason why a person may have been forced into committing an act or following a policy?

No

Yes

Step 3: Make an ethical decision.

The act or policy is *not* ethical

The act or policy *is* ethical

Figure 2.1
Model of Ethical Judgment Making[6]

submitting the alternative receipt is wrong under any circumstances.

Company Practices and Business Ethics

To discourage unethical and illegal activities, most companies have taken formal steps, such as setting up codes of conduct, developing clear ethical positions, and perhaps most effectively, demonstrating upper-management support of ethical standards. These policies contribute to a corporate culture that values ethical standards and announce that the firm is equally concerned with good citizenship and profits.

Two of the most common approaches to formalizing top management commitment to ethical business practices are *adopting written codes* and *instituting ethics programs*.

Adopting Written Codes Many companies have written codes that formally announce intent to do business ethically. The number of such companies has risen dramatically in the last three decades, and today almost all major corporations have written codes of ethics. Even Enron had a code of ethics, but managers must follow the code if it's going to work. On one occasion, Enron's board of directors voted to set aside the code in order to complete a deal that would violate it; after the deal was completed, they then voted to reinstate the code!

Instituting Ethics Programs Many examples suggest that ethical responses can be learned through experience. In the classic 1982 case of a corporate saboteur who poisoned Tylenol capsules and caused the deaths of several consumers, employees at Johnson & Johnson, the maker of Tylenol, didn't wait for instructions or a company directive before informing retailers and pulling the product from shelves. In retrospect, they reported simply knowing that this was what the company would want them to do. Business schools are important players in ethics education, but most analysts agree that companies must take the chief responsibility for educating employees.

More and more firms, like ExxonMobil and Boeing, require managers to periodically go through ethics training as a reminder of the importance of ethical decision making and to update them on current laws and regulations. Others, such as Texas Instruments, have ethics hotlines that employees may call to discuss the ethics of a particular problem or situation or to report unethical behavior or activities by others.

The Electronic Equivalent of Paper Shredding

In virtually every major corporate scandal of the last few years, the best-laid plans of managerial miscreants have come unraveled, at least in part, when e-mail surfaced as key evidence. For example, Citigroup analyst Jack Grubman changed stock recommendations in exchange for favors from CEO Sandy Weill and confirmed the arrangement via e-mail. Investigators found that David Duncan, Arthur Andersen's head Enron auditor, had deleted incriminating e-mails shortly after the start of the Justice Department's investigation. After Tim Newington, an analyst for Credit Suisse First Boston, refused to give in to pressure to change a client's credit rating, an e-mail circulated on the problem of Newington's troublesome integrity: "Bigger issue," warned an upper manager, "is what to do about Newington in general. I'm not sure he's salvageable at this point."

Many corporations are nervous about the potential liability that employee e-mails may incur. Software developer Omniva Policy Systems saw this concern as an opportunity. Their e-mail software allows users to send encrypted messages, specify an expiration date after which they can no longer be decrypted, and prevent resending or printing. In the event of a lawsuit or investigation, administrators can hit a "red button" that prevents any e-mail from being deleted.

"Our goal," says Omniva CEO Kumar Sreekanti, "is to keep the honest people honest. . . . We help organizations comply with regulations automatically so they don't have to rely on people to do it."

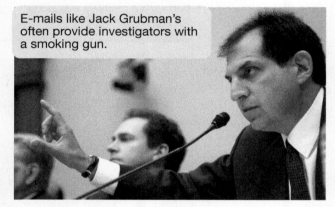

E-mails like Jack Grubman's often provide investigators with a smoking gun.

Social Responsibility

While ethics affect individual behavior in the workplace, **social responsibility** refers to the overall way in which a business attempts to balance its commitments to relevant groups and individuals in its social environment. These groups and individuals who are directly affected by the practices of an organization and have a stake in its performance are **organizational stakeholders**.[7]

The Stakeholder Model of Responsibility

Most companies that strive to be responsible to their stakeholders concentrate first and foremost on *customers*, *employees*, *investors*, *suppliers*, and *local communities*. They may then select other stakeholders who are particularly relevant or important to the organization and try to address their needs and expectations as well.

Customers Businesses that are responsible to their customers treat them fairly and honestly, charge fair prices, honor warranties, meet delivery commitments, and stand behind product quality. Apple, Wegmans Food Markets, UPS, and Lexus are among those companies with excellent reputations in this area.[8]

Employees Businesses that are socially responsible in their dealings with employees treat workers fairly, make them part of the team, and respect their dignity and

Apple has maintained a strong customer service reputation with features like the Apple Store's "Genius Bar," where Mac specialists answer questions for Mac users.

basic human needs. Many of these firms are also committed to hiring and promoting qualified minorities. The Container Store, Continental Airlines, and Whole Foods have excellent reputations for dealing with their employees in a fair and honest manner and for providing reasonable wages, benefits, and job security.

Investors A socially responsible stance toward investors means following proper accounting procedures, providing appropriate information about financial performance, and protecting shareholder rights and investments. Accurate and candid assessments of future growth and profitability are also important, as is avoiding even the appearance of impropriety in such sensitive areas as insider trading, stock-price manipulation, and the withholding of financial data. General Electric, 3M, and Hewlett-Packard are among the firms with exceptionally strong reputations for being open and candid with their investors.

Suppliers Relations with suppliers should also be managed with care, and firms should recognize the importance of mutually beneficial partnerships. A large corporation might easily take advantage of suppliers by imposing unrealistic delivery schedules and pushing for lower prices. Instead, it should keep suppliers informed about future plans, negotiate mutually agreeable delivery schedules and prices, and so forth. Toyota, Kroger, and Abercrombie & Fitch have excellent reputations for maintaining strong and positive relationships with their suppliers.

Local and International Communities Most businesses try to be socially responsible to local communities by contributing to local programs, getting involved in charities, and minimizing negative impact on communities. Target stores, for example, give over $2 million each week to local neighborhoods, programs, and schools.[9]

An organization should also recognize international stakeholders. The actions of international businesses affect their suppliers, employees, and customers in multiple countries. International businesses must also address their responsibilities in areas such as wages, working conditions, and environmental protection across different countries with varying regulatory laws and norms.

Contemporary Social Consciousness

Social consciousness and views toward social responsibility have been evolving since entrepreneurs such as John D. Rockefeller, J.P. Morgan, and Cornelius Vanderbilt raised concerns about abuses of power and led to the nation's first laws regulating basic business practices. In the 1930s, many blamed the Great Depression on a climate of business greed and lack of restraint. Out of this economic turmoil emerged new laws that dictated an expanded role for business in protecting and enhancing the general welfare of society, formalizing the concept of *accountability*.

In the 1960s and 1970s, business was again characterized negatively. Some charged that defense contractors had helped promote the Vietnam War to spur their own profits. Eventually, increased social activism prompted increased government regulation that led to changes such as health warnings on cigarette packaging and stricter environmental protection laws.

The general economic prosperity of the 1980s and 1990s led to another period of laissez-faire attitudes toward business. For the most part, business was viewed as a positive force. Many businesses continue to operate in enlightened and socially responsible ways: Wal-Mart and Target have policies against selling weapons, GameStop refuses to sell Mature-rated games to minors, and Anheuser-Busch promotes the concept of responsible drinking in its advertising.

Unfortunately, the recent spate of corporate scandals started to revive negative attitudes toward business and resulted in increased control and constraint of business practices by the government.[11] As just a single illustration, widespread moral outrage erupted when some of former Tyco CEO Dennis Kozlowski's extravagant perquisites were made public. In addition to the almost $300 million he made between 1998 and 2001 in salary, bonuses, and stock

Starbucks helps local farmers gain access to credit, works to develop and maintain sustainability of the coffee crop, and is building farmer support centers in Costa Rica, Ethiopia, and Rwanda to provide local farmers with agricultural and technical education and support.[10]

proceeds, his perks included a $50 million Florida mansion, an $18 million New York apartment, $11 million for antiques and furnishings, and a $2.1 million birthday party in Italy for his wife. In 2005, Kozlowski was sentenced to 25 years in prison for misappropriating Tyco funds.[12] The recession that began in 2008 and continued into 2009 provided additional fuel for growing negative attitudes toward business. Many people, for instance, blamed corporate greed and management neglect for the problems that beset banks, automobile companies, airlines, and retailers. Consequently, there has been increased pressure on the government to impose new regulations on business practices and to place limits on executive compensation.

2000 and 2005 and has pledged to reduce them another 5 percent by 2010.[14] Although cost concerns have created reluctance to "go green," the opportunity to make money by marketing green products to environmentally conscious consumers is becoming increasingly apparent.

Not all businesses make a sincere effort to adopt green policies and procedures. Some are guilty of **greenwashing**—using advertising to project a green image without adopting substantive environmentally friendly changes. In January 2008, the U.S. Federal Trade Commission (FTC) began a series of hearings to determine the veracity of many green marketing claims. No companies have been censured for false advertising as a result of these hearings, but increased regulation will likely result as the FTC catches up to new trends.[15]

Areas of Social Responsibility

When defining its sense of social responsibility, a firm typically confronts four areas of concern: responsibilities toward the *environment*, *customers*, *employees*, and *investors*.

Responsibility Toward the Environment

The devastating effects of increasing carbon dioxide (Figure 2.2) and other greenhouse gas emissions have begun to reveal themselves in the shrinking Arctic ice cap and the increase in severe weather incidents. With increased attention to global climate change comes pressure on business, both from governments and consumers, to control negative environmental impact.

Many socially responsible companies go beyond what government regulations require. For example, in addition to developing hydrogen fuel technologies, Honda reduced its own CO_2 emissions by 5 percent between

Responsibility Toward Customers

A company that does not act responsibly toward its customers will ultimately lose their trust and their business. To encourage responsibility, the FTC

Figure 2.2
CO_2 Emissions, Past and Future[13]

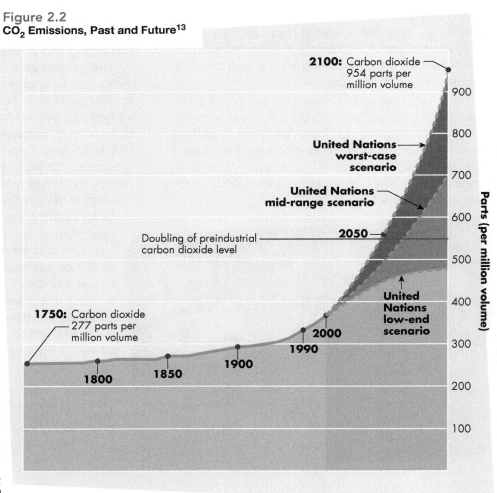

Green marketing (also environmental or ecological marketing)—the marketing of environmentally friendly goods—encompasses a wide variety of business strategies and practices.

- **Production Processes** Businesses, like Ford Motors and General Electric, modify their production processes to limit the consumption of valuable resources like fossil fuels by increasing energy efficiency and reduce their output of waste and pollution by cutting greenhouse gas emissions.

- **Product Modification** Products can be modified to use more environmentally friendly materials, a practice S.C. Johnson encourages with its Greenlist of raw materials classified according to their impact on health and the environment. Committed to only using the safest materials on this list, S.C. Johnson eliminated 1.8 million pounds of volatile organic compounds from its glass cleaner Windex.[17]

- **Carbon Offsets** Many companies are committed to offsetting the CO_2 produced by their products and manufacturing processes. In 2007, Volkswagen began a program of planting trees (which consume CO_2 during photosynthesis) in the so-called VW Forest in the lower Mississippi alluvial valley to offset the CO_2 emissions of every car they sell.[18]

- **Packaging Reduction** Reducing and reusing materials used in packaging products is another important strategy of green marketing, which Starbucks has pioneered. In 2004 the U.S. Food and Drug Administration gave the coffee retailer the first-ever approval to use recycled materials in its food and beverage packaging. Starbucks estimates that using cups composed of 10 percent recycled fibers reduces its packaging waste by more than 5 million pounds per year.[19]

- **Sustainability** Using renewable resources and managing limited resources responsibly and efficiently are important goals for any business pursuing a green policy. For example, Whole Foods Market is committed to buying food from farmers who use sustainable agriculture practices that protect the environment and agricultural resources, like land and water.

regulates advertising and pricing practices, and the FDA enforces labeling guidelines for food products. These government regulating bodies can impose penalties against violators, who may also face civil litigation. For example, in 2006, the FTC fined the social networking site Xanga $1 million for allowing children under the age of 13 to create accounts in clear violation of the Children's Online Privacy Protection Act.[16]

Consumer Rights Current interest in business responsibility toward customers can be traced to the rise of **consumerism**—social activism dedicated to protecting the rights of consumers in their dealings with businesses. The first formal declaration of consumer rights protection came in the early 1960s, when President John F. Kennedy identified four basic consumer rights. Since then, general agreement on two additional rights has emerged; these rights are described in Figure 2.3. The Consumer Bill of Rights is backed by numerous federal and state laws.

Merck provides an instructive example of what can happen to a firm that violates one or more of these consumer rights. For several years the firm aggressively marketed the painkiller Vioxx, which it was forced to recall in 2004 after clinical trials linked it to an increased risk of heart attacks and strokes. After the recall was announced, it was revealed that Merck had known about these risks as early as 2000 and downplayed them so that they could continue selling it. In 2007, Merck agreed to pay $4.85 billion to individuals or families of those who were injured or died as a result of taking the drug.[20]

Unfair Pricing Interfering with competition can take the form of illegal pricing practices. **Collusion** occurs when two or more firms collaborate on such wrongful acts as price fixing. In 2007, the European airlines Virgin and Lufthansa admitted to colluding with rivals to raise the prices of fuel surcharges on passenger flights as much as 12 times the regular price between August 2004 and January 2006. British Airways and Korean Air Lines were heavily fined, but in exchange for turning them in, Virgin and Lufthansa were not penalized.[21]

Firms can also come under attack for *price gouging*—responding to increased demand with overly steep (and often unwarranted) price increases. For

CONSUMERISM form of social activism dedicated to protecting the rights of consumers in their dealings with businesses

COLLUSION illegal agreement between two or more companies to commit a wrongful act

GREEN MARKETING marketing of environmentally friendly goods

Figure 2.3
Consumer Bill of Rights

Consumer Bill of Rights

1 Consumers have a right to safe products.

2 Consumers have a right to be informed about all relevant aspects of a product.

3 Consumers have a right to be heard.

4 Consumers have a right to choose what they buy.

5 Consumers have a right to be educated about purchases.

6 Consumers have a right to courteous service.

example, during threats of severe weather, people often stock up on bottled water and batteries. Unfortunately, some retailers take advantage of this pattern by marking up prices. Reports were widespread of gasoline retailers doubling or even tripling prices immediately after the events of September 11, 2001, and following the U.S. invasion of Iraq in 2003. Similar problems arose after hurricanes Katrina and Rita damaged oil refineries along the Gulf Coast in late 2005.

Ethics in Advertising In recent years, increased attention has been given to ethics in advertising and product information. Controversy arose when *Newsweek* magazine reported that Sony had literally created a movie critic who happened to be particularly fond of movies released by Sony's Columbia Pictures. When advertising its newest theatrical releases, the studio had been routinely using glowing quotes from a fictitious critic. After the story broke, Sony hastily stopped the practice and apologized.

The U.S.-based environmental group Nature Conservancy has recently teamed up with Indonesian logging company Sumalindo Lestari Jaya to help local villagers log a forest in a remote area of Indonesia. Why? The group believes that by working together with the company, it can better enforce sustainable practices.

Another issue concerns advertising that some consumers consider morally objectionable—for products such as underwear, condoms, alcohol, tobacco products, and firearms. Laws regulate some of this advertising (for instance, tobacco cannot be promoted in television commercials but can be featured in print ads in magazines), and many advertisers use common sense and discretion in their promotions. But some companies, such as Calvin Klein and Victoria's Secret, have come under fire for being overly explicit in their advertising.

Responsibility Toward Employees

Recruiting, hiring, training, promoting, and compensating are essential human resource management activities that provide the basis for social responsibility toward employees.

Legal and Social Commitments By law, businesses cannot discriminate against people in any facet of the employment relationship. For example, a company cannot refuse to hire someone because of ethnicity or pay someone a lower salary than someone else on the basis of gender. A company that provides its employees with equal opportunities without regard to race, sex, or other irrelevant factors is meeting both its legal and its social responsibilities. Firms that ignore these responsibilities risk losing good employees and leave themselves open to lawsuits.

Most would also agree that an organization should strive to ensure that the workplace is physically and socially safe. Companies with a heightened awareness of social responsibility also recognize an obligation to provide opportunities to balance work and life pressures and preferences, help employees maintain job skills, and, when terminations or layoffs are necessary, treat them with respect and compassion.

Ethical Commitments: The Special Case of Whistle-Blowers   Respecting employees as people also means respecting their behavior as ethical individuals. Ideally, an employee who discovers that a business has been engaging in illegal, unethical, or socially irresponsible practices should be able to report the problem to higher-level management and feel confident that managers will stop the questionable practices. However, if no one in the organization will take action, the employee might elect to drop the matter, or he or she may inform a regulatory agency or the media and become what is known as a **whistle-blower**—an employee who discovers and tries to put an end to a company's unethical, illegal, or socially irresponsible actions by publicizing them.[22]

Unfortunately, whistle-blowers may be demoted, fired, or, if they remain in their jobs, treated with mistrust, resentment, or hostility by coworkers. One recent study suggests that about half of all whistle-blowers eventually get fired, and about half of those who get fired subsequently lose their homes and/or families.[23] The law offers some recourse to employees who take action. The current whistle-blower law stems from the False Claims Act of 1863, which was designed to prevent contractors from selling defective supplies to the Union Army during the Civil War. With 1986 revisions to the law, the government can recover triple damages from fraudulent contractors. If the Justice Department does not intervene, a whistle-blower can proceed with a civil suit. In that case, the whistle-blower receives 25 to 30 percent of any money recovered.[24] Unfortunately, however, the prospect of large cash awards has generated a spate of false or questionable accusations.[25] In the wake of the Bernard Madoff investment scams, news broke that a Boston fraud investigator had for years been trying to convince the Securities and Exchange Commission (SEC) that Madoff was engaging in illegal and unethical practices. His warnings, though, had been ignored. This embarrassing revelation led to the SEC's recent announcement that it was reviewing all of its procedures regarding whistle-blowing and a pledge from the SEC chairman that new procedures would be put into place to safeguard against future problems.

Responsibility Toward Investors

Managers can abuse their responsibilities to investors in several ways. As a rule, irresponsible behavior toward shareholders means abuse of a firm's financial resources so that shareholder-owners do not receive their due earnings or dividends. Companies can also act irresponsibly toward shareholder-owners by misrepresenting company resources.

Improper Financial Management   Blatant financial mismanagement—such as paying excessive salaries to senior managers, sending them on extravagant "retreats" to exotic resorts, and providing frivolous perks—may be unethical but not necessarily illegal. In such situations, creditors and stockholders have few options for recourse. Forcing a management changeover is a difficult process

Because of controversies surrounding the potential misinterpretation of words and phrases, such as *light*, *reduced calorie*, *diet*, and *low fat*, food producers are now required to use a standardized format for listing ingredients on product packages.

that can drive down stock prices—a penalty that shareholders are usually unwilling to impose on themselves.

Insider Trading   **Insider trading** is using confidential information to gain from the purchase or sale of stocks.

Suppose, for example, that a small firm's stock is currently trading at $50 a share. If a larger firm is going to buy the smaller one, it might have to pay as much as $75 a share for a controlling interest. Individuals aware of the impending acquisition before it is publicly announced, such as managers of the two firms or the financial institution making the arrangements, could gain by buying the stock at $50 in anticipation of selling it for $75 after the proposed acquisition is announced.

Informed executives can also avoid financial loss by selling stock that's about to drop in value. Legally,

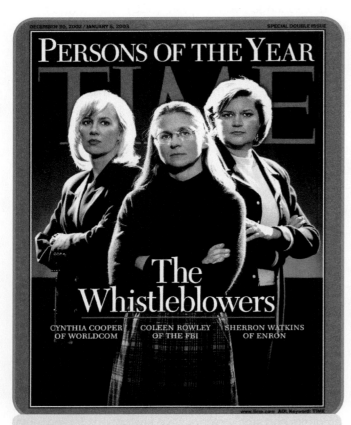

Enron's Sherron Watkins (right) reported concerns about the company's accounting practices well before the company's problems were made public, warning top management that Enron would "implode in a wave of accounting scandals." CEO Kenneth Lay commissioned a legal review of the firm's finances, but told his investigators not to "second-guess" decisions by Enron's auditor, accounting firm Arthur Andersen.[26]

stock can only be sold on the basis of public information available to all investors. Potential violations of this regulation were at the heart of the recent Martha Stewart scandal. Sam Waksal, president of ImClone, learned that the company's stock was going to drop in value and hastily tried to sell his own stock. He also allegedly tipped off close friend Martha Stewart, who subsequently sold her stock as well. Stewart, who argued that she never received Waksal's call and sold her stock only because she wanted to use the funds elsewhere, eventually pled guilty to other charges (lying to investigators) and served time in prison. Waksal, meanwhile, received a much stiffer sentence because his own attempts to dump his stock were well documented.

Misrepresentation of Finances   In maintaining and reporting its financial status, every corporation must conform to generally accepted accounting principles (GAAP; see Chapter 14). Unethical managers might project profits in excess of what they actually expect to earn, hide losses and/or expenses in order to boost paper profits, or slant financial reports to make the firm seem stronger than is really the case. In 2002, the U.S. Congress passed the *Sarbanes-Oxley Act*, which requires an organization's chief financial officer to personally guarantee the accuracy of all financial reporting (see Chapter 14).

Implementing Social Responsibility Programs

Opinions differ dramatically concerning social responsibility as a business goal. While some oppose any business activity that threatens profits, others argue that social responsibility must take precedence. Some skeptics fear that businesses will gain too much control over the ways social projects are addressed by society as a whole, or that they lack the expertise needed to address social issues. Still, many believe that corporations should help improve the lives of citizens because they are citizens themselves, often control vast resources, and may contribute to the very problems that social programs address.

Approaches to Social Responsibility

Given these differences of opinion, it is little wonder that corporations have adopted a variety of approaches to social responsibility. As Figure 2.4 illustrates, the four stances that an organization can take concerning its

Figure 2.4
Spectrum of Approaches to Corporate Social Responsibility

obligations to society fall along a continuum ranging from the lowest to the highest degree of socially responsible practices.

Obstructionist Stance The few organizations that take an **obstructionist stance** to social responsibility usually do as little as possible to solve social or environmental problems, have little regard for ethical conduct, and will go to great lengths to deny or cover up wrongdoing. For example, IBP, a leading meat-processing firm, has a long record of breaking environmental protection, labor, and food processing laws and then trying to cover up its offenses. Similarly, in 2009 a Georgia peanut processing plant owned by Peanut Corporation of America shipped products contaminated with salmonella. The firm's top manager allegedly knew that the products had failed safety tests but shipped them anyway in order to avoid losing money.

Defensive Stance Organizations that take a **defensive stance** will do everything that is legally required, including admitting to mistakes and taking corrective actions, but nothing more. Defensive stance managers insist that their job is to generate profits and might, for example, install pollution-control equipment dictated by law but not higher-quality equipment to further limit pollution.

Tobacco companies generally take this position in their marketing efforts. In the United States, they are legally required to include product warnings and to limit advertising to prescribed media. Domestically, they follow these rules to the letter of the law, but in many Asian and African countries, which don't have these rules, cigarettes are heavily promoted, contain higher levels of tar and nicotine, and carry few or no health warning labels.

DEFENSIVE STANCE approach to social responsibility by which a company meets only minimum legal requirements in its commitments to groups and individuals in its social environment

ACCOMMODATIVE STANCE approach to social responsibility by which a company, if specifically asked to do so, exceeds legal minimums in its commitments to groups and individuals in its social environment

Table 2.1 Top 10 Corporate Foundations[27]

Foundation	State	Total Giving (In U.S. Dollars)	Fiscal Date
1 Wal-Mart Foundation	NJ	$301 million	2007
2 Bank of America Foundation	NC	$211 million	2007
3 ExxonMobil Foundation	NY	$173 million	2007
4 Citigroup Foundation	CA	$146 million	2007
5 Johnson & Johnson Foundation	PA	$127 million	2007
6 Chevron Foundation	CA	$122 million	2007
7 AT&T Foundation	TX	$119 million	2007
8 General Electric Foundation	NY	$114 million	2007
9 Microsoft Foundation	WA	$110 million	2007
10 Wachovia Foundation	NC	$103 million	2007

Accommodative Stance A firm that adopts an **accommodative stance** meets and, in certain cases exceeds, its legal and ethical requirements. Such firms will agree to participate in social programs if solicitors convince them that given programs are worthy of their support. Both Shell and IBM, for example, will match contributions made by their employees to selected charitable causes.

Proactive Stance Firms with the highest degree of social responsibility exhibit the **proactive stance**; they take to heart the arguments in favor of social responsibility, view themselves as citizens in a society, indicate sincere commitment to improve the general social welfare, and surpass the accommodative stance by proactively seeking opportunities to contribute. The most common—and direct—way to implement this stance is to set up a foundation for providing direct financial support for various social programs. An excellent example of a proactive stance is the McDonald's Corporation's Ronald McDonald House program. These houses, located close to major medical centers, can be used for minimal cost by families while their sick children are receiving medical treatment nearby.

However, these categories are not sharply distinct: Organizations do not always fit neatly into one category or another. The Ronald McDonald House program has been widely applauded, but McDonald's has also been accused of misleading consumers about the nutritional value of its food products.

Managing Social Responsibility Program

A full commitment to social responsibility requires a carefully organized and managed program and managers who take steps to foster a companywide sense of social responsibility:[28]

1 *Social responsibility must start at the top and be considered a factor in strategic planning.* No program can succeed without the support of top management, who must embrace a strong stand on social responsibility and develop a policy statement outlining that commitment.

2 *A committee of top managers must develop a plan detailing the level of management support.* Companies may set aside percentages of profits for social programs or set specific priorities, such as supporting the arts.

3 *One executive must be put in charge of the firm's agenda.* Whether a separate job or part of an existing one, the selected individual must monitor the program and ensure implementation consistent with the firm's policy statement and strategic plan.

4 *The organization must conduct occasional **social audits**—systematic analyses of its success in using funds earmarked for its social responsibility goals.* Consider the case of a company whose strategic plan calls for spending $200,000 to train 300 unemployed people and to place 275 of them in jobs. If, at the end of a year, the firm has spent $198,000, trained 305 people, and filled 270 jobs, a social audit will confirm the program's success. But if the program has cost $350,000, trained only 190 people, and placed only 40 of them, the audit will reveal the program's failure. Such failure should prompt a rethinking of the program's implementation and its priorities.

Social Responsibility and the Small Business

Small-businesses owners are faced with similar ethical questions, although they may largely be a question of individual ethics. As the owner of a garden supply store, how would you respond to a building inspector's suggestion that a cash payment will speed your building permit application? As a liquor store manager, would you sell alcohol to a customer whose identification card looks forged? As the owner of a small laboratory, would you verify the license of your medical waste disposal company? Who will really be harmed if you pad your small firm's income statement to get a much-needed bank loan?

What about questions of social responsibility? Can your small business afford a social agenda? Should you sponsor Little League teams and donate to the United Way? Do joining the chamber of commerce and supporting the Better Business Bureau cost too much? Clearly, all managers in all organizations have to make decisions about ethics and social responsibility. One key to business success is to decide in advance how to respond to the issues that underlie all questions of ethical and social responsibility.

Questions for Review

1. What basic factors should be considered in any ethical decision?

2. Who are an organization's stakeholders? Who are the major stakeholders with which most businesses must be concerned?

3. What are the major areas of social responsibility with which businesses should be concerned?

4. What are the four basic approaches to social responsibility?

5. In what ways do you think your personal code of ethics might clash with the operations of some companies? How might you try to resolve these differences?

Questions for Analysis

6. What kind of wrongdoing would most likely prompt you to be a whistle-blower? What kind of wrongdoing would least likely cause you to blow the whistle? Why?

7. In your opinion, which area of social responsibility is most important? Why? Are there areas other than those noted in the chapter that you consider important?

8. Identify some specific ethical or social responsibility issues that might be faced by small-business managers and employees in each of the following areas: environment, customers, employees, and investors.

Application Exercises

9. Develop a list of the major stakeholders of your college or university. How do you think the school prioritizes these stakeholders? Do you agree or disagree with this prioritization?

10. Using newspapers, magazines, and other business references, identify and describe at least three companies that take a defensive stance to social responsibility, three that take an accommodative stance, and three that take a proactive stance.

Entrepreneurship, New Ventures, and Business Ownership

After reading this chapter, you should be able to:

1 Define *small business*, discuss its importance to the U.S. economy, and explain popular areas of small business.

2 Explain entrepreneurship and describe some key characteristics of entrepreneurial personalities and activities.

3 Describe the business plan and the start-up decisions made by small businesses and identify sources of financial aid available to such enterprises.

4 Discuss the trends in small business start-ups and identify the main reasons for success and failure among small businesses.

5 Explain sole proprietorships, partnerships, and cooperatives and discuss the advantages and disadvantages of each.

6 Describe corporations, discuss their advantages and disadvantages, and identify different kinds of corporations.

7 Explain the basic issues involved in managing a corporation and discuss special issues related to corporate ownership.

Harvard Dropout Turned Billionaire

In 2004, Mark Zuckerberg created the Web site Facebook for his Harvard classmates. Just a few years later, the social networking site had not only expanded beyond the Harvard campus, it had more than 40 million active users. By 2009, Zuckerberg was widely thought to be the richest 25-year-old in the world, with a net worth of over $1.5 billion. And it was all due to Facebook's success.

Zuckerberg's vision goes beyond a simple student directory. Facebook, which was made available to anyone with a valid e-mail address in 2006, allows users to re-create their network of social relationships online and facilitates their streamlined communication by, for example, sending newsfeed-style bulletins to everyone in a person's network whenever they make a change to their page, such as adding a friend or uploading a photograph. This feature caused privacy concerns and wasn't very popular when first introduced. But Zuckerberg listened to users, admitted he could have handled the launch better, and provided opt-out options and other new features. Now News Feed is one of Facebook's most popular features, and the service's ability to create instant word-of-mouth buzz among networks of friends has attracted software developers and advertisers. In fact, the site has done so well that it's attracted the attention of big-name corporations. Viacom and Yahoo have both expressed interest in buying Facebook, offering as much as $1 billion. But at this point, Zuckerberg isn't selling.

It takes more than a good idea to become rich at the ripe old age of 25, however. Zuckerberg worked long hours and even dropped out of Harvard to make his vision for Facebook a reality. Flexibility has also been important in allowing him to tailor the site to suit its always-expanding audience. Zuckerberg has also had to learn managerial skills on the job, but his willingness to make and learn from mistakes has served him well and helped Zuckerberg make Facebook the second-most-popular social networking site in the world.[1]

What's in It for Me?

Zuckerberg displayed many of the characteristics key to entrepreneurial success. This chapter will discuss these and additional elements important for starting and owning a business, including the business plan, reasons for success and failure, and the advantages and disadvantages of different kinds of ownership. First, we'll start by defining a small business and identifying its importance in the U.S. economy.

What Is a "Small" Business?

Locally owned and operated restaurants, dry cleaners, automobile repair shops, and hair salons are obviously small businesses, and giant corporations, such as Dell, Starbucks, Urban Outfitters, and Best Buy, are clearly big businesses. But between these extremes fall thousands of companies that cannot be easily categorized.

The U.S. Department of Commerce and the **Small Business Administration (SBA)**, a government agency that assists small businesses, define the size of a business based on its industry and number of employees. According to SBA standards, a small business can have as many as 1,500 employees. Because strict numerical terms sometimes lead to contradictory classifications, we will consider a **small business** to

---

Dell-ivering Innovation

Innovations are not always new products. Michael Dell didn't invent the PC; he developed an innovative way to build it (buy finished components and then assemble them) and an innovative way to sell it (directly to consumers, first by telephone and now via the Internet). Today, small businesses produce 13 times as many patents per employee as large patenting firms.[2]

---

be an independent (that is, not part of a larger business) business with relatively little influence in its market. A neighborhood grocer would be small, assuming it is not part of a chain and that the prices it pays to wholesalers and charges its customers are largely set by market forces. Dell was a small business when founded by Michael Dell in 1984, but today it's number one in the personal computer market and by no means small. Hence, it can negotiate from a position of strength with its suppliers and can set its prices with less consideration for what others are charging.

The Importance of Small Business in the U.S. Economy

As Figure 3.1 shows, most U.S. businesses employ fewer than 100 people, and most U.S. workers are employed by small business. Moreover, this same pattern exists across most free market economies. The contribution of small business can be measured in terms of *job creation*, *innovation*, and *contributions to big business*.

Job Creation Small businesses are an important source of new (and often well-paid) jobs. In recent years, small businesses have accounted for 40 percent of all new jobs in high-technology sectors.[3] Small firms often hire at a faster rate than big firms and are generally the first to hire in times of economic recovery. However, they also tend to cut jobs at a higher rate than big firms, which are generally the last to lay off workers during downswings.

Innovation Major innovations are as likely to come from small businesses (or individuals) as from big ones. Individuals, small

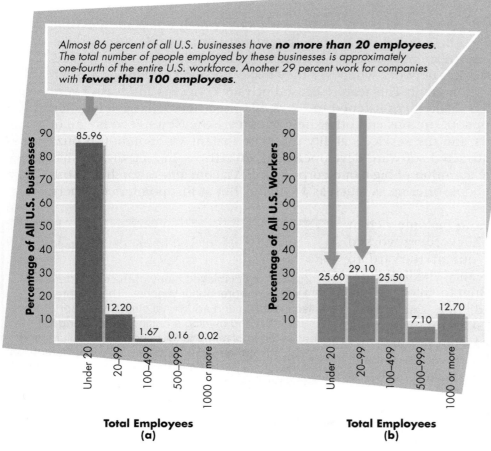

Almost 86 percent of all U.S. businesses have **no more than 20 employees**. The total number of people employed by these businesses is approximately one-fourth of the entire U.S. workforce. Another 29 percent work for companies with **fewer than 100 employees**.

Figure 3.1
The Importance of Small Business in the United States[4]

groups of people, or people working for small businesses invented the personal computer, the stainless-steel razor blade, the photocopier, the jet engine, and the self-developing photograph.

Contributions to Big Business Most of the products made by big businesses are sold to consumers by small businesses. For example, most dealerships that sell Fords, Toyotas, and Volvos are independently operated. Even as more shoppers turn to the Internet, many larger online retailers outsource the creation of their Web sites and the distribution of their products to small or regional firms. Smaller businesses also provide data-storage services, as well as other services and raw materials, for larger businesses. Microsoft, for instance, relies on hundreds of small firms located around the world to write most of its code.

Popular Areas of Small-Business Enterprise

Small businesses play a major role in services, retailing, construction, wholesaling, finance and insurance, manufacturing, and transportation. Generally, the more resources that are required, the harder a business is to start and the less likely an industry is dominated by small firms. Remember, too, that small is a relative term. The criteria (number of employees and total annual sales) differ among industries and are often meaningful only when compared with truly large businesses. Figure 3.2 shows the distribution of all U.S. businesses employing fewer than 20 people across industry groups.

Services About 50 percent of businesses with fewer than 20 employees are involved in the service industry,

Figure 3.2
Small Business by Industry[5]

Retailing 13.06%
Construction 12.70%
Services 50.07%
Wholesaling 6.00%
Finance and Insurance 4.11%
Manufacturing 4.40%
Other 6.90%
Transportation 2.76%

which ranges from marriage counseling to computer software, from management consulting to professional dog walking. Partly because they require few resources, service providers are the fastest-growing segment of small business.

Retailing Retailers, which sell products made by other firms directly to consumers, account for about 13 percent of these firms. Usually, people who start small retail businesses favor specialty shops—big men's clothing or gourmet coffees, for example—that let them focus limited resources on narrow or small market segments.

Construction About 13 percent of all U.S. businesses are involved in construction. Because many construction jobs are small local projects, like a homeowner adding a garage or remodeling a room, local contractors are often best suited to handle them.

Wholesaling Small-business owners often do well in wholesaling, which accounts for about 6 percent of businesses with fewer than 20 employees. Wholesalers buy products in bulk from manufacturers or other producers and store them in quantities and locations convenient for selling them to retailers.

Finance and Insurance Financial and insurance firms account for about 4 percent. Most of these businesses, such as local State Farm Insurance offices, are affiliates of or agents for larger national firms. Small locally owned banks are also common in

There are many areas in which small businesses excel. This enterprising entrepreneur, for example, has a lucrative business as a dog walker. A small business is much more likely than a large business to succeed in such a venture.

smaller communities and rural areas.

Manufacturing More than any other industry, manufacturing lends itself to big business, but it still accounts for about 4 percent of firms with fewer than 20 employees. Indeed, small manufacturers sometimes outperform big ones in such innovation-driven industries as electronics, equipment and machine parts, and computer software.

Transportation About 3 percent of these small companies are in transportation and related businesses, including many taxi and limousine companies, charter airplane services, and tour operators.

Other The remaining 7 percent or so are in other industries, such as small research-and-development laboratories and independent media companies, like start-up Web channels, small-town newspapers and radio broadcasters.

Entrepreneurship

Entrepreneurs are people who assume the risk of business ownership. **Entrepreneurship** is the process of seeking business opportunities under conditions of risk. However, not all entrepreneurs have the same goals.

Many entrepreneurs are driven to launch new businesses by the goal of gaining independence from working for someone else and securing a financial future for themselves, but they may not aspire to grow their businesses beyond their capacities to run them. Consider Jack Matz, who opened a photocopy and print service business after losing his job as a corporate executive when his firm merged with another. His goal is to earn enough money to lead a comfortable life until he retires. The term *small business* is most closely associated with these kinds of enterprises.

Others strive to grow and expand their ventures into large businesses. Terms such as *new ventures* and *start-ups* are often used to refer to these kinds of businesses. Moreover, there are also differences even among these businesses and the entrepreneurs who start them. Some, like Michael Dell, aspire to remain at the helm of

Managing in Turbulent Times

The Wide World of Risk

Globalization and the expanded reach and power of multinational companies require corporations to innovate, grow, and adapt to new markets and economic circumstances. In a highly interconnected world, it's often hard to figure out the complex ownership and organizational structures of many global corporations. Branding strategies and management structures may lead people to think that companies are local when, in fact, the real source of corporate power may lie thousands of miles away. One thing's for sure: if you're going to be dealing with a company overseas, you'd better have a good idea of where and how decisions are made, and who has the real power to make them.

Remember, too, that different cultures have different attitudes when it comes to entrepreneurship. Some countries and cultures, like that of the United States, promote a lively entrepreneurial spirit. Businesspeople are open to taking risks, and if they fail, they tend to pick themselves up and move on to something else. In some Asian countries, the entrepreneurial spirit is often tempered by the need for consensus. This approach requires

a lot of patience and the ability to compromise. Knowing the cultural forces that shape both a business organization and people's attitudes toward risk, success, and failure is an elementary but important component of international business.

their business even after it grows to be a gigantic corporation. Others may instead be more interested in starting a new business, demonstrating its potential for growth and profits, and then selling the business for a profit.

In some cases, an entrepreneur's goals may not always be clear in the early stages of business development. For instance, the founders of Google had no idea that their firm would grow to its present size. Others might start out with ambitious growth plans, but find that expected opportunities cannot be realized.

Entrepreneurial Characteristics

Many successful entrepreneurs share certain characteristics: resourcefulness, a concern for good customer relations, the ability to deal with uncertainty and risk, a desire to be their own bosses, to have greater control over their lives, and to build for their families.

Yesterday's entrepreneur was often stereotyped as "the boss"—self-reliant, male, and able to make quick, firm decisions. Today's entrepreneur is seen more often as an open-minded leader, just as likely to be male or female, who relies on networks, business plans, and consensus. Past and present entrepreneurs also have different views on such topics as how to succeed, how to automate business, and when to rely on experience in the trade or on basic business acumen.[6]

Consider Yoshiko Shinohara, who had lost her father by the age of 8, was divorced by the age of 28, and never received a college education. At the age of 70, she is president of Tempstaff, a Japanese temp agency that she started out of her one-room apartment more than 30 years ago. Fueled by Japan's need for temps during a period of stagnation in the 1990s and Shinohara's ambition, Tempstaff is now a $1.5 billion company with a high-rise headquarters in Tokyo.[7]

Among other things, Shinohara's story illustrates what is almost always a key element in entrepreneurship: risk. Interestingly, most successful entrepreneurs seldom see what they do as risky. Whereas others may focus on possibilities for failure and balk at gambling everything on a new venture, most entrepreneurs are so passionate about their ideas and plans that they see little or no likelihood of failure. For example, when Shinohara started Tempstaff, few Japanese businesses understood or had even heard of the temporary-worker concept. But Shinohara felt that she "had nothing to lose anyway" and preferred taking that risk to ending up "serving tea or just being a clerical assistant."[8]

Starting and Operating a New Business

Now more than ever, the Internet has made setting up a small business easier and faster, has created more potential opportunities, and has heightened the ability to gather and assess information. Would-be entrepreneurs must still decide whether to buy an existing business or build from the ground up and must know when to seek expert advice and where to find financing.

Crafting a Business Plan

Before investing time and money, the starting point for virtually every new entrepreneur is a **business plan** in which the entrepreneur thoroughly develops and describes her or his business strategy and demonstrates how it will be implemented.[9]

Setting Goals and Objectives A business plan describes the match between the entrepreneur's abilities and experiences and the requirements for producing and/or marketing a particular product. It defines strategies for production and marketing, legal elements and organization, and accounting and finance. It should specifically answer three questions: (1) What are the entrepreneur's goals and objectives? (2) What strategies will be used to obtain them? (3) How will these strategies be implemented?

Sales Forecasting Sales forecasts (also called revenue forecasts) must be based on sound logic and research and demonstrate an understanding of the current market, the strengths and weaknesses of existing firms, and the means by which the new venture will compete. For example, simply asserting that the new venture will sell 100,000 units per month is not credible without realistic market data to support that assertion.

Financial Planning Financial planning refers to the entrepreneur's plan for turning all other activities into dollars. It generally includes an income statement, balance sheets, a breakeven chart, and a cash budget, which shows how much money is needed before the business opens and how much is needed to keep the business going before it starts earning a profit.[10] Again, the critical requirement is that the financial plan be sound and realistic. Projecting huge profits after only a few weeks of operation, for example, is not likely to be very convincing.

Starting a Small Business

The first step to starting a new business is the individual's commitment to becoming a business owner. In preparing their business plans, entrepreneurs must come to understand the nature of the enterprises in which they are engaged.

Buying an Existing Business   Next, the entrepreneur must decide whether to buy an existing business or start from scratch. Because the odds are better, many experts recommend the first approach. If successful, an existing business has already proven its ability to attract customers and generate profit and has established relationships with lenders, suppliers, and other stakeholders. Moreover, potential buyers will have a much clearer picture of what to expect than any estimate of a start-up's prospects. For example, Ray Kroc bought McDonald's as an existing business, added entrepreneurial vision and business insight, and produced a multinational giant.

Franchising   Most Subway, 7-Eleven, RE/MAX, and Blockbuster outlets are franchises operating under licenses issued by parent companies to local owners. A

Entrepreneurs must study markets and answer the following questions:
- Who and where are my customers?
- How much will those customers pay for my product?
- How much of my product can I expect to sell?
- Who are my competitors?
- Why will customers buy my product rather than the product of my competitors?

franchise agreement involves two parties, a *franchisee* (the local owner) and a *franchiser* (the parent company).

Franchisees benefit from the parent corporation's experience and expertise. The franchiser may pick the store location, negotiate the lease, purchase equipment, and supply financing. Franchises offer the benefit of brand recognition, which can make it easier to attract customers and reduce the costs of advertising as well as increase the likelihood of success.

Perhaps the most significant disadvantage in owning a franchise is the start-up cost, which varies widely. The fee for a Curves fitness center is between $31,400 and $53,500, but a McDonald's franchise costs $506,000 to $1.6 million,[11] and professional sports teams cost an average of $957 million dollars.[12] Franchisees may also

"Eventually I'd like to have a business where the money rolls in and I wouldn't have to be there much."

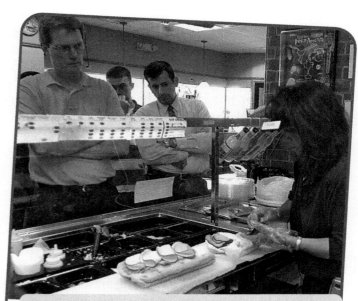

The ability of an entrepreneur to obtain adequate financing is a critical component in the potential success of a new venture. Many entrepreneurs rely on SBA financial programs, venture capital companies, or small-business investment companies to launch their businesses.

be obligated to contribute a percentage of sales to parent corporations. From the perspective of the parent company, some firms, such as Starbucks, choose not to franchise in order to retain more control over quality and earn more profits for themselves.

Starting from Scratch Despite the odds, some people seek the satisfaction that comes from planting an idea and growing it into a healthy business. A new business doesn't suffer the ill effects of a prior owner's errors, and the start-up owner is free to make all the choices. Of all new businesses begun in the past decade, 64 percent were started from scratch. Dell, Wal-Mart, Southwest Airlines, and Microsoft are among today's most successful businesses that were started from scratch by entrepreneurs.

However, new-business founders can only make projections about their prospects. Success or failure depends on identifying a genuine opportunity, such as a product for which many customers will pay well but which is currently unavailable.

Financing a Small Business

Although the choice of how to start a business is obviously important, it's meaningless without money. According to the National Federation of Independent Business, personal resources, including savings and money borrowed from friends and relatives, account for over two-thirds of all money invested in new small businesses, and one-half of that is used to purchase existing businesses. Getting money from banks, independent investors, and government agencies requires extra effort, like formulating business plans and meeting eligibility requirements. Moreover, lending institutions are more likely to help finance the purchase of an existing established business than a brand-new one. One of the many causes of the 2008–2009 recession was a sharp reduction in the availability of credit, including funds to help start new businesses. This credit crunch, in turn, limited both new start-up funding and funding for existing businesses wanting to make new investments.

Other Sources of Investment **Venture capital companies** are groups of small investors seeking to make profits on companies with rapid growth potential. Most of these firms do not lend money to start new businesses; they supply capital to fuel expansion of an existing firm in return for partial ownership, representation on boards of directors, and final approval of major decisions.

Small-business investment companies (SBICs) are federally licensed to borrow money from the SBA and to invest in or lend to small businesses with potential for rapid growth. Past beneficiaries of SBIC capital include Apple Computer, Intel, and FedEx. The government also sponsors *minority enterprise small-business investment companies (MESBICs)*, which target minority-owned businesses.

SBA Financial Programs Since its founding in 1953, the SBA has sponsored financing programs for small businesses that meet standards of size and independence and are unable to get private financing at reasonable terms. The most common form of SBA financing, its *7(a) loans programs*, allows small businesses to borrow from commercial lenders and guarantees to repay a maximum of 75 percent. The SBA's *special purpose loans* target businesses with specific needs, such as meeting international demands or implementing pollution-control measures. For loans under $35,000, the SBA offers the *micro-loan program*. The *Certified Development Company (504) program* offers fixed interest rates on loans from nonprofit community-based lenders to boost local economies.[13]

Other SBA Programs The SBA also helps entrepreneurs improve their management skills. The Service Corps of Retired Executives (SCORE) is made up of retired executives who volunteer to help entrepreneurs start new businesses. The **Small Business Development Center (SBDC)** program consolidates information from various disciplines and institutions for use by new and existing small businesses.

VENTURE CAPITAL COMPANY group of small investors who invest money in companies with rapid growth potential

SMALL-BUSINESS INVESTMENT COMPANY (SBIC) government-regulated investment company that borrows money from the SBA to invest in or lend to a small business

SMALL BUSINESS DEVELOPMENT CENTER (SBDC) SBA program designed to consolidate information from various disciplines and make it available to small businesses

Trends, Successes, and Failures in New Ventures

For every Sam Walton, Russell Simmons, Donald Trump, or Steve Jobs—entrepreneurs who transformed small businesses into big ones—there are many who fail. Each year, between 600,000 and 650,000 new businesses are launched in the United States, and between 500,000 and 600,000 fail.[14] In this section, we will look at a few key trends in small-business start-ups and examine some of the reasons for their success and failure.

Trends in Small-Business Start-ups

As noted previously, thousands of new businesses are started in the United States every year. Several factors

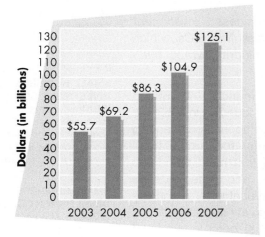

Figure 3.3
Growth of Online Retail Spending[15]

account for this trend, and in this section, we focus on five of them.

Emergence of E-Commerce The most significant recent trend is the rapid emergence of electronic commerce. Because the Internet provides fundamentally new ways of doing business, savvy entrepreneurs have created and expanded new businesses faster and easier than ever before. Figure 3.3 underscores this point by summarizing the growth in online retail spending from 2003 through 2007.

Crossovers from Big Business More businesses are being started by people who have opted to leave big corporations and put their experience to work for themselves.[16] John Chambers spent several years working at IBM and Wang Laboratories/ Wang Global before he signed on to help Cisco, then a small and struggling firm. Under his leadership and entrepreneurial guidance, Cisco has become one of the

Figure 3.4
Reasons Women Give for Starting Businesses[20]

largest and most important technology companies in the world.

Opportunities for Minorities and Women More small businesses are also being started by minorities and women.[17] The number of businesses owned by African Americans

increased by 48 percent during the most recent five-year period for which data are available and now totals about 1.2 million. The number of Hispanic-owned businesses has grown 31 percent and now totals about 1.6 million. Ownership among Asians has increased 24 percent and among Pacific Islanders 64 percent.[18]

Nearly 11 million businesses are now owned by women. Together, they generate a combined $2.5 trillion in revenue a year and employ 19 million workers.[19] Figure 3.4 shows some of the reasons women cite for starting their own businesses.

Global Opportunities Many entrepreneurs are also finding new opportunities in foreign markets. Doug Mellinger, founder and CEO of PRT Group, a software development company, had trouble finding trained programmers in the United States. So Mellinger set up shop on Barbados, where the government helps him attract foreign programmers. Today, PRT has customers and suppliers from dozens of nations.

Better Survival Rates More people are encouraged to test their skills as entrepreneurs because the small-business failure rate has declined. During the 1960s and 1970s, fewer than half of all new start-ups survived more than 18 months; only one in five lasted 10 years. Now, however, 44 percent can expect to survive for at least four years.[21]

Reasons for Failure

Unfortunately, over half of all new businesses will not enjoy long-term success. Although no set pattern is a reliable predictor, four general factors contribute to failure:

1. *Managerial incompetence or inexperience*. Some entrepreneurs put too much faith in common sense, overestimate their own managerial skills, or believe that hard work alone ensures success. Success will likely elude managers who don't know how to make basic business decisions or understand basic management principles.

2. *Neglect*. Starting a small business demands an overwhelming commitment of time and effort. Owners aren't likely to see success

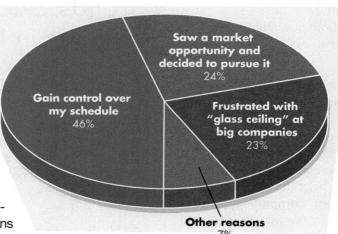

Saw a market opportunity and decided to pursue it
24%

Gain control over my schedule
46%

Frustrated with "glass ceiling" at big companies
23%

Other reasons
7%

The Road to Recovery

A homeless heroin addict at 24, Bob Williamson never would have expected a car accident to be the luckiest thing that ever happened to him. While recovering, he decided it was time to turn his life around. Although he may not have seemed the ideal hire, Williamson already had a work ethic that would carry him to his current position as CEO of Horizon Software International: "First one in, last to leave."

He lived by this code even when his job was just putting labels on paint cans in the basement at Glidden, which ended up promoting him eight times in two years. After working for two other paint companies, Williamson had the know-how to create a new formula for his

airbrushing hobby. His formula was a hit, and he started his own company, which he spun out into several others. Williamson overcame hard times again when he nearly faced bankruptcy after discovering his accountant was embezzling money.

But luck wasn't far behind him. Williamson started Horizon using the software that he just so happened to be writing as the software industry was about to boom. Once Williamson realized the value of his software, he rode that opportunity wherever it took him, and soon the company was selling the software to colleges, military bases, and hospitals. Now a 61-year-old CEO, Williamson is still "first one in, last to leave."[22]

---

if they try to launch ventures in their spare time or devote only limited time to new businesses.

3 *Weak control systems*. Effective control systems keep a business on track and alert managers to potential problems before they become serious. For instance, some businesses fail because they do a poor job of managing their credit-collection policies—anxious to grow, they may be too liberal in extending credit to their customers and then end up not being able to collect all the money that is owed to them.

4 *Insufficient capital*. Some entrepreneurs are overly optimistic about how soon they'll start earning profits. In most cases, it takes months or even years. Amazon.com didn't earn a profit for 10 years but obviously still required capital to pay employees and to cover other expenses. Experts say you need enough capital to operate at least six months to a year without earning a profit.[23]

Reasons for Success

Four basic factors are also typically cited to explain small-business success:

1 *Hard work, drive, and dedication*. Small-business owners must be committed to succeeding and willing to spend the time and effort to make it happen.

When Gladys Edmunds, a single mother in Pittsburgh, wanted to open a travel agency, she washed laundry, made chicken dinners to sell to cab drivers, and sold fire extinguishers door to door to earn start-up money. Today, Edmunds Travel Consultants earns about $6 million a year.[24]

2 *Market demand for the products or services being provided*. Careful analysis of market conditions can help small-business owners assess the probable reception of their products. Attempts to expand restaurants specializing in baked potatoes, muffins, and gelato have largely failed, but hamburger and pizza chains continue to expand.

3 *Managerial competence*. Successful owners may acquire competence through training or experience or by drawing on the expertise of others. Most spend time in successful companies or partner with others to bring expertise to a new business.[25]

4 *Luck*. After Alan McKim started Clean Harbors, an environmental cleanup firm in New England, he struggled to keep his business afloat. Then the U.S. government committed $1.6 billion to toxic-waste cleanup—McKim's specialty. Had the government fund not been created at just the right time, McKim might well have failed. Instead, he landed several government contracts.

SOLE PROPRIETORSHIP
business owned and usually operated by one person who is responsible for all of its debts

UNLIMITED LIABILITY
legal principle that holds owners responsible for paying off all debts of a business

GENERAL PARTNERSHIP
business with two or more owners who share in both the operation of the firm and the financial responsibility for its debts

Noncorporate Business Ownership

All entrepreneurs must decide which form of legal ownership best suits their goals: *sole proprietorship*, *partnership*, or *corporation*. Table 3.1 compares the most important differences among the three major ownership forms.

Sole Proprietorships

A **sole proprietorship** is owned and usually operated by one person. They account for about 72 percent of all U.S. businesses but only about 5 percent of total revenues.

Advantages of Sole Proprietorships   Sole proprietors answer to no one but themselves and can sometimes open up shop just by putting a sign on the door. Low start-up costs, the simplicity of legal setup procedures, and tax benefits make this form appealing. Further, the sole proprietor doesn't have to share the profits from the business with anyone.

Disadvantages of Sole Proprietorships   A major drawback is **unlimited liability**: a sole proprietor is personally liable for all debts incurred by the business. So, for example, if the business fails, creditors can make legal claims not only on the assets of the business but also on the personal assets of the proprietor, such as savings or the assets of other businesses owned by the individual. Another disadvantage is lack of continuity: a sole proprietorship legally dissolves when the owner dies. Additionally, sole proprietors often find it hard to borrow

money to start up or expand what many bankers see as risky businesses.

Partnerships

The most common type of partnership, the **general partnership**, is similar to a sole proprietorship but is owned by more than one person. Partners may invest equal or unequal sums of money. In most cases, partners share the profits equally or in proportion to their investment. In certain cases, though, the distribution of profits may be based on other things. A locally prominent athlete, for instance, may lend her or his name to the partnership and earn profits without actually investing funds. And sometimes one partner invests all of the funds needed for the business but plays no role in its management; this person is usually called a *silent partner*. Another partner might invest nothing but provide all the labor. In this case, the financial investor likely owns the entire business, and the labor partner owns nothing. But over time, and as specified in a contract, the labor partner gradually gains an ownership stake in the business (usually called *sweat equity*).

Advantages of Partnerships   The most striking advantage of general partnerships is the ability to grow by adding new talent and money. Because banks prefer to make loans to enterprises that are not dependent on single individuals, partnerships find it relatively easy to borrow and can invite new partners to invest as business opportunities expand.

Partnerships must begin with some kind of agreement that details who invested what sums and who will receive profit shares, how responsibilities are assigned, how the partnership may be dissolved and assets distributed, and how surviving partners will be protected from claims of a deceased partner's heirs. In all but two states, the Revised Uniform Limited Partnership Act requires the filing of specific information about the

Table 3.1   Comparative Summary: Three Forms of Business

Business Form	Liability	Continuity	Management	Sources of Investment
Proprietorship	Personal, unlimited	Ends with death or decision of owner	Personal, unrestricted	Personal
General Partnership	Personal, unlimited	Ends with death or decision of any partner	Unrestricted or depends on partnership agreement	Personal by partner(s)
Corporation	Capital invested	As stated in charter, perpetual or for specified period of years	Under control of board of directors, which is selected by stockholders	Purchase of stock

business and its partners. Partners may also agree to bind themselves in ways not specified by law. However, partners are still taxed as individuals.

Disadvantages of Partnerships   Unlimited liability is the greatest draw-back. Each partner may be liable for all business debts incurred by any of the partners. Partnerships also share with sole proprietorships the potential lack of continuity. When one partner dies or leaves, the original partnership dissolves, even if one or more of the others want it to continue. A related disadvantage is difficulty in transferring ownership. No partner may sell out, retire, or transfer interest without the others' consent.

Alternatives to General Partnerships   Because of these disadvantages, general partnerships are among the least popular forms of business. To resolve some of the problems inherent in general partnerships, some have tried alternative agreements. A **limited partnership** allows for **limited partners** who cannot take active roles in operations but invest money and are liable for debts only to the extent of their investments. For liability purposes, a limited partnership must have at least one **general (or active) partner** who runs the business and is responsible for its survival and growth.

Under a **master limited partnership**, an organization sells shares (partnership interests) to investors on public markets. Investors are paid back from profits. The master partner retains at least 50 percent ownership, runs the business, and provides detailed operating and financial reports to minority partners, who have no management voice.

Cooperatives

Groups of sole proprietorships or partnerships may agree to work together for their common benefit by forming **cooperatives**, which combine the freedom of sole proprietorships with the financial power of corporations. Although cooperatives make up only a minor segment of the U.S. economy, their role is especially important in agriculture. Ocean Spray, the Florida Citrus Growers, and Cabot Creamery are among the best-known cooperatives.

Corporations

The 4.93 million corporations in the United States account for about 20 percent of all U.S. businesses but generate about 85 percent of all sales revenues.[27]

Figure 3.5
Proportions of U.S. Firms in Terms of Organization Type and Sales Revenue[26]

Percentage of Businesses

20.2%
5.4%
71.6%
2.9%

Percentage of Sales Revenue

8.8%
1.7%
84.7%
4.9%

■ Sole proprietorships   ■ Corporations   ■ Partnerships   ■ Limited liability companies

CORPORATION business that is legally considered an entity separate from its owners and is liable for its own debts; owners' liabilities extend to the limits of their investments

LIMITED LIABILITY legal principle holding investors liable for a firm's debts only to the limits of their personal investments in it

TENDER OFFER offer to buy shares made by a prospective buyer directly to a target corporation's shareholders, who then make individual decisions about whether to sell

DOUBLE TAXATION situation in which taxes may be payable both by a corporation on its profits and by shareholders on dividend incomes

CLOSELY HELD (OR PRIVATE) CORPORATION corporation whose stock is held by only a few people and is not available for sale to the general public

PUBLICLY HELD (OR PUBLIC) CORPORATION corporation whose stock is widely held and available for sale to the general public

S CORPORATION hybrid of a closely held corporation and a partnership, organized and operated like a corporation but treated as a partnership for tax purposes

LIMITED LIABILITY CORPORATION (LLC) hybrid of a publicly held corporation and a partnership in which owners are taxed as partners but enjoy the benefits of limited liability

PROFESSIONAL CORPORATION form of ownership allowing professionals to take advantage of corporate benefits while granting them limited business liability and unlimited professional liability

The Corporate Entity

The very word *corporation* inspires images of size and power—a skyscraper for headquarters, large factories, and an army of workers. In reality, however, your corner newsstand has as much right to incorporate as a giant automaker, and they would share the characteristics of all **corporations**: legal status as separate entities, property rights and obligations, and indefinite life spans. As legal entities, like individuals, corporations can sue and be sued; buy, hold, and sell property; make and sell products; and commit crimes and be tried and punished for them.

Advantages of Incorporation

The biggest advantage of corporations is **limited liability**: investor liability is limited to personal investment in the corporation. If, for example, you invest $1,000 in stock in a corporation that ends up failing, you may lose your $1,000, but no more.

Another advantage is continuity. Shares of stock may be sold or passed on to heirs, and most corporations also benefit from the continuity provided by professional management. Finally, corporations have advantages in raising money. By selling stock, they expand the number of investors and the amount of available funds, and lenders are more willing to grant loans.

Disadvantages of Incorporation Although a chief attraction is ease of transferring ownership, this same

feature can create complications. For example, using a legal process called a **tender offer**—an offer to buy shares made by a prospective buyer directly to a corporation's shareholders—a corporation can be taken over against the will of its managers. Other disadvantages include more government regulations, high start-up costs, and complex legal requirements.

The biggest disadvantage, however, is **double taxation**. First, a corporation pays income taxes on company profits. Then, stockholders pay taxes on income (in the form of dividends) returned by their investments. Thus, the profits earned by corporations are taxed twice—at both the corporate and ownership levels.

The advantages and disadvantages of corporate ownership have inspired laws establishing different kinds of corporations intended to take advantage of the benefits of the corporate model without assuming all the disadvantages.

Types of Corporations

Within the broad categories of *public* or *private* are several specific types of corporations, some of which are summarized in Table 3.2.

■ Most smaller firms are **closely held (or private) corporations**. Stock is held by only a few people and isn't available for public sale. The controlling group of stockholders may be a family, a management group, or even the firm's employees.[28] So, even eager investors interested in buying shares of a private corporation are unable to do so.

■ Most large firms are **publicly held (or public) corporations**, in which shares are publicly issued. For instance, any investor with sufficient funds can buy shares of stock in Dell Computer, Gap, or Starbucks. These shares are "traded" (that is, bought and sold) through such forums as the New York Stock Exchange, e*Trade, brokerage houses, and similar forums.

■ An **S corporation** (*Subchapter S corporation*) is organized and operates like a corporation but treated like a partnership for tax purposes. S corporations must meet stringent eligibility requirements.

■ With a **limited liability corporation (LLC)**, owners are taxed like partners but also enjoy the benefits of limited liability. LLCs have grown in popularity in recent years, partially because of IRS rulings that allow corporations, partnerships, and foreign investors to be partial owners.

■ **Professional corporations** are most likely composed of doctors, lawyers, accountants, or other

Table 3.2 Types of Corporations

Type	Distinguishing Features	Examples
Closely Held	Stock held by only a few people	Blue Cross/Blue Shield
	Subject to corporate taxation	MasterCard
Publicly Held	Stock widely held among many investors	Dell Computer
	Subject to corporate taxation	Starbucks
		Texas Instruments
Subchapter S	Organized much like a closely held corporation	Minglewood Associates
	Subject to additional regulation	Entech Pest Systems
	Subject to partnership taxation	Frontier Bank
Limited Liability	Organized much like a publicly held corporation	Pacific Northwest Associates
	Subject to additional regulation	Global Ground Support
	Subject to partnership taxation	Ritz-Carlton
Professional	Subject to partnership taxation	Norman Hui, DDS & Associates
	Limited business liability	B & H Engineering
	Unlimited professional liability	Anderson, McCoy & Ortia
Multinational	Spans national boundaries	Toyota
	Subject to regulation in multiple countries	Nestlé
		General Electric

professionals. While the corporate structure protects from unlimited financial liability, members are not immune from unlimited liability. Professional negligence by a member can entail personal liability on the individual's part.

■ In a **multinational (or transnational) corporation**, stock may be traded on the exchanges of several countries, and managers are likely to be of different nationalities. For example, shares of Daimler AG, the German firm that makes Mercedes-Benz products, are traded on stock exchanges throughout Europe as well as in the United States and Japan. Of course, only large and reputable firms can manage to achieve multiple listings of this nature. They must also comply with regulatory requirements of every country where their stock is publicly traded.

Managing a Corporation

A corporation must be managed on the principles of **corporate governance**—the roles of shareholders, directors, and other managers in corporate decision making and accountability. In this section, we discuss the principles of *stock ownership* and *stockholders' rights*, describe the role of *boards of directors*, and examine some special issues related to corporate ownership.

Corporate Governance

Corporate governance is established by a firm's bylaws and usually involves three distinct bodies: **stockholders (or shareholders)**, the *board of directors*, and *officers*.

Stock Ownership and Stockholders' Rights Corporations sell shares, called *stock*, to investors who then become stockholders, or shareholders. Profits are distributed among stockholders in the form of *dividends*, and corporate managers serve at stockholders' discretion.

Boards of Directors The governing body of a corporation is its **board of directors**, which reports to stockholders and other stakeholders and sets policy on dividends, major spending, and executive compensation. Boards of directors are legally responsible and accountable for corporate actions and are increasingly being held personally liable for them. Members of the board of directors are elected by stockholders.

Officers Although board members oversee operations, most do not participate in day-to-day management. Rather, they hire a team of **officers**, usually headed by the firm's **chief executive officer (CEO)**, who is responsible for overall performance. Other

MULTINATIONAL (OR TRANSNATIONAL) CORPORATION form of corporation spanning national boundaries

CORPORATE GOVERNANCE roles of shareholders, directors, and other managers in corporate decision making and accountability

STOCKHOLDER (OR SHAREHOLDER) owner of shares of stock in a corporation

BOARD OF DIRECTORS governing body of a corporation that reports to its shareholders and delegates power to run its day-to-day operations while remaining responsible for sustaining its assets

OFFICERS top management team of a corporation

CHIEF EXECUTIVE OFFICER (CEO) top manager who is responsible for the overall performance of a corporation

STRATEGIC ALLIANCE strategy in which two or more organizations collaborate on a project for mutual gain

JOINT VENTURE strategic alliance in which the collaboration involves joint ownership of the new venture

MERGER union of two corporations to form a new corporation

ACQUISITION purchase of one company by another

DIVESTITURE strategy whereby a firm sells one or more of its business units

SPIN-OFF strategy of setting up one or more corporate units as new, independent corporations

officers typically include a *president*, who is responsible for internal management, and *vice presidents*, who oversee various functional areas such as marketing and operations.

Special Issues in Corporate Ownership

In recent years, several issues have grown in importance in the area of corporate ownership, including *joint ventures* and *strategic alliances*, *mergers* and *acquisitions*, and *divestitures* and *spin-offs*.

Joint Ventures and Strategic Alliances In a **strategic alliance**, two or more organizations collaborate on a project for mutual gain. When partners share ownership of what is essentially a new enterprise, it is called a **joint venture**. The number of strategic alliances has increased rapidly in recent years on both domestic and international fronts. For instance, Walt Disney Company

has an alliance with DreamWorks. Under the terms of the agreement, Disney distributes DreamWorks movies in return for a share of the revenue.

Mergers and Acquisitions (M&As) A **merger** occurs when two firms combine to create a new company. In an **acquisition**, one firm buys another outright. In general, when the two firms are roughly the same size, the combination is usually called a merger even if one firm is taking control of the other. When the acquiring firm is substantially larger than the acquired firm, the deal is really an acquisition. So-called M&As are an important form of corporate strategy for increasing product lines, expanding operations, going international, and creating new enterprises. Delta Air Lines recently acquired Northwest Airlines. Northwest planes are being repainted with Delta's logo, and Northwest employees are becoming Delta employees.

Divestitures and Spin-offs Sometimes a corporation decides to sell a part of its existing business operations or set it up as a new and independent corporation. If a firm sells off an unrelated and/or underperforming businesses to focus more specifically on its core businesses, the sale is called a **divestiture**. When a firm sells part of itself to raise capital or because it deems a business unit more valuable as a separate company, the strategy is known as a **spin-off**. For example, Morgan Stanley spun off its Discover Card

Joint ventures and strategic alliances have become increasingly popular in recent years. For example, these two executives are from General Motors and Toyota. They are shown here breaking ground on a new plant in California that will be managed as a joint venture.

division into a standalone company called Discover Financial Services. For every two shares of Morgan Stanley stock, shareholders received one share of Discover Financial Services. In effect, Morgan Stanley still owns Discover, but both companies are free to pursue separate and (hopefully) more profitable business strategies.[29]

Questions for Review

1. Why are small businesses important to the U.S. economy?

2. Which industries are easiest for start-ups to enter? Which are hardest? Why?

3. Describe the key components of a business plan. Why is it important for a new start-up to create a business plan?

4. What are the primary reasons for new business failure and success?

5. What are the basic forms of noncorporate business ownership? What are the key advantages and disadvantages of each?

6. What are the types of corporations? What are the key advantages and disadvantages of incorporation?

Questions for Analysis

7. Why might a closely held corporation choose to remain private? Why might it choose to be publicly traded?

8. If you were going to open a new business, what type would it be? Why?

9. Would you prefer to buy an existing business or franchise, or start from scratch? Why?

10. Under what circumstances might it be wise for an entrepreneur to reject venture capital? Under what circumstances might it be advisable to take more venture capital than he or she actually needs?

Application Exercises

11. Interview the owner/manager of a sole proprietorship or a general partnership. What characteristics of that business form led the owner to choose it? Does he or she ever contemplate changing the form of the business? If yes, what form would the owner choose, and why would he or she change it?

12. Identify two or three of the fastest-growing businesses in the United States during the last year. What role has entrepreneurship played in the growth of these firms?

The Global Context of Business

After reading this chapter, you should be able to:

1 Discuss the rise of international business and describe the major world marketplaces, trade agreements, and alliances.

2 Explain how differences in import–export balances, exchange rates, and foreign competition determine the ways in which countries and businesses respond to the international environment.

3 Discuss the factors involved in deciding to do business internationally and in selecting the appropriate levels of international involvement and organizational structure.

4 Describe some of the ways in which social, cultural, economic, legal, and political differences among nations affect international business.

A Truly Universal Studio

At first glance, things have not been going well for the U.S. film industry centered in Hollywood, California. Although U.S. theaters sell nearly $10 billion in tickets every year, the total number of tickets sold has been slowly but surely declining. Expensive, would-be blockbusters such as *Evan Almighty* and *Speed Racer* failed to turn a profit, and much-hyped sequels like *Spider-Man 3*, *Shrek the Third*, and *Pirates of the Caribbean: At World's End* all grossed significantly less than their predecessors.

From a broader perspective, however, Hollywood has been very successful in recent years. The take from domestic theaters is only half the story; the other half comes from foreign markets, where moviegoers almost as much as U.S. moviegoers on films distributed by the six major studios (Warner Bros., Disney, Fox, Paramount, Sony, and Universal). Taking worldwide grosses into account, *Spider-Man 3* was the most successful *Spider-Man* film yet. In a similar trend, international sales accounted for over $300 million (81 percent) of *The Golden Compass's* total earnings and over $650 million (68 percent) of total earnings for *Pirates of the Caribbean: At World's End*. Even *Speed Racer*, a domestic disaster that cost over $120 million to make, grossed only $43 million in the United States but earned over $50 million overseas.

The relationship between foreign markets and Hollywood's balance sheet is not a new one. With each new slate of releases, however, studio executives are reminded of the increasing importance of the international audience, which has set box office records in three of the past four years. The need to market a film to the broadest possible audience has even been blamed for what some perceive as a steady decline in the quality of Hollywood films. "What sells best overseas is a simple message, preferably one that is nonverbal and can be communicated with a single dominant image," argues Brooks Barnes of *The New York Times*. Whether this is itself an oversimplification remains debatable, but this much seems clear: the question of "what sells best overseas" will continue to generate lots of discussion in studio boardrooms. This pattern has also continued in 2009. *Wolverine* opened in the U.S. to $87 million but took in about $80 overseas. Other blockbusters such as *Star Trek* and *Angels and Demons*, and *2012* also did very well abroad.[1]

What's in It for Me?

Hollywood is hardly alone in its increasing dependence on the global marketplace. Businesses both large and small, across every industry, must understand how to reap the rewards and avoid the pitfalls of international trade. This chapter explores the various factors that influence a firm's decision to expand overseas, as well as the extent of that expansion. You, in turn, will better understand how global forces affect you as both a customer and an employee, and you will be better equipped to assess how global opportunities and challenges can affect you as a business owner and an investor.

The Contemporary Global Economy

The total volume of world trade is immense—over $9 trillion in merchandise trade each year. As more firms engage in international business, the world economy is fast becoming an interdependent system—a process called **globalization**.

We often take for granted the diversity of products we can buy as a result of international trade. Your television, your shoes, and even your morning coffee or juice are probably **imports**—products made or grown abroad and sold domestically in the United States. At the same time, the success of many U.S. firms depends on **exports**—products made or grown here, such as machinery, electronic equipment, and grains, and shipped for sale abroad. Several forces have combined to spark and sustain globalization. For one thing, governments and businesses are more aware of the benefits of globalization to businesses and shareholders. These benefits include the potential for higher standards of living and improved business profitability. New technologies have made international travel, communication, and commerce faster and cheaper than ever before. Finally, there are competitive pressures: Sometimes, a firm must expand into foreign markets simply to keep up with competitors.

Globalization is not without its detractors. Some critics charge that globalization allows businesses to exploit workers in less developed countries and bypass domestic environmental and tax regulations. For example, as smoking continues to decline in the United States, cigarette maker Philip Morris International (PMI) is aggressively pushing into countries like Russia, Japan, and China, where smoking is much more common. Indeed, China is home to one-third of the world's smokers and in that market PMI is free to advertise on television and employ other promotional strategies that are forbidden in the United States. They also charge that globalization leads to the loss of cultural heritages and often benefits the rich more than the poor. As a result, many international gatherings of global economic leaders are marked by protests and demonstrations.

The Major World Marketplaces

Managers involved with international businesses need to have a solid understanding of the global economy, including the major world marketplaces. This section examines some fundamental economic distinctions between countries based on wealth and then looks at some of the world's major international marketplaces.

Distinctions Based on Wealth The World Bank, an agency of the United Nations, uses per-capita income—average income per person—to make distinctions among countries. Its current classification method consists of four different categories of countries:[2]

1 *High-income countries.* Those with annual per-capita income greater than $11,115.

2 *Upper-middle-income countries.* Those with annual per-capita income of $11,115 or less but more than $3,595.

3 *Lower-middle-income countries.* Those with annual per-capita income of $3,595 or lower but more than $905.

4 *Low-income countries (often called developing countries).* Those with annual per-capita income of $905 or less.

Advocates of globalization argue that increased international commerce benefits all sectors of society and should be actively encouraged. But critics like these protestors argue that globalization benefits only big business and is eroding distinctive national cultures.

Geographic Clusters The world economy revolves around three major marketplaces: North America, Europe, and Pacific Asia. In general, these clusters include relatively more of the upper-middle and high-income nations but relatively few low- and lower-middle-income countries.

North America As the world's largest marketplace and most stable economy, the United States dominates the North American market. Canada also plays a major role in the international economy, and the United States and Canada are each other's largest trading partners.

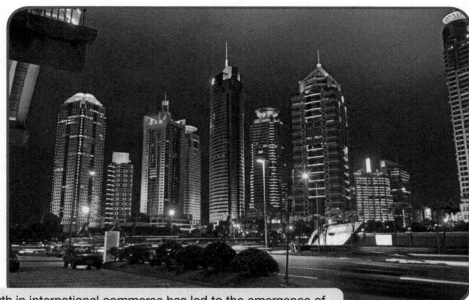

Mexico has become a major manufacturing center, especially along the U.S. border, where cheap labor and low transportation costs have encouraged many firms from the United States and other countries to build factories. However, Mexico's role as a low-cost manufacturing center may have peaked. The emergence of China as a low-cost manufacturing center may lead companies to begin to shift their production from Mexico to China.[3]

The growth in international commerce has led to the emergence of several major marketplaces. Much of the international commerce in these marketplaces, in turn, is generally managed from major cities. Traditional centers of international commerce include New York, London, Paris, Brussels, and Tokyo. In recent years, though, cities like Shanghai, Beijing, Hong Kong, Dubai, Vancouver, Bangalore, and Kuala Lumpur have taken on increased importance. For example, international business now defines the glittering skyline of Shanghai.

Europe Europe is often regarded as two regions—Western and Eastern. Western Europe, dominated by Germany, the United Kingdom, and France, has long been a mature but fragmented marketplace. The transformation of this region via the European Union (discussed later) into an integrated economic system has further increased its importance. E-commerce and technology have also become increasingly important in this region. There has been a surge in Internet start-ups in southeastern England, the Netherlands, and the Scandinavian countries; Ireland is now one of the world's largest exporters of software; Strasbourg, France, is a major center for biotech start-ups; Barcelona, Spain, has many flourishing software and Internet companies; and the Frankfurt region of Germany is dotted with software and biotech start-ups.

Eastern Europe, once primarily communist, has also gained in importance, both as a marketplace and as a producer. Such multinational corporations as Daewoo, Nestlé, General Motors, and ABB Asea Brown Boveri have all set up operations in Poland. Ford, General Motors, Suzuki, and Volkswagen have all built new factories in Hungary. On the other hand, governmental instability has hampered development in parts of Russia, Bulgaria, Albania, Romania, and other countries.

Pacific Asia Pacific Asia is generally agreed to consist of Japan, China, Thailand, Malaysia, Singapore, Indonesia, South Korea, Taiwan, the Philippines, and Australia. Fueled by strong entries in the automobile, electronics, and banking industries, the economies of these countries grew rapidly in the 1970s and 1980s. After a currency crisis in the late 1990s that slowed growth in virtually every country of the region, Pacific Asia was showing clear signs of revitalization until the global recession in 2009. Once the global economy regains its momentum, Pacific Asia is expected to again be on the forefront. This is especially true of Japan, which—led by firms such as Toyota, Toshiba, and Nippon Steel—dominates the region. South Korea (home to firms Samsung and Hyundai, among others), Taiwan (owner of Chinese Petroleum and the manufacturing home of many foreign firms), and Hong Kong (a major financial center) are also successful players in the international economy.

China, the world's most densely populated country, has emerged as an important market and now boasts the world's third-largest economy, behind only the European Union and the United States.[4] Although its per-capita income remains low, the sheer number of potential consumers makes it an important market. India, though not part of Pacific Asia, is also rapidly emerging as one of the globe's most important economies.

NORTH AMERICAN FREE TRADE AGREEMENT (NAFTA) agreement to gradually eliminate tariffs and other trade barriers among the United States, Canada, and Mexico

EUROPEAN UNION (EU) organization for economic, social, and security cooperation among European nations

ASSOCIATION OF SOUTHEAST ASIAN NATIONS (ASEAN) organization for economic, political, social, and cultural cooperation among Southeast Asian nations

GENERAL AGREEMENT ON TARIFFS AND TRADE (GATT) international trade agreement to encourage the multilateral reduction or elimination of trade barriers

WORLD TRADE ORGANIZATION (WTO) organization through which member nations negotiate trading agreements and resolve disputes about trade policies and practices

As in North America and Europe, technology promises to play an increasingly important role in the future of this region. In some parts of Asia, however, poorly developed electronic infrastructures, slower adoption of computers and information technology, and a higher percentage of lower-income consumers hamper the emergence of technology firms.

Trade Agreements and Alliances

Various legal agreements have sparked international trade and shaped the global business environment. Indeed, virtually every nation has formal trade treaties with other nations. A *treaty* is a legal agreement that specifies areas in which nations will cooperate with one another. Among the most significant treaties is the *North American Free Trade Agreement*. The *European Union*, the *Association of Southeast Asian Nations*, and the *World Trade Organization*, all governed by treaties, are also instrumental in promoting international business activity.

North American Free Trade Agreement The **North American Free Trade Agreement (NAFTA)** removes most tariffs and other trade barriers among the United States, Canada, and Mexico and includes agreements on environmental issues and labor abuses.

Most observers agree that NAFTA is achieving its basic purpose—to create a more active North American market. It has created several hundred thousand new jobs, although this number is smaller than NAFTA proponents had hoped. One thing is clear, though—the flood of U.S. jobs lost to Mexico predicted by NAFTA critics, especially labor unions, has not occurred.

The European Union The **European Union (EU)** includes most European nations, as shown in Figure 4.1. These nations have eliminated most quotas and set uniform tariff levels on

products imported and exported within their group. In 1992, virtually all internal trade barriers went down, making the EU the largest free marketplace in the world. The adoption of a common currency—the euro—by most member nations further solidified the EU's position in the world economy.

The Association of Southeast Asian Nations (ASEAN) The **Association of Southeast Asian Nations (ASEAN)** was founded in 1967 as an organization for economic, political, social, and cultural cooperation. In 1995, Vietnam became the group's first Communist member. Figure 4.2 shows a map of the ASEAN countries. Because of its relative size, ASEAN does not have the same global economic significance as NAFTA and the EU.

The World Trade Organization The **General Agreement on Tariffs and Trade (GATT)** was signed in 1947. Its purpose was to reduce or eliminate trade barriers, such as tariffs and quotas. It did so by encouraging nations to protect domestic industries within agreed-upon limits and to engage in multilateral negotiations. The GATT proved to be relatively successful. So, to further promote globalization, most of the world's countries joined to create the **World Trade Organization (WTO)**,

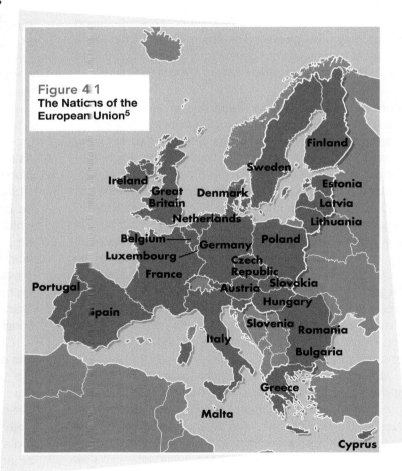

Figure 4.1
The Nations of the European Union[5]

Figure 4.2
The Nations of the Association of Southeast Asian Nations (ASEAN)[7]

value of all the products that it imports. A *positive balance of trade* results when a country exports (sells to other countries) more than it imports (buys from other countries). A *negative balance of trade* results when a country imports more than it exports.

Relatively small trade imbalances are common and are unimportant. Large imbalances, however, are another matter. The biggest concern about trade balances involves the flow of currency. When U.S. consumers and businesses buy foreign products, dollars flow from the United States to other countries; when U.S. businesses are selling to foreign consumers and businesses, dollars flow back into the United States. A large negative balance of trade means that many dollars are controlled by interests outside the United States.

Trade Deficits and Surpluses When a country's imports exceed its exports—that is, when it has a

which began on January 1, 1995. (The GATT is the actual treaty that governs the WTO). The 152 member countries are required to open markets to international trade, and the WTO is empowered to pursue three goals:[6]

1 Promote trade by encouraging members to adopt fair trade practices.

2 Reduce trade barriers by promoting multilateral negotiations.

3 Establish fair procedures for resolving disputes among members.

Import–Export Balances

Although international trade has many advantages, it can also pose problems if a country's imports and exports don't maintain an acceptable balance. Table 4.1 lists the major trading partners of the United States. The top part of the table shows the 10 largest markets for exported goods from the United States, while the bottom part of the table shows the 10 largest markets that import goods into the United States. Note that 9 of the 10 countries on both lists are the same.

In deciding whether an overall balance exists, economists use two measures: *balance of trade* and *balance of payments*.

Balance of Trade A country's **balance of trade** is the total economic value of all the products that it exports minus the economic

Table 4.1 **The Major Trading Partners of the United States[8]**

Top 10 U.S. Export Markets for Goods (2008)		
Rank	**Country**	**2008 Exports (in $ billions)**
1	Canada	261.4
2	Mexico	151.5
3	China	71.5
4	Japan	66.6
5	Federal Republic of Germany	54.7
6	United Kingdom	53.8
7	Netherlands	40.2
8	South Korea	34.8
9	Brazil	32.9
10	France	29.2
Top 10 U.S. Import Suppliers for Goods (2008)		
Rank	**Country**	**2008 Imports (in $ billions)**
1	China	337.8
2	Canada	335.6
3	Mexico	215.9
4	Japan	139.2
5	Federal Republic of Germany	97.6
6	United Kingdom	58.6
7	Saudi Arabia	54.8
8	Venezuela	51.4
9	South Korea	48.1
10	France	44

TRADE DEFICIT situation in which a country's imports exceed its exports, creating a negative balance of trade

TRADE SURPLUS situation in which a country's exports exceed its imports, creating a positive balance of trade

BALANCE OF PAYMENTS flow of all money into or out of a country

negative balance of trade—it suffers a **trade deficit**. When exports exceed imports, the nation enjoys a **trade surplus**. Several factors, such as general economic conditions and the effect of trade agreements, influence trade deficits and surpluses. For example, higher domestic costs, greater international competition, and con-

tinuing economic problems among some of its regional trading partners have slowed the tremendous growth in exports that Japan once enjoyed. But rising prosperity in China and India has led to strong increases in both exports from and imports to those countries.

Figures 4.3 and 4.4 highlight two series of events: (1) recent trends in U.S. exports and imports and (2) the resulting trade deficit. As Figure 4.3 shows, both U.S. imports and U.S. exports have, with minor variations, increased over the past eight years—a trend that's projected to continue.

Trade deficits between 2000 and 2007 are shown in Figure 4.4. There was a deficit in each of these eight years because more money flowed out to pay for foreign imports than flowed in to pay for U.S. exports. For example, in 2008, the United States exported $1,300.50 billion in goods and services and imported $2,100.4 billion in goods and services. Because imports exceeded exports, the United States

had a *trade deficit* of $800 billion (the difference between exports and imports). Note also that both experts and imports declined in 2008 from the previous year. This was due to the global economic slowdown.

Balance of Payments   The **balance of payments** refers to the flow of *money* into or out of a country. The money that a country pays for imports and receives for exports—its balance of trade—accounts for much of its balance of payments. Other financial exchanges are also factors. Money spent by tourists in a country, money spent by a country on foreign-aid programs, and money exchanged

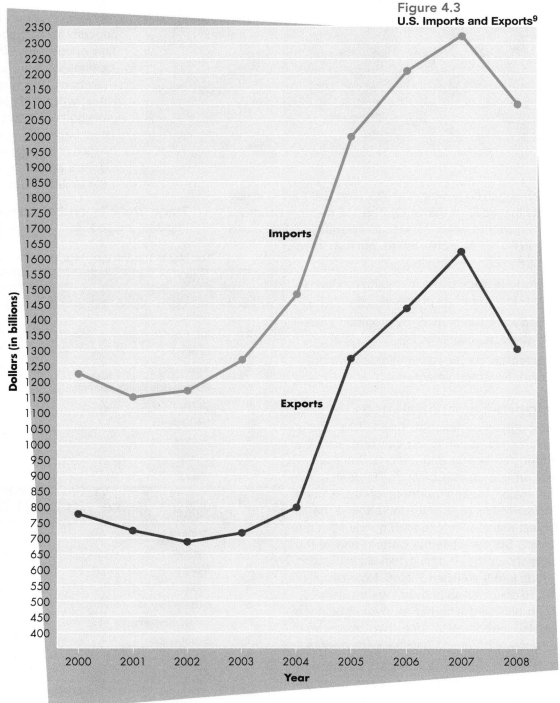

Figure 4.3
U.S. Imports and Exports[9]

by buying and selling currency on international money markets affect the balance of payments.

For instance, suppose that the United States has a negative balance of trade of $1 million. Now, suppose that this year, U.S. citizens travel abroad as tourists and spend a total of $200,000 in other countries. This amount gets added to the balance of trade to form the balance of payments, which is now a negative $1.2 million dollars. Now, further suppose that tourists from other countries come to the United States and spend the equivalent of $300,000 while they are here. This has the effect of reducing the negative balance of payments to $900,000. Then, further suppose that the United States then sends $600,000 in aid to help the victims of a tsunami-ravaged country in Asia. Because this represents additional dollars leaving the United States, the balance of payments is now a negative $1.5 million.

For many years, the United States enjoyed a positive balance of payments. Recently, however, the overall balance has become negative.

Exchange Rates

The balance of imports and exports between two countries is affected by the rate of exchange between their currencies. An **exchange rate** is the rate at which the currency of one nation can be exchanged for that of another. Suppose, for example, that the exchange rate between the U.S. dollar and the British pound was $2 to £1. This means that it costs £1 to "buy" $2 or $1 to "buy" £0.5. Stated differently, £1 and $2 have the same purchasing power, or £1 = $2.

At the end of World War II, the major nations of the world agreed to set *fixed exchange rates*. The value of any country's currency relative to that of another would remain constant. The goal was to allow the global economy to stabilize. Today, however, *floating exchange rates* are the norm, and the value of one country's currency relative to that of another varies with market conditions. For example, when many British citizens want to spend pounds to buy U.S. dollars (or goods), the value of the dollar relative to the pound increases. Demand for the dollar is high, and a currency is strong when demand for it is high. It's also strong when there's high demand for the goods manufactured with that currency. On a daily basis, exchange rates

fluctuate very little. Significant variations usually occur over longer time spans. Highly regulated economic systems like China are among the few that still use fixed exchange rates. The Chinese government regulates the flow of currency—its own as well as all others—into and out of China and determines the precise rate of exchange within its borders.

Exchange-rate fluctuation can have an important impact on balance of trade. Suppose you want to buy some English tea for £10 per box. At an exchange rate of $2 to £1, a box will cost you $20 (£10 × 2 = 20). But what if the pound is weaker? At an exchange rate of, say, $1.25 to £1, the same box would cost you only $12.50 (£10 × 1.25 = 12.50). If the dollar is strong in relation to the pound, the prices of all United States-made products will rise in England, and the prices of all English-made products will fall in the United States. The English would buy fewer U.S. products, and Americans would be prompted to spend more on English-made products. The result would probably be a U.S. trade deficit with England.

EXCHANGE RATE rate at which the currency of one nation can be exchanged for the currency of another nation

Figure 4.4
U.S. Trade Deficit[10]

One of the most significant developments in foreign exchange has been the introduction of the **euro**—the common currency of the European Union. The euro was officially introduced in 2002 and has replaced other currencies, such as the German Deutsche Mark and the French franc. The EU anticipates that the euro will become as important as the dollar and the yen in international commerce. When the euro was first introduced, its value was pegged as being equivalent to the dollar: €1 = $1. But because the dollar has been relatively weak in recent years, its value has eroded relative to that of the euro. In June 2009, for example, $1 was worth only about €0.71.

Companies with international operations must watch exchange-rate fluctuations closely because changes affect overseas demand for their products and can be a major factor in competition. In general, when the value of a country's currency rises—becomes stronger—companies based there find it harder to export products to foreign markets and easier for foreign companies to enter local markets. It also makes it more cost-efficient for domestic companies to move operations to lower-cost foreign sites. When the value of a currency declines—becomes weaker—the opposite occurs. As the value of a country's currency falls, its balance of trade usually improves because domestic companies should experience a boost in exports. There should also be less reason for foreign companies to ship products into the domestic market and less reason to establish operations in other countries.

Forms of Competitive Advantage

Before we discuss the fundamental issues involved in international business management, we must consider one last factor: forms of *competitive advantage*. Because no country can produce everything that it needs, countries tend to export what they can produce better or less expensively than other countries and use the proceeds to import what they can't produce as effectively. This principle doesn't fully explain why nations export and import what they do. Such decisions hinge partly on the advantages that a particular country enjoys regarding its abilities to create and/or sell certain products and resources.[11] Economists traditionally focused on absolute and comparative advantage to explain international trade. But because this approach focuses narrowly on such factors as natural resources and labor costs, a more contemporary view of national competitive advantage has emerged.

Absolute Advantage An **absolute advantage** exists when a country can produce something that is cheaper

---

Entrepreneurship and New Ventures

Rolling in the Worldwide Dough

Is any business more confined to a local market than a bakery? Breads and pastries get stale quickly, and even the largest operations, such as those that make buns for McDonald's, only move products over short distances. But a bakery in Paris has refused to accept geographic limitations and is now selling its famous bread in global markets.

When Lionel Poilâne took over the family business more than 30 years ago, he was determined to return breadmaking to its roots. Poilâne built clay ovens based on sixteenth-century plans and technology, trained his breadmakers in ancient techniques, and began selling old-style dark bread with a thick, chewy, fire-tinged flavor. It quickly became a favorite in Parisian bistros, and demand soared.

To help meet demand, Poilâne built two more bakeries in Paris; today they sell over 15,000 loaves of bread a day. Poilâne also opened a bakery in London, but his efforts to expand to Japan were stymied: Local ordinances prohibited wood-burning ovens, and Poilâne refused to compromise. During the negotiation process, however, he realized that he didn't really *want* to build new bakeries all over the world.

Instead, he turned to modern technology to expand his old-fashioned business. The key was the big FedEx hub at Paris Roissy Charles de Gaulle Airport near Poilâne's largest Paris bakery. After launching a Web site, Poilâne started taking international orders. New orders are packaged as the bread cools and then picked up by FedEx. A quick warm-up in the customer's oven gives it the same taste as it had when it came out of Poilâne's oven. Today, a loaf of bread baked in Paris in the morning can easily be reheated for tomorrow night's dinner in more than 25 countries.[12]

and/or of higher quality than any other country. Saudi oil, Brazilian coffee beans, and Canadian timber come close (because these countries have such abundant supplies of these resources), but examples of true absolute advantage are rare. For example, many experts say that the vineyards of France produce the world's finest wines. But the burgeoning wine business in California demonstrates that producers there can also make very good wine—wines that rival those from France but come in more varieties and at lower prices.

Comparative Advantage   A country has a **comparative advantage** in goods that it can produce more efficiently or better than other nations. If businesses in a given country can make computers more efficiently than they can make automobiles, then that nation has a comparative advantage in computer manufacturing.

In general, both absolute and comparative advantages translate into competitive advantage. Brazil, for instance, can produce and market coffee beans knowing full well that there are few other countries with the right mix of climate, terrain, and altitude to enter the coffee bean market. The United States has comparative advantages in the computer industry (because of technological sophistication) and in farming (because of large amounts of fertile land and a temperate climate). South Korea has a comparative advantage in electronics manufacturing because of efficient operations and cheap labor. As a result, U.S. firms export computers and grain to South Korea and import DVD players from South Korea. South Korea can produce food, and the United States can build DVD players, but each nation imports certain products because the other holds a comparative advantage in the relevant industry.

National Competitive Advantage   In recent years, a theory of national competitive advantage has become a widely accepted model of why nations engage in international trade.[13] **National competitive advantage** derives from four conditions:

1. *Factor conditions* are the factors of production we discussed in Chapter 1—*labor*, *capital*, *entrepreneurs*, *physical resources*, and *information resources*.

2. *Demand conditions* reflect a large domestic consumer base that promotes strong demand for innovative products.

3. *Related and supporting industries* include strong local or regional suppliers and/or industrial customers.

4. *Strategies*, *structures*, and *rivalries* refer to firms and industries that stress cost reduction, product quality, higher productivity, and innovative products.

When all attributes of national competitive advantage exist, a nation is likely to be heavily involved in international business. Japan, for instance, has an abundance of natural resources and strong domestic demand for automobiles. Its carmakers have well-oiled supplier networks, and domestic firms have competed intensely with one another for decades. These circumstances explain why Japanese car companies like Toyota and Honda are successful in foreign markets.

COMPARATIVE ADVANTAGE ability to produce some products more efficiently than others

NATIONAL COMPETITIVE ADVANTAGE international competitive advantage stemming from a combination of factor conditions, demand conditions, related and supporting industries, and firm strategies, structures, and rivalries

International Business Management

Regardless of where a firm is located, its success depends largely on how well it's managed. International business is so challenging because basic management tasks—planning, organizing, directing, and controlling—are much more difficult when a firm operates in markets scattered around the globe.

Managing means making decisions. In this section, we examine the three basic decisions that a company must make when considering globalization. The first decision is whether to go international at all. Once that decision has been made, managers must decide on the level of international involvement and on the organizational structure that will best meet the firm's global needs.

Going International

As the world economy becomes globalized, more firms are conducting international operations. U.S. firms are aggressively expanding abroad, while foreign companies such as BP and Nestlé continue to expand into foreign markets as well, including the U.S. market. This route, however, isn't appropriate for every company. If you buy and sell fresh fish, you'll find it more profitable to confine your activities to limited geographic areas because storage and transport costs may be too high to make international operations worthwhile. As Figure 4.5 shows, several factors affect the decision to go international.

Gauging International Demand   In considering international expansion, a company must consider whether there is a demand for its products abroad. Products that are successful in one country may be useless in another. Even when there is demand, advertising may still need to be adjusted. For example, bicycles are largely used for recreation in the United States but are seen as basic transportation in China. Hence, a bicycle maker would need to have different advertising strategies in each of these two countries. Market research and/or the prior market entry of competitors may indicate whether there's an international demand for a firm's products.

OUTSOURCING practice of paying suppliers and distributors to perform certain business processes or to provide needed materials or services

OFFSHORING practice of outsourcing to foreign countries

EXPORTER firm that distributes and sells products to one or more foreign countries

IMPORTER firm that buys products in foreign markets and then imports them for resale in its home country

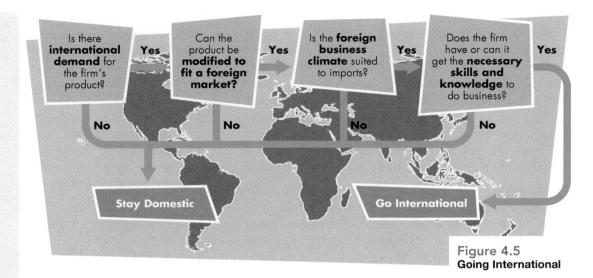

Is there **international demand** for the firm's product? → Yes → Can the product be **modified to fit a foreign market?** → Yes → Is the **foreign business climate** suited to imports? → Yes → Does the firm have or can it get the **necessary skills and knowledge** to do business? → Yes

No / No / No / No

Stay Domestic

Go International

Figure 4.5
Going International

Adapting to Customer Needs If its product is in demand, a firm must decide whether and how to adapt it to meet the special demands of foreign customers. For example, to satisfy local tastes, McDonald's sells wine in France, beer in Germany, and provides some vegetarian sandwiches in India. Likewise, consumer electronics companies have to be aware that different countries use different kinds of electric sockets and different levels of electric power. Therefore, regardless of demand, customer needs must still be considered.

Outsourcing and Offshoring Outsourcing—the practice of paying suppliers and distributors to perform certain business processes or to provide needed materials or services—has become a very popular option for going international. It has become so popular because (1) it helps firms focus on their core activities and avoid getting sidetracked on secondary activities, and (2) it reduces costs by locating certain business functions in areas where relevant costs are low.[14]

The practice of outsourcing to foreign countries is more specifically referred to as **offshoring**. Many companies today contract their manufacturing to low-cost factories in Asia. Similarly, many service call centers today are outsourced to businesses located in India. The 2008 Oscar winner *Slumdog Millionaire* featured a young Indian man who worked for an international call center in Mumbai.

Levels of International Involvement

After deciding to go international, a firm must determine the level of its involvement. Several levels are possible: A firm may act as an exporter

or importer, organize as an international firm, or (like most of the world's largest industrial firms) operate as a multinational firm.

Exporters and Importers An **exporter** makes products in one country to distribute and sell in others. An **importer** buys products in foreign markets and brings them home for resale. Both conduct most of their business in their home nations. Both entail the lowest level of involvement in international operations, and both are good ways to learn the fine points of global business.

While Toyota markets five different sport-utility vehicles in the United States, it sells only its two smallest ones at home in Japan, where crowded roads, narrow driveways, and scarce parking spaces make larger vehicles impractical.

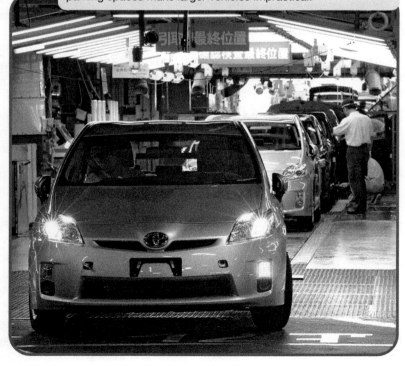

Table 4.2 The World's Largest Multinationals[17]

Rank	Company	Revenues ($ Millions)	Profits ($ Millions)
1	Royal Dutch Shell	458,361	26,277
2	ExxonMobil	442,851	45,220
3	Walmart Stores	405,607	13,400
4	BP	367,053	21,157
5	Chevron	263,159	23,931
6	Total	234,674.10	15,500.40
7	ConocoPhillips	230,764	−16,998
8	ING Group	226,577	−1,067
9	Sinopec	207,814.50	1,961.20
10	Toyota Motor	204,352.30	−4,349.30

INTERNATIONAL FIRM firm that conducts a significant portion of its business in foreign countries

MULTINATIONAL FIRM firm that designs, produces, and markets products in many nations

INDEPENDENT AGENT foreign individual or organization that agrees to represent an exporter's interests

Many large firms entered international business as exporters. IBM and Coke, among others, exported to Europe for several years before setting up production sites there.

International Firms As exporters and importers gain experience and grow, many move to the next level of involvement. **International firms** conduct a good deal of their business abroad and may even maintain overseas manufacturing facilities. An international firm may be large, but it's still basically a domestic company with international operations. Hershey, for instance, buys ingredients for its chocolates from several foreign suppliers, but makes all of its products in the United States. Moreover, while it sells its products in approximately 50 other countries, it generates most of its revenues from its domestic market.[15]

Multinational Firms Most **multinational firms**—firms that design, produce, and market products in many nations—such as ExxonMobil, Nestlé, IBM, and Ford, don't think of themselves as having domestic and international divisions. Headquarters locations are almost irrelevant, and planning and decision making are geared to international markets. The world's 10 largest multinationals in 2008 are shown in Table 4.2.

We can't underestimate the economic impact of multinational firms. Consider just the impact of the 500 largest multinationals: In 2008, these 500 firms generated $10.9 trillion in revenues and $615.4 billion in owner profits. They employed tens of millions of people, bought materials and equipment from literally thousands of other firms, and paid billions in taxes.[16] Moreover, their products affected the lives of hundreds of millions of consumers, competitors, investors, and even protestors.

International Organization Structures

Different levels of international involvement entail different kinds of organizational structure. A structure that would help coordinate an exporter's activities would be inadequate for those of a multinational. In this section, we consider the spectrum of organizational strategies, including *independent agents*, *licensing arrangements*, *branch offices*, *strategic alliances*, and *foreign direct investment*.

Independent Agents An **independent agent** is a foreign individual or organization that represents an exporter in foreign markets. Independent agents often act as sales representatives: They sell the exporter's products, collect payment, and make sure that customers are satisfied. They often represent several firms at once and usually

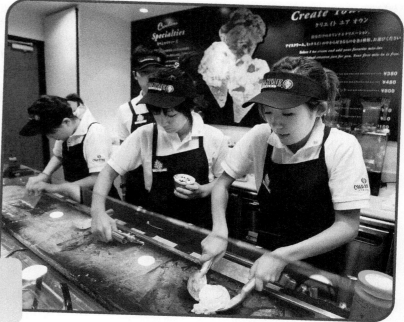

Since Cold Stone Creamery first went international in 2001, the Arizona-based ice cream seller has awarded franchises to firms in 20 countries, including Mexico, China, and Japan.[18]

don't specialize in a particular product or market. Peter So operates an import–export office in Hong Kong. He and his staff of three handle imports from about 15 foreign companies into Hong Kong and about 10 Hong Kong firms that export products abroad.

Licensing Arrangements Companies seeking more involvement may opt for **licensing arrangements**. Firms give foreign individuals or companies exclusive rights (called *licensing agreements*) to manufacture or market their products in that market. In return, the exporter receives a fee plus ongoing payments (royalties) that are calculated as a percentage of the license holder's sales. Franchising is an increasingly popular form of licensing. For example, McDonald's and Pizza Hut franchise around the world.

Branch Offices Instead of developing relationships with foreign agents or licensing companies, a firm may send its own managers to overseas **branch offices**, where the firm has more direct control than it does over agents or license holders. Branch offices also furnish a more visible public presence in foreign countries, and foreign customers tend to feel more secure when there's a local branch office. Halliburton, a Houston-based oil field supply and services company, recently opened a branch office in Dubai in order to more effectively establish relationships with customers in the Middle East.

Strategic Alliances In a **strategic alliance**, a company finds a partner in the country in which it wants to do business. Each party agrees to invest resources and capital into a new business or to cooperate in some

Managing in Turbulent Times

The Ups and Downs of Globalization

International business has been around for thousands of years. For example, as far back as 2000 B.C., tribes in northern Africa took dates and clothing to Babylonia and Assyria in the Middle East and traded them for spices and olive oil. By 500 B.C., Chinese merchants were actively exporting silk and jade to India and Europe, and trade routes were being established between many countries in Europe, Asia, and Africa.

But even as recently as 100 years ago, international trade was only a small part of the global economy. The effects of any given country's economy had a minimal effect on the rest of the world. Indeed, it wasn't until the Great Depression that swept the world in 1929 that experts realized how interdependent the global economy had become.

Globalization—the process through which the world's economy is becoming one interdependent system—brings with it both advantages and disadvantages. On the plus side, globalization has increased the standard of living of billions of people and has helped to create enormous wealth in many different parts of the globe. On the other hand, there are many people who have not shared in the benefits of globalization, and some critics believe that globalization has both hurt less developed countries and destroyed or damaged the unique cultures that exist in different parts of the world.

Globalization has also led to such a high degree of interdependence that no major country's economy is immune from what happens in the rest of the world. The recession of 2008–2009 demonstrated this fact once again: As the economy of the United States ground to a halt, so did the economies of virtually all major European and Asian countries as well. Global stock trading, real-time information available on the Internet, and worldwide financial networks combined to bring to a grinding halt just about every major business in the world.

Managers seeking to reverse the tide and get their businesses going again had to juggle more factors than ever before. Domestic forces such as consumer demand, interest rates, and production costs all had to be considered. But so too did international business conditions. And many businesses—Circuit City and Chrysler, for example—struggled mightily, and some failed. But those with managers and leaders who really understood the global economy did in fact regain their footing. And as global economic conditions improve, so too does the outlook for these businesses.

mutually beneficial way. This new business—the alliance—is owned by the partners, who divide its profits. Such alliances are sometimes called *joint ventures*, but the term *strategic alliance* has arisen because such partnerships are playing increasingly important roles in the strategies of major companies. In many countries, such as Mexico, India, and China, laws make alliances virtually the only way to do international business. Mexico, for example, requires that all foreign firms investing there have local partners.

In addition to easing the way into new markets, alliances give firms greater control over foreign activities than agents and licensees. Alliances also allow firms to benefit from the knowledge and expertise of foreign partners. Microsoft, for example, relies heavily on alliances as it expands into international markets. This approach has helped the firm learn the intricacies of doing business in China and India, two of the hardest emerging markets to crack.

Foreign Direct Investment **Foreign direct investment (FDI)** involves buying or establishing tangible assets in another country. Dell Computer, for example, has built assembly plants in Europe and China. Volkswagen has built a factory in Brazil. Each of these activities represents FDI by a firm in another country. Ford's purchase of Volvo, a Swedish company, is another kind of FDI, as is the acquisition of both Ben & Jerry's and SlimFast by the Dutch company Unilever.

Barriers to International Trade

Whether a business is truly multinational or sells to only a few foreign markets, several factors will affect its international operations. Success in foreign markets will depend largely on the ways it responds to *social*, *economic*, *legal*, and *political barriers* to international trade.

Social and Cultural Differences

Any firm planning to conduct business abroad must understand the social and cultural differences between host country and home country. Some differences are obvious. You must, for example, consider language factors when adjusting packaging, signs, and logos. Pepsi is the same product in Seattle and Moscow—except for the lettering on the bottle.

A wide range of subtle value differences can also affect operations. For example, many Europeans shop daily for groceries. To U.S. consumers accustomed to weekly supermarket trips, the European pattern may seem like a waste of time. For many Europeans, however, shopping is not just a matter of buying food; it's also an outlet for meeting friends and exchanging political views. Consider the implications of this difference for U.S. firms selling food and food-related products in European countries where gigantic American supermarkets are not the norm.

Economic Differences

Although cultural differences are often subtle, economic differences can be fairly pronounced. As we discussed in Chapter 1, in dealing with mixed market economies like those of France and Sweden, firms must know when—and to what extent—the government is involved in a given industry. The French government, for instance, is heavily involved in all aspects of airplane design and manufacturing. The impact of economic differences can be even greater in planned economies like those of China and Vietnam, where the government owns and operates many factors of production.

Legal and Political Differences

Governments can affect international business in many ways. They can set conditions for doing business within their borders and even prohibit doing business altogether. They can control the flow of capital and use tax legislation to discourage or encourage activity in a given industry. They can even confiscate the property of foreign-owned companies. In this section, we discuss some of the more common legal and political issues in international business: *quotas*, *tariffs*, and *subsidies*; *local content laws*; and *business practice laws*.

Quotas, Tariffs, and Subsidies Even free market economies, such as the United States, have some quotas and/or tariffs, both of which affect prices and quantities of foreign-made products. A **quota** restricts the number of products of a certain type that can be imported and, by reducing supply, raises the prices of those imports. Better terms are often given to friendly trading partners, and quotas are typically adjusted to protect domestic producers. For example, Honda can import 425,000 automobiles into the United States each year. (One reason companies like Honda have built manufacturing plants in the United States is that cars produced inside the United States don't count against the import quota.)

The ultimate quota is an **embargo**, a government order forbidding exportation and/or importation of a particular product—or even all products—from a specific country. Many nations control bacteria and disease by banning certain agricultural products. Because the United

FOREIGN DIRECT INVESTMENT (FDI) arrangement in which a firm buys or establishes tangible assets in another country

QUOTA restriction on the number of products of a certain type that can be imported into a country

EMBARGO government order banning exportation and/or importation of a particular product or all products from a particular country

TARIFF tax levied on imported products

SUBSIDY government payment to help a domestic business compete with foreign firms

PROTECTIONISM practice of protecting domestic business against foreign competition

LOCAL CONTENT LAW law requiring that products sold in a particular country be at least partly made there

BUSINESS PRACTICE LAW law or regulation governing business practices in given countries

CARTEL association of producers whose purpose is to control supply and prices

States has an embargo against Cuba, U.S. firms can't invest in their Cuban counterparts, and Cuban products can't legally be sold on U.S. markets. (The Obama administration has hinted at the possibility of removing or reducing this embargo but to date no real action has been taken.)

Tariffs are taxes on imported products. They raise the prices of imports by making consumers pay not only for the products but also for tariff fees. Tariffs take two forms. *Revenue tariffs* are imposed to raise money for governments, but most tariffs, called *protectionist tariffs*, are meant to discourage particular imports. French perfume makers pay a tariff on all products shipped into the United States for sale. Likewise, U.S. firms that export wine to Europe pay a tariff on each case shipped.

Quotas and tariffs are imposed for numerous reasons. The U.S. government aids domestic automakers by restricting the number of Japanese cars imported into this country. Because of national security concerns, we limit the export of technology (for example, computer and nuclear technology to China). The United States isn't the only country that uses tariffs and quotas. To protect domestic firms, Italy imposes high tariffs on electronic goods. As a result, CD players there are prohibitively expensive.

A **subsidy** is a government payment to help a domestic business compete with foreign firms. They're actually indirect tariffs that lower the prices of domestic goods rather than raise the prices of foreign goods. For example, many European governments subsidize farmers to help them compete against U.S. grain imports.

The Protectionism Debate In the United States, **protectionism**—the practice of protecting domestic business at the expense of free market competition—is controversial. Supporters argue that tariffs and quotas protect domestic firms and jobs as well as shelter new industries until they're able to compete internationally. They contend that we need such measures to counter steps taken by other nations. Other advocates justify protectionism in the name of national security. A nation, they argue, must be able to produce efficiently the goods needed for survival in case of war. Thus, the U.S. government requires the Air Force to buy planes only from U.S. manufacturers. As the global economy began to slide into recession in 2008,

there was widespread talk in numerous countries about the need to protect local businesses.

Critics cite protectionism as a source of friction between nations. They also charge that it drives up prices by reducing competition. They maintain that although jobs in some industries would be lost as a result of free trade, jobs in other industries (for example, electronics and automobiles) would be created if all nations abandoned protectionist tactics. Even though there was much discussion of protectionism during the 2008–2009 recession, few steps were actually taken to increase trade barriers.

Protectionism sometimes takes on almost comic proportions. Neither Europe nor the United States grows bananas, but both European and U.S. firms buy and sell bananas in foreign markets. Problems arose when the EU put a quota on bananas imported from Latin America—a market dominated by two U.S. firms, Chiquita and Dole—in order to help firms based in current and former European colonies in the Caribbean. To retaliate, the United States imposed a 100 percent tariff on certain luxury products imported from Europe, including Louis Vuitton handbags, Scottish cashmere sweaters, and Parma ham.

Local Content Laws Many countries, including the United States, have **local content laws**—requirements that products sold in a country be at least partly made there. Firms seeking to do business in a country must either invest there directly or take on a domestic partner. In this way, some of the profits from doing business in a foreign country stay there rather than flow to another nation.

Business Practice Laws Many businesses entering new markets encounter problems in complying with stringent regulations and bureaucratic obstacles. Such practices are affected by the **business practice laws** by which host countries govern business practices within their jurisdictions. For example, German law required Walmart to buy existing retailers rather than open brandnew stores and to stop refunding price differences on items sold for less by other stores. Of course, cooperating with foreign regulations does not guarantee global success—in 2006 Wal-Mart acknowledged that its German stores were losing too much money to remain competitive and pulled out of Germany completely.[19]

Cartels and Dumping Sometimes, a legal—even an accepted—practice in one country is illegal in another. In some South American countries, for example, it is legal to bribe business and government officials. The existence of **cartels**—associations of producers that control supply and prices—gives tremendous power to some nations, such as those belonging to the Organization of Petroleum Exporting Countries (OPEC). U.S. law forbids both bribery and cartels.

Finally, many (but not all) countries forbid **dumping**— selling a product abroad for less than the cost of production at home. U.S. antidumping legislation sets two conditions for determining whether dumping is being practiced:

1 Products are being priced at "less than fair value."

2 The result unfairly harms domestic industry. A few years ago Toyota was charged with dumping surplus minivans in the United States to get rid of surplus inventory. The U.S. government fined the firm and temporarily reduced its quota for importing minivans into the United States.

Questions for Review

1 How does the balance of trade differ from the balance of payments?

2 What are the three possible levels of involvement in international business? Give examples of each.

3 How does a country's economic system affect the decisions of foreign firms interested in doing business there?

4 What aspects of the culture in your state or region would be of particular interest to a foreign firm thinking about locating there?

Questions for Analysis

5 List all the major items in your bedroom, including furnishings. Try to identify the country in which each item was made. Offer possible reasons why a nation might have a comparative advantage in producing a given good.

6 Suppose that you're the manager of a small firm seeking to enter the international arena. What basic information would you need concerning the market that you're thinking of entering?

7 Do you support protectionist tariffs for the United States? If so, in what instances and for what reasons? If not, why not?

8 Do you think that a firm operating internationally is better advised to adopt a single standard of ethical conduct or to adapt to local conditions? Under what kinds of conditions might each approach be preferable?

Application Exercises

9 Interview the manager of a local firm that does at least some business internationally. Why did the company decide to go international? Describe the level of the firm's international involvement and the organizational structure(s) it uses for international operations.

10 Select a product familiar to you. Using library reference works to gain some insight into the culture of India, identify the problems that might arise in trying to market this product to Indian consumers.

5 chapter

Business Management

After reading this chapter, you should be able to:

1 Describe the nature of management and identify the four basic functions that constitute the management process.

2 Identify different types of managers likely to be found in an organization by level and area.

3 Describe the basic skills required of managers.

4 Explain the importance of strategic management and effective goal setting in organizational success.

5 Discuss contingency planning and crisis management in today's business world.

6 Describe the development and explain the importance of corporate culture.

Google Keeps Growing

Sergey Brin and Larry Page met at Stanford University in 1995, when both were graduate students in computer science. At the time, Page was working on a software-development project designed to create an index of Web sites by scouring sites for key words and other linkages. Brin joined him on the project, and when they were satisfied that they'd developed something with commercial value, they tried to license the technology to other search companies. As luck would have it, they couldn't find a buyer and settled instead for procuring enough investment capital to keep refining and testing their product.

In 2000, Brin and Page ran across the description of a business model based on the concept of selling advertising in the form of sponsored links and search-specific ads. They adapted it to their own concept and went into business for themselves, eventually building Google into the world's largest search engine, with an index of more than 10 billion Web pages and a user base of 380 million people per month in 112 different countries. Following an IPO in 2004, the company's market capitalization rose steadily; it stood at more than $157 billion by 2008, when Google controlled 61.5 percent of the U.S. search market (compared to Yahoo's 29.9 percent and Microsoft's 9.2 percent). Google, however, is much more than a mere search engine. Services include searches for news, shopping, local businesses, interactive maps, and discussion groups, as well as blogs, Web-based e-mail and voice mail, and a digital photo-management system. You can access the results of any Google search from the Google Web site, from your own user's toolbar, from your Windows taskbar, and from wireless devices such as phones and PDAs.

How did two young computer scientists build this astoundingly successful company, and where will they take it in the future? For one thing, Brin and Page remain in the forefront of Google's search for technological innovations. They believe in the power of mathematics and have developed unique algorithms for just about every form of activity in the firm. One of the most successful is an algorithm for auctioning advertising placements that ensures the highest possible prices.

What's in It for Me?

Sergey Brin and Larry Page are clearly effective managers, and they understand what it takes to build a business and then keep it at the forefront of its industry. In this chapter, we discuss these responsibilities and explore the relationship between effective management and organizational success. Along the way, we'll consider basic management skills and functions, including the need to establish and maintain a corporate culture. Understanding these things will help you better carry out various management responsibilities yourself and will allow you to assess and appreciate the quality of management in various companies.

Brin and Page have also been remarkably successful in attracting talented and creative employees and providing them with a work environment and culture that foster the kind of productivity and innovation for which they were hired. Finally, although the founders avoid formal strategic planning, they've managed to diversify extensively through acquisitions and key alliances. Typically, Google absorbs an acquired firm and then improves on its technology, thereby adding variety to its own online offerings. Recent acquisitions include YouTube, a leader in online video sharing (2006), Postini, a leader in communications-security products (2007), and Double Click, a leader in online advertising services (2008). Strategic alliances include those with foreign online service providers that offer Google searches on their sites.

For the future, Google plans on doing more of the same, competing head to head with financial-service providers for stock information and with iTunes for music and videos. Also committed to the in-house development of new features and services, Google spent $2.1 billion on R&D in 2007 (up from $1.2 billion in 2006) and another $1 billion to acquire new IT assets. Innovations in the works include an automated universal language translator for translating documents in any language into any other language and personalized home pages that will allow users to design automatic searches and display the results in personal "newspapers."

Nobody knows for sure what else is on the drawing board. In fact, outsiders—notably potential investors—often criticize Google for being a "black box" when they want a few more details about such topics of investor interest as long-range strategy. "We don't talk about our strategy," explains Page, "...because it's strategic. I would rather have people think we're confused than let our competitors know what we're going to do."[1]

Who Are Managers?

All corporations depend on effective management. Whether they run a multibillion-dollar business like Google or a small local fashion boutique, managers perform many of the same functions and have many of the same responsibilities. These include analyzing their competitive environments and planning, organizing, directing, and controlling day-to-day operations of their

(b)

(a)

(c)

As top managers, (a) Marjorie Scardino (CEO of Pearson PLC), (b) Kenneth Chenault (CEO of American Express), and (c) James Sinegal (co-founder and CEO of Costco) are important resources for their companies. In particular, they set the strategic direction for their companies and provide leadership to others. They are also accountable to shareholders, employees, customers, and other key constituents for the performance and effectiveness of their businesses.

business. Ultimately, they are also responsible for the performance and effectiveness of the teams, divisions, or companies that they head.

Although our focus is on managers in business settings, remember that the principles of management apply to all kinds of organizations. Managers work in charities, churches, social organizations, educational institutions, and government agencies. The prime minister of Canada, curators at the Museum of Modern Art, the dean of your college, and the chief administrator of your local hospital are all managers. Remember, too, that managers bring to small organizations much the same kinds of skills—the ability to make decisions and respond to a variety of challenges—that they bring to large ones. Regardless of the nature and size of an organization, managers are among its most important resources.

The Management Process

Management is the process of planning, organizing, leading, and controlling an organization's financial, physical, human, and information resources to achieve its goals. Managers oversee the use of all these resources in their respective firms. All aspects of a manager's job are interrelated. Any given manager is likely to be engaged in each of these activities during the course of any given day.

Planning

Determining what the organization needs to do and how best to get it done requires planning. **Planning** has three main components:

- Determine goals
- Develop a comprehensive *strategy* for achieving those goals
- Design *tactical and operational plans* for implementing the strategy

When Yahoo! was created, for example, its management set a strategic goal of becoming a top firm in the then-emerging market for Internet search engines. The company started by assessing the ways in which people actually use the Web and concluded

that users wanted to be able to satisfy a wide array of needs by going to as few sites as possible to find what they were looking for. The goal of partnering with other companies, whose resources could be accessed through Yahoo!'s comprehensive search engine, emerged as one set of *tactical plans* for moving forward.

Yahoo! managers then began fashioning alliances with such diverse partners as Reuters, Standard & Poor's, and the Associated Press (for news coverage), RE/MAX (for real estate information), and a wide array of information providers specializing in sports, weather, entertainment, shopping, and travel. The creation of individual partnership agreements with each of these partners represents a form of *operational planning*.

Organizing

Managers must also organize people and resources. Some businesses prepare charts that diagram the relationships among the various jobs within the company. These *organization charts* help everyone understand his or her role in the company. Some businesses go so far as to post their organization charts on an office wall. But in most larger businesses, roles and relationships, while important, may be too complex to draw as a simple box-and-line diagram.

> **MANAGEMENT** process of planning, organizing, leading, and controlling an organization's resources to achieve its goals
>
> **PLANNING** management process of determining what an organization needs to do and how best to get it done

Since 2000, Netflix CEO Reed Hastings has spent millions of dollars promoting charter schools and other educational reforms in an effort to break up what he calls "the last big government monopoly in America," the public school system. For Hastings, charter schools place the power to lead back in the hands of the teachers. With "more freedom to express their craft," he argues, "the innovators, the innovative teachers, are drawn to these schools."[2]

ORGANIZING management process of determining how best to arrange an organization's resources and activities into a coherent structure

LEADING management process of guiding and motivating employees to meet an organization's objectives

CONTROLLING management process of monitoring an organization's performance to ensure that it is meeting its goals

Consider the example of Hewlett-Packard (HP). Once one of the leading high-tech firms in the world, HP began to lose some of its luster a few years ago. Ironically, one of the major reasons for its slide could be traced back to what had once been a major strength. Specifically, HP had long prided itself on being little more than a corporate confederation of individual businesses. Sometimes, these businesses even ended up competing among themselves. This approach had been beneficial for much of the firm's history: It was easier for each business to make its own decisions quickly and efficiently, and the competition kept each unit on its toes. By the late 1990s, however, problems had become apparent, and no one could quite figure out what was going on.

Enter Ann Livermore, then head of the firm's software and services business. Livermore realized that the decentralized structure of loosely affiliated businesses, though it had served well in the past, was now holding the firm back. To regain its competitive edge, HP needed an integrated, organization-wide strategy. Livermore led the charge to create one organization united behind one strategic plan. Eventually, a new team of top managers was handed control of the company, and every major component of the firm's structure was reorganized. As a result, the firm appears to be back on solid footing and recently passed chief rival IBM in total revenues.[3] The process that was used to revive HP—determining the best way to arrange a business's resources and activities into a coherent structure—is called **organizing**. We explore organizing in more detail in Chapter 6.

Leading

Managers have the power to give orders and demand results. Leading, however, involves more complex activities. When **leading**, a manager works to guide and motivate employees to meet the firm's objectives. Legendary management figures like Walt Disney, Sam Walton (of Wal-Mart), and Herb Kelleher (of Southwest Airlines) had the capacity to unite their employees in a clear and targeted manner and motivate them to work in the best interests of their employers. Their employees respected them, trusted them, and believed that by working together, both the firm and themselves as individuals would benefit.

Other managers have been noticeably lacking in their ability to lead others. One of the most glaring examples in recent years resulted from Hurricane Katrina, when many of the top managers at the Federal Emergency Management Agency (FEMA) came under fire for their poor leadership and decision making that contributed to the loss of over 1,800 lives and $80 billion in damages.[4] We discuss leadership and decision making more fully in Chapter 9.

Controlling

Controlling is the process of monitoring a firm's performance to make sure that it is meeting its goals. All CEOs must pay close attention to costs and performance. Managers at Continental Airlines, for example, focus almost relentlessly on numerous indicators of performance that they can constantly measure and adjust. As a result, no single element of the firm's performance can slip too far before it's noticed and fixed.

Figure 5.1 illustrates the control process that begins when management establishes standards, often for financial performance. If, for example, a company sets a goal of increasing its sales by 20 percent over the next 10 years, an appropriate standard to assess progress toward the 20-percent goal might be an increase of about 2 percent a year. Managers then measure actual performance each year against standards. If the two amounts agree, the organization continues along its present course. If they vary significantly, however, one or the other needs adjustment.

Figure 5.1
The Control Process

Control can also show where performance is running better than expected and can serve as a basis for providing rewards or reducing costs. For example, after the distributor of the surprise 2005 hit movie *March of the Penguins* saw how popular the movie was becoming, the firm was able to increase advertising and distribution even more, turning the niche movie into a major commercial success.

Types of Managers

Although all managers plan, organize, lead, and control, not all managers have the same degree of responsibility for these activities. It is helpful to classify managers according to levels and areas of responsibility.

Levels of Management

As Table 5.1 illustrates, there are three basic levels of management: **top managers**, who are responsible for a firm's overall performance and effectiveness; **middle managers**, who implement the strategies and work toward the goals set by top managers; and **first-line managers**, who supervise the work of employees. Most firms have more middle managers than top managers and more first-line managers than middle managers. Both the power of managers and the complexity of their duties increase as they move up the ladder.

Areas of Management

In any large company, top, middle, and first-line managers work in a variety of areas, including human resources, operations, marketing, information, and finance.

Human Resource Managers Most companies have *human resource managers* who hire and train employees, evaluate performance, and determine compensation. At large firms, separate departments deal with recruiting and hiring, wage and salary levels, and labor relations. A smaller firm may have a single department—or a single person—responsible for all human resource activities. (We discuss some key issues in human resource management in Chapter 10.)

Operations Managers As we will see in Chapter 7, the term *operations* refers to the systems by which a firm produces goods and services. Among other duties, *operations managers* are responsible for production, inventory, and quality control. They may include *vice presidents for operations* (top managers), *plant managers* (middle managers), and *production supervisors* (first-line managers).

Marketing Managers As we will see in Chapter 11, marketing encompasses the development, pricing, promotion, and distribution of goods and services. *Marketing managers* are responsible for getting products from producers to consumers. Firms that manufacture consumer products, such as Procter & Gamble, Coca-Cola, and Levi Strauss, often have large numbers of marketing managers at several levels, including a *vice president for marketing* (top manager), *regional marketing managers* (middle managers), and *district sales managers* (first-line managers).

Information Managers Occupying a fairly new managerial position in many firms, *information managers* design and implement systems to gather, organize, and distribute information. Some firms have a top-management position for a *chief information officer* (*CIO*). Middle managers help design information systems for divisions or plants. Computer systems managers within smaller businesses are usually first-line managers. We'll discuss information management in more detail in Chapter 13.

TOP MANAGER manager responsible for a firm's overall performance and effectiveness

MIDDLE MANAGER manager responsible for implementing the strategies and working toward the goals set by top managers

FIRST-LINE MANAGER manager responsible for supervising the work of employees

Table 5.1   **The Three Levels of Management**

Level	Examples	Responsibilities
Top managers	President, vice president, treasurer, chief executive officer (CEO), chief financial officer (CFO)	• Responsible for the overall performance and effectiveness of the firm • Set general policies, formulate strategies, and approve all significant decisions • Represent the company in dealings with other firms and with government bodies
Middle managers	Plant manager, operations manager, division manager, regional sales manager	• Responsible for implementing the strategies and working toward the goals set by top managers
First-line managers	Supervisor, office manager, project manager, group leader, sales manager	• Responsible for supervising the work of employees who report to them • Ensure employees understand and are properly trained in company policies and procedures

TECHNICAL SKILLS skills needed to perform specialized tasks

HUMAN RELATIONS SKILLS skills in understanding and getting along with people

CONCEPTUAL SKILLS abilities to think in the abstract, diagnose and analyze different situations, and see beyond the present situation

Financial Managers Nearly every company has *financial managers* to plan and oversee its accounting functions and financial resources. Levels of financial management may include *CFO* or *vice president for finance* (top manager), a *division controller* (middle manager), and an *accounting supervisor* (first-line manager). We'll discuss financial management in more detail in Chapters 14 and 15.

Other Managers Some firms also employ other specialized managers. Many companies, for example, have public relations managers. Chemical and pharmaceutical companies such as Monsanto and Merck have research and development managers.

Basic Management Skills

Effective managers must develop *technical*, *human relations*, *conceptual*, *decision-making*, and *time management skills*.

Technical Skills

The skills needed to perform specialized tasks are called **technical skills**. Technical skills are especially important for first-line managers. Many of these managers spend considerable time helping employees solve work-related problems, training them in more efficient procedures, and monitoring performance. But many successful top managers, people like Sergey Brin and Larry Page, also stay abreast of current technologies that relate to their business.

Human Relations Skills

Human relations skills allow managers to understand and communicate with other people. A manager with poor human relations skills may have trouble getting along with subordinates, cause valuable employees to quit or transfer, and contribute to poor morale. Although human relations skills are important at all levels, they are probably most important for middle managers, who must often act as bridges between top managers, first-line managers, and managers from other areas of the organization. Sergey Brin and Larry Page use effective human relations skills to help attract the best and brightest people to Google.

Conceptual Skills

Conceptual skills refer to a person's ability to think in the abstract, to diagnose and analyze different situations, and to see beyond the present situation.

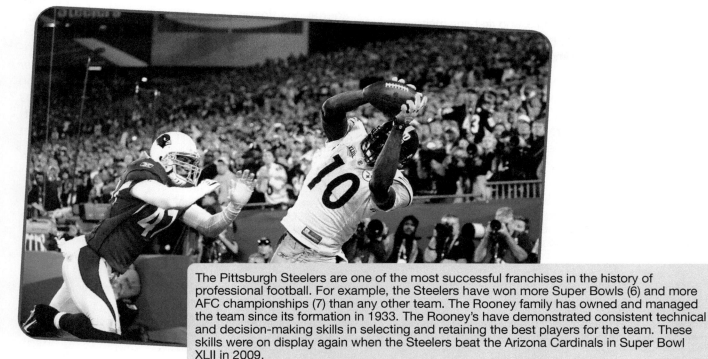

The Pittsburgh Steelers are one of the most successful franchises in the history of professional football. For example, the Steelers have won more Super Bowls (6) and more AFC championships (7) than any other team. The Rooney family has owned and managed the team since its formation in 1933. The Rooney's have demonstrated consistent technical and decision-making skills in selecting and retaining the best players for the team. These skills were on display again when the Steelers beat the Arizona Cardinals in Super Bowl XLII in 2009.

"I like to think of myself as a nice guy. Naturally, sometimes you have to step on a few faces."

Conceptual skills help managers recognize new market opportunities and threats. They can also help managers analyze the probable outcomes of their decisions. The need for conceptual skills differs at various management levels. Top managers depend most on conceptual skills, first-line managers least. Sergey Brin and Larry Page clearly have strong conceptual skills.

Decision-Making Skills

Decision-making skills include the ability to define problems and to select the best course of action. These skills involve gathering facts, identifying solutions, evaluating alternatives, and implementing the chosen alternative. Periodically following up on and evaluating the effectiveness of the choice are also part of the decision-making process. Sergey Brin and Larry Page need effective decision-making skills in order to assess potential acquisitions for Google. We'll discuss decision making more fully in Chapter 9.

Time Management Skills

Time management skills refer to the productive use that managers make of their time. To manage time effectively, managers must address four leading causes of wasted time:

1 *Paperwork.* Some managers spend too much time deciding what to do with letters and reports. Most documents of this sort are routine and can be handled quickly. Managers must learn to recognize those documents that require more attention.

2 *Telephone calls.* Experts estimate that the telephone interrupts managers every five minutes. To manage this time more effectively, experts suggest having an assistant screen all calls and setting aside a certain block of time each day to return the important ones. Unfortunately, the explosive use of cell phones seems to be making this problem even worse for many managers.

3 *Meetings.* Many managers spend as much as four hours a day in meetings. To help keep this time productive, the person handling the meeting should specify a clear agenda, start on time, keep everyone focused on the agenda, and end on time.

4 *E-mail.* Increasingly, managers are relying heavily on e-mail and other forms of electronic communication. Time is wasted when managers have to sort through spam and a variety of electronic folders, in-boxes, and archives.

> **DECISION-MAKING SKILLS** skills in defining problems and selecting the best courses of action
>
> **TIME MANAGEMENT SKILLS** skills associated with the productive use of time

Management Skills for the Twenty-first Century

Although the skills discussed in this chapter have long been important parts of every successful manager's career, new skill requirements continue to emerge. Today, most experts point to the growing importance of skills involving *global management* and *technology*.

Global Management Skills Tomorrow's managers must equip themselves with the special tools, techniques, and skills needed to compete in a global environment. They will need to understand foreign markets, cultural differences, and the motives and practices of foreign rivals. They also need to understand how to collaborate with others around the world on a real-time basis. In the past, most U.S. businesses hired local managers to run their operations in the various countries in which they operated. More recently, however, the trend has been to transfer U.S. managers to foreign locations. This practice helps firms transfer their corporate cultures to foreign operations and better prepares managers for international competition as they advance within the organization. The top management teams of large corporations today are also likely to include directors from other countries.

Management and Technology Skills Another significant issue facing tomorrow's managers is technology, especially as it relates to communication. New forms of technology have added to a manager's ability to process information while simultaneously making it even more important to organize and interpret an ever-increasing wealth of input.

Technology has also begun to change the way the interaction of managers shapes corporate structures.

To run its operations in China, MTV needed someone who understood both conservative Chinese television regulators and China's young urban elite. The company chose Li Yifei, a former Baylor University student, UN intern, and tai chi champion. She brought the Chinese MTV awards to state-owned TV, receiving a 7.9 percent rating—a whopping 150 million viewers.

Information now flows through elaborate computer networks to reach employees, clients, and customers simultaneously. As a result, decisions are made quicker, and more people are directly involved. E-mail, videoconferencing, and other forms of communication are breaking down bureaucracies, and the decision-making process is benefiting from group building and teamwork. We discuss the effects technology has on business in more detail in Chapter 13.

Strategic Management: Setting Goals and Formulating Strategy

Strategic management is the process of helping an organization maintain an effective alignment with its environment. For instance, if a firm's business environment is heading toward fiercer competition, the business may need to start cutting its costs and developing more products and services before the competition really starts to heat up. Likewise, if an industry is globalizing, a firm's managers may need to start entering new

markets and developing international partnerships during the early stages of globalization rather than waiting for its full effects.

The starting point in effective strategic management is setting **goals**—objectives that a business hopes and plans to achieve. Setting goals is only the first step for an organization, however. Managers must also make decisions about which actions will and will not achieve company goals. Decisions cannot be made on a problem-by-problem basis or merely to meet needs as they arise. In most companies, decisions are guided by a **strategy**, or broad set of organizational plans for implementing the decisions made for achieving organizational goals.

Setting Business Goals

Goals are performance targets—the means by which organizations and their managers measure success or failure at every level.

Purposes of Goal Setting We can identify four main purposes of organizational goal setting:

1 *Goal setting provides direction and guidance for managers at all levels*. If managers know precisely where the company is headed, there is less potential for error in the different units of the company.

Starbucks, for example, has a goal of increasing capital spending by 15 percent, with all additional expenditures devoted to opening new stores. This goal clearly informs everyone in the firm that expansion into new territories is a high priority.

2 *Goal setting helps firms allocate resources.* Areas that are expected to grow will get first priority. The company allocates more resources to new projects with large sales potential than it allocates to mature products with established but stagnant sales potential.

3 *Goal setting helps to define corporate culture.* For years, the goal at General Electric has been to push each of its divisions to first or second in its industry. The result is a competitive (and often stressful) environment and a corporate culture that rewards success and has little tolerance for failure.

4 *Goal setting helps managers assess performance.* If a unit sets a goal of increasing sales by 10 percent in a given year, managers in that unit who attain or exceed the goal can be rewarded. Units failing to reach the goal will also be compensated accordingly.

MISSION STATEMENT organization's statement of how it will achieve its purpose in the environment in which it conducts its business

Mission Statements Goals differ from company to company, depending on the firm's purpose and mission. Most companies articulate this in their **mission statements**—statements of how they will achieve their purposes in the environments in which they conduct their businesses.

Entrepreneurship and New Ventures

Samuel Adams Makes Headway

In 1984 James Koch was a high-flying management consultant earning over $250,000 a year. To the surprise of his family and friends, however, he quit this job and invested his life's savings to start a business from scratch and go head-to-head with international competitors in a market that had not had a truly successful specialty product in decades. To everyone's even greater surprise, he succeeded.

Koch's company is Boston Beer, and its flagship product is a premium beer called Samuel Adams. James set up shop in an old warehouse in Boston, bought some surplus equipment from a large brewery, and started operations. Because he used only the highest-quality ingredients, Koch had to price his product at about $1 more per case than such premium imports as Heineken. Most distributors, doubting consumers would pay $6 per six-pack for an American beer, refused to carry it. So Koch began selling directly to retailers and bars.

Samuel Adams founder James Koch takes a personal interest in his company's product.

His big break came when Samuel Adams Lager won the consumer preference poll at the Great American Beer Festival. Koch quickly turned this victory into an advertising mantra, proclaiming Samuel Adams "The Best Beer in America." As sales took off, national distributors came calling; to meet surging demand, Koch contracted parts of his brewing operations to facilities in Pittsburgh and Cincinnati.

During the early 1990s, annual sales of Samuel Adams products grew at a rate of over 50 percent and today exceed $340 million. The 2008 purchase of a brewery outside Philadelphia increased the firm's brewing capacity by over 1.6 million barrels per year. Boston Beer even exports Samuel Adams to Germany, where it's become popular among finicky beer drinkers. Koch, who retains controlling interest in the business, still oversees day-to-day brewing operations. Indeed, he claims to have sampled at least one of the firm's products every day.[5]

LONG-TERM GOAL goal set for an extended time, typically five years or more into the future

INTERMEDIATE GOAL goal set for a period of one to five years into the future

SHORT-TERM GOAL goal set for the very near future

CORPORATE STRATEGY strategy for determining a firm's overall attitude toward growth and the way it will manage its businesses or product lines

BUSINESS (OR COMPETITIVE) STRATEGY strategy, at the business-unit or product-line level, focusing on improving a firm's competitive position

FUNCTIONAL STRATEGY strategy by which managers in specific areas decide how best to achieve corporate goals through productivity

A company's mission is usually easy to identify, at least at a basic level. Starbucks sums up its mission very succinctly: the firm intends to "establish Starbucks as the premier purveyor of the finest coffee in the world while maintaining [its] uncompromising principles as [it] grow[s]." But businesses sometimes have to rethink their strategies and missions as the competitive environment changes. A few years ago, for example, Starbucks announced that Internet marketing and sales were going to become core business initiatives. Managers subsequently realized, however, that this initiative did not fit the firm as well as they first thought. As a result, they scaled back this effort and made a clear recommitment to their existing retail business.

Kinds of Goals   In addition to its mission, every firm also has long-term, intermediate, and short-term goals.

- **Long-term goals** relate to extended periods of time, typically five years or more. For example, Visa might set a long-term goal of doubling the number of participating merchants during the next 10 years. Kodak might adopt a long-term goal of increasing its share of the digital picture processing market by 10 percent during the next eight years.

- **Intermediate goals** are set for a period of one to five years. Companies usually set intermediate goals in several areas. For example, the marketing department's goal might be to increase sales by 3 percent in two years, while the production department might want to reduce expenses by 6 percent in four years.

- **Short-term goals** are set for perhaps one year and are developed for several different areas. Increasing sales by 2 percent this year, cutting costs by 1 percent next quarter, and reducing employee

turnover by 4 percent over the next 6 months are examples of short-term goals.

After a firm has set its goals, it then focuses attention on strategies to accomplish them.

Types of Strategies

There are three types of strategies that are usually considered by a company: *corporate strategy*, *business* (or *competitive*) *strategy*, and *functional strategy*.

Corporate Strategy   The purpose of **corporate strategy** is to determine what business or businesses a company will own and operate. A company may decide to *grow* by increasing its activities or investments or to *retrench* by reducing them.

Sometimes a corporation buys and operates multiple businesses in compatible industries as part of its corporate strategy. For example, the restaurant chains operated by Yum! (KFC, Pizza Hut, Taco Bell, and Long John Silver's) are clearly related to one another. This strategy is called *related diversification*. However, if the businesses are not similar, the strategy is called *unrelated diversification*. When Pearson PLC, a British media company, ran such unrelated businesses as publishing and a wax museum, it was following this approach. Under CEO Kenneth Chenault, AmEx corporate strategy calls for strengthening operations through a principle of growth called *e-partnering*—buying shares of small companies that can provide technology that AmEx itself does not have.

Business (or Competitive) Strategy   When a corporation owns and operates multiple businesses, it must develop strategies for each one. **Business (or competitive) strategy**, then, takes place at the level of the business unit or product line and focuses on improving a company's competitive position. For example, Pepsi has one strategy for its soft-drink business as it competes with Coca-Cola, a different strategy for its sports-drink business, and yet another strategy for its bottled-water line.

Functional Strategy   At the level of **functional strategy**, managers in specific areas such as marketing, finance, and operations decide how best to achieve corporate goals by performing their functional activities most effectively.

Formulating Strategy

Planning is often concerned with the nuts and bolts of setting goals, choosing tactics, and establishing schedules. In contrast, *strategy* is a broad concept that

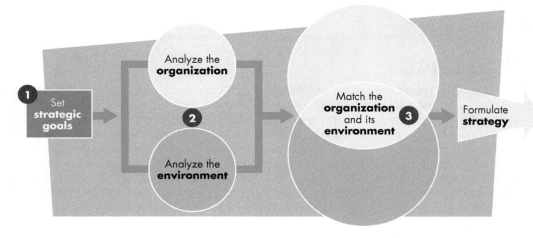

Figure 5.2
Strategy Formulation[6]

STRATEGY FORMULATION creation of a broad program for defining and meeting an organization's goals

STRATEGIC GOAL goal derived directly from a firm's mission statement

SWOT ANALYSIS identification and analysis of organizational strengths and weaknesses and environmental opportunities and threats as part of strategy formulation

ENVIRONMENTAL ANALYSIS process of scanning the business environment for threats and opportunities

ORGANIZATIONAL ANALYSIS process of analyzing a firm's strengths and weaknesses

describes an organization's intentions, outlines how it intends to meet its goals, and includes its responsiveness to new challenges and new needs. Because a well-formulated strategy is so vital to a business's success, most top managers devote substantial attention and creativity to this process. **Strategy formulation** involves the three basic steps summarized in Figure 5.2.

Step 1: Setting Strategic Goals **Strategic goals** are derived directly from a firm's mission statement. For example, Chipotle Mexican Grill promotes itself as serving "Food with Integrity." In the words of founder and CEO Steve Ells, this means "we can always do better in terms of the food we buy." This strategy—serving food that is "better tasting, coming from better sources, better for the environment, better for the animals, and better for the farmers who raise the animals and grow the produce"—seems to be working: in 2007 Chipotle's revenues exceeded $1 billion.[7]

Step 2: Analyzing the Organization and the Environment: SWOT Analysis After strategic goals have been established, managers usually attempt to assess both their organization and its environment. A common framework for this assessment is called a **SWOT analysis**. This process involves assessing organizational strengths and weaknesses (the **S** and **W**) and environmental opportunities and threats (the **O** and **T**).

Scanning the business environment for threats and opportunities is often called **environmental analysis**. Changing consumer tastes and hostile takeover offers are threats, as are new government regulations that will limit a firm's opportunities. Even more important threats come from new products and new competitors. For example, online music services like iTunes are a major threat to manufacturers of CDs and CD players. Opportunities, meanwhile, are areas in which a firm can potentially expand, grow, or take advantage of existing strengths.

In addition to analyzing external factors by performing an environmental analysis, managers must also examine internal factors. The purpose of such an **organizational analysis** is to better understand a company's strengths and weaknesses. Strengths might include surplus cash, a dedicated workforce, an ample supply of managerial talent, technical expertise, or little competition. A cash shortage, aging factories, a heavily unionized workforce, and a poor public image can all be important weaknesses.

Step 3: Matching the Organization and Its Environment The final step in strategy formulation is matching environmental threats and opportunities against corporate strengths and weaknesses. This matching process is at the heart of strategy formulation. That is, a firm should attempt to leverage its strengths so as to capitalize on opportunities and counteract threats; it should also attempt to shield its weaknesses or at least not allow them to derail other activities.

Understanding strengths and weaknesses may determine whether a firm typically takes risks or

Best Buy—Built to Last

Recent times have seen the demise of retailing giants like Circuit City and Linens-N-Things, as well as the weakening of others like Ann Taylor and Sears. But one industry stalwart, Best Buy, continues to thrive. Down the hall from the CEO's office at the Best Buy headquarters in Minneapolis, there's a row of hospital beds, each containing the effigy of an ailing or deceased U.S. retailer. Bedside charts reveal dire financial results. A nearby sign reads: "This is where companies go when their strategies get sick."

What are the keys to success at Best Buy? Former CEO Brad Anderson saw his job as keeping the company in strategic good health. So, for one thing, he went to great lengths to stay in tune with customer tastes and preferences. He also decided that the company would stop paying commissions to its sales staff and put these employees on salary instead. The move didn't go over well with the big suppliers who expected a retailer's salespeople to push their premium products, but customers appreciated the break from high-pressure sales tactics, and revenues at Best Buy jumped by 25 percent a year in the early 1990s.

Anderson also made the decision to buy a Minneapolis start-up that specialized in installing and fixing PCs. And by 2005, there was a Geek Squad presence in every store in the chain. Whether working at the customer's home, in a Best Buy outlet, over the phone, or online, the Geeks constitute a first line of defense against the technological frustrations that can sap the value out of an electronics purchase and the goodwill out of a customer experience. Anderson was confident from the first that the technical-services market would continue to grow, but perhaps more importantly, he realized that competitors like Wal-Mart and Costco would never offer the kind of customer service that Best Buy could offer through the Geek Squad. On sales of $1 billion, the Geek Squad now generates about $280 million in profits annually.

By far, however, Anderson's most ambitious strategic gambit has been the "customer-centricity"—or just plain "centricity"— initiative. The keys to centricity are demographics and segmentation. From store to store, the most valuable customers—the ones whose patronage is most lucrative—don't necessarily belong to the same group of people. At one outlet, for example, the most profitable customers might be affluent tech enthusiasts; elsewhere, they may be suburban mothers, price-conscious family guys, or youthful gadget fiends. Beginning in 2003, Anderson started "centrizing" Best Buy stores—realigning them to cater to their most profitable segments (or combination of segments). A given location, for instance, may be geared toward young gadget fiends, another toward suburban mothers. The first will have a broader range of video games and special stations for trying out accessories; the second will have a staff of personal shopping assistants to help a homemaker find the right digital camera for recording family activities. If a store caters to affluent tech enthusiasts (as about 40 percent of them do), there will be a home theater expert on hand.

In a sign of the volatile times, Best Buy announced in November 2008 that it expected revenues for fiscal 2009 to fall short of projections. When the smoke had cleared, however, sales had gone up 4 percent, thanks in part to another Brad Anderson gamble that had paid off: Although comparable-store sales (sales in stores that have been open for at least a year) had declined 6.8 percent, the losses were offset by revenues from 138 new stores that had been opened in the preceding 12 months. "While the environment continues to be as challenging as we expected," said Anderson, "consumers are being drawn to brands that they trust, and they are responding to our customer-centric model. In this light, we believe that the market-share gains we've been making will be sustained."[8]

behaves more conservatively. Either approach can be successful. Blue Bell, for example, is one of the most profitable ice-cream makers in the world, even though it sells its products in only a fifth of U.S. supermarkets.[9] Based in Brenham, Texas, the firm has resisted the temptation to expand too quickly. Its success is based on product freshness and frequent deliveries—strengths that may suffer if the company grows too large.

A Hierarchy of Plans

The final step in formulating strategy involves the creation of actual plans. Plans can be viewed on three levels: strategic, tactical, and operational. The levels constitute a hierarchy, because implementing plans is practical only when there is a logical flow from one level to the next.

- **Strategic plans** reflect decisions about resource allocations, company priorities, and the steps needed to meet strategic goals. They are usually created by the firm's top management team, but often rely on input from others in the organization.
- **Tactical plans** are shorter-term plans for implementing specific aspects of the company's strategic plans. They typically involve upper and middle management.
- **Operational plans,** which are developed by mid-level and lower-level managers, set short-term targets for daily, weekly, or monthly performance.

Contingency Planning and Crisis Management

Because business environments are often difficult to predict and because the unexpected can create major problems, even the best-laid plans sometimes do not work out. For instance, when Walt Disney announced plans to launch a cruise line replete with familiar Disney characters and themes, managers began aggressively marketing the new product. Three months before the first sailing, however, the shipyard constructing Disney's

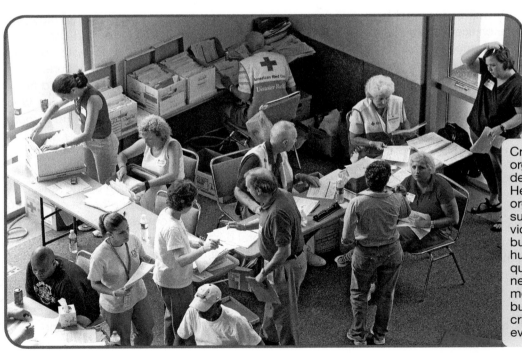

Crisis management involves an organization's methods for dealing with emergencies. Here, Red Cross volunteers organize and file paperwork submitted by Hurricane Katrina victims in Texas. Hundreds of businesses affected by the hurricane also had to respond quickly to events they had never anticipated. But today, most of those same businesses have much clearer crisis management plans in the event any disaster strikes.

ship notified the company that it was behind schedule and that delivery would be several weeks late. When similar problems befall other cruise lines, they can offer to rebook passengers on alternative itineraries. But because Disney had no other ship, it had no choice but to refund the money it had collected as prebooking deposits for its first 15 cruises.

Because managers know such things can happen, they often develop alternative plans in case things go awry. Two common methods of dealing with the unknown and unforeseen are *contingency planning* and *crisis management*.

Contingency Planning

Contingency planning seeks to identify in advance important aspects of a business or its market that might change. It also identifies the ways in which a company will respond to changes. Suppose, for example, that a company develops a plan to create a new division. It expects sales to increase at an annual rate of 10 percent for the next five years, and it develops a marketing strategy for maintaining that level. But suppose that sales have increased by only 5 percent by the end of the first year. Does the firm (1) abandon the venture, (2) invest more in advertising, or (3) wait to see what happens in the second year? Whichever choice the firm makes, its efforts will be more efficient if managers decide in advance what to do in case sales fall below planned levels.

Contingency planning helps them do exactly that. Disney learned from its mistake with its first ship—when the second ship was launched a year later, managers allowed for an extra two weeks between when the ship was supposed to be ready for sailing and its first scheduled cruise.

Crisis Management

A crisis is an unexpected emergency requiring immediate response. **Crisis management** involves an organization's methods for dealing with emergencies. Seeing the consequences of poor crisis management after the terrorist attacks of September 11, 2001, and the hurricanes that hit the Gulf Coast in 2005, many firms today are working to create new and better crisis management plans and procedures.

For example, both Reliant Energy and Duke Energy rely on computer trading centers where trading managers actively buy and sell energy-related commodities. If a terrorist attack or natural disaster were to strike their trading centers, they would essentially be out of business. Consequently, Reliant and Duke have created secondary trading centers at other locations. In the event of a shutdown at their main trading centers, these firms can quickly transfer virtually all their core trading activities to their secondary centers within 30 minutes or less.[10] Still, however many firms do not have comprehensive crisis management strategies. For example, as concerns grew about the outbreak of H1N1 (swine) flu in 2009 and some officials warned of a possible pandemic, a survey found that only about 57 percent of U.S. businesses had plans in place to deal with a flu pandemic.

Management and the Corporate Culture

Just as every individual has a unique personality, every company has a unique identity, a **corporate culture**: the shared experiences, stories, beliefs, and norms that characterize an organization. This culture helps define the work and business climate that exists in an organization.

A strong corporate culture directs employees' efforts and helps everyone work toward the same goals. It also helps newcomers learn accepted behaviors. If financial success is the key to a culture, newcomers quickly learn that they are expected to work long, hard hours and that the "winner" is the one who brings in the most revenue. But if quality of life is more fundamental, newcomers learn that balancing work and nonwork is encouraged.

Managing Change If an organization changes its culture, it must communicate the nature of the change to both employees and customers. According to the CEOs of several companies that have undergone radical change in the last decade or so, the process usually goes through three stages:

1 *At the highest level, analysis of the company's environment highlights extensive change as the most effective response to its problems.* Conflict and resistance typically characterize this period.

A business's founder or CEO plays a major role in shaping the company's culture. For example, Apple co-founder and CEO Steve Jobs helped establish an informal and laid-back culture at the company. Casual business attire and an open-door policy help him maintain that same culture today. And that culture, in turn, helps Apple continue to attract and retain talented people.

2 *Top management begins to formulate a vision of a new company*. Whatever that vision, it must include renewed focus on the activities of competitors and the needs of customers.

3 *The firm sets up new systems for appraising and compensating employees who enforce the firm's new values*. The purpose is to give the new culture solid shape from within the firm.

Questions for Review

1 Relate the five basic management skills (technical, human relations, conceptual, decision-making, and time management) to the four activities in the management process (planning, organizing, leading, and controlling). For example, which skills are most important in leading?

2 What are the four main purposes of setting goals in an organization?

3 Identify and explain the three basic steps in strategy formulation.

4 What is corporate culture? How is it formed? How is it sustained?

Questions for Analysis

5 Select any group of which you are a member (your company, your family, or a club or organization, for example). Explain how planning, organizing, leading, and controlling are practiced in that group.

6 Identify managers by level and area at your school, college, or university.

7 In what kind of company would the technical skills of top managers be more important than human relations or conceptual skills? Are there organizations in which conceptual skills are not important?

8 What differences might you expect to find in the corporate cultures of a 100-year-old manufacturing firm based in the Northeast and a 1-year-old e-commerce firm based in Silicon Valley?

Application Exercises

9 Interview the manager at any level of a local company. Identify that manager's job according to level and area. Show how planning, organizing, leading, and controlling are part of this person's job. Inquire about the manager's education and work experience. Which management skills are most important for this manager's job?

10 Compare and contrast the corporate cultures of two companies that do business in your community. Be sure to choose two companies in the same industry—for example, a Sears department store and a Wal-Mart discount store.

6 chapter

Organizing the Business

After reading this chapter, you should be able to:

1 Discuss the factors that influence a firm's organizational structure.

2 Explain specialization and departmentalization as two of the building blocks of organizational structure.

3 Describe centralization and decentralization, delegation, and authority as the key ingredients in establishing the decision-making hierarchy.

4 Explain the differences among functional, divisional, matrix, and international organizational structures and describe the most popular new forms of organizational design.

5 Describe the informal organization and discuss intrapreneuring.

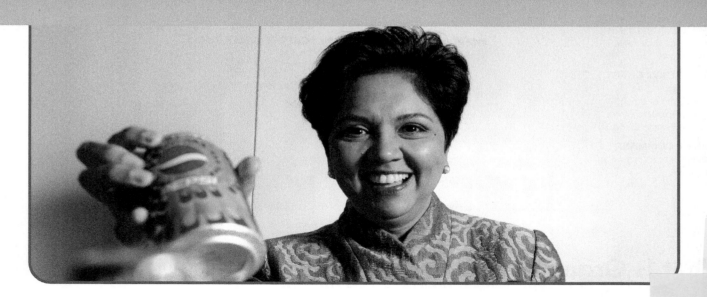

PepsiCo's Performance with Purpose

PepsiCo's chairman and CEO, Indra Nooyi, has been leading company reorganizations since she joined PepsiCo in 1994. During her career at PepsiCo she has served as strategy chief, mergers and acquisitions head, and CFO. Fueled by her unique style, global perspective, and nutritional goals, Nooyi has led PepsiCo to an annual revenue increase of 72 percent since 2000.

In her first bold response to the market, Nooyi spun off PepsiCo's restaurant business in 1997, a move that shrank the company by a third. She has since built it back up on a foundation of more nutritional foods with acquisitions such as Tropicana, Quaker Oats, and Naked Juice. To support the move in this direction, Nooyi appointed an endocrinologist as head of R&D and hired the company's first chief scientific officer. Nooyi has never shied away from change. In fact, she believes that "Companies today are bigger than many economies. We are little republics. We are engines of efficiency. If we don't do [responsible] things, who is going to? Why not start making change now?" This move away from being just another "ugly American company" has increased overseas sales, which grew 22 percent in 2007.

Since becoming CEO, Nooyi has reorganized the company to better reflect not only her management style but also the company's product share. She doubled the executive team to 29, which includes her former main challenger for the CEO job with whom she maintains a noncompetitive relationship. She also reorganized the company into three departmentalized units: Americas Foods, Americas Beverages, and International. Previously divided into North America and International departments, the new structure better reflects the company's focus on snack foods, which accounted for 46 percent of revenue in 2008.

These changes have all been in support of Nooyi's motto—Performance with Purpose—which guides how the organization, as well as the products, should function.[1]

What's in It for Me?

As PepsiCo illustrates, many factors that affect how a firm functions determine organizational structure. This chapter will further explore the factors that go into structuring an organization, the functions that must be determined, and the roles and responsibilities that must be defined. Elements that are increasingly relevant in today's business world, such as virtual and informal organizations and intrapreneuring, will also be discussed.

Figure 6.1
The Organization Chart

ORGANIZATIONAL STRUCTURE specification of the jobs to be done within an organization and the ways in which they relate to one another

ORGANIZATION CHART diagram depicting a company's structure and showing employees where they fit into its operations

CHAIN OF COMMAND reporting relationships within a company

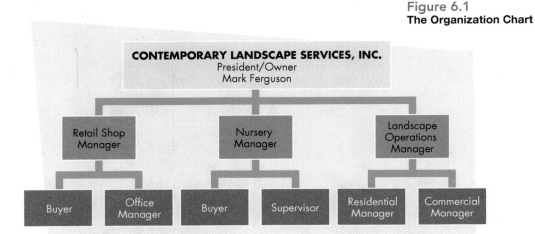

What Is Organizational Structure?

Organizational structure is the specification of the jobs within an organization and the ways they relate to one another. As organizations grow, it becomes increasingly important for managers to have a clear understanding of how responsibility and authority are distributed across different people and jobs. The mechanism used to establish these understandings is organizational structure. Perhaps the easiest way to understand this structure is in terms of an *organization chart.*

Organization Charts

Organization charts clarify structure and show employees where they fit into a firm's operations. Figure 6.1 is an organization chart for Contemporary Landscape Services, a small but thriving business in Bryan, Texas. Each box represents a job, and the lines represent how jobs relate to one another. The solid lines define the **chain of command**, or *reporting relationships*. For example, the retail shop, nursery, and landscape operations managers all report to the owner and president, Mark Ferguson. Within the landscape operation is one manager for residential accounts and another for commercial accounts. Similarly, there are other managers in the retail shop and the nursery.

Organization charts of large firms are often so complex that they may have one chart showing overall structure, separate charts for each division, and even more for individual departments or units. Virtually no two organizations will have the same structure: what works for one company may not work for another. For example, the American Red Cross will probably not have the same structure as Union Carbide or the University of Minnesota.

Determinants of Organizational Structure

Chief among the factors playing a part in determining an organization's optimal structure are *mission* and *strategy.* A dynamic and rapidly growing business, for example, needs an organizational structure that allows for flexibility and growth in response to environmental and strategic changes. A stable organization with only modest growth goals and a more conservative strategy will most likely function best with a different structure. A large corporation operating in a strongly competitive environment—for example, American Airlines or Hewlett-Packard—requires a different organizational structure than a local barbershop or video store. Even after an organizational structure has been created, it is rarely set in stone. Most organizations change their structures on an almost continuous basis.

Since it was first incorporated in 1903, Ford Motor Company has undergone dozens of major structural changes, hundreds of moderate changes, and thousands of minor changes. In the last decade alone, Ford has initiated several major structural changes. In 1994, the firm announced a major restructuring plan, Ford 2000, which was intended to integrate all of Ford's vast international operations into a single, unified structure by the year 2000.

By 1998, however, midway through implementation of the grand plan, top Ford executives announced major modifications, indicating that (1) additional changes would be made, (2) some previously planned changes would not be made, and (3) some recently realigned operations would be changed again. In early 1999, managers announced another set of changes intended to eliminate corporate bureaucracy, speed up decision making, and improve communication and working relationships among people at different levels of the organization. Early in 2001, Ford announced yet more sweeping changes intended to boost the firm's flagging bottom line and stem a decline in product quality. More significant changes followed in both 2003 and 2004, and in 2006, the firm announced several plant closings, resulting in even more changes.[2] And CEO Alan Mulally implemented more structural changes to help Ford survive the 2008–2009 recession.

The Building Blocks of Organizational Structure

The first step in developing the structure of any business, large or small, involves three activities:

1 *Specialization:* Determining who will do what

2 *Departmentalization:* Determining how people performing certain tasks can best be grouped together

3 *Establishment of a decision-making hierarchy:* Deciding who will be empowered to make which decisions and who will have authority over others

Specialization

The process of identifying the specific jobs that need to be done and designating the people who will perform them leads to **job specialization**. In a sense, all organizations have only one major "job," such as making cars (Ford), selling finished goods to consumers (PepsiCo), or providing telecommunications services (Verizon). Usually, that job is extremely complex in nature. For example, the "job" of Chaparral Steel is converting scrap steel (often salvaged from wrecked automobiles)

into finished steel products (such as beams and reinforcement bars).

Managers break down, or specialize, this one overall job into several smaller jobs. Thus, some workers transport the scrap steel to the company's mill. Others operate shredding equipment before turning raw materials over to the workers who then melt them into liquid. Other specialists oversee the flow of the liquid into molding equipment, where it is transformed into new products. Finally, others are responsible for moving finished products to a holding area before they are shipped to customers. When the overall job of the organization is broken down like this, workers can develop real expertise in their jobs, and employees can better coordinate their work with that done by others.

Specialization and Growth In a very small organization, the owner may perform every job. As the firm grows, however, so does the need to specialize jobs so that others can perform them. For example, when Walt Disney first opened his animation studio, he and his brother Roy did everything. When they created their very first animated feature, *Steamboat Willy*, they wrote the story, drew the pictures, transferred the pictures to film,

JOB SPECIALIZATION
process of identifying the specific jobs that need to be done and designating the people who will perform them

When Walt Disney and his brother Roy made Mickey Mouse's debut animated film, *Steamboat Willy*, they handled every step of the creative process. Today, it takes hundreds of people to create an animated film like 2009's *Up*.

DEPARTMENTALIZATION process of grouping jobs into logical units

PROFIT CENTER separate company unit responsible for its own costs and profits

PRODUCT DEPARTMENTALIZATION dividing of an organization according to specific products or services being created

PROCESS DEPARTMENTALIZATION dividing of an organization according to production processes used to create a good or service

FUNCTIONAL DEPARTMENTALIZATION dividing of an organization according to groups' functions or activities

provided the voices, and marketed the cartoon to theaters. Today, however, a Disney animated feature is made possible only through the efforts of hundreds of people. The job of one animator may be to create the face of a single character throughout an entire feature. Another artist may be charged with coloring background images in certain scenes. Others are responsible for the subsequent operations that turn individual computer-generated images into a moving picture or for the marketing of the finished product.

Job specialization is a natural part of organizational growth, and it has advantages and disadvantages. Specialized jobs can be learned and filled more easily and performed more efficiently than nonspecialized jobs. However, jobs at lower levels of the organization are especially susceptible to becoming too narrowly defined and overspecialized, which can cause employees to become bored and careless, to derive less satisfaction from their jobs, and to lose sight of their roles in the organization.[3]

Departmentalization

After jobs are specialized, they must be grouped into logical units, which is the process of **departmentalization**. With this division of activities, control and coordination are streamlined, and top managers can see easily how various units are performing.

Departmentalization allows the firm to treat each department as a **profit center**—a separate company unit responsible for its own costs and profits. Thus, Sears can calculate the profits it generates from men's clothing, appliances, home furnishings, and every other department within a given store separately. Managers can then use this information to make decisions about advertising and promotional events, space allocation, budgeting, and so forth.

In general, departmentalization may occur along *product*, *process*, *functional*, *customer*, or *geographic* lines (or any combination of these).

Product Departmentalization Manufacturers and service providers often opt for **product departmentalization**—dividing an organization according to the specific product or service being created. Kraft Foods uses this approach to divide departments: for example, the Oscar Mayer division focuses on hot dogs and lunch meats, the Kraft Cheese division focuses on cheese products, the Maxwell House and Post division focuses on coffee and breakfast cereal, and so on.[4] Because each division represents a defined group of products or services, managers at Kraft Foods are able—in theory—to focus on *specific* product lines in a clear and defined way.

Process Departmentalization Other manufacturers favor **process departmentalization**, in which the organization is divided according to production processes used to create a good or service. This principle is logical for Vlasic, which has three separate departments to transform cucumbers into either fresh-packed pickles, pickles cured in brine, or relishes. Cucumbers destined to become fresh-packed pickles must be packed into jars immediately, covered with a solution of water and vinegar, and prepared for sale. Those slated to be brined pickles must be aged in brine solution before packing. Relish cucumbers must be minced and combined with a host of other ingredients. Each process requires different equipment and worker skills, and different departments were created for each.

Functional Departmentalization Many service and manufacturing companies, especially smaller ones, use **functional departmentalization** to develop departments

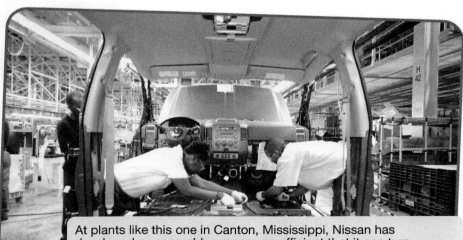

At plants like this one in Canton, Mississippi, Nissan has developed an assembly process so efficient that it can turn out a vehicle in up to 10 fewer hours than Ford. The key is the organization of the workstations. At this station, workers install just about everything that the driver touches inside the truck cab. Other stations take care of the whole vehicle frame, the entire electrical system, or completed doors.

according to a group's functions or activities. Such firms typically have production, marketing and sales, human resources, and accounting and finance departments. Departments may be further subdivided. For example, the marketing department might be divided into separate staffs for market research and advertising.

Customer Departmentalization   Retail stores actually derive their generic name—department stores—from the manner in which they are structured—a men's department, a women's department, a luggage department, a lawn and garden department, and so on. Each department targets a specific customer category (men, women, people who want to buy luggage, people who want to buy a lawn mower) by using **customer departmentalization** to create departments that offer products and meet the needs of–identifiable customer groups. Thus, a customer shopping for a baby's playpen at Sears can bypass lawn and garden supplies and head straight for children's furniture. In general, the store is more efficient,

and customers get better service because salespeople tend to specialize and gain expertise in their departments. Another illustration of customer departmentalization is reflected in most banks. A customer wanting a consumer loan goes to the retail banking office, whereas a small business owner goes to the commercial banking office.

Geographic Departmentalization **Geographic departmentalization** divides firms according to the areas of the country or the world that they serve. Levi Strauss, for instance, has one division for North and South America; one for Europe, the Middle East, and North Africa; and one for the Asia Pacific region.[5] Within the United States, geographic departmentalization is common among utilities. For

CUSTOMER DEPARTMENTALIZATION dividing of an organization to offer products and meet needs for identifiable customer groups

GEOGRAPHIC DEPARTMENTALIZATION dividing of an organization according to the areas of the country or the world served by a business

Managing in Turbulent Times

Force-feeding the Market

Some business crises hit quickly, like the 2008–2009 recession. Others come more slowly. PepsiCo is facing one of the slow kind but is taking rapid action to turn things around. For years, consumption of soft drinks has been slowly declining. Driven primarily by health concerns, consumers in most countries are simply drinking fewer cans and bottles of the stuff. While there are no-sugar versions available, of course, Pepsi and Coke just don't taste quite the same when preceded by the word "Diet." Pepsi, for instance, shipped about 1 billion cases of soft drinks in 2007, down 20 percent from 2000.

To compensate, PepsiCo has been heavily promoting its juice, bottled water, and fruity soda brands. But the 2008–2009 recession took its toll on those products as well. PepsiCo CEO Indra Nooyi knew action was needed, so she promoted Massimo F. d'Amore to the position of CEO of PepsiCo Americas Beverages and gave him a mandate: Get the beverage business back on track.

d'Amore, in turn, decided to use organization structure as the primary driver to fix things. When he took over, the three major brands at PepsiCo Americas Beverages were Pepsi, Gatorade, and Tropicana—each operating as an independent division. d'Amore concluded that this independence was actually a problem in that the three brands were competing for the same resources, that there was too little coordination between the divisions, and that all too often, market information that should have been

communicated across the divisions was instead treated as proprietary and not shared with others.

To help offset these problems, d'Amore created one large operating division for all three of the major brands, as well as four others. This move rankled some key executives, who saw it as a reduction in their own power, and a few left the company. But d'Amore stuck to his guns and has maintained this new structure. He believes that a unified and coordinated approach to brand management will be the key that revives growth at PepsiCo Americas Beverages and will help the firm establish increased market share across all product lines and in all markets the unit serves. And if he is right, he will also have staked a major claim as Indra Nooyi's successor when she decides it's time to step down.[6]

example, Southern Company organizes its power subsidiaries into four geographic departments—Alabama, Georgia, Gulf, and Mississippi Power.[7]

Multiple Forms of Departmentalization Because different forms of departmentalization have different advantages, larger companies tend to adopt different types of departmentalization for various levels. The company illustrated in Figure 6.2 uses functional departmentalization at the top level. At the middle level, production is divided along geographic lines. At a lower level, marketing is departmentalized by product group. Recall from the opening vignette that PepsiCo has adopted a structure that includes three broad divisions: Americas Foods, Americas Beverages, andInter national. The first two divisions are based on product families, the third on geography. The "Managing in Turbulent Times" feature highlights other structural changes at PepsiCo designed to help the firm be more competitive.

Establishing the Decision-Making Hierarchy

The third major building block of organizational structure is the establishment of a decision-making hierarchy. This is usually done by formalizing reporting relationships. When the focus is on the reporting relationships among individual managers and the people who report

to them, it is most commonly referred to as *delegation*. However, when the focus is on the overall organization, it becomes a question of *decentralization* versus *centralization*.

Distributing Authority: Centralization and Decentralization

Some managers make the conscious decision to retain as much decision-making authority as possible at the higher levels of the organizational structure; others decide to push authority as far down the hierarchy as possible. While we can think of these two extremes as anchoring a continuum, most companies fall somewhere between the middle of such a continuum and one end point or the other.

Centralized Organizations In a **centralized organization**, most decision-making authority is held by upper-level managers.[8] McDonald's practices centralization as a way to maintain standardization. All restaurants must follow precise steps in buying products and making and packaging menu items. Most advertising is handled at the corporate level, and any local advertising must be approved by a regional manager. Restaurants even have to follow prescribed schedules for facilities' maintenance and upgrades like floor polishing and parking lot cleaning. Centralized authority is most commonly found in companies that face relatively stable and predictable environments and is also typical of small businesses.

Decentralized Organizations As a company gets larger, more decisions must be made; thus, the company tends to adopt **decentralized organization**, in which much decision-making authority is delegated to levels of management at various points below the top. Decentralization is typical in firms that have complex and dynamic environmental conditions. It makes a company more responsive by allowing managers more

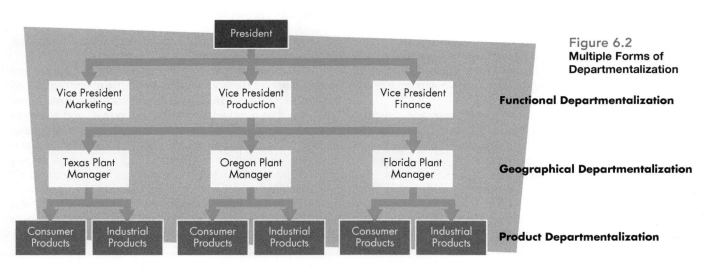

Figure 6.2
Multiple Forms of Departmentalization

Functional Departmentalization

Geographical Departmentalization

Product Departmentalization

The oil-industry giant ExxonMobil owns vast reserves of natural gas, like this field in the former Soviet republic of Turkmenistan. In most respects, ExxonMobil is a highly centralized company, but in this less stable market, which tends to innovate rapidly, many experts are skeptical about the company's ability to decentralize the control that management exercises over corporate operations.

discretion to make quick decisions in their areas of responsibility. For example, Urban Outfitters practices relative decentralization in that it allows individual store managers considerable discretion over merchandising and product displays.

Tall and Flat Organizations   Decentralized firms tend to have relatively fewer layers of management, resulting in a **flat organizational structure** like that of the hypothetical law firm shown in Figure 6.3(a). Centralized firms typically require multiple layers of management and thus **tall organizational structures**, as in the U.S. Army example in Figure 6.3(b). Because information, whether upward or downward bound, must pass through so many organizational layers, tall structures are prone to delays in information flow.

As organizations grow in size, it is both normal and necessary that they become at least somewhat taller. For instance, a small firm with only an owner-manager and a few employees is likely to have two layers—the owner-manager and the employees who report to that person. As the firm grows, more layers will be needed. A manager must ensure that he or she has only the number of layers his or her firm needs. Too few layers can create chaos and inefficiency, whereas too many layers can create rigidity and bureaucracy.

Span of Control   As you can see in Figure 6.3, the distribution of authority in an organization also affects the number of people who work for any individual manager. In a flat organizational structure, the number of people directly managed by one supervisor—the manager's **span of control**—is usually wide. In tall organizations, span of control tends to be narrower. Employees' abilities and the supervisor's managerial skills influence how

The Parts of Whole Foods

Whole Foods Market is an example of radical decentralization. Stores are broken up into small teams, which are responsible for making decisions on issues such as voting on which new staff members to hire and which products to carry based on local preferences. This practice taps into the idea that the people who will be most affected by decisions should be the ones making them.[9]

wide or narrow the span of control should be, as do the similarity and simplicity of tasks and the extent to which they are interrelated.

If lower-level managers are given more decision-making authority, their supervisors will have less work to do and may then be able to take on a widened span of control. Similarly, when several employees perform either the same simple task or a group of interrelated tasks, a wide span of control is possible and often desirable. For instance, because of the routine and interdependent nature of jobs on an assembly line, one supervisor may well control the entire line.

In contrast, when jobs are more diversified or prone to change, a narrow span of control is preferable. Consider how Electronic Arts develops video games. Design, art, audio, and software development teams have specialized jobs whose products must come together in the end to create a coherent game. Although related, the complexities involved with and the advanced skills required by each job mean that one supervisor can oversee only a small number of employees.[10]

DELEGATION process
through which a manager allocates work to subordinates

RESPONSIBILITY duty to perform an assigned task

AUTHORITY power to make the decisions necessary to complete a task

ACCOUNTABILITY obligation employees have to their manager for the successful completion of an assigned task

LINE AUTHORITY organizational structure in which authority flows in a direct chain of command from the top of the company to the bottom

LINE DEPARTMENT department directly linked to the production and sales of a specific product

Figure 6.3
Organizational Structure and Span of Control

The Delegation Process

Delegation is the process through which a manager allocates work to subordinates. In general, the delegation process involves:

1. Assigning **responsibility**, the duty to perform an assigned task

2. Granting **authority**, or the power to make the decisions necessary to complete the task

3. Creating **accountability**, the obligation employees have for the successful completion of the task

For the delegation process to work smoothly, responsibility and authority must be equivalent. Table 6.1 lists some common obstacles that hinder the delegation process, along with strategies for overcoming them.

Three Forms of Authority

As individuals are delegated responsibility and authority, a complex web of interactions develops in the form of *line*, *staff*, and *committee and team* authorities.

Line Authority The type of authority that flows up and down the chain of command is **line authority**. Most companies rely heavily on **line departments** linked directly to the production and sales of specific products. For example, in the division of Clark Equipment that produces forklifts and small earthmovers, line departments include purchasing, materials handling, fabrication, painting, and assembly (all of which are directly linked to production) along with sales and distribution (both of which are directly linked to sales).

As the doers and producers, each line department is essential to an organization's ability to sell and deliver finished goods. A bad decision by the manager in one department can hold up production for an entire plant. For example, the painting department manager at Clark Equipment changes a paint application on a batch of forklifts, which then show signs of peeling paint. The batch will have to be repainted (and perhaps partially reassembled) before the machines can be shipped.

Table 6.1 Learning to Delegate Effectively

I'm afraid to delegate because ...	Solution
My team doesn't know how to get the job done.	If members of your team are exhibiting opportunities for improved performance, offer them the training necessary for them to become more effective at their jobs.
I like controlling as many things as possible.	Recognize that trying to accomplish everything yourself while your team does nothing only sets you up for burnout and failure. As you begin to relinquish control, you will come to trust your team more as you watch your team members succeed.
I don't want anyone on my team outperforming me.	High-performing team members are a reflection of your success as a manager. Encourage them to excel, praise them for it, and share the success of *your* team with the rest of the organization.
I don't know how to delegate tasks effectively.	Consider taking a management training course or reading some books on the topic of delegating effectively.

Staff Authority Some companies also rely on **staff authority**, which is based on special expertise and usually involves advising line managers in areas such as law, accounting, and human resources. A corporate attorney, for example, may advise the marketing department as it prepares a new contract with the firm's advertising agency, but will not typically make decisions that affect how the marketing department does its job. **Staff members** help line departments make decisions, but do not usually have the authority to make final decisions.

Typically, the separation between line authority and staff responsibility is clearly delineated and is usually indicated in organization charts by solid lines (line authority) and dotted lines (staff responsibility), as shown in Figure 6.4. It may help to understand this separation by remembering that whereas *staff members* generally provide services to management, *line managers* are directly involved in producing the firm's products.

Committee and Team Authority Recently, more organizations have started to grant **committee and team authority** to groups that play central roles in daily operations. A committee, for example, may consist of top managers from several major areas. If the work of the committee is especially important and if the committee members will be working together for an extended time, the organization may even grant it special authority as a decision-making body beyond the individual authority possessed by each of its members.

At the operating level, many firms today use **work teams** that are empowered to plan, organize, and perform their work with minimal supervision and often with special authority as well. Most U.S. companies today use teams in at least some areas; some make widespread use of teams throughout every area of their operations.

**Figure 6.4
Line and Staff Organization**

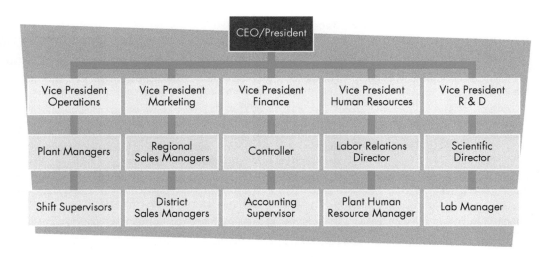

Figure 6.5
Functional Structure

Basic Forms of Organizational Structure

Organizations can structure themselves in an almost infinite number of ways. However, four basic forms reflect the trends followed by most firms: *functional*, *divisional*, *matrix*, and *international*.

Functional Structure

Under a **functional structure**, relationships between group functions and activities determine authority. Functional structure is used by most small to medium-sized firms, which are usually structured around basic business functions: a marketing department, an operations department, and a finance department. The benefits of this approach include specialization within functional areas and smoother coordination among them.

In large firms, coordination across functional departments becomes more complicated. Functional structure also fosters centralization (which can be desirable, but is usually counter to the goals of larger businesses) and

makes accountability more difficult. As organizations grow, they tend to shed this form and move toward one of the other three structures. Figure 6.5 illustrates a functional structure.

Divisional Structure

A **divisional structure** relies on product departmentalization. Organizations using this approach are typically structured around several product-based **divisions** that resemble separate businesses in that they produce and market their own products. The head of each division may be a corporate vice president or, if the organization is large enough, a divisional president. In addition, each division usually has its own identity and operates as a relatively autonomous business under the larger corporate umbrella. Figure 6.6 illustrates a divisional structure.

Johnson & Johnson, one of the most recognizable names in health care products, organizes its company into three major divisions: consumer health care products, medical devices and diagnostics, and pharmaceuticals. Each major division is then broken

Figure 6.6
Divisional Structure

down further. The consumer health care products division relies on product departmentalization to separate baby care, skin and hair care, topical health care, oral health care, women's health, over-the-counter medicines, and nutritionals. These divisions reflect the diversity of the company, which can protect it during downturns, such as the one in 2008 and 2009, which showed the slowest pharmaceutical growth in four decades. Because they are divided, the other divisions are protected from this blight and can carry the company through it.

Consider that Johnson & Johnson's over-the-counter pain management medicines are competition for their pain management pharmaceuticals. Divisions can maintain healthy competition among themselves by sponsoring separate advertising campaigns, fostering different corporate identities, and so forth. They can also share certain corporate-level resources (such as market research data). However, if too much control is delegated to divisional managers, corporate managers may lose touch with daily operations. Also, competition between divisions can become disruptive, and efforts in one division may duplicate those of another.[11]

Matrix Structure

Sometimes a **matrix structure**—a combination of two separate structures—works better than either simpler structure alone. This structure gets its matrix-like appearance, when shown in a diagram, by using one underlying "permanent" organizational structure (say, the divisional structure flowing up-and-down in the diagram), and then superimposing a different organizing framework on top of it (e.g., the functional form flowing side-to-side in the diagram). This highly flexible and readily adaptable structure was pioneered by NASA for use in developing specific space programs.

Suppose a company using a functional structure wants to develop a new product as a one-time special project. A team might be created and given responsibility for that product. The project team may draw members from existing functional departments, such as finance and marketing, so that all viewpoints are represented as the new product is being developed; the marketing member may provide ongoing information

MATRIX STRUCTURE organizational structure created by superimposing one form of structure onto another

---

Entrepreneurship and New Ventures

Making the Grade

In 1965, undistinguished Yale undergrad Fred Smith wrote a paper describing how automated technology necessitated quicker, more reliable transportation. According to legend, the paper received a poor grade. But Smith himself debunks this myth. "It's become a well-known story because everybody likes to flout authority. But to be honest, I don't really remember what grade I got."

Whatever the grade, the idea was a winner. After serving in Vietnam, Smith invested his own money to start the air transport business Federal Express. FedEx, as the firm is now named, was revolutionary in pioneering the hub-and-spoke system and using bar codes, handheld PDAs, and package tracking to compete with the monopolistic U.S. Postal Service.

When rival UPS entered the airfreight segment in 2000, FedEx acquired several key players in the ground transportation industry. "The economics of airplanes are such that we couldn't just keep taking prices down," Smith says. "We finally realized that if we wanted to grow, we had to get into surface transportation." FedEx's new fleet capitalized on the brand's reputation for speed and reliability: "People say 'FedEx this' when they mean 'Get it someplace fast,'" says investor Timothy M. Ghriskey. "No one says 'UPS this.'"

Although standardization is important, FedEx's commitment to decentralization breeds innovation. Managers are

encouraged and rewarded for questioning, challenging, and developing new ideas, which are always given serious consideration. Developments have included teaming up with Motorola and Microsoft to create a proprietary pocket-size PC, sending package information to cell phones, and creating software products for small business logistics. "Engage in constant change," is a mantra for CEO Smith, and he adds, "Companies that don't take risks—some of which are going to work and some of which aren't—are going to end up getting punched up by the marketplace."[12]

about product packaging and pricing issues, for instance, and the finance member may have useful information about when funds will be available.

In some companies, the matrix organization is a temporary measure installed to complete a specific project and affecting only one part of the firm. In these firms, the end of the project usually means the end of the matrix—either a breakup of the team or a restructuring to fit it into the company's existing line-and-staff structure. Ford, for example, uses a matrix organization to design new models, such as the newest Mustang. A design team composed of people with engineering, marketing, operations, and finance expertise was created to design the new car. After its work was done, the team members moved back to their permanent functional jobs.

In other settings, the matrix organization is a semipermanent fixture. Figure 6.7 shows how Martha Stewart Living Omnimedia has created a permanent matrix organization for its lifestyle business. As you can see, the company is organized broadly into media and merchandising groups, each of which has specific product and product groups. For instance, there is an Internet group housed within the media group. Layered on top of this structure are teams of lifestyle experts led by area specialists organized into groups, such as cooking, entertainment, weddings, crafts, and so forth. Although each group targets specific customer needs, they all work, as necessary, across all product groups. An area specialist in weddings, for example, might contribute to an article on wedding planning for an Omnimedia magazine, contribute a story idea for an Omnimedia cable television program, and supply content for an Omnimedia site. This same individual might also help select fabrics suitable for wedding gowns that are to be retailed.

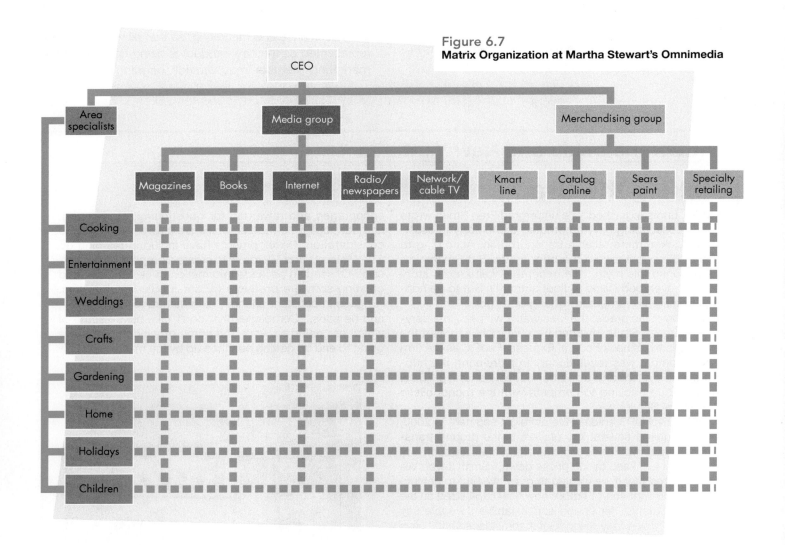

Figure 6.7
Matrix Organization at Martha Stewart's Omnimedia

International Structure

Several different **international organizational structures** have emerged in response to the need to manufacture, purchase, and sell in global markets.

For example, when Wal-Mart opened its first store outside the United States in 1992, it set up a special projects team. In the mid-1990s, the firm created a small international department to handle overseas expansion. By 1999 international sales and expansion had become such a major part of operations that a separate international division headed up by a senior vice president was created. By 2002, international operations had become so important that the international division was further divided into geographic areas, such as Mexico and Europe. And as the firm expands into more foreign markets, such as Russia and India, new units are created to oversee those operations.[13]

Some companies adopt a truly global structure in which they acquire resources (including capital), produce goods and services, engage in research and development, and sell products in whatever local market is appropriate, without consideration of national boundaries. Until a few years ago, General Electric (GE) kept its international business operations as separate divisions, as illustrated in Figure 6.8. Now, however, the company functions as one integrated global organization. GE businesses around the world connect and interact with each other constantly, and managers freely move back and forth among them. This integration is also reflected in GE's executive team, which includes executives from Spain, Japan, Scotland, Ireland, and Italy.[14]

Organizational Design for the Twenty-first Century

As the world grows increasingly complex and fast-paced, organizations also continue to seek new forms of organization that permit them to compete effectively. Among the most popular of these new forms are the *team organization*, the *virtual organization*, and the *learning organization*.

Team Organization *Team organization* relies almost exclusively on project-type teams, with little or no underlying functional hierarchy. People float from project to project as dictated by their skills and the demands of those projects. As the term suggests, team authority is the underlying foundation of organizations that adopt this organizational structure.

Virtual Organization Closely related to the team organization is the *virtual organization*. A virtual organization has little or no formal structure. Typically, it has only a handful of permanent employees, a very small staff, and a modest administrative facility. As the needs of the organization change, its managers bring in temporary workers, lease facilities, and outsource basic support services to meet the demands of each unique situation. As the situation changes, the temporary workforce changes in parallel, with some people leaving the organization and others entering. Facilities and the subcontracted services also change. In other words, the virtual organization exists only in response to its own needs.[15]

Figure 6.8
International Division Structure

INFORMAL ORGANIZATION network, unrelated to the firm's formal authority structure, of everyday social interactions among company employees

INTRAPRENEURING process of creating and maintaining the innovation and flexibility of a small-business environment within the confines of a large organization

This structure would be applicable to research or consulting firms that hire consultants based on the specific content knowledge required by each unique project. As the projects change, so too does the composition of the organization. Figure 6.9 illustrates a hypothetical virtual organization.

Learning Organization The so-called *learning organization* works to integrate continuous improvement with continuous employee learning and development. Specifically, a learning organization works to facilitate the lifelong learning and personal development of all of its employees while continually transforming itself to respond to changing demands and needs.

While managers might approach the concept of a learning organization from a variety of perspectives, the most frequent goals are superior quality, continuous improvement, and performance measurement. The idea is that the most consistent and logical strategy for achieving continuous improvement is to constantly upgrade employee talent, skill, and knowledge. For example, if each employee in an organization learns one new thing each day and can translate that knowledge into work-related practice, continuous improvement will logically follow. Indeed, organizations that wholeheartedly embrace this approach believe that only through constant employee learning can continuous improvement really occur. Shell Oil's Shell Learning Center boasts state-of-the-art classrooms and instructional technology, lodging facilities, a restaurant, and recreational amenities. Line managers rotate through the center to fulfill teaching assignments, and Shell employees routinely attend training programs, seminars, and related activities.

Informal Organization

The structure of a company, however, is by no means limited to the *formal organization* as represented by the organization chart and the formal assignment of authority. Frequently, the **informal organization**—everyday social interactions among employees that transcend

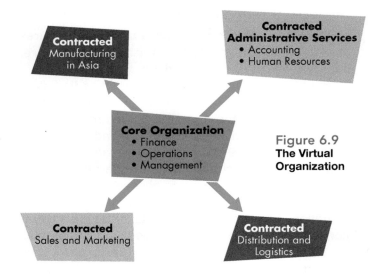

Figure 6.9
The Virtual Organization

formal jobs and job interrelationships—effectively alters a company's formal structure.[16] This level of organization is sometimes just as powerful—if not more powerful—than the formal structure. In 2005, Hewlett-Packard fired its CEO, Carly Fiorina. Much of the discussion that led to her firing took place outside formal structural arrangements in the organization—members of the board of directors, for example, held secret meetings and reached confidential agreements among themselves before Fiorina's future with the company was addressed in a formal manner.[17]

On the negative side, the informal organization can reinforce office politics that put the interests of individuals ahead of those of the firm and can disseminate distorted or inaccurate information. For example, if the informal organization is highlighting false information about impending layoffs, valuable employees may act quickly (and unnecessarily) to seek other employment.

Intrapreneuring

Good managers recognize that the informal organization exists whether they want it or not and can use it not only to reinforce the formal organization, but also to harness its energy to improve productivity.

Many firms, including Rubbermaid, 3M, and Xerox, support **intrapreneuring**—creating and maintaining the innovation and flexibility of a small-business environment within a large, bureaucratic structure. Historically, most innovations have come from individuals in small businesses. As businesses increase in size, however, innovation and creativity tend to become casualties in the battle for more sales and profits. In some large companies, new ideas are even discouraged, and champions of innovation have been stalled in midcareer. At Lockheed Martin, the Advanced Development Programs (ADP) encourages intrapreneurship in the tradition of Skunk Works, a legendary team developed in 1943 engineer Kelly Johnson's response to Lockheed's need for a powerful jet fighter. Johnson's innovative organization approach broke all the rules, and not only did it work, but it also taught Lockheed the value of encouraging that kind of thinking.[18]

Questions for Review

1. What is an organization chart? What purpose does it serve?

2. Explain the significance of size as it relates to organizational structure. Describe the changes that are likely to occur as an organization grows.

3. What is the difference between responsibility and authority?

4. Why do some managers have difficulties delegating authority? What solutions are available for managers with difficulties delegating authority?

5. What are the basic forms of organizational structure?

6. Why is a company's informal organization important? What are some of the drawbacks and benefits of the informal organization?

Questions for Analysis

7. Draw up an organization chart for your college or university. How would you describe the organizational structure of your college or university?

8. Describe a hypothetical organizational structure for a small printing firm. Describe changes that might be necessary as the business grows.

9. Compare and contrast the matrix and divisional approaches to organizational structure. How would you feel personally about working in a matrix organization in which you were assigned simultaneously to multiple units or groups?

Application Exercises

10. Interview the manager of a local service business, such as a fast-food restaurant. What types of tasks does this manager typically delegate? Is the appropriate authority also delegated in each case? What problems occur when authority is not delegated appropriately?

11. Using books, magazines, or personal interviews, identify a person who has succeeded as an intrapreneur. In what ways did the structure of the intrapreneur's company help this individual succeed? In what ways did the structure pose problems?

7 chapter

Operations Management and Quality

After reading this chapter, you should be able to:

1 Explain the meaning of the term *production* or *operations*.

2 Describe the three kinds of utility that operations processes provide for adding customer value.

3 Explain how companies with different business strategies are best served by having different operations capabilities.

4 Identify the major factors that are considered in operations planning and in operations control.

5 Discuss the information contained in four kinds of operations schedules—the master production schedule, detailed schedule, staff schedule, and project schedule.

6 Identify the activities and underlying objectives involved in total quality management.

7 Explain how a supply chain strategy differs from traditional strategies for coordinating operations among firms.

When Peanut Spreads Go Bad, Oh My!

They taste great—peanut butter crackers, nutrition bars, cookies, and ice cream—but surprisingly they can also be dangerous for consumers. Tasty family favorites are suspects in a nationwide salmonella outbreak that emerged in late 2008 and continued into 2009. By the time the first symptoms—cramping, fever, and diarrhea—had spread to some 700 reported sufferers, the outbreak may have caused nine deaths.

It started with one plant in Georgia shipping bulk peanut-butter paste to some 300 food producers, including General Mills, Kellogg Co., Abbott Nutrition, and Whole Foods, that use it in more than 2,000 products consumed by millions in the United States and beyond. Some U.S. products are sold in Mexico and as far away as Singapore and New Zealand. The consequences of producing poor quality in this case are widespread and potentially lethal.

Says Robert Brackett, of the Grocery Manufacturer's Association, "All it takes is a little company, and it has a huge ripple effect." In this case, a massive ripple spreads all the way from the consumer's table on back through each stage in the supply chain: Consumers must throw away products or return them to the store for a refund; retailers remove products from vending machines and store shelves, to be destroyed or returned to wholesale distributors; retailers suffer a plunge in sales; distributors' inventories (for supplying retailers) are shipped back to the companies that produced and packaged them; food producers isolate suspect bulk peanut paste and destroy it or return it to the bulk producer's plant at Blakely, Georgia.

Overall costs due to poor quality from just one producer are enormous. Medical bills are an obvious expense, and there are others, too. Transportation costs are multiplied by reshipments throughout the supply chain. Otherwise useful food is destroyed and disposed of. Productive resources are wasted—employee wages, equipment utilization, electricity and gas for production, packaging, shipping, and additional paperwork. All this waste can be avoided by assuring good quality instead of bad.[1]

What's in It for Me?

If—like the thousands of peanut-butter lovers disrupted by product recalls—you've ever been disappointed in a good or service that you bought, you'll find it easy to relate to the topics in this chapter. We'll explore the numerous ways companies align their operations processes with their business plans, and discuss how these decisions contribute to a firm's ability to create a high-quality product. Gaining an appreciation for the many steps it takes to bring high-quality goods and services to market will help make you a smarter consumer and more effective employee. And if you're a manager, understanding that production activities are pliable and should be reoriented to better support new business strategies will help you redefine your company and its marketplace over time.

What Does *Operations* Mean Today?

Although you're not always aware of it, you're constantly involved in business activities that provide goods and services to customers. You wake up to the sound of your favorite radio station, and on your bus ride to work or school you are texting on a cell phone. Your instructors, the bus driver, the messaging provider, and the morning radio announcer all work in **service operations** (or service production). They provide intangible and tangible service products, such as entertainment, transportation, education, and communications services. Firms that make only tangible products—radios, cell phones, buses, textbooks—are engaged in activities for **goods operations** (or goods production).

The term **operations** (or production) refers to all the activities involved in making products—goods and services—for customers. Although companies are typically classified as either goods producers or service providers, the distinction is often blurred. Consider General Electric. When you think of GE, you most likely think of appliances and jet engines. However, GE is not just a goods producer. According to its annual report, GE's "growth engines"—its most vibrant business activities—are service operations, including media and entertainment

(NBC Universal), consumer and commercial finance, investment, transportation services, and health care information, which account for over 80 percent of the company's revenues.[2]

Creating Value Through Operations

To understand a firm's production processes, we need to know what kinds of benefits its production provides, both for itself and for its customers. Production provides businesses with economic results: profits, wages, and goods purchased from other companies. At the same time, it adds customer value by providing **utility**—the ability of a product to satisfy a want or need—in terms of form, time, and place:

■ Production makes products available: By converting raw materials and human skills into finished goods and services, production creates *form utility*, as when Regal Cinemas combines building materials, theater seats, projection equipment, and food concessions to create entertainment.

■ When a theater offers mid-day, afternoon, and evening shows seven days a week, it creates *time utility*; that is, it adds customer value by making products available when consumers want them.

General Electric (GE) can be classified as both a goods producer (for example, of the GE Wind Turbine, shown here) and a service provider (for example, of media and entertainment shows such as *Saturday Night Live*).

- When a theater offers a choice of 15 movies, all under one roof at a popular location, it creates *place utility*: It makes products available where they are convenient for consumers.

Creating a product that customers value, then, is no accident, but instead results from organized effort. **Operations (production) management** is the systematic direction and control of the activities that transform resources into finished services and goods that create value for and provide benefits to customers. In overseeing production, **operations (production) managers** are responsible for ensuring that operations activities create what customers want and need.

Operations managers draw up plans to transform resources into products. First, they bring together basic resources: knowledge, physical materials, information, equipment, the customer, and human skills. Then they put them to effective use in a production facility. As demand for a product increases, they schedule and control work to produce the required amount. Finally, they control costs, quality levels, inventory, and facilities and equipment. In some businesses, the operations manager is one person. Typically, different employees work together to complete these different responsibilities.

Some operations managers work in factories; others work in offices, restaurants, theaters, and stores. Farmers are operations managers who create utility by transforming soil, seeds, fuel, and other inputs into soybeans, milk, and other outputs. They may hire crews of workers to plant and harvest, opt instead for automated machinery, or prefer some combination of workers and machinery. These decisions affect costs and determine the kinds of buildings and equipment in operations and the quality and quantity of goods produced.

Differences Between Service and Goods Manufacturing Operations

Both service and manufacturing operations transform raw materials into finished products. In service operations, however, the raw materials, or inputs, are not things like glass or steel. Rather, they are people who have either unsatisfied needs or possessions needing care or alteration. In service operations, finished products or outputs are people with needs met and possessions serviced.

Thus, there are several obvious differences between service and manufacturing operations. Four aspects of service operations can make them more complicated than simple goods production. These include (1) interacting with customers, (2) the intangible and unstorable nature of some services, (3) the customer's presence in the process, and (4) service quality considerations.

Interacting with Customers Manufacturing operations emphasize outcomes in terms of physical goods—for example, a new jacket. But the products of most *service* operations are really combinations of goods and services—both making a pizza *and* delivering (serving) it. Service workers need different skills. For example, gas company employees may need interpersonal skills to calm frightened customers who have reported gas leaks. Thus, the job includes more than just repairing pipes. In contrast, factory workers who install gas pipes in manufactured homes without any customer contact don't need such skills.

Services Can Be Intangible and Unstorable Two prominent characteristics—*intangibility* and *unstorability*—set services apart from physical goods:

- **Intangibility.** Often, services can't be touched, tasted, smelled, or seen, but they're still there. An important satisfier for customers, therefore, is the *intangible* value they receive in the form of pleasure, gratification, or a feeling of safety. For example, when you hire an attorney, you purchase not only the intangible quality of legal expertise but also the equally intangible reassurance that help is at hand.

- **Unstorability.** Many services—such as trash collection, transportation, child care, and house cleaning—can't be produced ahead of time and then stored for high-demand periods. If a service isn't used when available, it's usually wasted. Services, then, are typically characterized by a high degree of *unstorability*.

Customers' Presence in the Operations Process Because service operations transform customers or their possessions, the customer is often present in the operations process. To get a haircut, for example, most of us have to go to the barbershop or hair salon. As physical participants in the operations process, customers can affect it. As a customer, you expect the salon to be conveniently located (place utility), to be open for business at convenient times (time utility), to provide safe and comfortable facilities, and to offer high-quality grooming (form utility) at reasonable prices (value for money spent). Accordingly, the manager sets hours of operation, available services, and an appropriate number of employees to meet customer requirements. But what happens if a customer, scheduled to receive a haircut, also asks for additional services, such as highlights or a shave when he or she arrives? In this case, the service provider must adjust the schedule to provide customer satisfaction.

> **OPERATIONS (PRODUCTION) MANAGEMENT** systematic direction and control of the processes that transform resources into finished products that create value for and provide benefits to customers
>
> **OPERATIONS (PRODUCTION) MANAGERS** managers responsible for ensuring that operations processes create value and provide benefits to customers

High customer contact has the potential to affect the process significantly.

Intangibles Count for Service Quality Consumers use different measures to judge services and goods because services include intangibles, not just physical objects. Most service managers know that quality of work and quality of service are not necessarily the same thing. Your car, for example, may have been flawlessly repaired (quality of work), but you'll probably be unhappy with the service if you're forced to pick it up a day later than promised (quality of service).

Operations Processes

To better understand the diverse kinds of production in various firms and industries, it is helpful to classify production according to differences in operations processes. An **operations process** is a set of methods and technologies used to produce a good or a service. Banks, for example, use two processes—document shredding and data encryption—to protect confidential information. Automakers use precision painting methods to produce a glittering paint finish.

We can classify goods production into broad groupings, by asking whether its operations process has a "make-to-order" or a "make-to-stock" emphasis. We can classify services according to the extent of customer contact required.

Goods Production Processes: Make-to-Order Versus Make-to-Stock Processes Clothing, such as evening gowns, is available either off-the-shelf in department stores or custom-made at a designer/tailor shop. The designer/ tailor's **make-to-order operations** respond to one-of-a-kind gown requirements, including unique patterns, materials, sizes, and shapes, depending on customers' unique characteristics. **Make-to-stock operations**, in contrast,

produce standard gowns in large quantities to be stocked on store shelves or in displays for mass consumption. The production processes are quite different for the two settings, including procedures for designing gowns; planning for materials purchases; methods for cutting, sewing, and assembling gowns; and employee skills for production.

Service Production Processes: Extent of Customer Contact In classifying services, we may ask whether a service can be provided without the customer's being part of the production system. In answering this question, we classify services according to *extent of customer contact*.

Low-Contact Systems Consider the postal delivery operations at your local U.S. post office. Postal employees gather mail, sort it, and send it on its journey to addressees. This operation is a **low-contact system**: Customers are not in contact with the post office while the service is performed. They receive the service—mail sent and mail received—without setting foot in the processing center. Gas and electric companies, auto repair shops, and lawn-care services are other examples of low-contact systems.

High-Contact Systems Think about your local public transit system. The service is transportation, and when you purchase transportation, you board a bus or train. For example, the Bay Area Rapid Transit (BART) system, which connects San Francisco with outlying suburbs and, like all public transit systems, is a **high-contact system**: To receive the service, the customer must be part of the system. Thus, managers must worry about the cleanliness of trains and the appearance of stations.

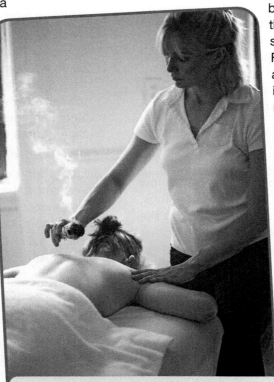

Because service operations transform customers or their possessions, the customer is often present in the operations process.

Business Strategy as the Driver of Operations

There is no one standard way for doing production. Rather, a company selects the kind of production that best achieves its larger business strategy.

Table 7.1   Business Strategies That Win Customers for Four Companies

Company	Strategy for Attracting Customers	What the Company Does to Implement Its Strategy
Toyota	Quality	Cars perform reliably, have an appealing fit and finish, and consistently meet or exceed customer expectations at a competitive price
Save-A-Lot	Low price	Foods and everyday items offered at savings up to 40 percent less than conventional food chains
3M	Flexibility	Innovation, with more than 55,000 products in a constantly changing line of convenience items for home and office
FedEx	Dependability	Every delivery is fast and on time, as promised

> **OPERATIONS CAPABILITY (PRODUCTION CAPABILITY)** special ability that production does especially well to outperform the competition

The Many Faces of Production Operations

Consider the four firms listed in Table 7.1. Two are in goods production (Toyota and 3M), and two are in services. Each company has identified a business strategy that it can use for attracting customers in its industry. For Toyota, *quality* was chosen as the strategy for competing in selling autos. Save-A-Lot grocery stores, in contrast to others in the grocery industry, offer customers *lower prices*. The *flexibility* strategy at 3M emphasizes new product development in an ever-changing line of products for home and office. FedEx captures the overnight delivery market by emphasizing delivery *dependability*, first and foremost.

Business Strategy Determines Operations Capabilities Successful firms design their operations to support the company's business strategy.[3] In other words, production operations are adjusted to support the firms' target markets. Since our four firms use different business strategies, we should expect to see differences in their operations, too. The top-priority **operations capability (production capability)**—the special ability that production does especially well to outperform the competition—is listed for each firm in Table 7.2, along with key operations characteristics for implementing

Table 7.2   Operations Capabilities and Characteristics for Four Companies

Operations Capability	Key Operations Characteristics
Quality (Toyota)	• High-quality standards for materials suppliers • Just-in-time materials flow for lean manufacturing • Specialized, automated equipment for consistent product build-up • Operations personnel are experts on continuous improvement of product, work methods, and materials
Low Cost (Save-A-Lot)	• Avoids excessive overhead and costly inventory (no floral departments, sushi bars, or banks that drive up costs) • Limited assortment of products, staples, in one size only for low-cost restocking, lower inventories, and less paperwork • Many locations; small stores—less than half the size of conventional grocery stores—for low construction and maintenance costs • Reduces labor and shelving costs by receiving and selling merchandise out of custom shipping cartons
Flexibility (3M)	• Maintains some excess (expensive) production capacity available for fast start on new products • Adaptable equipment/facilities for production changeovers from old to new products • Hires operations personnel who thrive on change • Many medium- to small-sized facilities in diverse locations, which enhances creativity
Dependability (FedEx)	• Customer automation: uses electronic and online tools with customers to shorten shipping time • Wireless information system for package scanning by courier, updating of package movement, and package tracking by customer • Maintains a company air force, global weather forecasting center, and ground transportation for pickup and delivery, with backup vehicles for emergencies • Each of 30 automated regional distribution hubs processes up to 45,000 packages per hour for next-day deliveries

that capability. Each company's operations capability matches up with its business strategy so that the firm's activities—from top to bottom—are focused in a particular direction.

For example, because Toyota's top priority focuses on quality, its operations—the resource inputs for production, the transformation activities, and the outputs from production—are devoted first and foremost to that characteristic. Its car designs and production processes emphasize appearance, reliable performance, and desirable features at a reasonable price. All production processes, equipment, and training are designed to build better cars. The entire culture supports a quality emphasis among employees, suppliers, and dealerships. Had Toyota instead chosen to compete as the low-price car in the industry, as some successful car companies do, then a cost-minimization focus would have been appropriate, giving Toyota's operations an altogether different form. Toyota's operations support its chosen business strategy, and do it successfully.

Expanding into Additional Capabilities Finally, it should be noted that excellent firms learn, over time,

how to achieve more than just one competence. Our four example firms eventually became excellent in several capabilities. FedEx, for example, in addition to dependability, is noted for world-class service quality and cost containment, too. But in the earlier start-up years, its primary and distinguishing capability, which set it apart from the competition, was dependability, the foundation upon which future success was built.

Operations Planning

Let's turn now to a discussion of production activities and resources that are considered in every business organization. Like all good managers, we start with planning. Managers from many departments contribute to decisions about operations. As Figure 7.1 shows, however, no matter how many decision makers are involved, the process is a logical sequence of decisions.

The business plan and forecasts developed by top managers provide guidance for long-term operations

Entrepreneurship and New Ventures

From a Missouri Garage to Hollywood

The feature films *The Red Canvas* and the upcoming *Way of the Guardian* were not developed by your typical Hollywood production team. For starters, one of the films' co-creators lives and works in Missouri. Adam Boster and his partner, Ken Chamitoff, started Photo-Kicks—a marketing company specializing in action photography—in their garages in 2002. From their beginnings photographing students at local martial arts schools, Boster and Chamitoff built Photo-Kicks into a multimillion-dollar business employing photographers, graphic designers, and marketers throughout the United States and Canada. In 2007 Photo-Kicks came in at number 592 on *Inc.* magazine's list of the 5,000 fastest-growing private companies in America.

Just a quick glance at the many photographs on display at the Photo-Kicks Web site (http://photo-kicks.com) provides an eye-opening introduction to action photography. Athletes young and old punch, kick, and leap their way across the frames. But it's the countless other services that Photo-Kicks provides its customers that have allowed it to grow so rapidly. Photo-Kicks bills itself as "a fully equipped graphic design and marketing organization," creating such products as customized logos, brochures, Web sites, posters, and trading cards.

Then, of course, there are the movies. *Way of the Guardian* began as a card game and animated series also

developed by Boster and Chamitoff. *The Red Canvas*, a 2008 award-winning action film, is more personal. It tells the story of a struggling immigrant who finds success and redemption in the sport of mixed martial arts. Chamitoff acknowledges that the film could not have happened without the years he and Boster spent traveling the country photographing martial arts students. "I learned the stories of every person I encountered," said Chamitoff. Those stories shaped not only *The Red Canvas*, but Photo-Kicks as well.[4]

plans. Covering a two- to five-year period, the operations plan anticipates the number of plants or service facilities and the amount of labor, equipment, transportation, and storage needed to meet future demand for new and existing products. The planning activities fall into five categories: *capacity*, *location*, *layout*, *quality*, and *methods planning*.

Capacity Planning

The amount of a product that a company can produce under normal conditions is its **capacity**. A firm's capacity depends on how many people it employs and the number and size of its facilities. A supermarket's capacity for customer checkouts, for instance, depends on its number of checkout stations. A typical store has excess capacity—more cash registers than it needs—on an average day, but on Saturday morning or during the three days before Thanksgiving, they'll all be running at full capacity.

Long-range capacity planning considers both current and future requirements. If capacity is too small for demand, the company must turn away customers—a situation that cuts into profits and alienates both customers and salespeople. If capacity greatly exceeds demand, the firm is wasting money by maintaining facilities that are too large, keeping excess machinery online, or employing too many workers.

Location Planning

Because location affects production costs and flexibility, sound location planning is crucial for factories, offices, and stores. Depending on its site, a company may be able to produce low-cost products, or it may find itself at a cost disadvantage relative to its competitors.

Consider the reasons why Slovakia is fast becoming known as "Detroit East." The central European country is an ideal place to produce cars. It has a good railroad system and nearby access to the Danube River, meaning economical transportation for incoming materials and outgoing cars once auto factories are in operation. The area also has skilled, hard-working laborers, and wages lower than those of surrounding countries.[5]

In contrast to manufacturing, consumer services concentrate on being located near customers. Thus, fast-food restaurants, such as Taco Bell and McDonald's, are located in areas with high traffic, such as dormitories, hospital cafeterias, and shopping malls. At retail giant Wal-Mart, managers of the company's huge distribution centers regard Wal-Mart outlets as their customers. To ensure that truckloads of merchandise flow quickly to stores, distribution centers are located near the hundreds of Wal-Mart stores that they supply, not near the companies that supply them.

CAPACITY amount of a product that a company can produce under normal conditions

CUSTOM-PRODUCTS LAYOUT physical arrangement of production activities that groups equipment and people according to function

Layout Planning

Layout is the physical location or floor plan for machinery, equipment, and supplies. It determines whether a company can respond efficiently to demand for more and different products or whether it finds itself unable to match competitors' speed and convenience. Among the many layout possibilities, two well-known alternatives—*custom-products layouts and same-steps layouts*—are presented here to illustrate how different layouts serve different purposes for operations.

Custom-Products Layouts In a **custom-products layout**, which is well suited to *make-to-order shops* (or

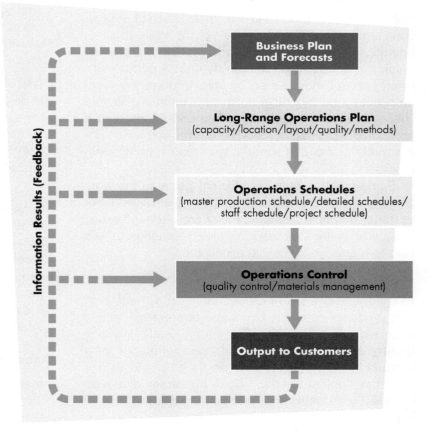

Figure 7.1
Operations Planning and Control

job shops) specializing in custom work, equipment and people are grouped according to function. Kinko's Copy Centers, for example, use custom-products layouts to accommodate a variety of custom jobs. Specific activities, such as photocopying, computing, binding, photography, and laminating, are performed in separate, specialized areas of the store.

The main advantage of custom-products layouts is flexibility—at any time, the shop can process individual customer orders, each requiring different kinds of work. Depending on its work requirements, a job may flow through three activity areas, another through just one area, and still others through four or more work zones. Machining, woodworking, and dry cleaning shops, as well as health clinics and physical fitness studios, are among the many facilities using custom-products layouts.

Same-Steps Layouts A **same-steps layout** is set up to make one type of product in a fixed sequence of production steps. It is efficient for large-volume make-to-stock operations that mass-produce many units of a product quickly, often using an **assembly line**: A partially finished product moves step by step through the plant on conveyor belts or other equipment, often in a straight line, as it passes through each stage until the product is completed. Automobile, food-processing, and television-assembly plants use same-steps layouts, as do mail-processing facilities, such as UPS or FedEx.

Same-steps layouts are efficient because the work skill is built into the equipment, allowing unskilled labor to perform simple tasks. But they are often inflexible, especially where they use specialized equipment that's hard to rearrange for new applications.

Quality Planning

Every operations plan includes activities for ensuring that products meet the firm's and customers' quality standards. The American Society for Quality defines **quality** as the combination of "characteristics of a product or service that bear on its ability to satisfy stated or implied needs."[6] Such characteristics may include a reasonable price and dependability in delivering the benefits it promises.

Planning for quality begins when products are being designed. Early in the process, goals are established for both performance and consistency. **Performance** refers to how well the product does what it is supposed to do. For loyal buyers of Godiva premium chocolates, performance includes such sensory delights as aroma, flavor, color, and texture. Superior performance helps Godiva remain one of the world's top brands.[7]

In addition to performance, quality also includes **consistency**—the sameness of product quality from unit to unit. Business travelers using Courtyard by Marriott, for example, enjoy high consistency with each overnight stay, which is one reason Courtyard by Marriott is among the best-selling brands in the lodging industry. This is achieved by maintaining the same features at all of Marriott's nearly 700 U.S. locations. Designed for business travelers, most guest rooms include a Courtyard Suite with high-speed internet access, meeting space, and access to an exercise room, restaurant and lounge, swimming pool, and 24-hour access to food. The layout of the suites is identical at many locations, the rooms are always clean, and check-in/check-out procedures are identical so that lodgers know what to expect with each overnight stay. This consistency is achieved by monitoring for uniformity of materials and supplies, encouraging conscientious work, training employees, and maintaining equipment.

In addition to product design, quality planning includes employees deciding what constitutes a high-quality product—for both goods and services—and determining how to measure these quality characteristics.

Methods Planning

In designing operations systems, managers must identify each production step and the specific methods for performing it. They can then reduce waste and inefficiency by examining procedures on a step-by-step basis—an approach called *methods improvement*.

Improving Process Flows Improvements for operations begin by documenting current production practices. A detailed description, often using a diagram called a *process flowchart*, is helpful in organizing and recording information. The flowchart identifies the sequence of production activities, movements of materials, and work performed at each stage of the process. It can then be analyzed to isolate wasteful activities, sources of delay, and other inefficiencies in both goods and services operations. The final step is implementing improvements.

Improving Customer Service Consider, for example, the traditional checkout method at hotels. The process flowchart in Figure 7.2 shows five stages of customer

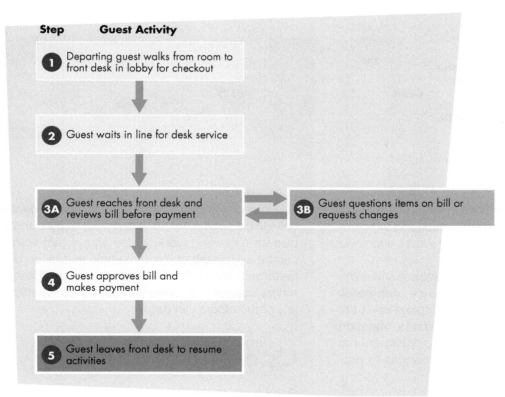

Step   **Guest Activity**

1. Departing guest walks from room to front desk in lobby for checkout

2. Guest waits in line for desk service

3A. Guest reaches front desk and reviews bill before payment

3B. Guest questions items on bill or requests changes

4. Guest approves bill and makes payment

5. Guest leaves front desk to resume activities

Figure 7.2
Flowchart of Traditional Guest Checkout

MASTER PRODUCTION SCHEDULE schedule showing which products will be produced and when, in upcoming time periods

DETAILED SCHEDULE schedule showing daily work assignments with start and stop times for assigned jobs

STAFF SCHEDULE assigned working times in upcoming days for each employee on each work shift

activities. A more efficient checkout method was developed that eliminates steps 1, 2, 3A, and 5. Customers now scan their bills on television in the privacy of their rooms any time before departure. If the bill is correct, no further checkout is required, and the hotel submits the charges against the credit card that the customer submitted during check-in.

Operations Scheduling

Once operations plans have been determined, managers then develop timetables for implementing them. This aspect of operations, called *operations scheduling*, identifies times when specific production activities will occur.

The Master Production Schedule

Scheduling of production occurs at different levels. First, a top-level **master production schedule** shows which products will be produced, and when, in upcoming time periods. Logan Aluminum, for example, makes coils of aluminum that it supplies to five customer companies that use it to make beverage cans. Logan's master schedule, with a format like the partial schedule shown in Figure 7.3, covers production for 60 weeks in which more than 300,000 tons will be produced. For various

types of coils (products), it specifies how many tons will be produced each week, helping managers determine the kinds of materials, equipment, and other resources that will be needed for each week's production.

Detailed Schedules

While the master production schedule is the backbone for overall scheduling, additional information comes from **detailed schedules**—schedules showing daily work assignments with start and stop times for assigned jobs at each work station. Logan's production personnel need to know the locations of all coils in the plant and their various stages of completion. Start and stop times must be assigned, and employees need scheduled work assignments daily, not just weekly. Detailed short-term schedules allow managers to use customer orders and information about equipment status to update sizes and the variety of coils to be made each day.

Staff Schedules and Computer-Based Scheduling

Scheduling is useful for employee staffing in service companies, too, including restaurants, hotels, transportation, and landscaping. **Staff schedules**, in general, specify assigned working times in upcoming days—perhaps for

GANTT CHART production schedule that breaks down large projects into steps to be performed and specifies the time required to perform each step

OPERATIONS CONTROL process of monitoring production performance by comparing results with plans and taking corrective action when needed

Figure 7.3
Example Partial Master Production Schedule (Tons of Each Product to Be Produced)

Coil # (Product)	8/6/07	8/13/07	8/20/07	...	11/5/07	11/12/07
TC016	1,500	2,500			2,100	600
TC032	900		2,700		3,000	
TR020	300		2,600			1,600

as many as 30 days or more—for each employee on each work shift. They consider employees' needs and the company's efficiency and costs, including the ebbs and flows of demand for production.

Computer-based scheduling, using tools such as the *ABS Visual Staff Scheduler PRO* software, can easily handle multi-shift activities for many employees—both part-time and full-time. It accommodates vacation times, holiday adjustments, and daily adjustments in staffing for unplanned absences and changes in production schedules.

Project Scheduling

Special projects, such as new business construction or redesigning a product, require close coordination and precise timing among many activities. In these cases, project management is facilitated by project scheduling tools, including graphical methods such as the Gantt chart (named after its developer, Henry Gantt).

A **Gantt chart** breaks down large projects into steps to be performed and specifies the time required to perform each one. The project manager lists all activities needed to complete the work, estimates the time required for each step, records the progress on the chart, and checks the progress against the time scale on the chart to keep the project moving on schedule. If work is ahead of schedule, some employees may be shifted to another project. If it's behind schedule, workers may be added or completion delayed.

Figure 7.4 shows a Gantt chart for the renovation of a college classroom. It shows progress to date and schedules for remaining work. It also shows that some steps can be performed at the same time (e.g., step D can be performed during the same time as steps C and E), but others cannot (e.g., step A must be completed before any of the others can begin).

Operations Control

Once long-range plans have been put into action and schedules have been drawn up, **operations control** requires managers to monitor performance by comparing results with detailed plans and schedules. If schedules or quality standards aren't met, managers can take

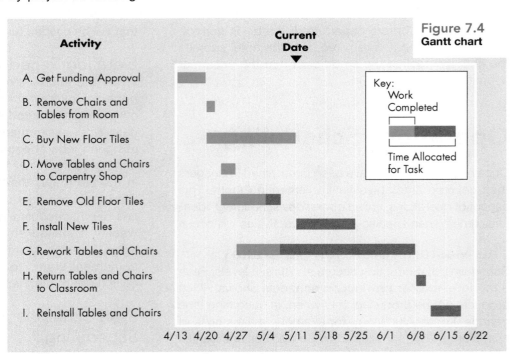

Figure 7.4
Gantt chart

corrective action. **Follow-up**—checking to ensure that production decisions are being implemented—is a key and ongoing facet of operations.

Operations control includes *materials management* and *quality control*. Both activities ensure that schedules are met and products delivered, both in quantity and in quality.

Materials Management

Most of us have difficulty keeping track of personal items now and then—clothes, books, DVDs, and so on. Imagine keeping track of thousands or even millions of things at any one time. That's the challenge in **materials management**—the process by which managers plan, organize, and control the flow of materials from sources of supply through distribution of finished goods. For manufacturing firms, typical materials costs make up 50 to 75 percent of total product costs. For service firms, too, the materials stakes are high. UPS delivers 16 million packages every day and promises that all of them will arrive on schedule. It keeps this promise by tracking the locations, schedules, and on-time performance of 600 aircraft and 100,000 vehicles as they carry packages through the delivery system.

Materials Management Activities Once a product has been designed, successful materials flows depend on five activities. From selecting suppliers on through the distribution of finished goods, materials managers engage in the following areas that compose materials management:

- **Supplier selection** means finding and choosing suppliers of services and materials to buy from. It includes evaluating potential suppliers, negotiating terms of service, and maintaining positive buyer–seller relationships.

- **Purchasing** is the acquisition of all the raw materials and services that a company needs to produce its products. Most large firms have purchasing departments to buy proper materials in the amounts needed.

FOLLOW-UP operations control activity for ensuring that production decisions are being implemented

MATERIALS MANAGEMENT process of planning, organizing, and controlling the flow of materials from sources of supply through distribution of finished goods

SUPPLIER SELECTION process of finding and choosing suppliers from whom to buy

LEAN PRODUCTION SYSTEM production system designed for smooth production flows that avoid inefficiencies, eliminate unnecessary inventories, and continuously improve production processes

JUST-IN-TIME (JIT) PRODUCTION type of lean production system that brings together all materials at the precise time they are required at each production stage

PURCHASING acquisition of the materials and services that a firm needs to produce its products

It's All in the Timing

Lean production systems, pioneered by Toyota, are designed for smooth production flows that avoid inefficiencies, eliminate unnecessary inventories, and continuously improve production processes. **Just-in-time (JIT) production**, a type of lean system, brings together all needed materials at the precise moment they are required for each production stage, not before, thus creating fast and efficient responses to customer orders. All resources flow continuously—from arrival as raw materials to final assembly and shipment of finished products.

JIT production reduces to practically nothing the number of goods in process (goods not yet finished). It minimizes inventory costs, reduces storage space requirements for inventories, and saves money by replacing stop-and-go production with smooth movement. Once smooth flow is the norm, disruptions are more visible and are resolved more quickly. Finding and eliminating disruptions by the continuous improvement of production is a major objective of JIT production.

Quality control means
taking action to ensure that
operations produce
products that meet specific
quality standards.

■ **Transportation** includes the means of transporting resources to the producer and finished goods to buyers.

■ **Warehousing** is the storage of both incoming materials for production and finished goods for distribution to customers.

■ **Inventory control** includes the receiving, storing, handling, and counting of all raw materials, partly finished goods, and finished goods. It ensures that enough materials inventories are available to meet production schedules, while at the same time avoiding expensive excess inventories.

Quality Control

Quality control means taking action to ensure that operations produce goods or services that meet specific quality standards. At a bank, for example, quality control for teller services might require supervisors to observe employees periodically and evaluate their work according to a checklist. The results would then be reviewed with employees and would either confirm proper performance or indicate changes for bringing performance up to standards.

The quality of customer-employee interactions is no accident in firms that monitor customer encounters and provide training for employee skills development. Many managers realize that without employees trained in customer-relationship skills, quality suffers, and businesses, such as airlines and hotels, can lose customers to better-prepared competitors.

Quality Improvement and Total Quality Management

It is not enough to *control* quality by inspecting products and monitoring service operations as they occur, like when a supervisor listens in on a catalog sales service representative's customer calls. Businesses must also consider *building* quality into products and services. In order to compete on a global scale, U.S. companies continue to emphasize a quality orientation. All employees, not just managers, participate in quality efforts, and firms have embraced new methods to measure progress and to identify areas for improvement. In many organizations, quality improvement has become a way of life.

Managing for Quality

Total quality management (TQM) includes all the activities necessary for getting high-quality goods and services into the marketplace. It must consider all aspects of a business, including customers, suppliers, and employees. To marshal the interests of all these stakeholders, TQM first evaluates the costs of poor quality. It then involves assigning and accepting responsibility for quality improvement.

The Cost of Poor Quality As seen in this chapter's opener, poor quality of foods produced from contaminated peanut-butter paste was dangerous and costly in various ways to many consumers and producers. As with goods producers, service providers and

---

Managing in Turbulent Times

Will Leaner Operations Restore the U.S. Auto Industry?

General Motors and Chrysler, suffering grave financial losses, need to demonstrate that they can survive and repay the bridge loans received from the U.S. Department of the Treasury. Under the guise of restructuring or reorganization, the steps automakers are considering can be summarized in just two words: *leaner operations*. GM, Chrysler, and Ford are adopting business strategies that Japanese producers have been using (and have mastered) for three decades to simplify production and capture a greater market share.

A reduction in product offerings is the foundation for leaner operations: A smaller number of makes, models, and options such as colors, engine sizes, trims, etc. simplifies product design, production, and distribution. It leads to lower costs, higher quality, and better customer service. Because it's easier to design a few rather than many different products, design and engineering requirements are vastly lowered. Designers strive for commonality of component parts so that all models use the same parts [e.g., all use the same door handles] rather than having separate designs for each model. Parts reductions simplify the supply chain, too: Fewer suppliers are needed, communications are easier and faster, and closer relationships with suppliers provide faster supplier responses on short notice.

Design simplification is a blessing for assembly operations, too, because fewer production steps are required, and when quality problems arise, they are easier to find and are quickly corrected. Because fewer components require less inventory space and equipment, smaller factories—which are less costly and easier to maintain—become possible. Production scheduling is simpler, as are materials movements during production, so there is less work stoppage and there are fewer mistakes, product quality improves, and on-time deliveries to customers increase.

The company's distribution network is simplified, too, when some of its auto brands are eliminated. Fewer brands means some auto dealerships are no longer needed, thus lowering distribution costs. With speedier product designs and production operations, newer products get into the marketplace more quickly than those of competitors, and customer service improves. When the benefits of lower costs, higher quality, and lower prices are added together, it becomes apparent that lean production systems offer significant competitive advantages. Causing it to happen, and quickly, at GM, Chrysler, and Ford is a massive challenge for survival in turbulent times.

customers, too, suffer financial distress from poor-quality service products. The banking industry is a current example. As a backbone of the U.S. financial system, banks and their customers are still suffering because of bad financial products, most notably home mortgage loans. Lenders during "good times" began relaxing (or even ignoring altogether) traditional lending standards for determining whether borrowers are credit worthy (are they qualified to borrow and likely to repay mortgage loans?). Lenders in some cases intentionally overstated property values so customers could borrow more money than the property justified. Borrowers were sometimes encouraged to overstate (falsify) their incomes and were not required to present evidence of income or even employment. Some borrowers, unaware of the terms of their loan agreements and, after an initial time lapse, were surprised when a much higher interest rate (and monthly payment) suddenly kicked in. Unable to meet their payments, borrowers had to abandon their homes. Meanwhile, banks were left holding foreclosed properties, unpaid (defaulted) loans, and no cash. With shortages of bank funds threatening to shut down the entire financial system, the entire nation felt the widespread costs of poor quality.

Quality Ownership: Taking Responsibility for Quality To assure high-quality goods and services, many firms assign responsibility for some aspects of TQM to specific departments or positions. These specialists and experts may be called in to assist with quality-related problems in any department, and they keep everyone informed about the latest developments in quality-related equipment and methods. They also monitor quality-control activities to identify areas for improvement.

The backbone of TQM, however, and its biggest challenge, is motivating all employees throughout the company and its suppliers to achieve quality goals. Leaders of the quality movement use various methods and resources to foster a quality focus—training, verbal encouragement, teamwork, and tying compensation to work quality. When those efforts succeed, employees and suppliers will ultimately accept **quality ownership**—the idea that quality belongs to each person who creates it while performing a job.

Tools for Total Quality Management

Hundreds of tools have proven useful for quality improvement, ranging from statistical analysis of product data, to satisfaction surveys of customers, to **competitive product analysis**—a process by which a company analyzes a competitor's products to identify desirable improvements. In this section, we survey five of the most commonly used tools for TQM: *value-added analysis*, *quality improvement teams*, *getting closer to the customer*, *the ISO series*, and *business process reengineering*.

Value-Added Analysis **Value-added analysis** refers to the evaluation of all work activities, materials flows, and paperwork to determine the value that they add for customers. It often reveals wasteful or unnecessary activities that can be eliminated without jeopardizing customer service.

Quality Improvement Teams Companies throughout the world have adopted **quality improvement teams** patterned after the successful Japanese concept of *quality circles*: collaborative groups of employees from various work areas who meet regularly to define, analyze, and solve common production problems. Their goal is to improve both their own work methods and the products they make. Quality improvement teams organize their own work, select leaders, and address problems in the workplace.

Getting Closer to the Customer Successful businesses take steps to know what their customers want in the products they consume. On the other hand, struggling companies have often lost sight of customers as the driving force behind all business activity. Such companies waste resources by designing products that customers do not want. Sometimes, they ignore customer reactions to existing products or fail to keep up with changing tastes.

Identifying Customers—Internal and External Improvement projects are undertaken for both external and internal customers. Internal suppliers and internal customers exist wherever one employee or activity relies on others. For example, marketing managers rely on internal accounting information—costs for materials, supplies, and wages—to plan marketing activities for coming months. The marketing manager is a customer of the firm's accountants—the information user relies on the information supplier. Accountants in a TQM environment recognize this supplier–customer connection and take steps to improve information for marketing.

The ISO Series Perhaps you've driven past companies proudly displaying large banners announcing, "This Facility Is ISO Certified." The ISO (pronounced ICE-oh) label is a mark of quality achievement that is respected throughout the world and, in some countries, it's a requirement for doing business.

ISO 9000 **ISO 9000** is a certification program attesting that a factory, a laboratory, or an office has met the rigorous quality management requirements set by the International Organization for Standardization. Today, more than 140 countries have adopted ISO 9000 as a national standard. To become certified, companies must document the procedures followed by workers during every stage of production. The purpose is to ensure that a company's processes can create products exactly the same today as it did yesterday and as it will tomorrow.

ISO 14000 The **ISO 14000** program certifies improvements in environmental performance by requiring a firm to develop an *environmental management system*: a plan documenting how the company has acted to improve its performance in using resources (such as raw materials) and in managing pollution. A company must not only identify hazardous wastes that it expects to create, but it must also stipulate plans for treatment and disposal.

Business Process Reengineering Every business consists of processes—activities that it performs regularly and routinely in conducting business, such as receiving and storing materials from suppliers, billing patients for medical treatment, and filing insurance claims for auto accidents.

Business process reengineering focuses on improving a business process—rethinking each of its steps by starting from scratch. *Reengineering* is the fundamental rethinking and radical redesign of business processes to achieve dramatic improvements as measured by cost, quality, service, and speed. As companies conduct an increasing amount of their business online, old processes must be reengineered to utilize the power of the Internet.

Adding Value Through Supply Chains

The term *supply chain* refers to the group of companies and stream of activities that work together to create a product. A **supply chain** (or **value chain**) for any product is the flow of information, materials, and services that starts with raw-materials suppliers and continues adding value through other stages in the network of firms until the product reaches the end customer.

Figure 7.5 shows the chain of activities for supplying baked goods to consumers. Each stage adds value for the final customer. This bakery example begins with raw materials (grain harvested from the farm). It also includes storage and transportation activities, factory operations for baking and wrapping, and distribution to retailers. Each stage depends on the others for success in getting freshly baked goods to consumers. However, a failure by any link can spell disaster for the entire chain, as in the case of the contamination of peanut-butter paste.

The Supply Chain Strategy

Traditional strategies assume that companies are managed as individual firms rather than as members of a coordinated supply system. Supply chain strategy is based on the idea that members of the chain will gain competitive advantage by working as a coordinated unit.

A traditionally managed bakery, for example, would focus simply on getting production inputs from flour millers and paper suppliers and supplying baked goods to distributors. Unfortunately, this approach limits the chain's performance and doesn't allow for possible improvements when activities are more carefully coordinated. Proper management and better coordination of the supply chain can provide fresher baked goods at lower prices.

ISO 9000 program certifying that a factory, laboratory, or office has met the quality management standards set by the International Organization for Standardization

ISO 14000 certification program attesting to the fact that a factory, laboratory, or office has improved its environmental performance

BUSINESS PROCESS REENGINEERING rethinking and radical redesign of business processes to improve performance, quality, and productivity

SUPPLY CHAIN (VALUE CHAIN) flow of information, materials, and services that starts with raw-materials suppliers and continues adding value through other stages in the network of firms until the product reaches the end customer

Supply Chain Management

Supply chain management (SCM) looks at the chain as a whole to improve the overall flow through a system composed of companies working together. Because customers ultimately get better value, supply chain management gains competitive advantage for each of the chain's members.

An innovative supply chain strategy was the heart of Michael Dell's vision when he established Dell Inc. Dell's concept improves performance by sharing information among chain members. Dell's long-term production plans and up-to-the-minute sales data are available to suppliers via the Internet. The process starts when customer orders are automatically translated into updated production schedules in the factory. These schedules are used not only by operations managers at Dell but also by such parts suppliers as Sony, which adjust their own production and shipping activities to better meet Dell's production needs. In turn, parts suppliers' updated schedules are transmitted to their materials suppliers, and so on up the chain. As Dell's requirements change, suppliers up and down the chain synchronize their schedules to produce only the right materials and parts. As a result, Dell's prices are low and turnaround time for shipping PCs to customers is reduced to a matter of hours instead of days.

Reengineering Supply Chains for Better Results Process improvements and reengineering often are applied in supply chains to lower costs, speed up service, and coordinate flows of information and material. Because the smoother flow of accurate information along the chain reduces unwanted inventories and transportation, avoids delays, and cuts supply times, materials move faster to business customers and individual consumers. Faster deliveries result in lower costs than customers could get if each member acted only according to its own operations requirements.

Outsourcing and Global Supply Chains

Outsourcing is the strategy of paying suppliers and distributors to perform certain business processes or to provide needed materials or services. The decision to outsource expands supply chains and creates new

Figure 7.5
Supply Chain for Baked Goods

operations jobs for supply chain management. Maytag, for example, had to develop its own internal global operations expertise before it could decide to open a new refrigerator factory in Mexico, import refrigerators from South Korea's Daewoo, and get laundry appliances from South Korea's Samsung Electronics. Global communications technologies are also essential. Although manufacturing operations are located remotely, they are closely integrated with the firm's home-base activities. That tightness of integration demands on-site operations expertise on both sides of the outsourcing equation.

Questions for Review

1 What are the major differences between goods-production operations and service operations?

2 What are the major differences between high-contact and low-contact service systems?

3 What are the five major categories of operations planning?

4 What are the major activities in materials management?

5 What activities are involved in total quality management?

Questions for Analysis

6 What are the input resources and finished products in the following services: a real estate firm, a child care facility, a bank, and a hotel?

7 Choose a consumer item and trace its supply chain. Identify at least four upstream stages in the chain. Based on your familiarity with the product and the supply chain stages you identified, what recommendations would you make to improve the supply chain?

8 Develop a list of internal customers and internal suppliers for some business that you use frequently (or where you work). Identify areas of potential quality improvement in these internal customer-supplier activity relationships.

Application Exercises

9 Think of an everyday activity, either personal or professional, that you would like to streamline for faster performance or more convenience. It could be something like gassing up your car, going to work or school, enrolling in classes at school, or any other activity that involves several stages with which you are familiar. Describe how you would use methods planning as described in the chapter to improve the activity. Draw a process flowchart that shows the stages in the activity you chose, then tell how you would use it.

10 Interview the manager of a local service business, or speak to a food service, bookstore, or other manager at your school. Identify the major decisions involved in planning that business's service operations.

Employee Behavior and Motivation

After reading this chapter, you should be able to:

1 Identify and discuss the basic forms of behaviors that employees exhibit in organizations.

2 Describe the nature and importance of individual differences among employees.

3 Explain the meaning and importance of psychological contracts and the person–job fit in the workplace.

4 Identify and summarize the most important models and concepts of employee motivation.

5 Describe some of the strategies and techniques used by organizations to improve employee motivation.

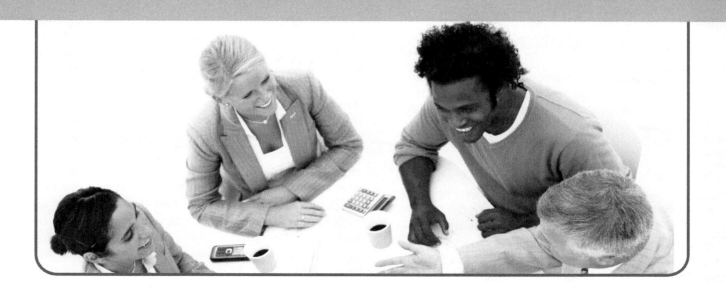

What's the Deal about Work?

The stereotypical overworked, underpaid, and unhappy worker is too often a reality caused by competitive environments, pressure to do more with less, economic uncertainty, and [?] connectivity.

Consequences for businesses include low retention, efficiency, and morale, or worse: employ[?] have filed lawsuits against Electronic Arts for routinely making them work 65–85 hours a week without overtime pay. Consequences for workers are even direr. White-collar injuries, illnesses, and even suicides related to work reportedly continue to rise. One study found that 23 percent of male stockbrokers were clinically depressed, three times the national average for U.S. men. Other studies find that many workers feel overworked and constantly worry about both their job security and financial stability. In Japan, there is even a term for "death by overwork"—*karoshi*, which is a legally recognized cause of death.[1]

Yet many find happiness at work. One study finds that an overall average of 47 percent of U.S. workers are very satisfied with their jobs.[2] For college professors, nurses, and others, happiness often comes from satisfying intellectual curiosity or helping others. Others redefine their jobs to make them more satisfying. As publisher of *Forbes* magazine, Richard Karlgaard's job primarily involved the mundane task of assessing and managing the reporting of financial data. So, he gave himself a new set of responsibilities as an editor-at-large writing about technology and left the financial reporting to others.

For those without the power to change their responsibilities, looking elsewhere is often the best option. Sandor Zombori walked away from his engineering job and invested his savings into what would become his award-winning restaurant. Mary Lou Quinlan quit her job as CEO of a New York advertising agency to start a small consulting business. The pay is less, but she is happier: "Finally," she says, "I'm doing something I can picture doing for a long, long time."

What's in It for Me?

At the extremes, some people truly love their jobs, while others just as truly hate them. Most people, however, fall somewhere in between. This chapter will discuss the factors related to how people feel about their jobs, including different forms of behaviors that employees exhibit and different methods of employee motivation. By understanding the basic elements of this chapter, you will develop a better understanding of your own and others' feelings toward work from the perspective of employees and managers.

Forms of Employee Behavior

Employee behavior is the pattern of actions by the members of an organization that directly or indirectly influences the organization's effectiveness. *Performance behaviors* directly contribute to productivity and performance. Other employee behaviors, referred to as *organizational citizenship*, provide positive benefits to the organization in more indirect ways. *Counterproductive behaviors* detract from performance and actually cost the organization.

Managers can help promote profitability and competitiveness if they have a clear understanding of these behaviors. They should then strive to motivate employees to enhance their performance behaviors. Organizational citizenship is also of value and should be encouraged. And counterproductive behaviors, of course, should be discouraged and punished. Let's look at each of these types of behavior in a bit more detail.

Performance Behaviors

Performance behaviors are the total set of work-related behaviors that the organization expects employees to display. Essentially, these are the behaviors directly targeted at performing a job. For some jobs, performance behaviors can be narrowly defined and easily measured. For example, an assembly-line worker who sits by a moving conveyor and attaches parts to a product as it passes by has relatively few performance behaviors. He or she is expected to remain at the workstation for a predetermined number of hours and correctly attach the parts. Such performance can often be assessed quantitatively by counting the percentage of parts correctly attached.

For many other jobs, however, performance behaviors are more diverse and difficult to assess. For example, a research-and-development scientist at Merck Pharmaceuticals works in a lab trying to discover breakthroughs with commercial potential. The scientist must apply knowledge and experience gained from previous research. Intuition and creativity are also important. But even with all the scientist's abilities and

effort, a desired breakthrough may take months or even years to accomplish.

Organizational Citizenship

Employees can also engage in **organizational citizenship**—positive behaviors and overall contributions that do not directly contribute to the bottom line.[3] Consider, for example, an employee who does work that is highly acceptable in terms of both quantity and quality. However, she refuses to work overtime, won't help newcomers learn the ropes, and is generally unwilling to make any contribution beyond the strict performance requirements of her job. This person may be seen as a good performer, but she is not likely to be seen as a good organizational citizen. Another employee may exhibit a comparable level of performance but may be seen as a better organizational citizen because she often works late when the boss asks her to, takes time to help newcomers learn their way around, and is perceived as helpful and committed to the organization's success.

A number of factors, including individual, social, and organizational variables, play roles in promoting or minimizing organizational citizenship behaviors. For example, the personality, attitudes, and needs of the individual may cause some to be more helpful than others. Similarly, the individual's work group may encourage or discourage such behaviors. And the organization itself, especially its corporate culture, may or may not promote, recognize, and reward these types of behaviors.

Counterproductive Behaviors

Counterproductive behaviors are those that detract from, rather than contribute to, organizational

For some jobs, performance behaviors can be narrowly defined and easily measured. For many other jobs, such as those held by scientists or doctors, however, performance behaviors are less objective, more diverse, and more difficult to assess.

performance. **Absenteeism** occurs when an employee does not show up for work. Some absenteeism has a legitimate cause, such as illness, jury duty, or death or illness in the family. Other times, the employee may feign a legitimate cause as an excuse to stay home. When an employee is absent, legitimately or not, his or her work does not get done, a substitute must be hired to do it, or others in the organization must pick up the slack. In any event, absenteeism results in direct costs to a business.

Turnover occurs when people quit their jobs for various reasons, including aspects of the job, the organization, the individual, the labor market, and family influences. A poor person–job fit (which we'll discuss later in the chapter) is also a likely cause of turnover. An organization usually incurs costs as a result of turnover—lost productivity while seeking a replacement, training someone new, etc. There are some employees whose turnover doesn't hurt the business; however, when productive employees leave an organization, it does reflect counterproductive behavior.

Other forms of counterproductive behavior may be even more costly for an organization. *Theft and sabotage*, for example, result in direct financial costs. *Discriminatory harassment* also costs an organization, both indirectly (by lowering morale, producing fear, and driving off valuable employees) and directly (through financial liability if the organization responds inappropriately). *Workplace aggression and violence* are also of growing concern.

Managing in Turbulent Times

Tragedy in the Workplace

A few years ago, James Davis walked through the doors of the Union Butterfield tool company in Asheville, North Carolina. He had been fired by Union Butterfield just two days before, and now he wanted revenge for what he felt was a grave injustice. To extract that revenge, Davis carried a semiautomatic rifle and a pistol. Once inside the doors, he opened fire, getting off about 50 shots and killing 3 of his former co-workers. After he finished shooting, Davis lit a cigarette and calmly waited for the police to arrive; then he quietly surrendered and was led away in handcuffs.

Unfortunately, tragedies such as this one are not all that uncommon. According to recent statistics, 1 employee is killed at a U.S. workplace by a current or former co-worker an average of once each week. In addition, another 25 are seriously injured by violent assaults. Overall, some 2 million U.S. workers are victims of some form of workplace violence each year.

The National Institute for Occupational Safety and Health (NIOSH) defines *workplace violence* as any physical assault, threatening behavior, or verbal abuse that occurs in a work setting. Experts also suggest that U.S. businesses lose billions of dollars each year in lost work time and productivity, litigation expenses, and security measures in the aftermath of workplace violence. Among the most common reasons often given for increasing workplace violence are economic fears regarding job security, heightened concerns for personal safety after the September 11, 2001, terrorist attacks, and generalized stress and anxiety among workers.

The recession of 2008–2009 only served to heighten these concerns. Massive layoffs, few prospects for new jobs, a spike in home foreclosures—any one of these might push a desperate person over the edge. But many people have encountered all three of these setbacks at the same time.

Fortunately, most people are resilient and on a relative basis, few resort to the type of twisted revenge James Davis used.

Still, though, managers should be aware of how they treat people. Probably the most important advice is to always treat people with respect, dignity, fairness, and honesty; this applies in all conditions, of course, not just during an economic downturn. When it becomes necessary to cut jobs or reduce pay and/or work hours, managers should provide as much advance information as possible so the cuts do not come as a surprise. They should also make sure each person who is being laid off or taking a cut in pay understands the basis for the decision—job performance, seniority, and so forth.

People should also be given a reasonable severance package. Two weeks of pay was once the standard for hourly workers, but some companies in recent times have provided no pay at all. Displaced workers should be informed about future prospects—does the company expect to hire again in the future, and if so, will they be considered for reemployment? Many larger firms also have additional security on site when large layoffs are being announced.

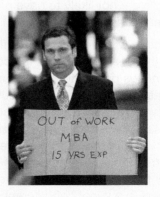

INDIVIDUAL DIFFERENCES personal attributes that vary from one person to another

PERSONALITY relatively stable set of psychological attributes that distinguish one person from another

"BIG FIVE" PERSONALITY TRAITS five fundamental personality traits especially relevant to organizations

EMOTIONAL INTELLIGENCE (EMOTIONAL QUOTIENT, EQ) extent to which people are self-aware, can manage their emotions, can motivate themselves, express empathy for others, and possess social skills

Individual Differences among Employees

What causes some employees to be more productive, better citizens, or more counterproductive than others? As we already noted, every individual is unique. **Individual differences** are personal attributes that vary from one person to another and may be physical, psychological, and emotional. The individual differences that characterize a specific person make that person unique. As we see in the sections that follow, basic categories of individual differences include *personality* and *attitudes*.

Personality at Work

Personality is the relatively stable set of psychological attributes that distinguish one person from another. In recent years, researchers have identified the fundamental *"big five" personality traits* that are especially relevant to organizations. *Emotional intelligence*, while not part of the "big five," also plays a large role in employee personality.

The "Big Five" Personality Traits   The **"big five" personality traits** can be summarized as follows.

■ *Agreeableness* is a person's ability to get along with others. A person with a *high* level of agreeableness is gentle, cooperative, forgiving, understanding, and good-natured in their dealings with others. A person with a *low* level of agreeableness is often irritable, short-tempered, uncooperative, stubborn, and generally antagonistic toward other people. Highly agreeable people are good at developing good working relationships with co-workers, whereas less agreeable people are not likely to have particularly good working relationships.

■ *Conscientiousness* in this context is a reflection of the number of things a person tries to accomplish. *Highly conscientious* people tend to focus on relatively few tasks at one time, as a result they're likely to be organized, responsible, and self-disciplined. *Less conscientious* people tend to pursue a wider array of tasks, so they are often more disorganized, irresponsible, and less self-disciplined. Highly conscientious people tend to be relatively higher performers in a variety of different jobs.

■ *Emotionality* refers to the degree to which people tend to be positive or negative in their outlook and behaviors toward others. People with *positive* emotionality are relatively poised, calm, and resilient; people with *negative* emotionality are more excitable, insecure, reactive, and moody. People with positive emotionality might be expected to better handle job stress. Their stability might also lead them to be seen as being more reliable than their less-stable counterparts.

■ *Extraversion* refers to a person's comfort level with relationships. *Extraverts* are sociable, assertive, and open to establishing new relationships. *Introverts* are much less sociable and assertive, and more reluctant to begin new relationships. Extraverts tend to be higher overall job performers than introverts and are more likely to be attracted to jobs based on personal relationships, such as sales and marketing positions.

■ *Openness* reflects how open or rigid a person's beliefs are. People with *high* levels of openness are curious and willing to consider and accept new ideas. People with *low* levels of openness tend to be less receptive to new ideas and less willing to change their minds. People with more openness are often more flexible and better accepted by others.

The "big five" framework continues to attract the attention of both researchers and managers. The potential value of this framework is that it encompasses an integrated set of traits that appear to be valid predictors of certain behaviors in certain situations. Thus, managers who can both understand the framework and assess these traits in their employees are in a good position to understand how and why they behave as they do.[4]

Emotional Intelligence   The concept of emotional intelligence has also been identified in recent years and provides some interesting insights into personality. **Emotional intelligence**, or **emotional quotient (EQ)**, refers to the extent to which people are self-aware, manage their emotions, motivate themselves, express empathy for others, and possess social skills.[5] These various dimensions can be described as follows.

■ *Self-awareness* refers to a person's capacity for understanding how she is feeling. In general, more self-awareness allows people to more effectively guide their own lives and behaviors.

■ *Managing emotions* refers to a person's capacity to avoid letting anxiety, fear, anger, and other emotions interfere with getting things accomplished.

■ *Motivating oneself* refers to a person's ability to remain optimistic and to continue striving toward goals in the face of obstacles and failure.

- *Empathy* refers to a person's ability to understand and have compassion for how others are feeling.

- *Social skills* refers to a person's ability to get along with others and to establish positive relationships.

Research suggests that people with high EQs may perform better than others, especially in jobs that require a high degree of interpersonal interaction and that involve influencing or directing the work of others. EQ appears to be something that people lacking these skills can work on and develop.[6]

Attitudes at Work

People's attitudes also affect their behavior in organizations. **Attitudes** are the mechanisms through which we express our beliefs and feelings about ideas, situations, or people. An employee's comment that he feels underpaid by the organization reflects his feelings about his pay. Similarly, when a manager says that she likes the new advertising campaign, she is expressing her feelings about the organization's marketing efforts.

People in an organization form attitudes about many different things. Employees are likely to have attitudes about salary, promotion opportunities, bosses, benefits, and so on. Especially important attitudes are *job satisfaction* and *organizational commitment*.

- **Job satisfaction**, or *morale*, reflects the extent to which people have positive attitudes toward their jobs. A satisfied employee tends to have low absenteeism, to be a good organizational citizen, and to stay with the organization. Dissatisfied employees may be absent more often, may experience stress that disrupts co-workers, and may be continually looking for another job. While high job satisfaction does not guarantee high productivity, employees with low morale are unlikely to exhibit high productivity.

- **Organizational commitment**, sometimes called *job commitment*, reflects an individual's identification with the organization and its mission. A highly committed person will probably feel included in the organization and refer to it in personal terms, overlook minor sources of dissatisfaction, and see herself as a long-term member of the organization. A less committed person is more likely to see himself as an outsider and refer to the organization in impersonal terms, to express more dissatisfaction, and to see himself as a temporary member of the organization.

By treating employees fairly, providing fair rewards and job security, allowing employees a say in how things are done, and designing stimulating jobs, managers can foster satisfaction and commitment in employees. Another key element is understanding and respecting what experts call *psychological contracts*, which we will discuss in the next section.

ATTITUDES person's beliefs and feelings about specific ideas, situations, or people

JOB SATISFACTION degree of enjoyment that people derive from performing their jobs

ORGANIZATIONAL COMMITMENT individual's identification with the organization and its mission

PSYCHOLOGICAL CONTRACT set of expectations held by an employee concerning what he or she will contribute to an organization (referred to as contributions) and what the organization will in return provide the employee (referred to as inducements)

Matching People and Jobs

Given the differences among individual employees and their behaviors within the organization, matching people to the jobs they perform is important. Two key methods for helping to understand how this match can be better understood are *psychological contracts* and the *person–job fit*.

Psychological Contracts

A **psychological contract** is the set of expectations held by employees and the organization regarding what employees will contribute and what the organization will provide in return. Unlike a business contract, a psychological contract is not written, nor are all of its terms explicitly negotiated.

Figure 8.1 illustrates the essential nature of a psychological contract. The individual makes a variety of *contributions* to the organization, such as effort, ability, loyalty, skills, and time. These contributions satisfy the employee's obligation under the contract. For example, Jill Henderson, a branch manager for Merrill Lynch, uses her knowledge of financial markets and investment opportunities to help her clients make profitable investments. Her MBA in finance, coupled with hard work and motivation,

Contributions from the Individual
- effort
- ability
- loyalty
- skills
- time
- competency

Inducements from the Organization
- pay
- benefits
- job security
- status
- promotion opportunities
- career opportunities

Figure 8.1
The Psychological Contract

have led her to become one of the firm's most promising young managers. The firm believed she had these attributes when it hired her and expected that she would use them to contribute to the firm's success. In return for these contributions, the organization satisfies its contract obligation by providing *inducements* to the individual. Some inducements, such as pay and career opportunities, are tangible rewards. Others, such as job security and status, are more intangible. Jill Henderson started at Merrill Lynch at a very competitive salary and has received a salary increase each of the six years she has been with the firm. She has also been promoted twice and expects another promotion in the near future.

When employer and employee perceive that the psychological contract is equitable, both will be satisfied with the relationship and will do what they can to continue it. In other situations, however, either party may see an inequity in the contract and initiate a change. The employee might ask for a pay raise or promotion, put forth less effort, or look for a better job elsewhere. The organization can also initiate change by training the worker to improve his skills, transferring him to another job, or firing him.

All organizations face the basic challenge of managing psychological contracts. They want value from their employees, and they need to give employees the right inducements. For instance, underpaid employees may perform poorly, leave for better jobs elsewhere, or even steal from the company.

Recent trends in downsizing and cutbacks have complicated the process of managing psychological contracts. For example, many organizations used to offer at least reasonable assurances of job permanence as a fundamental inducement to employees. Now, however, job permanence is less likely, so alternative inducements, like training opportunities and flexible work schedules, may be used.

The Person–Job Fit

The **person–job fit** refers to the extent to which a person's contributions and the organization's inducements match one another. A good person–job fit is one in which the employee's contributions match the inducements the organization offers. In theory, each employee has a specific set of needs that she wants fulfilled and a set of job-related behaviors and abilities to contribute. If the organization can use those behaviors and abilities and fulfill her needs, it will have achieved a perfect person–job fit, which can result in higher performance and more positive attitudes. A poor person–job fit, though, can have the opposite effects.

Basic Motivation Concepts and Theories

Broadly defined, **motivation** is the set of forces that causes people to behave in certain ways.[7] One worker may be motivated to work hard to produce as much as possible, whereas another may be motivated to do just enough to get by. Managers must understand these differences in behavior and the reasons for them.

Over the years, a steady progression of theories and studies has attempted to address these issues. This section surveys the major studies and theories of employee motivation with particular focus on three approaches to human relations in the workplace that reflect a basic chronology of thinking in the area: (1) *classical theory* and *scientific management*, (2) *early behavioral theory*, and (3) *contemporary motivational theories*.

Classical Theory

According to the **classical theory of motivation**, workers are motivated solely by money. In his 1911 book, *The Principles of Scientific Management*, industrial engineer Frederick Taylor proposed a way for both companies and workers to benefit from this widely accepted view of life in the workplace: If workers are motivated by money, paying them more based on how much they produce (for example, paying $1 per product completed) should prompt them to produce more. Meanwhile, the firm that analyzed jobs and found the most efficient ways to perform them would be able to produce goods more cheaply, make higher profits, and pay and motivate workers better than its competitors.

Taylor's approach is known as *scientific management*. Many managers in the early twentieth century bought into his ideas, and manufacturing plants across the United States began hiring experts to perform time-and-motion studies. Industrial engineering techniques were applied to each facet of a job to determine how to perform it most efficiently. These studies were the first scientific attempts to break down jobs into easily repeated components and to devise more efficient tools and machines for performing them.[8]

Early Behavioral Theory

In 1925, a group of Harvard researchers began a study at the Hawthorne Works of Western Electric outside Chicago. With an eye to increasing productivity, they wanted to examine the relationship between changes in the physical environment and worker output.

The results of the experiment were unexpected, even confusing. For example, increased lighting levels improved productivity. For some reason, however, so did lower lighting levels. Moreover, against all expectations, increased pay failed to increase productivity. Gradually,

Table 8.1   Theory X and Theory Y

Theory X	Theory Y
People are lazy.	People are energetic.
People lack ambition and dislike responsibility.	People are ambitious and seek responsibility.
People are self-centered.	People can be selfless.
People resist change.	People want to contribute to business growth and change.
People are gullible and not very bright.	People are intelligent.

HAWTHORNE EFFECT tendency for productivity to increase when workers believe they are receiving special attention from management

THEORY X theory of motivation holding that people are naturally lazy and uncooperative

THEORY Y theory of motivation holding that people are naturally energetic, growth-oriented, self-motivated, and interested in being productive

HIERARCHY OF HUMAN NEEDS MODEL theory of motivation describing five levels of human needs and arguing that basic needs must be fulfilled before people work to satisfy higher-level needs

the researchers pieced together the puzzle. The explanation lay in the workers' response to the attention they were receiving. The researchers concluded that productivity rose in response to almost any management action that workers interpreted as special attention. This finding—known today as the **Hawthorne effect**—had a major influence on human relations theory, although in many cases it amounted simply to convincing managers that they should pay more attention to employees.

Following the Hawthorne studies, managers and researchers alike focused more attention on the importance of good human relations in motivating employee performance. Stressing the factors that cause, focus, and sustain workers' behavior, most motivation theorists became concerned with the ways in which management thinks about and treats employees. The major motivation theories include the *human resources model*, the *hierarchy of needs model*, and the *two-factor theory*.[9]

Human Resources Model: Theories X and Y Behavioral scientist Douglas McGregor concluded that different managers had radically different beliefs about how best to use the human resources employed by a firm. He also believed that these different beliefs represented two relatively distinct views about employee behavior at work. He classified these beliefs into sets of assumptions that he labeled "Theory X" and "Theory Y." The basic differences between these two theories are shown in Table 8.1.

Managers who subscribe to **Theory X** tend to believe that people are naturally lazy and uncooperative and must be either punished or rewarded to be made productive. Managers who accept **Theory Y** tend to believe that people are naturally energetic, growth-oriented, self-motivated, and interested in being productive.

McGregor argued that Theory Y managers are more likely to have satisfied and motivated employees. Theory X and Y distinctions are somewhat simplistic and offer little concrete basis for action. Their value lies primarily in

their ability to highlight and classify the behavior of managers in light of their attitudes toward employees.

Maslow's Hierarchy of Needs Model Psychologist Abraham Maslow's **hierarchy of human needs model** proposes that people have several different needs that they attempt to satisfy in their work. Maslow classified these needs into five basic types and suggested that they be arranged in the hierarchy of importance shown in Figure 8.2. According to Maslow, needs are hierarchical because lower-level needs must be met before a person will try to satisfy higher-level needs.

Once a set of needs has been satisfied, it ceases to motivate behavior. For example, if you feel secure in your job, your security needs have been met, so additional opportunities to achieve even more security, such as being assigned to a long-term project, will probably be less

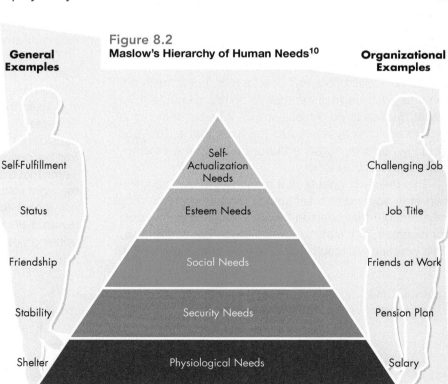

Figure 8.2
Maslow's Hierarchy of Human Needs[10]

General Examples

General Examples		Organizational Examples
Self-Fulfillment	Self-Actualization Needs	Challenging Job
Status	Esteem Needs	Job Title
Friendship	Social Needs	Friends at Work
Stability	Security Needs	Pension Plan
Shelter	Physiological Needs	Salary

important to you than the chance to fulfill social or esteem needs, such as working with a mentor or becoming the member of an advisory board.

If, however, a lower-level need suddenly becomes unfulfilled, most people immediately refocus on that lower level. Suppose, for example, you are seeking to meet your self-esteem needs by working as a divisional manager at a major company. If you learn that your division and, consequently, your job may be eliminated, you might very well find the promise of job security at a new firm as motivating as a promotion once would have been at your old company.

Two-Factor Theory After studying a group of accountants and engineers, psychologist Frederick Herzberg concluded that job satisfaction and dissatisfaction depend on two factors: *hygiene factors*, such as working conditions, and *motivation factors*, such as recognition for a job well done.

According to Herzberg's **two-factor theory**, hygiene factors affect motivation and satisfaction only if they are absent or fail to meet expectations. For example, workers will be dissatisfied if they believe they have poor working conditions. If working conditions are improved, however, they will not necessarily become satisfied; they will simply not be dissatisfied. On the other hand, if workers receive no recognition for successful work, they may be neither dissatisfied nor satisfied. If recognition is provided, they will likely become more satisfied.

Figure 8.3 illustrates the two-factor theory. Note that motivation factors lie along a continuum from satisfaction to no satisfaction. Hygiene factors, in contrast, are likely to produce feelings that lie on a continuum from dissatisfaction to no dissatisfaction. Whereas motivation factors are directly related to the work that employees actually perform, hygiene factors refer to the environment in which they work.

This theory suggests that managers should follow a two-step approach to enhancing motivation. First, they must ensure that hygiene factors—working conditions, for example, or clearly stated policies—are acceptable. This practice will result in an absence of dissatisfaction.

Figure 8.3
Two-Factor Theory of Motivation

Then they must offer motivation factors—recognition or added responsibility—as a way to improve satisfaction and motivation.

Contemporary Motivation Theory

Recently, other more complex models of employee behavior and motivation have been developed.[11] Two of the more interesting and useful ones are *expectancy theory* and *equity theory*.

Expectancy Theory **Expectancy theory** suggests that people are motivated to work toward rewards that they want and that they believe they have a reasonable chance—or expectancy—of obtaining. A reward that seems out of reach is likely to be undesirable even if it is intrinsically positive. Figure 8.4 illustrates expectancy theory in terms of issues that are likely to be considered by an individual employee.

Consider the case of an assistant department manager who learns that her firm needs to replace a retiring division manager three levels above her in the organization. Even though she wants the job, she does not apply because she doubts she will be selected. In this case, she considers the performance-reward issue: she believes that her performance will not get her the position. She also learns that the firm is looking for a production manager on the night shift. She thinks she could get this job but does not apply because she does not want to work nights (the rewards-personal goals issue). Finally, she learns of an opening one level higher—department manager—in her own division. She may well apply for this job because she both wants it and thinks that she has a good chance of

Figure 8.4
Expectancy Theory Model

getting it. In this case, her consideration of all the issues has led to an expectancy that she can reach a goal.

Expectancy theory helps explain why people whose salaries are based purely on seniority may not work as hard as they can. Paying employees the same whether they work very hard or just hard enough to get by removes the financial incentive for them to work harder. In other words, they ask themselves, "If I work harder, will I get a pay raise?" (the performance-reward issue) and conclude that the answer is no. Similarly, if hard work will result in one or more undesirable outcomes—for example, a transfer to another location or a promotion to a job that requires unpleasant travel (the rewards-personal goal issue)—employees will not be motivated to work hard.

Equity Theory **Equity theory** focuses on social comparisons—people evaluating their treatment by the organization relative to the treatment of others. This approach holds that people analyze their individual inputs to the organization (what they contribute to their jobs in terms of time, effort, education, and experience) relative to individual outcomes they receive from the organization (what they receive in return—salary, benefits, recognition, and

security). This comparison is very similar to the psychological contract. As viewed by equity theory, the result is a ratio of contribution to return. Then they compare their own ratios with those of other employees and ask whether their ratios are equal to, greater than, or less than those of others. Depending on their assessments, they experience feelings of equity or inequity. Figure 8.5 illustrates the three possible results of such an assessment.

> **EQUITY THEORY** theory of motivation holding that people evaluate their treatment by the organization relative to the treatment of others

For example, suppose a new college graduate gets a starting job at a large manufacturing firm. His starting salary is $45,000 a year, he gets an inexpensive company car, and he shares an assistant with another new employee. If he later learns that another new employee has received the same salary, car, and staff arrangement, he will feel equitably treated (result 1 in Figure 8.5). If the other newcomer, however, has received $70,000, a more expensive company car, and a personal assistant, he may feel inequitably treated (result 2 in Figure 8.5).

Note, however, that for an individual to feel equitably treated, the two ratios do not have to be identical, only equitable. Assume, for instance, that our new employee has a bachelor's degree and two years of work experience. Perhaps he learns subsequently that the other new employee has an advanced degree and ten years of experience. After first feeling inequity, the new employee may conclude that the person with whom he compared himself is actually contributing more to the organization (based on higher levels of education and greater experience). That employee is equitably entitled, therefore, to receive more in return (result 3 in Figure 8.5).

When people feel they are being inequitably treated, they may do various constructive and some not-so-constructive things to restore fairness. For example, they may speak to their boss about the perceived inequity. Or (less constructively) they may demand a raise, reduce their efforts, work shorter hours, or just complain to co-workers. They may also rationalize ("Management succumbed to pressure to promote a minority"), find different people with whom to compare themselves, or leave their jobs.

Strategies and Techniques for Enhancing Motivation

Understanding what motivates workers is only one part of the manager's job. The other part is applying that knowledge. Experts have suggested—and many companies have implemented—a range of programs designed to make jobs more interesting and rewarding, to make the work environment more pleasant, and to motivate employees to work harder.

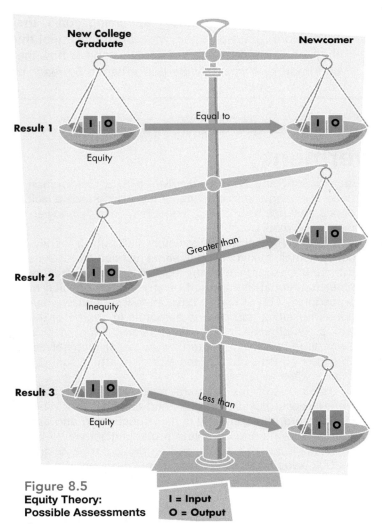

Figure 8.5
Equity Theory:
Possible Assessments

I = Input
O = Output

Reinforcement/ Behavior Modification

Some companies try to control workers' behavior through systematic rewards and punishments for specific behaviors. Such companies first try to define the specific behaviors that they want their employees to exhibit (working hard, being courteous to customers, and stressing quality) and the specific behaviors they want to eliminate (wasting time, being rude to customers, and ignoring quality). Then they try to shape employee behavior by linking positive reinforcement with desired behaviors and punishment with undesired behaviors.

Positive reinforcement is used when a company or manager provides a reward when employees exhibit desired behaviors. When rewards are tied directly to performance, they serve as positive reinforcement. For example, paying large cash bonuses to salespeople who exceed quotas prompts them to work even harder during the next selling period. John Deere has adopted a reward system based on positive reinforcement. The firm gives pay increases when its workers complete college courses and demonstrate mastery of new job skills.

Punishment is designed to change behavior by presenting people with unpleasant consequences if they exhibit undesired behaviors. Employees who are repeatedly late for work, for example, may be suspended or have their pay docked. Similarly, when the National Football League or Major League Baseball fines or suspends players found guilty of substance abuse, the organization is seeking to change players' behaviors.

Using Goals to Motivate Behavior

Performance goals are also commonly used to direct and motivate behavior. **Management by objectives (MBO)** is a system of collaborative goal setting that extends from the top of an organization to the bottom. MBO involves managers and subordinates in setting goals and evaluating progress. After the organization specifies its overall goals and plans, managers collaborate with each of their subordinates to set individual goals accordingly. Managers meet periodically to review progress toward individual goals, and then, usually on an annual basis, goal achievement is evaluated and used as a basis for starting the cycle over again.

According to many experts, motivational impact is the biggest advantage of MBO. When employees sit down with managers to set upcoming goals, they learn more about companywide objectives, feel that they are an important part of a team, and see how they can improve companywide performance by reaching

Entrepreneurship and New Ventures

Extreme Employee Empowerment

In the mid-1980s, Roger Sant and Dennis Bakke decided to take advantage of the Public Utility Regulatory Policy Act and establish what would become a huge international energy company built on the values of social responsibility, integrity, fairness, and fun. To achieve these

Dennis Bakke, co-founder of AES Corporation, speaks worldwide about the advantages of the Public Utility Regulatory Policy Act.

ideals, Sant and Bakke established AES Corporation under a management structure, or more accurately a lack of one, that has been called "adhocracy" and "empowerment gone mad."

Under an organizational structure AES dubs a "honeycomb," small, multifunctional teams manage themselves without the assistance of any legal, human resources, or other functional department or any written policies or procedures. AES strives to have as few supervisory layers as possible, and no one person is in charge of the teams. Employees make HR decisions, such as how much time to take for maternity leave, for themselves, and they consult outside experts on matters such as finance when necessary.

As a result of this structure, employees are empowered, flexible, multidimensional, and constantly learning. Furthermore, the company is high-functioning and can make decisions and complete projects efficiently. AES continues to adapt to its increasing growth, though, and in 2002 added five executive officer positions and has since expanded its corporate leaders while remaining true to its honeycomb roots.[12]

"O.K., I messed up. He didn't have to rub my nose in it."

their own goals. If an MBO system is used properly, employees should leave meetings not only with an understanding of the value of their contributions but also with fair rewards for their performances. They should also accept and be committed to the moderately difficult and specific goals they have helped set for themselves.[13]

Participative Management and Empowerment

In **participative management and empowerment**, employees are given a voice in how they do their jobs and in how the company is managed—they become empowered to take greater responsibility for their own performance. Not surprisingly, participative empowerment often makes employees feel more committed to organizational goals they have helped to shape.

Participation and empowerment can be used in large or small firms with managers and operating employees. For example, sports gear company And1 allows its designers considerable latitude in testing new ideas—a designer can make a few prototypes of a new product, distribute them to kids on a neighborhood basketball court, and then get their feedback.

Although some employees thrive in participative programs, such programs are not for everyone. People may be frustrated by responsibilities they are not equipped to handle by a symbolic rather than substantive invitation to participate. One key, say

most experts, is to invite participation only to the extent that employees want to have input and only if participation will have real value for an organization.

Team Structures

We have already noted the increased use of teams in organizations. Yet another benefit that some companies get from using teams is increased motivation and enhanced job satisfaction. Although teams are often less effective in traditional and rigidly structured bureaucratic organizations, they often help smaller, more flexible organizations make decisions more quickly and effectively, enhance companywide communication, and encourage members to feel more like a part of an organization. In turn, these attitudes usually lead to higher levels of both employee motivation and job satisfaction.[14]

But managers should remember that teams are not for everyone. Levi Strauss, for example, encountered major problems when it tried to use teams. Individual workers previously performed repetitive, highly specialized tasks, such as sewing zippers into jeans, and were paid according to the number of jobs they completed each day. In an attempt to boost productivity, company management reorganized everyone into teams of 10 to 35 workers and assigned tasks to the entire group. Each team member's pay was determined by the team's level of productivity. In practice, however, faster workers became resentful of slower workers because they reduced the group's total output. Slower workers, meanwhile, resented the pressure put on them by faster-working co-workers. As a result, motivation, satisfaction, and morale all dropped, and Levi Strauss eventually abandoned the teamwork plan altogether.

Job Enrichment and Job Redesign

Whereas goal setting and MBO programs and empowerment can work in a variety of settings, *job enrichment* and *job redesign* programs are generally used to increase satisfaction in jobs significantly lacking in motivating factors.[15]

Job Enrichment Programs **Job enrichment** is designed to add one or more motivating factors to job activities. For example, *job rotation* programs expand growth opportunities

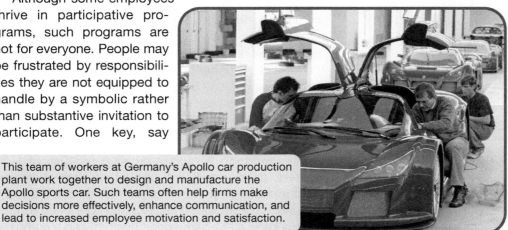

This team of workers at Germany's Apollo car production plant work together to design and manufacture the Apollo sports car. Such teams often help firms make decisions more effectively, enhance communication, and lead to increased employee motivation and satisfaction.

JOB REDESIGN method of increasing job satisfaction by designing a more satisfactory fit between workers and their jobs

WORK SHARING (JOB SHARING) method of increasing job satisfaction by allowing two or more people to share a single full-time job

FLEXTIME PROGRAMS method of increasing job satisfaction by allowing workers to adjust work schedules on a daily or weekly basis

TELECOMMUTING form of flextime that allows people to perform some or all of a job away from standard office settings

by rotating employees through various positions in the same firm. Workers gain not only new skills but also broader overviews of their work and their organization. Other programs focus on increasing responsibility or recognition. At Continental Airlines, for example, flight attendants now have more control over their own scheduling. The jobs of flight service managers were enriched when they were given more responsibility and authority for assigning tasks to flight crew members.

Job Redesign Programs **Job redesign** acknowledges that different people want different things from their jobs. By restructuring work to achieve a more satisfactory fit between workers and their jobs, job redesign can motivate individuals with strong needs for career growth or achievement. Job redesign is usually implemented through one of three ways:

■ *Combining tasks* involves enlarging jobs and increasing their variety to make employees feel that their work is meaningful and, in turn, become more motivated. For example, the job done by a programmer who maintains computer systems might be redesigned to include some system design and system development work. While developing additional skills, the programmer also gets involved in the overall system development.

Best Buy is taking the modified schedules and alternative workplaces to new extremes with its corporate "results-only work environment" or ROWE. Under ROWE, Best Buy employees can work anytime, anywhere, as long as they achieve results. The program has been so successful that Best Buy has begun introducing the program into its retail stores in 2007.

■ *Forming natural work groups* allows people who do different jobs on the same projects to help employees see their place and importance in the total structure of the firm. They are valuable to management because the people working on a project are usually the most knowledgeable about it and the most capable problem solvers.

■ *Establishing client relationships* means letting employees interact with customers to increase job variety and give workers both a greater sense of control and more performance feedback. For example, software writers at Microsoft watch test users work with programs and discuss problems with them directly rather than receive feedback from third-party researchers.

Modified Work Schedules

As another way of increasing job satisfaction, many companies are experimenting with *modified work schedules*—different approaches to working hours.[16]

Work-Share Programs At Steelcase, the country's largest maker of office furnishings, two very talented women in the marketing division both wanted to work only part-time. The solution: they now share a single full-time job and each work 2.5 days a week to get the job done well. The practice, known as **work sharing** (or **job sharing**), has "brought sanity back to our lives," according to at least one Steelcase employee.

Job sharing usually benefits both employees and employers. Employees tend to appreciate the organization's attention to their personal needs, while the company can reduce turnover and save on the cost of benefits. On the negative side, job-share employees generally receive fewer benefits than their full-time counterparts and may be the first to be laid off when cutbacks are necessary.

Flextime Programs and Alternative Workplace Strategies **Flextime programs** allow people to choose their working hours by adjusting a standard work schedule on a daily or weekly basis. Often, there are limits to flextime: Steelcase, for instance, requires all employees to work certain core hours during which everyone works and can communicate. Employees can then decide whether to make up the rest of the standard eight-hour day by coming in and leaving early or late. Companies may also allow employees to choose the number of days during which to work each week, provided they still complete 40 hours of work.

Telecommuting A rapidly growing number of U.S. workers do a significant portion of their work via **telecommuting**—performing some or all of a job away from standard office settings. Working from a home office outfitted with a PC, high-speed Internet, and a company intranet connection, telecommuters can keep abreast of everything going on at the office. In 2004, at least 14 million U.S. workers spent at least part of their working hours telecommuting. This trend is on the rise: in 2005, 44 percent of U.S. companies offered some telecommuting options, up from 32 percent in 2001.[17] And in 2008 almost 80 percent of white collar and other professional workers in the United States performed at least some of their work from a location other than their office.

Advantages and Disadvantages of Modified Work Schedules and Alternative Workplaces Flextime gives employees more freedom in their professional and personal lives by allowing them to plan around family schedules. Studies show that the increased sense of freedom and control reduces stress and improves individual productivity. Companies also benefit in other ways. In urban areas, for example, such programs can reduce traffic congestion and similar problems that contribute to stress and lost work time, and employers benefit from higher levels of commitment and job satisfaction. John Hancock Insurance, Atlantic Richfield, and Metropolitan Life are among the major U.S. corporations that have successfully adopted some form of flextime.

Conversely, flextime sometimes complicates coordination because people are working different schedules. In addition, if workers are paid by the hour, flextime may make it difficult for employers to keep accurate records of when employees are actually working.

As for telecommuting, it may not be for everyone. For example, consultant Gil Gordon points out that telecommuters are attracted to the ideas of "not having to shave and put on makeup or go through traffic, and sitting in their blue jeans all day." However, he suggests that would-be telecommuters ask themselves several other questions: "Can I manage deadlines? What will it be like to be away from the social context of the office five days a week?" One study has shown that even though telecommuters may be producing results, those with strong advancement ambitions may miss out on day-to-day networking opportunities.

Another obstacle to establishing a telecommuting program is convincing management of its benefits. Telecommuters may have to fight the perception from both bosses and co-workers that if they are not being supervised, they are not working. Managers, admits one experienced consultant, "usually have to be dragged kicking and screaming into this. They always ask 'How can I tell if someone is working when I can't see them?' " But, he adds, "that's based on the erroneous assumption that if you can see them, they are working." Most experts agree that clear expectations, reeducation, and constant communication are requirements of a successful telecommuting arrangement. Both managers and employees must determine expectations in advance.

Questions for Review

1. Describe the psychological contract you currently have or have had in the past with an employer. If you have never worked, describe the psychological contract that you have with the instructor in this class.

2. Do you think that most people are relatively satisfied or dissatisfied with their work? What factors do you think most contribute to satisfaction or dissatisfaction?

3. Compare and contrast the hierarchy of human needs with the two-factor theory of motivation.

4. How can participative management programs enhance employee satisfaction and motivation?

Questions for Analysis

5. Some evidence suggests that recent college graduates show high levels of job satisfaction. Levels then drop dramatically as they reach their late twenties, only to increase gradually once they get older. What might account for this pattern?

6. Under what sort of circumstances might you, as a manager, apply each of the theories of motivation discussed in this chapter? Which would be easiest to use? Which would be hardest? Why?

7. Suppose you realize one day that you are dissatisfied with your job. Short of quitting, what might you do to improve your situation?

8. Describe what you would tell a low-skill worker performing a simple and routine job who wants more challenge and enjoyment from work.

Application Exercises

9. Assume that you are about to start your own business. What might you do from the very beginning to ensure that your employees will be satisfied and motivated?

10. Interview the manager of a local manufacturing company. Identify as many different strategies for enhancing job satisfaction at that company as you can. Are the strategies effective at enhancing employee job satisfaction? Why or why not?

Leadership and Decision Making

After reading this chapter, you should be able to:

1 Define *leadership* and distinguish it from management.

2 Summarize early approaches to the study of leadership.

3 Discuss the concept of situational approaches to leadership.

4 Describe transformational and charismatic perspectives on leadership.

5 Identify and discuss leadership substitutes and neutralizers.

6 Discuss leaders as coaches and examine gender and cross-cultural issues in leadership.

7 Describe strategic leadership, ethical leadership, and virtual leadership.

8 Relate leadership to decision making and discuss both rational and behavioral perspectives on decision making.

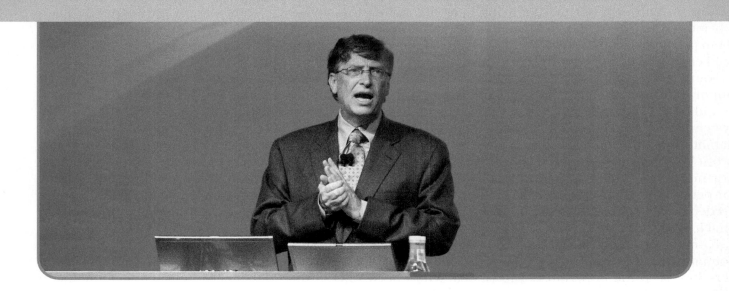

Leadership Stretched to the Brink

It isn't easy leading a U.S. business today. Leaving aside the global recession (at least for a moment), the passion for "lean and mean" operations means that there are fewer workers to do more work. Globalization requires keeping abreast of cross-cultural differences. Knowledge industries present unique leadership challenges, requiring better communication skills and greater flexibility. Advances in technology have opened unprecedented channels of communication. Now more than ever before, leaders must be able to do just about everything—and more of it. As U.S. senator and former presidential candidate John McCain puts it, "[Leadership is] a game of pinball, and you're the ball." Fortunately, a few of corporate America's veteran leaders have some tips for those who still want to follow their increasingly treacherous path.

Carlos Ghosn, who's currently president of Renault *and* CEO of Nissan, believes in regular breaks. "I don't bring my work home. I play with my four children and spend time with my family on weekends," says Ghosn. "I come up with good ideas as a result of becoming stronger after being recharged." Google VP Marissa Mayer admits, "I can get by on four to six hours of sleep," but she also takes a weeklong vacation three times a year. Many leaders report that playing racquetball, running marathons, practicing yoga, or getting regular exercise helps them to recover from overwork.

Effective leaders also take control of information flow—which means managing it, not reducing the flow until it's as close to a trickle as you can get it. Ghosn, whose schedule requires weekly intercontinental travel, uses bilingual assistants to screen and translate information—one assistant for information from Europe (home of Renault), one for information from Japan (home of Nissan), and one for information from the United States (where Ghosn often has to be when he doesn't have to be in Europe or Japan). Clothing designer Vera Wang also uses an assistant to filter information. "The barrage of calls is so enormous," she says, "that if I just answered calls I'd do nothing else. . . . If I were to go near e-mail, there'd be even more obligations, and I'd be in [a mental hospital] with a white jacket on."

What's in It for Me?

It is time to examine in detail how leaders—who may or may not also be managers such as Carlos Ghosn or Marissa Mayer—actually go about affecting employee behavior and motivating their performance. We shall place these strategies and tactics in the context of various approaches to leadership throughout the years, including the situational perspective accepted today. Understanding these concepts will help you function more effectively as a leader and give you more insight into how your manager or boss strives to motivate you through his or her own leadership.

Bill Gates also knows how important it is to motivate and retain talented individuals who (at least under normal circumstances) have other options for employment. In fact, he once stated that if the 20 smartest people at Microsoft left the company, it would shrivel into an insignificant dot on the corporate map. Obviously, then, executives who employ thousands of such workers are under enormous pressure to keep them productive and happy. Mayer holds office hours at a regularly scheduled time every day so that she can field employee complaints and concerns.

Some leaders go a step further and use a time of upheaval, such as the 2008–2009 recession, as an opportunity to rethink a company's reward system. At Boeing, for example, CEO Jim McNerney replaced an old bonus system based on something that managers can't control (the company's stock price) with a system based on something they *can* control—profit. He rewards people who improve the firm's profitability by better managing its capital. So, if a manager can figure out how to generate $10 million in profit by spending $1 million instead of $2 million, he or she now gets to keep some of the savings. One organizational psychologist adds that if you're the top person at your company, "the last thing you want is for people to perceive that you're in it for yourself." In December 2008, for example, when FedEx founder Frederick W. Smith was forced to make broad salary cuts, he started with himself, slashing his own paycheck by 20 percent.

Former Starbucks CEO Jim Donald makes a fairly simple recommendation: "Communicate, communicate, communicate. Especially at a time of crisis," he advises, "make sure your message reaches all levels, from the very lowest to the uppermost." Kip Tindell, who's been CEO of the Container Store since its founding in 1978, agrees. That's why his managers "run around like chickens relentlessly trying to communicate everything to every single employee at all times." He admits that it's an impossible task, but he's also convinced that the effort is more important in times of crisis than at any other time. He also contends that his company is in a better position to ride out the economic storm "because we're so dedicated to the notion that communication and leadership are the same thing." At the very least, he says, "we're fortunate to be minus the paranoia that goes with employees who feel they don't know what's going on."

LEADERSHIP the processes and behaviors used by someone, such as a manager, to motivate, inspire, and influence the behaviors of others

The Nature of Leadership

Because *leadership* is a term that is often used in everyday conversation, you might assume that it has a common and accepted meaning. It is also, however, a word that is often misused. We define **leadership** as the processes and behaviors used by someone, such as a manager, to motivate, inspire, and influence the behaviors of others. One of the biggest errors people make is assuming that leadership and management mean the same thing when they are really different concepts. A person can be a manager, a leader, both, or neither.[1] Some of the basic distinctions between the two are summarized in Table 9.1. The first column lists four dimensions that differentiate leadership from management. The second and third columns show how each dimension differs when considered from the perspectives of managers versus leaders. For example, when they are executing plans, managers focus on monitoring results and identifying deviations. In contrast, leaders focus on energizing people to overcome bureaucratic hurdles to reach goals.

Consider the various roles of managers and leaders in a hospital setting. The chief of staff (chief physician) of a large hospital, though clearly a manager by virtue of his position, may not be respected or trusted by others and may have to rely solely on the authority vested in the position to get people to do things. On the other hand, an emergency-room nurse with no formal authority may be quite effective at taking charge of a chaotic situation and directing others in dealing with specific patient problems. The chief of staff is a manager but not really a leader, while the nurse is a leader but not really a manager.

Finally, the head of pediatrics, supervising a staff of 20 other doctors, nurses, and attendants, may also enjoy the staff's complete respect, confidence, and trust. They readily take her advice and follow directives without question, and often go far beyond what is necessary to help carry out the unit's mission. Thus, the head of pediatrics is both a manager (by virtue of the position she occupies) and a leader (by virtue of the respect she commands from others and their willingness to follow her direction).

Organizations need both management and leadership if they are to be effective. Management in conjunction with leadership can help achieve planned orderly change, and leadership in conjunction with management can keep the organization properly aligned with its environment.

Table 9.1 Kotter's Distinctions Between Management and Leadership[2]

Activity	Management	Leadership
Creating an agenda	**Planning and budgeting.** Establishing detailed steps and timetables for achieving needed results; allocating the resources necessary to make those needed results happen.	**Establishing direction.** Developing a vision of the future, often the distant future, and strategies for producing the changes needed to achieve that vision.
Developing a human network for achieving the agenda	**Organizing and staffing.** Establishing some structure for accomplishing plan requirements, staffing that structure with individuals, delegating responsibility and authority for carrying out the plan, providing policies and procedures to help guide people, and creating methods or systems to monitor implementation.	**Aligning people.** Communicating the direction by words and deeds to all those whose cooperation may be needed to influence the creation of teams and coalitions that understand the vision and strategies and accept their validity.
Executing plans	**Controlling and problem solving.** Monitoring results vs. plan in some detail, identifying deviations, and then planning and organizing to solve these problems.	**Motivating and inspiring.** Energizing people to overcome major political, bureaucratic, and resource barriers to change by satisfying very basic, but often unfulfilled, human needs.
Outcomes	Produces a degree of predictability and order and has the potential to consistently produce major results expected by various shareholders (e.g., for customers, always being on time; for stockholders, being on budget).	Produces change, often to a dramatic degree, and has the potential to produce extremely useful change (e.g., new products that customers want, new approaches to labor relations that help make a firm more competitive).

Early Approaches to Leadership

Although leaders and leadership have profoundly influenced history, careful scientific study of them began only about a century ago. Early studies focused on the *traits*, or personal characteristics, of leaders. Later research shifted to examine actual leader *behaviors*.

Trait Approaches to Leadership

Early researchers believed that notable leaders had some unique set of qualities or traits that distinguished them from their peers and endured throughout history. This **trait approach to leadership** led researchers to focus on identifying the essential leadership traits, including intelligence, dominance, self-confidence, energy, activity (versus passivity), and knowledge about the job. Unfortunately, the list of potential leadership traits quickly became so long that it lost any practical value. In addition, the results of many studies were inconsistent. For example, one argument stated that the most effective leaders were tall, like Abraham Lincoln. But critics were quick to point out that neither Napoleon Bonaparte nor Adolf Hitler was tall, but both were effective leaders in their own way.

Although the trait approach was all but abandoned several decades ago, in recent years, it has resurfaced. For example, some researchers have again started to focus on a limited set of traits. These traits include

emotional intelligence, mental intelligence, drive, motivation, honesty and integrity, self-confidence, knowledge of the business, and charisma. Some people even believe that biological factors, such as appearance or height, may play a role in leadership. However, it is too early to know whether these traits really do relate to leadership.

Behavioral Approaches to Leadership

In the late 1940s, most researchers began to shift away from the trait approach and to look at leadership as a set of actual behaviors. The goal of the **behavioral approach to leadership** was to determine what *behaviors* were employed by effective leaders. These researchers assumed that the behaviors of effective leaders differed somehow from the behaviors of less effective leaders, and that the behaviors of effective leaders would be the same across all situations.

This research led to the identification of two basic forms of leader behavior. While different researchers applied different names, the basic leader behaviors identified during this period were

■ **Task-focused leader behavior**: Task-focused leader behavior occurs when a leader focuses on how tasks

TRAIT APPROACH TO LEADERSHIP approach focused on identifying the essential traits that distinguished leaders

BEHAVIORAL APPROACH TO LEADERSHIP approach focused on determining what behaviors are employed by leaders

TASK-FOCUSED LEADER BEHAVIOR leader behavior focusing on how tasks should be performed in order to meet certain goals and to achieve certain performance standards

Leaders have always played important roles in society. For instance, even though Abraham Lincoln, Mohandas Gandhi, and Eleanor Roosevelt lived at different times and worked in different areas, each is recognized as an exemplary leader. Early approaches to leadership attempted to identify the key traits or behaviors that characterized these and other leaders.

should be performed in order to meet certain goals and to achieve certain performance standards.

■ **Employee-focused leader behavior**: Employee-focused leader behavior occurs when a leader focuses on the satisfaction, motivation, and well-being of his or her employees.

During this period, people believed that leaders should always try to engage in a healthy dose of both behaviors, one to increase performance and the other to increase job satisfaction and motivation. Experts also began to realize that they could train managers to engage in these behaviors in a systematic manner. But they also discovered that there were other leader behaviors that needed to be considered, and that there were circumstances in which different combinations of leader behavior might be more effective than other combinations.

For instance, suppose a new manager takes over a work site that is plagued by low productivity and whose workers, while perhaps satisfied, are not motivated to work hard. The leader should most likely focus on task-focused behaviors in order to improve lagging productivity. But now suppose the situation is different—productivity is very high, but workers are stressed out about their jobs and have low levels of job satisfaction. In this instance, the manager should most likely concentrate on employee-focused behaviors to help improve job satisfaction. This line of thinking led to the creation of *situational theories*.

The Situational Approach to Leadership

The **situational approach to leadership** assumes that appropriate leader behavior varies from one situation to another. This approach was first proposed as a continuum of leadership behavior, which is shown in Figure 9.1. This continuum ranges from the one extreme of having the leader make decisions alone to the other extreme of having employees make decisions with only minimal guidance from the leader. Each point on the continuum is influenced by *characteristics of the leader*, *his or her subordinates*, and the *situation*.

Leadership characteristics include the manager's value system, confidence in subordinates, personal inclinations, and feelings of security. Subordinate characteristics include the subordinates' need for independence, readiness to assume responsibility, tolerance for ambiguity, interest in the problem, understanding of

Boss-Centered Leadership

Use of Authority by Manager

Use of Freedom for Subordinates

Subordinate-Centered Leadership

| Manager makes decision and announces it. | Manager "sells" decision. | Manager presents ideas and invites questions. | Manager presents tentative decision subject to change. | Manager presents problem, gets suggestions, makes decision. | Manager defines limits, asks group to make decision. | Manager permits subordinates to function within limits defined by superior. |

Figure 9.1
The Leadership Continuum[3]

goals, knowledge, experience, and expectations. Situational characteristics that affect decision making include the type of organization, group effectiveness, the problem itself, and time pressures.

Leadership through the Eyes of Followers

Another recent perspective that has been adopted by some leadership experts focuses on how leaders are seen through the eyes of their followers. The two primary approaches to leadership through the eyes of followers are *transformational leadership* and *charismatic leadership*. Barrack Obama's successful bid for the U.S. presidency in 2008 was fueled in part by many people's perceptions that he was both a transformational and charismatic leader. Indeed, during the campaign, he frequently talked about the need to transform the way the United States addressed issues such as health care, education, and foreign policy. And his personal charisma undoubtedly attracted support from many people as well.

Transformational Leadership

Transformational leadership focuses on the importance of leading for change (as opposed to leading during a period of stability). According to this view, much of what a leader does involves carrying out what might be thought of as basic management "transactions"—assigning work, evaluating performance, making decisions, and so forth. Occasionally, however, the leader has to engage in transformational leadership to initiate and manage major change, such as managing a

merger, creating a new work team, or redefining the organization's culture.

Thus, **transformational leadership** is the set of abilities that allows a leader to recognize the need for change,

> **TRANSFORMATIONAL LEADERSHIP** set of abilities that allows a leader to recognize the need for change, to create a vision to guide that change, and to execute the change effectively

Rupert Murdoch, CEO of News Corp., has used transformational leadership to expand and consolidate his media empire of newspapers, film, and television. He will need to strike a balance between transformational and transactional leadership as he manages his newest acquisition, the *Wall Street Journal*.

Under New Ownership

Some leaders are able to adopt either transformational or transactional perspectives, depending on their circumstances. For instance, Rupert Murdoch, CEO of News Corp., has a long history of transforming the media properties he acquires in order to expand their reach and turn a profit. Early in his career Murdoch relaunched *The Sun*, a British daily newspaper, as a tabloid notorious for its sensationalistic focus on sex. On the other hand, he has generally avoided retooling another of his British acquisitions, the well-regarded *Times*. When he purchased the struggling *Wall Street Journal* in 2007, he pledged to remain a hands-off manager. In the months since, the paper's signature coverage of U.S. business news has decreased to make room for increased coverage of politics and foreign events, and it remains to be seen how Murdoch will balance transformational and transactional leadership at the *Journal*.[4]

to create a vision to guide that change, and to execute the change effectively. Some experts believe that change is such a vital organizational function that even successful firms need to change regularly to avoid becoming complacent and stagnant. In contrast, **transactional leadership** is essentially the same as management in that it involves routine, regimented activities. Only a leader with tremendous influence can hope to perform both functions successfully. Some experts believe that change is such a vital organizational function that even successful firms need to change regularly to avoid becoming complacent and stagnant; accordingly, leadership for change is extremely important.

Charismatic Leadership

Charismatic leadership is a type of influence based on the leader's charisma, a form of interpersonal attraction that inspires support and acceptance. Charismatic leaders are likely to have a lot of confidence in their beliefs and ideals and a strong need to influence people. They also tend to communicate high expectations about follower performance and to express confidence in their followers. Many of the most influential leaders in history have been extremely charismatic, including entrepreneurs Mary Kay Ash, Steve Jobs, and Ted Turner; civil rights leader Martin Luther King, Jr.; and Pope John Paul II. Unfortunately, charisma can also empower leaders in other directions. Adolf Hitler, for instance, had strong charismatic qualities.

Most experts today acknowledge three crucial elements of charismatic leadership:[5]

1 Charismatic leaders *envision* likely future trends and patterns, set high expectations for themselves and for others, and behave in ways that meet or exceed those expectations.

2 Charismatic leaders *energize* others by demonstrating personal excitement, personal confidence, and consistent patterns of success.

3 Charismatic leaders *enable* others by supporting them, empathizing with them, and expressing confidence in them.

Charismatic leadership ideas are quite popular among managers today and are the subject of numerous books and articles.[6] Unfortunately, few studies have specifically attempted to test the meaning and impact of charismatic leadership. Lingering ethical concerns about charismatic leadership also trouble some people. They stem from the fact that some charismatic leaders inspire such blind faith in their followers that they may engage in inappropriate, unethical, or even illegal behaviors just

Highly charismatic leaders often achieve great success. Vince Lombardi's charisma helped lead the Green Bay Packers to win five league championships and two Super Bowls. Succeeding a charismatic leader can be difficult, however; Lombardi's successor Phil Bengtson was fired after following up Lombardi's successes with two losing seasons.

Table 9.2 Leadership Substitutes and Neutralizers

Individual factors	• Individual professionalism
	• Individual ability, knowledge, and motivation
	• Individual experience and training
	• Indifference to rewards
Job factors	• Structured/automated
	• Highly controlled
	• Intrinsically satisfying
	• Embedded feedback
Organization factors	• Explicit plans and goals
	• Rigid rules and procedures
	• Rigid reward system not tied to performance
	• Physical distance between supervisor and subordinate
Group factors	• Group performance norms
	• High level of group cohesiveness
	• Group interdependence

because the leader instructed them to do so. This tendency likely played a role in the unwinding of both Enron and Arthur Andersen, as people followed orders from their charismatic bosses to hide information, shred documents, and mislead investigators.

Taking over a leadership role from someone with substantial personal charisma is also a challenge. For instance, the immediate successors to very successful and charismatic athletic coaches like Vince Lombardi (Green Bay Packers) and Phil Jackson (Chicago Bulls) each failed to measure up to their predecessors' legacies and were subsequently fired.

Special Issues in Leadership

Another interesting perspective on leadership focuses on *alternatives* to leadership. In some cases, certain factors may actually *substitute* for leadership, making actual leadership unnecessary or irrelevant. In other cases, factors may exist that *neutralize* or negate the influence of a leader even when that individual is attempting to exercise leadership.

Leadership Substitutes
Leadership substitutes are individual, task, and organizational characteristics that tend to outweigh the

need for a leader to initiate or direct employee performance. In other words, if certain factors are present, the employee will perform his or her job capably, without the direction of a leader. Table 9.2 identifies several basic leadership substitutes.

Consider, for example, what happens when an ambulance with a critically injured victim screeches to the door of a hospital emergency room. Do the ER employees stand around waiting for someone to take control and instruct them on what to do? The answer is no—they are highly trained and well-prepared professionals who know how to respond and work together as a team without someone playing the role of leader. When a U.S. Airways flight crashed into the Hudson River in 2009, all members of the flight crew knew exactly what to do, without waiting for orders. As a result of their effective and prompt actions, a disaster was averted, and all passengers on the plane were quickly rescued.

LEADERSHIP SUBSTITUTES individual, task, and organizational characteristics that tend to outweigh the need for a leader to initiate or direct employee performance

LEADERSHIP NEUTRALIZERS factors that may render leader behaviors ineffective

Leadership Neutralizers
In other situations, even if a leader is present and attempts to engage in various leadership behaviors, those behaviors may be rendered ineffective—or neutralized—by various factors that can be called **leadership neutralizers**. Suppose, for example, that a relatively new and inexperienced leader is assigned to a work group composed of very experienced employees with long-standing performance norms and a high level of group cohesiveness. The norms and cohesiveness of the group may be so strong that there is nothing the new leader can do to change things.

In addition to group factors, elements of the job itself may also limit a leader's ability to "make a difference." Consider, for example, employees working on a moving assembly line. Employees may only be able to work at the pace of the moving line, so performance quantity and quality are constrained by the speed of the line and simplicity of each individual task.

Finally, organizational factors can also neutralize at least some forms of leader behavior. Suppose a new leader is accustomed to using merit pay increases as a way to motivate people. But in his or her new job, pay increases are dictated by union contracts and are based primarily on employee seniority and cost of living. The leader's previous approach to motivating people would be neutralized, and new approaches would have to be identified.

No More Secrets?

As the public faces of their companies, CEOs are subject to intense scrutiny and take the heat from critics and consumer advocates for any company fault or misdeed. As a result, many CEOs take a very cautious and calculated approach to communicating with consumers. Many companies have strict guidelines regarding employees' blogging and reporting on internal issues. This kind of closed-doors approach keeps competitors in the dark and presumably minimizes public scrutiny.

However, a realistic evaluation of today's limitless capacity for information dissemination might lead a CEO to doubt the effectiveness of this policy. Some CEOs have embraced a philosophy of accessibility. In lieu of a carefully worded press release, they are using blogs and Web sites like YouTube to personally deliver messages to the public. In a YouTube video, the CEO of Jet Blue apologized to passengers who had been trapped for hours in planes grounded by bad weather, and Microsoft now allows its engineers to write about current projects in blogs. Glenn Kelman, CEO of the real estate brokerage firm Redfin, started a blog to air his frustrations regarding real estate sales practices that he judged unfair to the consumer. His blog elicited angry responses in the comments section, to which he posted his own rebuttals. Redfin's customer base expanded, suggesting that Kelman's personal approach made his sympathy for the consumer more believable.

A strategy of transparency may have a humanizing effect on a company, making it more sympathetic to consumers who feel alienated by the trend toward an increasingly automated customer service experience. All firms have flaws and commit errors, and an admission of culpability, frustration, or weakness can make a company more relatable. Responsive, accessible CEOs may not be able to prevent criticism or scrutiny, but they may take a little air out of free-swinging critics used to hammering faceless offenders. Occasionally, the CEO may even beat the critics to the punch. And, indeed, people today are increasingly expecting managers to be forthright and candid when problems arise. Some employees of a national pizza chain recently made a disgusting video in which they were shown appearing to add unsavory ingredients to pizzas. When this video attracted national attention after it was posted on YouTube, the company did not respond for several days. Many critics were angered by the lack of response, and in the eyes of some experts the public damage was greater than if the firm had responded immediately. So, the challenge for managers during turbulent times is to find the right blend of timely candor and considered deliberation. And sometimes, only the leader's instincts can serve as a guide.[7]

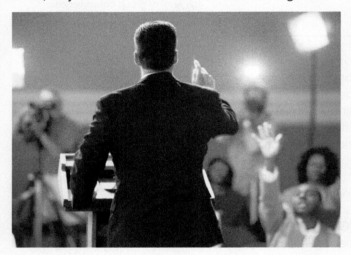

The Changing Nature of Leadership

Various alternatives to leadership aside, many settings still call for at least some degree of leadership, although the nature of that leadership continues to evolve. Among the recent changes in leadership that managers should recognize are the increasing role of *leaders as coaches* as well as *gender and cross-cultural patterns* of leader behavior.

Leaders as Coaches

We noted in Chapter 6 that many organizations today are using teams. Many other organizations are attempting to become less hierarchical—that is, to eliminate the old-fashioned command-and-control mentality often inherent in bureaucratic organizations and to motivate and empower individuals to work independently. In each case, the role of leaders is also changing. Whereas leaders were once expected to control situations, direct work, supervise people, closely monitor performance, make decisions, and structure activities, many leaders today are being asked to change how they manage people. Perhaps the best description of this new role is for the leader to become a *coach* instead of an *overseer*.[8]

From the standpoint of a business leader, a coaching perspective would call for the leader to help select and train team members and other new employees, to provide some general direction, and to help the team get the information and other resources it needs. Coaches from different teams may play important roles in linking the activities and functions of their respective teams. Some leaders may function as *mentors*, helping less experienced employees learn the ropes and better preparing them to advance within the organization; they may also help resolve conflicts among team members and mediate other disputes that arise. But beyond these activities, the leader keeps a low profile and lets the group get its work done with little or no direct oversight, just as during a game an athletic coach trusts his or her players to execute the plays successfully.

Gender and Leadership

Another factor that is clearly altering the face of leadership is the growing number of women advancing to higher levels in organizations. Given that most leadership theories and research studies have focused on male leaders, developing a better understanding of how women lead is clearly an important next step. Some early observers, for instance, predicted that (consistent with prevailing stereotypes) female leaders would be relatively warm, supportive, and nurturing as compared to their male counterparts. But research suggests that female leaders are not necessarily more nurturing or supportive than male leaders. Likewise, male leaders are not systematically harsher, more controlling, or more task focused than female leaders.

The one difference that has arisen in some cases is that women may be slightly more democratic in making decisions, whereas men have a tendency to be more autocratic.[9] However, much more work needs to be done in order to better understand the dynamics of gender and leadership. In the meantime, high-profile and successful female leaders, such as Andrea Jung (CEO of Avon Products) and Angela Merkel (chancellor of Germany), continue to demonstrate the effectiveness with which women can be exceptional leaders.

Cross-Cultural Leadership

Another changing perspective on leadership relates to cross-cultural issues. In this context, *culture* is used as a broad concept to encompass both international differences and diversity-based differences within one culture. For instance, Japan is generally characterized by *collectivism* (group before individual), whereas the United States is based more on *individualism* (individual before group). So when a Japanese firm sends an executive to head up the firm's operation in the United States, that person will likely find it necessary to recognize the importance of individual contributions and rewards and the differences in individual and group roles that exist in Japanese and U.S. businesses.

Similarly, cross-cultural factors also play a growing role in organizations as their workforces become more diverse. As African Americans, Asian Americans, Hispanics, and

Andrea Jung (left), CEO of Avon Products, and Angela Merkel (right), chancellor of Germany, are demonstrating the effectiveness with which women can be exceptional leaders. For instance, Jung has transformed Avon and made it a real powerhouse in its industry, and Merkel was recently named to *TIME Magazine*'s list of "people who shape our world."

members of other ethnic groups achieve leadership positions, it may be necessary to reassess how applicable current theories and models of leadership are when applied to an increasingly diverse pool of leaders.

Emerging Issues in Leadership

Finally, there are also three emerging issues in leadership that warrant discussion. These issues are *strategic leadership*, *ethical leadership*, and *virtual leadership*.

Strategic Leadership

Strategic leadership is a new concept that explicitly relates leadership to the role of top management. **Strategic leadership** is a leader's ability to understand the complexities of both the organization and its environment and to lead change in the organization so as to enhance its competitiveness.

To be effective as a strategic leader, a manager needs to have a thorough and complete understanding of the organization—its history, its culture, its strengths, and its weaknesses. In addition, the leader needs a firm grasp of the organization's external environment. This needs to include current business and economic conditions and circumstances as well as significant trends and issues on the horizon. The strategic leader also needs to recognize the firm's current strategic advantages and shortcomings.

Entrepreneurship and New Ventures

An Apple a Day

As CEO of Apple Computer, Steve Jobs has developed a reputation for brilliance, originality, and charm. His leadership style has been criticized as well. One industry observer portrayed Jobs as intimidating and power hungry, while others said he commanded "a cult-like following from employees and consumers." Yet Jobs is clearly a leader who can deliver success in businesses that are evolving, highly technical, and demanding. Writer Steven Berglas says, "Jobs, the *enfant terrible* widely reputed to be one of the most aggressive egotists in Silicon Valley, has an unrivaled track record when it comes to pulling development teams through start-ups."

But how do Jobs's charisma, confidence, and vision shape his leadership style during times of prosperity and success? In a recent interview, Jobs discussed how his passion and focus enable the company to succeed in any type of situation or environment. "Lots of companies have tons of great engineers and smart people," said Jobs. "But ultimately, there needs to be some gravitational force that pulls it all together. . . . That's what was missing at Apple for a while. There were bits and pieces of interesting things floating around, but not that gravitational pull."

Today, Jobs is riding high, as he focuses on bringing Apple's unique blend of hi-tech gadgetry and cool design to applications reaching far beyond the computers that first made his fortune. The company has released several versions of the iPod, its hugely popular digital music player, supported by Apple's online music store, iTunes. The iPhone, a mobile phone that connects to the Internet, was named 2007's Invention of the Year by *TIME Magazine*. And Jobs's confidence and excitement for the future are only growing. "Apple is doing the best work in its history," he says, "and there's a lot more coming."[10]

Ethical Leadership

Most people have long assumed that business leaders are ethical people. But in the wake of recent corporate scandals at firms like Enron, Boeing, and AIG, faith in business leaders has been shaken. Perhaps now more than ever, high standards of ethical conduct are being held up as a prerequisite for effective leadership. More specifically, business leaders are being called on to maintain high ethical standards for their own conduct, to unfailingly exhibit ethical behavior, and to hold others in their organizations to the same standards—in short, to practice **ethical leadership**.

The behaviors of top leaders are being scrutinized more than ever, and those responsible for hiring new leaders for a business are looking more closely at the backgrounds of those being considered. And the emerging pressures for stronger corporate governance models are likely to further increase the commitment to select only those individuals with high ethical standards for leadership positions in business and to hold them more accountable than in the past for both their actions and the consequences of those actions.

Virtual Leadership

Finally, **virtual leadership** is also emerging as an important issue for organizations. In earlier times, leaders and their employees worked together in the same physical location and engaged in face-to-face interactions on a regular basis. But in today's world, both leaders and their employees may work in locations that are far from one another. Such arrangements might include people telecommuting from a home office one or two days a week to people actually living and working far from company headquarters.

Increasingly, then, communication between leaders and their subordinates happens largely by telephone and e-mail. One implication may be that leaders in these situations must work harder at creating and maintaining relationships with their employees that go beyond words on a computer screen. While nonverbal communication, such as smiles and handshakes, may not be possible online, managers can instead make a point of adding a few personal words in an e-mail (whenever appropriate) to convey appreciation, reinforcement, or constructive feedback.

Leadership, Management, and Decision Making

We noted earlier the differences and similarities between managing and leading. **Decision making** is another important related concept. Indeed, decision making is a fundamental component of both leadership and management managers and leaders must frequently make decisions.

Rational Decision Making

Managers and leaders should strive to be rational in making decisions. Figure 9.2 shows the steps in the rational decision-making process.

Recognizing and Defining the Decision Situation

The first step in rational decision making is recognizing that a decision is necessary—that is, there must be some stimulus or spark to initiate the process. The stimulus for a decision may be either positive or negative. Managers who must decide how to invest surplus funds, for example, face a positive decision situation. A negative financial stimulus could involve having to trim budgets because of cost overruns.

Inherent in making such a decision is the need to define precisely what the problem is. Consider the situation currently being faced in the international air travel industry. Because of the growth of international travel related to business, education, and tourism, global carriers need to increase their capacity. Because most major international airports are already operating at or near capacity, adding a significant number of new flights to existing schedules is not feasible. As a result, the most logical alternative is to increase capacity on existing flights. Thus, Boeing and Airbus, the world's only manufacturers of large commercial aircraft, recognized an important opportunity and defined their decision situations as how best to respond to the need for increased global travel capacity.[11]

Identifying Alternatives

Once the decision situation has been recognized and defined, the second step is to identify alternative courses of effective action. Developing both obvious, standard alternatives and creative, innovative alternatives is useful. In general, the more important the decision, the more attention is directed to developing alternatives. Although managers should seek creative solutions, they must also recognize that various constraints often limit their alternatives. Common constraints include legal restrictions, moral and ethical norms, and constraints imposed by the power and authority of the manager, available technology, economic considerations, and unofficial social norms. After assessing the question of how to increase international airline capacity, Boeing and Airbus identified three

ETHICAL LEADERSHIP
leader behaviors that reflect high ethical standards

VIRTUAL LEADERSHIP
leadership in settings where leaders and followers interact electronically rather than in face-to-face settings

DECISION MAKING
choosing one alternative from among several options

Step	Detail	Example
1. Recognizing and defining the decision situation	Some stimulus indicates that a decision must be made. The stimulus may be positive or negative.	The plant manager sees that employee turnover has increased by 5 percent.
2. Identifying alternatives	Both obvious and creative alternatives are desired. In general, the more important the decision, the more alternatives should be generated.	The plant manager can increase wages, increase benefits, or change hiring standards.
3. Evaluating alternatives	Each alternative is evaluated to determine its feasibility, its satisfactoriness, and its consequences.	Increasing benefits may not be feasible. Increasing wages and changing hiring standards may satisfy all conditions.
4. Selecting the best alternative	Consider all situational factors and choose the alternative that best fits the manager's situation.	Changing hiring standards will take an extended period of time to cut turnover, so increase wages.
5. Implementing the chosen alternative	The chosen alternative is implemented into the organizational system.	The plant manager may need permission from corporate headquarters. The human resource department establishes a new wage structure.
6. Following up and evaluating the results	At some time in the future, the manager should ascertain the extent to which the alternative chosen in step 4 and implemented in step 5 has worked.	The plant manager notes that six months later, turnover dropped to its previous level.

Figure 9.2
Steps in the Rational Decision-Making Process[12]

different alternatives: they could independently develop new large planes, they could collaborate in a joint venture to create a single new large plane, or they could modify their largest existing planes to increase their capacity.

Evaluating Alternatives The third step in the decision-making process is evaluating each of the alternatives. Some alternatives may not be feasible because of legal or financial barriers. Limited human, material, and information resources may make other alternatives impractical. Managers must thoroughly evaluate all the alternatives in order to increase the chances that the alternative finally chosen will be successful. For example, Airbus felt it would be at a disadvantage if it tried simply to enlarge its existing planes because the Boeing 747 was at the time already the largest aircraft being made and could readily be expanded to remain

the largest. Boeing, meanwhile, was seriously concerned about the risk inherent in building a new and even larger plane, even if it shared the risk with Airbus as a joint venture.

Selecting the Best Alternative Choosing the best available alternative is the real crux of decision making. Even though many situations do not lend themselves to objective, mathematical analysis, managers and leaders can often develop subjective estimates and weights for choosing an alternative. Decision makers should also remember that finding multiple acceptable alternatives may be possible; selecting just one alternative and rejecting all the others might not be necessary. For example, Airbus proposed a joint venture with Boeing. Boeing, meanwhile, decided that its best course of action was to modify its existing 747 to increase its capacity. As a result, Airbus decided to proceed on its own to develop and manufacture a new jumbo jet. Boeing then decided that in addition to modifying its 747, it would develop a new plane to offer as an alternative, albeit one not as large as the 747 or the proposed Airbus plane.

Implementing the Chosen Alternative After an alternative has been selected, managers and leaders must put it into effect. Boeing set its engineers to work expanding the capacity of its 747 by adding 30 feet to the plane's body; the firm also began developing another plane intended for international travel, the 787. Airbus engineers, meanwhile, developed design concepts for a new jumbo jet equipped with escalators and elevators and capable of carrying 655 passengers. Airbus's development costs alone were estimated to exceed $12 billion.

Managers must also consider people's resistance to change when implementing decisions. The reasons for such resistance include insecurity, inconvenience, and fear of the unknown. Managers should anticipate potential resistance at various stages of the implementation process. However, even when all alternatives have been evaluated as precisely as possible and the consequences of each alternative have been weighed, unanticipated consequences are still likely. Employees may resist or protest change; they may even quit rather than agree to it. Other factors, such as unexpected cost increases, a less-than-perfect fit with existing organizational subsystems, or unpredicted effects on cash flow or operating expenses, could develop after implementation has begun. Both Boeing and Airbus were plagued by production delays that pushed back delivery of their respective aircrafts by years and could end up costing each company billions of dollars. Airbus got its plane to market first (it began flying in late 2007), but profits have been pushed far into the future as the global recession of 2008–2009 caused many airlines to cancel or delay orders for several years.

After a long decision-making process, Airbus decided to design its own jumbo jet. The Airbus A380's design allows seating for up to 850 people, and major airports around the world have been building new runways and terminal areas to accommodate the behemoth. Boeing, meanwhile, went through a similar decision-making process but concluded that the risks were too great to gamble on such an enormous project. Instead, the firm decided to modify its existing 747 design and develop a new fuel-efficient aircraft, the 787.

Following Up and Evaluating the Results The final step in the decision-making process requires that managers and leaders evaluate the effectiveness of their decision—that is, they should make sure that the chosen alternative has served its original purpose. If an implemented alternative appears not to be working, they can respond in several ways. Another previously identified alternative (the original second or third choice, for instance) could be adopted. Or they might recognize that the situation was not correctly defined to begin with and start the process all over again. Finally, managers and leaders might decide that the original alternative is in fact appropriate but either has not yet had time to work or should be implemented in a different way.

At this point, both Boeing and Airbus are nearing the crucial period when they will learn whether they made good decisions. Airbus's A380 made its first commercial flight in 2007, though delays continue to push back its production schedule. Meanwhile, Boeing's 787 continues to face delays, and widespread use of the plane is not unexpected until at least 2010. The expanded 747 is on schedule, however, and should be in service by 2010. Most airlines seem willing to wait patiently for the 787s, which are designed to be much more fuel efficient than other international airplanes. Given the

COALITION informal alliance of individuals or groups formed to achieve a common goal

INTUITION innate belief about something, often without conscious consideration

ESCALATION OF COMMITMENT condition in which a decision maker becomes so committed to a course of action that she or he stays with it even when it appears to have been wrong

RISK PROPENSITY extent to which a decision maker is willing to gamble when making a decision

dramatic surge in fuel costs in recent years, a fuel-efficient option like the 787 could be an enormous success. Indeed, Airbus has begun developing its own fuel-efficient jet, the A350.[13]

Behavioral Aspects of Decision Making

If all decision situations were approached as logically as described in the previous section, more decisions would prove successful. Yet decisions are often made with little consideration for logic and rationality. Some experts have estimated that U.S. companies use rational decision-making techniques less than 20 percent of the time. Of course, even when organizations try to be logical, they sometimes fail. For example, when Starbucks opened its first coffee shops in New York, it relied on scientific marketing research, taste tests, and rational deliberation in making a decision to emphasize drip over espresso coffee. However, that decision proved wrong, as it became clear that New Yorkers strongly preferred the same espresso-style coffees that were Starbucks mainstays in the West. Hence, the firm had to reconfigure its stores hastily to meet customer preferences.

On the other hand, sometimes a decision made with little regard for logic can still turn out to be correct.[14] Important ingredients in how these forces work are behavioral aspects of decision making. These include *political forces*, *intuition*, *escalation of commitment*, and *risk propensity*.

Political Forces in Decision Making

Political forces contribute to the behavioral nature of decision making. One major element of politics, *coalitions*, is especially relevant to decision making. A **coalition** is an informal alliance of individuals or groups formed to achieve a common goal. This common goal is often a preferred decision alternative. For example, coalitions of stockholders frequently band together to force a board of directors to make a certain decision.

When these coalitions enter the political arena and attempt to persuade lawmakers to make decisions favorable to their interests, they are called *lobbyists*. Lobbyists may also donate money to help elect a candidate who is more likely to pursue their agendas. A recurring theme in U.S. politics is the damaging influence these special interest groups have on politicians, who may feel unduly obligated to favor campaign donors when making decisions.

Intuition **Intuition** is an innate belief about something, often without conscious consideration. Managers sometimes decide to do something because it "feels right" or they have a hunch. This feeling is usually not arbitrary, however. Rather, it is based on years of experience and practice in making decisions in similar situations. Such an inner sense may help managers make an occasional decision without going through a full-blown rational sequence of steps.

That said, all managers, but most especially inexperienced ones, should be careful not to rely too heavily on intuition. If rationality and logic are continually flouted for "what feels right," the odds are that disaster will strike one day.

Escalation of Commitment Another important behavioral process that influences decision making is **escalation of commitment** to a chosen course of action. In particular, decision makers sometimes make decisions and then become so committed to the course of action suggested by that decision that they stay with it, even when it appears to have been wrong.[16] For example, when people buy stock in a company, they sometimes refuse to sell it even after repeated drops in price. They choose a course of action—buying the stock in anticipation of making a profit—and then stay with it even in the face of increasing losses. Moreover, after the value drops they may rationalize that they can't sell at such a low price because they will lose money.

Risk Propensity and Decision Making The behavioral element of **risk propensity** is the extent to which a decision maker is willing to

> ### Major League Deal
>
> The New York Yankees once contacted three major sneaker manufacturers—Nike, Reebok, and Adidas—and informed them that they were looking to make a sponsorship deal. While Nike and Reebok were carefully and rationally assessing the possibilities, managers at Adidas quickly realized that a partnership with the Yankees made a lot of sense for them. They responded very quickly to the idea and ended up hammering out a contract while the competitors were still analyzing details.[15]

gamble when making a decision. Some managers are cautious about every decision they make. They try to adhere to the rational model and are extremely conservative in what they do. Such managers are more likely to avoid mistakes, and they infrequently make decisions that lead to big losses. Others are extremely aggressive in making decisions and willing to take risks.[17] They rely heavily on intuition, reach decisions quickly, and often risk big investments on their decisions. As in gambling, these managers are more likely than their conservative counterparts to achieve big successes with their decisions; they are also more likely to incur greater losses.[18] The organization's culture is a prime ingredient in fostering different levels of risk propensity.

Questions for Review

1. What are the basic differences between management and leadership?

2. Summarize the basic premises underlying the trait, behavioral, and situational approaches to leadership.

3. What are leadership substitutes and neutralizers?

4. List and briefly explain the steps in rational decision making.

Questions for Analysis

5. Identify five people you would consider to be excellent leaders. Explain why you feel that way about each person.

6. What factors are present in your job that motivate you to perform without the direction of a leader? Are there factors that neutralize the efforts of your leader?

7. The impact of virtual leadership is likely to grow in the future. As a potential "follower" in a virtual leadership situation, what issues would be of most concern to you? What would the issues be from the perspective of the "leader" role in such a situation?

8. Identify and discuss examples of how your decision making has been affected by at least two of the behavioral processes noted in the chapter.

Application Exercises

9. Interview a senior manager at a local company. Ask that manager if he or she believes that leadership can be taught. What are the key implications of his or her position?

10. Review the running example in the textbook regarding the decisions made by Airbus and Boeing regarding new long-haul aircraft. Research the most current information available about the status of both planes. Based on the information you have available, which firm seems to have made the better decision?

Human Resource Management and Labor Relations

After reading this chapter, you should be able to:

1 Define *human resource management* and explain how managers plan for their organization's human resource needs.

2 Identify the tasks in staffing a company and discuss ways in which organizations select, develop, and appraise employee performance.

3 Describe the main components of a compensation system and describe some of the key legal issues involved in hiring, compensating, and managing workers in today's workplace.

4 Discuss workforce diversity, the management of knowledge workers, and the use of a contingent workforce as important changes in the contemporary workplace.

5 Explain why workers organize into labor unions and describe the collective bargaining process.

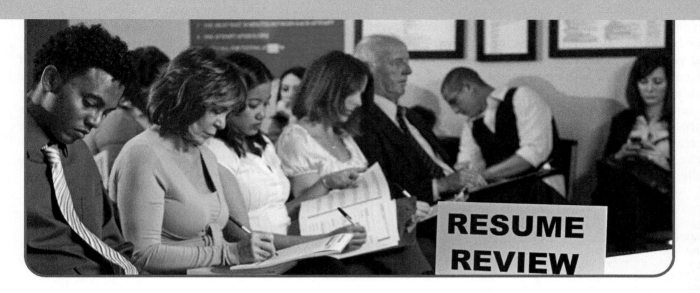

The Temping of America

A few years ago New Yorker Diana Bloom logged on to Craigslist, an online network that posts free classified ads, and offered her services as a tutor, an editor, and a translator. She's been making a living on the short-term jobs that come her way from the Web site ever since. A former English professor who couldn't find secure long-term employment, Bloom works out of her home in order to take care of a young son. Temp work is also appealing, she says, because "I'm not very outgoing, and getting my foot in the door to companies would have been hard."

Craigslist works in the other direction, too, with employers posting openings for jobs both permanent and temporary. Another New Yorker, Simone Sneed, scours the Craigslist "Gigs" section for jobs that last for perhaps a day, often for just a few hours. Whether as a backup singer or a grant writer, she's turned the strategy of patching together "gigs" into a convenient way to supplement the income from her full-time job. "I'll use the extra money to pay off my school loan," she says. "Every little bit helps."

In the economic climate of 2008–2009, unfortunately, overall job postings were down on Craigslist and everywhere else, except for short-term jobs—those that usually include no health benefits, sick days, or paid vacations. If you're employed short term or part time for economic reasons (probably because you got laid off), the Bureau of Labor Statistics (BLS) classifies you as "underemployed." You're on a list that added nearly 800,000 names in February 2009, for a total of 8.6 million, up from 4.9 million in February 2008—2 percent to 4 percent of the overall workforce.

Interestingly, for some people, the adjustment to current labor-market conditions isn't necessarily very traumatic. A recent survey conducted by the temporary-staffing agency Kelly Services found that as many as 26 percent of employed U.S. adults regarded themselves as "free agents" when it comes to the type of job they're willing to take (up from 19 percent in 2006). Of all those polled, only 10 percent said that they were doing temporary work because they'd been laid off from permanent jobs; 90 percent said they were doing it because they liked the variety and flexibility that temping afforded them.

What's in It for Me?

Effectively managing human resources is the lifeblood of an organization. Successful firms develop clear, consistent approaches to staffing, training, evaluating, and compensating employee performance, whether those employees number in the tens or the tens of thousands. In this chapter we'll explore these various approaches. We'll also look at some key legal issues involved in human resources management, and consider why workers organize into labor unions. Whether employee or employer, your company's HR policies will shape your working experience greatly. This chapter will help you understand the rationale behind those policies.

In fact, temping offers several advantages. You can learn something not only about a given company but about the industry in which it operates. Even if the job doesn't work out, you can acquire some skills and beef up your résumé; you may also come away with better ideas about what you want in a job or a boss. Temp work can also provide income during career transitions, and it's a good way to exercise a little control over the balance between work and the rest of life. Further, temp work can be a path to a permanent job.

If you're a U.S. employer, you've always been able to get temp workers at a relatively good price. As of December 2008, according to the BLS, the average cost of a full-time worker in private industry was $21.64 per hour in wages plus $9.43 in benefits, for a total of $31.07 in compensation. In contrast, the average wages for a temp were $12.04, and the average benefits were $3.28, for total compensation of $15.32. One of the results of this differential in cost has been a long-term increase in the number of temp workers that far outstrips the increase in jobs occupied by full-time workers. Between 1990 and 2006, for example, the number of temp jobs in the United States more than doubled, from 1.2 million to 2.6 million. Total employment in key sectors, meanwhile, went up by only 26 percent.

The Foundations of Human Resource Management

Human resource management (HRM) is the set of organizational activities directed at attracting, developing, and maintaining an effective workforce.

The Strategic Importance of HRM

Human resources (or *personnel*, as the department is sometimes called) has a substantial impact on a firm's bottom-line performance. Consequently, the chief HR executive of most large businesses is a vice president directly accountable to the CEO, and many firms are developing strategic HR plans that are integrated with other strategic planning activities.

HR Planning

As you can see in Figure 10.1, the starting point in attracting qualified human resources is planning. Specifically, HR planning involves job analysis and forecasting the demand for, and supply of, labor.

Job Analysis   **Job analysis** is a systematic analysis of jobs within an organization. A job analysis results in two things:

■ The **job description** lists the duties and responsibilities of a job; its working conditions; and the tools, materials, equipment, and information used to perform it.

■ The **job specification** lists the skills, abilities, and other credentials and qualifications needed to perform the job effectively.

Job analysis information is used in many HR activities. For instance, knowing about job content and job requirements is necessary to develop appropriate selection methods, to create job-relevant performance appraisal systems, and to set equitable compensation rates.

Forecasting HR Demand and Supply   After managers comprehend the jobs to be performed within an organization, they can start planning for the organization's future HR needs. The manager starts by assessing trends in past HR usage, future organizational plans, and general economic trends.

Figure 10.1
The HR Planning Process

Conduct Job Analysis

Forecast Demand for Labor

Forecast Internal Supply of Labor

Forecast External Supply of Labor

Develop Plan to Match Demand with Supply

Forecasting the supply of labor is really two tasks:

1. Forecasting *internal supply*—the number and type of employees who will be in the firm at some future date.

2. Forecasting *external supply*—the number and type of people who will be available for hiring from the labor market at large.

Replacement Charts   At higher levels of an organization, managers plan for specific people and positions. The technique most commonly used is the **replacement chart**, which lists each important managerial position, who occupies it, how long that person will probably stay in it before moving on, and who is now qualified or soon will be qualified to move into it. (In larger firms, of course, this information is computerized today.) This technique allows ample time to plan developmental experiences for people identified as potential successors for critical managerial jobs. Halliburton, for instance, has a detailed replacement system that the firm calls its Executive Succession System (ESS). When a manager has his or her performance reviewed each year, notations are placed in the system about the person's readiness for promotion, potential positions for promotion, and what development activities are needed to order to prepare the individual for promotion. Other managers throughout the firm can access the system whenever they have vacant positions available.

Skills Inventories   To facilitate both planning and identifying people for transfer or promotion, some organizations also have **employee information systems (skills inventories)** that contain information on each employee's education, skills, work experience, and career aspirations. Such a system can quickly locate every employee who is qualified to fill a position.

Forecasting the external supply of labor is a different problem altogether. Planners must rely on information from outside sources, such as state employment commissions, government reports, and figures supplied by colleges on the numbers of students in major fields.

Matching HR Supply and Demand   After comparing future demand and internal supply, managers can make plans to manage predicted shortfalls or overstaffing. If a shortfall is predicted, new employees can be hired, present employees can be retrained and transferred into understaffed areas, individuals approaching retirement can be convinced to stay on, or labor-saving or productivity-enhancing systems can be installed. If overstaffing is expected to be a problem, the main options are transferring the extra employees, not replacing individuals who quit, encouraging early retirement, and laying off workers. During the 2008–2009 recession, many firms found it necessary to reduce the size of their workforces through layoffs. Others accomplished the same thing by reducing the number of hours their employees worked.

Staffing the Organization

When managers have determined that new employees are needed, they must then turn their attention to recruiting and hiring the right mix of people. This involves two processes: acquiring staff from outside the company and promoting staff from within. Both external and internal staffing, however, start with effective *recruiting*.

Recruiting Human Resources

Recruiting is the process of attracting qualified persons to apply for the jobs that are open.

Internal Recruiting   **Internal recruiting** means considering present employees as candidates for openings. Promotion from within can help build morale and keep high-quality employees from leaving. For higher-level positions, a skills inventory system may be used to identify internal candidates, or managers may be asked to recommend individuals to be considered.

External Recruiting   **External recruiting** involves attracting people outside the organization to apply for jobs. External recruiting methods include posting jobs on the company Web site or other job sites, such as Monster.com; holding campus interviews for potential college recruits; using employment agencies or executive search firms to scout out potential talent; seeking referrals by present employees; advertising in print publications; and hiring "walk-ins" (unsolicited applicants).

Selecting Human Resources

Once the recruiting process has attracted a pool of applicants, the next step is to select someone to hire. The intent of the selection process is to gather from applicants the information that will predict job success and then to hire the candidates likely to be most successful.

REPLACEMENT CHART list of each management position, who occupies it, how long that person will likely stay in the job, and who is qualified as a replacement

EMPLOYEE INFORMATION SYSTEM (SKILLS INVENTORY) computerized system containing information on each employee's education, skills, work experiences, and career aspirations

RECRUITING process of attracting qualified persons to apply for jobs an organization is seeking to fill

INTERNAL RECRUITING process of considering present employees as candidates for openings

EXTERNAL RECRUITING process of attracting persons outside the organization to apply for jobs

Moving People to Move Movies

Selling movies to consumers is a dynamic and challenging industry today. The market is evolving so rapidly that even the basic business model, product, and technology are unresolved. Is streaming media the right way to deliver content? Are movies best viewed on a television, PC monitor, PDA, or cell phone? Should the consumer rent the content or own it? What is the role of advertising? Netflix is one of the companies at the forefront of addressing these questions.

In order to cope with the many complex issues the company faces, Netflix CEO and founder Reed Hastings recruited a team of top performers in fields as diverse as marketing, content management, and Web site operations. Then the company had to find a way to motivate these stars to fulfill their potential. Netflix uses monetary rewards as a motivator. "We're unafraid to pay high," says Hastings. However, the company achieves its greatest results by focusing on employee needs.

One important set of needs that Netflix fulfills is the desire to work with friends, be part of a team, and belong. Employees recommend people they've enjoyed working with at other jobs. The atmosphere is casual and collaborative. However, the company avoids patronizing its employees. As Michelle Conlin of *BusinessWeek* puts it, "Netflix is no frat party with beer bashes and foosball tables." The Netflix values statement says, "The benefit of a high-performance culture is that you work with consistently outstanding colleagues, which is exhilarating. We're a high-performance team, not a family. A strong family is together forever, no matter what. A strong company, on the other hand, is more like a professional sports team, which is built to win."[1]

Netflix works to fulfill employees' needs for esteem by providing an employer that is well liked. The job pages of the company's Web site say, "It is satisfying to work at a company that people love. We're ranked number one in customer satisfaction across the entire Internet, narrowly besting such great companies as Apple and Amazon."

Another set of fulfilled needs is related to employees' passion to achieve. The "best in class" personnel at this firm of just 400 workers are attracted by the opportunity to have a significant impact on a successful and ever-changing company. Before founding Netflix, Hastings started Pure Software. At first the start-up was an exciting place to work, but it became more humdrum and bureaucratic as it grew. When Pure was sold to IBM, Hastings vowed to never repeat that mistake. The Netflix values statement summarizes Hastings's viewpoint, saying, "Rules inhibit creativity and entrepreneurship, leading to a lack of innovation. Our solution to increased complexity is to increase talent density. Great people make great judgment calls, despite ambiguity. We believe in freedom and responsibility, not rules."

Clearly, the Netflix motivation scheme is not for everyone. "At most companies, average performers get an average raise," says Hastings. "At Netflix, they get a generous severance package." However, the company is doing a good job of motivating stellar workers. Netflix is depending on wringing maximum performance from those workers to win competitive advantage over top competitors such as Apple, Blockbuster, and Amazon.

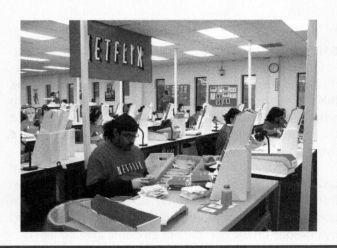

Application Forms The first step in selection is usually asking the candidate to fill out an application. An application form is an efficient method of gathering information about the applicant's previous work history, educational background, and other job-related demographic data. Application forms are seldom used for upper-level jobs; candidates for such positions usually provide the same information on their résumé. Most applications for larger firms are now prepared electronically and submitted at the firm's Web site.

Tests Employers sometimes ask candidates to take tests during the selection process. Tests of ability, skill, aptitude, or knowledge relevant to a particular job are usually the best predictors of job success, although tests of general intelligence or personality are occasionally useful as well. Some companies use a test of the "big five" personality dimensions discussed in Chapter 8 to predict success.

Interviews *Interviews* are a very popular selection device, although they are sometimes a poor predictor

A Simulating Experience

A variation of off-site training is **vestibule training**, which takes place in simulated work environments that make the off-the-job training more realistic; increasingly, these simulations are computerized or Web-based. American Airlines, for example, trains flight attendants at a vestibule training site that resembles the interior cabin of an airplane; it also uses simulation software to help acquaint its pilots with new instrumentation that is added to its aircraft.[2]

of job success. For example, biases inherent in the way people perceive and judge others on first meeting affect subsequent evaluations. Interview validity can be improved by training interviewers to be aware of potential biases and by tightening the structure of the interview. In a structured interview, questions are written in advance, and all interviewers follow the same question list with each candidate. For interviewing managerial or professional candidates, a somewhat less structured approach can be used. Although question areas and information-gathering objectives are still planned in advance, specific questions vary with the candidates' backgrounds. Sometimes, companies are looking for especially creative employees and may try to learn more about the individual's creativity during an interview.

Other Techniques Organizations also use other selection techniques that vary with circumstances. Polygraph

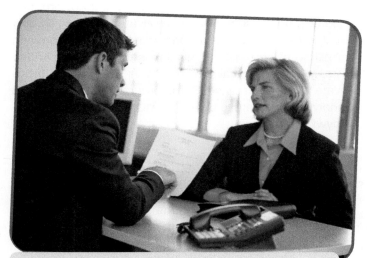

Interviews are a very popular selection device. In a structured interview, such as the kind that typically takes place during a job fair, questions are written in advance, and all interviewers follow the same question list with each candidate.

tests, once popular, are declining in popularity. On the other hand, organizations occasionally require applicants to take physical exams (being careful that their practices are consistent with the Americans with Disabilities Act). More organizations are using drug tests, especially in situations in which drug-related performance problems could create serious safety hazards. Some organizations also run credit checks on prospective employees. Reference checks with previous employers are also used, but have been shown to have limited value because individuals are likely to only provide the names of references that will give them positive recommendations.

VESTIBULE TRAINING off-the-job training conducted in a simulated environment

ON-THE-JOB TRAINING training, sometimes informal, conducted while an employee is at work

OFF-THE-JOB TRAINING training conducted in a controlled environment away from the work site

PERFORMANCE APPRAISAL evaluation of an employee's job performance in order to determine the degree to which the employee is performing effectively

Developing the Workforce

After a company has hired new employees, it must acquaint them with the firm and their new jobs. Managers also take steps to train employees and to further develop necessary job skills. In addition, every firm has some system for performance appraisal and feedback.

Training

As its name suggests, **on-the-job training** occurs while an employee is at work. **Off-the-job training** takes place at locations away from a work site. This approach offers a controlled environment and allows focused study without interruptions. Training is a necessary practice if the organization wants to maintain a qualified and effective workforce. Moreover, many employees see training as a benefit—it allows them to keep their job skills current and to learn new skills to prepare them for the jobs of tomorrow.

Performance Appraisal

Performance appraisals are designed to show workers precisely how well they are doing their jobs. Typically, the appraisal process involves a written assessment issued on a regular basis. As a rule, however, the written evaluation is only one part of a multistep process.

The appraisal process begins when a manager defines performance standards for an employee. The manager then observes the employee's performance. For some jobs, a rating scale like the abbreviated one in

COMPENSATION SYSTEM total package of rewards that organizations provide to individuals in return for their labor

WAGES compensation in the form of money paid for time worked

SALARY compensation in the form of money paid for discharging the responsibilities of a job

INCENTIVE PROGRAM special compensation program designed to motivate high performance

BONUS individual performance incentive in the form of a special payment made over and above the employee's salary

MERIT SALARY SYSTEM individual incentive linking compensation to performance in nonsales jobs

Figure 10.2 is useful in providing a basis for comparison. Comparisons drawn from such scales form the basis for written appraisals and for decisions about raises, promotions, demotions, and firings. The process is completed when the manager and employee meet to discuss the appraisal.

Compensation and Benefits

People who work for a business expect to be paid, and most workers today also expect certain benefits from their employers. Indeed, a major factor in retaining skilled workers is a company's **compensation system**—the total package of rewards that it offers employees in return for their labor. Finding the right combination of compensation elements is always complicated by the need to make employees feel valued, while holding down company costs.

Wages and Salaries

Wages and salaries are the dollar amounts paid to employees for their labor. **Wages** are paid for time worked. A **salary** is paid for performing a job. A salaried executive earning $100,000 per year is paid to achieve results even if that means working 5 hours one day and 15 the next. Salaries are usually expressed as an amount paid per year.

In setting wage and salary levels, a company may start by looking at its competitors' levels. Firms must also decide how their internal wage and salary levels will compare for different jobs. Although two employees may do exactly the same job, the employee with more experience may earn more.

The recession of 2008–2009 prompted some firms to reduce the wages and salaries they were paying in order to lower costs. For example, Hewlett-Packard reduced the salaries of all but its top performers by amounts ranging from 2.5 to 20 percent. CareerBuilder.com reduced all employee pay but also began giving all employees Friday afternoons off.

Figure 10.2
Sample Performance Evaluation Form

Incentive Programs

As we discussed in Chapter 8, studies have shown that beyond a certain point, more money will not produce better performance. Money motivates employees only if it is tied directly to performance. The most common method of establishing this link is the use of **incentive programs**—special pay programs designed to motivate high performance. Some programs are available to individuals, whereas others are distributed on a companywide basis.

Individual Incentives   A sales bonus is a typical incentive. Employees receive a **bonus**—special payments above their salaries—when they sell a certain number or certain dollar amount of goods for the year. Employees who fail to reach this goal earn no bonuses. **Merit salary systems** link pay raises to performance levels in non-sales jobs.

Executives commonly receive stock options as incentives. Halliburton CEO David Lesar, for example,

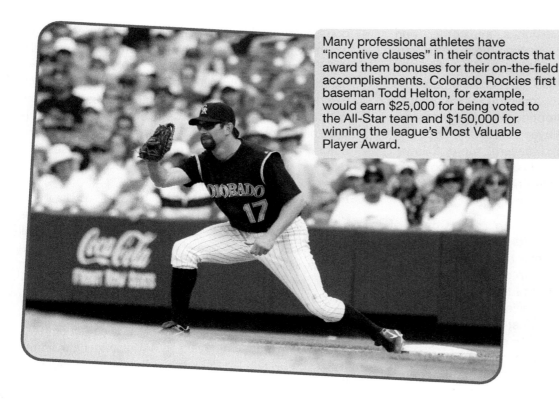

Many professional athletes have "incentive clauses" in their contracts that award them bonuses for their on-the-field accomplishments. Colorado Rockies first baseman Todd Helton, for example, would earn $25,000 for being voted to the All-Star team and $150,000 for winning the league's Most Valuable Player Award.

PAY FOR PERFORMANCE (VARIABLE PAY) individual incentive that rewards a manager for especially productive output

PROFIT-SHARING PLAN incentive plan for distributing bonuses to employees when company profits rise above a certain level

GAINSHARING PLAN incentive plan that rewards groups for productivity improvements

PAY-FOR-KNOWLEDGE PLAN incentive plan to encourage employees to learn new skills or become proficient at different jobs

BENEFITS compensation other than wages and salaries

WORKERS' COMPENSATION INSURANCE legally required insurance for compensating workers injured on the job

can buy several thousand shares of company stock each year at a predetermined price. If his managerial talent leads to higher profits and stock prices, he can buy the stock at a price lower than the market value for which, in theory, he is largely responsible. He is then free to sell the stock at market price, keeping the profits for himself.

A newer incentive plan is called **pay for performance** (or **variable pay**). In essence, middle managers are rewarded for especially productive output—for producing earnings that significantly exceed the cost of bonuses. The number of variable pay programs in the United States has been growing consistently for the last decade, and most experts predict that they will continue to grow in popularity. Many firms say that variable pay is a better motivator than merit raises because the range between generous and mediocre merit raises is usually quite small.

Companywide Incentives Some incentive programs apply to all the employees in a firm. Under **profit-sharing plans**, for example, profits earned above a certain level are distributed to employees. Also, **gainsharing plans** distribute bonuses to employees when a company's costs are reduced through greater work efficiency. **Pay-for-knowledge plans** pay workers to learn new skills and to become proficient at different jobs.

Benefits Programs

Benefits—compensation other than wages and salaries and other incentives offered by a firm to its workers—account for an increasing percentage of most compensation budgets. Most companies are required by law to pay tax for Social Security retirement benefits and provide **workers' compensation insurance** (insurance for compensating workers injured on the job). Most businesses also provide health, life, and disability insurance for their workers, as well as paid time off for vacations and holidays. Many also allow employees to use payroll deductions to buy stock at discounted prices. Counseling services for employees with alcohol, drug, or emotional problems are also becoming more common, as are on-site child-care centers. Some companies even provide reduced membership fees at gyms and health clubs, as well as insurance or other protection for identity theft.[3]

Retirement Plans Retirement plans (or pension plans) constitute another important—and sometimes controversial—benefit that is available to many employees. Most company-sponsored retirement plans are set up to pay pensions to workers when they retire. In some cases, the company contributes all the money to the pension fund. In others, contributions are made by both the company and employees. In recent years, some companies have run into problems because they have not set aside enough money to cover the retirement funds they have agreed to provide. Both FedEx and Goodyear, for instance, recently announced that they were freezing their pension programs in order to transition workers to riskier 401(k)s, in which payroll deductions are invested

CAFETERIA BENEFITS PLAN benefit plan that sets limits on benefits per employee, each of whom may choose from a variety of alternative benefits

EQUAL EMPLOYMENT OPPORTUNITY legally mandated nondiscrimination in employment on the basis of race, creed, sex, or national origin

PROTECTED CLASS set of individuals who by nature of one or more common characteristics is protected under the law from discrimination on the basis of that characteristic

EQUAL EMPLOYMENT OPPORTUNITY COMMISSION (EEOC) federal agency enforcing several discrimination-related laws

in stocks and other non-guaranteed funds.[4] This trend increased during the 2008–2009 recession. For example, 16 major U.S. employers stopped contributing to employee retirement accounts, and several more followed suit in 2009. Among these were Anheuser-Busch, Wells-Fargo, and Saks.

Containing the Costs of Benefits As the range of benefits has increased, so has concern about containing the costs of these benefits. Many companies are experimenting with cost-cutting plans while still attracting and retaining valuable employees. One approach is the **cafeteria benefits plan**. A certain dollar amount of benefits per employee is set aside so that each employee can choose from a variety of alternatives.

Another area of increasing concern is health care costs. Medical expenses have increased insurance premiums, which have increased the cost to employers of maintaining benefits plans. Many employers are looking for new ways to cut those costs. One increasingly popular approach is for organizations to create their own networks of health care providers. These providers agree to charge lower fees for services rendered to employees of member organizations. In return, they enjoy established relationships with large employers and, thus, more clients and patients. Insurers also charge less to cover the employees of network members because they make lower reimbursement payments.

The Legal Context of HRM

Federal law and judicial review heavily influence HRM as much or more than any area of business. In this section, we summarize some of the most important and far-reaching areas of HR regulation.

Equal Employment Opportunity

The basic goal of all **equal employment opportunity** regulation is to protect people from unfair or inappropriate discrimination in the workplace.[5] Let's begin by noting that discrimination in itself is not illegal. Whenever

one person is given a pay raise and another is not, for example, the organization has made a decision to distinguish one person from another. As long as the basis for this discrimination is purely job related (made, for example, on the basis of performance or seniority) and is applied objectively and consistently, the action is legal and appropriate. Problems arise when distinctions among people are not job related. In such cases, the resulting discrimination is illegal.

Protected Classes in the Workplace To combat illegal discrimination, laws have been passed to protect various classes of individuals. A **protected class** consists of all individuals who share one or more common characteristics as indicated by a given law. The most common criteria for defining protected classes include race, color, religion, gender, age, national origin, disability status, and status as a military veteran.[6] One recent illustration of this protection is the Americans with Disabilities Act of 1990. This law requires employers to not discriminate on the basis of physical limitations and to provide reasonable work-related modifications to help disabled individuals do their jobs.

Enforcing Equal Employment Opportunity The enforcement of equal opportunity legislation is handled by two agencies. The **Equal Employment Opportunity Commission (EEOC)** is a division of the Department of Justice. It was created by Title VII of the 1964 Civil Rights Act and has specific responsibility for enforcing Title VII, the Equal Pay Act, and the Americans with Disabilities Act.

The other agency charged with monitoring equal employment opportunity legislation is the *Office of Federal Contract Compliance Programs* (OFCCP). The OFCCP is responsible for enforcing executive orders that apply to companies doing business with the federal

"I see by your résumé that you're a woman."

government. A business with government contracts must have on file a written **affirmative action plan**— that is, a written statement of how the organization intends to actively recruit, hire, and develop members of relevant protected classes.

Legal Issues in Compensation As noted earlier, most employment regulations are designed to provide equal employment opportunity. Some

Managing in Turbulent Times

In Good Times and Bad

Sometimes the worst brings out the best in both people and businesses. When Hurricane Katrina struck the Gulf Coast in 2005, for instance, millions of people lost everything they had, and to make matters worse, the response of the federal government was fraught with bureaucratic blundering. Fortunately, many businesses stepped forward to come to the aid of Katrina victims. Dozens of companies, including Apple, Citigroup, Enterprise Rent-a-Car, and the Gap, made contributions of $1 million, and some gave much more, with Wal-Mart's $17 million topping the list.

Some employers made funds available to match employee contributions, and other firms donated goods or services. Abbott donated infant formula, and AT&T donated calling cards. Clorox supplied 50,000 gallons of bleach to aid in removing mold. Albertson's donated $9 million in food, and pharmaceutical firms furnished medicines. Some companies made more unusual offers. A few banks, for example, offered home equity loans, even for homes that weren't inhabitable. DIRECTV launched a Hurricane Katrina information channel. KB Home, a national builder, committed to building thousands of new houses.

The outpouring of support went a long way toward helping New Orleans residents and other Gulf Coast residents rebuild shattered lives. That support, however, took forms other than corporate financial resources: In many cases, it took the form of corporate human resources. Consider the response of Entergy, the country's third-largest electric utility, which serves 2.7 million customers in the Gulf Coast region. When Katrina hit, more than 1 million Entergy customers were left without power—including 1,500 Entergy employees. CEO Wayne Leonard immediately began organizing repair efforts, but his goal was to restore more than electricity. Leonard firmly believes that he and his employees "do a lot more than make electricity and money. We cool [people's] homes in the summer and warm their homes in the winter. We allow people to cook their food. We clean the environment and educate their children."

Using optimistic (and sometimes emotional) e-mails, Leonard motivated Entergy employees by appealing to a company culture based on his conviction that the people who work for an organization "want to know that what they do makes a difference." "We have a great passion for the difference we make in other people's lives," he told his workforce." "We provide a commodity that sustains life." Working 16-hour days, Entergy crews had restored power to 550,000 people by the end of the first week, and by the end of September, nearly every Entergy customer had electricity. In the third week of September, when Hurricane Rita

followed hard on the heels of Katrina, knocking out power to 750,000 customers, Entergy employees—many of whom had barely had time to check up on their own families—were back at work with the same levels of commitment and teamwork.

Employees were also a major focus of disaster response at the Domino Sugar refinery located in St. Bernard Parish, east of New Orleans. Virtually the entire parish was flooded, leaving most of the plant's 332 employees homeless. At the refinery itself, floodwaters melted 6.5 million pounds of sugar into huge lakes of sugar syrup. Because 19 percent of the nation's sugar supply comes through the St. Bernard facility, it was imperative for officials to get it up and running again as quickly as possible. "We can fix anything," says VP for operations Mickey Seither. "We can rebuild everything. But," he adds, "if we don't have employees, it's for naught." From the outset, Seither recalls, "we decided the one thing we have to really concentrate on is fixing the situation that our employees are in."

So Domino managed to get 200 mobile homes from the Federal Emergency Management Agency within two weeks and immediately set up a mobile home park on the grounds of the refinery. Other companies in the area also set up mobile home parks, but Domino was the only employer to house employees' families as well. Not every household was comfortable, but each mobile home had hot water and a microwave for cooking. Said one worker who lived in 28-foot mobile home with his wife and five children, "We, as employees, appreciate it because, if not, we'd be . . . at my brother-in-law's house with 15 people." Within 6 months, the refinery was operating at nearly full capacity, providing 300 well-paying jobs and working to function as a catalyst for further recovery in the parish. During the entire period, according to the company, not one employee lost an hour of pay.

OCCUPATIONAL SAFETY AND HEALTH ACT OF 1970 (OSHA) federal law setting and enforcing guidelines for protecting workers from unsafe conditions and potential health hazards in the workplace

SEXUAL HARASSMENT unwelcome sexual advances in the workplace

QUID PRO QUO HARASSMENT form of sexual harassment in which sexual favors are requested in return for job-related benefits

HOSTILE WORK ENVIRONMENT form of sexual harassment deriving from off-color jokes, lewd comments, and so forth

EMPLOYMENT AT WILL principle, increasingly modified by legislation and judicial decision, that organizations should be able to retain or dismiss employees at their discretion

legislation, however, deals with other issues such as compensation. For example, the Fair Labor Standards Act (passed in 1938) established a minimum hourly wage, whereas the Employee Retirement Income Security Act of 1974 sets standards by which companies must manage pension funds.

Contemporary Legal Issues in HRM

In addition to these established areas of HR legal regulation, several emerging legal issues will likely become more important in the future. These include employee safety and health, various emerging areas of discrimination law, employee rights, and employment at will.

Employee Safety and Health The **Occupational Safety and Health Act of 1970 (OSHA)** is the single most comprehensive piece of legislation ever passed regarding worker safety and health. OSHA holds that every employer has an obligation to furnish each employee with a place of employment that is free from hazards that cause or are likely to cause death or physical harm. It is generally enforced through inspections of the workplace by OSHA inspectors. Serious or willful and repeated violations may incur fines up to $10,000 per incident.

Emerging Areas of Discrimination Law Managers must also be familiar with several emerging areas of discrimination law.

AIDS in the Workplace Although AIDS is considered a disability under the Americans with Disabilities Act of 1990, the AIDS situation itself is severe enough that it warrants special attention. Employers cannot legally require an HIV test or any other medical examination as a condition for making an offer of employment. Organizations must accommodate or make a good-faith effort to accommodate individuals with HIV, maintain the confidentiality of all medical records, and try to educate coworkers about AIDS.

Sexual Harassment **Sexual harassment** is defined by the EEOC as unwelcome sexual advances in the work environment. If the conduct is indeed unwelcome and occurs with sufficient frequency to create an abusive work environment, the employer is responsible for changing the environment by warning, reprimanding, or perhaps firing the harasser.[7]

The courts have defined two types of sexual harassment:

1 In cases of **quid pro quo harassment**, the harasser offers to exchange something of value for sexual favors. A male supervisor, for example, might tell or suggest to a female subordinate that he will recommend her for promotion or give her a raise in exchange for sexual favors.

2 The creation of a **hostile work environment** is a subtler form of sexual harassment. A group of male employees who continually make off-color jokes and lewd comments and perhaps decorate the work environment with inappropriate photographs may create a hostile work environment for a female colleague, who may become uncomfortable working in that environment.

In recent years, the concept of harassment has been expanded to encompass unwelcome or inappropriate behaviors regarding ethnicity, religion, and age.

Employment at Will The concept of **employment at will** holds that both employer and employee have the mutual right to terminate an employment relationship at any time for any reason, with or without advance notice to the other. Over the last two decades, however, terminated employees have challenged the employment-at-will doctrine by filing lawsuits against former employers on the grounds of wrongful discharge.

In the last several years, such suits have put limits on employment-at-will provisions in certain circumstances. In the past, for example, organizations were guilty of firing employees who filed workers' compensation claims or took "excessive" time off to serve on jury duty. More recently, however, the courts have ruled that employees may not be fired for exercising rights protected by law.

The Patriot Act In response to the terrorist attacks of September 11, 2001, the U.S. government passed legislation that increases its powers to investigate and prosecute suspected terrorists. This legislation, known as the Patriot Act, has several key implications for HRM. For instance, certain "restricted" individuals (including ex-convicts and aliens from countries deemed by the State Department to have "repeatedly provided support for acts of international terrorism") are ineligible to work with potentially dangerous biological agents. More controversial are sections granting government investigators access to previously confidential personal and financial records.[8]

New Challenges in the Changing Workplace

In addition to the challenges we have already considered, HR managers face several new challenges reflecting the changing economic and social environments of business.

Managing Workforce Diversity

One extremely important set of HR challenges centers on **workforce diversity**—the range of workers' attitudes, values, beliefs, and behaviors that differ by gender, race, age, ethnicity, physical ability, and other relevant characteristics. In the past, organizations tended to work toward homogenizing their workforces, getting everyone to think and behave in similar ways. Partly as a result of affirmative action efforts, however, many U.S. organizations are now creating more diverse workforces than ever before.

Figure 10.3 projects the racial and ethnic composition of the U.S. workforce through 2050. The picture is clearly one of increasing diversity. The number of white Americans as a percentage of the total workforce is declining steadily, offset by increases in every other racial group. Most striking are the growing numbers of people of Hispanic origin (who may be members of any racial group). By 2050 the U.S. Department of Labor estimates that nearly a quarter of the workforce will be Hispanic.

Today, organizations are recognizing that diversity can be a competitive advantage. For example, by hiring the best people available from every single group rather than hiring from just one or a few groups, a firm can develop a higher-quality labor force. Similarly, a diverse workforce can bring a wider array of information to bear on problems and can provide insights on marketing products to a wider range of consumers.

Managing Knowledge Workers

Traditionally, employees added value to organizations because of what they did or because of their experience. In the information age, however, many employees add value because of what they *know*.

The Nature of Knowledge Work Employees who add value because of what they know are usually called **knowledge workers**. Knowledge workers—including computer scientists, engineers, physical scientists, and game developers—typically require extensive and highly specialized training; once they are on the job, retraining and training updates are critical to prevent their skills from becoming obsolete. It has been suggested, for example, that the half-life of a technical education in engineering is about three years.

A firm's failure to update the skills of its knowledge workers will not only result in the loss of competitive advantage, it will also increase the likelihood that those workers will go to other firms that are more committed to updating their skills. Hence, HR managers must ensure that the proper training is prepared to enable knowledge workers to stay current while also making sure they are compensated at market rates.

Contingent and Temporary Workers

A final contemporary HR issue of note involves the use of contingent and temporary workers. In recent years there has been an explosion in the use of such workers by organizations. Recall, for instance, the anecdotes and examples provided in this chapter's opening case.

Trends in Contingent and Temporary Employment A **contingent worker** is a person who works for an organization on something other than a permanent or full-time basis. Categories of contingent workers include independent contractors, on-call workers, temporary employees (usually hired through outside agencies), and contract and leased employees. Another category is part-time workers.

Managing Contingent and Temporary Workers One key to managing contingent workers effectively is careful planning and analysis. Rather than having to call in workers sporadically, and with no prior notice, organizations try to bring in specified numbers of workers for well-defined periods of time. Firms should also be able to document the labor-cost savings of using contingent workers.

A second key is recognizing what can and cannot be achieved by using contingent and temporary workers. For instance, these workers may lack the firm-specific knowledge to perform as effectively as a permanent employee would perform. They are also less committed

> **WORKFORCE DIVERSITY**
> the range of workers' attitudes, values, beliefs, and behaviors that differ by gender, race, age, ethnicity, physical ability, and other relevant characteristics
>
> **KNOWLEDGE WORKERS**
> employees who are of value because of the knowledge they possess
>
> **CONTINGENT WORKER**
> employee hired on something other than a full-time basis to supplement an organization's permanent workforce

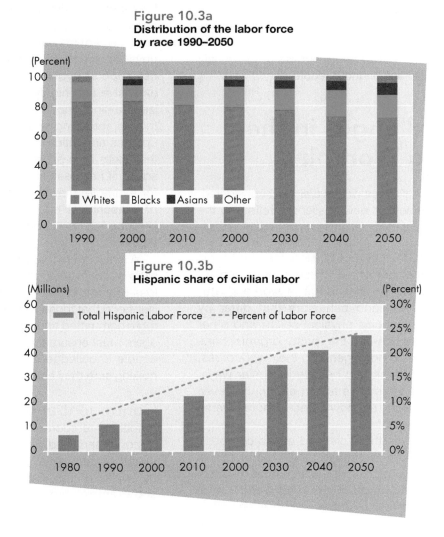

LABOR UNION group of individuals working together to achieve shared job-related goals, such as higher pay, shorter working hours, more job security, greater benefits, or better working conditions

LABOR RELATIONS process of dealing with employees who are represented by a union

Figure 10.3a
Distribution of the labor force by race 1990–2050

(Percent)

☐ Whites ☐ Blacks ☐ Asians ☐ Other

1990 2000 2010 2000 2030 2040 2050

Figure 10.3b
Hispanic share of civilian labor

(Millions) (Percent)

☐ Total Hispanic Labor Force - - - Percent of Labor Force

1980 1990 2000 2010 2000 2030 2040 2050

to the organization and less likely to engage in organizational citizenship behaviors.

Finally, managers must make decisions about how to integrate contingent workers into the organization. These decisions may be as simple as whether to invite contingent workers to the holiday party, or they may be more complicated, such as whether to grant contingent workers access to such employee benefits as counseling services and child care.

Dealing with Organized Labor

A **labor union** is a group of individuals working together to achieve shared job-related goals, such as higher pay, shorter working hours, more job security, greater benefits, or better working conditions. **Labor relations** refers to the process of dealing with employees who are represented by a union.

Unionism Today

In the years immediately following World War II and continuing through the mid-1960s, most unions routinely won certification elections. In recent years, however, labor unions have been winning certification less than 50 percent of the times that workers are called upon to vote. As a result, although millions of workers still belong to unions, union membership as a percentage of the total workforce has steadily declined. In 2007, only 12.1 percent of U.S. workers belonged to a labor union, down from 20.1 percent in 1983, when the U.S. Department of Labor first began compiling data.[9] We should note, however, that union membership took a jump in 2009, in part due to workers concerns about job security during the 2008–2009 recession.

The Future of Unions Even though several of its members withdrew from the parent organization in 2005, the American Federation of Labor and Congress of Industrial Organizations (AFL-CIO), as well as independent major unions such as the Teamsters and the

Knowledge workers such as Ann Quinn, a self-employed marketing consultant, often prefer to work independently. However, this arrangement may make it difficult for them to secure adequate health care coverage. Consequently, nonprofit organizations have stepped forward to assist. Quinn insures herself, her daughter, and her husband through Freelancers Union, a nonprofit that furnishes portable, affordable health insurance to freelance workers in New York and many other states. *Source:* Joyce Dopkeen/New York Times

National Education Association (NEA), still play a major role in U.S. business. Unions in the traditional strong-holds of goods-producing industries continue to wield considerable power as well. The United Auto Workers (UAW), was for decades one of the largest unions in the United States. But it, too, seems to be entering a period of decline. The traumas experienced by the U.S. auto industry in 2008–2009, for instance, required the UAW to make many major concessions in order to help Ford, DaimlerChrysler, and General Motors survive. In addition, auto plant closures will dramatically reduce the number of auto jobs in the years to come.

Collective Bargaining

The power of unions comes from collective action—forcing management to listen to the demands of all workers rather than to just the few who speak out. **Collective**

bargaining is the process by which labor and management negotiate conditions of employment for union-represented workers and draft a labor contract.

Reaching Agreement on Contract Terms

The collective bargaining process begins when the union is recognized as the exclusive negotiator for its members and union leaders meet with management representatives to agree on a contract. By law, both parties must sit down at the bargaining table and negotiate in good faith.

Sometimes, this process goes quite smoothly. At other times, the two sides cannot agree. Resolving the impasse depends in part on the nature of the contract issues, the willingness of each side to use certain tactics, such as strikes, and the prospects for mediation or arbitration.

Contract Issues

The labor contract itself can address an array of different issues. Issues that are typically most important to union negotiators include *compensation*, *benefits*, and *job security*. Certain management rights, such as control over hiring policies and work assignments, are also negotiated in most bargaining agreements. Other possible issues might include such specific details as working hours, overtime policies, rest period arrangements, differential pay plans for shift employees, the use of temporary workers, grievance procedures, and allowable union activities (dues collection, union bulletin boards, and so forth).

Compensation Compen-sation includes both current and future wages. One common tool for securing wage increases is a **cost-of-living adjustment (COLA)**. Most COLA clauses tie future raises to the *Consumer Price Index (CPI)*, a government statistic that reflects changes in consumer purchasing power. Almost half of all labor contracts today include COLA clauses.

A union might be uncomfortable with a long-term contract based solely on COLA wage increases. One solution is a **wage reopener clause**, which allows wage rates to be renegotiated at preset times during the life of the contract.

COLLECTIVE BARGAINING process by which labor and management negotiate conditions of employment and draft a labor contract for union-represented workers

COST-OF-LIVING ADJUSTMENT (COLA) labor contract clause tying future raises to changes in consumer purchasing power

WAGE REOPENER CLAUSE clause allowing wage rates to be renegotiated during the life of a labor contract

STRIKE labor action in which employees temporarily walk off the job and refuse to work

PICKETING labor action in which workers publicize their grievances at the entrance to an employer's facility

BOYCOTT labor action in which workers refuse to buy the products of a targeted employer

WORK SLOWDOWN labor action in which workers perform jobs at a slower than normal pace

LOCKOUT management tactic whereby workers are denied access to the employer's workplace

STRIKEBREAKER worker hired as a permanent or temporary replacement for a striking employee

MEDIATION method of resolving a labor dispute in which a third party suggests, but does not impose, a settlement

ARBITRATION method of resolving a labor dispute in which both parties agree to submit to the judgment of a neutral party

Benefits   Employee benefits are also an important component in most labor contracts. Unions typically want employers to pay all or most of the costs of insurance for employees. Other benefits commonly addressed during negotiations include retirement benefits, paid holidays, and working conditions. Due to surging health care costs, employee health insurance premiums have become a major point of contention in recent years. For example, many employees have much larger co-pays today when they visit their doctor than was the case a few years ago. (A *co-pay* is the dollar amount a patient pays to the doctor; insurance then pays the remainder.)

Job Security   Job security also remains an important agenda item in many bargaining sessions today. In some cases, a contract may dictate that if the workforce is reduced, seniority will be used to determine which employees keep their jobs. Unions are setting their sights on preserving jobs for workers in the United States in the face of business efforts to outsource production in some sectors to countries where labor costs are cheaper. For example, the AFL-CIO has been an outspoken opponent of efforts to normalize trade relations with China, fearing that more businesses might be tempted to move jobs there to take advantage of lower wage levels.

When Bargaining Fails

An impasse occurs when, after a series of bargaining sessions, management and labor have failed to agree on a new contract or a contract to replace an agreement that is about to expire. Although it is generally agreed that both parties suffer when an impasse is reached and some action by one part against the other is taken, each side can use several tactics to support its cause until the impasse is resolved.

Union Tactics   Historically, one of the most common union tactics has been the **strike**, which occurs when

employees temporarily walk off the job and refuse to work. Far fewer strikes occur today than in previous years. From 1960 to 1980, for example, an average of 281 strikes occurred per year. Since 1990, however, the annual number of strikes has ranged from a high of 45 (in 1994) to a low of 14 (in 2003).[10]

To support a strike, a union faced with an impasse has recourse to additional legal activities:

- In **picketing**, workers march at the entrance to the employer's facility with signs explaining their reasons for striking.

- A **boycott** occurs when union members agree not to buy the products of a targeted employer. Workers may also urge consumers to boycott the firm's products.

- Another alternative to striking is a **work slowdown**. Instead of striking, workers perform their jobs at a much slower pace than normal. A variation is the *sickout*, during which large numbers of workers call in sick.

Management Tactics   Like workers, management can respond forcefully to an impasse with the following:

- **Lockouts** occur when employers deny employees access to the workplace. Lockouts are illegal if they are used as offensive weapons to give management a bargaining advantage. However, they are legal if management has a legitimate business need (for instance, avoiding a buildup of perishable inventory).

- A firm can also hire temporary or permanent replacements called **strikebreakers**. However, the law forbids the permanent replacement of workers who strike because of unfair practices. In some cases, an employer can obtain legal injunctions that either prohibit workers from striking or prohibit a union from interfering with its efforts to use replacement workers.

Mediation and Arbitration   Rather than wield these often unpleasant weapons against one another, labor and management can agree to call in a third party to help resolve the dispute:

- In **mediation**, the neutral third party (the mediator) can suggest, but cannot impose, a settlement on the other parties.

- In **arbitration**, the neutral third party (the arbitrator) dictates a settlement between the two sides, which have agreed to submit to outside judgment. In some disputes, such as those between the government and public employees, arbitration is compulsory, or required by law.

Managing an organization's human resources is both a complex and an important undertaking. Most businesses can buy the same equipment and use the same technology as their competitors. But differences in employee talent and motivation are not easily copied. Consequently, most well-managed companies today recognize the value provided by their employees and strive to insure that the HR function is managed as efficiently and effectively as possible.

Questions for Review

1. What are the advantages and disadvantages of internal and external recruiting? Under what circumstances is each more appropriate?

2. Why is the formal training of workers so important to most employers? Why don't employers simply let people learn about their jobs as they perform them?

3. What different forms of compensation do firms typically use to attract and keep productive workers?

4. What tactics do unions use to overcome an impasse at the bargaining table? What tactics does management use?

Questions for Analysis

5. What are your views on drug testing in the workplace? What would you do if your employer asked you to submit to a drug test?

6. Workers at Ford, GM, and DaimlerChrysler are represented by the UAW. However, the UAW has been unsuccessful in its attempts to unionize U.S. workers employed at Toyota, Nissan, and Honda plants in the United States. Why do you think this is so?

7. What training do you think you are most likely to need when you finish school and start your career?

8. How much will benefit considerations affect your choice of an employer after graduation?

Application Exercises

9. Interview an HR manager at a local company. Focus on a position for which the firm is currently recruiting applicants and identify the steps in the selection process.

10. Interview the managers of two local companies, one unionized and one nonunionized. Compare the wage and salary levels, benefits, and working conditions of employees at the two firms.

chapter 11

Marketing Processes and Consumer Behavior

After reading this chapter, you should be able to:

1 Explain the concept of marketing and identify the five forces that constitute the external marketing environment.

2 Explain market segmentation and how it is used in target marketing.

3 Describe the key factors that influence the consumer buying process.

4 Discuss the three categories of organizational markets.

5 Explain the definition of a product as a value package and classify goods and services.

6 Describe the key considerations in the new product development process, and explain the importance of branding and packaging.

7 Discuss the challenges that arise in adopting an international marketing mix.

Starbucks Brews a New Marketing Mix

For lovers of upscale coffee products, Starbucks has long been the standout brand with a premium image as the "home of affordable luxury." With its well-established line of tasty lattes and Frappuccinos—some priced above $4 and all presented by service-savvy baristas—Starbucks gained great popularity in the connoisseur coffee market. Seeking to tap the market's full potential, Chairman and CEO Howard Schultz spearheaded an ambitious expansion dream for 40,000 retail outlets globally, creating a massive network of stores dispensing Starbucks products, along with an infusion of Starbucks's "romance, warmth and theater," to millions of coffee gourmets. All of that changed, however, with the sting of the 2008–2009 recession.

To stay afloat, Starbucks is reconsidering all aspects of its marketing strategy, including downsizing the distribution network of retail stores, refashioning its line of products and prices, and promoting a repositioned Starbucks image. The new strategy—presenting Starbucks as being more affordable—reflects the company's tighter budget and realignment with the target market, as consumers adjust to the realities of a down-turning economy. Instead of adding 2,500 locations annually, hundreds of the existing 17,000 locations will be closed, especially in areas such as Florida and California that have seen widespread home foreclosures. The strategy also refocuses its products back onto what made Starbucks great—coffee—instead of side-tracking into movies and music. New entries in the product mix include a line of instant coffee (once shunned by Starbucks). In a competitive response to McDonald's (with its own new specialty coffee drinks) and Dunkin' Donuts, Starbucks has presented a new line of recession-friendly value meals, including a choice of breakfast sandwich paired with a coffee product, at a reduced-price savings of as much as $1.20. To keep its customers and bolster sales, the company launched Starbucks Card Rewards, a customer loyalty promotion that gets you free coffee refills and other extras, all to support the affordability image.[1]

Will it work? Can Starbucks reposition the brand so it appeals to the convenience market without tarnishing the company's premium image? Some observers note that the new approach may attract some cost-conscious customers at the same time that it alienates others in the coffee connoisseur segment. It's a marketing risk that Starbucks is taking.

What's in It for Me?

Adjusting its marketing strategy is an example of how a company can apply marketing basics in an innovative way to appeal to the forces of the external marketing environment. This chapter discusses these basics along with the marketing plan and components of the marketing mix, as well as target marketing and market segmentation. It also explores key factors that influence consumer and organizational buying processes, as well as how new products are developed and how they are defined by branding and packaging. By grasping the marketing methods and ideas in this chapter, you will not only be better prepared as a marketing professional, but also as an informed consumer.

What Is Marketing?

MARKETING activity, set of institutions, and processes for creating, communicating, delivering, and enhancing offerings that have value for customers, clients, partners, and society at large

VALUE relative comparison of a product's benefits versus its costs

UTILITY ability of a product to satisfy a human want or need

CONSUMER GOODS physical products purchased by consumers for personal use

INDUSTRIAL GOODS physical products purchased by companies to produce other products

SERVICES products having nonphysical features, such as information, expertise, or an activity that can be purchased

What comes to mind when you think of marketing? Most of us think of marketing as advertisements for detergents and soft drinks. Marketing, however, encompasses a much wider range of activities. The American Marketing Association defines **marketing** as "the activity, set of institutions, and processes for creating, communicating, delivering, and exchanging offerings that have value for customers, clients, partners, and society at large."[2] Let's see this definition in action.

Providing Value and Satisfaction

Although our desires for the many goods and services available to us may be unbounded, limited financial resources force most of us to be selective. Accordingly, customers buy products that offer the best value when it comes to meeting their needs and wants.

Value and Benefits   The **value** of a product compares its benefits with its costs. Benefits include not only the functions of the product, but also the emotional satisfaction associated with owning, experiencing, or possessing it. But every product has costs, including sales price, the expenditure of the buyer's time, and even the emotional costs of making a purchase decision. A satisfied customer perceives the benefits derived from the purchase to be greater than its costs. Thus, the simple but important ratio for value is derived as follows:

$$Value = \frac{Benefits}{Costs}$$

The marketing strategies of leading firms focus on increasing value for customers. Marketing resources are deployed to add benefits and decrease costs of products to provide greater value. To satisfy customers, a company may:

■ Develop an entirely new product that performs better (provides greater performance benefits) than existing products;

■ Keep a store open longer hours during a busy season (adding the benefit of greater shopping convenience);

■ Offer price reductions (the benefit of lower costs).

Value and Utility   To understand how marketing creates value for customers, we need to know the kind of benefits that buyers get from a firm's goods or services. Those benefits provide customers with **utility**—the ability of a product to satisfy a human want or need. Marketing strives to provide utility in the following ways:

■ *Form utility.* Marketing has a voice in designing products with features that customers want.

■ *Time utility.* Marketing creates sales agreements that stipulate when products will be delivered to customers.

■ *Place utility.* Marketing creates sales agreements that stipulate where products will be delivered to customers.

■ *Ownership utility.* Marketing arranges for transferring product ownership to customers by setting selling prices, setting terms for customer credit payments, and providing ownership documents.

Because they determine product features, and the timing, place, and terms of sale that provide utility and add value for customers, marketers must understand customers' wants and needs. Their methods for creating utility are described in this and the following chapter.

Goods, Services, and Ideas

The marketing of tangible goods is obvious in everyday life. It applies to two types of customers: those who buy consumer goods and those who buy industrial goods. Think of the products that you bought the last time you went to the mall or the grocery store. These products are all **consumer goods**: tangible goods that you, the consumer, may buy for personal use. Firms that sell goods to consumers for personal consumption are engaged in consumer marketing.

Marketing also applies to **industrial goods**: physical items used by companies to produce other products. Firms that sell goods to other companies are engaged in industrial marketing.

But marketing techniques are also applied to **services**—products with intangible (nonphysical) features. Service marketing—the application of marketing for services—continues to be a major growth area in the United States. Insurance companies, airlines, and health clinics all engage in service marketing, both to individuals (consumer markets) and to other companies (industrial markets). Thus, the terms consumer marketing and industrial marketing include services as well as goods.

Finally, marketers also promote ideas. Ads in theaters, for example, warn us against copyright infringement and

Managing the Information Overload

Marketers rely on technology to build better relationships with customers and to predict what customers will want and buy. The compiling and storage of customer data, known as data warehousing, provides the raw materials from which marketers can extract information that enables them to better know their customers and supply more of what they need. Data mining automates the massive analysis of data by using computers to sift, sort, and search for previously undiscovered clues about what customers look at, react to, and how they might be influenced. The hoped-for result is a clearer picture of how marketing can use resources more effectively to build closer relationships with customers.

piracy. Other ads stress the advantages of avoiding fast foods, wearing our seat belts, or quitting smoking.

Relationship Marketing Although marketing often focuses on single transactions for products, services, or ideas, marketers also take a longer-term perspective. Thus, **relationship marketing** emphasizes building lasting relationships with customers and suppliers. Stronger relationships— including stronger economic and social ties—can result in greater long-term satisfaction, customer loyalty, and customer retention.[3] Starbucks's Card Rewards attracts return customers with free coffee refills and other extras.

The Marketing Environment

Marketing strategies are not determined unilaterally by any business—rather, they are strongly influenced by powerful outside forces. Every marketing program must recognize the factors in a company's external environment, which is everything outside an organization's boundaries that might affect it.

Political-Legal Environment Political activities, both global and domestic, have profound effects on marketing. For example, environmental legislation has determined the destinies of entire industries. The political push for alternative energy sources is creating new markets and products for emerging companies such as India's Suzlon Energy Limited (large wind turbines), wind-powered electric generators by Germany's Nordex AG, and wind farms and power plants by Spain's Gamesa Corporation. Marketing managers try to maintain favorable political and legal environments in several ways. To gain public support for products and activities, marketers use ad campaigns to raise public awareness of important issues. Companies contribute to political candidates and frequently support the activities of political action committees (PACs) maintained by their respective industries.

Sociocultural Environment Changing social values force companies to develop and promote new products for both individual consumers and industrial customers. Just a few years ago, organic foods were available only in specialty food stores like Whole Foods. Today, in response to a growing demand for healthy foods, Target's Archer Farms product line brings affordable organic food to a much larger audience. New industrial products, too, reflect changing social values: A growing number of wellness programs are available to companies for improving employees' health. Quest Diagnostics, for example, a B2B company, supplies a "Blueprint for Wellness" service that assesses employee health-care risks in client companies and recommends programs for reducing those risks. This and other trends reflect the values, beliefs, and ideas that shape society.

Technological Environment New technologies create new goods and services. New products make existing products obsolete, and many products change our values and lifestyles. In turn, lifestyle changes often stimulate new products not directly related to the new technologies themselves. Cell phones, for example, facilitate business

> **RELATIONSHIP MARKETING** marketing strategy that emphasizes lasting relationships with customers and suppliers

Marketing strategies are strongly influenced by powerful outside forces. For example, new technologies create new products, such as the Chinese cell phone "gas station" kiosk shown here. Called *shouji jiayouzhan* in Chinese, these kiosks enable customers to recharge their cell phones just as they would refuel their cars. The screens on the kiosks also provide marketers with a new way to display ads to waiting customers.

Managing in Turbulent Times

Feeling the Pressure for "Green"

Today's marketers are struggling with pressures from several outside forces: The political-legal, sociocultural, technological, and economic environments are all pushing for change. Industries ranging from autos to energy to housing are grappling with a common environmental theme: green. Public sentiment turned decidedly toward alternatives to gas-guzzling cars when consumers choked on $4-plus for a gallon of gasoline. Home buyers, too, want energy-efficient heating and cooling, such as geothermal heat, in their next home. Environmentalists are pushing for alternative energy sources, notably wind and solar power, to replace fossil fuels. Local utilities are offering incentives for construction using environmentally sensitive building designs to conserve utilities services. In Washington, the Obama administration and Congress are struggling to reverse severe economic conditions and meet commitments for a cleaner environment by pressuring financially troubled companies to reorient toward lower-cost energy-saving technologies.

These outside pressures present challenges to all areas of marketing, from identifying the new target markets, to designing new products for those markets and, in some cases, finding technologies to make those products. Success depends on coordinating the various marketing activities—making them compatible with one another. Marketers need to present a convincing rationale for a product's pricing and demonstrate how the product provides the benefits sought by the target markets. Distribution methods—delivering products and after-services to customers—have to match up with promises in the promotional message so that, together, the marketing activities provide a persuasive package that delivers the desired value and benefits. Further, this integrated marketing strategy must be coordinated with financial management and production operations to provide timely customer satisfaction.

The marketing blueprint for Toyota's Prius automobile utilized an integrated marketing mix for meeting the challenge of *going green*. While developing the fuel-efficient hybrid technology, Toyota identified niche target markets of users in some 40 countries and determined a price range compatible with the company's performance reliability and quality reputation. Promotion in the U.S. market started two years before the car was released so customers could view and purchase a Prius. One pre-launch promotion involved teaming up with the Sierra Club; in addition, lending the Prius to environmentally sensitive Hollywood superstars provided exposure and allowed car testing in the target market. The main ad campaign to general audiences emphasized that consumers can still have speed and comfort along with environmental friendliness. And pre-orders were delivered on time to buyers. As a result, the Prius is the most successful hybrid automobile in the United States and the rest of the world.[4]

communication just as prepackaged meals provide convenience for busy household cooks. Both products also free up time for recreation and leisure.

Economic Environment Because they determine spending patterns by consumers, businesses, and governments, economic conditions influence marketing plans for product offerings, pricing, and promotional strategies. Marketers are concerned with such economic variables as inflation, interest rates, and recession. Thus, they monitor the general business cycle to anticipate trends in consumer and business spending.

The interconnected global economy has become an increasingly important concern for marketers worldwide—for example, in 2008, rising oil prices broke records on an almost daily basis. Fed up with gas prices, U.S. drivers drove less, decreasing the demand and prices for gasoline. As the global economy continued to

sour, the Canadian government demanded its auto makers reduce production costs and auto prices to qualify for the government's bailout fund. Money-strapped U.S. consumers, meanwhile, shifted to used cars instead of buying new. This product shift by consumers affects all areas of marketing—target markets, pricing, promotion, and distribution—for used cars.[5]

Competitive Environment In a competitive environment, marketers must convince buyers that they should purchase one company's products rather than those of some other seller. Because both consumers and commercial buyers have limited resources, every dollar spent on one product is no longer available for other purchases. Each marketing program, therefore, seeks to make its product the most attractive. Expressed in business terms, a failed program loses the buyer's dollar forever (or at least until it is time for the next purchase decision).

Wenner Media Chair and CEO Jann Wenner (above) is hoping that his strategy for greater differentiation between his *Us Weekly* magazine and rival *People* will continue to pay off. *People* is news driven, reporting on ordinary people as well as celebrities, whereas *Us Weekly* features more coverage of celebrity sex and glitter.

To promote products effectively, marketers must first understand which of three types of competition they face:

- *Substitute products* may not look alike or they may seem very different from one another, but they can fulfill the same need. For example, your cholesterol level may be controlled with either of two competing products: a physical fitness program or a drug regimen. The fitness program and the drugs compete as substitute products.

- *Brand competition* occurs between similar products and is based on buyers' perceptions of the benefits of products offered by particular companies.

- *International competition* matches the products of domestic marketers against those of foreign competitors. The intensity of international competition has been heightened by the formation of alliances, such as the European Union and NAFTA. In 2009 the U.S. Air Force opened bidding to foreign manufacturers for three new planes to replace the existing Presidential Air Force One fleet (made by Boeing). If Europe's Airbus wins the contract it will be the first time a U.S. President has flown in a non-U.S. made Air Force One.[6]

Having identified the kind of competition, marketers can then develop a strategy for attracting more customers.

Strategy: The Marketing Mix

A company's **marketing managers** are responsible for planning and implementing all the activities that result in the transfer of goods or services to its customers. These activities culminate in the **marketing plan**—a detailed strategy for focusing marketing efforts on customers' needs and wants. Therefore, marketing strategy begins when a company identifies a customer need and develops a product to meet it.

In planning and implementing strategies, marketing managers develop the four basic components (often called the "Four Ps") of the **marketing mix**: product, pricing, place, and promotion.

Product Marketing begins with a **product**—a good, a service, or an idea designed to fill a customer's need or want. Conceiving and developing new products is a constant challenge for marketers, who must always consider the factor of change—changing technology, changing wants and needs of customers and changing economic conditions. Meeting these changing conditions often means changing existing products to keep pace with emerging markets and competitors.

PRODUCT DIFFERENTIATION creation of a product feature or product image that differs enough from existing products to attract customers

PRICING process of determining the best price at which to sell a product

DISTRIBUTION (PLACE) part of the marketing mix concerned with getting products from producers to consumers

PROMOTION aspect of the marketing mix concerned with the most effective techniques for communicating information about products

INTEGRATED MARKETING STRATEGY strategy that blends together the Four Ps of marketing to ensure their compatibility with one another and with the company's non-marketing activities as well

TARGET MARKET group of people that have similar wants and needs and can be expected to show interest in the same products

MARKET SEGMENTATION process of dividing a market into categories of customer types, or "segments"

Product Differentiation Producers often promote particular features of products in order to distinguish them in the marketplace. **Product differentiation** is the creation of a feature or image that makes a product differ enough from existing products to attract customers.

Pricing The **pricing** of a product—selecting the best price at which to sell it—is often a balancing act. On the one hand, prices must support a variety of costs—operating, administrative, research costs, and marketing costs. On the other hand, prices can't be so high that customers turn to competitors. Successful pricing means finding a profitable middle ground between these two requirements.

Place (Distribution) In the marketing mix, *place* refers to **distribution**. Placing a product in the proper outlet—for example, a retail store—requires decisions about several activities, all of which are concerned with getting the product from the producer to the consumer. Decisions about warehousing and inventory control are distribution decisions, as are decisions about transportation options.

Promotion The most visible component of the marketing mix is no doubt **promotion**, which refers to techniques for communicating information about products. The most important promotional tools include advertising, personal selling, sales promotions, publicity, and public relations.

Blending It All Together: Integrated Strategy An **integrated marketing strategy** ensures that the Four Ps blend together so that they are compatible with one another and with the company's non-marketing activities as well. Toyota's auto superiority, for example, stems from a coherent marketing mix that is tightly integrated with its production strategy. Offering a relatively small number of different models, Toyota targets auto customers that want high quality, excellent performance reliability, and moderate prices (a good value for the price). With a smaller number of different models than U.S. automakers, fewer components and parts are needed, purchasing costs are lower, and less factory space is required for inventory and assembly in Toyota's lean production system. Lean production's assembly simplicity yields higher quality, the factory's cost savings lead to lower product prices, and speedy production gives shorter delivery times in Toyota's distribution system. Taken together, this integrated strategy is completed when Toyota's advertising communicates its message of industry-high customer satisfaction.[7]

Target Marketing and Market Segmentation

Marketers have long known that products cannot be all things to all people. The emergence of the marketing concept and the recognition of customers' needs and wants led marketers to think in terms of **target markets**—groups of people or organizations with similar wants and needs and who can be expected to show interest in the same products. Selecting target markets is usually the first step in the marketing strategy.

Target marketing requires **market segmentation**—dividing a market into categories of customer types or "segments." Once they have identified segments, companies may adopt a variety of strategies. Some firms market products to more than one segment. General Motors, for example, once offered automobiles with various features and at various price levels.

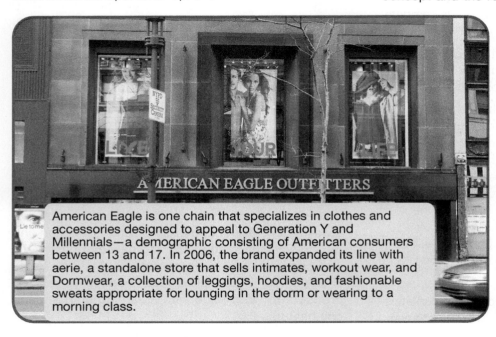

American Eagle is one chain that specializes in clothes and accessories designed to appeal to Generation Y and Millennials—a demographic consisting of American consumers between 13 and 17. In 2006, the brand expanded its line with aerie, a standalone store that sells intimates, workout wear, and Dormwear, a collection of leggings, hoodies, and fashionable sweats appropriate for lounging in the dorm or wearing to a morning class.

GM's past strategy was to provide an automobile for nearly every segment of the market. The financial crisis, however, is forcing GM's changeover to fewer target markets and associated brands by closing Saturn, phasing out Pontiac, and selling or shutting down Hummer and Saab.

In contrast, some businesses offer a narrower range of products, such as Ferrari's high-priced sports cars, aiming at just one segment. Note that segmentation is a strategy for analyzing consumers, not products. Once a target segment is identified, the marketing of products for that segment begins. The process of fixing, adapting, and communicating the nature of the product itself is called **product positioning**.

Identifying Market Segments

By definition, members of a market segment must share some common traits that affect their purchasing decisions. In identifying consumer segments, researchers look at several different influences on consumer behavior. Here are three of the most important variables:

Geographic Segmentation   Many buying decisions are affected by the places people call home. Urban residents don't need agricultural equipment, and sailboats sell better along the coasts than on the Great Plains. **Geographic variables** are the geographic units, from countries to neighborhoods, that may be considered in a segmentation strategy.

Demographic Segmentation   **Demographic variables** describe populations by identifying traits, such as age, income, gender, ethnic background, marital status, race, religion, and social class, as detailed in Table 11.1. Depending on the marketer's purpose, a demographic segment can be a single classification (ages 20–34) or a combination of categories (ages 20–34, married without children, earning $25,000– $44,999 a year).

Psychographic Variables   Markets can also be segmented according to such **psychographic variables** as lifestyles, interests, and attitudes. Psychographics are particularly important to marketers because, unlike demographics and geographics, they can be changed by marketing efforts. For example, Polish companies have overcome consumer resistance by promoting the safety and desirability of using credit cards rather than depending solely on cash.[8]

Understanding Consumer Behavior

Although marketing managers can tell us what features people want in a new refrigerator, they cannot tell us why they buy particular refrigerators. What desire are

PRODUCT POSITIONING process of fixing, adapting, and communicating the nature of a product

GEOGRAPHIC VARIABLES geographic units that may be considered in developing a segmentation strategy

DEMOGRAPHIC VARIABLES characteristics of populations that may be considered in developing a segmentation strategy

PSYCHOGRAPHIC VARIABLES consumer characteristics, such as lifestyles, opinions, interests, and attitudes that may be considered in developing a segmentation strategy

"I'd get out of children and into older people."

Table 11.1   **Demographic Variables**

Age	Under 5, 5–11, 12–19, 20–34, 35–49, 50–64, 65+
Education	Grade school or less, some high school, graduated high school, some college, college degree, advanced degree
Family Life Cycle	Young single, young married without children, young married with children, older married with children under 18, older married without children under 18, older single, other
Family Size	1, 2–3, 4–5, 6+
Income	Under $9,000, $9,000–$14,999, $15,000–$24,999, $25,000–$34,999, $35,000–$45,000, over $45,000
Nationality	African, American, Asian, British, Eastern European, French, German, Irish, Italian, Latin American, Middle Eastern, Scandinavian
Race	Native American, Asian, African American, Caucasian
Religion	Buddhist, Catholic, Hindu, Jewish, Muslim, Protestant
Sex	Male, female

CONSUMER BEHAVIOR study of the decision process by which people buy and consume products

BRAND LOYALTY pattern of regular consumer purchasing based on satisfaction with a product's performance

consumers fulfilling? Is there a psychological or sociological explanation for why they purchase one product and not another? These questions and many others are addressed in the study of **consumer behavior**—the study of the decision process by which people buy and consume products.

Influences on Consumer Behavior

To understand consumer behavior, marketers draw heavily on such fields as psychology and sociology. By identifying which influences are most active in certain circumstances, marketers try to explain consumer choices and predict future buying behavior.

1 Psychological influences include an individual's motivations, perceptions, ability to learn, and attitudes.

2 Personal influences include lifestyle, personality, and economic status.

3 Social influences include family, opinion leaders (people whose opinions are sought by others), and such reference groups as friends, co-workers, and professional associates.

4 Cultural influences include culture (the way of living that distinguishes one large group from another), subculture (smaller groups with shared values), and social class (the cultural ranking of groups according to such criteria as background, occupation, and income).

Although these factors can have a strong impact on a consumer's choices, their effect on actual purchases is sometimes weak or negligible. Some consumers, for example, exhibit high **brand loyalty**—they regularly purchase products because they are satisfied with their performance. Such people are less subject to influence and stick with preferred brands.[9] On the other hand, the clothes you wear and the food you eat often reflect social and psychological influences on your consumer behavior.

The Consumer Buying Process

Students of consumer behavior have constructed various models to help show how consumers decide to buy products. Figure 11.1 presents one such model. At the core of this and similar models is an awareness of the many influences that lead to consumption. Ultimately, marketers use this information to develop marketing plans.

Problem/Need Recognition This process begins when the consumer recognizes a problem or need. Need recognition also occurs when you have a chance to change your buying habits. When you obtain your first job after graduation, your new income may let you buy things that were once too expensive for you. You may find that you need professional clothing, apartment furnishings, and a car. American Express and Citi cater to such shifts in needs when they market credit cards to college students.

Information Seeking Having recognized a need, consumers often seek information. The search is not always extensive, but before making major purchases, most people seek information from personal sources, public sources, and experience.

Evaluation of Alternatives By analyzing product attributes (price, prestige, quality), consumers compare products before deciding which one best meets their needs.

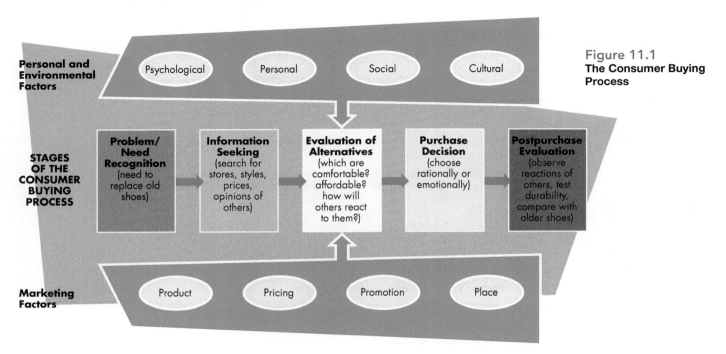

Figure 11.1
The Consumer Buying Process

Purchase Decision Ultimately, consumers make purchase decisions. "Buy" decisions are based on rational motives, emotional motives, or both. **Rational motives** involve the logical evaluation of product attributes: cost, quality, and usefulness. **Emotional motives** involve nonobjective factors and include sociability, imitation of others, and aesthetics.

Postpurchase Evaluation Marketing does not stop with the sale of a product. What happens after the sale is important. Marketers want consumers to be happy after buying products so that they are more likely to buy them again. Because consumers do not want to go through a complex decision process for every purchase, they often repurchase products they have used and liked. Not all consumers are satisfied with their purchases. These buyers are not likely to purchase the same product(s) again and are much more apt to broadcast their experiences than are satisfied customers.

Organizational Marketing and Buying Behavior

In the consumer market, buying and selling transactions are visible to the public. Equally important, though far less visible, are organizational (or commercial) markets. Marketing to organizations that buy goods and services used in creating and delivering consumer products involves various kinds of markets and buying behaviors different from those in consumer markets.

Business Marketing

Business marketing involves organizational or commercial markets that fall into three B2B (business-to-business) categories: industrial, reseller, and government/institutional markets. Taken together, the B2B markets do over $25 trillion in business annually—more than two times the amount done in the U.S. consumer market.[10]

Industrial Market The **industrial market** includes businesses that buy goods to be converted into other products or that are used up during production. It includes farmers, manufacturers, and some retailers.

Reseller Market Before products reach consumers, they pass through a **reseller market** consisting of intermediaries, including wholesalers and retailers, that buy and resell finished goods.

Government and Institutional Market In addition to federal and state governments, there are some 87,000 local governments in the United States. State and local governments annually spend nearly $7 trillion for durable goods, nondurables, services, and construction.[11]

The **institutional market** consists of nongovernmental organizations, such as hospitals, churches, museums, and charities, that also use supplies and equipment as well as legal, accounting, and transportation services.

B2B Buying Behavior

In some respects, organizational buying behavior bears little resemblance to consumer buying practices. Differences include the buyers' purchasing skills and an emphasis on buyer-seller relationships.

Differences in Buyers Unlike most consumers, organizational buyers are professional, specialized, and well informed.

- As professionals, B2B buyers are trained in methods for negotiating purchase terms. Once buyer-seller agreements have been reached, they also arrange formal contracts.

- As a rule, industrial buyers are company specialists in a line of items. As one of several buyers for a large bakery, for example, you may specialize in food ingredients. Another buyer may specialize in baking equipment (industrial ovens and mixers), whereas a third may buy office equipment and supplies.

- Industrial buyers are often experts about the products they buy. On a regular basis, organizational buyers study competing products and alternative suppliers by attending trade shows, reading trade magazines, and conducting technical discussions with sellers' representatives.

Differences in the Buyer-Seller Relationship Consumer-seller relationships are often impersonal, short-lived, one-time interactions. In contrast, B2B situations often involve frequent and enduring buyer-seller relationships. The development of a long-term relationship provides each party with access to the technical strengths of the other as well as the security of knowing what future business to expect. Thus, a buyer and a supplier may form a design team to create products to benefit both parties. Accordingly, industrial sellers emphasize personal selling by trained representatives who understand the needs of each customer.

RATIONAL MOTIVES reasons for purchasing a product that are based on a logical evaluation of product attributes

EMOTIONAL MOTIVES reasons for purchasing a product that are based on nonobjective factors

INDUSTRIAL MARKET organizational market consisting of firms that buy goods that are either converted into products or used during production

RESELLER MARKET organizational market consisting of intermediaries that buy and resell finished goods

INSTITUTIONAL MARKET organizational market consisting of such nongovernmental buyers of goods and services as hospitals, churches, museums, and charitable organizations

Table 11.2 **Categories of Consumer Products**

CATEGORY	DESCRIPTION	EXAMPLES
Convenience goods and services	• Consumed rapidly and regularly • Inexpensive • Purchased often and with little input of time and effort	• Milk • Newspaper • Fast food
Shopping goods and services	• Purchased less often • More expensive • Consumers may shop around and compare products based on style, performance, color, price, and other criteria.	• Television set • Tires • Car insurance
Specialty goods and services	• Purchased infrequently • Expensive • Consumer decides on a precise product and will not accept substitutions and spends a good deal of time choosing the "perfect" item.	• Jewelry • Wedding gown • Catering

PRODUCT FEATURES tangible and intangible qualities that a company builds into its products

VALUE PACKAGE product marketed as a bundle of value-adding attributes, including reasonable cost

CONVENIENCE GOOD/CONVENIENCE SERVICE inexpensive good or service purchased and consumed rapidly and regularly

SHOPPING GOOD/SHOPPING SERVICE moderately expensive, infrequently purchased good or service

SPECIALTY GOOD/SPECIALTY SERVICE expensive, rarely purchased good or service

EXPENSE ITEM industrial product purchased and consumed rapidly and regularly for daily operations

CAPITAL ITEM expensive, long-lasting, infrequently purchased industrial good, such as a building, or industrial service, such as building maintenance

PRODUCT MIX group of products that a firm makes available for sale

PRODUCT LINE group of products that are closely related because they function in a similar manner or are sold to the same customer group who will use them in similar ways

What Is a Product?

In developing the marketing mix for any product, whether goods or services, marketers must consider what customers really want when they purchase products. Only then can these marketers plan strategies effectively.

The Value Package

Whether it is a physical good, a service, or some combination of the two, customers get value from the various benefits, features, and even intangible rewards associated with a product. **Product features** are the qualities, tangible and intangible, that a company builds into its products. However, as we discussed earlier, to attract buyers, features must also provide benefits, or intangible rewards.

Today's customer regards a product as a bundle of attributes—benefits and features—that, taken together, marketers call the **value package**. Increasingly, buyers expect to receive products with greater value—with more benefits and features at reasonable costs—so firms must compete on the basis of enhanced value packages. They find that the addition of a new service often pleases customers far beyond the cost of providing it. Just making the purchase transaction faster and more convenient, for example, adds value by sparing customers long waits and cumbersome paperwork.

Classifying Goods and Services

We can classify products according to expected buyers, who fall into two groups: buyers of consumer products and buyers of organizational products. Marketing products to consumers is vastly different from marketing products to companies and other organizations.

Classifying Consumer Products Consumer products are commonly divided into three categories that reflect buyer behavior: **convenience goods and services**, **shopping goods and services**, and **specialty goods and services**. These are outlined in Table 11.2.

Classifying Organizational Products Depending on how much they cost and how they will be used, organizational products can be divided into two categories: **expense items** and **capital items**. These are explained in Table 11.3.

The Product Mix

The group of products that a company makes available for sale, whether consumer, industrial, or both, is its **product mix**. Black & Decker, for example, makes toasters, vacuum cleaners, electric drills, and a variety of other appliances and tools.

Product Lines Many companies begin with a single product. Over time, they find that the initial product fails to suit every customer shopping for the product type. To meet market demand, they introduce similar products designed to reach more customers. A group of products that are closely related because they function in a similar manner or are sold to the same customer group who will use them in similar ways is a **product line**.

Companies may extend their horizons and identify opportunities outside existing product lines. The

Table 11.3 Organizational Products

CATEGORY	DESCRIPTION	EXAMPLES
Expense items	• Goods or services that are consumed within a year by firms producing other goods or supplying other services • Goods used directly in the production process	• Loads of tea processed into tea bags • Oil and electricity for machines
Capital items	• Permanent (expensive and long-lasting) goods and services • Life expectancy of more than a year • Purchased infrequently so transactions often involve decisions by high-level managers	• Buildings (offices, factories) • Fixed equipment (water towers, baking ovens) • Accessory equipment (computers, airplanes) • Building maintenance • Legal services

SPEED TO MARKET strategy of introducing new products to respond quickly to customer or market changes

result—multiple (or diversified) product lines—is evident at Starbucks. Beyond just serving beverages to customers at coffee bars, Starbucks has lines of home-brewing equipment, supermarket products, music products, and industry services. Multiple product lines allow a company to grow rapidly and can help offset the consequences of slow sales in any one product line.

Developing New Products

To expand or diversify product lines—in fact, just to survive—firms must develop and introduce streams of new products. Faced with competition and shifting customer preferences, no firm can count on a single successful product to carry it forever. Even products that have many firms have research and development (R&D) departments for exploring new product possibilities. Why do they devote so many resources to exploring product possibilities, rejecting many seemingly good ideas along the way?

Product Mortality Rates

It is estimated that it takes 50 new product ideas to generate one product that finally reaches the market. Even then, only a few of these survivors become successful products. Many seemingly great ideas have failed as products. Creating a successful new product has become increasingly difficult—even for the most experienced marketers. Why? The number of new products hitting the market each year has increased dramatically; more than 180,000 new household, grocery, and drugstore items are introduced annually. In 2008 the U.S. consumer packaged goods industry alone launched 20,000 new products (snacks, school supplies, paper products).[12] At any given time, however, the average supermarket carries a total of only 20,000 to 40,000 different items. Because of lack of

space and customer demand, about 9 out of 10 new products will fail. Those with the best chances are innovative and deliver unique benefits.

Speed to Market The more rapidly a product moves from the laboratory to the marketplace, the more likely it is to survive. By introducing new products ahead of competitors, companies establish market leadership. They become entrenched in the market before being challenged by newer competitors. How important is **speed to market**—that is, a firm's success in responding to customer demand or market changes? One study reports that a product that is only three months late to market (three months behind the leader) loses 12 percent of its lifetime profit potential. At six months, it will lose 33 percent.

At Equity Marketing, engineers like Mark Barbato and Frank Kautzman used to design toys by sculpting models out of clay. Now they use "rapid prototyping," a technology that allows several employees to work simultaneously on 3D "models" that can then be e-mailed to clients for instant review. It now takes five days instead of three weeks to make an initial sculpture.

Product Life Cycle

When a product reaches the market, it enters the **product life cycle (PLC)**: a series of stages through which it passes during its commercial life. Depending on the product's ability to attract and keep customers, its PLC may be a matter of months, years, or decades.

Stages in the PLC The life cycle for both goods and services is a natural process in which products are born, grow in stature, mature, and finally decline and die. Look at the two graphics in Figure 11.2. In Figure 11.2(a), the four phases of the PLC are applied to several products with which you are familiar:

1 *Introduction.* This stage begins when the product reaches the marketplace. Marketers focus on making potential customers aware of the product and its benefits. Extensive promotional and development costs erase all profits.

2 *Growth.* If the new product attracts enough customers, sales start to climb rapidly. Marketers lower price slightly and continue promotional expenditures to increase sales. The product starts to show a profit, and other firms move rapidly to introduce their own versions.

3 *Maturity.* Sales growth starts to slow. Although the product earns its highest profit level early in this stage, increased competition eventually forces price-cutting, increasing advertising and promotional expenditures, and lower profits. Toward the end of the stage, sales start to fall.

4 *Decline.* Sales and profits continue to fall, as new products in the introduction stage take away sales. Firms end or reduce promotional support (ads and salespeople), but may let the product linger to provide some profits.

Figure 11.2(b) plots the relationship of the PLC to a product's typical sales, costs, and profits or losses. Although the early stages of the PLC often show financial losses, increased sales for successful products recover earlier losses and continue to generate profits until the decline stage. For most products, profitable life spans are short—thus, the importance placed by so many firms on the constant replenishment of product lines.

Identifying Products

Marketers must also identify products so that consumers recognize them. Two important tools for this task are branding and packaging.

Figure 11.2
Products in the Life Cycle: Stage, Sales, Cost, and Profit[13]

Branding Products

Branding is a process of using names and symbols, like Coca-Cola or McDonald's golden arches, to communicate the qualities of a particular product made by a particular producer. Brands are designed to signal uniform quality; customers who try and like a product can return to it by remembering its name or its logo.

Several benefits result from successful branding, including brand loyalty and **brand awareness**— the brand name that first comes to mind when you consider a particular product category. What company, for example, comes to mind when you need to ship a document a long way on short notice? For many people, FedEx has the necessary brand awareness.

Gaining Brand Awareness The expensive, sometimes fierce struggle for brand recognition is perhaps nowhere more evident than in branding battles among dot-com firms. Collectively, the top Internet brands—Google, Yahoo!, eBay, and Amazon.com—spend billions a year, even though only Google (ranked twentieth) and eBay (forty-sixth) have cracked the ranks of the top 50 global brands.[14] Moreover, the mounting costs of establishing a brand identity mean that many more would-be e-businesses do and will probably fail.

With its growing importance in nearly every industry, marketers are finding more effective, less expensive ways to gain brand awareness. Recent successes have been found with several methods, including product placements, buzz marketing, viral marketing, and social networking.

Product Placements Television commercials can be a real turnoff for many viewers, but entertainment programming gets our full attention. And that's when marketers are turning up the promotional juice with **product placement**—a promotional tactic for brand exposure in which characters in television, film, music, magazines, or video games use a real product with a brand visible to viewers.

Product placements are effective because the message is delivered in an attractive setting that holds the customer's interest. When used in successful films and TV shows, the brand's association with famous performers is an implied celebrity endorsement. The idea is to legitimize the brand in the mind of the customer. In all, nearly $5 billion is spent annually on product placements, especially in television, and major marketers are putting more into product placements instead of television advertisements. A Minute Maid beverage and Clorox make appearances in the hit movie *Madea Goes to Jail*. In print placements, Hewlett-Packard computers appear in the photo layouts in the IKEA catalog. Television placements are widespread, especially as digital video recorders (DVRs) gain popularity. Viewers can use their DVRs to skip commercials in recorded shows, but product placements are unavoidable.

Buzz Marketing One method for increasing brand awareness is **buzz marketing** which relies on word-of-mouth to spread "buzz" about a particular product or idea. Buzz marketing agencies provide volunteer participants with new products to try and ask them to share the buzz with their friends, family, co-workers, and others in their social network. Here's the key—most companies running word-of-mouth campaigns require full disclosure, which means the participants should let people know they are participating in a campaign. This is essential so that those on the receiving end of the "buzz" don't feel tricked or taken advantage of.

Viral Marketing and Social Networking **Viral marketing** is a form of buzz marketing that relies on social networking on the Internet to spread information like a "virus" from person to person. Messages about new cars, sports events, and numerous other goods and services flow via networks among potential customers who pass the information on to others. Using various

BRANDING process of using symbols to communicate the qualities of a product made by a particular producer

BRAND AWARENESS extent to which a brand name comes to mind when a consumer considers a particular product category

PRODUCT PLACEMENT a promotional tactic for brand exposure in which characters in television, film, music, magazines, or video games use a real product with its brand visible to viewers

BUZZ MARKETING promotional method that relies on word of mouth to create buzz about products and ideas

VIRAL MARKETING type of buzz marketing that relies on the Internet to spread information like a "virus" from person to person about products and ideas

How many of these brand logos are you able to recognize?

social network formats—games, contests, chat rooms, blogs, and bulletin boards—marketers encourage potential customers to try out products and tell other people about them. Marketers—including such giants as Bank of America, McDonald's, eBay, and Cisco—are using **corporate blogs** increasingly for public relations, branding, and otherwise spreading messages that stimulate chat about products to target markets.[15]

How effective can it be? Viral marketing can lead to consumer awareness faster and with wider reach than traditional media messages—and at a lower cost. It works for two reasons. First, people rely on the Internet for information that they used to get from newspapers, magazines, and television. Equally important, however, is the interactive element: The customer becomes a participant in the process of spreading the word by forwarding information to other Internet users. Success of the movie *The Dark Knight* is credited to Warner Bros.' use of pre-release viral tactics for stimulating public awareness of the blockbuster movie.

Types of Brand Names   Just about every product has a brand name. Generally, different types of brand names—national, licensed, or private—increase buyers' awareness of the nature and quality of competing products. When customers are satisfied with a product, marketers try to build brand loyalty among the largest possible segment of repeat buyers.

National Brands   **National brands** are produced by, widely distributed by, and carry the name of the manufacturer. These brands are often widely recognized by customers because of national advertising campaigns, and they are, therefore, valuable assets. Because the costs of developing a national brand are high, some companies use a national brand on several related products. Procter & Gamble now markets Ivory Shampoo, capitalizing on the name of its bar soap and dishwashing liquid.

Licensed Brands   We have become used to companies (and even personalities) selling the rights to put their names on products. These are called **licensed brands**. For example, the popularity of auto racing is generating millions in revenues for the NASCAR brand, which licenses its name on car accessories, ladies and men's apparel, headsets, and countless other items with the names of popular drivers. Marketers exploit brands because of their public appeal—the image and status that customers hope to gain by associating with them.

Private Brands   When a wholesaler or retailer develops a brand name and has a manufacturer put it on a product, the resulting name is a **private brand** (or **private label**). Sears, which carries such lines as Craftsman tools, Canyon River Blues denim clothing, and Kenmore appliances, is a well-known seller of private brands.

Packaging Products

With a few exceptions, products need some form of **packaging** to reduce the risk of damage, breakage, or spoilage, and to increase the difficulty of stealing small products. A package also serves as an in-store advertisement that makes the product attractive, displays the brand name, and identifies features and benefits. Also, packaging features, such as no-drip bottles of Clorox bleach, add utility for consumers.

The International Marketing Mix

Marketing internationally means mounting a strategy to support global business operations. Foreign customers, for example, differ from domestic buyers in language, customs, business practices, and consumer behavior. If they go global, marketers must reconsider each element of the marketing mix—product, pricing, place, and promotion.

International Products

Some products can be sold abroad with virtually no changes. Budweiser, Coca-Cola, and Marlboros are the same in Peoria, Illinois, and Paris, France. In other cases, U.S. firms have had to create products with built-in flexibility—for example, an electric shaver that is adaptable to either 115- or 230-volt outlets, so travelers can use it in both U.S. and European electrical outlets. Frequently, however, domestic products require a major redesign for buyers in foreign

Before creating an international advertisement like this Chinese ad for Coca-Cola, it is crucial to research what disparities, such as meaning of words, traditions, and taboos, exist between different societies. For example, German manufacturers of backpacks label them as "body bags," not terribly enticing to the U.S. consumer. Can you guess why Gerber baby food is not sold in France? The French translation of Gerber is "to vomit"! Effective marketing does not just involve knowledge of culture abroad, but also requires a general sensitivity to social trends and language.

U.S. promotional tactics do not succeed in other countries. Many Europeans believe that a product must be inherently shoddy if a company resorts to any advertising, particularly the American hard-sell variety.

International marketers are ever more aware of cultural differences that can cause negative reactions to improperly advertised products. Some Europeans, for example, are offended by TV commercials that show weapons or violence. Meanwhile, cigarette commercials that are banned from U.S. television thrive in many Asian and European markets. Product promotions must be carefully matched to local customs and cultural values.

Because of the need to adjust the marketing mix, success in international markets is hard won. But whether a firm markets in domestic or international markets, the basic principles of marketing still apply; only their implementation changes.

markets. To sell computers in Japan, for example, Apple had to develop a Japanese-language operating system.

International Pricing

When pricing for international markets, marketers must consider the higher costs of transporting and selling products abroad. For example, because of the higher costs of buildings, rent, equipment, and imported meat, a McDonald's Big Mac costs more in Switzerland than in the United States.

International Distribution

In some industries, delays in starting new international distribution networks can be costly. Therefore, companies with existing distribution systems often enjoy an advantage. Many companies have avoided time delays by buying existing businesses with already-established distribution and marketing networks.

International Promotion

Occasionally, a good ad campaign is a good campaign just about anywhere. Quite often, however,

Small Business and the Marketing Mix

Many of today's largest firms were yesterday's small businesses. Behind the success of many small firms lie a skillful application of the marketing concept and an understanding of each element in the marketing mix.

Small-Business Products Some new products and firms are doomed at the start because few customers want or need what they have to offer. Many fail to estimate realistic market potential, and some offer new products before they have clear pictures of their target segments. In contrast, a thorough understanding of what customers want has paid off for many small firms. Take, for example, the case of Little Earth Productions, a company that makes fashion accessories, such as handbags. Originally, the company merely considered how consumers would use its handbags. But after examining shopping habits, Little Earth Productions redesigned for better in-store display. Because stores

Social Networking for Job Opportunities in Tough Times

If you're out of work, looking for a job, and wondering where to turn, help is as close as your PC. While troubled times have dampened demand for many products, others are getting a boost. Service products such as social networking sites are an example. While popular entertainment sites—including Facebook and MySpace—began as cyber highways for recreational and friendship interactions, social networking is no longer just for entertainment. In today's economy, there's a different kind of traffic—professional networking for career transition—joining the list of new cyber networking products for job-hunting assistance.

LinkedIn, started by five co-founders in the living room of Reid Hoffman in 2002, is an example of an interconnected network that now serves professionals in 200 countries and some 170 industries. Officially founded in 2003, this Mountain View, California, start-up had 4,500 members in the network after just one month. Today, profiles from more than 36 million members include executives from all *Fortune 500* companies. Users can post résumés, search companies, and find job openings. However, the key attraction of the network is personal connections: One member knows other LinkedIn users, who link with still others, and so on as information flows to those looking for good candidates until they find a word-of-mouth prospect that looks good. The system is based on trusted relationships and connections, and it works: LinkedIn is the world's largest business network, and it connects a huge pool of talent that keeps on growing.

Help is available to get new members started in LinkedIn, familiarizing them with tools that help build a network from frequent contacts, manage LinkedIn contacts, stay connected to a network, and search. Lisa Hendrickson, manager of LinkedIn Minnesota, for example, started *Project: Link It Forward* to give free monthly LinkedIn workshops to job-hunting professionals. She emphasizes that the system is effective because it gets the job-seeker's profile to the person who does the

hiring. Hendrickson adds, "Five years ago we did not have tools like LinkedIn to help find work. That's why LinkedIn is so prevalent now. It works."[16]

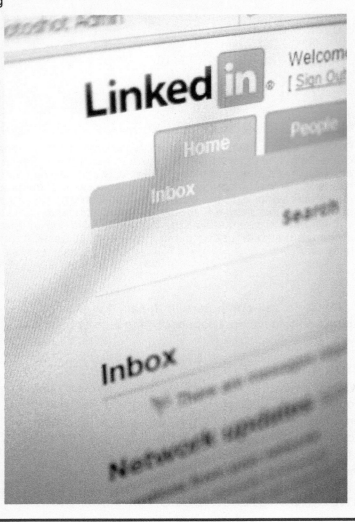

can give handbags better visibility by hanging them instead of placing them on floors or low countertops, Little Earth Productions added small handles specifically for that purpose.

Small-Business Pricing   Haphazard pricing can sink a firm with a good product. Small-business pricing errors usually result from a failure to estimate operating expenses accurately. But when small businesses set

prices by carefully assessing costs, many earn satisfactory profits.

Small-Business Distribution   The ability of many small businesses to attract and retain customers depends partly on the choice of location, especially for new service businesses.

In distribution as in other aspects of the marketing mix, however, smaller companies may have advantages over larger competitors. A smaller company may be able to address customer's needs more quickly and efficiently with an added personal touch. Everex Systems of Fremont, California, sells personal computers to wholesalers and dealers through a system that the company calls *zero response time*. Because Everex Systems is small and flexible, phone orders can be reviewed every two hours and factory assembly adjusted to match demand.

Small-Business Promotion Successful small businesses plan for promotional expenses as part of start-up costs. Some hold down costs by using less expensive promotional methods, like publicity in local newspapers. Other small businesses identify themselves and their products with associated groups, organizations, and events. Thus, a crafts gallery might join with a local art league to organize public showings of their combined products.

Questions for Review

1. What are the key similarities and differences between consumer buying behavior and B2B buying behavior?

2. Why and how is market segmentation used in target marketing?

3. What are the various classifications of consumer and industrial products? Give an example of a good and a service for each category other than those discussed in the text.

Questions for Analysis

4. Select an everyday product (personal fitness training, CDs, dog food, cell phones, or shoes, for example). Show how different versions of your product are aimed toward different market segments. Explain how the marketing mix differs for each segment.

5. Select a second everyday product and describe the consumer buying process that typically goes into its purchase.

6. Consider a service product, such as transportation, entertainment, or health care. What are some ways that more customer value might be added to this product? Why would your improvements add value for the buyer?

7. How would you expect the branding and packaging of convenience, shopping, and specialty goods to differ? Why? Give examples to illustrate your answers.

Application Exercises

8. Interview the marketing manager of a local business. Identify the degree to which this person's job is focused on each element in the marketing mix.

9. Select a product made by a foreign company and sold in the United States. What is the product's target market? What is the basis on which the target market is segmented? Do you think that this basis is appropriate? How might another approach, if any, be beneficial? Why?

10. Choose a product that could benefit from word-of-mouth buzz marketing. Then create a marketing campaign kit for participants to spread the word about this product.

12 chapter

Pricing, Distributing, and Promoting Products

After reading this chapter, you should be able to:

1 Identify the various pricing objectives that govern pricing decisions, and describe the price-setting tools used in making these decisions.

2 Discuss pricing strategies that can be used for different competitive situations and identify the pricing tactics that can be used for setting prices.

3 Explain the meaning of *distribution mix*, identify the different channels of distribution, and describe the major activities in the physical distribution process.

4 Describe the role of wholesalers and explain the different types of retailing.

5 Describe how online shopping agents and online retailers add value for advertisers and consumers on the Internet.

6 Identify the important objectives of promotion, discuss the considerations in selecting a promotional mix, and discuss advertising promotions.

7 Outline the tasks involved in personal selling, describe the various types of sales promotions, and distinguish between publicity and public relations.

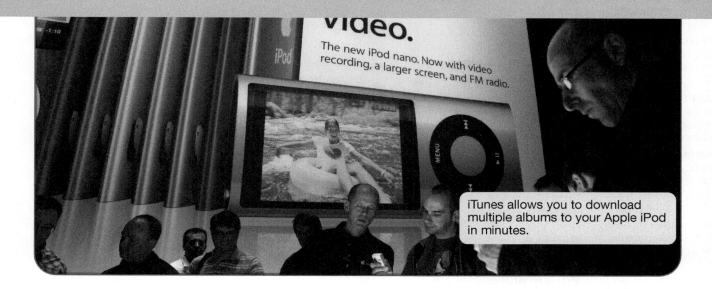

iTunes allows you to download multiple albums to your Apple iPod in minutes.

iTunes Is It

In 2008, iTunes became the number-one music retailer in the United States, with a 19 percent market share. As of early 2009, iTunes had sold over 6 billion songs to more than 75 million customers and held 70 percent of the market share for global digital downloads.

Apple has perfected the art of creating a buzz by coupling iTunes's massive music library with stylish, must-have gadgets like the iPod and iPhone. TV ads feature products showing off their groundbreaking functionality to the soundtrack of songs so infectious you can hardly resist shelling out $.69 (for most songs), $.99, or $1.25 (top hits) each for them at the iTunes music store. That three-tier pricing policy is part of Apple CEO Steve Jobs's plan to keep a customer base of loyal purchasers from resorting to piracy. He has criticized the "greedy" music industry for its push to raise digital download prices. But don't assume that Jobs is all generosity—his contentment with a relatively meager profit from the iTunes music store is more than made up for by the more than $6 billion Apple raked in last quarter from sales of its own iTunes-compatible MP3 players.[1]

iTunes has also capitalized on the fastest method of product delivery—high-speed Internet—and the tech savvy of its target teen market. The result has been that fewer than 48 percent of U.S. teens didn't purchase a single CD in 2008 and brick-and-mortar retailers like Wal-Mart have reduced the amount of physical store space devoted to CDs.[2] As gadgets and software become increasingly affordable and user-friendly, teens aren't the only demographic flooding the market. Baby Boomers can tap into iTunes's increasing supply of classic music titles to replace their worn-out vinyl. Even older generations can download books and informational podcasts through iTunes and its latest venture iTunes U, which offers downloadable lectures and other educational programs.

What's in It for Me?

To become the number-one retailer in any market takes a solid understanding of how best to set prices to achieve profit and market share objectives, and how to promote and distribute products to customers. This chapter also describes different types of wholesalers, retailers, and intermediaries, as well as how the online marketplace has changed the nature of how companies do business. By understanding this chapter's methods for pricing, distributing, and promoting products, you'll have a clearer picture of how to sort out and identify the different kinds of people that are targeted by various companies, products, and advertising campaigns. You'll also be prepared to evaluate a company's marketing programs, distribution methods, and competitive potential.

Sidebar Definitions

PRICING process of determining what a company will receive in exchange for its products

PRICING OBJECTIVES the goals that sellers hope to achieve in pricing products for sale

MARKET SHARE company's percentage of the total industry sales for a specific product type

COST-ORIENTED PRICING pricing that considers the firm's desire to make a profit and its need to cover production costs

MARKUP amount added to an item's purchase cost to sell it at a profit

Determining Prices

After deciding what *products* a company will offer to customers, the second major component of the marketing mix is **pricing**—determining what the customer pays and the seller receives in exchange for a product. Setting prices involves understanding how they contribute to achieving the firm's sales objectives.

Pricing to Meet Business Objectives

Pricing objectives are the goals that sellers hope to achieve in pricing products for sale. Some companies have *profit-maximizing pricing objectives*, while others have *market share pricing objectives*. Pricing decisions are also influenced by the need to compete in the marketplace, by social and ethical concerns, and even by corporate image. Most recently we've seen how prices of financial products—loans and other borrowing—are determined by the government's persuasion and its control of interest rates in times of crisis.

Profit-Maximizing Objectives The seller's pricing decision is critical for determining the firm's revenue, which is the selling price times the number of units sold.

$$\text{Revenue} = \text{Selling price} \times \text{Units sold}$$

Companies that set prices to maximize profits want to set the selling price to sell the number of units that will generate the highest possible total profits. If a company sets prices too low, it will probably sell many units but may miss out on additional profits on each unit (and may even lose money on each exchange). If a company sets prices too high, it will make a large profit on each item but will sell fewer units. Again, the firm loses money, and it may also be left with excess inventory.

In calculating profits, managers weigh sales revenues against costs for materials and labor, as well as capital resources (plant and equipment) and marketing costs

(such as maintaining a large sales staff). To use these resources efficiently, many firms set prices to cover costs and achieve a targeted level of return for owners.

Market Share (Market Penetration) Objectives In the long run, a business must make a profit to survive. Because they are willing to accept minimal profits, even losses, to get buyers to try products, companies may initially set low prices for new products to establish **market share** (or **market penetration**)—a company's percentage of the total industry sales for a specific product type.

Price-Setting Tools

Before deciding on final prices, managers can use *cost-oriented pricing* and *breakeven analysis* to measure potential impact.

Cost-Oriented Pricing **Cost-oriented pricing** considers a firm's desire to make a profit and its need to cover production costs.

$$\text{Selling price} = \text{Seller's costs} + \text{Profit}$$

A video store manager would price DVDs by calculating the cost of making them available to shoppers. Thus, price would include the costs of store rent, employee wages, utilities, product displays, insurance, and the DVD manufacturer's price.

If the manufacturer's price is $8 per DVD and the store sells DVDs for $8, the store won't make any profit. Nor will it make a profit if it sells DVDs for $8.50 each—or even $10 or $11. To be profitable, the company must charge enough to cover product and other costs. Together, these factors determine the **markup**—the amount added to an item's purchase cost to sell it at a profit. In this case, a reasonable markup of $7 over the purchase cost means a $15 selling price. The following equation calculates the markup percentage and determines what percent of every dollar of revenue is gross profit:

$$\text{Markup percentage} = \frac{\text{Markup}}{\text{Sales price}} \times 100\%$$

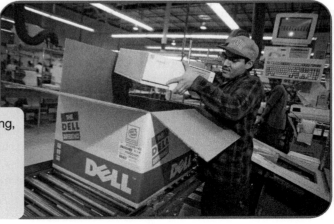

Using low-cost, direct-to-consumer selling and market share pricing, Dell profitably dominated the personal computer market, while its competitors—Apple, IBM, Compaq, and Hewlett-Packard—sold through retailers, adding extra costs that prevented them from matching Dell's low prices. Competitors have switched to direct-to-consumer sales, but Dell is strongly anchored as the industry's number-two PC maker (after Hewlett-Packard).[3]

Figure 12.1
Breakeven Analysis

400,000

350,000

300,000

Total revenue
(units sold x $15)   Profits

Dollars

250,000

Total cost
(fixed cost + $8 per DVD)

Breakeven Point

200,000

150,000

100,000

Losses

Fixed costs = $100,000

50,000

0

5,000   10,000   15,000   20,000   25,000

Units Sold (DVDs)

For our DVD retailer, the markup percentage is 46.7:

$$\text{Markup percentage} = \frac{\$7}{\$15} \times 100\% = 46.7\%$$

For experienced price setters, an even simpler method uses a standard cost-of-goods percentage to determine the markup amount. Many retailers, for example, use 100 percent of cost-of-goods as the standard markup. If the manufacturer's price is $8 per DVD, the markup (100 percent) is also $8, so the selling price is $16.

Breakeven Analysis: Cost-Volume-Profit Relationships   Using cost-oriented pricing, a firm will cover **variable costs**—costs that change with the number of units of a product produced and sold, such as raw materials, sales commissions, and shipping. Firms also need to pay **fixed costs**—costs, such as rent, insurance, and utilities, that must be paid *regardless of the number of units produced and sold*.

Costs, selling price, and the number of units sold determine how many units a company must sell before all costs, both variable and fixed, are covered, and it begins to make a profit. **Breakeven analyses** assess costs versus revenues for various sales volumes and show, at any particular selling price, the amount of loss or profit for each possible volume of sales.

If you were the manager of a video store, how would you determine how many DVDs you needed to sell to break even? We know that the *variable cost* of buying each DVD from the manufacturer is $8. This means that the store's annual variable costs depend on how many DVDs are sold—the number of DVDs

sold times the $8 cost for each DVD. Say that *fixed costs* for keeping the store open for 1 year are $100,000 (no matter how many DVDs are sold). At a selling price of $15 each, how many DVDs must be sold *so that total revenues exactly cover both* fixed and variable costs? The answer is the **breakeven point**, which is 14,286 DVDs:

$$\text{Breakeven point (in units)} = \frac{\text{Total Fixed Cost}}{\text{Price} - \text{Variable Cost}}$$

$$= \frac{\$100,000}{\$15 - \$8} = 14,286 \text{ DVDs}$$

Look at Figure 12.1. If the store sells fewer than 14,286 DVDs, it loses money for the year. If sales go over 14,286, profits grow by $7 for each additional DVD. If the store sells exactly 14,286 DVDs, it will cover all its costs but earn zero profit.

Zero profitability at the breakeven point can also be seen by using the profit equation:

$$\text{Profit} = \text{Total Revenue} - \left(\begin{array}{c} \text{Total} \\ \text{Fixed} + \\ \text{Cost} \end{array} \begin{array}{c} \text{Total} \\ \text{Variable} \\ \text{Cost} \end{array} \right)$$

$$= (14,286 \text{ DVDs} \times \$15) - (\$100,000 \text{ Fixed Cost}$$
$$+ [14,286 \text{ DVDs} \times \$8 \text{ Variable Cost}])$$

$$\$0 = (\$214,290) - (\$100,00 + \$114,288)$$

(rounded to the nearest whole DVD)

Pricing Strategies and Tactics

The pricing tools discussed in the previous section help managers set prices on specific goods. They do not, however, help them decide on pricing philosophies for diverse competitive situations. In this section, we discuss pricing *strategy* (pricing as a planning activity) and some basic pricing *tactics* (ways in which managers implement a firm's pricing strategies).

Pricing Strategies

Pricing is an extremely important element in the marketing mix, as well as a flexible marketing tool: it is certainly easier to change prices than to change products or distribution channels. This section will look at how pricing strategies can result in widely differing prices for very similar products.

Pricing Existing Products   A firm has three options for pricing existing products:

1. Pricing above prevailing market prices for similar products to take advantage of the common assumption that higher price means higher quality

2. Pricing below market prices while offering a product of comparable quality to higher-priced competitors

3. Pricing at or near market prices

Pricing New Products When introducing new products, companies must often choose between very high prices or very low prices. **Price skimming**—setting an initial high price to cover development and introduction costs and generate a large profit on each item sold—works only if marketers can convince customers that a new product is truly different from existing products. In contrast, **penetration pricing**—setting an initial low price to establish a new product in the market—seeks to create customer interest and stimulate trial purchases.

Startup firms often use one-price, fixed pricing for launching new products. Carbonite, Inc., started its online backup service in 2006 with "one-flat-low price," no matter how much space you needed to back up your PC files.[4] To date the company has backed up more than 2.5 billion files, using a $54.95-per-year one-price strategy. The initial policy of Apple's iTunes was to use one low price per song, $.99, to attract and build a customer base in the first five years. In 2009, with 75 million customers, a new three-tier pricing was adopted to reflect differences in value among songs. Older or obscure tunes of lesser value are priced at $.69, while current hot songs are priced at $1.29, and still others sell for $.99.

Fixed Versus Dynamic Pricing for Online Business The digital marketplace has introduced a highly variable pricing system as an alternative to conventional fixed pricing for both consumer and business-to-business (B2B) products. At present, fixed pricing, used by iTunes and Carbonite, is still the most common option for cybershoppers. In contrast, dynamic pricing, like eBay's traditional auction bidding, uses flexibility between buyers and sellers in setting a price and uses the Web to instantly notify millions of buyers of product availability and price changes.

Reverse auction allows sellers to alter prices privately on an individual basis. At Priceline.com, for example, consumers set a price (below the published fixed price) they are willing to pay for airfare (or a rental car or a hotel room); then an airline can complete the sale by accepting the bid price. For B2B purchases, MediaBids.com uses reverse advertising auctions to sell ad space. A company will notify MediaBids that it is going to spend $1,000 for advertising. Publications then use their ad space as currency to place bids for the advertising dollars. The company can then accept the bid that offers the most ad exposure in the best publication.[5]

Pricing Tactics

Regardless of its pricing strategy, a company may adopt one or more *pricing tactics*. Companies selling multiple items in a product category often use **price lining**—offering all items in certain categories at a limited number of prices. A department store, for example, might predetermine $175, $250, and $400 as the *price points* for men's suits, so all men's suits would be set at one of these three prices.

Psychological pricing takes advantage of the fact that customers are not completely rational when making buying decisions. One type, **odd-even pricing**, is based on the theory that customers prefer prices that are not stated in even dollar amounts. Thus, customers regard prices of $1,000, $100, $50, and $10 as significantly higher than $999.95, $99.95, $49.95, and $9.95, respectively. Finally, sellers must often resort to price reductions—**discounts**—to stimulate sales.

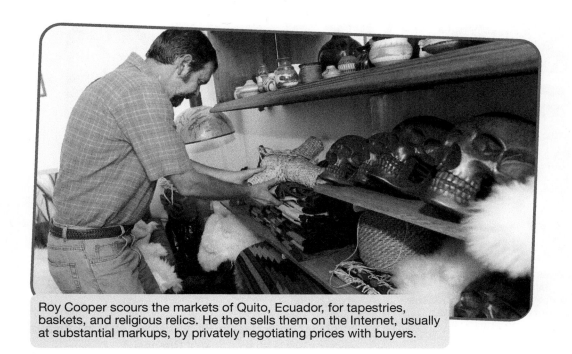

Roy Cooper scours the markets of Quito, Ecuador, for tapestries, baskets, and religious relics. He then sells them on the Internet, usually at substantial markups, by privately negotiating prices with buyers.

The Distribution Mix

In addition to a good product mix and effective pricing, the success of any product also depends on its **distribution mix**—the combination of distribution channels by which a firm gets products to end users.

Intermediaries and Distribution Channels

Once called *middlemen*, **intermediaries** help to distribute goods, either by moving them or by providing information that stimulates their movement from sellers to customers. **Wholesalers** are intermediaries who sell products to other businesses for resale to final consumers. **Retailers** sell products directly to consumers.

Distribution of Goods and Services   A **distribution channel** is the path a product follows from producer to end user. Figure 12.2 shows how four popular distribution channels can be identified according to the channel members involved in getting products to buyers.

Channel 1: Direct Distribution In a **direct channel**, the product travels from the producer to the consumer or organizational buyer without intermediaries. Avon, Dell, GEICO, and Tupperware, as well as many companies on the Internet, use this channel. Most business goods, especially those bought in large quantities, are sold directly by the manufacturer to the industrial buyer.

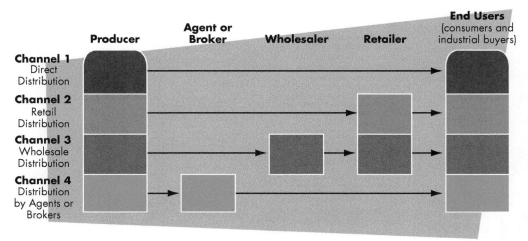

Figure 12.2
Channels of Distribution

At the plant of the world's largest auto parts supplier, Delphi Automotive Systems, Jessica V. Prince assembles fuel pumps according to a process that she helped engineers and consultants design. The auto parts are shipped from the plant to an auto manufacturer, illustrating a direct (producer to consumer) channel of distribution.

Channel 2: Retail Distribution In Channel 2, producers distribute consumer products through retailers. Goodyear, for example, maintains its own system of retail outlets. Levi's has its own outlets but also produces jeans for other retailers. Large outlets, such as Wal-Mart, buy merchandise directly from producers. Many industrial buyers, such as businesses buying office supplies at Staples, rely on this channel.

Channel 3: Wholesale Distribution Once the most widely used method of nondirect distribution, Channel 2 requires a large and costly amount of floor space for storing and displaying merchandise. Wholesalers relieve the space problem by storing merchandise and restocking store displays frequently. With approximately 90 percent of its space used to display merchandise and only 10 percent left for storage and office facilities, the combination convenience store/gas station's use of wholesalers is an example of Channel 3.

Channel 4: Distribution by Agents or Brokers Sales agents or brokers represent producers and receive commissions on the goods they sell to consumers or industrial users. **Sales agents**, including many travel agents, generally deal in the related product lines of a few producers to meet the needs of many customers. **Brokers**, in such industries as real estate and stock exchanges, match numerous sellers and buyers as needed, often without knowing in advance who they will be.

The Pros and Cons of Nondirect Distribution One downfall of nondirect distribution is higher prices: The more members in the channel—the more intermediaries making a profit by charging a markup or commission—the higher the final price. Intermediaries, however, can provide *added value* by providing time-saving information and making the right quantities of products available where and when consumers need them. Figure 12.3 illustrates

Figure 12.3
The Value-Adding Intermediary

Tomato Producer	Chili Powder Producer	Beef Producer	Beans Producer

Consumer 1	Consumer 2	Consumer 3	Consumer 4

Tomato Producer	Chili Powder Producer	Beef Producer	Beans Producer

Supermarket

Consumer 1	Consumer 2	Consumer 3	Consumer 4

the problem of making chili without the benefit of a common intermediary—the supermarket. As a consumer, you would obviously spend a lot more time, money, and energy if you tried to gather all the ingredients from separate producers.

Wholesaling

Most wholesalers are independent operations that buy products from manufacturers and sell them to various consumers or other businesses. They usually provide storage, delivery, and additional value-adding services, including credit, marketing advice, and merchandising services, such as marking prices and setting up displays.

Unlike wholesalers, agents and brokers do not own their merchandise. Rather, they serve as sales and merchandising arms for producers or sellers who do not have their own sales forces. The value of agents and brokers lies in their knowledge of markets and their merchandising expertise. They show sale items to potential buyers and, for retail stores, they provide such services as shelf and display merchandising and advertising layout. They remove open, torn, or dirty packages; arrange products neatly; and generally keep goods attractively displayed.

Retailing

There are more than 3 million brick-and-mortar retail establishments in the United States. Many consist only of owners and part-time help. Indeed, over one-half of the nation's retailers account for less than 10 percent of all retail sales. Retailers also include huge operations, such as Wal-Mart, the world's largest corporate employer, and Home Depot. Although there are large retailers in many other countries—Metro in Germany, Carrefour in France, and Daiei in Japan—most of the world's largest retailers are U.S. businesses.

Types of Retail Outlets

U.S. retail operations vary widely by type as well as size. They can be classified by their pricing strategies, location, range of services, or range of product lines. Choosing the right types of retail outlets is a crucial aspect of distribution strategy. This section describes U.S. retail stores by using three classifications: *product-line retailers*, *bargain retailers*, and *convenience stores*.

Product Line Retailers   Retailers featuring broad product lines include **department stores**, which are organized into specialized departments: shoes, furniture, women's petite sizes, and so on. Stores are usually large, handle a wide range of goods, and offer a variety of services, such as credit plans and delivery. Similarly, **supermarkets** are divided into departments of related products: food products, household products, and so forth. They stress low prices, self-service, and wide selection.

In contrast, **specialty stores**, like Lids—a retailer selling athletic fashion headwear—are small, serve specific market segments with full product lines in narrow product fields, and often feature knowledgeable sales personnel.

Bargain Retailers **Bargain retailers** carry wide ranges of products at low prices. **Discount houses** began by selling large numbers of items at substantial price reductions to cash-only customers. As name-brand items became more common, they offered better product assortments while still transacting cash-only sales in low-rent facilities. As they became firmly entrenched, they began moving to better locations, improving decor, selling better-quality merchandise at higher prices, and offering services such as credit plans and noncash sales.

Catalog showrooms mail catalogs to attract customers into showrooms to view display samples, place orders, and wait briefly while clerks retrieve orders from attached warehouses. **Factory outlets** are manufacturer-owned stores that avoid wholesalers and retailers by selling merchandise directly from factory to consumer. **Wholesale clubs**, like Costco, offer large discounts on a wide range of brand-name merchandise to customers who pay annual membership fees.

Convenience Stores **Convenience store** chains, such as 7-Eleven and Circle K stores, stress easily accessible locations, extended store hours, and speedy service. They differ from most bargain retailers in that they do not feature low prices.

DEPARTMENT STORE large product-line retailer characterized by organization into specialized departments

SUPERMARKET large product-line retailer offering a variety of food and food-related items in specialized departments

SPECIALTY STORE retail store carrying one product line or category of related products

BARGAIN RETAILER retailer carrying a wide range of products at bargain prices

DISCOUNT HOUSE bargain retailer that generates large sales volume by offering goods at substantial price reductions

CATALOG SHOWROOM bargain retailer in which customers place orders for catalog items to be picked up at on-premises warehouses

FACTORY OUTLET bargain retailer owned by the manufacturer whose products it sells

WHOLESALE CLUB bargain retailer offering large discounts on brand-name merchandise to customers who have paid annual membership fees

CONVENIENCE STORE retail store offering easy accessibility, extended hours, and fast service

Doing Good in a Bad Economy: wowOwow!

The five founders of a new social networking service in 2008 had no idea that wowOwow.com would reinvigorate the talents of midlife professionals into new, more promising careers in the economic downturn. The site's business concept is simple: (a) Women over 40 enjoy social networking but with different interests than the younger crowd. (b) The fame and sophistication of its founders' personal lives, interests, and experiences is an attraction for the target audience. Plus, a contributing cast, including Whoopi Goldberg, Candice Bergen, and Lily Tomlin, provides added punch. (c) The $1 million start-up investment is shared equally among its media-savvy founders; all are pace-setting veteran businesswomen: Lesley Stahl (broadcast journalist), Mary Wells (advertising executive), Joni Evans (publishing executive), Peggy Noonan (political commentator), and Liz Smith (gossip columnist). (d) Branding—the distinctive wowOwow.com (for Women on the Web)—signifies the site's mature audience and its goal of sharing professional and personal experiences to encourage one another and to make the world better. (e) The price is right for social networkers: Sign-up is free. Revenues from advertisers will be firmed up later, after wowOwow demonstrates that it can attract a massive audience: Grow the audience, and advertisers will come. (f) Publicity gives wowOwow's message a powerful boost, including interviews on National Public Radio, prominent articles in *The New York Times* and *The Los Angeles Times*, and television features on NBC's *Today Show*.

The surprising career-change twist came with wowOwow.com's Executive Intern Program, begun in late 2008. It's not for newcomer youth interns but, rather, for experienced businesswomen with marketable skills, who, in the business downturn, especially in media industries, need new skills leading to another job. With more and more newspapers and magazines moving online, newer print-Web skills are required, while traditional print media personnel are being displaced. That was the situation for the first intern (unpaid), who at age 55 started listening, watching, and learning by doing and asking for help from much younger tech-savvy Web writers at WOW's offices. She learned new skills in writing URLs, tags, headlines, subheads, and links in story development for wowOwow.com content. Positive buzz created by the internship program confirms that wowOwow's social network endorses the site's goal of sharing professional and personal experiences to encourage others and to make the world better.[6]

Commenting on potential contributions by mature women, co-founder Liz Smith says, "A long time ago, Margaret Mead, the great anthropologist, said that there was nothing to equal the power of the menopausal woman. And I think she is right."

DIRECT-RESPONSE RETAILING form of nonstore retailing in which firms directly interact with customers to inform them of products and to receive sales orders

MAIL ORDER (CATALOG MARKETING) form of nonstore retailing in which customers place orders for catalog merchandise received through the mail

TELEMARKETING form of nonstore retailing in which the telephone is used to sell directly to consumers

Nonstore Retailing

Some of the largest retailers sell all or most of their products without brick-and-mortar stores. Certain types of products—snack foods, pinball, jukeboxes, pool, and cigarettes—sell well from coin-operated machines. But even at $110 billion per year, vending machine sales still make up less than 3 percent of all U.S. retail sales.[7]

Nonstore retailing also includes **direct-response retailing**, in which firms contact customers directly to inform them about products and to receive sales orders. **Mail order** (or **catalog marketing**) is a popular form of direct-response retailing practiced by Crate & Barrel and Sharper Image. Less popular in recent years due to do-not-call registries, **telemarketing** uses phone calls to sell directly to consumers. Finally, more

Table 12.1 **Top 10 Online Retailers**

Rank	Online Retailer	Headquarters	Main Product
1	Amazon.com	Seattle, Washington	Books
2	eBay.com	San Jose, California	Auction
3	Walmart.com	Bentonville, Arkansas	General merchandise
4	BestBuy.com	Richfield, Minnesota	Electronics
5	JCPenney.com	Plano, Texas	Apparel
6	Target.com	Minneapolis, Minnesota	General merchandise
7	Google.com	Mountainview, California	Information
8	Overstock.com	Salt Lake City, Utah	General merchandise
9	Kohls.com	Menomonee Falls, Wisconsin	Apparel
10	Sears.com	Hoffman Estates, Illinois	General merchandise

Source: "Favorite 50: The Online Retailers Shoppers Like Most," Stores, October 2008

DIRECT SELLING form of nonstore retailing typified by door-to-door sales

SHOPPING AGENT (E-AGENT) e-intermediary (middleman) in the Internet distribution channel that assists users in finding products and prices but does not take possession of products

ELECTRONIC RETAILING nonstore retailing in which information about the seller's products and services is connected to consumers' computers, allowing consumers to receive the information and purchase the products in the home

E-CATALOG nonstore retailing in which the Internet is used to display products

ELECTRONIC STOREFRONT commercial Web site at which customers gather information about products and buying opportunities, place orders, and pay for purchases

than 600 U.S. companies, including Mary Kay cosmetics, use **direct selling** to sell door-to-door or through home-selling parties. Avon Products, the world's largest direct seller, has 6 million door-to-door sales representatives in more than 100 countries.[8]

Online Shopping Agents

Shopping agents (e-agents), like PriceSCAN.com, rapidly gather, sort, and present accurate information to help Internet consumers compare Web sites, stores, prices, and product features.

Electronic Retailing

Over 85 percent of the world's online population—over 1 billion consumers—have made purchases on the Internet. iTunes has outsold brick-and-mortar music retailers, and Amazon.com is the world's largest online retailer, with annual sales of $19 billion.[9] **Electronic retailing (online retailing)** allows sellers to inform, sell to, and distribute to consumers via the Web. The largest U.S. "e-tailers" are shown in Table 12.1. In addition to large companies, millions of small businesses around the globe have their own Web sites.

Electronic Catalogs

E-catalogs use online displays of products to give millions of retail and business customers instant access to product information. The seller avoids mail distribution and printing costs, and once an online catalog is in place, there is little cost in maintaining and accessing it. About 90 percent of all catalogers are now on the Internet, with sales via Web sites accounting for nearly 50 percent of all catalog sales.[10]

Electronic Storefronts and Cybermalls Each seller's Web site is an **electronic storefront** (or *virtual storefront*) from which shoppers collect information about products and buying opportunities, place orders, and pay for purchases. Producers of large product lines, such as Dell, dedicate storefronts to their own product lines. Other sites, such as Newegg.com, which offers computer and other electronics equipment, are category sellers whose storefronts feature products from many manufacturers.

QVC host Bob Bowersox is getting ready to offer bedding made by Northern Lights, which distributes regularly through the TV home-shopping channel. Northern Lights markets through such electronic-retailing outlets as eBay and Shopping.com as well as QVC, which also sells online through its Web site and through six outlet stores.

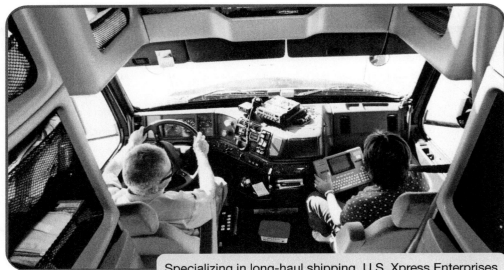

Specializing in long-haul shipping, U.S. Xpress Enterprises employs nearly 6,000 drivers to operate 5,300 trucks and 12,000 trailers. Trucks have satellite capabilities, anticollision radar, vehicle-detection sensors, computers for shifting through 10 speeds, and roomy cabs with sleepers, refrigerators, and microwaves.

Search engines like Yahoo! serve as **cybermalls**—collections of virtual storefronts representing diverse products and offering speed, convenience, 24-hour access, and efficient searching. After entering a cybermall, shoppers can navigate by choosing from a list of stores (L.L. Bean or Macy's), product listings (computers or MP3 players), or departments (apparel or bath/beauty).

Interactive and Video Marketing Today, both retail and B2B customers interact with multimedia sites using voice, graphics, animation, film clips, and access to live human advice. As an example of **interactive marketing**, LivePerson.com is a leading provider of real-time sales and customer service that allows customers to enter a live chat room with a service operator who can answer their specific product questions.

Video marketing, a long-established form of interactive marketing, lets viewers shop at home from channels on their TVs. QVC, for example, displays and demonstrates products and allows viewers to phone in or e-mail orders.

Physical Distribution

Physical distribution refers to the activities needed to move products from manufacturer to customer and includes *warehousing* and *transportation operations*. Its purpose is to make goods available when and where customers want them, keep costs low, and provide services to satisfy customers. Because of its importance for customer satisfaction, some firms have adopted distribution as their marketing strategy of choice.

Warehousing Operations

Storing, or **warehousing**, is a major part of distribution management. In selecting a strategy, managers must keep in mind both the different characteristics and costs of warehousing operations. **Private warehouses** are owned by a single manufacturer, wholesaler, or retailer that deals in mass quantities and needs regular storage.

Independently owned and operated **public warehouses**, which rent to companies only the space they need, are popular with firms needing storage only during peak periods and with manufacturers who need multiple storage locations to get products to multiple markets.

Transportation Operations

Physically moving a product creates the highest cost many companies face. In addition to transportation methods, firms must also consider the nature of the product, the distance it must travel, the speed with which it must be received, and customer wants and needs.

Transportation Modes Differences in cost among the major transportation modes—trucks, railroads, planes, digital transmission, water carriers, and pipelines—are usually most directly related to delivery speed.

Trucks With more than 3 million drivers, trucks haul more than two-thirds of all tonnage carried by all modes of U.S. freight transportation. The advantages of trucks include flexibility for any-distance distribution, fast service, and dependability. Increasing truck traffic, however, is raising safety and courtesy concerns.

Planes   Air is the fastest and most expensive mode of transportation for physical goods. Airfreight customers benefit from lower inventory costs by eliminating the need to store items that might deteriorate. Shipments of fresh fish, for example, can be picked up by restaurants each day, avoiding the risk of spoilage from packaging and storing.

High-Speed Digital Transmission   iTunes's transportation mode of choice, online transmission is newer, faster, and less expensive than all other modes. It is also restricted to products—such as music, images, movies, and software—that exist as digital bits that can be transmitted over communication channels.

Water Carriers   Aside from high-speed digital transmission, water is the least expensive mode but, unfortunately, also the slowest. Networks of waterways—oceans, rivers, and lakes—let water carriers reach many areas throughout the world. Boats and barges are used mostly for moving bulky products (such as oil, grain, and gravel).

Railroads   Railroads can economically transport high-volume, heavy, bulky items, such as cars, steel, and coal. However, their delivery routes are limited by fixed, immovable rail tracks.

Pipelines   Pipelines are slow and lack flexibility and adaptability, but for specialized products, like liquids and gases, they provide economical and reliable delivery.

Distribution as a Marketing Strategy
Instead of just offering advantages in product features, quality, price, and promotion, many firms have turned to distribution as a cornerstone of business strategy.

Managing in Turbulent Times

Getting a Stimulus Boost with Pricing and Promotion

"We're not trying to make a profit; we just want to cover costs and keep our employees." This broadcast message illustrates how a construction company is using reduced pricing coupled with coordinated advertising promotions to stimulate demand in a slow economy. Unusual marketing conditions sometimes call for uncommon actions, including changes in pricing and promotions for attracting customers in different ways than usual. Some of these methods seem simple and straightforward, but others are downright creative and unique.

Price discounts and free shipping are among the ordinary pricing attractions, but even those won't work without integrated promotions that get the cost-savings message to customers. Online B2B clothing wholesaler Apparelus.com offers free shipping to clothing merchants, as does retailer LLBean.com, with its wide-ranging line of consumer products. Both, however, highlight free shipping in Internet marketing campaigns that can also include online chats for stimulating buzz that informs customers about the cost savings.[11]

Auto dealers, too, are adopting newer, more radical tactics, with promotions that shift costs, such as increasing gasoline prices, from customers to the dealers: "Buy a new car now, and if gas prices exceed $2, we'll pay the gas bill." Even more extreme, as a safety net against rising job losses, in 2009 Ford and General Motors announced protection when customers buy a new vehicle and then lose their job. Ford will make monthly payments up to $700 for up to one year. GM will cover payments up to $500 per month for up to nine months. Hyundai Motor Co. allows buyers to return a new car within a year due to the buyer's job loss and, in the event of a layoff, Hyundai will make payments for up to three months. All of these offers are coordinated with advertising promotions—on radio, television, and the Internet—along with public relations and widespread publicity to boost sagging auto sales.[12]

Want to take a vacation, but your portfolio's gone south in the stock-market downfall? It's too late now, but Elite Island Resorts may have had the answer you needed. In December 2008 and January 2009 you could have booked a deluxe Caribbean vacation by paying up to $5,000 per room with stock instead of credit cards. Elite Island promoted the unique "Roll Back Your Stock's Value" offer, accepting a list of some 100 stocks at their higher mid-2008 market values for payment. For example, Elite Island accepted American Express at its earlier value of $40 per share although its value at the time had fallen to less than $22, and Goldman Sachs at $177 although its current value at the time was less than $72. By transferring the stock as payment, the resort was betting that the stock would eventually regain its value, and customers enjoyed the same price benefit as when their portfolio had been more valuable.[13]

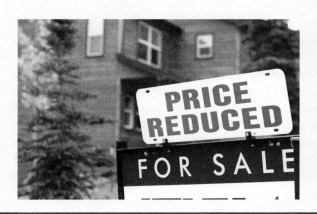

PROMOTION aspect of the marketing mix concerned with the most effective techniques for communicating information about and selling a product

POSITIONING process of establishing an identifiable product image in the minds of consumers

PROMOTIONAL MIX combination of tools used to promote a product

This approach means assessing and improving the entire stream of activities—wholesaling, warehousing, and transportation—involved in getting products to customers.

Consider, for example, the distribution system of National Semiconductor, one of the world's largest microchip makers. Finished microchips are produced in plants around the world and shipped to 1,700 customers, such as IBM, Toshiba, and Hewlett-Packard, which also run factories around the globe. Chips originally traveled 20,000 different routes on as many as 12 airlines and sat waiting at one location after another—on factory floors, at customs, in distributors' facilities, and in warehouses—before reaching customers. National has streamlined the system and now airfreights ship worldwide from a single center in Singapore. Every activity—storage, sorting, and shipping—is run by FedEx. By outsourcing the activities, National's distribution costs have fallen, delivery times have been reduced by half, and sales have increased.

The Importance of Promotion

Promotion refers to techniques for communicating information about products and is part of the *communication mix*—the total message any company sends to customers about its product. Promotional techniques, especially advertising, must communicate the uses, features, and benefits of products, and marketers use an array of tools for this purpose.

Promotional Objectives

The ultimate objective of any promotion is to increase sales. In addition, marketers may use promotion to *communicate information*, *position products*, *add value*, and *control sales volume*.

Positioning is the process of establishing an easily identifiable product image in the minds of consumers by fixing, adapting, and communicating the nature of the product itself. First, a firm must identify which market segments are likely to purchase its product and how its product measures up against competitors. Then, it can focus on promotional choices for differentiating its product and positioning it in the minds of the target audience.

Promotional mixes are often designed to communicate a product's *value-added benefits* to distinguish it from the competition. Mercedes automobiles and Ritz-Carlton Hotels, for example, promote their products as upscale goods and services featuring high quality, style, and performance, all at a higher price.

The Promotional Mix

Four of marketing's most powerful promotional tools are *advertising*, *personal selling*, *sales promotions*, and *publicity and public relations*. The best combination of these tools—the best **promotional mix**—depends on many factors. The most important is the target audience. As an example, two generations from now, 25 percent of the U.S. workforce will be Hispanic. The rise in Latinos' disposable income has made them a potent economic force, and marketers are scrambling to redesign and promote products to appeal to them. Spanish-language media is one obvious outlet: the audience for programming from Univision, the biggest Spanish-language media company in the United States—with television, radio, music, and Internet—has ballooned by 50 percent since 2001 to become the number five network in the United States.[14]

The Target Audience: Promotion and the Buyer Decision Process In establishing a promotional mix, marketers match promotional tools with the five stages in the buyer decision process:

1 When buyers first recognize the need to make a purchase, marketers use advertising and publicity to make sure buyers are aware of their products.

2 As buyers search for information about available products, advertising and personal selling are important methods to educate them.

3 Personal selling can become vital as buyers compare competing products. Sales representatives can demonstrate product quality, features, and performance in comparison with competitors' products.

4 When buyers are ready to purchase products, sales promotion can give consumers an incentive to buy. Personal selling can help by bringing products to convenient purchase locations.

5 After making purchases, buyers evaluate products and note (and remember) their strengths and deficiencies. Advertising and personal selling can remind customers that they made wise purchases.

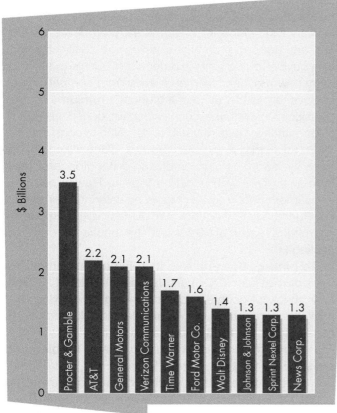

Figure 12.4
Top 10 U.S. National Advertisers[16]

Advertising Promotions

Advertising is paid, nonpersonal communication by which an identified sponsor informs an audience about a product. In 2007, U.S. firms spent $157 billion on advertising—nearly $19 billion of it by just 10 companies.[15] Figure 12.4 shows U.S. advertising expenditures for the top-spending firms. Let's take a look at the different types of advertising media, noting some of the advantages and limitations of each.

Advertising Media Consumers tend to ignore the bulk of advertising messages that bombard them; they pay attention to what interests them. Moreover, the advertising process is dynamic, reflecting the changing interests and preferences of both customers and advertisers. A 2008 customer survey, for example, reports that mail ads are rated as most irritating and boring, while newspaper and magazine ads are least annoying. Yet, while newspaper ads are rated as more informative and useful than some other media, advertisers continue to shift away, using instead more online, cell phone, and PDA advertising because newsprint readership (the audience) is dwindling.[17]

Real-Time Ad Tracking Advertisers always want better information about who looks at ads and for how long. Which target audiences and demographics are more attracted to various ad contents? Accurate ad-watching behavior of shoppers in malls, theaters, and grocery stores is on the increase with assistance from high-tech real-time surveillance. As passing consumers watch ads on video screens, cameras watch the shoppers, while software analyzes the viewers' demographics and reactions to various ad contents and formats. The makers of the tracking system claim accuracy of up to 90 percent for determining gender, approximate age, and ethnicity. Once perfected, the system might measure your demographics, identify you with a target audience, then instantly change the presentation to a preferred product and visual format to attract and hold your attention.[18] Marketers must find out, then, who their customers are, which media they pay attention to, what messages appeal to them, and how to get their attention. Thus, marketers use several different **advertising media**—specific communication devices for carrying a seller's message to potential customers. The combination of media through which a company advertises is called its **media mix**. Table 12.2 shows the relative sizes of media usage and their strengths and weaknesses.

Personal Selling

In the oldest and most expensive form of sales, **personal selling**, a salesperson communicates one-on-one with potential customers to identify their needs and align them with the product. Salespeople gain credibility by investing a lot of time getting acquainted with potential customers and answering their questions.

Salespeople must be adept at performing three basic tasks of personal selling. In **order processing**, a salesperson receives an order and sees to its handling and delivery. When potential customers are not aware that they need or want a product, **creative selling** involves

ADVERTISING promotional tool consisting of paid, nonpersonal communication used by an identified sponsor to inform an audience about a product

ADVERTISING MEDIA variety of communication devices for carrying a seller's message to potential customers

MEDIA MIX combination of advertising media chosen to carry a message about a product

PERSONAL SELLING promotional tool in which a salesperson communicates one-on-one with potential customers

ORDER PROCESSING personal-selling task in which salespeople receive orders and see to their handling and delivery

CREATIVE SELLING personal-selling task in which salespeople try to persuade buyers to purchase products by providing information about their benefits

MISSIONARY SELLING personal-selling task in which salespeople promote their firms and products rather than try to close sales

SALES PROMOTION short-term promotional activity designed to encourage consumer buying, industrial sales, or cooperation from distributors

COUPON sales-promotion technique in which a certificate is issued entitling the buyer to a reduced price

PREMIUM sales-promotion technique in which offers of free or reduced-price items are used to stimulate purchases

POINT-OF-SALE (POS) DISPLAY sales-promotion technique in which product displays are located in certain areas to stimulate purchase or to provide information on a product

TRADE SHOW sales-promotion technique in which various members of an industry gather to display, demonstrate, and sell products

providing information and demonstrating product benefits to persuade buyers to complete a purchase. Finally, a salesperson may use **missionary selling** to promote a company and its products rather than simply to close a sale. Pharmaceutical companies often use this method to make doctors aware of the company and its products so they will recommend the company's products to others.

Sales Promotions

Sales promotions are short-term promotional activities designed to encourage consumer buying, industrial sales, or cooperation from distributors. They can increase the likelihood that buyers will try products, enhance product recognition, and increase purchase size and sales revenues.

Types of Sales Promotions Most consumers have taken part in a variety of sales promotions such as free *samples* (giveaways), which let customers try products without risk, and **coupon** promotions, which use certificates entitling buyers to discounts in order to encourage customers to try new products, lure them away from competitors, or induce them to buy more of a product. **Premiums** are free or reduced-price items, such as pencils, coffee mugs, and six-month low-interest credit cards, given to consumers in return for buying a specified product. *Contests* can boost sales by rewarding high-producing distributors and sales representatives with vacation trips to Hawaii or Paris. Consumers, too, may win prizes by entering their cats in the Purina Cat Chow calendar contest, for example, by submitting entry blanks from the backs of cat-food packages.

To grab customers' attention in stores, companies use **point-of-sale (POS) displays** at the ends of aisles or near checkout counters to ease finding products and to eliminate competitors from consideration. In addition to physical goods, POS pedestals also provide services, namely information for consumers. Bank lobbies and physicians' waiting rooms, for example, have computer-interactive kiosks inviting clients to learn more about bank products and educational information about available treatments on consumer-friendly touch-screen displays. For B2B promotions, industries sponsor **trade shows** where companies rent booths to display

Table 12.2 Measured Media Usage, Strengths, and Weaknesses[19]

Advertising Medium	Percentage of Advertising Outlays	Strengths	Weaknesses
Television	37%	Program demographics allow for customized ads Large audience	Most expensive
Magazines	18%	Often reread and shared Variety of ready market segmentation	Require advanced planning Little control over ad placement
Newspapers	15%	Broad coverage Ads can be changed daily	Quickly discarded Broad readership limits ability to target specific audience
Direct mail	15%	Targeted audience Personal messages Predictable results	Easily discarded Environmentally irresponsible
Internet	7%	Targeted audience Measurable success	Nuisance to consumers Easy to ignore
Radio	6%	Inexpensive Large audience Variety of ready market segmentation	Easy to ignore Message quickly disappears
Outdoor	2%	Inexpensive Difficult to ignore Repeat exposure	Presents limited information Little control over audience

A combination of additional unmeasured media—catalogs, sidewalk handouts, skywriting, telephone calls, ads on PDAs, special events, movies, and door-to-door communication—are not included.

and demonstrate products to customers who have a special interest or who are ready to buy.

Publicity and Public Relations

Publicity is information about a company, a product, or an event transmitted by the general mass media to attract public attention. While publicity is free, marketers have no control over the content media reporters and writers disseminate, and because it is presented in a news format, consumers often regard it as objective and credible. In 2005, for example, U.S. fast-food patrons were horrified when a customer said she found a human fingertip in a bowl of Wendy's chili. The publicity nightmare immediately bruised the food chain's reputation and cost about $15 million in lost sales in just six weeks.[20]

In contrast to publicity, **public relations** is company-influenced information that seeks either to build good relations with the public—by publicizing the company's charitable contributions, for example—or to deal with unfavorable events. In the Wendy's case, CEO Jack Schuessler's public relations response was decisive and focused: protect the brand and tell the truth. That meant there would be no payoff or settlement to keep it out of the news. Instead, Wendy's enlisted cooperation with the health department and police, did visual inspections, polygraphed employees, publicly announced a hotline for tips, and offered a reward for information, all leading to the conclusion that the reported episode was a hoax. Energetic public relations was an effective promotional tool for clearing the Wendy's name and preserving the company's reputation.[21]

Questions for Review

1 How does breakeven analysis help managers measure the potential impact of prices?

2 Discuss the goal of price skimming and penetration pricing.

3 Identify the channels of distribution. In what key ways do they differ from one another?

4 Explain how e-agents or e-brokers differ from traditional agents or brokers.

5 Select four advertising media and compare the advantages and disadvantages of each.

Questions for Analysis

6 Suppose that a small publisher selling to book distributors has fixed operating costs of $600,000 each year and variable costs of $3.00 per book. How many books must the firm sell to break even if the selling price is $6.00?

7 Choose two advertising campaigns: one that you think is effective and one that you think is ineffective. What makes one campaign better than the other?

8 Give examples of two products that typify the products sold to shoppers through each form of nonstore retailing. Explain why different products are best suited to each form of nonstore retailing.

Application Exercises

9 Select a product and analyze pricing objectives for it. What information would you want if you were to adopt a profit-maximizing objective or a market share objective?

10 Select a product and identify the media used in its promotion. On the whole, do you think the campaign is effective? Why or why not? If the campaign is not effective, what changes would you suggest to improve it?

Information Technology for Business

After reading this chapter, you should be able to:

1 Discuss the impacts information technology has had on the business world.

2 Identify the IT resources businesses have at their disposal and how these resources are used.

3 Describe the role of information systems, the different types of information systems, and how businesses use such systems.

4 Identify the threats and risks information technology poses on businesses.

5 Describe the ways in which businesses protect themselves from the threats and risks information technology poses.

Online Pirates Feast on Economic Downturn

"*Start a 'work-at-home' job as an 'international sales representative' or a 'shipping manager,' with excellent pay. Simply open a new bank account in your name, accept money transfers into the account, then forward the money to our customers at locations around the globe.*" For out-of-work computer users, this e-mail message can be quite appealing. In reality, the victim is tricked into becoming a "mule" in a money-laundering racket. The new "employee" provides anonymous racketeers a safe way to launder stolen or otherwise illegal money. As Internet money transfers arrive, the mule relays them (illegally) to a global network of recipient racketeers. With rising unemployment, the volume of mule e-mails is growing; more job-seekers seem willing to take the risk of being arrested.

Financial fears are a boon to scammers, as businesses and consumers grasp at schemes that are ordinarily ignored. Fake Web sites, cell phones, and Internet-based phones boast high-paying jobs, low-cost loans, and can't-miss lotteries. Cell phone text messages lure bank customers into telephoning account information, saying victims' credit cards have been de-activated. Internet-based phone users receive fake caller-IDs of real hospitals, government agencies, banks, and other businesses in a new form of telephone phishing that talks victims into revealing personal information. Perhaps most impressive, cyber-thieves are using marketing techniques—most notably "targeting"—to reach specific audiences. Also known as "spear phishing," with targeting, scammers do research to identify wealthy individuals, families, and professional money managers. Victims receive friendly-sounding e-mails containing contaminated attachments that, once opened, infect their computers, exposing bank account and other identity information to scammers. While computer security devices—spam filters, data encryption, firewalls, and anti-virus software—catch a vast number of intrusions, the threat remains.[1]

What's in It for Me?

Protecting against cyber-terrorism is an extreme example of the way the Internet and related technologies are reshaping the business landscape. But even the most traditional businesses must change with the times, whether those times are defined by paper and pencil, telephone and fax machine, or digital language translators and Wi-Fi. Indeed, it may seem like the times are changing more rapidly with each passing year, and it is in this context that our discussion of the various kinds of information technology, their functions, and the benefits and risks associated with each assumes particular importance. By understanding the material in this chapter, you'll have a clearer picture of how technology is used by and affects business, and how you can use it to your best advantage.

IT Impacts

The effect of **information technology (IT)** on business has been immeasurable. In fact, IT—the various appliances and devices for creating, storing, exchanging, and using information in diverse modes, including visual images, voice, multimedia, and business data—has altered the very structure of business organizations, radically changing the way employees and customers interact. **E-commerce** (short for *electronic commerce*)—the use of the Internet and other electronic means for retailing and business-to-business transactions—has created new market relationships around the globe. In this section, we'll look at how businesses are using IT to bolster productivity, improve operations and processes, create new opportunities, and communicate and work in ways not possible before.

Creating Portable Offices: Providing Remote Access to Instant Information

IT appliances such as the BlackBerry messaging device feature wireless Internet access and PC-style office applications, saving businesses time and travel expenses by enabling employees, customers, and suppliers to communicate from any location. No longer is work done only at the office or the factory, nor are all of a company's operations performed at one place; employees take the office with them. When using such devices, off-site employees have continuous access to information, instead of being forced to be at a desk to access their files and the Internet. Such benefits have attracted 21 million enthusiastic subscribers to BlackBerry, making it the leader in the handheld wireless industry.[2]

Enabling Better Service by Coordinating Remote Deliveries

Meanwhile, with access to the Internet, company activities may be geographically scattered but remain coordinated through a networked system that provides better service for customers. Many businesses, for example, coordinate activities from one centralized location, but their deliveries flow from several remote locations, often at lower cost. When you order furniture—for example, a chair, a sofa, a table, and two lamps—from an Internet storefront, the chair may come from a warehouse in Philadelphia and the lamps from a manufacturer in California; the sofa and table may be shipped direct from different suppliers in North Carolina. Beginning

with the customer's order, activities are coordinated through the company's network, as if the whole order were being processed at one place. This avoids the expensive in-between step of first shipping all the items to a central location.

Creating Leaner, More Efficient Organizations

Networks and technology are also leading to leaner companies with fewer employees and simpler structures. Because networks enable firms to maintain information linkages among both employees and customers, more work and customer satisfaction can be accomplished with fewer people. For example, truck drivers used to return to a shipping terminal to receive instructions from supervisors on reloading freight for the next delivery. Today, one dispatcher using IT has replaced several supervisors. Instructions to the fleet arrive on electronic screens in trucks on the road so drivers know in advance the next delivery schedule, while satellite navigation services, such as the XM NavTraffic, alert drivers of traffic incidents ahead so they can reroute to avoid delivery delays.[3]

Enabling Increased Collaboration

Collaboration among internal units and with outside firms is greater when firms use collaboration software and other IT communications devices, which we'll discuss later in this chapter. Companies are learning that complex problems can be better solved through IT-supported collaboration, either with formal teams or spontaneous interaction among people and departments. The design of new products, for example, was

Barack Obama's Blackberry uses an encrypted system for secure e-mailing with advisors and colleagues.

once an engineering responsibility. Now it is a shared activity using information from people in marketing, finance, production, engineering, and purchasing who, collectively, determine the best design. For example, the design of Boeing's 787 Dreamliner aircraft is the result of collaboration, not just among engineers, but also from passengers (who wanted electric outlets to recharge personal electronic devices), cabin crews (who wanted more bathrooms and wider aisles), and air-traffic controllers (who wanted larger, safer air brakes).

Enabling Global Exchange

The global reach of IT is enabling business collaboration on a scale that was unheard of before. Consider Lockheed Martin's contract for designing and supplying thousands of Joint Strike Fighters in different versions for the United States, Britain, Italy, Denmark, Canada, and Norway. Lockheed can't do the job alone—over the project's 20-year life, more than 1,500 firms will supply everything from radar systems to engines to bolts. Web collaboration on a massive scale is essential for coordinating design, testing, and construction while avoiding delays, holding down costs, and maintaining quality.[4]

Improving Management Processes

IT has also changed the nature of the management process. The activities and methods of today's manager differ significantly from those that were common just a few years ago. At one time, upper-level managers didn't concern themselves with all of the detailed information filtering upward from the workplace because it was expensive to gather, slow in coming, and quickly became out of date. Workplace management was delegated to middle and first-line managers.

With databases, specialized software, and networks, however, instantaneous information is accessible and useful to all levels of management. For example, consider *enterprise resource planning (ERP)*: an information system for organizing and managing a firm's activities across product lines, departments, and geographic locations. The ERP stores real-time information on work status and upcoming transactions and notifies employees when action is required if certain schedules are to be met. It coordinates internal operations with activities of outside suppliers and notifies customers of upcoming deliveries and billings. Consequently, more managers use it routinely for planning and controlling company-wide operations. Today, a manager at Hershey Foods, for example, uses ERP to check on the current status of any customer order for Kisses or Jolly Ranchers, inspect productivity statistics for each workstation, and analyze

the delivery performance on any shipment. Managers can better coordinate company-wide performance. They can identify departments that are working well together and those that are lagging behind schedule and creating bottlenecks.

Providing Flexibility for Customization

IT networks and other IT advances also create new manufacturing capabilities that enable businesses to offer customers greater variety, customizable options, and faster delivery cycles. Many designs at Ponoko.com can be altered to suit each buyer's tastes. Similarly, at San Francisco–based Timbuk2's Web site, you can "build your own" custom messenger bag at different price levels with your choice of size, fabric, color combination, accessories, liner material, strap, and even left- or right-hand access.[5] This principle is called **mass-customization**: Although companies produce in large volumes, IT allows each unit to feature the unique options the customer prefers. With IT, the old standardized assembly line has become quickly adaptable because workers have instantaneous access to assembly instructions for all the product options, and equipment can be changed quickly for each customer's order.

As shown in Figure 13.1, flexible production and speedy delivery depend on an integrated network of information to coordinate all the activities among customers, manufacturers, suppliers, and shippers.

Providing New Business Opportunities

Not only is IT improving existing businesses, it is creating entirely new businesses where none existed before. For big businesses, this means developing new products, offering new services, and reaching new clients. Only a few years ago, the multibillion-dollar behemoth known as Google was a fledgling search engine. Today, that company boasts not just a search engine but instant messaging, e-mail, and online software services including photo editing and document creation.

The IT landscape has also presented small-business owners with new e-business opportunities. More than 600 online marketplaces allow entrepreneurs to sell directly to consumers, bypassing conventional retail outlets, and enable B2B selling and trading with access to a worldwide customer base. To assist start-up businesses, eBay's services network is a ready-made online business model, not just an auction market. Services range from credit financing to protection from fraud and misrepresentation, information security, international currency exchanges, and post-sales management. These features

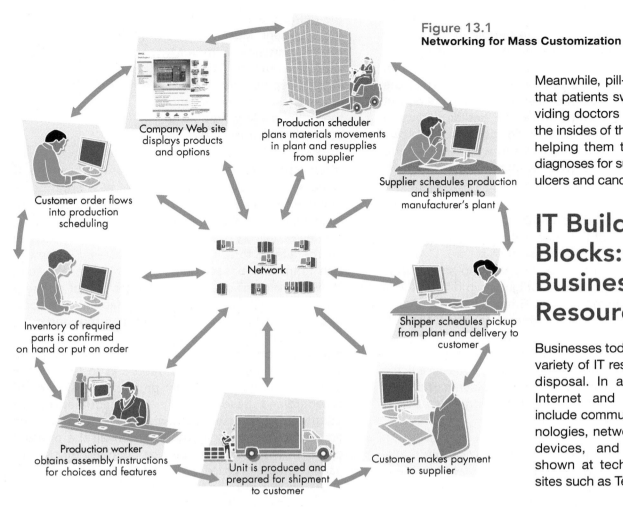

Figure 13.1
Networking for Mass Customization

Company Web site displays products and options

Production scheduler plans materials movements in plant and resupplies from supplier

Supplier schedules production and shipment to manufacturer's plant

Customer order flows into production scheduling

Network

Inventory of required parts is confirmed on hand or put on order

Shipper schedules pickup from plant and delivery to customer

Production worker obtains assembly instructions for choices and features

Unit is produced and prepared for shipment to customer

Customer makes payment to supplier

Meanwhile, pill-sized cameras that patients swallow are providing doctors with images of the insides of the human body, helping them to make better diagnoses for such ailments as ulcers and cancer.[7]

IT Building Blocks: Business Resources

Businesses today have a wide variety of IT resources at their disposal. In addition to the Internet and e-mail, these include communications technologies, networks, hardware devices, and software, as shown at technology media sites such as TechWeb.com.

enable users to complete sales transactions, deliver merchandise, and get new merchandise for future resale, all from the comfort of their own homes.

Improving the World and Our Lives

Can advancements in IT really make the world a better place? Hospitals and medical equipment companies certainly think so. For example, when treating combat injuries, surgeons at Walter Reed Army Medical Center now rely on high-tech imaging systems that convert two-dimensional photographs of their patients' anatomies into three-dimensional physical models for presurgical planning. These 3-D mockups of shoulders, femurs, and facial bones give doctors the opportunity to see and feel the anatomy as it will be seen in the operating room, before they even use their scalpels.

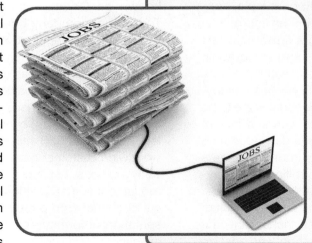

Social Networking as a Service

The many forms of social media—blogs, chats, and networks such as LinkedIn, Twitter, and Facebook—are no longer just playthings for gossips and hobbyists. They're also active tools for getting a job. With the economic meltdown, millions of job seekers have turned to online networking—tapping leads from friends, colleagues, and acquaintances—for contacts with companies that may be hiring. Peers and recruiters are networking using electronic discussion forums and bulletin boards at Web sites of professional associations and trade groups, technical schools, and alumni organizations. Some social sites provide occupation-specific career coaching and job tips: Scientists are connecting with Epernicus, top managers use Meet the Boss, and graduate students are connecting with Graduate Junction.[6]

After this capsule is swallowed, the camera inside it can transmit almost 50,000 images during its eight-hour journey through the digestive tract.

The Internet and Other Communication Resources

The **Internet** is a gigantic system of interconnected computers—more than 100 million computers in over 100 countries make up the Internet we know today.[8] These computers are connected by numerous applications utilizing different communications protocols. The most familiar Internet protocols are **hypertext transfer protocol (HTTP)**—which is used for the **World Wide Web**, a branch of the Internet consisting of interlinked hypertext documents, or Web pages— and **simple message transfer protocol (SMTP)** and **post office protocol (POP)**, which are used to send and receive e-mail. For thousands of businesses, the Internet has replaced the telephone, fax machine, and standard mail as the primary communications tool.

The Internet has spawned a number of other business communications technologies, including *intranets*, *extranets*, *electronic conferencing*, and *VSAT satellite communications*.

Intranets Many companies have extended Internet technology by maintaining internal Web sites linked throughout the firm. These private networks, or

intranets, are accessible only to employees and may contain confidential information on benefits programs, a learning library, production management tools, or product design resources. For firms such as Ford Motor Company, whose intranet is accessible to 200,000 people daily, sharing information on engineering, distribution, and marketing has reduced the lead time for getting new models into production and has shortened customer delivery times.[10]

Extranets Extranets allow outsiders limited access to a firm's internal information network. The most common application allows buyers to enter a system to see which products are available for sale and delivery, thus providing convenient product-availability information. Industrial suppliers are often linked into customers' information networks so that they can see planned production schedules and prepare supplies for customers' upcoming operations. The extranet at Chaparral Steel, for example, lets customers

INTERNET gigantic system of interconnected computers—more than 100 million computers in over 100 countries

HYPERTEXT TRANSFER PROTOCOL (HTTP) communications protocol used for the World Wide Web, in which related pieces of information on separate Web pages are connected using hyperlinks

WORLD WIDE WEB branch of the Internet consisting of interlinked hypertext documents, or Web pages

SIMPLE MESSAGE TRANSFER PROTOCOL (SMTP) basic communications protocol used to send e-mail

POST OFFICE PROTOCOL (POP) one of the basic communications protocols used to receive e-mail

INTRANET organization's private network of internally linked Web sites accessible only to employees

EXTRANET system that allows outsiders limited access to a firm's internal information network

In this map of the Internet, each line represents a connection between computers or other network devices.[9]

shop electronically through its storage yards and gives them electronic access to Chaparral's planned inventory of industrial steel products.

Electronic Conferencing **Electronic conferencing** allows groups of people to communicate simultaneously from various locations via e-mail, phone, or video, thereby eliminating travel time and saving money. One form, called *dataconferencing*, allows people in remote locations to work simultaneously on one document. *Videoconferencing* allows participants to see one another on video screens while the conference is in progress. For example, Lockheed Martin's Joint Strike Fighter project, discussed earlier, uses Internet collaboration systems with both voice and video capabilities. Although separated by oceans, partners can communicate as if they were in the same room for redesigning components and production schedules. Electronic conferencing is attractive to many businesses because it eliminates travel and saves money.

VSAT Satellite Communications Another Internet technology businesses use to communicate is **VSAT satellite communications**. VSAT (short for *very small aperture terminal*) systems have a transmitter-receiver (*transceiver*) that sits outdoors with a direct line of sight to a satellite. The hub—a ground-station computer at the company's headquarters—sends signals to and receives signals from the satellite, exchanging voice, video, and data transmissions. An advantage of VSAT is privacy. A company that operates its own VSAT system has total control over communications among its facilities, no matter their location, without dependence on other companies. A firm might use VSAT to exchange sales and inventory information, advertising messages, and visual presentations between headquarters and store managers at remote sites.

Networks: System Architecture

A **computer network** is a group of two or more computers linked together, either hardwired or wirelessly, to share data or resources, such as a printer. The most common type of network used in businesses is a **client-server network**. In client-server networks, *clients* are usually the laptop or desktop computers through which users make requests for information or resources. *Servers* are the computers that provide the services shared by users. In big organizations, servers are usually assigned a specific task. For example, in a local university or college network, an *application server* stores the word-processing, spreadsheet, and other programs used by all computers connected to the network. A *print server* controls the printers, stores printing requests from client computers, and routes jobs as the printers become available. An *e-mail server* handles all incoming and outgoing e-mail. With a client-server system, users can share resources and Internet connections—and avoid costly duplication.

Networks can be classified according to geographic scope and means of connection (either wired or wireless).

Wide Area Networks (WANs) Computers that are linked over long distances—statewide or even nationwide—through telephone lines, microwave signals, or satellite communications make up what are called **wide area networks (WANs)**. Firms can lease lines from communications vendors or maintain private WANs. Wal-Mart, for example, depends heavily on a private satellite network that links thousands of U.S. and international retail stores to its Bentonville, Arkansas, headquarters.

Local Area Networks (LANs) In **local area networks (LANs)**, computers are linked in a smaller area such as an office or a building. For example, a LAN unites hundreds of operators who enter call-in orders at TV's Home Shopping Network facility. The arrangement requires only one computer system with one database and one software system.

Wireless Networks Wireless networks use airborne electronic signals to link network computers and devices. Like wired networks, wireless networks can reach across long distances or exist within a single building or small area. For example, the BlackBerry system shown in Figure 13.2 consists of devices that send and receive transmissions on the **wireless wide area networks (WWANs)** of more than 100 service providers—such as Cellular One (United States), T-Mobile (United Kingdom and United States), and Vodafone (Italy)—in countries throughout the world. The wireless format that the system relies on to control wireless messaging is supplied by Research in Motion (RIM), the company that makes the BlackBerry, and is

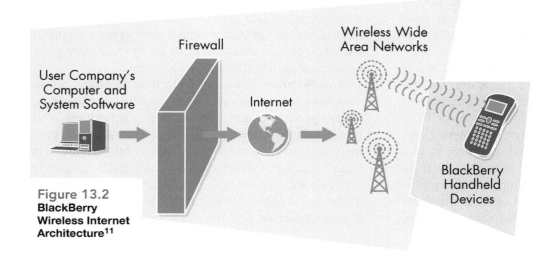

Figure 13.2
BlackBerry Wireless Internet Architecture[11]

WI-FI technology using a wireless local area network

WIRELESS LOCAL AREA NETWORK local area network with wireless access points for PC users

HARDWARE physical components of a computer network, such as keyboards, monitors, system units, and printers

installed on the user-company's computer. A *firewall* provides privacy protection. We'll discuss firewalls in more detail later in the chapter.

Wi-Fi You've no doubt heard of "hotspots"—more than 25,000 U.S. locations, such as coffee shops, hotels, and airports that provide wireless Internet connections for people on the go. Each hotspot, or **Wi-Fi** (a play on audio recording term Hi-Fi) access point, uses its own small network, called a **wireless local area network (wireless LAN or WLAN)**. Although wireless service is free at some hotspots, others charge a fee—a daily or hourly rate—for the convenience of Wi-Fi service.

The benefit of Wi-Fi is that you're not tethered to a wire for accessing the Internet. Employees can wait for a delayed plane in the airport and still be connected to the Internet through their wireless-enabled laptops. However, as with every technology, Wi-Fi has limitations, including a short range of distance. This means that your laptop's Internet connection can be severed if you move farther than about 300 feet from the hotspot. In addition, thick walls, construction beams, and other obstacles can interfere with the signals sent out by the network. So, while a city may have hundreds of hotspots, your laptop must remain near one to stay connected. *WiMAX (Worldwide Interoperability for Microwave Access)*, the next step in wireless advancements, will improve this distance limitation with its wireless range of 30 miles.

Hardware and Software

Any computer network or system needs **hardware**—the physical components, such as keyboards, monitors, system units, and printers. In addition to the laptops, desktop computers, and BlackBerrys mentioned earlier, *handheld computers* are also used often in businesses. For example, Target employees roam the store aisles using handhelds to identify, count, and order items; track deliveries; and

Apple's latest iPhone includes a rotation feature with a larger keyboard, and it downloads movies, TV shows, and audiobooks from the iTunes store. In addition to capturing voice memos, it has applications for cutting, copying, and pasting text and Web images.

update backup stock at distribution centers to keep store shelves replenished with merchandise.

The other essential in any computer system is **software**: programs that tell the computer how to function. Software includes *system software*, such as Microsoft Windows Vista for PCs, which tells the computer's hardware how to interact with the software, what resources to use, and how to use them. It also includes *application software*, such as Microsoft Excel and Adobe Photoshop, which are programs that meet the needs of specific users. Some application programs are used to address such common, long-standing needs as database management and inventory control, whereas others have been developed for a variety of specialized tasks ranging from mapping the underground structure of oil fields to analyzing the anatomical structure of the human body.

Finally *groupware*—software that connects group members for e-mail distribution, electronic meetings, message storing, appointments and schedules, and group writing—allows people to collaborate from their own desktop PCs, even if they're remotely located. It is especially useful when people work together regularly and rely heavily on information sharing. Groupware systems include IBM Lotus Domino, Microsoft Exchange Server, and Novell GroupWise.

Managing in Turbulent Times

When Cash Gets Scarce, Businesses Switch to Internet Bartering

For many companies, the economic downturn involves tighter credit, a drop in sales revenues, and a shortage of cash for doing business. Without cash and credit, companies can't buy the materials, services, and supplies needed to produce products for customers, so business prospects grow even dimmer. Or do they? Enter an unexpected liberator—bartering. This ancient trade practice survives even today, but in an Internet-enhanced form with global reach and instantaneous access to a vast network of swap agreements. And best of all, it can be done without cash: For example, Firm A provides an advertising program for Firm B that, in return, has vacant building space needed by Firm A. Thus, the needs of both are met, and a cashless swap is born. As the recession has deepened, the popularity of bartering is booming. Craigslist.org, the free online classified ad service, reports a 100 percent increase in barter traffic for 2009 compared to 2008. Activity has tripled at U-Exchange.com, where its "Barter 101" gets you started, and you can barter as much as you like at no cost. Overall, the electronically based barter business has grown to a $600 billion industry.[12]

Whether it's B2B or business-to-consumer, online bartering is an efficient way around the recession's credit crunch because it enables companies and individuals to get goods and services without using cash. Restaurants, for example, can trade meals or catering for advertising or for cooking equipment. Bartering can also be a good way to move excessive inventory and get needed benefits in return. An unemployed electrician bartered with homeowners who needed electrical wiring; in return, the homeowners gave up unneeded furniture and laptops that the electrician later sold to make mortgage payments.

For avid swappers of services, Web sites such as People TradingServices.com make it easy for small business owners to find barter matchups with hundreds of kinds of services, ranging from gardeners to songwriters to clergy. As a barter matchmaker, PeopleTradingServices.com posts members' profiles, lists services they trade, and provides a convenient way to contact member professionals online. Along with endless trading possibilities, the cash conservation can be a life-saver for any cash-strapped small business during troubled times.[13]

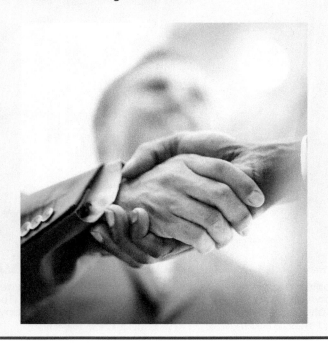

Information Systems: Harnessing the Competitive Power of IT

Business today relies on information management in ways that no one could foresee a decade ago. Managers now treat IT as a basic organizational resource for conducting daily business. At major firms, every activity—designing services, ensuring product delivery and cash flow, and evaluating personnel—is linked to *information systems*. An **information system (IS)** is a system that uses IT resources and enables managers to take **data**—raw facts and figures that, by themselves, may not have much meaning—and turn that data into **information**—the meaningful, useful interpretation of data. Information systems also enable managers to collect, process, and transmit that information for use in decision making.

One company well-known for its strategic use of information systems is Wal-Mart. The nerve center for company operations is a centralized IS in Bentonville, Arkansas. The IS drives costs down and raises efficiency because the same methods and systems are applied for all 5,000-plus stores in Europe, Asia, and the Americas. Data on the billions of sales transactions—time, date, and place—flows to Bentonville. The information system tracks nearly 700 million stock-keeping units (SKUs) weekly, enforces uniform reordering and delivery procedures for more than 30,000 suppliers, and regulates the flow of merchandise through its distribution centers and stores.

Beyond the firm's daily operations, information systems are also crucial in planning. Managers routinely use the IS to decide on products and markets for the next 5 to 10 years. The company's vast database enables marketing managers to analyze demographics, and it is also used for financial planning, materials handling, and electronic funds transfers with suppliers and customers.

Wal-Mart, like most businesses, regards its information as a private resource—an asset that's planned, developed, and protected. Therefore, it's not surprising that they have **information systems managers** who operate the systems used for gathering, organizing, and distributing information, just as they have production, marketing, and finance managers. These managers use many of the IT resources we discussed earlier—the Internet, communications technologies, networks, hardware, and software—to sift through information and apply it to their jobs.

Leveraging Information Resources: Data Warehousing and Data Mining

Almost everything you do leaves a trail of information about you. Your preferences in movie rentals, television viewing, Internet sites, and groceries; the destinations of your phone calls, your credit card charges, your financial status; personal information about age, gender, marital status, and even your health are just a few of the items about each of us that are stored in scattered databases. The behavior patterns of millions of users can be traced by analyzing files of information gathered over time from their Internet usage and in-store purchases.

The collection, storage, and retrieval of such data in electronic files is called **data warehousing**. For managers, the data warehouse is a goldmine of information about their business. Indeed, Kroger Co., the Ohio-based grocery chain, collects data on customer shopping

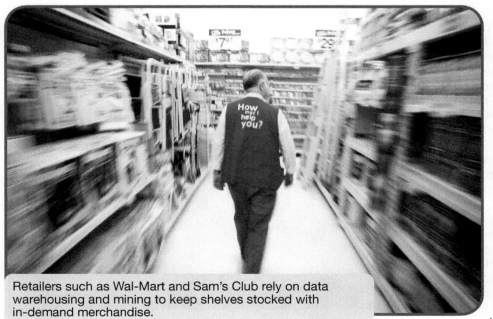

Retailers such as Wal-Mart and Sam's Club rely on data warehousing and mining to keep shelves stocked with in-demand merchandise.

INFORMATION SYSTEM (IS) system that uses IT resources to convert data into information and to collect, process, and transmit that information for use in decision making

DATA raw facts and figures that, by themselves, may not have much meaning

INFORMATION meaningful, useful interpretation of data

INFORMATION SYSTEMS MANAGERS managers who operate the systems used for gathering, organizing, and distributing information

DATA WAREHOUSING the collection, storage, and retrieval of data in electronic files

DATA MINING the application of electronic technologies for searching, sifting, and reorganizing pools of data to uncover useful information

habits to find ways to gain greater customer loyalty. As part owner of a data-mining firm, Kroger accumulates information from its shopper cards, analyzes the data to uncover shopping patterns, and sends money-saving coupons to regular customers for the specific products they usually buy. Kroger's precision targeting pays off, especially in the recession economy. With a rate of coupon usage up to as much as 50 times the industry average, it's a money-saver for Kroger customers and boosts the company's sales, too.[14]

Data Mining After collecting information, managers use **data mining**—the application of electronic technologies for searching, sifting, and reorganizing pools of data to uncover useful information. Data mining helps managers plan for new products, set prices, and identify trends and

shopping patterns. By analyzing what consumers actually do, businesses can determine what subsequent purchases they are likely to make and then send them tailor-made ads. The *Washington Post*, for example, uses data-mining software to analyze census data and target households likely to respond to sales efforts.[15]

Information Linkages with Suppliers The top priority for Wal-Mart's IS—improving in-stock reliability—requires integration of Wal-Mart's and suppliers' activities with store sales. That's why P&G, Johnson & Johnson, and other suppliers connect into Wal-Mart's information system to observe up-to-the-minute sales data on individual items, by store. They can use the system's computer-based tools—spreadsheets, sales forecasting, and weather information—to forecast sales demand and plan delivery schedules. Coordinated planning avoids excessive inventories, speeds up deliveries, and holds down costs throughout the supply chain while keeping shelves stocked for retail customers.

Entrepreneurship and New Ventures

LaidOffCamp: Silver Lining in a Stormy Recession?

Chris Hutchins is not an ordinary Gen Y entrepreneur; he's a self-described technology enthusiast, a results-oriented team player, and an avid rock climber with seemingly endless ideas for sharing the latest trends in technology for applications in business strategy, marketing, finance, and social networking. Hutchins was laid off in December 2008, one month after being reassigned from New York to San Francisco as a business strategy consultant. Like thousands of other young, bright professionals, Hutchins turned to the Internet as a source for reemployment. Unlike others, however, he grasped a positive side to massive unemployment, seeing both a need and an opportunity for mutual assistance, professional growth, and encouragement among the talented unemployed. He decided to build an organization to connect other people who were out of work. Thus was born LaidOffCamp, launched in February 2009 as a gathering ". . . of unemployed and nontraditionally employed people (. . . including entrepreneurs and startups), who want to share ideas and learn from each other."[16]

The camps—informal local gatherings—started in San Francisco; they quickly spread nationwide to Dallas, Los Angeles, New York, Miami, and other U.S. cities. Each location is self-organized, usually by people connected via social networking sites, including LinkedIn, Facebook, and Twitter. The LaidOffCamp Web site lists steps for organizing a camp, including venue selection, job fairs, creating a home page, and other start-up details. Attendees decide which topics should be presented, from job seeking, to personal budgeting, to starting a business. LaidOffCamp's

Web site gets open participation by encouraging all users to edit the LaidOffCamp wiki as they see fit.[17]

LaidOffCamp became an instant smash hit on the Internet, aided by massive buzz on popular social networking sites, even before the date and venue for the first camp were known. One report noted, "On Twitter, some users informally proclaimed LaidOffCamp to be 'the biggest *retweet* of the day.'"[18]

In addition to having founded LaidOffCamp, Hutchins is also co-founder of three Internet-based start-ups. Although he doesn't expect LaidOffCamp to be an immediate money-maker, Hutchins is confident it puts him at the leading edge for a new yet-to-be-developed venture with future returns.

Types of Information Systems

Employees have a variety of responsibilities and decision-making needs, and a firm's *information system* may actually be a set of several systems that share information while serving different levels of the organization, different departments, or different operations. Because they work on different kinds of problems, managers and their employees have access to the specialized information systems that satisfy their different information needs.

In addition to different types of users, each business *function*—marketing, human resources, accounting, production, or finance—has its own information needs, as do groups working on major projects. Each user group and department, therefore, may need a special IS.

Information Systems for Knowledge Workers As we discussed in Chapter 10, *knowledge workers* are employees for whom information and knowledge are the raw materials of their work, such as engineers, scientists, and IT specialists who rely on IT to design new products or create new processes. These workers require **knowledge information systems**, which provide resources to create, store, use, and transmit new knowledge for useful applications—for instance, databases to organize and retrieve information, and computational power for data analysis.

Specialized support systems have also increased the productivity of knowledge workers. **Computer-aided design (CAD)** helps knowledge workers—and now ordinary people too, as we saw at the beginning of this chapter—design products ranging from cell phones to jewelry to auto parts by simulating them and displaying them in 3-D graphics. The older method—making handcrafted prototypes from wood, plastic, or clay—is replaced with faster, cheaper prototyping: the CAD system electronically transfers instructions to a computer-controlled machine that builds the prototypes.

In archaeology, CAD is helping scientists uncover secrets hidden in fossils using 3-D computer models of skeletons, organs, and tissues constructed with digital data from CT (computed tomography) scans of dinosaur fossils. From these models, scientists have learned, for example, that the giant apatosaurus's neck curved downward, instead of high in the air as once thought. By seeing how the animals' bones fit together with cartilage, ligaments, and vertebrae, scientists are discovering more about how these prehistoric creatures interacted with their environment.[19]

Information Systems for Managers Each manager's information activities and IS needs vary according to his or her functional area (accounting or marketing and so forth) and management level. The following are some popular information systems used by managers for different purposes.

Management Information Systems Management information systems (MIS) support managers by providing reports, schedules, plans, and budgets that can then be used for making decisions, both short- and long-term. For example, at Walsworth Publishing Company, managers rely on detailed information—current customer orders, staffing schedules, employee attendance, production schedules, equipment status, and materials availability—for moment-to-moment decisions during the day. They require similar information to plan such mid-range activities as personnel training, materials movements, and cash flows. They also need to anticipate the status of the jobs and projects assigned to their departments. Many MIS—cash flow, sales, production scheduling, and shipping—are indispensable for helping managers complete these tasks.

For longer-range decisions involving business strategy, Walsworth managers need information to analyze trends in the publishing industry and overall company performance. They need both external and internal information, current and future, to compare current performance data to data from previous years and to analyze consumer trends and economic forecasts.

KNOWLEDGE INFORMATION SYSTEM information system that supports knowledge workers by providing resources to create, store, use, and transmit new knowledge for useful applications

COMPUTER-AIDED DESIGN (CAD) IS with software that helps knowledge workers design products by simulating them and displaying them in three-dimensional graphics

MANAGEMENT INFORMATION SYSTEM (MIS) computer system that supports managers by providing information—reports, schedules, plans, and budgets—that can be used for making decisions

The 3-D computer model of this dinosaur is constructed from digital scans of fossilized tissue.

Decision Support Systems
Managers who face a particular kind of decision repeatedly can get assistance from **decision support systems (DSS)**—interactive systems that create virtual business models and test them with different data to see how they respond. When faced with decisions on plant capacity, for example, Walsworth managers can use a capacity DSS. The manager inputs data on anticipated sales, working capital, and customer-delivery requirements. The data flow into the DSS processor, which then simulates the plant's performance under the proposed data conditions. After experimenting with various data conditions, the DSS makes recommendations on the best levels of plant capacity for each future time period.

IT Risks and Threats

As with other technologies throughout history, IT has attracted abusers set on doing mischief, with severity ranging from mere nuisance to outright destruction. Eager IT users everywhere are finding that even social networking and cell phones have a "dark side"—privacy invasion. Facebook postings of personal information about users can be intercepted and misused by intruders.

Beacon caused a public uproar when it published peoples' online purchases publicly on their Facebook newsfeeds. And with cellular technology, some features of Bluetooth connections allow savvy intruders to read a victim's text messages, listen in on live conversations, and even view unwary users' photos.[20]

Businesses, too, are troubled with IT's "dark side." Hackers break into computers, stealing personal information and company secrets, and launching attacks on other computers. Meanwhile, the ease of information sharing on the Internet has proven costly for companies who are having an increasingly difficult time protecting their intellectual property, and viruses that crash computers have cost companies millions. In this section, we'll look at these and other IT risks. In the next section, we'll discuss ways in which businesses are protecting themselves from these risks.

Hackers

Breaking and entering no longer refers merely to physical intrusion. Today, it applies to IT intrusions as well. **Hackers** are cybercriminals who gain unauthorized access to a computer or network, either to steal information, money, or property or to tamper with data. Another common hacker activity is to launch *denial of service (DoS) attacks*. DoS attacks flood networks or Web sites with bogus requests for information and resources, thereby shutting the networks or Web sites down and preventing legitimate users from accessing them.

Wireless mooching is a profitable industry for cybercriminals. In just five minutes, a *St. Petersburg Times* (Florida) reporter using a laptop found six unprotected wireless networks that were wide open to outside users.[21] Once inside

Of Pirates and Profits

Hackers often break into company networks to steal company or trade secrets. But it's not just hackers who are doing the stealing. Because the chances of getting caught seem slim, home users continue, illegally, to download unpaid-for movies, music, and other resources from file-swapping networks. A recent study shows that sound piracy costs the United States $12.5 billion and 71,060 jobs annually. However, these losses also showcase what can happen to businesses who fail to adapt to changes in technology. The recording industry has been reluctant to embrace the Internet as a path for distribution, preferring to prosecute pirates rather than offer them legal online alternatives. On the other hand, Apple has benefitted immensely from its online distribution models, with over 6 billion songs sold—some analysts predict that by 2012 Apple's iTunes music store will account for 28% of all music sold throughout the world.[22]

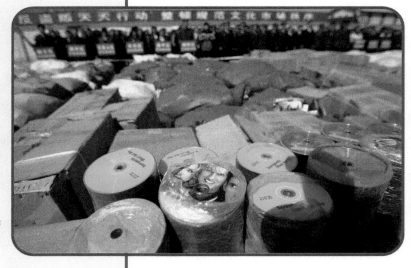

an unsecured wireless network, hackers use it to commit identity theft and to steal credit card numbers, among other things. When police officers try to track down these criminals, they're long gone, leaving you, the network host, exposed to criminal prosecution.

Identity Theft

Once inside a computer network, hackers are able to commit **identity theft**, the unauthorized stealing of personal information (such as Social Security number and address) to get loans, credit cards, or other monetary benefits by impersonating the victim.

Not all identity theft is committed by hackers, though. Clever crooks get information on unsuspecting victims by digging in trash, stealing mail, or using *phishing* or *pharming* schemes to lure Internet users to bogus Web sites. For instance, a cybercriminal might send an American Online subscriber an e-mail notifying him or her of a billing problem with his or her account. When the customer clicks on the AOL Billing Center link, he or she is transferred to a spoofed (falsified) Web page, modeled after AOL's. The customer then submits the requested information—credit card number, Social Security number, and PIN—into the hands of the thief.

Intellectual Property Theft

Nearly every company faces the dilemma of protecting product plans, new inventions, industrial processes, and other **intellectual property**: something produced by the intellect or mind that has commercial value. Its ownership and right to its use may be protected by patent, copyright, trademark, and other means.

Computer Viruses, Worms, and Trojan Horses

Another IT risk facing businesses is rogue programmers who disrupt IT operations by contaminating and destroying software, hardware, or data files. Viruses, worms, and Trojan horses are three kinds of malicious programs that, once installed, can shut down any computer system. A *computer virus* exists in a file that attaches itself to a program and migrates from computer to computer as a shared program or as an e-mail attachment. It does not infect the system unless the user opens the contaminated file, and users typically are unaware they are spreading the virus by file sharing. It can, for example, quickly copy itself over and over again, using up all available memory and effectively shutting down the computer.

Worms are a particular kind of virus that travel from computer to computer within networked computer systems, without your needing to open any software to spread the contaminated file. In a matter of days,

the notorious Blaster worm infected some 400,000 computer networks, destroying files and even allowing outsiders to take over computers remotely. The worm replicates itself rapidly, sending out thousands of copies to other computers in the network. Traveling through Internet connections and e-mail address books in the network's computers, it absorbs system memory and shuts down network servers, Web servers, and individual computers.

Unlike viruses, a *Trojan horse* does not replicate itself. Instead, it most often comes into the computer, at your request, masquerading as a harmless, legitimate software product or data file. Once installed, the damage begins. For instance, it may simply redesign desktop icons or, more maliciously, delete files and destroy information.

Spyware

As if forced intrusion isn't bad enough, Internet users unwittingly invite spies—masquerading as a friendly file available as a giveaway or shared among individual users on their PCs. This so-called **spyware** is downloaded by users that are lured by "free" software. Once installed, it crawls around to monitor the host's computer activities, gathering e-mail addresses, credit card numbers, passwords, and other inside information that it transmits back to someone outside the host system. Spyware authors assemble incoming stolen information to create their own "intellectual property" that they then sell to other parties to use for marketing and advertising purposes or for identity theft.[23]

Spam

Spam—junk e-mail sent to a mailing list or a newsgroup (an online discussion group)—is a greater nuisance than postal junk mail because the Internet is open to the public, e-mail costs are negligible, and massive mailing lists are accessible through file sharing or by theft. Spam operators send unwanted messages ranging from explicit pornography to hate mail to advertisements, and even destructive computer viruses. In addition to wasting users' time, spam also consumes a network's bandwidth, thereby reducing the amount of data that can be transmitted in a fixed amount of time

IDENTITY THEFT
unauthorized use of personal information (such as Social Security number and address) to get loans, credit cards, or other monetary benefits by impersonating the victim

INTELLECTUAL PROPERTY something produced by the intellect or mind that has commercial value

SPYWARE program unknowingly downloaded by users that monitors their computer activities, gathering e-mail addresses, credit card numbers, and other information that it transmits to someone outside the host system

SPAM junk e-mail sent to a mailing list or a newsgroup

for useful purposes. U.S. industry experts estimate spam's damage in lost time and productivity at more than $140 billion worldwide in 2008 alone.[24]

IT Protection Measures

Security measures against intrusion and viruses are a constant challenge. Most systems guard against unauthorized access by requiring users to have protected passwords. Other measures include firewalls, special software, and encryption.

Preventing Unauthorized Access: Firewalls

Firewalls are security systems with special software or hardware devices designed to keep computers safe from hackers. A firewall is located where two networks—for example, the Internet and a company's internal network—meet. It contains two components for filtering each incoming data:

■ The company's *security policy*—Access rules that identify every type of data that the company doesn't want to pass through the firewall.

■ A *router*—A table of available routes or paths; a "traffic switch" that determines which route or path on the network to send each piece of data after it is tested against the security policy.

Only that information that meet the conditions of the user's security policy is routed through the firewall and permitted to flow between the two networks. Data that fail the access test are blocked and cannot flow between the two networks.

Preventing Identity Theft

While foolproof prevention is impossible, steps can be taken to avoid being victimized. A visit to the Identity Theft Resource Center (http://www.idtheftcenter.org) is a valuable first step to get information on everything from scam alerts to victim issues to legislation such as the Fair and Accurate Credit Transactions Act (FACTA). FACTA,

which took effect in 2005, strengthens identity-theft protections by specifying how organizations must destroy information instead of dropping it in a dumpster. When a company disposes of documents that contain credit or Social Security information, they must be shredded, pulverized, or burned, and all electronic records (in computers and databases) must be permanently removed to keep them out of the hands of intruders.[25]

Preventing Viruses: Anti-Virus Software

Combating viruses, worms, and Trojan horses has become a major industry for systems designers and software developers. Installation of any of hundreds of **anti-virus software** products protects systems by searching incoming e-mail and data files for "signatures" of known viruses and virus-like characteristics. Contaminated files are discarded or placed in quarantine for safekeeping.

Many viruses take advantage of weaknesses in operating systems, such as Microsoft Windows, in order to spread and propagate. Network administrators must make sure that the computers on their systems are using the most up-to-date operating system that includes the latest security protection.

Protecting Electronic Communications: Encryption Software

Security for electronic communications is another concern for businesses. Unprotected e-mail can be intercepted, diverted to unintended computers, and opened, revealing the contents to intruders. Protective software is available to guard against those intrusions, adding a layer of security by encoding e-mails so that only intended recipients can open them. An **encryption system** works by scrambling an e-mail message so that it looks like garbled nonsense to anyone who doesn't possess the key.

Avoiding Spam and Spyware

To help their employees avoid privacy invasion and to improve productivity, businesses often install anti-spyware and spam-filtering software on their systems. While dozens of anti-spyware products provide protection—software such as Webroot Spy Sweeper and Microsoft Windows Defender—they must be continually updated to keep pace with new spyware techniques.

The federal CAN-SPAM Act of 2003 requires the Federal Trade Commission to shield the public from falsified header information, sexually explicit e-mails that are not so labeled, Internet spoofing (using trickery to make a message appear as if it came from a trusted source), and hijacking of computers through worms or Trojan horses. While it cannot be prevented entirely, spam is abated by many Internet service providers (ISPs) that ban the spamming of ISP subscribers. In a now-classic punishment, an ISP in Iowa was awarded $1 billion in a lawsuit against 300 spammers that jammed the ISP system with an astounding 10 million e-mails a day. Anti-spam groups, too, promote the public's awareness of known spammers. The Spamhaus Project (http://www.spamhaus.org), for example, maintains a list—the Register of Known Spam Operators (ROKSO)—of over 100 professional spammers that are responsible for over 80 percent of spam traffic in North America and Europe.

Questions for Review

1 Why must a business manage information as a resource?

2 How can electronic conferencing increase a company's productivity and efficiency?

3 Why do different users in an organization need different kinds of information from the information system?

4 Why has the BlackBerry become a popular tool among business people?

5 What is the definition of *intellectual property*? List three examples of intellectual property.

Questions for Analysis

6 Describe how a company might use data warehousing and data mining in its information system to better plan for new products.

7 Aside from the eBay example in this chapter, describe one or more ways that IT presents new business opportunities for small businesses.

8 Give three examples (other than those in this chapter) of how a company can become leaner and more efficient by adopting IT.

Application Exercises

9 Consider your daily activities—as a consumer, student, parent, friend, homeowner or renter, car driver, employee, etc.—and think about the ways that you are involved in transactions with IT systems. Make a list of your recent IT encounters and then recall instances in those encounters that you revealed personal information that could be used to steal your identity. Are some encounters on your list riskier than others? Why or why not?

10 Describe the computer network at your school. Identify its components and system architecture. What features either promote or inhibit intrusions from hackers? What features either promote or inhibit intellectual property theft? What features either promote or inhibit computer viruses and spam?

14 chapter

The Role of Accountants and Accounting Information

After reading this chapter, you should be able to:

1 Explain the role of accountants and distinguish between the kinds of work done by public accountants, private accountants, management accountants, and forensic accountants.

2 Explain how the accounting equation is used.

3 Describe the three basic financial statements and show how they reflect the activity and financial condition of a business.

4 Explain the key standards and principles for reporting financial statements.

5 Describe how computing financial ratios can help users get more information from financial statements to determine the financial strengths of a business.

6 Discuss the role of ethics in accounting.

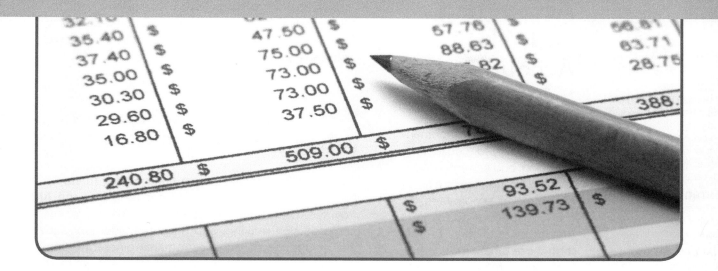

CSI: Wall Street

In the aftermath of major accounting scandals, such as the infamous $65 billion Bernard Madoff Ponzi scheme, many companies are showing an urgent interest in the field of forensic accounting: the use of accounting for legal purposes. The expansion of the forensic accounting field—the Association of Certified Fraud Examiners (ACFE) has experienced a surging membership, reaching 50,000 professionals in 2009—is due to increased vigilance as a result of recent scandals, as well as a strong desire on the part of companies to protect themselves from accounting fraud.

Fraud examiners typically begin an investigation of a company by interviewing high-level executives. Team members pursue tips from employees or outsiders, then comb through e-mails, searching for suspicious words and phrases. The combination of interviews and e-mails may lead investigators to specific accounting files or ledger entries. According to Al Vondra, a Certified Fraud Examiner at PricewaterhouseCoopers, some of the most common fraudulent practices involve hiding revenues and expenses under phony categories such as "Total Noncurrent Assets" or "Other Current Liabilities." At India's Satyam Computer Services Ltd., for example, founder and former CEO Ramalinga Raju is under arrest after admitting he falsified accounts, thus deceiving investors for years. The government's Serious Fraud Investigation Office is searching to identify collaborators who falsely reported more than $1 billion in cash and assets that didn't exist at India's fourth largest software company.[1]

Although accounting scandals have always existed, they spike upward in economic recessions. Data from the ACFE indicate that corporate fraud cases began increasing significantly early in the current recession, reaching an estimated $994 billion in 2008. Fraud-related reports and whistle-blowing at U.S. firms jumped dramatically in early 2009. ACFE members believe the increase stems from heavier financial pressures: When employees feel less secure, they may falsify data to show better performance, or they may take greater risks that need to be covered up to show financial success. Forensic accounting professor Tommie Singleton states, "The cases of fraud will only climb as the country sinks into recession, and with that so will the demand for highly skilled, specialized forensic accountants to help prevent, detect and prosecute those looking to cheat the system."[2]

What's in It for Me?

For most of us, the words and ideas in accounting can seem like a foreign language. As we have seen, the specialized terminology can be used to mask fraud and corruption. However, it's also a necessary tool that allows professionals in every industry to analyze growth, understand risk, and communicate complex ideas about a firm's financial health. This chapter will cover the fundamental concepts of accounting and apply them to familiar business situations. By grasping the basic accounting vocabulary you will be able to participate when the conversation turns to the financial matters that constitute so great a part of a firm's daily operations.

What Is Accounting, and Who Uses Accounting Information?

Accounting is a comprehensive system for collecting, analyzing, and communicating financial information to a firm's owners and employees, to the public, and to various regulatory agencies. To perform these functions, accountants keep records of taxes paid, income received, and expenses incurred—a process called **bookkeeping**—and they assess the effects of these transactions on business activities.

Because businesses engage in thousands of transactions, ensuring consistent, dependable financial information is mandatory. This is the job of the **accounting information system (AIS)**—an organized procedure for identifying, measuring, recording, and retaining financial information so that it can be used in accounting statements and management reports. The system includes all of the people, reports, computers, procedures, and resources that are needed to compile financial transactions.[3]

Users of accounting information are numerous:

- *Business managers* use it to develop goals and plans, set budgets, and evaluate future prospects.

- *Employees and unions* use it to plan for and receive compensation and such benefits as health care, vacation time, and retirement pay.

- *Investors and creditors* use it to estimate returns to stockholders, determine growth prospects, and decide whether a firm is a good credit risk.

- *Tax authorities* use it to plan for tax inflows, determine the tax liabilities of individuals and businesses, and ensure that correct amounts are paid on time.

- *Government regulatory agencies* rely on it to fulfill their duties toward the public. The Securities and Exchange Commission (SEC), for example, requires firms to file financial disclosures so that potential investors have valid information about their financial status.

Who Are Accountants and What Do They Do?

The **controller**, or chief accounting officer, manages a firm's accounting activities by ensuring that the AIS provides the reports and statements needed for planning, decision making, and other management activities. This range of activities requires different types of accounting specialists. In this section, we begin by distinguishing between the two main fields of accounting: *financial* and *managerial*. Then, we discuss the different functions and activities of *certified public accountants*, *private accountants*, *management accountants*, and *forensic accountants*.

Financial Versus Managerial Accounting

In any company, the two fields of accounting—financial and managerial—can be distinguished by the users they serve: those outside the company and those within.[4]

Financial Accounting A firm's **financial accounting** system is concerned with external information users: consumer groups, unions, stockholders, suppliers, creditors, and government agencies. It prepares reports such as income statements and balance sheets that focus on the activities of the company as a whole rather than on individual departments or divisions.[5]

Managerial Accounting **Managerial (management) accounting** serves internal users. Managers at all levels need information to make departmental decisions, monitor projects, and plan future activities. Other employees also need accounting information. To set performance goals, for example, salespeople need past sales data organized by geographic region.

Certified Public Accountants

Certified public accountants (CPAs) offer accounting services to the public. They are licensed by a state after passing an exam prepared by the American Institute of Certified Public Accountants (AICPA), which also provides technical support and discipline in matters of ethics. Whereas some CPAs work as individual

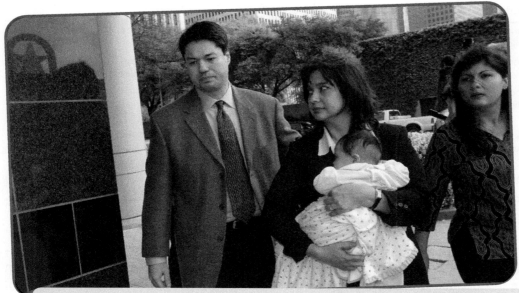

Sometimes, companies ignore GAAP and accountants fail to disclose violations. Jamie Olis (left) was a mid-level executive at Texas-based energy producer Dynegy. To cover up the company's financial difficulties and dodge $79 million in federal taxes, Olis helped devise an accounting scheme to disguise a $300 million loan as cash flow. He was sentenced to 24 years in jail, though the judge later reduced it to six years.

practitioners, many form or join existing partnerships or professional corporations.

CPA Services Virtually all CPA firms, whether large or small, provide auditing, tax, and management services. Larger firms such as Deloitte Touche Tohmatsu and Ernst & Young earn much of their revenue from auditing services, though consulting (management advisory) services constitute a major growth area. Smaller firms earn most of their income from tax and management services.

Auditing An **audit** examines a company's AIS to determine whether financial reports reliably represent its operations.[6] Organizations must provide audit reports when applying for loans, selling stock, or when going through a major restructuring. Independent auditors who do not work for the company must ensure that clients' accounting systems follow **generally accepted accounting principles (GAAP)**, which are formulated by the Financial Accounting Standards Board (FASB) of the AICPA and govern the content and form of financial reports.[7] The Securities and Exchange Commission (SEC) is the U.S. government agency that legally enforces accounting and auditing rules and procedures.

Tax Services **Tax services** include assistance not only with tax-return preparation but also with tax planning. A CPA's advice can help a business structure (or restructure) operations and investments and perhaps

save millions of dollars in taxes. Staying abreast of tax-law changes is no simple matter. Some critics charge that tax changes have become a full-time vocation among some state and federal legislators who add increasingly complicated laws and technical corrections on taxation each year.

Management Advisory Services As consultants, accounting firms provide **management advisory services** ranging from personal financial planning to planning corporate mergers. Other services include production scheduling, computer-feasibility studies, AIS design, and even executive recruitment. The staffs of the largest CPA firms include engineers, architects, mathematicians, and psychologists, all of whom are available for consulting.

Noncertified Public Accountants Many accountants don't take the CPA exam; others work in the field while getting ready for it or while meeting requirements for state certification. Many small businesses, individuals, and even larger firms rely on these noncertified public accountants for income-tax preparation, payroll accounting, and financial-planning services.

The CPA Vision Project The recent talent shortage in accounting has led the profession to rethink its culture and lifestyle.[8] With grassroots participation from CPAs, educators, and industry leaders, the AICPA, through its CPA Vision Project, is redefining the role of

Table 14.1   Core Competencies for Accounting[9]

Strategic and Critical Thinking Skills	The accountant can provide competent advice for strategic action by combining data, knowledge, and insight.
Communications and Leadership Skills	The accountant can exchange information meaningfully in a variety of business situations with effective delivery and interpersonal skills.
Focus on the Customer, Client, and Market	The accountant can meet the changing needs of clients, customers, and employers better than the competition and can anticipate those needs better than competitors.
Skills in Interpreting Converging Information	The accountant can interpret new meaning by combining financial and nonfinancial information into a broader understanding that adds more business value.
Technology Skills	The accountant can use technology to add value to activities performed for employers, customers, and clients.

the accountant for today's world economy. The Vision Project identifies a unique combination of skills, technology, and knowledge—called **core competencies for accounting**—that will be necessary for the future CPA. As Table 14.1 shows, those skills—which include communication, critical thinking, and leadership—go far beyond the ability to "crunch numbers." They include certain communications skills, along with skills in critical thinking and leadership. Indeed, the CPA Vision Project foresees CPAs who combine specialty skills with a broad-based orientation in order to communicate more effectively with people in a wide range of business activities.

Private Accountants and Management Accountants

To ensure integrity in reporting, CPAs are always independent of the firms they audit. However, many businesses also hire their own salaried employees—**private accountants**—to perform day-to-day activities.

Private accountants perform numerous jobs. An internal auditor at ConocoPhillips might fly to the North Sea to confirm the accuracy of oil-flow meters on offshore petroleum drilling platforms. A supervisor responsible for $2 billion in monthly payouts to vendors and employees may never leave the executive suite, with duties such as hiring and training, assigning projects, and evaluating performance of accounting personnel. Large businesses employ specialized accountants in such areas as budgeting, financial planning, internal auditing, payroll, and taxation. In small businesses, a single person may handle all accounting tasks.

Most private accountants are **management accountants** who provide services to support managers in various activities (marketing, production, engineering, and so forth). Many hold the **certified management accountant (CMA)** designation, awarded by the Institute of Management Accountants (IMA), recognizing qualifications of professionals who have passed IMA's experience and examination requirements.

Forensic Accountants

The fastest growing area in accounting is **forensic accounting**—the use of accounting for legal purposes.[10] Forensic accountants may be called upon—by law enforcement agencies, insurance companies, law firms, and business firms—for both investigative accounting and litigation support in crimes against companies, crimes by companies, and civil disagreements. Civil cases often require investigating and quantifying claims of personal injury loss due to negligence and analyzing financial issues in matrimonial disputes. Forensic accountants also assist business firms in tracing and recovering lost assets from employee business fraud or theft.

Investigative Accounting   A forensic accountant may be asked to investigate a trail of financial transactions behind a suspected crime, as in a money-laundering scheme or an investment swindle. Try your hand, for example, at "Catch Me If You Can," the popular interactive forensic accounting game sponsored by the AICPA (at **www.startheregoplaces.com**). The forensic accountant, being familiar with the legal concepts and procedures of the case, identifies and analyzes pertinent financial evidence—documents, bank accounts, phone calls, computer records, and people—and presents accounting conclusions and their legal implications.

Litigation Support   Forensic accountants assist in the application of accounting evidence for judicial proceedings by preparing and preserving evidence for these

Table 14.2 Selected Provisions of the Sarbanes-Oxley Act[11]

- Creates a national Accounting Oversight Board that, among other activities, must establish the ethics standards used by CPA firms in preparing audits.
- Requires that auditors retain audit working papers for specified periods of time.
- Requires auditor rotation by prohibiting the same person from being the lead auditor for more than five consecutive years.
- Requires that the CEO and CFO certify that the company's financial statements are true, fair, and accurate.
- Prohibits corporations from extending personal loans to executives and directors.
- Requires that the audited company disclose whether it has adopted a code of ethics for its senior financial officers.
- Requires that the SEC regularly review each corporation's financial statements.
- Prevents employers from retaliating against research analysts that write negative reports.
- Imposes criminal penalties on auditors and clients for falsifying, destroying, altering, or concealing records (10 years in prison).
- Imposes a fine or imprisonment (up to 25 years) on any person that defrauds shareholders.
- Increases penalties for mail and wire fraud from 5 to 20 years in prison.
- Establishes criminal liability for failure of corporate officers to certify financial reports.

CERTIFIED FRAUD EXAMINER (CFE) professional designation administered by the Association of Certified Fraud Examiners in recognition of qualifications for a specialty area within forensic accounting

SARBANES-OXLEY ACT OF 2002 (SARBOX) enactment of federal regulations to restore public trust in accounting practices by imposing new requirements on financial activities in publicly traded corporations

ACCOUNTING EQUATION Assets = Liabilities + Owners' Equity; used by accountants to balance data for the firm's financial transactions at various points in the year

proceedings. They also assist by presenting visual aids to support trial evidence, by testifying as expert witnesses, and, especially, in determining economic damages in any case before the court.

Certified Fraud Examiners The **Certified Fraud Examiner (CFE)** designation, administered by the Association of Certified Fraud Examiners, is awarded to those with expertise in fraud-related issues and investigations. Many CFEs, like Al Vondra from our opening story, find employment in corporations seeking to prevent fraud from within. The CFE examination covers four areas:

1 Criminology and ethics. Includes theories of fraud prevention and ethical situations

2 Financial transactions. Examines types of fraudulent financial transactions incurred in accounting records

3 Fraud investigation. Pertains to tracing illicit transactions, evaluating deception, and interviewing and taking statements

4 Legal elements of fraud. Includes rules of evidence, criminal and civil law, and rights of the accused and accuser

Federal Restrictions on CPA Services and Financial Reporting: Sarbox

The financial wrongdoings associated with firms such as ImClone Systems, Tyco, WorldCom, Enron, Arthur Andersen, and others have not gone unnoticed in legislative circles. Federal regulations, in particular the **Sarbanes-Oxley Act of 2002** (**Sarbox** or **SOX**),

have been enacted to restore public trust in corporate accounting practices.

Sarbox restricts the kinds of nonaudit services that CPAs can provide. Under the new law, for example, a CPA firm cannot help design a client's financial information system if it also does the client's auditing. By prohibiting CPAs from providing auditing and nonauditing services to the same client, Sarbox encourages audits that are independent and unbiased.

Sarbox Compliance Requirements Sarbox imposes new requirements on virtually every financial activity in publicly traded corporations, as well as severe criminal penalties for persons committing or concealing fraud or destroying financial records. Table 14.2 provides brief descriptions of several of Sarbox's many provisions.

The Accounting Equation

All accountants rely on record keeping to enter and track transactions. Underlying all record-keeping procedures is the most basic tool of accounting—the **accounting equation**:

$$\boxed{\text{Assets} = \text{Liabilities} + \text{Owners' Equity}}$$

After each financial transaction (e.g., payments to suppliers, sales to customers, wages to employees), the accounting equation must be in balance. If it isn't, then an accounting error has occurred. To better understand

ASSET any economic resource expected to benefit a firm or an individual who owns it

LIABILITY debt owed by a firm to an outside organization or individual

OWNERS' EQUITY amount of money that owners would receive if they sold all of a firm's assets and paid all of its liabilities

FINANCIAL STATEMENT any of several types of reports summarizing a company's financial status to stakeholders and to aid in managerial decision making

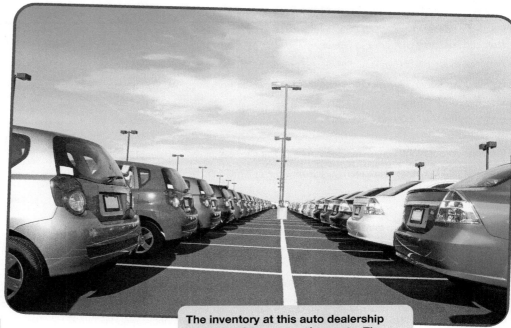

The inventory at this auto dealership is among the company's assets: The cars constitute an economic resource because the firm will benefit financially as it sells them.

the importance of this equation, we must understand the terms *assets*, *liabilities*, and *owners' equity*.

Assets and Liabilities An **asset** is any economic resource that is expected to benefit a firm or an individual who owns it. Assets include land, buildings, equipment, inventories, and payments due the company (accounts receivable). Google, the Internet search and information provider, for example, held assets amounting to $31.768 billion at year-end 2008.[12]

A **liability** is a debt that a firm owes to an outside party. The total of Google's liabilities—all the debt owed to others—was $3.529 billion at the end of 2008.

Owners' Equity **Owners' equity** is the amount of money that owners would receive if they sold all of a company's assets and paid all of its liabilities. Google's financial reports for 2008 declared shareholders' equity of $28.239 billion. For the Google example, we see that the accounting equation is in balance, as it should be.

> Assets = Liabilities + Owners' Equity
> $31.768 = $3.529 + $28.239 billion

We can rewrite the equation to highlight how owners' equity relates to assets and liabilities.

> Assets − Liabilities = Owners' Equity

Another term for this is *net worth*: the difference between what a firm owns (assets) minus what it owes (liabilities) is its net worth, or owners' equity. If a company's assets exceed its liabilities, owners' equity is

positive. If the company goes out of business, the owners will receive some cash (a gain) after selling assets and paying off liabilities. If liabilities outweigh assets, owners' equity is *negative*; assets are insufficient to pay off all debts, and the firm is bankrupt. If the company goes out of business, the owners will get no cash, and some creditors won't be paid.

Owners' equity is meaningful for both investors and lenders. Before lending money to owners, for example, lenders want to know the amount of owners' equity in a business. A larger owners' equity indicates greater security for lenders. Owners' equity consists of two sources of capital:

1 The amount that the owners originally invested

2 Profits (also owned by the owners) earned by and reinvested in the company

Financial Statements

As noted previously, accountants summarize the results of a firm's transactions and issue reports to help managers make informed decisions. Among the most important reports are **financial statements**, which fall into three broad categories: *balance sheets*, *income statements*, and *statements of cash flows*.

Balance Sheets

Balance sheets supply detailed information about the accounting equation factors: *assets*, *liabilities*, and *owners' equity*. Because they also show a firm's financial condition at one point in time, they are sometimes called *statements of financial position*. Figure 14.1 is a simplified presentation of the balance sheet for Google, Inc.

Assets From an accounting standpoint, most companies have three types of assets: *current*, *fixed*, and *intangible*.

Current Assets **Current assets** include cash and assets that can be converted into cash within a year. The act of converting something into cash is called *liquidating*. Assets are normally listed in order of **liquidity**—the ease of converting them into cash. Debts, for example, are usually paid in cash. A company that needs but cannot generate cash—a company that's not "liquid"—may be forced to sell assets at reduced prices or even to go out of business.

By definition, cash is completely liquid. *Marketable securities* purchased as short-term investments are slightly less liquid but can be sold quickly. These include stocks or bonds of other companies, government securities, and money market certificates. Many companies hold other nonliquid assets such as *merchandise inventory*—the cost of merchandise that's been acquired for sale to customers and is still on hand.

Fixed Assets **Fixed assets** (such as land, buildings, and equipment) have long-term use or value, but as buildings and equipment wear out or become obsolete, their value decreases. Accountants use **depreciation** to spread the cost of an asset over the years of its useful life. To reflect decreasing value, accountants calculate an asset's useful life in years, divide its worth by that many years, and subtract the resulting amount each year. Every year, therefore, the remaining value (or net value) decreases on the books.

Intangible Assets Although their worth is hard to set, **intangible assets** have monetary value in the form of expected benefits, which may include fees paid by others for obtaining rights or privileges—including patents,

BALANCE SHEET financial statement that supplies detailed information about a firm's assets, liabilities, and owners' equity

CURRENT ASSET asset that can or will be converted into cash within a year

LIQUIDITY ease with which an asset can be converted into cash

FIXED ASSET asset with long-term use or value, such as land, buildings, and equipment

DEPRECIATION accounting method for distributing the cost of an asset over its useful life

INTANGIBLE ASSET nonphysical asset, such as a patent or trademark, that has economic value in the form of expected benefit

Figure 14.1
Google's Balance Sheet[13]

Google, Inc.
Summary of Balance Sheet (condensed)
as of December 31, 2008
(in millions)

Assets		Liabilities and Shareholders' Equity	
Current assets:		Current liabilities:	
Cash	$8,656.67	Accounts payable	$178.00
Marketable securities	7,189.10	Other	2,124.09
Other	4,332.41	**Total current liabilities**	**$2,302.09**
Total current assets	**$20,178.18**		
		Long-term liabilities:	
Fixed assets:		All long-term debts	0.00
Property and equipment, net	$5,233.84	Other	1,226.62
Other	519.02	**Total long-term liabilities**	**$1,226.62**
Total fixed assets	**$5,752.86**		
		Total liabilities	**$3,528.71**
Intangible assets:			
Intangible assets	996.69	Shareholders' equity:	
Goodwill	4,839.85	Paid-in capital	$14,677.24
Total intangible assets	**$5,836.54**	Retained earnings	13,561.63
		Total shareholders' equity	**$28,238.87**
Total assets	**$31,767.58**		
		Total liabilities and shareholders' equity	**$31,767.58**

Google's balance sheet for year ended December 31, 2008. The balance sheet shows clearly that the firm's total assets are equal to its total liabilities and owners' equity.

GOODWILL amount paid for an existing business above the value of its other assets

CURRENT LIABILITY debt that must be paid within one year

ACCOUNTS PAYABLE (PAYABLES) current liability consisting of bills owed to suppliers, plus wages and taxes due within the coming year

LONG-TERM LIABILITY debt that is not due for at least one year

PAID-IN CAPITAL money that is invested in a company by its owners

RETAINED EARNINGS earnings retained by a firm for its use rather than paid out as dividends

INCOME STATEMENT (PROFIT-AND-LOSS STATEMENT) financial statement listing a firm's annual revenues and expenses so that a bottom line shows annual profit or loss

REVENUES funds that flow into a business from the sale of goods or services

Figure 14.2
Google's Income Statement[14]

Google, Inc.
Summary of Income Statement (condensed)
as of December 31, 2008
(in millions)

Revenues (gross sales)		$21,795.55
Cost of revenues	8,621.51	
Gross profit		13,174.04
Operating expenses:		
Sales and marketing	1,946.24	
Administrative and general	4,595.83	
Total operating expenses		**$6,542.07**
Operating income (before taxes)		6,631.97
Income taxes*		2,405.11
Net income		**$4,226.86**

*approximated

Google's income statement for year ended December 31, 2008. The final entry on the income statement, the bottom line, reports the firm's profit or loss.

trademarks, copyrights, and franchises—to your products. **Goodwill** is the amount paid for an existing business beyond the value of its other assets. A purchased firm, for example, may have a particularly good reputation or location.

Liabilities Like assets, liabilities are often separated into different categories. **Current liabilities** are debts that must be paid within one year. These include **accounts payable (payables)**—unpaid bills to suppliers for materials as well as wages and taxes that must be paid in the coming year. **Long-term liabilities** are debts that are not due for at least a year. These normally represent borrowed funds on which the company must pay interest.

Owners' Equity The final section of the balance sheet in Figure 14.1 shows owners' equity broken down into *paid-in capital* and *retained earnings*. **Paid-in capital** is money invested by owners, such as purchases of Google's initial public offering of stock in 2004. **Retained earnings** are net profits kept by a firm rather than paid out as dividend payments to stockholders.

The balance sheet for any company, then, is a barometer for its financial condition at one point in time. By comparing the current balance sheet with those of previous years, creditors and owners can better interpret the firm's financial progress and future

prospects in terms of changes in its assets, liabilities, and owners' equity.

Income Statements

The **income statement** is sometimes called a **profit-and-loss statement** because its description of revenues and expenses results in a figure showing the firm's annual profit or loss. In other words,

$$\boxed{\text{Revenues} - \text{Expenses} = \text{Profit (or Loss)}}$$

Popularly known as the *bottom line*, profit or loss is probably the most important figure in any business enterprise. Figure 14.2 shows the 2008 income statement for Google, whose bottom line was $4.23 (rounded) billion. The income statement is divided into four major categories: *revenues*, *cost of revenues*, *operating expenses*, and *net income*. Unlike a balance sheet, which shows the financial condition at a specific *point in time*, an income statement shows the financial results that occurred during a *period of time*, such as a month, quarter, or year.

Revenues When a law firm receives $250 for preparing a will or a supermarket collects $65 from a grocery shopper, both are receiving **revenues**—the funds that flow into a business from the sale of goods or services. In 2008, Google reported revenues of $21.80 (rounded) billion from the sale of advertising and Web-search services to Google Network members, such as AOL.

Cost of Revenues (Cost of Goods Sold) In the Google income statement, the **cost of revenues** section shows the costs of obtaining the revenues from other companies during the year. These are fees Google must pay its network members—revenue sharing from advertising income—and also include expenses arising from the operation of Google's data centers, including labor, energy, and costs of processing customer transactions.

While cost of revenues is a relevant income statement category for service providers like Google, goods producers do not use it. Instead, income statements for manufacturing firms such as Procter & Gamble use the corresponding category, **cost of goods sold**: costs of obtaining materials to make products sold during the year.

Gross Profit Managers are often interested in **gross profit**, a preliminary, quick-to-calculate profit figure that considers just two pieces of data—revenues and cost of revenues (the direct costs of getting those revenues)—from the income statement. To calculate gross profit, subtract cost of revenues from revenues obtained by selling the firm's products.

Operating Expenses In addition to costs directly related to generating revenues, every company has general expenses ranging from erasers to the CEO's salary. Like cost of revenues and cost of goods sold, **operating expenses** are resources that must flow out of a company if it is to earn revenues.

Sales and marketing expenses result from activities related to selling goods or services, such as salesforce salaries and advertising expenses. *Administrative and general expenses*, such as management salaries and maintenance costs, are related to the general management of the company.

Operating and Net Income
Operating income compares the gross profit from operations against operating expenses. This calculation for Google ($13.17 billion – $6.54 billion) reveals an operating income, or income before taxes, of $6.63 billion. Subtracting income taxes from operating income ($6.63 billion – $2.40 billion) reveals

net income (net profit or net earnings). Google's net income for the year was $4.23 billion (rounded).

The step-by-step information in an income statement shows how a company obtained its net income for the period, making it easier for shareholders and other stakeholders to evaluate the firm's financial health.

Statements of Cash Flows

Some companies prepare only balance sheets and income statements. However, the SEC requires all firms whose stock is publicly traded to issue a third report, the **statement of cash flows**, which shows the effects on cash of three aspects of a business: *operating activities*, *investing activities*, and *financing activities*. Google's 2008 statement of cash flows is reproduced in Figure 14.3.

Figure 14.3
Google's Statement of Cash Flows[15]

Google, Inc.
Summary of Statement of Cash Flows (condensed)
as of December 31, 2008
Increase (Decrease) in Cash
(in millions)

Net cash provided by operating activities		**$7,852.86**
Cash flows from investment activities:		
Payment for purchase of property, equipment, and securities	(5,319.42)	
Net cash used in investing activities		**(5,319.42)**
Cash flows from financing activities:		
Proceeds from sale of stock (IPO)	0.00	
Other	41.64	
Net cash provided by financing activities		**41.64**
Net increase in cash		2,575.08
Cash at beginning of year		6,081.59
Cash at end of year		**$8,656.67**

Google's statement of cash flows for year ended December 31, 2008. The final entry shows year-end cash position resulting from operating activities, investing activities, and financing activities.

BUDGET detailed statement of estimated receipts and expenditures for a future period of time

■ Cash Flows from Operations. This first section of the statement concerns main operating activities: cash transactions involved in buying and selling goods and services. For the Google example, it reveals how much of the year's cash balance results from the firm's main line of business—sales of advertising and Web-search services.

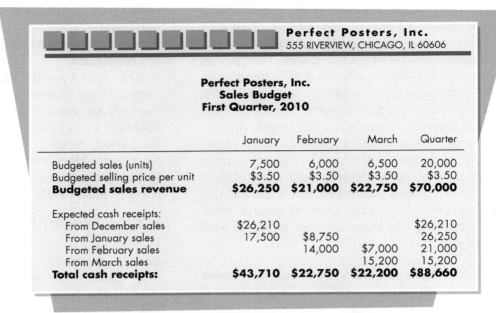

Perfect Posters, Inc.				
555 RIVERVIEW, CHICAGO, IL 60606				

Perfect Posters, Inc.
Sales Budget
First Quarter, 2010

	January	February	March	Quarter
Budgeted sales (units)	7,500	6,000	6,500	20,000
Budgeted selling price per unit	$3.50	$3.50	$3.50	$3.50
Budgeted sales revenue	**$26,250**	**$21,000**	**$22,750**	**$70,000**
Expected cash receipts:				
From December sales	$26,210			$26,210
From January sales	17,500	$8,750		26,250
From February sales		14,000	$7,000	21,000
From March sales			15,200	15,200
Total cash receipts:	**$43,710**	**$22,750**	**$22,200**	**$88,660**

Figure 14.4
Perfect Posters' Sales Budget

■ Cash Flows from Investing. The second section reports net cash used in or provided by investing. It includes cash receipts and payments from buying and selling stocks, bonds, property, equipment, and other productive assets. These sources of cash are not the company's main line of business. A cash outflow is shown in parentheses.

■ Cash Flows from Financing. The third section reports net cash from all financing activities. It includes cash inflows from borrowing or issuing stock, as well as outflows for payment of dividends and repayment of borrowed money.

The overall change in cash from these three sources is added to or subtracted from the beginning cash (year-end cash from the 2007 balance sheet) to arrive at the end-of-year cash position. When creditors and stockholders know how a firm obtained and used funds during the course of a year, it's easier for them to interpret year-to-year changes in the balance sheet and income statement.

The Budget: An Internal Financial Statement

For planning, controlling, and decision making, the most important internal financial statement is the **budget**—a detailed report on estimated receipts and expenditures for a future period of time. Although that period is usually one year, some companies also prepare three- or five-year budgets, especially when considering major capital expenditures. The budget differs from the other statements we have discussed in that budgets are not shared outside the company; hence the "internal financial statement" title.

Although the accounting staff coordinates the budget process, it needs input from many areas regarding proposed activities and required resources. Figure 14.4 is a sales budget for a hypothetical wholesaler, Perfect Posters. In preparing the budget, accounting must obtain from the sales group projections for units to be sold and expected expenses for the coming year. Then, accounting draws up the final budget and, throughout the year, compares the budget to actual expenditures and revenues. Discrepancies signal potential problems and spur action to improve financial performance.

Reporting Standards and Practices

Accountants follow standard reporting practices and principles when they prepare external reports. The common language dictated by standard practices and spelled out in GAAP is designed to give external users confidence in the accuracy and meaning of financial information. Forensic accountants such as PricewaterhouseCoopers's Al Vondra watch for deviations from GAAP as indicators of possible fraudulent practices.

Revenue Recognition and Activity Timing The reporting of revenue inflows, and the timing of other transactions, must abide by accounting principles that govern financial statements. **Revenue recognition**, for example, is the formal recording and reporting of revenues at the appropriate time. Although a firm earns revenues continuously as it makes sales, earnings are not reported until the *earnings cycle* is completed. This cycle is complete under two conditions:

1 The sale is complete and the product delivered.

2 The sale price has been collected or is collectible (accounts receivable).

The end of the earnings cycle determines the timing for revenue recognition in a firm's financial statements. Suppose a toy company in January signs a sales contract to supply $1,000 of toys to a retail store, with delivery scheduled in February. Although the sale is completed in January, the $1,000 revenue should not then be recognized because the toys have not been delivered and the sale price is not yet collectible, so the earnings cycle is incomplete. Revenues are recorded in the accounting period—February—in which the product is delivered and collectible (or collected).

Full Disclosure To help users better understand the numbers in a firm's financial statements, GAAP requires that financial statements also include management's interpretations and explanations of those numbers. This is known as the **full disclosure** principle. Because they

REVENUE RECOGNITION formal recording and reporting of revenues at the appropriate time

FULL DISCLOSURE guideline that financial statements should not include just numbers but should also furnish management's interpretations and explanations of those numbers

Managing in Turbulent Times

The "Fairness" Dilemma: What's an Asset's Real Value?

Think of a personal possession, such as a car. What is its monetary worth, or value? Is it the amount you paid, or what you could get by selling it today, or what you would expect if you sell two years from now? Businesses face similar questions when valuing assets on the balance sheet. Consider the Boston home buyer who paid $475,000 in 2006 when a bank generously valued the property at more than $525,000, allowing the new homeowner to borrow the full amount of the purchase price. The bank's asset (the mortgage loan) was valued at $475,000 and the borrower's property was valued at $525,000. Today, the borrower has vacated the house, unable to make payments. The bank holds the repossessed the property; it is unsellable at a $360,000 asking price. In the event of future economic recovery, the bank expects that the property will be worth at least $500,000. So, what should be the asset value on the balance sheet—$475,000 or $360,000 or $500,000? Many other firms in addition to banks are grappling with such questions in the plunging economy.[16]

The core problem is market shutdown: In a recession, there is no functioning market that sets a "fair market price" for many assets. With no buyers, once-valuable properties and financial investments have become "toxic assets": They are unsellable, often having no current market value. Difficulty worsens when market shutdown runs headlong into an accounting rule known as "mark-to-market," resulting in potential business closures.[17]

Mark-to-market—or "fair value accounting"—requires that assets be priced on balance sheets at current market value. That forces a major write-down for toxic assets at companies facing inactive markets for housing, cars, and financial securities, and it forces accounting losses that may cause "bleeding" companies to fold. Advocates for relaxing mark-to-market argue that presently distressed assets will become more valuable later, as the economy recovers, so currently depressed values are not at all "fair" indicators of their worth. Instead, they say, mark-to-market exaggerates the scale of their losses in the economic crisis.[18]

Relief for some troubled firms came in early 2009, with unusual action by the U.S. Financial Accounting Standards Board (FASB), an independent organization that sets accounting guidelines. FASB relaxed mark-to-market accounting for financial institutions. Banks now have more flexibility for valuing toxic assets, using estimates from their internal computer models instead of reporting assets at currently distressed market prices. Opponents to the change, however, warn that relaxed rules could let banks hide the true, low value of assets and deceive investors at a time when trust in financial reporting is most needed.[19]

know about events inside the company, managers prepare additional information to explain certain events or transactions or to disclose the circumstances behind certain results.

Analyzing Financial Statements

Financial statements present a lot of information in the form of data. This data, when applied to various *ratios* (comparative numbers), reveals trends that can be used to evaluate a firm's financial health, its progress, and its prospects for the future.

Ratios are normally grouped into three major classifications:

1 **Solvency ratios** for estimating short-term and long-term risk

2 **Profitability ratios** for measuring potential earnings

3 **Activity ratios** for evaluating management's use of assets

Depending on the decisions to be made, a user may apply none, some, or all of these ratios.

Solvency Ratios: Borrower's Ability to Repay Debt

What are the chances that a borrower will be able to repay a loan and the interest due? Solvency ratios provide measures of a firm's ability to meet its debt obligations.

The Current Ratio and Short-Term Solvency **Short-term solvency ratios** measure a company's liquidity and its ability to pay immediate debts. The most commonly used of these is the **current ratio**, or "banker's ratio." This measures a firm's ability to generate cash to meet current obligations through the normal, orderly process of selling inventories and collecting revenues from customers. It is calculated by dividing current assets by current liabilities. The higher a firm's current ratio, the lower the risk to investors.

As a rule, a current ratio is satisfactory at 2:1 or higher—that is, if current assets more than double

current liabilities. A smaller ratio may indicate that a firm will have trouble paying its bills.

How does Google measure up? Look again at the balance sheet in Figure 14.1. Judging from current assets and current liabilities at the end of 2008, we see that

$$\frac{\text{Current assets}}{\text{Current liabilities}} = \frac{\$20.18 \text{ billion}}{\$2.30 \text{ billion}} = 8.8$$

The industry average for companies that provide business services is 1.4. Google's current ratio of 8.8 indicates the firm is a good short-run credit risk.

Long-Term Solvency A firm that can't meet its long-term debt obligations is in danger of collapse or takeover—a risk that makes creditors and investors quite cautious. To evaluate a company's risk of running into this problem, creditors turn to the balance sheet to see the extent to which a firm is financed through borrowed money. Long-term solvency is calculated by dividing **debt**—total liabilities—by owners' equity. The lower a firm's debt, the lower the risk to investors and creditors. Companies with more debt may find themselves owing so much that they lack the income needed to meet interest payments or to repay borrowed money.

Leverage Sometimes, high debt can be not only acceptable, but also desirable. Borrowing funds gives a firm **leverage**—the ability to make otherwise unaffordable investments. In *leveraged buyouts*, firms have willingly taken on sometimes huge debts to buy out other companies. If owning the purchased company generates profits above the cost of borrowing the purchase price, leveraging

"It's up to you now, Miller. The only thing that can save us is an accounting breakthrough."

often makes sense. Unfortunately, many buyouts have caused problems because profits fell short of expected levels or because rising interest rates increased payments on the buyer's debt.

Profitability Ratios: Earnings Power for Owners

It's important to know whether a company is solvent in both the long and the short term, but risk alone is not an adequate basis for investment decisions. Investors also want some indication of the returns they can expect. Evidence of earnings power is available from profitability ratios, such as *earnings per share*.

Earnings per Share   Defined as net income divided by the number of shares of common stock outstanding, **earnings per share** determines the size of the

dividend that a firm can pay shareholders. As the ratio goes up, stock value increases because investors know that the firm can better afford to pay dividends. Naturally, stock loses market value if financial statements report a decline in earnings per share. For Google, we can use the net income total from the income statement in Figure 14.2, together with the number of outstanding shares of stock, to calculate earnings per share as follows:

$$\frac{\text{Net income}}{\text{Number of common shares outstanding}} = \frac{\$4,226.9 \text{ million}}{315.9 \text{ million shares of stock}} = \frac{\$13.38}{\text{per share}}$$

Entrepreneurship and New Ventures

How Will Twitter Turn Tweets into Treasure?

Widely accepted accounting measurements provide useful information about established firms but are a bit foggier with startups. Consider the continuing questions from the investment community about Twitter's ambiguous financial status. Profitability, for example, is a key indicator of any firm's worth. With several firms interested in buying Twitter, how can they know its value, variously estimated between $300 million and $700 million, without solid financial data? As to its profitability, Twitter reports, "we spend more money than we make." Since Twitter was launched in 2006, its total losses have not been reported publicly. When (and how) will losses blossom into profitability? As stated by co-founder and CEO Evan Williams, "We will make money, and I can't say exactly how because . . . we can't predict how the businesses we're in will work." And until they know *how*, they don't know *when* profits will occur.[20]

Twitter's balance sheet is another source of ambiguity. The accounting equation requires a fixed relationship among three items: Assets = Liabilities + Owners' Equity. Twitter insiders have a clear accounting of its outstanding liabilities. Paid-in capital (a part of shareholders' equity) is known, too: It includes the co-founders' personal investments plus a recent $35 million venture capital infusion, bringing the total to at least $55 million.

Questions also arise for valuing assets. For example, Twitter acquired the assets of *Values of n* to get needed technology and intellectual property into its operations. Exactly how Twitter will use them is unknown, so how should they be valued? Twitter's greatest asset is a massive

loyal customer base with a phenomenal growth rate—17 million visitors in one recent month alone—and its enormous advertising potential. Celebrities, media, politicians, and companies such as Apple, JetBlue, and Dell are using Twitter for sales and marketing promotions. Should this untapped advertising potential be recognized as an intangible asset? At what value? While the company's market, customer base, and products are just emerging, how should its many assets—tangible and intangible—be valued? On what basis can those valuations be justified? Clearly, these issues at Twitter are less well settled than at well-established firms.[21]

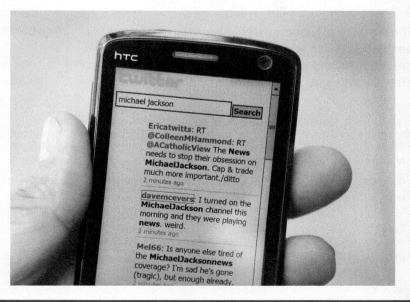

Table 14.3 Overview of the Code of Ethics for CPAs[22]

Membership in the American Institute of Certified Public Accountants is voluntary. By accepting membership, a certified public accountant assumes an obligation of self-discipline above and beyond the requirements of laws and regulations.

Responsibilities	In carrying out their responsibilities as professionals, members should exercise sensitive professional and moral judgments in all their activities.
The Public Interest	Members should accept the obligation to act in a way that will serve the public interest, honor the public trust, and demonstrate commitment to professionalism.
Integrity	To maintain and broaden public confidence, members should perform all professional responsibilities with the highest sense of integrity.
Objectivity and Independence	A member should maintain objectivity and be free of conflicts of interest in discharging professional responsibilities. A member in public practice should be independent in fact and appearance when providing auditing and other attestation services.
Due Care	A member should observe the profession's technical and ethical standards, strive continually to improve competence and the quality of services, and discharge professional responsibility to the best of the member's ability.
Scope and Nature of Services	A member in public practice should observe the Principles of the Code of Professional Conduct in determining the scope and nature of services to be provided.

This means that Google had net earnings of $13.38 (rounded) for each share of stock during 2008. In contrast, Time Warner's recent earnings were −$11.31 per share, while Microsoft earned $0.33.

Activity Ratios: How Efficiently Is the Firm Using Its Resources?

The efficiency with which a firm uses resources is linked to profitability. As a potential investor, you want to know which company gets more mileage from its resources. Information obtained from the income statement can be used for *activity ratios* to measure this efficiency. For example, two firms use the same amount of resources or assets to perform a particular activity, such as advertising or inventory management. If Firm A generates greater profits or sales, it has used its resources more efficiently and so enjoys a better activity ratio. It means that Firm A is getting more bang for the buck.

Bringing Ethics into the Accounting Equation

The purpose of ethics in accounting is to maintain public confidence in business institutions, financial markets, and the products and services of the accounting profession. Without ethics, all of accounting's tools and methods would be meaningless because their usefulness depends, ultimately, on veracity in their application.

Why Accounting Ethics?

Amidst a flurry of unscrupulous activity, ethics remains an area where one person who is willing to "do the right thing" can make a difference—and people do, every day. Refusing to turn a blind eye to unethical accounting around her at Enron, Lynn Brewer tried to alert people inside about misstatements of the company's assets. When that failed, she, along with colleagues Sherron Watkins and Margaret Ceconi, talked with the U.S. Committee on Energy and Commerce to voice concerns about Enron's condition. To Brewer, maintaining personal and professional integrity was an overriding concern, and she acted accordingly.

AICPA's Code of Professional Conduct   The **code of professional conduct** for public accountants in the United States is maintained and enforced by the AICPA. The institute identifies six ethics-related areas—listed in Table 14.3—with which accountants must comply

Table 14.4 Examples of Unethical and Illegal Accounting Actions[23]

Corporation	Accounting Violation
AOL Time Warner	America Online (AOL) inflated ad revenues to keep stock prices high before and after merging with Time Warner.
Cendant	Inflated income in financial statements by $500 million through fraud and errors.
HCA, Columbia/HCA	Defrauded Medicare, Medicaid, and TRICARE through false cost claims and unlawful billings (must pay $1.7 billion in civil penalties, damages, criminal fines, and penalties).
Tyco	CEO Dennis Kozlowski illegally used company funds to buy expensive art for personal possession (he received an 8- to 25-year prison sentence).
Waste Management	Overstated income in financial statements (false and misleading reports) by improperly calculating depreciation and salvage value for equipment.
WorldCom	Hid $3.8 billion in expenses to show an inflated (false) profit instead of loss in an annual income statement.

to maintain certification. Comprehensive details for compliance in each area are spelled out in the AICPA Code of Professional Conduct. The IMA maintains a similar code to provide ethical guidelines for the management accounting profession.

In reading the AICPA's Code, you can see that it forbids misrepresentation and fraud in financial statements. Deception certainly violates the call for exercising moral judgments (in "Responsibilities"), is contrary to the public interest (by deceiving investors) and does not honor the public trust (in "The Public Interest"). Misleading statements destroy the public's confidence in the accounting profession and in business in general. While the Code prohibits such abuses, its success depends, ultimately, on its acceptance and use by the professionals it governs.

Violations of Accounting Ethics and GAAP Unethical and illegal accounting violations have dominated the popular press in recent years. Some of the more notorious cases, listed in Table 14.4, violated the public's trust, ruined retirement plans for thousands of employees, and caused shutdowns and lost jobs. As you read each case, you should be able to see how its violation relates to the presentation of balance sheets and income statements in this chapter. In each case, adversity would have been prevented if employees had followed the code of professional conduct. In each case, nearly all of the code's six ethics-related areas were violated. And in every case, "professionals" willingly participated in unethical behavior. Such was the impetus for Sarbox.

Questions for Review

1 Who are the users of accounting information, and for what purposes do they use it?

2 Identify the three types of services performed by CPAs.

3 Explain the ways in which financial accounting differs from managerial (management) accounting.

4 Discuss the activities and services performed by forensic accountants.

5 What are the three basic financial statements, and what major information does each contain?

6 Explain how financial ratios allow managers to gain additional information from financial statements.

Questions for Analysis

7 If you were planning to invest in a company, which of the three types of financial statements would you most want to see? Why?

8 Suppose that you, as the manager of a company, are making changes to fully comply with provisions of the Sarbanes-Oxley Act. Your company traditionally has relied on CPA firms for auditing, tax services, and management services. What major changes will your company need to make?

Application Exercises

9 Interview an accountant at a local firm. How does the firm use budgets? How does budgeting help managers plan business activities? How does budgeting help them control activities? Give examples.

10 Interview the manager of a local retailer, wholesale business, or manufacturing firm about the role of ethics in that company's accounting practices. Is ethics in accounting an important issue to the manager? If the firm has its own private accountants, what measures are taken for ensuring ethical practices internally? What steps, if any, does the company take to maintain ethical relationships in its dealings with CPA firms?

Money and Banking

After reading this chapter, you should be able to:

1 Define *money* and identify the different forms that it takes in the nation's money supply.

2 Describe the different kinds of financial institutions that compose the U.S. financial system and explain the services they offer.

3 Explain how financial institutions create money and describe the means by which they are regulated.

4 Discuss the functions of the Federal Reserve System and describe the tools that it uses to control the money supply.

5 Identify three important ways in which the money and banking system is changing.

6 Discuss some of the institutions and activities in international banking and finance.

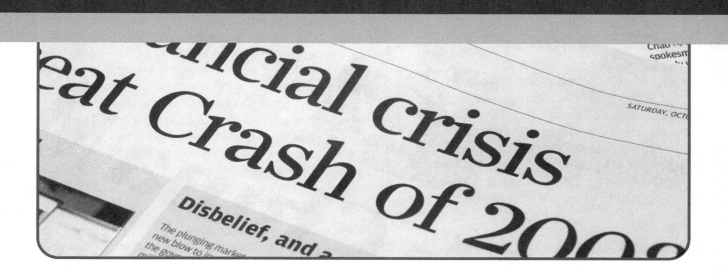

Banking Systems Crash in "Perfect Storm"

The U.S. financial system was rocked when Los Angeles–based IndyMac Bank, one of the nation's largest banks, was seized by the Federal Deposit Insurance Corporation (FDIC) and closed in July 2008. Banks around the globe, strapped with bad loans ("toxic assets," or "troubled assets") in floundering economies, fell into financial distress. More than 115 U.S. banks were closed—in 2009 alone. The nation's remaining 8,000 lenders, too, were shaken by the recession and housing market collapse. As uncollectable loans increased, banks were left with unsellable foreclosed properties, and housing values continued to fall.

Along with industry giants, some 940 smaller U.S. banks faced potential additional losses of $200 billion through 2010 on commercial loans for office buildings, shopping malls, and apartment projects, as well as on bad home loans. Revenues lost from uncollectable loans were unavailable to lend, and the growing shortage of capital looked as though it could be fatal. Banks were trying to shore up cash by selling off assets, cutting costs, or hording funds rather than making loans. As cash dwindled, financial losses foreshadowed more bank closures.

With the global credit crisis threatening to top $4 trillion, governments from London to Berlin were using massive injections of money to shore up banks and public confidence. The Troubled Asset Relief Program (TARP) allowed the U.S. Department of the Treasury to inject up to $700 billion into financial institutions by buying the banks'"troubled assets." By mid-2009, $600 billion had been allocated, mostly to financial institutions for new lending. Similarly, the European Central Bank (ECB) pumped a record-setting €442 billion ($622 billion) into euro zone financial markets via low-interest loans to its banks. Only time would tell if these interventions were enough to thaw out frozen credit markets, boost real estate markets, and restore confidence in the financial institutions and economies around the globe.[1]

What's in It for Me?

Dealing in matters of money is vastly more complicated than counting the cash and coins in your pocket, especially when technology and globalization come into play. At its core are questions about where money comes from, how national economies depend on it, and the public's trust in its value. This chapter will give you a solid understanding of the different forms of money and how its supply is created and controlled by different kinds of financial institutions and government regulations.

What Is Money?

When someone asks you how much money you have, do you count the dollar bills and coins in your pockets? Do you include your checking and savings accounts? What about stocks and bonds? Do you count your car? Taken together, the value of all these combined is your personal wealth. Not all of it, however, is "money." This section considers more precisely what *money* is and does.

The Characteristics of Money

Modern money generally takes the form of stamped metal or printed paper issued by governments. Theoretically, however, just about anything *portable*, *divisible*, *durable*, and *stable* can serve as **money**. To appreciate these qualities, imagine using something that lacks them—for example, a 1,000-pound cow used as a unit of exchange in ancient agrarian economies.

- **Portability.** Try lugging 1,000 pounds of cow from shop to shop. In contrast, modern currency is light and easy to handle.

- **Divisibility.** How would you divide your cow if you wanted to buy a hat, a book, and a radio from three different stores? Is a pound of head worth as much as a pound of leg? Modern currency is easily divisible into smaller parts with fixed values—for example, a dollar for ten dimes.

- **Durability.** Your cow will lose value every day (and eventually die). Modern currency, however, neither dies nor spoils, and if it wears out, it can be replaced. It is also hard to counterfeit—certainly harder than cattle breeding.

- **Stability.** If cows were in short supply, you might be able to make quite a deal for yourself. In the middle of an abundant cow year, however, the market would be flooded with cows, so their value would fall. The value of our paper money also fluctuates, but it is considerably more stable and predictable.

The Functions of Money

Imagine a successful cow rancher who needs a new fence. In a *barter economy*—one in which goods are exchanged directly for one another—he or she would have to find someone who is willing to exchange a fence for a cow (or parts of it). If no fence maker wants a cow, the rancher must find someone else—for example, a wagon maker—who does want a cow. Then, the rancher must hope that the fence maker will trade for a new wagon. In a money economy, the rancher would sell his or her cow, receive money, and exchange the money for such goods as a new fence.

Money serves three functions:

1. **It is a medium of exchange.** Like the rancher "trading" money for a new fence, money is used to buy and sell things. Without money, we would be bogged down in a system of barter.

2. **It is a store of value.** Pity the rancher whose cow gets sick on Monday and who wants to buy some clothes on the following Saturday, by which time the cow may have died and lost its value. In the form of currency, however, money can be used for future purchases and "stores" value.

3. **It is a measure of worth.** Money lets us measure the relative values of goods and services. It acts as a measure of worth because all products can be valued and accounted for in terms of money. For example, the concepts of $1,000 worth of clothes or $500 in labor costs have universal meaning.

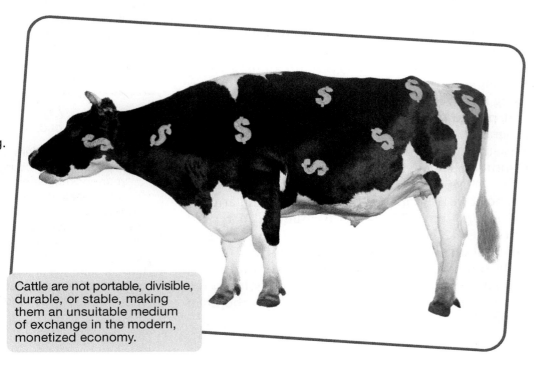

Cattle are not portable, divisible, durable, or stable, making them an unsuitable medium of exchange in the modern, monetized economy.

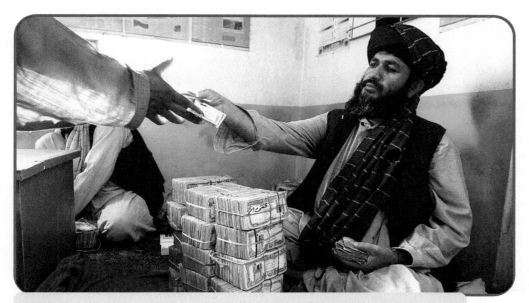

Instead of using a modern monetary system, traders like Muhammed Essa in Quetta, Pakistan, transfer funds through handshakes and code words. The ancient system is called *hawala*, which means *trust* in Arabic. The worldwide *hawala* system, though illegal in most countries, moves billions of dollars past regulators annually and is alleged to be the system of choice for terrorists because it leaves no paper trail.

M-1: The Spendable Money Supply

For money to serve its basic functions, both buyers and sellers must agree on its value, which depends in part on its *supply*—how much money is in circulation. When the money supply is high, the value of money drops. When it is low, that value increases.

Unfortunately, there is no single agreed-upon measure of the supply of money. The oldest and most basic measure, **M-1**, counts only the most liquid, or spendable, forms of money—cash, checks, and checking accounts.

■ Paper money and metal coins are **currency (cash)** issued by the government and widely used for small exchanges. Law requires creditors to accept it in payment of debts.

■ A **check** is essentially an order instructing a bank to pay a given sum to a payee. Checks are usually, but not always, accepted because they are valuable only to specified payees and can be exchanged for cash.

■ **Checking accounts**, or **demand deposits**, are money because their funds may be withdrawn at any time on demand.

These are all noninterest-bearing or low–interest-bearing forms of money. As of May 2009, M-1 in the United States totaled $1.60 trillion.[2]

M-2: M-1 Plus the Convertible Money Supply

M-2, a second measure of the money supply, is often used for economic planning by businesses and government agencies. **M-2** includes everything in M-1 plus other forms of money that are not quite as liquid—short-term investments that are easily converted to spendable forms—including *time deposits*, *money market mutual funds*, and *savings accounts*. Totaling $8.35 trillion in May 2009, M-2 accounts for most of the nation's money supply.[3] As this overall level increases, more money is available for consumer purchases and business investments. When the supply is tightened, less money is available; financial transactions, spending, and business activity slow down.

Unlike demand deposits, **time deposits**, such as certificates of deposit (CDs), have a fixed term, are intended to be held to maturity, cannot be transferred by check, and pay higher interest rates. Time deposits in M-2 include only accounts of less than $100,000 that can be redeemed on demand, with penalties for early withdrawal.

With **money market mutual funds**, investment companies buy a collection of short-term, low-risk financial securities. Ownership of and profits (or losses) from the sale of these securities are shared among the fund's investors.

M-1 measure of the money supply that includes only the most liquid (spendable) forms of money

CURRENCY (CASH) government-issued paper money and metal coins

CHECK demand deposit order instructing a bank to pay a given sum to a specified payee

CHECKING ACCOUNT (DEMAND DEPOSIT) bank account funds, owned by the depositor, that may be withdrawn at any time by check or cash

M-2 measure of the money supply that includes all the components of M-1 plus the forms of money that can be easily converted into spendable forms

TIME DEPOSIT bank funds that have a fixed term of time to maturity and cannot be withdrawn earlier or transferred by check

MONEY MARKET MUTUAL FUND fund of short-term, low-risk financial securities purchased with the pooled assets of investor-owners

Figure 15.1 shows how M-1 and M-2 have grown since 1969. For many years, M-1 was the traditional measure of liquid money. Because it was closely related to gross domestic product, it served as a reliable predictor of the nation's economic health. This situation changed in the early 1980s, with the introduction of new types of investments and the easier transfer of money among investment funds to gain higher interest returns. As a result, M-2 today is regarded as a more reliable measure than M-1.

The U.S. Financial System

Many forms of money depend on the existence of financial institutions that provide money-related services to both individuals and businesses. The sections that follow explain their role as creators of money and discuss the regulation of the U.S. banking system.

Financial Institutions

The main function of financial institutions is to ease the flow of money from users with surpluses to those with deficits by attracting funds into checking and savings accounts. Incoming funds will be loaned to individuals and businesses and perhaps invested in government securities. U.S. consumers have access to more than 89,000 U.S. branches and offices of *commercial banks*, *savings institutions*, *credit unions*, and various *nondeposit institutions*.

Commercial Banks Federally insured **commercial banks** accept deposits, make loans, earn profits, and pay interest and dividends. Commercial banks range from the very largest institutions in New York, such as Citigroup, Bank of America, and JPMorgan Chase, to tiny banks dotting the rural landscape. Bank liabilities—holdings owed to others—include checking accounts and savings accounts.

Savings Institutions Savings institutions include mutual savings banks and savings and loan associations. They are also called *thrift institutions* because they were established decades ago to promote the idea of savings among the general population.

Savings and Loan Associations Like commercial banks, **savings and loan associations (S&Ls)** accept deposits, make loans, and are owned by investors. Most S&Ls were created to encourage savings habits and provide financing for homes; they did not offer check services. Many have ventured into a variety of other investments.

Mutual Savings Banks In a **mutual savings bank**, all depositors are considered owners of the bank. All profits are divided proportionately among depositors, who receive dividends. Some 800 U.S. mutual savings banks attract most of their funds in the form of savings deposits, and funds are loaned out in the form of mortgages.

Credit Unions A **credit union** is a nonprofit, cooperative financial institution

Figure 15.1
Money Supply Growth[4]

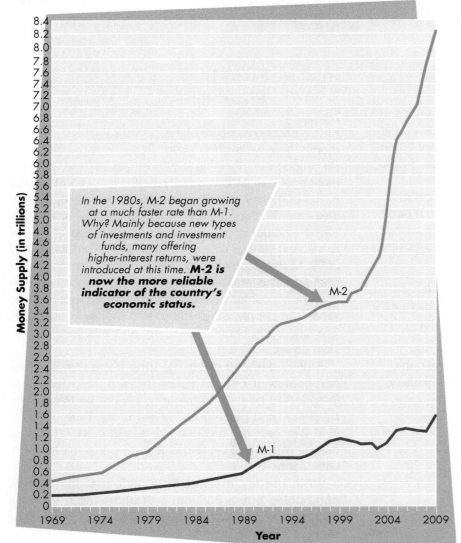

In the 1980s, M-2 began growing at a much faster rate than M-1. Why? Mainly because new types of investments and investment funds, many offering higher-interest returns, were introduced at this time. **M-2 is now the more reliable indicator of the country's economic status.**

owned and run by its members. Its purpose is to promote *thrift*—careful management of one's money or resources—and to provide members with a safe place to save and borrow at reasonable rates. Members pool their funds to make loans to one another. Each credit union decides whom it will serve, such as a group of employees, people in a particular community, or members of an association. Most universities, for example, have credit unions, as does the U.S. Navy.

Nondeposit Institutions   A variety of other organizations take in money, provide interest or other services, and make loans. Unlike commercial banks, these *nondeposit institutions* use inflowing funds for purposes other than earning interest for depositors. Four of the most important are *pension funds*, *insurance companies*, *finance companies*, and *securities investment dealers*.

1 A **pension fund** is a pool of funds that is managed to provide retirement income for its members. *Public pension funds* include Social Security and $2 trillion (down from $3 trillion before the recession started in 2007) in retirement programs for state and local government employees. *Private pension funds*, operated by employers, unions, and other private groups, cover about 44 million people and have total assets of $12 trillion, down from $15 trillion during the recession.[5]

2 **Insurance companies** accumulate money from premiums charged for coverage. They invest these funds in stocks, real estate, and other assets. Earnings pay for insured losses, such as death benefits, automobile damage, and healthcare expenses.

3 **Finance companies** specialize in making loans to businesses and consumers. *Commercial finance companies* lend to businesses needing capital or long-term funds. *Consumer finance companies* devote most of their resources to providing small noncommercial loans to individuals.

4 **Securities investment dealers (brokers)**, such as Merrill Lynch and A. G. Edwards Inc., buy and sell stocks and bonds for client investors. They also invest in securities—they buy stocks and bonds for their own accounts in hopes of reselling them later at a profit. These companies hold large sums of money for transfer between buyers and sellers. (We discuss the activities of brokers and investment bankers more fully in Chapter 16.)

PENSION FUND nondeposit pool of funds managed to provide retirement income for its members

INSURANCE COMPANY nondeposit institution that invests funds collected as premiums charged for insurance coverage

FINANCE COMPANY nondeposit institution that specializes in making loans to businesses and consumers

SECURITIES INVESTMENT DEALER (BROKER) financial institution that buys and sells stocks and bonds both for investors and for its own accounts

PRIME RATE interest rate available to a bank's most creditworthy customers

The Growth of Financial Services

The finance business today is highly competitive. No longer is it enough for commercial banks to accept deposits and make loans. Most, for example, also offer bank-issued credit cards, safe-deposit boxes, ATMs, and electronic money transfer. In addition, many offer pension, trust, international, and brokerage services and financial advice.

The Prime Rate

Every bank receives a major portion of its income from interest paid on loans by borrowers. As long as terms and conditions are clearly revealed to borrowers, banks may set their own interest rates, within limits set by each state. Traditionally, banks only offered the lowest rate, or **prime rate**, to their most creditworthy commercial customers. Most commercial loans are set at markups over prime, like prime + 1, which means 1 percent over the prime rate.

To remain competitive with lower-interest foreign banks, U.S. banks now offer some commercial loans at rates below prime. Figure 15.2 shows the changes in the prime rate since 1999. Lower rates in 2008–2009 encouraged banks to continue lending in the recession.

Figure 15.2
The Prime Rate[6]

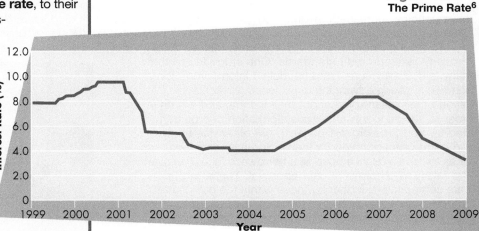

INDIVIDUAL RETIREMENT ACCOUNT (IRA) tax-deferred pension fund that wage earners set up to supplement retirement funds

TRUST SERVICES management by a bank of an estate, investments, or other assets on behalf of an individual

LETTER OF CREDIT bank promise, issued for a buyer, to pay a designated firm a certain amount of money if specified conditions are met

BANKER'S ACCEPTANCE bank promise, issued for a buyer, to pay a designated firm a specified amount at a future date

Pension and Trust Services

Individual retirement accounts (IRAs) are tax-deferred pension funds that wage earners and their spouses can set up to supplement other retirement funds. Advantages and drawbacks to various kinds of IRAs—*traditional, Roth, and education*—are discussed in Appendix III.

Many commercial banks offer **trust services**—the management of funds left in the bank's trust. In return for a fee, the trust department will perform such tasks as making your monthly bill payments and managing your investment portfolio. Trust departments also manage the estates of deceased persons.

International Services Suppose a U.S. company wants to buy a product from a Japanese supplier. For a fee, it can use one or more of three services offered by its bank:

"And, hey, don't kill yourself trying to pay it back. You know our motto—'What the hell, it's only money.'"

1 Currency Exchange: It can exchange U.S. dollars for Japanese yen to pay the supplier.

2 Letters of Credit: It can pay its bank to issue a **letter of credit**—a promise by the bank to pay the Japanese firm a certain amount if specified conditions are met.

3 Banker's Acceptances: It can pay its bank to draw up a **banker's acceptance**, which promises that the bank will pay some specified amount at a future date.

Managing in Turbulent Times

Getting Serious with Credit Standards

While banks try to avoid drowning in troubled assets—bad loans—borrowers and lenders alike are questioning how the banks got into the current financial mess. Many observers blame subprime mortgage lending. Unlike prime mortgages, subprime loans are made to high-risk borrowers—those with bad credit histories, excessive debt, inadequate income, or other indicators that they will not repay the lender. In return for riskier loans, borrowers pay higher interest rates. As the housing market tumbled, delinquencies skyrocketed on millions of subprime loans. Whereas about 6 percent of mortgage loans were uncollectable from 2000 to 2005, thereafter delinquencies increased, nearing 30 percent by 2008. Lenders extended too much credit to weak borrowers.[7]

Reports indicate that the subprime crisis can be traced to overly relaxed credit standards. One study found that many loan applications listed fraudulent information. Some borrowers, taking advantage of lax lending practices to live beyond their means, lied about their income and assets in order to secure loans. Other misinformation can be attributed to mortgage brokers eager to get otherwise unqualified borrowers approved for loans. Some lenders went so far as to have a relative pose as a borrower's fake employer and falsify W-2 forms to gain approval. These problems were compounded further by those within the banking and finance system who knew that rampant fraud was occurring but looked the other way, as long as profits kept rolling in.[8]

Now stuck with uncollectable loans, unsellable foreclosed properties, and big financial losses, the industry is tightening credit standards and lending practices. Federal bank examiners, for example, are insisting that loan officers use greater caution and judgment to identify credit-worthy borrowers and avoid weak loans. Lenders are switching to independent real estate appraisers who have no direct contact with loan officers, to get accurate rather than inflated property appraisals. Along with eliminating loans with zero or very low down payments, home equity lending is shrinking as home values continue to fall. Lenders are also reducing credit card limits. With a dire lesson learned, it appears that tighter standards are here for the foreseeable future.[9]

A banker's acceptance requires payment by a particular date. Letters of credit are payable only after certain conditions are met. The Japanese supplier, for example, may not be paid until shipping documents prove that the merchandise has been shipped from Japan.

Financial Advice and Brokerage Services Many banks, both large and small, help their customers manage their money. Depending on the customer's situation, the bank, in its role as financial advisor, may recommend different investment opportunities. The recommended mix might include CDs, mutual funds, stocks, and bonds. Many banks also serve as securities intermediaries, using their own stockbrokers to buy and sell securities and their own facilities to hold them.

Electronic Funds Transfer **Electronic funds transfer (EFT)** provides for payments and collections by transferring financial information electronically. Consumers using debit cards instead of writing personal checks enjoy EFT's convenience and speed at the checkout. In addition, EFT systems provide automatic payroll deposit, ATM transactions, bill payment, and automatic funds transfer. Such systems can help a businessperson close an important business deal by transferring money from San Francisco to Miami within a few seconds. The U.S. Treasury reports that it costs $1.03 to issue a check payment, but only $0.105 to issue an EFT payment.[10]

Automated Teller Machines **Automated teller machines (ATMs)** allow customers to withdraw money, make deposits, transfer funds between accounts, and access information on their accounts. About 360,000 machines are located in U.S. bank buildings and other locations.[11] Increasingly, ATMs have become multilingual global fixtures. As Figure 15.3 shows, among the world's more than 2 million ATMs, most are located outside the United States, and many U.S. banks now offer international ATM services.

and banks are allowed to loan out 90 percent of all their deposits, then your bank will hold $10 in reserve and loan $90 of your money to borrowers. (You still have $100 on deposit.) Meanwhile, a borrower—or the people paid—will deposit the $90 loan in a bank. The borrower's bank will then have $81 (90 percent of $90) available for new loans. The banks, therefore, have turned your original $100 into $271 ($100 + $90 + $81). The chain continues, with borrowings from one bank becoming deposits in the next.

Regulation of the Banking System

Because commercial banks are essential to the creation of money, the government regulates them to ensure a sound and competitive financial system. Federal and state agencies regulate banks to ensure that the failure of some will not cause the public to lose faith in the banking system itself.

Federal Deposit Insurance Corporation The **Federal Deposit Insurance Corporation (FDIC)** supervises banks and insures deposits in banks and thrift institutions. The FDIC is a government agency, created by President Franklin D. Roosevelt to restore public confidence in banks during the Depression era. More than 99 percent of the nation's commercial banks and savings institutions pay fees for membership in the FDIC. In return, the FDIC guarantees the safety of all deposits of every account owner up to the current maximum of $100,000. If a bank collapses, the FDIC promises to pay each depositor for

Financial Institutions as Creators of Money

Financial institutions provide a special service to the economy: they create money. They don't mint bills and coins, but by taking in deposits and making loans, they expand the money supply.

As Figure 15.4 shows, the money supply expands because banks are allowed to loan out most (although not all) of the money they take in from deposits. If you deposit $100 in your bank

Figure 15.3
Global Dispersion of ATMs

- Asia
- North America
- Western Europe
- Latin America
- Other

26%
20%
32%
11%
11%

Deposit	Money Held in Reserve by Bank	Money to Lend	Total Supply
$100.00	$10.00	$90.00	**$190.00**
90.00	9.00	81.00	**271.00**
81.00	8.10	72.90	**343.90**
72.90	7.29	65.61	**409.51**
65.61	6.56	59.05	**468.56**

Figure 15.4
How Banks Create Money

losses up to $100,000. In 2008, however, a temporary increase to $250,000 maximum was implemented through 2013 to ensure public confidence in bank safety. A person with more money can establish accounts in more than one bank to protect sums in excess of $250,000. (A handful of the nation's 7,000 commercial banks are insured by states rather than by the FDIC.) To insure against multiple bank failures, the FDIC maintains the right to examine the activities and accounts of all member banks.

The Role of the FDIC in Bank Failures What happens with banks that fail, such as the more than 115 U.S. banks that failed in the recession year 2009? The FDIC becomes responsible for disposing of failed banks. One option is to sell them to other banks that are then responsible for the liabilities of the failed banks. Alternatively, the FDIC can seize the assets of the failed banks and undertake two activities: (1) Pay insurance to depositors and (2) dispose of the banks' assets and settle their debts, all at the lowest cost to the FDIC's insurance deposit fund. The resulting net gain (or loss) is put into (or paid from) the insurance deposit fund. As the recession of 2007–2009 deepened, this fund had dwindled to $13 billion in 2009, down from $45 billion in 2008. With more bank closures expected, the FDIC was raising assessments against member banks to restore the fund's reserves.[12]

The Federal Reserve System

Perched atop the U.S. financial system and regulating many aspects of its operation is the **Federal Reserve System (the Fed)**, the nation's central bank, established by Congress in 1913. This section describes the structure of the Fed, its functions, and the tools it uses to control the nation's money supply.

The Structure of the Fed

The Fed consists of a board of governors, a group of reserve banks, and member banks. As originally established by the Federal Reserve Act of 1913, the system consisted of 12 relatively autonomous banks and a seven-member committee whose powers were limited to coordinating the activities of those banks. By the 1930s, however, both the structure and function of the Fed had changed dramatically.

The Board of Governors The Fed's board of governors consists of seven members appointed by the president for overlapping terms of 14 years. The chair of the board serves on major economic advisory

Devout Muslims can't pay or receive interest—a fact that tends to complicate banking operations. Because money has to work in order to earn a return, institutions like the Shamil Bank in Bahrain invest deposits directly in such ventures as real estate and pay back profit shares rather than interest.

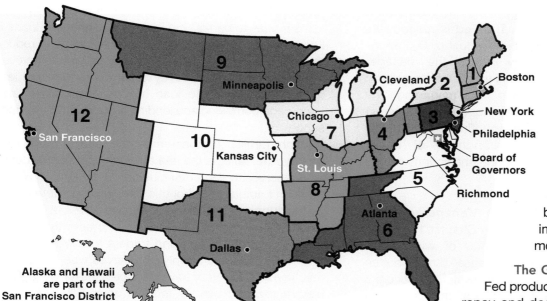

Figure 15.5
The Twelve Federal Reserve Districts[13]

committees and works actively with the administration to formulate economic policy. The board plays a large role in controlling the money supply. It alone determines the reserve requirements, within statutory limits, for depository institutions. It also works with other members of the Fed to set discount rates and handle the Fed's sale and purchase of government securities.

Reserve Banks The Fed consists of 12 districts, as shown in Figure 15.5. Each Federal Reserve Bank holds reserve deposits from and sets the discount rate for commercial banks in its geographic region. Reserve Banks also play a major role in the nation's check-clearing process.

Open Market Committee The Federal Open Market Committee is responsible for formulating the Fed's monetary policies to promote economic stability and growth by managing the nation's money supply. Its members include the Board of Governors, the president of the Federal Reserve Bank of New York, and the presidents of four other Reserve Banks, who serve on a rotating basis.

Member Banks All nationally chartered commercial banks and some state-chartered banks are members of the Fed. The accounts of all member bank depositors are automatically covered by the FDIC.

Other Depository Institutions Although many state-chartered banks, credit unions, and S&Ls do not belong to the Fed, they are subject to its regulations, pay deposit insurance premiums, and are covered

by the FDIC or the National Credit Union Administration (NCUA).

The Functions of the Fed

In addition to chartering national banks, the Fed serves as the federal government's bank and the "bankers' bank," regulating a number of banking activities. Most importantly, it controls the money supply.

The Government's Bank The Fed produces the nation's paper currency and decides how many bills to produce and destroy. It also lends money to the government by buying bonds issued by the Treasury Department to help finance the national deficit.

The Bankers' Bank Individual banks can borrow from the Fed and pay interest on the loans. In addition, the Fed provides storage for commercial banks, which are required to keep funds on reserve at a Federal Reserve Bank.

Check Clearing

The Fed also clears checks for commercial banks to ensure that cash is deducted from the check writer's bank account and deposited into the check receiver's account. With electronic payments, however, the number of paper checks processed is falling, with 33 billion written in 2007, down from a peak of 60 billion in 2000. Consumers prefer the convenience of debit and credit cards and electronic transactions such as direct deposits and online payments. Even with paper checks, however, the clearing is faster because banks can now send the Fed electronic images to be processed (instead of shipping the checks). As a result, the Fed plans to have just one full-service check-processing site by the end of 2009, instead of the 45 locations needed as recently as 2003.[14]

Controlling the Money Supply The Fed is responsible for the conduct of U.S. **monetary policy**—the management of the nation's economic growth by managing the money supply and interest rates to influence the ability and willingness of banks throughout the country to loan money.

Inflation Management As defined in Chapter 1, *inflation* is a period of widespread price increases throughout an economic system. It occurs if the money supply grows too large. Demand for goods and services increases, and the prices of everything rise. In contrast, *deflation* occurs when the supply of goods outpaces the supply of money, so demand for goods and services falls. Decreasing prices lead businesses to cut output, and unemployment rises. The Fed, with its goal of economic stability, uses the money supply to avoid extreme inflation or deflation. Because commercial banks are the main creators of money, much of the Fed's management of the money supply takes the form of regulating the supply of money through commercial banks.

The Tools of the Fed

According to the Fed's original charter, its primary duties were to supervise banking and to manage the nation's currency. The duties of the Fed have evolved to include an emphasis on the broad economic goals as discussed in Chapter 1, especially growth and stability. The Fed's role in controlling the nation's money supply stems from its role in setting policies to help reach these goals. To control the money supply, the Fed uses *reserve requirements*, *interest rate controls*, and *open-market operations*.

Reserve Requirements The **reserve requirement** is the percentage of its deposits that a bank must hold, in cash or on deposit, with a Federal Reserve Bank. High requirements mean that banks have less money to lend and the money supply is reduced. Conversely, low requirements permit the supply to expand.

Interest Rate Controls As the bankers' bank, the Fed loans money to banks. The interest rate on these loans is known as the **discount rate**. If the Fed wants to reduce the money supply, it increases the discount rate, making it more expensive for banks to borrow money and less attractive for them to loan it. Conversely, low rates encourage borrowing and lending and expand the money supply.

More familiar to consumers, the **federal funds rate** (or **key rate**) reflects the rate at which commercial banks lend reserves to each other, usually overnight. While the Fed can't actually control this rate, which is determined by the supply and demand of bank reserves, it can control the supply of those reserves to create the desired rate. By instructing its bond traders to buy fewer government bonds, the supply of reserves was decreased, resulting in a series of key rate increases—from a then-historic low of 1 percent in 2004 up to 5.25 percent in 2006—to slow a booming U.S. economy. The Fed then reversed its policy as the economy lost momentum, cutting the target rate gradually down to its current record low, 0.25 percent in 2008 to boost the economy during the recession.[15]

Open-Market Operations **Open-market operations** refer to the Fed's sale and purchase of securities (usually U.S. Treasury notes and short-term bonds) in the open market, as directed by the open-market committee. Open-market operations are particularly effective because they act quickly and predictably on the money supply. The Fed buys securities from a dealer, whose bank account is credited for the transaction. Its bank has more money to lend, so this transaction expands the money supply.

The opposite happens when the Fed sells securities. Selling treasury securities to investors allows the U.S. government to raise money and contract the money supply. These securities are usually bought at a price below face value and mature to face value within a few weeks to a year for T-bills, between 2 and 10 years for T-notes, and in 30 years for T-bonds. Treasury securities are highly liquid because they are actively traded on the secondary market, and are considered a risk-free investment because they are backed by the U.S. government.[16]

Fed Uses Massive Bond Purchases to Stem Recession In 2009, the Fed launched its most aggressive buying of long-term Treasury bonds in history—$300 billion—to fight the recession. The purchases were intended to push up market prices for Treasuries and thereby drive down interest rates. As long-term Treasury rates fell, other interest rates soon followed, including rates for home mortgages, business loans, and consumer loans. Overall lower interest rates were expected to encourage more widespread borrowing and lending to get the economy moving again.[17]

The Changing Money and Banking System

The U.S. money and banking systems continue to change today. Government emergency intervention aims to stabilize a troubled financial system. Enforcement of anti-terrorism regulations deters criminal misuse of the financial system. And with the expansion of banking services, electronic technologies affect how you obtain money and how much interest you pay for it.

Government Intervention for Stabilizing the U.S. Financial System

The financial world was shaken with the 2008 collapse of Lehman Brothers, the leading U.S. investment bank. Lehman's bankruptcy was soon followed by the threat of another giant's demise, as Bear Stearns teetered and then was bought by JPMorgan Chase. But JPMorgan Chase's purchase of Bear Stearns became possible only when the Federal Reserve stepped forward with $26 billion to guarantee potential losses on Bear Stearns's assets. With a goal of stabilizing the fractured financial system, the government had begun its unprecedented infusion of funding for U.S. financial institutions.

Government Emergency Investment By mid-2009, the Fed's investments reached nearly $300 billion, mostly in lending programs to commercial banks. Banks used the loans to get rid of bad mortgages and other hard-to-sell assets, thereby gaining cash for lending to bank customers. Another source of funds, the Troubled Asset Relief Program (TARP), a temporary program under the U.S. Treasury, was included in the government's bailout efforts. TARP support included $15 billion to auto-financing companies at risk of failure and $235 billion in direct investments to some 600 banks to encourage lending. Other government sources provided $85 billion to rescue Freddie Mac and Fannie Mae, two government-sponsored enterprises on the verge of financial failure. Freddie Mac and Fannie Mae buy home mortgages from the original lenders—for example, from banks—and hold them or resell them. In 2008, they bought 80 percent of U.S. home mortgages, many of which turned bad in the collapsing housing market.[18]

Assurances of Repayment In return for its investments, the government imposes various kinds of assurances. The Fed's loans to banks, for example, are secured by the banks' assets. That is, the Fed holds some of the banks' assets, such as commercial loans, residential mortgages, and asset-backed securities as collateral until the banks repay the Fed. In return for TARP funds, the U.S. Treasury holds preferred stock (dividend-paying ownership shares) of the banks. The Treasury also holds *warrants*—which give the right to buy shares of the banks' stock in the future at a preset price. In addition to creating the government's precedent-setting part ownership, TARP also imposes stricter executive compensation requirements. In the bailout of Freddie Mac and Fannie Mae, both firms were taken over by the Federal Housing Finance Agency (FHFA) because the failure of either would severely damage global financial markets along with the U.S. economy. FHFA took full control over the two firms' assets and operations.[19]

Anti-Crime and Anti-Terrorism Regulations

Under provisions of the *Bank Secrecy Act (BSA)*, the U.S. Department of the Treasury imposed a $24 million fine on the New York branch of a Jordan-based Arab Bank for failing to implement required monitoring and record-keeping methods to deter funding of crimes. The enforcement of BSA regulations includes tracking and reporting on suspicious transactions, such as a sudden increase in wire transfers or cash transactions exceeding $10,000, to cut off funding of criminal and terrorist activities.[20]

Banks are subject to prosecution when they fail to maintain systems for identifying and reporting suspicious activities that indicate possible drug transactions and money laundering. In violation of the BSA, a Miami, Florida, bank agreed to pay a $55 million penalty to the U.S. government following charges that it did not operate an effective anti-money laundering program. A Puerto Rico bank was assessed a $21 million penalty for not filing suspicious activity reports when repeated cash deposits were made into one account, often in paper bags in small denominations, totaling $20 million. A California bank was cited for not maintaining an effective anti-money laundering program when proceeds from cocaine sales were transferred from Mexico for deposit into accounts at the bank.[21]

The *USA PATRIOT Act*, passed in 2001 and designed to reduce terrorism risks, requires banks to obtain and verify every customer's name, address, date of birth, and Social Security (or tax identification) number. They must also implement a *customer identification program (CIP)* to verify identities, keep records of customer activities, and compare identities of new customers with government terrorist lists.

The Impact of Electronic Technologies

Banks are increasingly adopting technology to improve efficiency and customer service. In addition to EFT systems, banks offer telephone, TV, and Internet banking, which allow customers to make around-the-clock transactions. Each business day, more than $4 trillion exists in and among banks and other financial institutions in purely electronic form. Each year, the Fed's Fedwire funds transfer system—the world's largest electronic payments system—processes about $800 trillion in transactions for some 9,300 financial institutions.

Automated Clearing House (ACH) Network   ACH is a growing electronic funds transfer system that provides interbank clearing of electronic payments for participating

---

Entrepreneurship and New Ventures

Sowing the Seeds for a Green Bank

While dozens of cash-strapped banks flounder in the deep recession, is the time ripe for opening a new bank? Yes, say founders Frank Baldassarre, Jr., and Sandy Wiggins, especially when you color it "green," where *green* means more than just the color of money. The key word here is "environmental" green. Departing from the industry's traditional direction, e3bank takes a different path by using "the triple bottom line (TBL)" for evaluating projects. TBL considers enterprise, environment, and social equity instead of judging a project on just its economic returns. "All the decisions we make are passed through three lenses," says president and CEO Baldassarre. How will each decision affect the bank's profitability? How will it affect the environment? What will be its effect on the people involved?

"We want our customers to know how we're putting their money to work," says Wiggins, chairman of e3bank and former head of the U.S. Green Building Council. Specialized real-estate loans, for example, are focused on buildings certified by Leadership in Energy and Environmental Design (LEED). Buildings that receive higher levels of LEED certification get lower-interest loans because they are expected to last longer and save energy. Discounted interest rates are also given on loans for energy-efficient cars. These loans return a profit to the bank, while also having a positive impact on people and the environment, thus meeting the TBL requirement. TBL applies to other decision areas, too: Philadelphia-based e3bank doesn't have branches, its customer center is located near mass transit, and it limits the number of paper checks, all to keep a low environmental footprint. Environmental

and operating costs are reduced by communicating with customers online, transferring funds electronically, receiving deposits using scanners and software (instead of handling physical checks), and using remote digital signatures so customers don't have to sign papers at the bank.

While this may seem like a bad time to start a bank, Wiggins believes the opposite. Existing banks are suffering because they hold lots of bad loans, whereas e3bank is starting with a clean slate. And with the government touting a stimulus package to encourage green projects for consumers and businesses, e3bank is posturing for the economy's rebound. Will its TBL approach become a winner? Green-minded supporters who want to become investors can buy shares by visiting **e3bank.com**.[22]

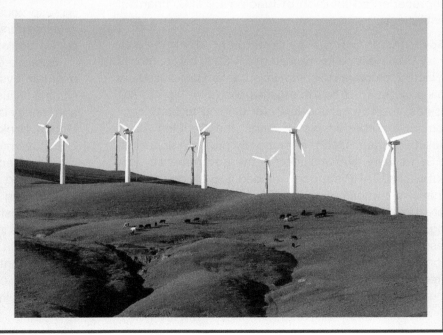

financial institutions. The ACH network allows businesses, government, and consumers to choose an electronic-over-paper alternative for payments (instead of written checks); the system is green, safe, and efficient.

ACH payments include:

- Internet-initiated debit and credit payments by businesses and consumers
- B2B electronic payments
- Direct deposit of payroll, Social Security benefits, and tax refunds
- Federal, state, and local tax payments
- E-checks
- Direct payment of consumer bills: mortgages, loans, utility bills, and insurance premiums
- E-commerce payments

In 2008, the ACH system processed some 18 billion payments that were initiated or received by customers at 15,000 U.S. financial institutions. Those payments totaled nearly $30 trillion. With the federal government's use of ACH, each direct deposit that replaces a check saves $0.925. With more than 1 billion direct deposits for 2008, the federal savings was more than $925 million.

The ACH system is governed by NACHA—The Electronic Payments Association—which administers and enforces the association's strict *NACHA Operating Rules* for sound risk management practices. Although NACHA was formed within the American Bankers Association, it later became an independent not-for-profit association that launched the Accredited ACH Professional program and established the system's operating rules.[23]

Check 21: Making the Paper Check Go Away The *Check Clearing for the 21st Century Act (Check 21)*, which became federal law in 2004, allows a receiving bank to make an electronic image of a paper check and electronically send the image to the paying bank for instant payment instead of waiting days for the paper check to wind its way back to the sender. More banks are adopting check image processing (Check 21) and benefitting from its speed and cost efficiency: less paper handling, reduced reliance on physical transportation, faster collection times, and elimination of expensive float. The days of writing a check, mailing it, and having several days to put money in the account to cover it are numbered, so check writers need to be aware of faster check clearing.[24]

Blink Credit Card "Blink" technology uses a computer chip that sends radio-frequency signals in place of the magnetic strips that have been embedded in credit cards for the past 30 years. The "contactless" payment system lets consumers wave the card in front of a merchant's terminal, at a gas pump or in a department store, without waiting to swipe and sign. Radio-frequency identification,

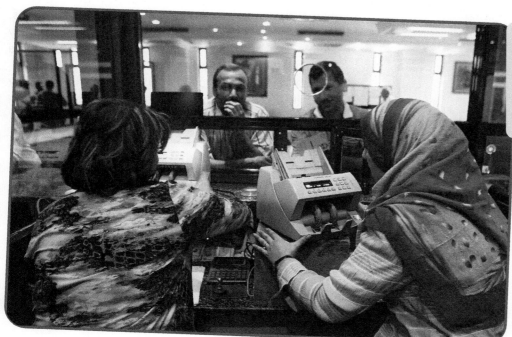

Tellers at the Bank of Baghdad in the capital's Karrada neighborhood work with customers to convert Iraqi dollars into euros for sending payments from Iraq to a French seller.

while new to credit cards, is familiar on toll roads with electronic passes that allow drivers to avoid waiting in line to pay.

Debit Cards Unlike credit cards, **debit cards** do not increase the funds at an individual's disposal but allow users only to transfer money between accounts to make retail purchases. Debit cards are used as payment for more than 30 percent of all U.S. consumer transactions, as compared with 21 percent for credit-card payments.[25]

Many stores use **point-of-sale (POS) terminals** to communicate relevant purchase information with a customer's bank. A customer inserts a card, and the bank automatically transfers funds from the customer's account to the store's account.

Smart Cards A **smart card** has an embedded computer chip that can be programmed with "electronic money." Also known as *electronic purses* or *stored-value cards*, smart cards have existed for more than a decade. They are most popular in gas-pump payments, followed by prepaid phone service, ATMs, self-operated checkouts, vending machines, and automated banking services.[26]

International Banking and Finance

Electronic technologies permit nearly instantaneous financial transactions around the globe. The *international payments process* that moves money between buyers and sellers on different continents is not subject to any worldwide policy system beyond loosely structured agreements among countries.

The International Payments Process

Financial settlements between buyers and sellers in different countries are simplified through services provided by banks. For example, payments from U.S. buyers start at a local bank that converts them from dollars into the seller's currency—for example, into euros to be sent to a seller in Greece. At the same time, payments and currency conversions from separate transactions also are flowing between Greek businesses and U.S. sellers in the other direction.

If trade between the two countries is in balance—if money inflows and outflows are equal for both countries—then *money does not actually have to flow between the two countries*. If inflows and outflows are not in balance at the U.S. bank (or at the Greek bank), then a flow of money—either to Greece or to the United States—is made to cover the difference.

International Bank Structure

There is no worldwide banking system comparable, in terms of policy making and regulatory power, to the system of any industrialized nation. Worldwide banking stability relies on a loose structure of agreements among individual countries or groups of countries.

Two United Nations agencies, the World Bank and the International Monetary Fund, help to finance international trade. Unlike true banks, the **World Bank** (technically, the International Bank for Reconstruction and Development) provides only a very limited scope of services. For instance, it funds national improvements by making loans to build roads, schools, power plants, and hospitals. The resulting improvements eventually enable borrowing countries to increase productive capacity and international trade.

Another U.N. agency, the **International Monetary Fund (IMF)**, is a group of some 150 nations that have combined resources for the following purposes:

- To promote the stability of exchange rates

- To provide temporary, short-term loans to member countries

- To encourage members to cooperate on international monetary issues

- To encourage development of a system for international payments

The IMF makes loans to nations suffering from temporary negative trade balances. By making it possible for these countries to continue buying products from other countries, the IMF facilitates international trade. However, some nations have declined IMF funds rather than accept the economic changes that the IMF demands. For example, some developing countries reject the IMF's requirement that they cut back social programs and spending in order to bring inflation under control.

Questions for Review

1 Explain the four characteristics of money.

2 What are the components of M-1 and M-2?

3 Explain the roles of commercial banks, savings and loan associations, credit unions, and nondeposit institutions in the U.S. financial system.

4 Describe the structure of the Federal Reserve System.

5 Show how the Fed uses the discount rate to manage inflation in the U.S. economy.

Questions for Analysis

6 Do you think credit cards should be counted in the money supply? Why or why not? Support your argument by using the definition of *money*.

7 Should commercial banks be regulated, or should market forces be allowed to determine the kinds of loans and the interest rates for loans and savings deposits? Why?

8 Customers who deposit their money in online-only checking and savings accounts can expect to get much higher interest rates than at brick-and-mortar banks. Why do you think that online banks can offer these rates? What might be some drawbacks to online-only banking?

Application Exercises

9 Start with a $1,000 deposit and assume a reserve requirement of 15 percent. Now trace the amount of money created by the banking system after five lending cycles.

10 Interview the manager of a local commercial bank. Identify the ways in which the bank has implemented requirements of the Bank Secrecy Act and the USA PATRIOT Act. What costs has the bank incurred to implement the federal requirements?

Managing Finances

After reading this chapter, you should be able to:

1 Explain the concept of the time value of money and the principle of compound growth.

2 Identify the investment opportunities offered by mutual funds and exchange-traded funds.

3 Describe the role of securities markets and identify the major stock exchanges and stock markets.

4 Explain how securities markets are regulated and tracked.

5 Describe the risk–return relationship and discuss the use of diversification and asset allocation for investments.

6 Describe the various ways that firms raise capital and identify the pros and cons of each method.

7 Identify the reasons a company might make an initial public offering of its stock and explain how stock value is determined.

Investing in Green

Traders are accustomed to using financial markets for investing in just about everything, ranging from pig bellies to movie production, in hopes of gaining a profit. New financial markets for commodities known as carbon credits, however, are driven, not just by profit motive, but by a sense of social responsibility. The economic incentives of emissions trading (ET) bring together both environmental polluters and green investors in an effort to both turn a profit and save the planet. In 2009, the U.S. Congress proposed a version of ET called Cap and Trade.

Here's how ET works: Regulators in various countries are setting limits on the amounts of industrial pollutants that can be released. A leading example, the European Union's Emissions Trading Scheme (ETS), was started by the European Commission in 2005 to meet carbon reductions in accordance with the Kyoto Protocol on Climate Change. The ETS annually sets a cap for the total amount of carbon dioxide (CO_2) emissions allowed for each EU member state and company. The state totals and the EU total cannot exceed the caps.

Companies are issued a permit containing a number of "credits" (or certificates) representing the right to emit a certain amount of CO_2. Any company producing below its CO_2 cap can sell its surplus credits to other, more pollution-prone companies that need more credits to keep operating. That's where trading comes into play—it's like a stock exchange that quickly matches up buyers and sellers of emissions credits.

With emissions trading, environmentally oriented companies (so-called green companies) sell unneeded emissions allowances and gain a financial return on past investments for reducing pollution. Such companies view environmental cleanup not as an expense, but as a responsible investment. Other companies, finding it cheaper to avoid such investments, are facing higher costs as they bid for others' unused carbon credits. The trading scheme is adding a new financial incentive for cleaner industries that reduce carbon emissions and other greenhouse gases.[1]

What's in It for Me?

Emissions trading is just one of countless activities drawing investors of every kind to the world's financial markets. Businesses from all over the world, representing every industry, converge there each day, seeking funds that can be used to finance their endeavors and pay off their debts. Individual investors gather as well, in person or—increasingly—online, looking to make their money "work" for them. This chapter will help you understand the various ways this is possible, whether your goals are short- or long-term, whether you are motivated by the desire for profit or security, or simply because you enjoy the challenges inherent in the successful raising and investing of capital.

TIME VALUE OF MONEY
principle that invested money grows, over time, by earning interest or some other form of return

COMPOUND GROWTH
compounding of interest over time—with each additional time period, interest returns accumulate

STOCK portion of ownership of a corporation

COMMON STOCK
most basic form of ownership, including voting rights on major issues, in a company

Figure 16.1
Amount to Which an Initial $10,000 Investment Grows

Maximizing Capital Growth

Wise investments are the key to growing your money, especially if you are seeking to build capital to start your own business. In searching for investment opportunities, a number of concepts come into play for evaluating alternative investments and sorting out the good from the bad.

The Time Value of Money

The **time value of money**, perhaps the single most important concept in business finance, recognizes the basic fact that, while it's invested, money grows by earning interest or yielding some other form of return. Time value stems from the principle of **compound growth**—the compounding of interest paid to the investor over given time periods. With each additional time period, interest payments accumulate and earn more interest, thus multiplying the earning capacity of the investment.

Making Better Use of Your Time Value What if you invested $10,000 at seven percent interest for one year? You would earn $700 on your $10,000 investment. If you re-invested the principal amount plus the interest you earned during the first year, and re-invested interest annually for another 4 years, you'd end up with $14,025. Now, if you were planning for retirement and reinvested that money at the same interest rate for another 25 years, you could retire with $76,122—almost eight times the amount you started with!

Figure 16.1 illustrates how the returns from an initial investment of $10,000 accumulate substantially over longer periods of time. Notice that the gains for the last 10 years are much greater than for the first 10 years, illustrating the power of compound growth. Each year, the interest rate is applied to a larger sum. Notice also the larger gains from higher interest rates. Even a seemingly small increase in interest rates, from 7% to 8%, results in much larger accumulations.

Common Stock

As you can see from Figure 16.1, the best way to take advantage of the time value of money is to obtain a high rate of return on your investment. One way to achieve a high rate of return is to invest in the stock market. A **stock** is a portion of the ownership of a corporation. The company's total ownership is divided into small parts, called *shares*, that can be bought and sold to determine how much of the company (how many shares of stock) is owned by each shareholder.

While several types of stock exist, common stock is the most prominent. A share of **common stock** is the most basic form of ownership in a company. Individuals and other companies purchase a firm's

---

The Rule of 72

How long does it take to double an investment? A handy rule of thumb is called the "Rule of 72." You can find the number of years needed to double your money by dividing the annual interest rate (in percent) into 72. If, for example, you re-invest annually at 8 percent, you'll double your money in about 9 years:

$$\frac{72}{8} = 9 \text{ years to double the money}$$

The Rule of 72 can also calculate how much interest you must get if you want to double your money in a given number of years: Simply divide 72 by the desired number of years. If you want to double your money in 10 years, you need to get 7.2 percent:

$$\frac{72}{10} = 7.2 \text{ percent interest needed to double the money}$$

The lesson for the investor is clear: seek *higher* interest rates because money will double more frequently.

---

common stock in the hope that it will increase in value and provide dividend income; in addition, each common share has a vote on major issues that are brought before the shareholders.

Stock values are usually expressed in two different ways: as market value and book value.

1 A stock's real value is its **market value**—the current price of a share in the stock market. Market value reflects the amount that buyers are willing to pay for a share of the company's stock.

2 The **book value** for a share of common stock is determined as the firm's owners' equity (from the balance sheet) divided by the number of common shares owned by all shareholders. Book value is used as a comparison indicator because the market value for successful companies is usually greater than its book value. Thus, when market price falls to near book value, some profit-seeking investors buy the stock on the principle that it is underpriced and will increase in the future.

Investment Traits of Common Stock Common stocks are among the riskiest of all investments. Uncertainties about the stock market itself can quickly change a given stock's value. Furthermore, when companies have unprofitable years, or when economic conditions go sour, potential investors become wary of future stock values, so share price drops. U.S. stocks, for example, lost over half their value in the recession years 2008 and early 2009. On the upside, however, common stocks offer high growth potential; when a company's performance brightens, because of public acceptance of a hot new product, for example, share price can sharply increase.

Dividends A **dividend** is a payment to shareholders, on a per-share basis, from the company's earnings. Dividend payments are optional and variable—the corporation's board of directors decides whether and when a dividend will be paid, as well as the amount that is best for the future of the company and its shareholders. Many companies distribute between 30 and 70 percent of their profits to shareholders. However, some firms, especially fast-growing companies, do not pay dividends; instead, they use cash earnings for expanding the company so that future earnings can grow even faster. What's more, any company can have a bad year and decide to reduce or omit dividend payments to stockholders.

Mutual Funds and Exchange-Traded Funds

As an alternative to buying stock, mutual funds and exchange-traded funds are popular because they offer attractive investment opportunities for various financial objectives and often do not require large sums of money for entry. In addition, the simple and easy transaction process makes them accessible to the public.

Mutual funds are created by companies such as T. Rowe Price and Vanguard that pool cash investments from individuals and organizations to purchase a portfolio of stocks, bonds, and other securities. The portfolio is expected to appreciate in market value and otherwise produce income for the mutual fund and its investors.

Reasons for Investing It's relatively easy to open a mutual fund account by e-mail or phone. There are numerous funds that meet any chosen financial objective. Three of the most common objectives are financial stability, conservative growth, and aggressive growth.

■ **Stability and Safety** Funds stressing safety seek only modest growth with little fluctuation in principal value regardless of economic conditions. They include *money market mutual funds* and other funds that preserve the fund holders' capital and reliably pay current income. Typical assets of these funds include lower-risk U.S. corporate bonds, U.S.

MARKET VALUE current price of a share of stock in the stock market

BOOK VALUE value of a common stock expressed as the firm's owners' equity divided by the number of common shares

DIVIDEND payment to shareholders, on a per-share basis, out of the company's earnings

MUTUAL FUND company that pools cash investments from individuals and organizations to purchase a portfolio of stocks, bonds, and other securities

PROSPECTUS registration statement filed with the SEC, containing information for prospective investors about a security to be offered and the issuing company

INSIDER TRADING illegal practice of using special knowledge about a firm for profit or gain

---

The Securities and Exchange Commission

The U.S. Securities and Exchange Commission (SEC) is the regulation and enforcement agency that oversees the markets' activities, including the ways securities are issued. The SEC was created in 1934 to prevent the kinds of abuses that led to the stock market crash of 1929. The SEC regulates the public offering of new securities by requiring that all companies file prospectuses before proposed offerings commence. To protect investors from fraudulent issues, a **prospectus** contains pertinent information about both the offered security and the issuing company. False statements are subject to criminal penalties.

The SEC also enforces laws against **insider trading**—the use of special knowledge about a firm for profit or gain. It is illegal, for example, for an employee of a firm to tell others about an anticipated event that may affect the value of that firm's stock, such as an acquisition or a merger, before news of that event is made public. Those in possession of such insider knowledge would have an unfair advantage over other investors.

government bonds, and other safe short-term securities that provide stable income from interest and dividends.

■ **Conservative Capital Growth** Mutual funds that stress preservation of capital and current income, but also seek some capital appreciation, are called *balanced funds*. Typically, these funds hold long-term municipal bonds, corporate bonds, and common stocks with good dividend-paying records and potential for market appreciation (higher market value), though there is always the risk of price declines if the general stock market falls.

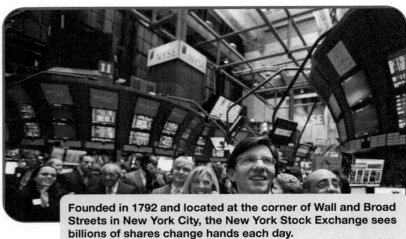

Founded in 1792 and located at the corner of Wall and Broad Streets in New York City, the New York Stock Exchange sees billions of shares change hands each day.

■ **Aggressive Growth** *Aggressive growth funds* seek maximum long-term capital growth. They sacrifice current income and safety by investing in stocks of new (and even troubled) companies, firms developing new products and technologies, and other high-risk securities. They are designed for investors who can accept the risk of loss inherent in common stock investing with severe price fluctuations, but also the potential for superior returns over time.

Most Mutual Funds Don't Match the Market Many, but not all, mutual funds are managed by "experts" who select the fund's stocks and other securities that provide the fund's income. Unfortunately, some estimates indicate that up to 80% of these managed funds do not perform as well as the average return of the overall stock market, due to costly management expenses and underperforming stocks.[2] This underperformance disadvantage has resulted in the emergence of passively managed mutual funds such as index funds, which nearly match the performance of a particular market. The selection of which stocks to purchase in an index fund is relatively automatic—it holds many of the same stocks as the market it tracks—and requires little human input, thus reducing management expenses.

Exchange-Traded Funds As with an index mutual fund, an **exchange-traded fund (ETF)** is a bundle of stocks (or bonds) that are in an index that tracks the overall movement of a market; unlike a mutual fund, however, an ETF can be traded like a stock. Each share of an ETF rises and falls as market prices change continuously for the market being tracked.

Advantages of ETFs ETFs offer three areas of advantage over mutual funds: They can be traded throughout the day like a stock, they have low operating expenses, and they do not require high initial investments. Because they are traded on stock exchanges (hence, "exchange traded"), ETFs can be bought and sold—priced continuously—any time throughout the day. This *intraday trading* means you can time your transaction during the day to buy or sell when (or if) the market reaches a desired price. Mutual fund shares, in contrast, are priced once daily, at the end of the day. Thus, when you buy or sell during the day, you don't find out the share price until after the day has ended.

Whereas many mutual funds pass the costs of expensive active management onto shareholders, an ETF is bound by a rule that specifies what stocks will be purchased and when; once the rule is established, little or no active human decisions are involved. The *lower annual operating expenses* mean that, for the buy-and-hold investor, annual fees for ETFs are as low as 0.09 percent of assets; annual fees for mutual funds average 1.4 percent.[3]

Finally, unlike mutual funds, ETFs require no minimum investment, meaning they offer *ease of entry* for investors getting started without much money.[4] On the other hand, because ETFs must be bought and sold through a broker, they require payment of a brokerage commission (transaction fees). Traders who buy and sell frequently can end up paying more in transactions fees, even surpassing a mutual fund's high management expenses.[5]

The Business of Trading Securities

Stocks, bonds, and mutual funds are known as **securities** because they represent *secured*, or financially valuable claims on the part of investors. The markets in which stocks and bonds are sold are called **securities markets**. Mutual funds, on the other hand, are not bought and sold on securities markets, but are managed by financial professionals in the investment companies that create, buy, and sell the funds.

Primary and Secondary Securities Markets

In **primary securities markets**, new stocks and bonds are bought and sold by firms and governments. Sometimes, new securities are sold to single buyers or small groups of buyers. These so-called *private placements* are desirable because they allow issuers to keep their plans confidential.

Most new stocks and some bonds are sold on the wider public market. To bring a new security to market, the issuing firm must get approval from the U.S. **Securities and Exchange Commission (SEC)**—the government agency that regulates U.S. securities markets. The firm also relied, traditionally, on the services of an **investment bank**—a financial institution that specialized in issuing and reselling new securities. All that changed, however, in the financial collapse of 2008, when Lehman Brothers's became the largest bankruptcy in U.S. history, Bear Stearns was purchased by JPMorgan Chase, and the two remaining large U.S. investment banks—Morgan Stanley and Goldman Sachs—were allowed to become bank holding companies (much like a commercial bank).[6] Although the companies' structures have changed, they still provide three important investment banking services:

1. They advise companies on the timing and financial terms of new issues.

2. They *underwrite*—that is, assume liability for—new securities, thus providing the issuing firms with 100% of the money (less commission). The inability to resell the securities is a risk that the banks must bear.

3. They create distribution networks for moving new securities through groups of other banks and brokers into the hands of individual investors.

New securities, however, represent only a small portion of traded securities. *Existing* stocks and bonds are sold in the much larger **secondary securities market**, which is handled by such familiar bodies as the New York Stock Exchange and, more recently, by online trading with electronic communication networks.

Stock Exchanges

Most of the buying and selling of stocks, historically, has been handled by organized stock exchanges. A **stock exchange** is an organization of individuals coordinated to provide an institutional auction setting in which stocks can be bought and sold.

The Trading Floor

Each exchange regulates the places and times at which trading may occur. The most important difference between traditional exchanges and the electronic market is the geographic location of the trading activity. Brokers at an exchange trade face-to-face on the *trading floor* (also referred to as an *outcry market*). The electronic market, on the other hand, conducts trades electronically among thousands of dealers in remote locations around the world.

Trading floors today are equipped with vast arrays of electronic communications equipment for displaying buy and sell orders or confirming completed trades. A variety of news services furnish up-to-the-minute information about world events and business developments. Any change in these factors, then, may be swiftly reflected in share prices.

The Major Stock Exchanges

Among the stock exchanges that operate on trading floors in the United States, the New York Stock Exchange is the largest. Today it faces stiff competition from both the electronic market in the United States—NASDAQ—and large foreign exchanges, such as those in London and Tokyo.

The New York Stock Exchange   For many people, "the stock market" means the *New York Stock Exchange (NYSE)*. Founded in 1792, the NYSE is the model for exchanges worldwide. The merger with Euronext in 2007 formed NYSE Euronext, bringing together marketplaces across Europe and the United States. Only firms meeting certain minimum requirements—earning power, total value of outstanding stock, and number of shareholders—are eligible for listing on the NYSE.[7]

Today's NYSE is a *hybrid market* that utilizes both floor and electronic trading. When a client places an order through a brokerage house or online, it is transmitted to a broker on the NYSE floor. Floor brokers who want to trade that stock meet together to agree upon a trading price based on supply and demand, and the order is executed. Alternatively, buyers can use the NYSE's Direct+ service to automatically execute trades electronically.

Other, smaller, U.S. exchanges include the American Stock Exchange (AMEX), also located in New York City, and several regional stock exchanges organized over a century ago to serve investors in places other than New York—including Chicago, Los Angeles, San

PRIMARY SECURITIES MARKET market in which new stocks and bonds are bought and sold by firms and governments

SECURITIES AND EXCHANGE COMMISSION (SEC) government agency that regulates U.S. securities markets

INVESTMENT BANK financial institution that specializes in issuing and reselling new securities

SECONDARY SECURITIES MARKET market in which existing (not new) stocks and bonds are sold to the public

STOCK EXCHANGE an organization of individuals to provide an institutional auction setting in which stocks can be bought and sold

Francisco, Cincinnati, and Spokane.

Global Stock Exchanges

As recently as 1980, the U.S. market accounted for more than half the value of the world market in traded stocks. Market activities, however, have shifted as the value of shares listed on foreign exchanges continues to grow. Table 16.1 identifies several stock exchanges and the volume of shares traded each day. While new exchanges are flourishing in cities from Shanghai to Warsaw, others are merging or partnering in different regions. NYSE Euronext, for example, gained a valuable presence in the Middle East by joining with Qatar Exchange, which enables Qatar to become a stronger international exchange.[8]

The NASDAQ Market

The **National Association of Securities Dealers Automated Quotation (NASDAQ) system**, the world's oldest electronic stock market, was established in 1971. Whereas buy and sell orders to the NYSE are gathered on the trading floor, NASDAQ orders are gathered and executed on a computer network connecting 350,000 terminals worldwide. Currently, NASDAQ is working with officials in an increasing number of countries in replacing the trading floors of traditional exchanges with electronic networks like NASDAQ's.

The stocks of some 3,800 companies, both emerging and well known, are traded by NASDAQ. Although the volume of shares traded surpasses that of the New York Stock Exchange, the total market value of NASDAQ's U.S. stocks is less than that of the NYSE.

International Consolidation and Cross-Border Ownership

A wave of technological advances, along with regulatory and competitive factors, is propelling the consolidation of stock exchanges and the changeover from physical to electronic trading floors across international borders. Electronic communication networks have opened the door to around-the-clock and around-the-globe trading. Every major European stock exchange had gone electronic by the close of the twentieth century, and the United States is catching up. Stock exchanges that don't have enough savvy with electronic technologies to stay competitive are merging or partnering with those having more advanced trading systems. The intensified competition among stock exchanges is resulting in speedier transactions and lower transaction fees for investors.[10]

Table 16.1 Selected Global Stock Exchanges and Markets[9]

Country	Stock Exchange	Total Value of Trades January–May 2009 (millions of U.S. dollars)
Australia	Australian Securities Exchange	273,206
Brazil	Sao Paulo Stock Exchange	191,926
Canada	Toronto Stock Exchange	490,912
China	Shanghai Stock Exchange	1,685,862
Hong Kong	Hong Kong Stock Exchange	519,466
Japan	Tokyo Stock Exchange	1,561,889
United Kingdom	London Stock Exchange	1,483,263
United States	New York Stock Exchange	7,986,836

Non-Exchange Trading: Electronic Communication Networks

The SEC in 1998 authorized the creation of **electronic communication networks (ECNs)**—electronic trading systems that bring buyers and sellers together outside of traditional stock exchanges by automatically matching buy and sell orders at specified prices. ECNs have gained rapid popularity because the trading procedures are fast and efficient, often lowering transactions costs per share to mere pennies. They also allow after-hours trading (after traditional markets have closed for the day) and protect traders' anonymity.[11]

ECNs must register with the SEC as broker-dealers. The ECN then provides service to subscribers, that is, other broker-dealers and institutional investors. Subscribers can view all orders at any time on the system's Web site to see information on what trades have taken place and at what times.[12] Individual investors must open an account with a subscriber (a broker-dealer) before they can send buy or sell orders to the ECN system.

Individual Investor Trading

Some of the many individual investors who buy and sell securities are novices who seek the advice of experienced professionals, or brokers. Investors who are well informed and experienced, however, often prefer to invest independently without outside guidance.

Stock Brokers

Stock brokers earn commissions by executing buy and sell orders for outside customers. Although they match buyers with sellers, brokers do not own the securities. They earn commissions from the individuals and organizations for whom they place orders.

Discount Brokers As with many other products, brokerage assistance can be purchased at either discount or at full-service prices. Discount brokers offer well-informed individual investors who know what they want to buy or sell a fast, low-cost way to participate in the market. Sales personnel receive fees or salaries, not commissions. Unlike many full-service brokers, they do not offer in-depth investment advice or person-to-person sales consultations. They do, however, offer automated online services, such as stock research, industry analysis, and screening for specific types of stocks.

Full-Service Brokers Despite the growth in online investing, full-service brokers remain an important resource, both for new, uninformed investors and for experienced investors who don't have time to keep up with all the latest developments. Full-service firms such as Merrill Lynch offer clients consulting advice in personal financial planning, estate planning, and tax strategies, along with a wider range of investment products. In addition to delivering and interpreting information, financial advisors can point clients toward investments that might otherwise be lost in an avalanche of online financial data.

Online Investing The popularity of online trading stems from convenient access to the Internet, fast, no-nonsense transactions, and the opportunity for self-directed investors to manage their own investments while paying low fees for trading.

Online investors buy into and sell out of the stocks of thousands of companies daily. Consequently, keeping track of who owns what at any given time has become a monumental burden. Relief has come from **book-entry ownership**. Historically, shares of stock have been issued as physical paper certificates; now they are simply recorded in the companies' books, thereby eliminating the costs of storing, exchanging, and replacing certificates.

Tracking the Market Using Stock Indexes

For decades investors have used stock indexes to measure market performance and to predict future movements of stock

markets. Although not indicative of the status of individual securities, **market indexes** provide useful summaries of overall price trends, both in specific industries and in the stock market as a whole. Market indexes, for example, reveal bull and bear market trends. **Bull markets** are periods of rising stock prices, generally lasting 12 months or longer; investors are motivated to buy, confident they will realize capital gains. Periods of falling stock prices, usually 20% off peak prices, are called **bear markets**; investors are motivated to sell, anticipating further falling prices.

As Figure 16.2 shows, the past three decades have been characterized primarily by bull markets, including the

BOOK-ENTRY OWNERSHIP procedure that holds investors' shares in book-entry form, rather than issuing a physical paper certificate of ownership

MARKET INDEX statistical indicator designed to measure the performance of a large group of stocks or track the price changes of a stock market

BULL MARKET period of rising stock prices, lasting 12 months or longer, featuring investor confidence for future gains and motivation to buy

BEAR MARKET period of falling stock prices marked by negative investor sentiments with motivation to sell ahead of anticipated losses

Figure 16.2
Bull and Bear Markets

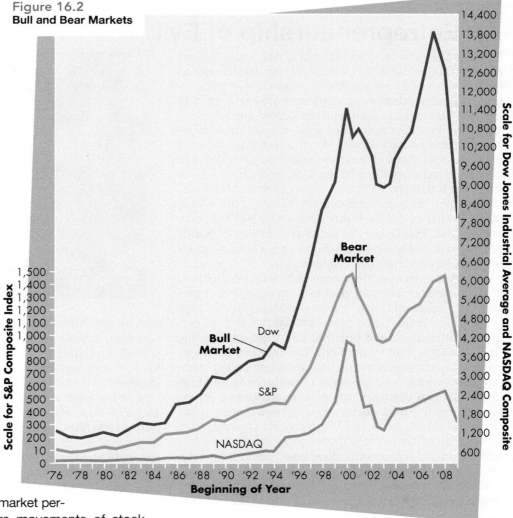

longest in history, from 1981 to the beginning of 2000. In contrast, the period 2000 to 2003 was characterized by a bear market. The period 2007–2009 was the second-worst bear market of all time, exceeded only by that of 1929–1932.[13] The data that characterize such periods are drawn from three leading market indexes: the Dow Jones, Standard & Poor's, and NASDAQ Composite.

The Dow The **Dow Jones Industrial Average (DJIA)** is the oldest and most widely cited U.S. market index. It measures the performance of the industrial sector of the U.S. stock markets by focusing on just 30 blue-chip, large-cap companies as reflectors of the economic health of the many similar U.S. firms. The Dow is an average of the stock prices for these 30 large firms, and traders and investors use it as a traditional barometer of the market's overall movement.

Over the decades, the Dow has been revised and updated to reflect the changing composition of U.S. companies and industries. Recent modifications occurred in 2008–2009, when three companies were added—Kraft Foods, insurance giant Travelers Companies, and technology titan Cisco Systems—replacing insurance company American International Group, banker Citigroup, and auto icon General Motors. Replacing the three outgoing firms, all facing substantial financial and restructuring upheavals, the new additions better represent today's food- and technology-based economy and the prominence of the financials industry.[15]

The S&P 500 Because it considers very few firms, the Dow is a limited gauge of the overall U.S. stock market. The **S&P 500** is a broader report, considered by many

Entrepreneurship and New Ventures

An Entrepreneurship of Evil

Bernard Madoff's scheme was not a new idea; it dates back to 1899, when a New Yorker, William Miller, cheated investors out of $1 million. Miller's method was popularized by Boston businessman Charles Ponzi, who, in 1919 to 1920, swindled millions of dollars from unsuspecting investors; he expected to net a 50 percent profit in 90 days. Madoff's contribution to Ponzi-scheme history is the enormity of its size and duration: It reached more than $50 billion and lasted perhaps 10 years. So convincing was his sales pitch that the $100,000 minimum investment was paid willingly by a star-studded list, including the Wilpon family (owner of the New York Jets), actor Kevin Bacon, actress Zsa Zsa Gabor, Baseball Hall of Famer Sandy Koufax, and Steven Spielberg, along with a host of banks, universities, churches, and charities.

Ponzi victims over the decades fit a certain pattern: Many are unsophisticated investors, do not rely on a professional representative, believe that unusually high returns are realistic, and place unfounded faith in personal relationships and tips that lure them into making bad decisions. That's how Ponzi connivers operate—by offering abnormally large returns, deflecting prying questions and doubts with personal re-assurances and high dividends, and bolstering the scheme's allure by paying high returns to early investors by using new money raised from new clients. As word of high payoffs spreads, more new investors are attracted; otherwise, the scheme falls apart, and the investments disappear. Without an ever-growing pool of new clients, the payoff money runs dry.

Madoff's scheme collapsed when nervous investors, worried about the economic downturn in 2008, asked to

withdraw their money. As new money ran dry, the fraud was soon exposed; a federal judge ordered that Bernard Madoff Investment Securities LLC be liquidated, and Madoff was sentenced to a 150-year prison term. Meanwhile, victims have filed more than 15,000 claims against the fraud. Investor claims may be eligible for up to $500,000 each from the Securities Investment Protection Corporation (SIPC), a private fund authorized by Congress to protect securities investors. Some of the massive losses, but certainly not all, may be recovered from the liquidated company's assets. Meanwhile, the end question from Madoff's evil remains unanswered: What percentage of losses will be recovered?[14]

to be the best single indicator of the U.S. equities market. It consists of 500 large-cap stocks, including companies from various sectors—such as information technology, energy, industrials, financials, health care, consumer staples, and telecommunications—for a balanced representation of the overall large-cap equities market.

The NASDAQ Composite Because it considers more stocks, some Wall Street observers regard the **NASDAQ Composite Index** as one of the most useful of all market indexes. Unlike the Dow and the S&P 500, all NASDAQ-listed companies, not just a selected few, are included in the index for a total of some 3,800 firms across six continents. However, it includes a high proportion of technology companies, including small-company stocks, and a smaller representation of other sectors—financial, consumer products, and industrials.

The Russell 2000 Investors in the U.S. small-cap market are interested in the **Russell 2000 Index**—a specialty index that measures the performance of the smallest U.S. companies based on market capitalization. As the most quoted index focusing on the small-cap portion of the U.S. economy, its stocks represent a range of sectors such as financials, consumer discretionary, health care, technology, materials, and utilities.

Index-Matching ETFs Countless other specialty indexes exist for specific industries, countries, and economic sectors to meet investors' diverse needs. Additionally, many exchange-traded funds are available to investors for duplicating (or nearly duplicating) the market performance of popular stock-market indexes. For example, one ETF, Standard & Poor's Depository Receipts (SPDRS, known as *Spiders*), owns a portfolio of stocks that matches the composition of the S&P 500 index. Similarly the Fidelity® NASDAQ Composite Index® Tracking Stock holds a portfolio

of equities for tracking the NASDAQ Composite Index.

The Risk-Return Relationship

Each type of investment has a **risk–return (risk-reward) relationship**: Whereas safer investments tend to offer lower returns, riskier investments tend to offer higher returns (rewards).

Figure 16.3 shows the general risk–return relationship for various financial instruments, along with the types of investors they attract. Thus, conservative investors, who have a low tolerance for risk, will opt for no-risk U.S. Treasury Bills, or even intermediate-term high-grade corporate bonds that rate low in terms of risk on future returns, but also low on the size of expected returns. The reverse is true of aggressive investors who prefer the higher risks and potential returns from long-term junk bonds and common stocks.

NASDAQ COMPOSITE INDEX market index that includes all NASDAQ-listed companies, both domestic and foreign, with a high proportion of technology companies and small-cap stocks

RUSSELL 2000 INDEX specialty index that uses 2000 stocks to measure the performance of the smallest U.S. companies

RISK-RETURN (RISK-REWARD) RELATIONSHIP principle that safer investments tend to offer lower returns whereas riskier investments tend to offer higher returns (rewards)

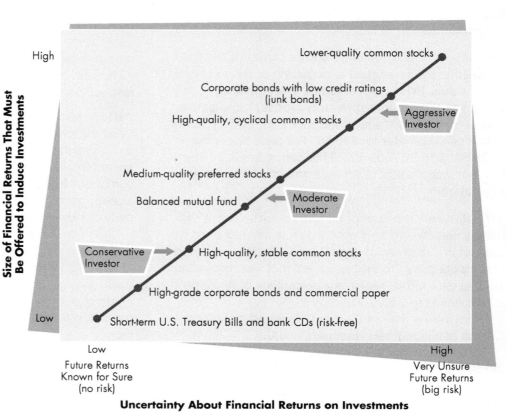

Figure 16.3
Potential Financial Returns Rise with Riskier Investments[16]

Investment Dividends (or Interest), Appreciation, and Total Return

In evaluating potential investments, investors look at returns from dividends (or from interest), returns from price appreciation, and total return.

Dividends The returns from stock dividends are commonly referred to as the **current dividend yield** (or, in the case of interest from a loan, the **interest dividend yield**), and are figured by dividing the yearly dollar amount of dividend income by the investment's current market value. In 2008, for example, each share of GE stock was receiving annual dividends payments of $1.24. If, on a particular day, the share price was $33.82, the current yield would be 3.66% ($1.24/$33.82 × 100). This dividend can then be compared against current yields from other investments. Larger dividend yields, of course, are preferred to smaller returns.

Price Appreciation Another source of returns depends on whether the investment is increasing or decreasing in dollar value. **Price appreciation** is an increase in the dollar value of an investment. Suppose, for example, you purchased a share of GE stock for $33.82, then sold it one year later for $36.50. The price appreciation is $2.68 ($36.50 − 33.82). This profit, realized from the increased value of an investment, is known as a **capital gain**.

Total Return The sum of an investment's current dividend (interest) yield and capital gain is referred to as its total return. Total return cannot be accurately evaluated until it's compared to the investment that was required to get that return. Total return as a percentage of investment is calculated as follows:

Total return (%) = (Current dividend payment + Capital gain)/Original investment × 100.

To complete our GE example, the total return as a percentage of our one-year investment would be 11.59% [($1.24 + $2.68)/$33.82 × 100]. Note that larger total returns are preferred to smaller ones.

Reducing Risk with Diversification and Asset Allocation

Investors seldom take an extreme approach—total risk or total risk avoidance—in selecting their investments. Extreme positions attract extreme results; instead, most investors select a mixed portfolio of investments—some riskier and some more conservative—that, collectively, provides the overall level of risk and financial returns that feel comfortable. After determining the desired *risk-return* balance, they then achieve it in two ways: through *diversification* and *asset allocation*.

Diversification **Diversification** means buying several different kinds of investments rather than just one. For example, diversification as applied to common stocks means that you invest in stocks of several different companies. The risk of loss is reduced by spreading the total investment across different stocks because although any one stock may tumble, the chances are less that all of them will fall at the same time. More diversification is gained when assets are spread across a variety of investment alternatives—stocks, bonds, mutual funds, precious metals, real estate, and so on.

Asset allocation **Asset allocation** is the proportion—the relative amounts—of funds invested in (or allocated to) each of the investment alternatives. You may decide for example, to allocate 50% of your funds to common stocks, 25% to a money market mutual fund, and 25% to a U.S. Treasury bond mutual fund. Ten years later, with more concern for financial safety, you may decide on a less risky asset allocation of 20%, 40%, and 40% in the same investment categories, respectively.

Performance Differences for Different Portfolios Once an investment objective with acceptable risk level is chosen, the tools of diversification and asset allocation are put to use in the investor's portfolio. A **portfolio** is the combined holdings of all the financial investments—stocks, bonds, mutual funds, real estate—of any company or individual.

Just like investors, investment funds have different investment objectives—ranging from aggressive growth/high risk to stable income/low volatility—and their holdings are diversified accordingly among hundreds of company stocks, corporate bonds, or government bonds that provide the desired orientation. The money in a diversified portfolio is allocated in different proportions among a variety of funds; if all goes according to plan, most of these funds will meet their desired investment objectives and the overall portfolio will increase in value.

Financing the Business Firm

If you invest wisely, you may earn enough money to start your own firm—but that's only the first step in the complicated process of financing a business. Every company needs cash to function. Although a business owner's savings may be enough to get a firm up and running, businesses depend on sales revenues to survive. When current sales revenues are insufficient to pay for expenses, firms tap into various other sources of funds, typically starting with the owners' savings—as discussed in Chapter 14, owners contribute funds, or paid-in capital, from their own pockets. If a firm needs more money, they can turn to borrowing from banks, soliciting cash from private outside investors, or selling bonds to the public.

Secured Loans for Equipment

Money to purchase new equipment often comes in the form of loans from commercial banks. In a **secured loan** the borrower guarantees repayment of the loan by pledging the asset as **collateral** to the lender. That is, if the borrower defaults, or fails to repay the loan, the bank can take possession of his or her assets and sell them to recover the outstanding debt. However, as we learned in the 2007–2009 recession, assets from loans defaulted by businesses and home buyers may have little or no value.

Principal and Interest Rates   The amount of money that is loaned and must be repaid is called the **loan principal**. However, borrowers also pay the lender an additional fee, called **interest**, for the use of the borrowed funds. The amount of interest owed depends on an **annual percentage rate (APR)** that is agreed upon between the lender and borrower. The interest amount is found by multiplying the APR by the loan principal.

Working Capital and Unsecured Loans from Banks

Firms need more than just fixed assets for daily operations; they need current, liquid assets available to meet short-term operating expenses such as employee wages and marketing expenses. The firm's ability to meet these expenses is measured by its working capital:

Working capital = Current assets – Current liabilities

Positive working capital means the firm's current assets are large enough to pay off current liabilities (see Chapter 14). Negative working capital means the firm's current liabilities are greater than current assets, so it may need to borrow money from a commercial bank. With an **unsecured loan**, the borrower does not have to put up collateral. In many cases, however, the bank requires the borrower to maintain a *compensating balance*—the borrower must keep a portion of the loan amount on deposit with the bank in a non–interest-bearing account.

Firms with bad credit scores typically cannot get unsecured loans. Because access to such loans requires a good credit history, many firms establish a relationship with a commercial bank and, over time, build a good credit record by repaying loan principal and interest on time.

In extreme conditions, however, even a good credit history may not be enough. With the deepening recession, the cash shortages at most banks have prevented loans of nearly any kind to business customers, thereby slowing down the economy even more. Even after vast injections of cash from TARP and other government sources, banks lagged far behind in supplying loans to meet working-capital needs of cash-strapped business borrowers.

Angel Investors and Venture Capital

Once a business has been successfully launched it needs additional capital for growth. Outside individuals who provide such capital are called **angel investors**. In return for their investment, angel investors typically expect a sizable piece of ownership in the company (up to 50 percent of its equity). They may also want a formal say in how the company is run. If the firm is bought by a larger company or if it sells its stock in a public offering, the angel may receive additional payments.

Angel investors help many firms grow rapidly by providing what is known as **venture capital**—private funds from wealthy individuals or companies (see Chapter 3) that seek investment opportunities in new

SECURED LOAN (ASSET-BACKED LOAN) loan to finance an asset, backed by the borrower pledging the asset as collateral to the lender

COLLATERAL asset pledged for the fulfillment of repaying a loan

LOAN PRINCIPAL amount of money that is loaned and must be repaid

INTEREST fee paid to a lender for the use of borrowed funds; like a rental fee

ANNUAL PERCENTAGE RATE (APR) one-year rate that is charged for borrowing, expressed as a percentage of the borrowed principal

UNSECURED LOAN loan for which collateral is not required

ANGEL INVESTORS outside investors who provide new capital for firms in return for a share of equity ownership

VENTURE CAPITAL private funds from wealthy individuals seeking investment opportunities in new growth companies

CORPORATE BOND formal pledge obligating the issuer (the company) to pay interest periodically and repay the principal at maturity

BOND INDENTURE legal document containing complete details of a bond issue

MATURITY DATE (DUE DATE) future date when repayment of a bond is due from the bond issuer (borrower)

FACE VALUE (PAR VALUE) amount of money that the bond buyer (lender) lent the issuer and that the lender will receive upon repayment

DEFAULT failure of a borrower to make payment when due to a lender

BONDHOLDERS' CLAIM request for court enforcement of a bond's terms of payment

BANKRUPTCY court-granted permission for a company to not pay some or all debts

Table 16.2 Bond Rating Systems

Rating System	High Grades	Medium Grades (Investment Grades)	Speculative	Poor Grades
Moody's	Aaa, Aa	A, Baa	Ba, B	Caa to C
Standard & Poor's	AAA, AA	A, BBB	BB, B	CCC to D

growth companies. In most cases, the growth firm turns to venture capital sources because they have not yet built enough credit history to get a loan from commercial banks or other lending institutions.

Sale of Corporate Bonds

Corporations can raise capital by issuing bonds. A **corporate bond** is a formal pledge (an IOU) obligating the issuer to pay interest periodically and repay the principal at maturity (a preset future date) to the lender. The federal government also issues bonds to finance projects and meet obligations, as do state and local governments (called *municipal bonds*).

Characteristics of Corporate Bonds The bondholder (the lender) has no claim to ownership of the company and does not receive dividends. However, interest payments and repayment of principal are financial obligations; payments to bondholders have priority over dividend payments to stockholders in cases of financial distress.

Each new bond issue has specific terms and conditions spelled out in a **bond indenture**—a legal document identifying the borrower's obligations and the financial returns to lenders. One of the most important details is the **maturity date** (or **due date**), when the firm must repay the bond's **face value** (also called **par value**, or the amount purchased) to the lender.

Corporate bonds have been traditionally issued to fund outstanding debts and major projects for various lengths of time. Short-term bonds mature in less than five years after they are issued. Bonds with 5- to 10-year lives are considered intermediate term, while anything over

10 years is considered long term. Longer-term corporate bonds are somewhat riskier than shorter-term bonds because they are exposed to greater unforeseen economic conditions that may lead to default.

Default and Bondholders' Claim A bond is said to be in **default** if the borrower fails to make payment when due to lenders. Bondholders may then file a **bondholders' claim**—a request for court enforcement of the bond's terms of payment. When a financially distressed company cannot pay bondholders, it may seek relief by filing for **bankruptcy**—the court-granted permission not to pay some or all debts. After a restructured General Motors emerged from bankruptcy in 2009, the holders of GM's $24 billion in bonds wondered how much payment, if any, they would recover from the financially-strapped company.

Risk Ratings To aid investors in making purchase decisions, several services measure the default risk of bonds. Table 16.2, for example, shows the rating systems of two well-known services, Moody's and Standard & Poor's. The highest grades are AAA and Aaa, and the lowest are C and D. Low-grade bonds are usually called *junk bonds*. Negative ratings do not necessarily keep issues from being successful. Rather, they raise the interest rates that issuers must offer to attract lenders.

Flawed Ratings Misread Recession Risks The financial meltdown of 2008 has raised questions about whether any good purpose is being served by credit-rating agencies. Among other investors, California Public Employees Retirement Fund (Calpers), the nation's largest public pension fund, has filed a suit against the three top agencies—Moody's, Standard & Poor's, and Fitch—charging losses caused by "wildly inaccurate and unreasonably high" credit ratings. Calpers officials relied on ratings for investments that turned sour—many failing altogether. Skepticism of agencies' ratings has soared following the collapse of highly rated giants such as Lehman Brothers, Goldman Sachs, and Citigroup, along with high ratings on billions of dollars of mortgage-backed securities that eventually became toxic.[17]

Highly-Rated Securities Turn Toxic Mortgage-backed securities (MBS) became a trillion-dollar investment industry during the pre-2007 housing market boom years. Financial institutions bundled home mortgages into packages and resold them as securities to eager investors who trusted in the securities' risk ratings given by Moody's, Standard & Poor's, and Fitch. Each MBS is a group of mortgages bundled together to form a debt obligation—a bond—that entitles the holder (investor) to the cash that flows in from the mortgages. Unknown to investors, some $3 trillion of MBSs contained subprime mortgages—high-risk loans to applicants with bad credit, low income, and low down payments—most of whom had received very high ratings (AAA) by credit-rating agencies. With flawed risk assessments, investors were left with little or nothing when the housing and financial markets collapsed.[18]

Becoming a Public Corporation

Initial public offerings (IPOs)—the first sale of a company's stock to the general public—are a major source of funds that fuel continued growth for many

---

Managing in Turbulent Times

Staying Afloat in a Sea of Falling Home Values

While questions remain on causes of the U.S. credit crisis, consensus has emerged that two financial giants—Fannie Mae and Freddie Mac—contributed significantly to the downfall. Senator John McCain said the companies were the "catalyst—the match that started this forest fire." Representative Henry Waxman, citing irresponsible investments and ignoring credit risks, noted that the companies' "own risk managers warned time after time of the dangers of investing in the subprime market."[19]

In 2008, to support the housing market, the U.S. government took over these two companies, which had losses totaling over $100 billion and which owned or guaranteed nearly $6 trillion in outstanding home mortgage debt. The top executives at both companies were fired, and day-to-day operations were placed under control of the Federal Housing Finance Agency. The government also committed up to $200 billion in bailout funds to each firm, if needed, to avoid further meltdown.[20]

Freddie Mac and Fannie Mae, also known as FM2, are federally backed, publicly traded companies chartered by Congress. They were created decades ago to keep the housing market flowing by making home mortgage money more available. FM2 buy mortgage loans from loan-making financial institutions, then bundle them together into securities that are insured by FM2 and sold to investors. Before 1992, FM2 applied stricter credit standards, refusing to buy and resell subprime mortgages; banks that made subprime loans had to accept the risks by holding them. When lenders failed to repay, the failed loans became the bank's loss. Since 1992, with FM2's acceptance of subprime mortgages, lending risks have been transferred from banks to FM2 on a massive scale. By selling their subprime loans to FM2, banks receive new cash to lend without being saddled with the risky subprimes. As housing values continue to fall and loan defaults grow, the mortgage-backed securities issued by FM2 are under increasing risk of default, and the U.S. government faces prospects of repaying an ocean of money to insured securities investors.[21]

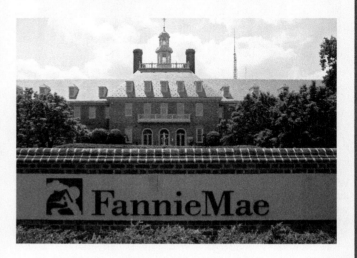

---

firms, as well as introduce numerous considerations and complexities inherent in running a public company.

Going Public Means Selling Off Part of the Company

Private owners lose some control of the company when shares are sold to the public. Common shareholders usually have voting rights in corporate governance, so they elect the board of directors and vote on major issues put forth at the company's annual shareholders' meeting. Anyone owning a large proportion of the company's shares gains a powerful position in determining who runs the corporation and how.

At an extreme, a **corporate raider**—an investor conducting a type of hostile (unwanted) takeover—buys shares on the open market, attempting to seize control of the company and its assets. The raider then sells off those assets at a profit, resulting in the company's disappearance.

A company is ripe for raiding when its stock price falls so shares can be cheaply bought, although its assets still have high value.

Stock Valuation

There are many factors that affect a stock's value, which in turn affect the value of the business. In addition, different investors measure value differently, and their measurements may change according to circumstance. Because of the uncertainties involved in stock prices, investment professionals believe day-to-day prices to be a generally poor indicator of any stock's real value. Instead, a long-run perspective considers the company's financial health, past history of results and future forecasts, its record for managerial performance, and overall prospects for competing successfully in the coming years. Accordingly, any stock's value today looks beyond the current price and is based on expectations of the financial returns it will provide to shareholders during the long run.

Why Shares Are Different Prices In June 2008 the price of Google Inc. was about $570 per share on the New York Stock Exchange, while GE shares traded at about $29, and Delta Airlines shares were priced at about $5.30. Berkshire Hathaway shares traded for $127,000.[22]

Why such differences? One reason is supply and demand for each company's shares; another is because some corporations want the shares to sell within a particular price range, say between $20 and $80, believing it will attract a larger pool of investors. If the price gets too high, the company can restore it to the desired range by a **stock split**—a stock dividend paid in additional shares to shareholders. Here's how it works. Suppose company X has 100,000 common shares outstanding that are trading at $100 per share, but the company wants it priced in the $20 to $80 range. X can declare a 2-for-1 stock split, meaning the company gives shareholders one additional share for each share they own. Now X has 200,000 shares outstanding but its financial performance has not

With an initial public offering in 2004, Google began selling its stock to the public, thus creating additional funds that were needed for expansion. The IPO raised proceeds of $1.9 billion from selling 22.5 million shares at $85 per share.

Comparing Prices of Different Stocks

Consider a typical pre-recession day when PepsiCo's share price was $70, while Coca-Cola was $58 per share. Does the price difference mean that PepsiCo is a better company than Coca-Cola, because its shares are more expensive? Or does it mean that Coke shares are a better value because they can be bought at a lower price than PepsiCo's? In fact, neither of these two reasons is correct. Share prices alone do not provide enough information to determine which is the better investment. Table 16.3 can help us make a better comparison.

First, earnings per share (EPS) are greater for PepsiCo. Even though you pay more to own a PepsiCo share, earnings per dollar of investment are greater as well ($3.42 earnings/$70 investment = $0.049; versus $2.16 earnings/$58 investment = $0.037): PepsiCo's earnings were nearly 5 cents for each dollar of its share price, whereas Coca-Cola earned less than 4 cents. PepsiCo generated more earnings power for each dollar of shareholder investment.

Now consider annual dividends paid to shareholders. The dividend yield from Coca-Cola was 2.32%. That is, the dividend payment amounted to a 2.32% return on the shareholder's $58 investment, or $1.35 ($58 × 2.32%). PepsiCo's dividend payment was about $1.50 ($70 × 2.14%), though this represents a somewhat smaller return (yield) on shareholder investment than Coca-Cola.

Based on this limited information, it's not clear which of the two companies is the better investment. A more complete evaluation would compare historical performance consistency over a period of several years, along with indicators of each firm's prospects for the future.

changed, so the stock price immediately falls to $50 per share. Every shareholder's investment value, however, is unchanged: they previously owned one share at $100, and now they own two shares at $50 each.

Market Capitalization

A widely used measure of corporate size and value is known as **market capitalization (market cap)**—the total dollar value of all the company's outstanding shares, calculated as the current stock price multiplied by the number of shares outstanding. As indicated in Table 16.4, the investment industry categorizes firms according to size of capitalization.

Investors typically regard larger market caps as less risky, and firms with small market caps (small-cap firms) as being particularly risky investments.

"Our stock just went up ten points on the rumor that I was replacing you all with burlap sacks stuffed with straw."

Table 16.3 **Financial Comparison: Coca-Cola and PepsiCo**[23]

	Coca-Cola	PepsiCo
Recent price	$58	$70
EPS	$2.16	$3.42
Dividend yield	2.32%	2.14%

Table 16.4 **Corporation Sizes Based on Capitalization**

Capitalization Category	Range of Capitalization
Micro-Cap	below $250 million
Small-Cap	$250–$2 billion
Mid-Cap	$2 billion–$10 billion
Large-Cap	over $10 billion

Choosing Equity versus Debt Capital

Firms can meet their capital needs through two sources: debt financing (from outside the firm) or equity financing (putting the owners' capital to work).

Pros and Cons for Debt Financing

Long-term borrowing from sources outside the company—**debt financing**—via loans or the sale of corporate bonds is a major component in most U.S. firms' financial planning.

Long-Term Loans Long-term loans are attractive for several reasons:

- Because the number of parties involved is limited, loans can often be arranged very quickly.

- The firm need not make public disclosure of its business plans or the purpose for which it is acquiring the loan. (In contrast, the issuance of corporate bonds requires such disclosure.)

  Long-term loans also have some disadvantages. Borrowers, for example, may have trouble finding lenders to supply large sums. Long-term borrowers may also face restrictions as conditions of the loan. For example, they may have to pledge long-term assets as collateral or agree to take on no more debt until the loan is paid.

Corporate Bonds Bonds are attractive when firms need large amounts for long periods of time. The issuing company gains access to large numbers of lenders through nationwide bond markets. On the other hand, bonds entail high administrative and selling costs. They may also require stiff interest payments, especially if the issuing company has a poor credit rating. Bonds also impose binding obligations on the firm, in many cases for up to 30 years, to pay bondholders a stipulated sum of annual or semiannual interest, even in times of financial distress. If the company fails to make a bond payment, it goes into default.

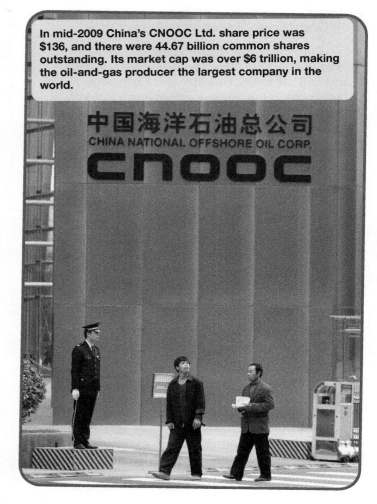

In mid-2009 China's CNOOC Ltd. share price was $136, and there were 44.67 billion common shares outstanding. Its market cap was over $6 trillion, making the oil-and-gas producer the largest company in the world.

Pros and Cons for Equity Financing

Although debt financing often has strong appeal, **equity financing**—looking inside the company for long-term funding—is sometimes preferable. Equity financing includes either issuing common stock or retaining the firm's earnings.

The Expense of Common Stock The use of equity financing by means of common stock can be expensive because paying dividends is more expensive than paying bond interest. Interest paid to bondholders is a business expense and therefore a tax deduction for the firm. Payments of cash dividends to shareholders are not tax deductible.

Retained Earnings as a Source of Capital As presented in Chapter 14, *retained earnings* are net profits retained for the firm's use rather than paid out in dividends to stockholders. If a company uses retained earnings as capital, it will not have to borrow money and pay interest. If a firm has a history of reaping profits by reinvesting retained earnings, it may be very attractive to some investors. Retained earnings, however, mean smaller dividends for shareholders. This practice may decrease the demand for—and the price of—the company's stock.

Questions for Review

1 Explain the concept of the *time value of money*.

2 What do mutual funds and exchange-traded funds offer, and how do they work?

3 Identify the various characteristics of corporate bonds.

4 How does the market value of a stock differ from the book value of a stock?

5 How do firms meet their needs through debt financing and equity financing?

Questions for Analysis

6 After researching several stocks online, you notice that they have continually fluctuated in price. What might be the reason for this? Is a higher-priced stock a better investment than a lower-priced stock? What factors would you consider in purchasing stocks?

7 Which type of fund do you think you would invest in, a mutual fund or an exchange traded fund? What is the difference, and why would you favor one over the other?

8 Suppose that you are a business owner and you need new equipment and immediate funds to meet short-term operating expenses. From what sources could you gain the capital you need, and what are some of the characteristics of these sources?

Application Exercises

9 Go to http://www.sec.gov to research how a new security is approved by the Securities and Exchange Commission. What is the process involved and how long would it take? Next, contact a financial institution such as Merrill Lynch and request information about their procedures for issuing or reselling new securities. Share this information with your classmates.

10 If you are not currently involved in investing, imagine that you are analyzing potential investments to build your portfolio. Create a mock portfolio with the investments you would obtain. How would you apply diversification and asset allocation to assure that your risk-return balance is at a point at which you are comfortable?

Risk Management

In this appendix, we describe other types of risks that businesses face, and analyze some of the ways in which they typically manage them.

Coping with Risk

Businesses constantly face two basic types of **risk**—uncertainty about future events. **Speculative risks**, such as financial investments, involve the possibility of gain or loss. **Pure risks** involve only the possibility of loss or no loss. Designing and distributing a new product, for example, is a speculative risk—the product may fail, or it may succeed and earn high profits. In contrast, the chance of a warehouse fire is a pure risk.

For a company to survive and prosper, it must manage both types of risk in a cost-effective manner. We can define the process of **risk management** as conserving the firm's earning power and assets by reducing the threat of losses due to uncontrollable events. In every company, each manager must be alert for risks to the firm and their impact on profits.

The risk-management process usually involves five steps:

Step 1: Identify Risks and Potential Losses Managers analyze a firm's risks to identify potential losses.

Step 2: Measure the Frequency and Severity of Losses and Their Impact To measure the frequency and severity of losses, managers must consider both history and current activities. How often can the firm expect the loss to occur? What is the likely size of the loss in dollars?

Step 3: Evaluate Alternatives and Choose the Techniques That Will Best Handle the Losses Having identified and measured potential losses, managers are in a better position to decide how to handle them. They generally have four choices:

- A firm opts for **risk avoidance** by declining to enter or by ceasing to participate in a risky activity.

- When avoidance is not practical or desirable, firms can practice **risk control**—the use of loss-prevention techniques to minimize the frequency or severity of losses.

- When losses cannot be avoided or controlled, firms must cope with the consequences. When such losses are manageable and predictable, the firm may decide to cover them out of company funds. The firm is said to assume or retain the financial consequences of the loss; hence, the practice is known as **risk retention**.

- When the potential for large risks cannot be avoided or controlled, managers often opt for **risk transfer** to another firm—namely, an insurance company—to protect itself.

Step 4: Implement the Risk-Management Program The means of implementing risk-management decisions depend on both the technique chosen and the activity being managed.

- Risk avoidance for certain activities can be implemented by purchasing those activities from outside providers.

- Risk control might be implemented by training employees and designing new work methods and equipment for on-the-job safety.

- For situations in which risk retention is preferred, reserve funds can be set aside from revenues.

- When risk transfer is needed, implementation means selecting an insurance company and buying the appropriate policies.

RISK uncertainty about future events

SPECULATIVE RISK risk involving the possibility of gain or loss

PURE RISK risk involving only the possibility of loss or no loss

RISK MANAGEMENT process of conserving the firm's earning power and assets by reducing the threat of losses due to uncontrollable events

RISK AVOIDANCE practice of avoiding risk by declining or ceasing to participate in an activity

RISK CONTROL practice of minimizing the frequency or severity of losses from risky activities

RISK RETENTION practice of covering a firm's losses with its own funds

RISK TRANSFER practice of transferring a firm's risk to another firm

Step 5: Monitor Results New types of risks emerge with changes in customers, facilities, employees, and products. Insurance regulations change, and new types of insurance become available. Consequently, managers must continuously monitor a company's risks, reevaluate the methods used for handling them, and revise them as necessary.

Insurance as Risk Management

To deal with some risks, both businesses and individuals may choose to purchase insurance. Insurance is purchased by paying **insurance premiums**—payments to an insurance company to buy a policy and keep it active. In return, the insurance company issues an **insurance policy**—a formal agreement to pay the policyholder a specified amount in the event of certain losses. In some cases, the insured party must also pay a **deductible**, an agreed-upon amount of the loss that the insured must absorb prior to reimbursement. Buyers find insurance appealing because they are protected against large, potentially devastating losses in return for a relatively small sum of money.

With insurance, individuals and businesses share risks by contributing to a fund from which those who suffer losses are paid. Insurance companies are willing to accept these risks because they make profits by taking in more premiums than they pay out to cover policyholders' losses. Although many policyholders are paying for protection against the same type of loss, by no means will all of them suffer such a loss.

Insurable Versus Uninsurable Risks Like every business, insurance companies must avoid certain risks. Insurers divide potential sources of loss into *insurable risks* and *uninsurable risks.* They issue policies only for insurable risks. Although there are some exceptions, an insurable risk must meet the following four criteria:

1 *Predictability*: The insurer must be able to use statistical tools to forecast the likelihood of a loss. This forecast also helps insurers determine premiums charged to policyholders.

2 *Casualty*: A loss must result from an *accident,* not from an intentional act by the policyholder. To avoid paying in cases of fraud, insurers may refuse to cover losses when they cannot determine whether policyholders' actions contributed to them.

3 *Unconnectedness*: Potential losses must be random and must occur independently of other losses. No insurer can afford to write insurance when a large percentage of those who are exposed to a particular

kind of loss are likely to suffer such a loss. By carefully choosing the risks that it will insure, an insurance company can reduce its chances of a large loss or insolvency.

4 *Verifiability*: Insured losses must be verifiable as to cause, time, place, and amount.

Special Forms of Insurance for Business Businesses have special insurable concerns—*liability*, *property*, *business interruption*, *key person insurance*, and *business continuation agreements*.

Liability Insurance Liability means responsibility for damages in case of accidental or deliberate harm to individuals or property. **Liability insurance** covers losses resulting from damage to people or property when the insured party is judged liable.

A business is liable for any injury to an employee when the injury arises from activities related to the occupation. When workers are permanently or temporarily disabled by job-related accidents or disease, employers are required by law to provide **workers' compensation coverage** for medical expenses, loss of wages, and rehabilitation services.

Property Insurance A firm purchases **property insurance** to cover injuries to itself resulting from physical damage to or loss of real estate or personal property. Property losses may result from fire, lightning, wind, hail, explosion, theft, vandalism, or other destructive forces.

Business Interruption Insurance In some cases, loss to property is minimal in comparison to loss of income. If a firm is forced to close down for an extended time, it will not be able to generate income. During this time, however, certain expenses—such as taxes, insurance premiums, and salaries for key personnel—may

INSURANCE PREMIUM fee paid to an insurance company by a policyholder for insurance coverage

INSURANCE POLICY formal agreement to pay the policyholder a specified amount in the event of certain losses

DEDUCTIBLE amount of the loss that the insured must absorb prior to reimbursement

LIABILITY INSURANCE insurance covering losses resulting from damage to people or property when the insured party is judged liable

WORKERS' COMPENSATION COVERAGE coverage provided by a firm to employees for medical expenses, loss of wages, and rehabilitation costs resulting from job-related injuries or disease

PROPERTY INSURANCE insurance covering losses resulting from physical damage to or loss of the insured's real estate or personal property

BUSINESS INTERRUPTION INSURANCE insurance covering income lost during times when a company is unable to conduct business

KEY PERSON INSURANCE special form of business insurance designed to offset expenses entailed by the loss of key employees

BUSINESS CONTINUATION AGREEMENT special form of business insurance whereby owners arrange to buy the interests of deceased associates from their heirs

continue. To cover such losses, a firm may buy **business interruption insurance**.

Key Person Insurance Many businesses choose to protect themselves against loss of the talents and skills of key employees, as well as the recruitment costs to find a replacement and training expenses once a replacement is hired. **Key person insurance** is designed to offset both lost income and additional expenses.

Business Continuation Agreements Who takes control of a business when a partner or associate dies? Surviving partners are often faced with the possibility of having to accept an inexperienced heir as a management partner. This contingency can be handled in **business continuation agreements**, whereby owners make plans to buy the ownership interest of a deceased associate from his or her heirs. The value of the ownership interest is determined when the agreement is made. Special policies can also provide survivors with the funds needed to make the purchase.

Appendix II
The Legal Context of Business

In this appendix, we describe the basic tenets of U.S. law and show how these principles work through the court system. We'll also survey a few major areas of business-related law.

The U.S. Legal and Judicial Systems

Laws are the codified rules of behavior enforced by a society. In the United States, laws fall into three broad categories according to their origins: *common*, *statutory*, and *regulatory*.

Types of Law

Law in the United States originated primarily with English common law. U.S. law includes the U.S. Constitution, state constitutions, federal and state statutes, municipal ordinances, administrative agency rules and regulations, executive orders, and court decisions.

Common Law Court decisions follow *precedents*, or the decisions of earlier cases. Following precedent lends stability to the law by basing judicial decisions on cases anchored in similar facts. This principle is the keystone of **common law**—the body of decisions handed down by courts ruling on individual cases.

Statutory Law Laws created by constitutions or by federal, state, or local legislative acts constitute **statutory law**. Under the U.S. Constitution, federal statutes take precedence over state and local statutes.

Regulatory Law Statutory law and common law have long histories. Relatively new is **regulatory (or administrative) law**—law made by the authority of administrative agencies.

Although Congress retains control over the scope of agency action, regulations have the force of statutory law once passed. Government regulatory agencies act as a secondary judicial system, determining whether regulations have been violated and then imposing penalties.

Much agency activity consists of setting standards for safety or quality and monitoring the compliance of businesses.

Congress has created many new agencies in response to pressure to address social issues. In some cases, agencies were established in response to public concern about corporate behavior. The activities of these agencies have sometimes forced U.S. firms to consider the public interest almost as routinely as they consider their own financial performance.

LAWS codified rules of behavior enforced by a society

COMMON LAW body of decisions handed down by courts ruling on individual cases

STATUTORY LAW law created by constitution(s) or by federal, state, or local legislative acts

REGULATORY (ADMINISTRATIVE) LAW law made by the authority of administrative agencies

DEREGULATION elimination of rules that restrict business activity

Keeping an Eye on Business Today a host of agencies regulate U.S. business practices, including:

- Equal Employment Opportunity Commission (EEOC)
- Environmental Protection Agency (EPA)
- Food and Drug Administration (FDA)
- Federal Trade Commission (FTC)
- Occupational Safety and Health Administration (OSHA)

Trends in Deregulation and Regulation Although government regulation has benefited U.S. business in many ways, it is not without its drawbacks. Businesspeople complain—with some justification—that government regulations require too much costly paperwork. Many people in both business and government support broader **deregulation**—the elimination of rules that restrict business activity. Deregulation, they argue, is a primary incentive to innovation; deregulated industries are forced to innovate in order to survive in fiercely competitive industries. Those firms that are already conditioned to compete by being more creative will outperform firms that have been protected by regulatory climates in their home countries.

TRIAL COURT general court that hears cases not specifically assigned to another court

APPELLATE COURT court that reviews case records of trials whose findings have been appealed

CONTRACT agreement between two or more parties enforceable in court

CAPACITY competence required of individuals entering into a binding contract

CONSIDERATION item of value exchanged between parties to create a valid contract

However, it appears likely that there will be a trend back toward more regulation in the United States, at least for the near future. For one thing, the Democratic party tends to support a larger role for government. Given that the Democrats control both the White House and Congress, more regulation is likely. In addition, many critics blame the financial crisis and economic recession of 2008–2009 on the uncontrolled actions of major U.S. banks and have been calling for more regulation to help prevent a future recurrence of the same mistakes.

The U.S. Judicial System

Much of the responsibility for law enforcement falls to the courts. Litigation is a significant part of contemporary life, and we have given our courts a voice in a wide range of issues, some touching personal concerns, some ruling on matters of public policy that affect all our lives.

The Court System There are three levels in the U.S. judicial system—*federal*, *state*, and *local*. Federal courts hear cases on questions of constitutional law, disputes relating to maritime laws, and violations of federal statutes. They also rule on regulatory actions and on such issues as bankruptcy, postal law, and copyright or patent violation. Both the federal and most state systems embody a three-tiered system of *trial*, *appellate*, and *supreme courts*.

Trial Courts At the lowest level of the federal court system are the **trial courts**, the general courts that hear cases not specifically assigned to another court. Every state has at least one federal trial court, called a *district court*.

Trial courts also include special courts and administrative agencies. Special courts hear specific types of cases, such as cases involving tax evasion, fraud, international disputes, or claims against the U.S. government. Within their areas of jurisdiction, administrative agencies also make judgments much like those of courts.

Courts in each state deal with the same issues as their federal counterparts. However, they may rule only in areas governed by state law. For example, a state special court would hear a case involving state income tax laws. Local courts in each state system also hear cases on municipal ordinances, local traffic violations, and similar issues.

Appellate Courts A losing party may disagree with a trial court ruling. If that party can show grounds for review, the case may go before a federal or state **appellate court**. These courts consider questions of law, such as possible errors of legal interpretation made by lower courts. They do not examine questions of fact.

Supreme Courts Cases still not resolved at the appellate level can be appealed to the appropriate state supreme courts or to the U.S. Supreme Court. If it believes that an appeal is warranted or that the outcome will set an important precedent, the U.S. Supreme Court also hears cases appealed from state supreme courts.

Business Law

Most legal issues confronted by businesses fall into one of six basic areas: *contract*, *tort*, *property*, *agency*, *commercial*, or *bankruptcy law*. These areas cover a wide range of business activity.

Contract Law

A **contract** is any agreement between two or more parties that is enforceable in court. As such, it must meet six conditions. If all these conditions are met, one party can seek legal recourse from another if the other party breaches, or violates, the terms of the agreement.

1 *Agreement.* Agreement is the serious, definite, and communicated offer and acceptance of the same terms.

2 *Consent.* A contract is not enforceable if any of the parties has been affected by an honest mistake, fraud, or pressure.

3 *Capacity.* To give real consent, both parties must demonstrate legal **capacity** (competence). A person under legal age (usually 18 or 21) cannot enter into a binding contract.

4 *Consideration.* An agreement is binding only if it exchanges **considerations**—items of value. Note that items of value do not necessarily entail money. Contracts need not be rational, nor must they provide the best possible bargain for both sides. They need only include legally sufficient consideration. The terms are met if both parties receive what the contract details.

5 *Legality.* A contract must be for a lawful purpose and must comply with federal, state, and local laws and regulations.

6 *Proper form.* A contract may be written, oral, or implied from conduct. It must be written, however, if it involves the sale of land or goods worth more than $500. It must be written if the agreement requires more than a year to fulfill. All changes to written contracts must also be in writing.

Breach of Contract   Contract law offers a variety of remedies designed to protect the reasonable expectations of the parties and, in some cases, to compensate them for actions taken to enforce the agreement. As the injured party to a breached contract, any of the following actions might occur:

■ You might cancel the contract and refuse to live up to your part of the bargain.

■ You might sue for damages up to the amount that you lost as a result of the breach.

■ If money cannot repay the damage you suffered, you might demand specific performance, or require the other party to fulfill the original contract.

Tort Law

Tort law applies to most business relationships *not governed by contracts.* A **tort** is a *civil*—that is, noncriminal—injury to people, property, or reputation for which compensation must be paid. Trespass, fraud, defamation, invasion of privacy, and even assault can be torts, as can interference with contractual relations and wrongful use of trade secrets. There are three classifications of torts: *intentional, negligence,* and *product liability.*

Intentional Torts   **Intentional torts** result from the deliberate actions of another person or organization. To remedy torts, courts will usually impose **compensatory damages**—payments intended to redress an injury actually suffered. They may also impose **punitive damages**—fines that exceed actual losses suffered by plaintiffs and are intended to punish defendants.

Negligence Torts   Most suits involve charges of **negligence**—conduct that falls below legal standards for protecting others against unreasonable risk.

Product Liability Torts   In cases of **product liability**, a company may be held responsible for injuries caused by its products.

Strict Product Liability   Since the early 1960s, businesses have faced a number of legal actions based on

the relatively new principle of **strict product liability**—the principle that liability can result not from a producer's negligence but from a defect in the product itself. An injured party need only show the following:

1 The product was defective.

2 The defect was the cause of injury.

3 The defect caused the product to be unreasonably dangerous.

Because plaintiffs need not demonstrate negligence or fault, these suits have a good chance of success.

Property Law

Property is anything of value to which a person or business has sole right of ownership. Legally speaking, the right of ownership is itself property.

Within this broad general definition, we can divide property into four categories:

1 **Tangible real property** is land and anything attached to it.

2 **Tangible personal property** is any movable item that can be owned, bought, sold, or leased.

3 **Intangible personal property** cannot be seen but exists by virtue of written documentation.

4 **Intellectual property** is created through a person's creative activities.

Protection of Intellectual Rights   The U.S. Constitution grants protection to intellectual property by means of copyrights, trademarks, and patents. Copyrights and patents apply to the tangible expressions of an idea, not to the ideas themselves.

TORT civil injury to people, property, or reputation for which compensation must be paid

INTENTIONAL TORT tort resulting from the deliberate actions of a party

COMPENSATORY DAMAGES monetary payments intended to redress injury actually suffered because of a tort

PUNITIVE DAMAGES fines imposed over and above any actual losses suffered by a plaintiff

NEGLIGENCE conduct that falls below legal standards for protecting others against unreasonable risk

PRODUCT LIABILITY tort in which a company is responsible for injuries caused by its products

STRICT PRODUCT LIABILITY principle that liability can result not from a producer's negligence but from a defect in the product itself

PROPERTY anything of value to which a person or business has sole right of ownership

TANGIBLE REAL PROPERTY land and anything attached to it

TANGIBLE PERSONAL PROPERTY any movable item that can be owned, bought, sold, or leased

INTANGIBLE PERSONAL PROPERTY property that cannot be seen but that exists by virtue of written documentation

INTELLECTUAL PROPERTY property created through a person's creative activities

COPYRIGHT exclusive ownership right belonging to the creator of a book, article, design, illustration, photo, film, or musical work

TRADEMARK exclusive legal right to use a brand name or symbol

PATENT exclusive legal right to use and license a manufactured item or substance, manufacturing process, or object design

EMINENT DOMAIN principle that the government may claim private land for public use by buying it at a fair price

AGENT individual or organization acting for and in the name of another party

PRINCIPAL individual or organization authorizing an agent to act on its behalf

EXPRESS AUTHORITY agent's authority, derived from written agreement, to bind a principal to a certain course of action

IMPLIED AUTHORITY agent's authority, derived from business custom, to bind a principal to a certain course of action

APPARENT AUTHORITY agent's authority, based on the principal's compliance, to bind a principal to a certain course of action

UNIFORM COMMERCIAL CODE (UCC) body of standardized laws governing the rights of buyers and sellers in transactions

WARRANTY seller's promise to stand by its products or services if a problem occurs after the sale

Copyrights **Copyrights** give creators exclusive ownership rights to their intellectual property. Copyrights extend to creators for their entire lives and to their estates for 70 years thereafter.

Trademarks Because the development of products is expensive, companies must prevent other firms from using their brand names. Often, they must act to keep competitors from seducing consumers with similar or substitute products. A producer can apply to the U.S. government for a **trademark**—the exclusive legal right to use a brand name.

Trademarks are granted for 20 years and may be renewed indefinitely if a firm continues to protect its brand name. If a firm allows the brand name to lapse into common usage, it may lose protection. Common usage takes effect when a company fails to use the ® symbol to indicate that its brand name is a registered trademark. It also takes effect if a company seeks no action against those who fail to acknowledge its trademark.

Patents **Patents** provide legal monopolies for the use and licensing of manufactured items, manufacturing processes, substances, and designs for objects. A patentable invention must be *novel, useful*, and *nonobvious*. Patents are valid for 20 years, with the term running from the date on which the application was *filed*, not the date on which the patent itself was *issued*.

Restrictions on Property Rights Property rights are not always absolute. For example, rights may be compromised under the following circumstances:

- Utility companies typically have rights called *easements*, such as the right to run wire over private property or to lay cable or pipe under it.
- Under the principle of **eminent domain**, the government may, upon paying owners fair prices, claim private land to expand roads or erect public buildings.

Agency Law

The transfer of property often involves agents. An **agent** is a person who acts for and in the name of another party, called the **principal**. Courts have ruled that both a firm's employees and its outside contractors may be regarded as its agents.

Authority of Agents Agents have the authority to bind principals to agreements. They receive that authority, however, from the principals themselves; they cannot create their own authority. An agent's authority to bind a principal can be **express**, **implied**, or **apparent**.

Responsibilities of Principals Principals have several responsibilities to their agents. They owe agents reasonable compensation, must reimburse them for related business expenses, and should inform them of risks associated with their business activities. Principals are liable for actions performed by agents *within the scope of their employment.* If agents make untrue claims about products or services, the principal is liable for making amends. Employers are similarly responsible for the actions of employees. Firms are often liable in tort suits because the courts treat employees as agents. Businesses are also increasingly being held accountable for *criminal* acts by employees. Court findings have argued that firms are expected to be aware of workers' negative propensities, to check their employees' backgrounds, and to train and supervise employees properly.

Commercial Law

Managers must be well acquainted with the most general laws affecting commerce. Specifically, they need to be familiar with the provisions of the **Uniform Commercial Code (UCC)**, which describes the rights of buyers and sellers in transactions. One key area of coverage by the UCC, contracts, was discussed earlier. Another key area is warranties.

A **warranty** is a seller's promise to stand by its products or services if a problem occurs after the sale. Warranties may be express or implied. The seller specifically states the terms of an **express warranty**, while an **implied warranty** is dictated by law. Implied warranties embody the principle that a product should (1) fulfill the promises made by advertisements and (2) serve the purpose for which it was manufactured and sold. It is important to note, however, that warranties, unlike most contracts, are easily limited, waived, or disclaimed. Consequently, they are the source of tort action more often, as dissatisfied customers seek redress from producers.

Bankruptcy Law

Both organizations and individuals can seek debt relief by filing for bankruptcy—the court-granted permission not to pay some or all incurred debts. Many individuals and businesses file for bankruptcy each year, and their numbers continue to increase. Three main factors account for the increase in bankruptcy filings:

1 The increased availability of credit

2 The "fresh-start" provisions in current bankruptcy laws

3 The growing acceptance of bankruptcy as a financial tactic

In some cases, creditors force an individual or firm into **involuntary bankruptcy** and press the courts to award them payment of at least part of what they are owed. Far more often, however, a person or business chooses to file for court protection against creditors. In general, individuals and firms whose debts exceed total assets by at least $1,000 may file for **voluntary bankruptcy**.

Business Bankruptcy   One of three plans resolves a business bankruptcy:

1 Under a *liquidation plan*, the business ceases to exist. Its assets are sold and the proceeds are used to pay creditors.

2 Under a *repayment plan*, the bankrupt company simply works out a new payment schedule to meet its obligations. The time frame is usually extended, and payments are collected and distributed by a court-appointed trustee.

3 *Reorganization* is the most complex form of business bankruptcy. The company must explain the sources of its financial difficulties and propose a new plan for remaining in business. Reorganization may include a new slate of managers and a new financial strategy. A judge may also reduce the firm's debts to ensure its survival.

Legislation passed since 1994 restricts how long a company can protect itself in bankruptcy while continuing to do business. Critics have charged that many firms have succeeded in operating for many months under bankruptcy protection. During that time, they were able to cut costs and prices, not only competing with an unfair advantage, but also dragging down overall industry profits. The new laws place time limits on various steps in the filing process. The intended effect is to speed the process and prevent assets from being lost to legal fees.

The International Framework of Business Law

Laws vary from country to country, and many businesses today have international markets, suppliers, and competitors. Managers need a basic understanding of the international framework of business law that affects the ways in which they can do business. Issues, such as pollution across borders, are matters of **international law**— the very general set of cooperative agreements and guidelines established by countries to govern the actions of individuals, businesses, and nations themselves.

International law has several sources. One source is custom and tradition. Among countries that have been trading with one another for centuries, many customs and traditions governing exchanges have gradually evolved into practice. Although some trading practices still follow ancient unwritten agreements, there has been a clear trend in more recent times to approach international trade within a more formal legal framework. Key features of that framework include a variety of formal trade agreements.

Another important source of international law is the formal trade treaties that nations negotiate with one another. Governing such entities as the WTO and the EU, for instance, also provide legal frameworks within which participating nations agree to abide.

EXPRESS WARRANTY warranty whose terms are specifically stated by the seller

IMPLIED WARRANTY warranty, dictated by law, based on the principle that products should fulfill advertised promises and serve the purposes for which they are manufactured and sold

INVOLUNTARY BANKRUPTCY bankruptcy proceedings initiated by the creditors of an indebted individual or organization

VOLUNTARY BANKRUPTCY bankruptcy proceedings initiated by an indebted individual or organization

INTERNATIONAL LAW general set of cooperative agreements and guidelines established by countries to govern the actions of individuals, businesses, and nations

FINANCIAL PLANNING
process of looking at one's current financial condition, identifying one's goals, and anticipating requirements for meeting those goals

PERSONAL NET WORTH
value of one's total assets minus one's total liabilities (debts)

Dealing with personal finances is a lifelong job involving a crucial choice between two options:

1 Committing to the rational management of your personal finances by controlling them, helping them grow, and therefore enjoying greater personal satisfaction and financial stability.

2 Letting the financial chips fall where they may and hoping for the best (which seldom happens) and therefore inviting frustration, disappointment, and financial distress.

Personal finance management requires consideration of cash management, financial planning and control, investment alternatives, and risk. Let's start by looking at one key factor in success: the personal financial plan. We'll then discuss the steps in the planning process and show how you can make better decisions to manage your personal finances.

Building Your Financial Plan

Financial planning is the process of looking at your current financial condition, identifying your goals, and anticipating steps toward meeting those goals. Because your goals and finances will change as you get older, your plan should always allow for revision. Figure AIII.1 summarizes a step-by-step approach to personal financial planning.

Assessing Your Current Financial Condition

The first step in developing a personal financial plan is assessing your current financial position. Your **personal net worth** is the value of all your assets minus all your liabilities (debts) *at the present time*. The worksheet in Figure AIII.2 provides some sample calculations for developing your own personal "balance sheet." Because assets and liabilities change over time, updating your balance sheet not only allows you to monitor changes, but also provides more accurate information for realistic budgeting and planning.

Develop Your Financial Goals

Step 2 involves setting three different types of future goals: *immediate* (within one year), *intermediate* (within five years), and *long-term* (more than five years). The worksheet in Figure AIII.3 will help you establish these goals. By thinking about your finances in three different time frames, you'll be better able to

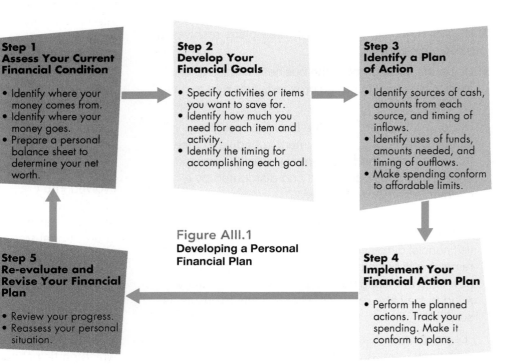

Step 1
Assess Your Current Financial Condition

- Identify where your money comes from.
- Identify where your money goes.
- Prepare a personal balance sheet to determine your net worth.

Step 2
Develop Your Financial Goals

- Specify activities or items you want to save for.
- Identify how much you need for each item and activity.
- Identify the timing for accomplishing each goal.

Step 3
Identify a Plan of Action

- Identify sources of cash, amounts from each source, and timing of inflows.
- Identify uses of funds, amounts needed, and timing of outflows.
- Make spending conform to affordable limits.

Step 4
Implement Your Financial Action Plan

- Perform the planned actions. Track your spending. Make it conform to plans.

Step 5
Re-evaluate and Revise Your Financial Plan

- Review your progress.
- Reassess your personal situation.

Figure AIII.1
Developing a Personal Financial Plan

Making Better Use of the Time Value of Money

Assets: What You Own	Example Numbers	Your Numbers
LIQUID ASSETS:		
1. Cash $	300	
2. Savings +	3,700	
3. Checking +	1,200	
INVESTMENTS:		
4. IRAs +	12,400	
5. Securities +	500	
6. Retirement Plan +	—	
7. Real Estate (other than primary residence) +	—	
HOUSEHOLD:		
8. Cars (market value) +	18,000	
9. House (market value) +	—	
10. Furniture +	3,400	
11. Personal Property +	6,600	
12. Other assets	—	
13. Total Assets (add lines 1-12)	**= $46,100**	
Liabilities (Dept): What You Owe		
CURRENT LIABILITIES:		
14. Credit-card balance $	1,300	
15. Unpaid bills due +	1,800	
16. Alimony and child support +	—	
LONG-TERM LIABILITIES:		
17. Home mortgage +	—	
18. Home equity loan +	—	
19. Car loan +	4,100	
20. Student loan +	3,600	
21. Other liabilities +	2,400	
22. Total Liabilities (add lines 14-21)	**= $13,200**	
Net Worth		
23. Total Assets (line 13)	$46,100	
24. Less: Total Debt (line 22) −	13,200	
25. Results: Net Worth	**= $32,900**	

Figure AIII.2
Worksheet for Calculating Net Worth

set measurable goals and completion times, or to set priorities for rationing your resources if, at some point, you're not able to pursue all of your goals.

Because step 3 (identifying a plan of action) and step 4 (implementing your plan) will affect your assets and liabilities, your balance sheet will change over time. As a result, step 5 (reevaluating and revising your plan) needs periodic updating.

As discussed in Chapter 16, the value of time with any investment stems from the principle of compound growth—the compounding of interest received over several time periods. With each additional time period, interest receipts accumulate and earn even more interest, thus, multiplying the earning capacity of the investment. Whenever you make everyday purchases, you're giving up interest that you could have earned with the same money if you'd invested it instead. From a financial standpoint, "idle" or uninvested money, which could be put to work earning more money, is a wasted resource.

Planning for the Golden Years

The sooner you start saving, the greater your financial power will be—you will have taken advantage of the time value of money for a longer period of time. Consider co-workers Ellen and Barbara, who are both planning to retire in 25 years, as can be seen in Figure AIII.4. Over that period, each can expect a 10 percent annual return on investment (the U.S. stock market has averaged more than 10 percent for the past 75 years). Their savings strategies, however, are different: Barbara begins saving immediately, while Ellen plans to start later but invest larger sums. Barbara will invest $2,000 annually for each of the next 5 years (years 1 through 5), for a total investment of $10,000. Ellen, meanwhile, wants to live a little larger by spending rather than saving for the next 10 years. Then, for years 11 through 20, she'll start saving $2,000 annually, for a total investment of $20,000. They will both allow annual returns to accumulate until they retire in year 25. Ellen expects to have a larger retirement

Name the Goal	Financial Requirement (amount) for This Goal	Time Frame for Accomplishing Goal	Importance (1= highest, 5 = lowest)
Immediate Goals:			
Live in a better apartment	_____	_____	_____
Establish an emergency cash fund	_____	_____	_____
Pay off credit-card debt	_____	_____	_____
Other	_____	_____	_____
Intermediate Goals:			
Obtain adequate life, disability, liability, property insurance	_____	_____	_____
Save for wedding	_____	_____	_____
Save to buy new car	_____	_____	_____
Establish regular savings program (5% of gross income)	_____	_____	_____
Save for college for self	_____	_____	_____
Pay off major outstanding debt	_____	_____	_____
Make major purchase	_____	_____	_____
Save for home remodeling	_____	_____	_____
Save for down payment on a home	_____	_____	_____
Other	_____	_____	_____
Long-Term Goals:			
Pay off home mortgage	_____	_____	_____
Save for college for children	_____	_____	_____
Save for vacation home	_____	_____	_____
Increase personal net worth to $___ in ___ years.	_____	_____	_____
Achieve retirement nest egg of $ __ in ___ years.	_____	_____	_____
Accumulate fund for travel in retirement	_____	_____	_____
Save for long-term care needs	_____	_____	_____
Other	_____	_____	_____

Figure AIII.3
Worksheet for Setting Financial Goals

fund than Barbara because she has contributed twice as much, but she is in for a surprise. Barbara's retirement wealth will be much larger—$90,364 versus Ellen's $56,468—even though she invested only half as much. Barbara's advantage lies in the length of her savings program. Her money is invested longer—over a period of 21 to 25 years—with interest compounding over that range of time. Ellen's earnings are compounded over a shorter period—6 to 15 years. Granted, Ellen may have had more fun in years 1 to 10, but Barbara's retirement prospects look brighter.

Time Value as a Financial-Planning Tool

A good financial plan takes into account future needs, the sources of funds for meeting those needs, and the time needed to develop those funds. When you begin your financial plan, you can use various time-based tables to take into account the time value of money. Figure AIII.5 shows how much a $1.00 investment will grow over different lengths of time and at different interest rates.

A timetable like this can determine the factor at which your money will multiply over a given period of

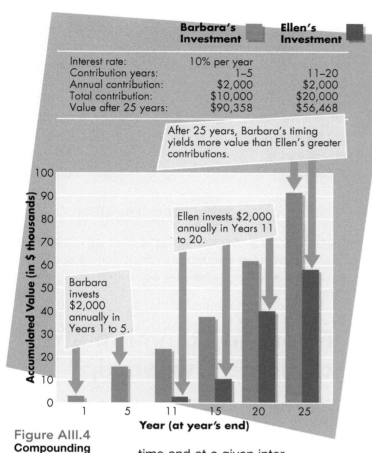

	Barbara's Investment	Ellen's Investment
Interest rate:	10% per year	
Contribution years:	1–5	11–20
Annual contribution:	$2,000	$2,000
Total contribution:	$10,000	$20,000
Value after 25 years:	$90,358	$56,468

After 25 years, Barbara's timing yields more value than Ellen's greater contributions.

Ellen invests $2,000 annually in Years 11 to 20.

Barbara invests $2,000 annually in Years 1 to 5.

Figure AIII.4
Compounding Money over Time

time and at a given interest rate. It can also help you determine how long and at what interest rate you will need to invest to meet your financial goals. For example, if you wanted to double your money in less than 10 years, you would have to find an interest rate of return of at least 8%. The catch is that to obtain a high interest rate, you will have to make riskier investments, such as buying stocks. Because higher interest rates carry greater risks, it is unwise to "put all your eggs in one basket." A sound financial plan will include more conservative investments, such as a bank savings account, to mitigate the risks of more speculative investments.

Conserving Money by Controlling It

A major pitfall in any financial plan is the temptation to spend too much, especially when credit is so easy to get. Because many credit-card issuers target college students and recent graduates with tempting offers appealing to the desire for financial independence, it is important that you arm yourself with a solid understanding of the financial costs entailed by credit cards. The same lessons apply equally to other loans—home mortgages, cars, and student financial aid.

Credit Cards: Keys to Satisfaction or Financial Handcuffs?

Although some credit cards don't charge annual fees, all of them charge interest on unpaid (outstanding) balances. Figure AIII.6 reprints part of a page from Bankrate.com's credit-card calculator at **www.bankrate.com/brm/calc/MinPayment.asp**. Using the table as a guide, suppose you owe $5,000 for credit-card purchases, and your card company requires a minimum monthly payment (minimum payment due [MPD]) of 5 percent of the unpaid balance. The interest rate is 18 percent APR (annual percentage rate) on the outstanding balance.

If you pay only the monthly minimum, it will take you 115 months—over 9 1/2 years—to pay off your credit-card debt. During this time you

n	1%	2%	4%	6%	8%	10%
1	1.010	1.020	1.040	1.060	1.080	1.100
2	1.020	1.040	1.082	1.124	1.166	1.210
3	1.030	1.061	1.125	1.191	1.260	1.331
4	1.041	1.082	1.170	1.262	1.360	1.464
5	1.051	1.104	1.217	1.338	1.469	1.611
6	1.062	1.126	1.265	1.419	1.587	1.772
7	1.072	1.149	1.316	1.504	1.714	1.949
8	1.083	1.172	1.369	1.594	1.851	2.144
9	1.094	1.195	1.423	1.689	1.999	2.358
10	1.105	1.219	1.480	1.791	2.159	2.594
15	1.161	1.346	1.801	2.397	3.172	4.177
20	1.220	1.486	2.191	3.207	4.661	6.727
25	1.282	1.641	2.666	4.292	6.848	10.834
30	1.348	1.811	3.243	5.743	10.062	17.449

Note:
n = Number of time periods
% = Various interest rates

Figure AIII.5
Timetable for Growing $1.00

will pay $2,096.70 in interest, almost half again the principal balance! Repayment takes so long because you are making only the MPD, which decreases with each monthly payment.

Save Your Money: Lower Interest Rates and Faster Payments

| Balance = $5,000 | MPD 3% | | MPD 5% | | MPD 10% | |
APR	Months	Costs	Months	Costs	Months	Costs
6%	144	$5,965.56	92	$5,544.58	50	$5,260.74
9%	158	$6,607.24	96	$5,864.56	51	$5,401.63
12%	175	$7,407.50	102	$6,224.26	53	$5,550.32
18%	226	$9,798.89	115	$7,096.70	55	$5,873.86
21%	266	$11,704.63	123	$7,632.92	57	$6,050.28

Note:
MPD = Minimum Payment Due
APR = Annual Percentage Rate

Figure AIII.6
Paying Off Credit-Card Debt

Figure AIII.6 confirms two principles for saving money that you can apply when borrowing from any source, not just credit cards: Look for lower interest rates and make faster repayments.

Seeking Lower Interest Rates Look again at Figure AIII.6 and compare the cost of borrowing $5,000 at 18 percent with the cost of borrowing it at 9 percent. If you assume the same 5 percent minimum monthly payment, a 9 percent APR will save you $1232.14 in interest during the repayment period—a nearly 59 percent savings.

Making Faster Payments Because money has a time value, lenders charge borrowers according to the length of time for which they borrow it. In general, longer lending periods increase the cost, while shorter periods are cheaper. Using Figure AIII.6, compare the costs of the 5 percent MPD with the faster 10 percent MPD. The faster schedule cuts the repayment period from 115 to 55 months and, at 18 percent APR, reduces interest costs by $1,222.84.

Combining both faster repayment and the lower interest rate cuts your total interest cost to $450.30—a savings of $1,695.07 over the amount you'd pay if you made slower repayments at the higher rate.

Declining Asset Value: A Borrower's Regret

Financially speaking, nothing's more disappointing than buying an expensive item and then discovering that it's not worth what you paid. For example, if you buy a $5,000 used car with a credit card at 18 percent APR and make only the MPD, as in the example above, you'll end up spending a total of $7,407.50 over 9 1/2 years. By that time, however, the car you bought will be worth less than $1,000. Some of this loss in asset value can be avoided through realistic planning and spending—by knowing and staying within your financial means.

Financial Commitments of Home Ownership

Deciding whether to rent or buy a home involves a variety of considerations, including life stage, family needs, career, financial situation, and preferred lifestyle. If you decide to buy, you have to ask yourself what you can afford, and that requires asking yourself questions about your personal financial condition and your capacity for borrowing. Figure AIII.7 summarizes the key considerations in deciding whether to rent or buy.

How Much House Can You Afford?

Buying a home is the biggest investment most people ever make. Unfortunately, many make the mistake of buying a house that they can't afford, resulting in unnecessary stress and even devastating financial loss. This happened on a massive scale in the housing downfall of 2007–2009; millions of home buyers had borrowed beyond their means by getting larger loans than they could afford. Borrowers were aided by lenders using loose credit standards, unlike the time-proven standards presented below, leading to unrealistic re-payment requirements. Borrowers' incomes were too small to meet monthly payments, especially when interest rates (and thus payments) increased, and when unemployment increased in the recession. They lost their homes.

In addition to loan payments, the typical demands of ownership—time and other resources for maintaining and improving a home—tend to cut into the money left

Renting	Buying
• No down payment to get started	• Must make payments for mortgage, property taxes, and insurance
• Flexibility to leave	• Equity builds up over time
• No obligation for upkeep or improvements	• More privacy
• No groundskeeping	• Value of property may increase
• Easy cash-flow planning (a single monthly payment)	• Lower income taxes: mortgage-interest and property tax payments reduce taxable income
• May provide access to recreation and social facilities	• Financial gains from selling house can be exempt from taxes
• Rental conditions may be changed by owner	• Greater control over use of property and improvements
• Timing for repairs controlled by owner	• The home can become a source of cash by refinancing with another mortgage loan or a home-equity loan

Figure AIII.7
To Buy or Not to Buy

over for recreation, eating out, taking vacations, and so on. You can reduce the financial pressure by calculating in advance a realistic price range—one that not only lets you buy a house but also lets you live a reasonably pleasant life once you're in it.

Most people need a loan to buy a house, apartment, or condominium. A **mortgage loan** is secured by the property—the home—being purchased. Because the size of a loan depends on the cost of the property, both borrowers and lenders want to know whether the buyer can afford the house he or she wants. To determine how much you can afford, one time-tested (though somewhat conservative) rule recommends keeping the price below 2 1/2 times your annual income. If your income is $48,000, look for a house priced below $120,000.

Any such calculation, however, will give you just a rough estimate of what you can afford. You should also consider how much money you have for a down payment and how much you can borrow. Lending institutions want to determine a buyer's borrowing capacity—the borrower's ability to meet the *recurring costs* of buying and owning.

PITI Every month, the homeowner must pay **p**rincipal (pay back some of the borrowed money), along with **i**nterest, **t**axes, and homeowner's **i**nsurance— PITI, for short. As Figure AIII.8 shows, the size of principal and interest payments depends on (1) the mortgage amount, (2) the

length of the mortgage loan, and (3) the interest rate.

MORGAGE LOAN loan secured by property (the home) being purchased

In evaluating loan applications, lenders use PITI calculations to estimate the buyer's ability to meet monthly payments. To determine how much someone is likely to lend you, calculate 28 percent of your gross monthly income (that is, before taxes and other deductions). If your PITI costs don't exceed that figure, your loan application probably will receive favorable consideration. With a monthly gross income of $4,000, for example, your PITI costs shouldn't exceed $1,120 (28 percent of $4,000). Additional calculations show a house price of $162,382 is the most this borrower can afford. Figure AIII.9 gives a sample calculation, and you should be able to make step-by-step computations by plugging your own numbers into the worksheet.

Figure AIII.8
Monthly Payments on a $10,000 Loan

| Interest Rate (%) | Length of Loan | | | | |
	3 Years	5 Years	10 Years	20 Years	30 Years
5.0	$299.71	$188.71	$106.07	$66.00	$53.68
6.0	304.22	193.33	111.02	71.64	59.96
6.5	306.49	195.66	113.55	74.56	63.21
7.0	308.77	198.01	116.11	77.53	66.53
8.0	313.36	202.76	121.33	83.65	73.38
9.0	318.00	207.58	126.68	89.98	80.47
10.0	322.67	212.47	132.16	96.51	87.76
11.0	327.39	217.42	137.76	103.22	95.24
12.0	332.14	222.44	143.48	110.11	102.86

**TRADITIONAL
INDIVIDUAL
RETIREMENT ACCOUNT
(IRA)** provision allowing
individual tax-deferred
retirement savings

Other Debt In evaluating financial capacity, lenders also look at any additional outstanding debt, such as loans and credit-card bills. They will generally accept indebtedness (including PITI) up to 36 percent of gross income. Because PITI itself can be up to 28 percent, you might be allowed as little as 8 percent in other long-term debt. With your $4,000 monthly gross income, your total debt should be less than $1,440 ($1,120 for PITI and $320 for other debt). If your total debt exceeds $1,440, you may have to settle for a smaller loan than the one you calculated with the PITI method. Web sites such as **http://mortgages.interest. com** provide mortgage calculators for testing interest rates, lengths of loans, and other personal financial information.

ASSUMPTIONS:

30-year mortgage
Closing costs (fees for property, survey, credit report, title search,
   title insurance, attorney, interest advance, loan origination) = $5,000
Funds available for closing costs and down payment = $25,000
Interest rate on mortgage = 6½% per year
Estimated real estate taxes = $200 per month
Estimated homeowner's insurance = $20 month

Example Numbers   Your Numbers

1. Monthly income, gross (before taxes or deductions)........$4,000   _____
2. Apply PITI ratio (0.28 x amount on line 1) to determine
   borrower's payment capacity:
   0.28 x $4,000 = ...$1,120   _____
3. Determine mortgage payment (principal and interest)
   by subtracting taxes and insurance from
   PITI (line 2)...–$ 220   _____
**4. Result: Maximum mortgage payment
   (principal and interest)..................................... $900**   _____

5. Using Table Figure AIII.11, find the monthly mortgage payment
   on a $10,000 loan at 6½% interest for
   30 years.. $63.21
6. Since each $10,000 loan requires a $63.21 monthly payment,
   how many $10,000 loans can the borrower afford
   with the $900 payment capacity? The answer is
   determined as follows:
       $900.00/$63.21 =
       14.2382 loans of $10,000 each   _____

7. Result: Maximum allowable mortgage loan [calculated
   as follows:
       14.2382 loans (from line 6 above)
       x $10,000 per loan] = ...**$142,382**   _____

**8. Result: Maximum house price borrower can afford
   using PITI** (amount of house that can be bought with
   available funds):

       From loan...........................$142,382   _____
       From down payment............$ 25,000   _____
       Less closing cost.................–$ 5,000   _____
                               ....**$162,382**   _____

Cashing Out from Tax Avoidance (Legally)

Personal expenditures always require cash outflows; some also reduce your tax bill and save you some cash. Individual retirement accounts (IRAs) and some education savings accounts have this effect. (Before you commit any money to these instruments or activities, check with an expert on tax regulations; they change from time to time.)

The IRA Tax Break

With a **traditional individual retirement account (IRA)**, you can make an annual tax-deductible savings deposit

of up to $5,000, depending on your income level. IRAs are long-term investments, intended to provide income after age 59 1/2. For distant future savings, an IRA boasts immediate cash advantages over a typical savings account because it reduces your current taxable income by the amount of your contribution.

Here's how it works: You're a qualified employee with a federal income tax rate of 20 percent in year 2008. If you contribute $4,000 to an IRA, you avoid $800 in income taxes (0.20 × $4,000 = $800). Your untaxed contributions and their accumulated earnings will be taxed later when you withdraw money from your IRA. The tax break is based on the assumption that, after you retire, you're likely to have less total income and will have to pay less tax on the money withdrawn as income from your IRA.

IRA Risks If you underestimate your future cash requirements and have to withdraw money before you reach 59 1/2, you'll probably get hit with a 10 percent penalty. You can, however, make penalty-free withdrawals under certain circumstances: buying a first home, paying college expenses, and paying large medical bills.

The unpredictability of future income tax rates also poses a financial risk. If tax rates increase substantially, future IRA withdrawals may be taxed at higher rates, which may offset your original tax savings.

Roth IRA versus Traditional IRA The **Roth IRA** is the reverse of the traditional IRA in that contributions are not tax deductible, withdrawals on initial contribution are not penalized, and withdrawals on accumulated earnings after the age of 59 1/2 are not taxed.

Figure AIII.10 shows the significant advantage of this last feature. Accumulated earnings typically far outweigh the initial contribution, so although you pay an extra $1,285 in front-end taxes, you get $40,732 in additional cash at retirement—and even more if income-tax rates have increased.

IRAs and Education Depending on your income level, you can contribute up to $2,000 annually to a Coverdell Education Savings Account (also known as an *Education IRA*) for each child under age 18. As with the Roth IRA, your initial contribution is not tax deductible, your earnings are tax-free, and you pay no tax on withdrawals to pay for qualified education expenses. However, the Education IRA requires that you use the money by the time your child reaches age 30. Funds that you withdraw but don't use for stipulated education expense are subject to taxation plus a 10 percent penalty.

ROTH IRA provision allowing individual retirement savings with tax-free accumulated earnings

Protecting Your Net Worth

With careful attention, thoughtful saving and spending, and skillful financial planning (and a little luck), you can build up your net worth over time. Every financial plan should also consider steps for preserving it. One approach involves the risk–return relationship discussed in Chapter 16. Do you prefer to protect your current assets, or are you willing to risk them in return for greater growth? At various life stages and levels of wealth, you should adjust your asset portfolio to conform to your risk and return preferences: conservative, moderate, or aggressive.

Why Buy Life Insurance? You can think of life insurance as a tool for financial preservation. As explained in Appendix I, a life insurance policy is a promise to pay

Figure AIII.10
Cash Flows: Roth IRA versus Traditional IRA

Assumptions:
Initial contribution and earnings average 10 percent growth annually.
Initial contribution and earnings remain invested for 40 years.
Income tax rate is 30 percent.

	Traditional IRA	Roth IRA
Initial cash contribution to IRA	$3,000	$3,000
Income tax paid initially: $4,285 income x 30% tax rate = $1,285 tax	0	1,285
Total initial cash outlay	**$3,000**	**$4,285**
Accumulated earnings (40 years)	$132,774	$132,774
Initial contribution	+ 3,000	+ 3,000
Total available for distribution after 40 years	= $135,774	= $135,774
Income tax at time of distribution	− $40,732	0
After-tax distribution (cash)	**= $95,042**	**= $135,774**

beneficiaries after the death of the insured party who paid the insurance company premiums during his or her lifetime.

What Does Life Insurance Do?   Upon the death of the policyholder, life insurance replaces income on which someone else is dependent. The amount of insurance you need depends on how many other people rely on your income. For example, while insurance makes sense for a married parent who is a family's sole source of income, a single college student with no financial dependents needs little or no insurance.

How Much Should I Buy?   The more insurance you buy, the more it's going to cost you. To estimate the amount of coverage you need, begin by adding up all of your annual expenses—rent, food, clothing, transportation, schooling, debts to be paid—that you pay for the dependents who'd survive you. Then multiply the total by the number of years that you want the insurance to cover them. Typically, this sum will amount to several times— even 10 to 20 times—your current annual income.

Why Consider Term Insurance?   *Term insurance* pays a predetermined benefit when death occurs during the stipulated policy term. If the insured outlives the term, the policy loses its value and simply ceases. Term-life premiums are significantly lower than premiums for whole-life insurance.

Unlike term life, *whole-life insurance*—also known as *cash-value insurance*—remains in force as long as premiums are paid. In addition to paying a death benefit, whole life accumulates cash value over time—a form of savings. Paid-in money can be withdrawn; however, whole-life savings earn less interest than most alternative forms of investment.

How Much Does It Cost?   The cost of insurance depends on how much you buy, your life expectancy, and other statistical risk factors. To get the best match between your policy and your personal situation, you should evaluate the terms and conditions of a variety of policies. You can get convenient comparisons on Web sites such as **www.intelliquote.com**.

Notes, Sources, and Credits

Reference Notes

Chapter 1

[1] Energy Information Administration. "Short Term Energy Outlook," May 6, 2008, at http://www.eia.doe.gov/steo; "Why the World Is One Storm away from Energy Crisis," *Wall Street Journal*, September 24, 2005, A1, A2; "Price of Oil Spurts to 42.90 a Barrel," *USA Today*, July 29, 2004, 1B; "Higher and Higher— Again: Gasoline Prices Set a Record," *USA Today*, May 25, 2004, 1B; Brad Foss, "Drivers Pay Price for Imported Gas," Associated Press Wire Story, May 22, 2004; Allan Sloan, "Why $2 Gas Isn't the Real Energy Problem," *Newsweek*, May 24, 2004, 40; "Who Wins and Loses When Gas Prices Skyrocket?" *Time*, May 8, 2006, 28.

[2] See Paul Heyne, Peter J. Boetke, and David L. Prychitko, *The Economic Way of Thinking*, 11th ed. (Upper Saddle River, NJ: Prentice Hall, 2005), 171–176.

[3] "100 Best Companies to Work for 2008," *Fortune*, February 4, 2008 (May 28, 2008), at http://money.cnn.com/magazines/fortune/bestcompanies/2008/snapshots/7.html.

[4] See Karl E. Case and Ray C. Fair, *Principles of Economics*, 8th ed., updated (Upper Saddle River, NJ: Prentice Hall, 2007), 103–105.

[5] Adapted from Karl E. Case and Ray C. Fair, *Principles of Economics*, 8th ed., updated (Upper Saddle River, NJ: Prentice Hall, 2007).

[6] See Henry R. Cheeseman, *Business Law: Legal, E-Commerce, Ethical, and International Environments*, 7th ed. (Upper Saddle River, NJ: Prentice Hall, 2007), 920–923, 928–930.

[7] United States Department of Labor Bureau of Labor and Statistics. "National Employment Matrix," (May 2, 2008), at http://www.bls.gov/oco/ocos285.htm#projections_data.

[8] U.S. Department of Commerce Bureau of Economic Analysis, May 2008, http://www.doc.gov.

[9] Case and Fair, *Principles of Economics*, 432–433.

[10] The World Factbook: United States. (May 28, 2008), at https://www.cia.gov/library/publications/the-world-factbook/print/us.html.

[11] Ibid.

[12] Data obtained from U.S. Department of Commerce Bureau of Economic Analysis, http://www.bea.gov/bea/dn/gdplev.xls; U.S. Census Bureau, www.census.gov/popest/states/tables/NST-EST2005–01.xls; www.census.gov/popest/archives/1990s/; National Economic Accounts, at http://www.bea.gov/national/nipaweb/TableView.asp#Mid; From World Bank Development Indicators 2007–Feb 2008: International Comparison Program (May 29, 2008), at http://www.finfacts.com/biz10/globalworldincomepercapita.htm.

[13] See Olivier Blanchard, *Macroeconomics*, 4th ed. (Upper Saddle River, NJ: Prentice Hall, 2005), 24–26.

[14] Data obtained from Big Mac Index Review 2007 (May 29, 2008), at http://www.woopidoo.com/reviews/news/big-mac-index.htm.

[15] See Jay Heizer and Barry Render, Operations Management, 8th ed. (Upper Saddle River, NJ: Prentice Hall, 2006), 14.

[16] Data obtained from U.S. Census Bureau (June 19, 2008), at http://www.census.gov/foreign-trade/balance/c0004.html#2005.

[17] This section is based on Paul Heyne, Peter J. Boetke, and David L. Prychitko, *The Economic Way of Thinking*, 11th ed. (Upper Saddle River, NJ: Prentice Hall, 2005), 491–493.

[18] This section follows Ronald M. Ayers and Robert A. Collinge, *Economics: Explore and Apply*, (Upper Saddle River, NJ: Prentice Hall, 2004), 163–167.

[19] See Heyne, Boetke, and Prychitko, *The Economic Way of Thinking*, 403–409, 503–504.

[20] See "The New Fed," *BusinessWeek*, November 7, 2005, pp. 30–34.

Chapter 2

[1] "Oil Company BP Pleads Guilty to Environmental Crime," *International Herald Tribune* (November 29, 2007), at http://www.iht.com/articles/ap/2007/11/30/business/NA-FIN-US-BP-Settlement-Alaska.php?page=1; Michael Hawthorne, "BP Gets Break on Dumping in Lake," *Chicago Tribune* (July 15, 2007), at http://www.chicagotribune.com/news/nationworld/chi-pollute_15jul15,1,386727; Terry Macalister "Greenpeace Calls BP's Oil Sands Plan an Environmental Crime," *guardian.co.uk* (December 7, 2007), at http://www.guardian.co.uk/business/2007/dec/07/bp; Sharon Epperson, "BP's Fundamental But Obscured Energy Contradiction," cnbc.com (May 21, 2008), at http://www.cnbc.com/id/24758394; Brad Hem, "10 plaintiffs in BP Case Will Seek $950 Million," *Houston Chronicle* (May 23, 2008), at http://www.chron.com/disp/story.mpl/headline/biz/5797579.html.

[2] William G. Symonds, Geri Smith, "The Tax Games Tyco Played," *BusinessWeek* (July 1, 2002), 40–41.

[3] "Tyco Votes to Stay Offshore," *BBC News* (March 6, 2003), at http://news.bbc.co.uk/2/hi/business/2827683.stm.

[4] This section follows the logic of Gerald F. Cavanaugh, *American Business Values: A Global Perspective*, 5th ed. (Upper Saddle River, NJ: Prentice Hall, 2006), Chapter 3.

[5] Manuel G. Velasquez, *Business Ethics: Concepts and Cases*, 6th ed. (Upper Saddle River, NJ: Prentice Hall, 2006), Chapter 2. See also John R. Boatright, *Ethics and the Conduct of Business*, 4th ed. (Upper Saddle River, NJ: Prentice Hall, 2003), 34–35, 57–59.

[6] Based on Gerald S. Cavanaugh, *American Business Values: With International Perspectives*, 4th ed. (Upper Saddle River, NJ: Prentice Hall, 1998) 71, 84.

[7] Jeffrey S. Harrison, R. Edward Freeman, "Stakeholders, Social Responsibility, and Performance: Empirical Evidence and Theoretical Perspectives," *Academy of Management Journal*, 1999, vol. 42, no. 5, 479–485. See also David P. Baron, *Business and Its Environment*, 5th ed.

(Upper Saddle River, NJ: Prentice Hall, 2006), Chapter 18.

8 http://bwnt.businessweek.com/interactive_reports/customer_satisfaction/index.asp, accessed May 30, 2008.

9 http://target.com/target_group/community_giving/index.jhtml, accessed January 15, 2006.

10 Starbucks About Us, at http://www.starbucks.com/aboutus/origins.asp, accessed May 30, 2008; "Starbucks to Open Regional Farmer Support Center in Rwanda," (December 1, 2007), at http://www.csrwire.com/News/10275.html.

11 Gerald Seib, "What Could Bring 1930s-Style Reform of U.S. Business?" *Wall Street Journal* (July 24, 2002), A1, A8.

12 William G. Symonds, Geri Smith, "The Tax Games Tyco Played," *Business Week*, July 1, 2002, 40–41; "Tyco Titan Charged with Tax Violations," *CBSNews.com* (June 4, 2002), at http://www.cbsnew.com/stories/2002/06/04/national/main511051.shtm; Nicholas Varchaver, "CEOs Under Fire," *Fortune.com* (December 6, 2002), at http://www.fortune.com/fortune/ceo/articles/0,15114,442883,00.html; "Kozlowski Gets up to 25 Years," *money.cnn.com* (September 19, 2005).

13 Based on Andrew C. Revkin, "Who Cares about a Few Degrees?" *New York Times*, December 12, 1997, F1.

14 http://money.cnn.com/galleries/2007/fortune/0703/gallery.green_giants.fortune/index.html, accessed May 30, 2008.

15 Louise Story, "F.T.C. Asks if Carbon-Offset Money Is Well Spent," *New York Times* (January 8, 2008), at http://www.nytimes.com/2008/01/09/business/09offsets.html?_r=2&ei=5088&en=05dc8be5247f9737&ex=1357707600&oref=slogin&partner=rssnyt&emc=rss&pagewanted=print.

16 Bob Sullivan, "FTC Fines Xanga for Violating Kids' Privacy," (September 7, 2006), at http://www.msnbc.msn.com/id/14718350.

17 http://money.cnn.com/galleries/2007/fortune/0703/gallery.green_giants.fortune/7.html, accessed May 30, 2008; http://www.scjohnson.com/environment/growing_1.asp, accessed May 30, 2008.

18 http://www.nytimes.com/2008/01/09/business/09offsets.html?_r=1&ex=1357707600&en=05dc8be5247f9737&ei=5088&partner=rssnyt&emc=rss&oref=slogin, accessed May 30, 2008.

19 http://www.starbucks.com/csrnewsletter/winter06/csrEnvironment.asp, accessed May 30, 2008.

20 Alex Berenson, "Merck Agrees to Pay $4.85 Billion in Vioxx Claims," *New York Times,* (November 9, 2007), at http://www.nytimes.com/2007/11/09/business/09cnd-merck.html?ref=business; Rita Rubin, "How Did Vioxx Debacle Happen?" *USA Today*, (October 12, 2004), at http://www.usatoday.com/news/health/2004-10-12-vioxx-cover_x.htm.

21 "British Airways and Korean Air Lines Fined in Fuel Collusion," *New York Times* (August 2, 2007), at http://www.nytimes.com/2007/08/02/business/worldbusiness/02air.html?scp=2&sq=british+airways+price+fixing&st=nyt.

22 Jerald Greenberg and Robert A. Baron, *Behavior in Organizations: Understanding and Managing the Human Side of Work*, 8th ed. (Upper Saddle River, NJ: Prentice Hall, 2003), 410–413.

23 Cora Daniels, "It's a Living Hell," *Fortune* (April 15, 2002), 367–368.

24 Henry R. Cheeseman, *Business Law: Legal, E-Commerce, Ethical, and International Environments*, 5th ed. (Upper Saddle River, NJ: Prentice Hall, 2004), 128–129.

25 http://www.usdoj.gov/usao/iln/pr/chicago/2008/pr0318_01.pdf, accessed May 30, 2008; Jacob Goldstein, "CVS to Pay $37.5 Million to Settle Pill Switching Case," *Wall Street Journal* (March 18, 2008), at http://blogs.wsj.com/health/2008/03/18/cvs-to-pay-375-million-to-settle-pill-switching-case.

26 Greg Farrell, "Enron Law Firm Called Accounting Practices Creative," *USA Today*, January 2002, 1B.

27 http://foundationcenter.org/gainknowledge/research/pdf/keyfacts_corp_2007.pdf, accessed May 30, 2008.

28 Michael E. Porter and Mark R. Kramer, "Philanthropy's New Agenda: Doing Well by Doing Good," *Sloan Management Review* (Winter 2000), 75–85.

Chapter 3

1 Fred Vogelstein, "How Mark Zuckerberg Turned Facebook into the Web's Hottest Platform," *Wired* (September 6, 2007), at http://www.wired.com/techbiz/startups/news/2007/09/ff_facebook?currentPage=3; Ellen McGirt, "Hacker. Dropout. CEO," *Fast Company* (May 2007), at http://www.fastcompany.com/magazine/115/open_features-hacker-dropout-ceo.html.

2 See http://www.sba.gov/aboutsba.

3 See http://www.sba.gov.

4 Data from http://www.sba.gov, accessed 3/6/2006, and U.S. Census Bureau, "Statistics About Business Size (including Small Business) from the U.S. Census Bureau," at http://www.census.gov/epcd/www/smallbus.html, accessed 4/25/2007.

5 U.S. Census Bureau, "Statistical Abstract of the United States," at http://www.census.gov/prod/www/statistical-abstract.html.

6 "A New Generation Re-Writes the Rules," *Wall Street Journal* (May 22, 2002), R4; See also Mark Henricks, "Up to the Challenge," *Entrepreneur* (February 2006), 64–67.

7 "Special Report—Stars of Asia," *Business Week* (July 12, 2004), at http://www.businessweek.com/magazine/content/04_28/b3891412.htm?chan=search.

8 "Special Report—Stars of Asia," *Business Week* (July 12, 2004), at http://www.businessweek.com/magazine/content/04_28/b3891413.htm?chan=search.

9 See Thomas Zimmerer and Norman Scarborough, *Essentials of Entrepreneurship and Small Business Management*, 5th ed. (Upper Saddle River, NJ: Prentice Hall, 2008).

10 Ibid.

11 "2008 Franchise 500 Rankings," Entrepreneur.com, http://www.entrepreneur.com/franchises/rankings/franchise500-115608/2008,.html, accessed 6/3/2008.

12 Kurt Badenhausen, Michael K. Ozanian, and Christina Settimi, "The Business of Football," Forbes.com (September 13, 2007), at http://www.forbes.com/home/business/2007/09/13/nfl-team-valuations-biz-07nfl_cz_kb_mo_cs_0913nfl_land.html.

[13] U.S. Small Business Administration, "Finance Primer: A Guide to SBA's Loan Guaranty Programs," http://app1.sba.gov/training/sbafp/, accessed 6/9/2008.

[14] Ibid.

[15] Zimmerer and Scarborough, 16.

[16] Jim Hopkins, "The New Entrepreneurs: Americans Over 50," *USA Today* (January 18, 2005), 1A, 2A.

[17] U.S. Census Bureau, "1997 Economic Census Surveys of Minority- and Women-Owned Business Enterprises," at http://www.census.gov/csd/mwb.

[18] Peter Hoy, "Minority- and Women-Owned Businesses Skyrocket," *Inc.* (May 1, 2006), at http://www.inc.com/news/articles/200605/census.html.

[19] Zimmerer and Scarborough, 20.

[20] Ibid.

[21] See U.S. Small Business Administration, "Frequently Asked Questions," at http://app1.sba.gov/faqs/faqIndexAll.cfm?areaid=24, accessed 7/9/2008.

[22] John Tozzi, "From Junkie to Software Success," *BusinessWeek* (May 12, 2008), at http://www.businessweek.com/smallbiz/content/may2008/sb20080512_133843.htm?chan=search.

[23] Zimmerer and Scarborough.

[24] See "Gladys Edmunds Biography," at http://biography.jrank.org/pages/2404/Edmunds-Gladys.html, accessed 6/6/2008.

[25] See Chris Penttila, "Keep it Simple," *Entrepreneur* (February 2006), 60–63.

[26] Zimmerer and Scarborough, 161.

[27] Ibid.

[28] Emily Thornton, "A Little Privacy, Please," *BusinessWeek* (May 24, 2004), 74–75.

[29] "Morgan Stanley Announces Record and Distribution Dates for Spin-off of Discover," Morgan Stanley Press Release (June 1, 2007), at http://www.morganstanley.com/about/press/articles/4984.html.

Chapter 4

[1] All box office data taken from http://www.imdb.com, accessed May 14, 2008; Media By Numbers, "Full-Year Box-office & Attendance Since 1990" at http://www.mediabynumbers.com/userfiles/file/MEDIA%20BY%20NUMBERS%20HISTORICAL%20AND%20YTD%20BOX-OFFICE%20-%202008(10).pdf, accessed May 14, 2008; Box Office Mojo,

"2007 Worldwide Grosses" at http://www.boxofficemojo.com/yearly/chart/?view2=worldwide&yr=2007&p=.htm, accessed May 14, 2008; Brooks Barnes, "Moviegoers in Seoul Will Love This Film," *The New York Times*, (January 27, 2008), at http://www.nytimes.com/2008/01/27/business/27steal.html?_r=1&pagewanted=print&oref=slogin; Dave McNary, "Foreign Box Office Hits Record Levels," *Variety* (January 1, 2008), at http://www.variety.com/article/VR1117978262.html?categoryid=1236&cs=1&query=%22resident+evil%22; Ian Mohr, "Box Office, Admissions Rise in 2006," *Variety* (March 6, 2007), at http://www.variety.com/article/VR1117960597.html?categoryid=13&cs=1; Edward Jay Epstein, "Send in the Aliens," *Slate.com* (August 29, 2005), at http://www.slate.com/id/2125153/.

[2] Ricky W. Griffin and Michael W. Pustay, *International Business: A Managerial Perspective,* 6th ed. (Upper Saddle River, NJ: Prentice Hall, 2009); The World Bank: "Data & Statistics," at http://web.worldbank.org/WBSITE/EXTERNAL/DATASTATISTICS/0,,contentMDK:20420458~isCURL:Y~menuPK:1277382~pagePK:64133150~piPK:64133175~theSitePK:239419,00.html, accessed May 14, 2008.

[3] Thomas Friedman, *The World Is Flat* (New York: Farrar, Straus, and Giroux, 2005).

[4] Brian Love, "Weak Dollar Costs U.S. Economy Its No. 1 Spot," (March 14, 2008), at http://www.reuters.com/article/idUSL1491971920080314; International Monetary Fund (April 2008), at http://www.imf.org/external/pubs/ft/weo/2008/01/weodata/weorept.aspx?sy=2006&ey=2013&scsm=1&ssd=1&sort=country&ds=.&br=1&c=924%2C158%2C111&s=NGDP_R%2CNGDP_RPCH%2CNGDP%2CNGDPD%2CPPPGDP&grp=0&a=&pr.x=51&pr.y=14.

[5] Europe, at http://europa.eu/abc/maps/index_en.htm, accessed June 4, 2008.

[6] World Trade Organization, at http://www.wto.org/English/thewto_e/whatis_e/tif_e/org6_e.htm, accessed June 4, 2008.

[7] Association of Southeast Asian Nations, at http://www.aseansec.org/74.htm, accessed June 4, 2008.

[8] http://census.gov/foreign-trade/statistics/highlights/top/top0812.html.

[9] U.S. Census Bureau: "Foreign Trade Statistics," at http://www.census.gov/foreign-trade/statistics/highlights/annual.html, accessed May 14, 2008.

[10] Ibid.

[11] Griffin and Pustay, *International Business: A Managerial Perspective*, 125–127. See also Steven Husted and Michael Melvin, *International Economics*, 5th ed. (Boston: Addison Wesley Longman, 2001), 54–61; and Karl E. Case and Ray C. Fair, *Principles of Economics*, 8th ed. (Upper Saddle River, NJ: Prentice Hall, 2007), 700–708.

[12] Ron Lieber, "Give Us This Day Our Global Bread," *Fast Company*, March 2001, 164–167; Poilâne: "Our History," at http://www.poilane.fr/pages/en/company_univers_histoire.php, accessed May 14, 2008; "Les Boulangeries-Pâtisseries de Paris: Poilâne," (June 14, 2006), at http://louisrecettes.blogspot.com/2006/06/les-boulangeries-ptisseries-de-paris.html.

[13] This section is based on Michael Porter, *The Competitive Advantage of Nations* (Boston: Addison-Wesley Longman, 2001), 54–61; and Case and Fair, *Principles of Economics*, 669–677.

[14] Lee J. Krajewski, Manoj Malhotra, and Larry P. Ritzman, *Operations Management: Processes and Value Chains*, 8th ed. (Upper Saddle River, NJ: Prentice Hall, 2007), 401–403.

[15] *Hoover's Handbook of American Business 2006* (Austin, Texas: Hoover's Business Press, 2006), 432–433; Hershey Foods (HSY), at http://www.wikinvest.com/stock/Hershey_Foods_(HSY), accessed May 14, 2008; The Hershey Company, at http://library.corporate-ir.net/library/11/115/115590/items/283950/10K_Hershey%5b1%5d.pdf, accessed May 14, 2008.

[16] Christopher Tkaczyk and David Goldman, "Fortune 500 - Big Business Battles It Out," *Fortune* (April 21, 2008), at http://finance.yahoo.com/career-work/article/104864/Fortune-500-Big-Business-Battles-It-Out.

[17] "Fortune Global 500," *Fortune* (July 23, 2007), at http://money.cnn.com/magazines/fortune/global500/2007/full_list/index.html.

[18] Cold Stone Creamery, at http://www.coldstonecreamery.com/franchises/international.html, accessed June 4, 2008.

[19] Louisa Schaefer, "World's Biggest Retailer Wal-Mart Closes Up Shop in

Germany," *DW-World.de* (July 28, 2006), at http://www.goethe-bytes.de/dw/article/0,2144,21b12746,00.html.

Chapter 5

[1] Google, "Corporate Information," May 10, 2009, at http://www.google.com; "The Secret to Google's Success," *BusinessWeek*, March 6, 2008, http://www.businessweek.com; "In Search of the Real Google," *Time*, February 20, 2007, http://www.time.com.

[2] Jason Riley, "Movie Man," *Wall Streeet Journal Online* (February 9, 2008), at http://online.wsj.com/article/SB120251714532955425.html?mod=googlenews_wsj.

[3] *Hoover's Handbook of American Business 2006* (Austin, Texas: Hoover's Business Press, 2006); "HP Reaches $100 Billion Revenue Mark for the Fiscal 2007," CBR Online (November 21, 2007), at http://www.cbronline.com/article_news.asp?guid=C4927745-C588-4832-B8A1-92C3B77DDFE0.

[4] Richard D. Knabb, Jamie R. Rhome, and Daniel P. Brown, "Tropical Cyclone Report: Hurricane Katrina," National Hurricane Center (December 20, 2005), at http://www.nhc.noaa.gov/pdf/TCR-AL122005_Katrina.pdf.

[5] "Sam Adams Beer to Expand Cincinnati Brewery," *USA Today* (January 6, 2005); Christopher Edmunds, "Bottom of the Barrel: Boston Beer's Winning Formula," RealMoney.com (March 5, 2003), http://www.thestreet.com/realmoney; Gary Hamel, "Driving Grassroots Growth," *Fortune* (September 4, 2002), 173–187; Ronald Lieber, "Beating the Odds," *Fortune* (March 31, 2002), 82–90; The Boston Beer Company, Inc.: Investor Relations Center, "The Boston Beer Company Announces Agreement with Diageo to Acquire Pennsylvania Brewery," at http://www.bostonbeer.com/phoenix.zhtml?c=69432&p=irol-newsArticle&ID=1035844&highlight, accessed 6/18/2008; Income Statement for Boston Beer Co. Inc., Yahoo! Finance, at http://finance.yahoo.com/q/is?s=SAM&annual, accessed 5/19/2008; "Boston Beer Company - Company Profile, Information, Business Description, History, Background Information on Boston Beer Company," at http://www.referenceforbusiness.com/history2/74/Boston-Beer-Company.html, accessed 5/19/2008.

[6] Based on Stephen P. Robbins and Mary Coulter, *Management*, 9th ed. (Upper Saddle River, NJ: Prentice Hall, 2007), 199.

[7] See Chipotle, "F.W.I," at http://www.chipotle.com/#flash/fwi_story; Income Statement for Chipotle Mexican Grill, Inc., Yahoo! Finance, at http://finance.yahoo.com/q/is?s=CMG&annual, accessed 5/19/2008.

[8] Matthew Boyle, "Best Buy's Giant Gamble," Fortune, April 3, 2006, http://money.cnn.com; Kristina Bell, "Q&A with Best Buy CEO Brad Anderson," *Time*, June 12, 20; "How to Break Out of Commodity Hell," BusinessWeek, March 27, 2006, http://www.businessweek.com on May 10, 2009; "Best Buy Reports December Revenue of $7.5 Billion, Continues Market Share Gains," Best Buy Inc., news release, January 9, 2009, http://www.bestbuyinc.com.

[9] See Blue Bell Creamery, "Our History," at http://www.bluebell.com/The_Little_Creamery/history.aspx, accessed 5/19/2008.

[10] Del Jones, "Next Time," *USA Today* (October 4, 2005), 1B, 2B.

Chapter 6

[1] Betsy Morris, "The Pepsi Challenge," *Fortune*, February 19, 2008 (June 19, 2008), at http://money.cnn.com/2008/02/18/news/companies/morris_nooyi.fortune/index.htm; Flex News, "PepsiCo Unveils New Organizational Structure, Names CEOs of Three Principal Operating Units," May 11, 2007 (June 19, 2008), at http://www.flex-news-food.com/pages/12058/pepsi/pepsico-unveils-new-organizational-structure-names-ceos-three-principal-operating-units.html; Diane Brady, "Indra Nooyi: Keeping Cool In Hot Water," *BusinessWeek*, June 11, 2007 (June 19, 2008), at http://www.businessweek.com/magazine/content/07_24/b4038067.htm.

[2] Joann S. Lublin, "Place vs. Product: It's Tough to Choose a Management Model," *Wall Street Journal*, June 27, 2001, A1, A4; Joann Muller, "Ford: Why It's Worse Than You Think," *BusinessWeek*, June 25, 2001, at http://www.businessweek.com/magazine/content/01_26/b3738001.htm; "Can This Man Save the American Auto Industry?" *Time*, January 30, 2006, pp. 38–48.

[3] Amy Wrzesniewski and Jane Dutton, "Crafting a Job: Revisioning Employees as Active Crafters of Their Work," *Academy of Management Review*, 2001, 26 (2): 179–201.

[4] AllBusiness.com, "Kraft Foods North America Announces New Management Structure," September28, 2000 (June 19, 2008), at http://www.allbusiness.com/food-beverage/food-beverage-overview/6505848-1.html.

[5] See Levi Strauss & Co., at http://www.levistrauss.com/Company/WorldwideRegions.aspx.

[6] See Southern Company, http://investor.southerncompany.com/governance.cfm.

[7] "Blowing Up Pepsi," *BusinessWeek*, April 27, 2009, pp. 32–36; *Hoover's Handbook of American Business 2009* (Austin, Texas: Hoover's Business Press, 2009), pp. 643–644.

[8] Michael E. Raynor and Joseph L. Bower, "Lead From the Center," *Harvard Business Review*, May 2001, 93–102.

[9] Gary Hamel, "What Google, Whole Foods Do Best," *Fortune*, September 27, 2007 (June 19, 2008), at http://money.cnn.com/2007/09/26/news/companies/management_hamel.fortune/index.htm.

[10] See http://www.ea.com/.

[11] *Hoover's Handbook of American Business 2006* (Austin, Texas: Hoover's Business Press, 2006); Brian Dumaine, "How I Delivered the Goods," *Fortune Small Business*, October 2002 (*quote); Charles Haddad, "FedEx: Gaining on the Ground," *BusinessWeek*, December 16, 2002, 126–128; Claudia H. Deutsch, "FedEx Has Hit the Ground Running, but Will Its Legs Tire?" *New York Times*, October 13, 2002, BU7; http://www.Forbes.com/finance (February 16, 2006); PBS.org, "Who Made America" (June 19, 2008), at http://www.pbs.org/wgbh/theymadeamerica/whomade/fsmith_hi.html.

[12] John Simons, "Prognosis Looks Good for J&J," *Fortune*, November 16, 2007 (June 19, 2008), at http://money.cnn.com/2007/11/16/news/companies/simons_JnJ.fortune/index.htm; Johnson & Johnson, "Company Structure" (June 19, 2008), at http://www.jnj.com/connect/about-jnj/company-structure/.

[13] "Wal-Mart Acquires Interspar," *Management Ventures* (July 20, 2001), at http://www.mvi-insights.com/Index.aspx; Kerry Capell et al., "Wal-Mart's Not-So-Secret British Weapon," *BusinessWeek Online* (July 20, 2001), at http://www.businessweek.com/2000/00_04/b3665095.htm; Brent Schlender, "Wal-Mart's $288 Billion Meeting," *Fortune*, April 18, 2005, 90–106; see http://walmartstores.com.

[14] Thomas A. Stewart, "See Jack. See Jack Run," *Fortune*, September 27, 1999, 124–271; Jerry Useem, "America's Most Admired Companies," *Fortune*, March 7, 2005, 67–82; See GE.com, "Executive Leaders," at http://www.ge.com/company/leadership/executives.html.

[15] Leslie P. Willcocks and Robert Plant, "Getting from Bricks to Clicks," *Sloan Management Review*, Spring 2001, 50–60.

[16] "The Office Chart That Really Counts," *BusinessWeek*, February 27, 2006, 48–49.

[17] Carol Loomis, "How the HP Board KO'd Carly," *Fortune*, March 7, 2005, 99–102.

[18] Lockheed Martin, "Skunk Works" (June 19, 2008), at http://www.lockheedmartin.com/aeronautics/skunkworks/index.html.

Chapter 7

[1] Julie Schmit and Elizabeth Weise, "Peanut Product Recalls Spread Fast," *USA Today*, Feb. 2, 2009, page 1B; Associated Press, "Makers Join Growing Peanut Butter Foods Recall," *Columbia Daily Tribune*, Jan. 20. 2009, page 6B; Jennifer Corbett Dooren, "Problems at Peanut Plant Prompt Expansion of Recall," *Wall Street Journal*, January 29, 2009, page A5.

[2] General Electric Company, *Annual Report for Year Ended Dec. 31, 2008, FORM 10-K*, (U.S. Securities and Exchange Commission, February 19, 2009).

[3] Terry Hill, *Manufacturing Strategy*, 3rd edition (Boston: Irwin McGraw-Hill, 2000), Chapters 2–4; James A. Fitzsimmons, Mona J. Fitzsimmons, *Service Management: Operations Strategy, Information Technology*, 6th edition (Boston: Irwin McGraw-Hill, 2008), 46–48.

[4] Photo-Kicks.com, at http://photo-kicks.com/content/view/10/21/, accessed June 5, 2008; Inc.com 5000, at http://www.inc.com/inc5000/2007/company-profile.html?id=200705920, accessed June 8, 2008.

[5] Gail Edmondson, Willam Boston, Andrea Zammert, "Detroit East," *BusinessWeek* (July 25, 2005), at http://www.businessweek.com/print/magazine/content/05_30/b3944003.htm?chan=gl/.

[6] American Society for Quality, "ASQ Glossary of Terms," http://www.asq.org/glossary/q.html, accessed April 10, 2009.

[7] "Savoring Fine Chocolates," at http://www.godiva.com/godivacollection/guideToGodiva.aspx, accessed April 10, 2009.

Chapter 8

[1] "Death by Overwork in Japan," *The Economist*, December 19, 2007, (June 4, 2008), at http://www.economist.com/world/asia/displaystory.cfm?story_id=10329261.

[2] Smith, Tom W. "Job Satisfaction in the United States," April 17, 2007, (June 4, 2008), at http://www.norc.org/NR/rdonlyres/2874B40B-7C50-4F67-A6B2-26BD3B06EA04/0/JobSatisfactionintheUnitedStates.pdf.

[3] Mark Bolino and William Turnley, "Going the Extra Mile: Cultivating and Managing Employee Citizenship Behavior," *Academy of Management Executive*, 2003, vol. 17, no. 3, 60–70.

[4] See Carl Thoresen, Jill Bradley, Paul Bliese, and Joseph Thoresen, "The Big Five Personality Traits and Individual Job Performance," *Journal of Applied Psychology*, 2004, vol. 89, no. 5, 835–853.

[5] See Daniel Goleman, *Emotional Intelligence: Why It Can Matter More Than IQ* (New York: Bantam Books, 1995); see also Kenneth Law, Chi-Sum Wong, and Lynda Song, "The Construct and Criterion Validity of Emotional Intelligence and Its Potential Utility for Management Studies," *Journal of Applied Psychology*, 2004, vol 89, no. 3, 483–596.

[6] Daniel Goleman, "Leadership That Gets Results," *Harvard Business Review*, March–April 2000, 78–90.

[7] See Ricky W. Griffin and Gregory Moorhead, *Organizational Behavior*, 8th ed. (Boston: Houghton Mifflin Company), 2007.

[8] See Daniel Wren, *The History of Management Thought*, 5th ed. (New York: John Wiley & Sons), 2004.

[9] Ibid.

[10] A. H. Maslow, *Motivation and Personality*, 2nd ed. (Upper Saddle River, NJ: Prentice Hall, 1970). Reprinted by permission of Prentice Hall Inc.

[11] Lyman Porter, Gregory Bigley, and Richard Steers, *Motivation and Work Behavior*, 7th ed. (New York: McGraw-Hill), 2003.

[12] Gary P. Latham, "The Importance of Understanding and Changing Employee Outcome Expectancies for Gaining Commitment to an Organizational Goal," *Personnel Psychology*, 2001, vol. 54, 707–720.

[13] Grant, Robert M. "AES Corporation: Rewriting the Rules of Management," *Cotemporary Strategy Analysis* (Hoboken: Wiley, John & Sons, 2007), (June 4, 2008), at http://www.blackwellpublishing.com/grant/docs/17AES.pdf.

[14] Russ Forrester, "Empowerment: Rejuvenating a Potent Idea," *Academy of Management Executive*, 2002, vol. 14, no. 1, 67–78.

[15] Ricky W. Griffin and Gary C. McMahan, "Motivation Through Job Design," in Jerald Greenberg (ed.), *Organizational Behavior: State of the Science* (New York: Lawrence Erlbaum and Associates, 1994), 23–44.

[16] Stephanie Armour, "Working 9-to-5 No Longer," *USA Today*, December 6, 2004, 1B, 2B.

[17] Foss, Brad. "Telecommuters Tout Perks of Lifestyle," *Boston Globe*, March 14, 2006, (June 4, 2008), at http://www.boston.com/business/personalfinance/articles/2006/03/14/telecommuters_tout_perks_of_lifestyle/?page=2.

Chapter 9

[1] See John Kotter, "What Leaders Really Do," *Harvard Business Review*, December 2001, 85–94.

[2] Reprinted by permission of The Free Press, a division of Simon & Schuster Adult Publishing Group, from *A Force for Change: How Leadership Differs From Management* by John P. Kotter. © 1990 by John P. Kotter, Inc. All rights reserved.

[3] Reprinted by permission of *Harvard Business Review*. Exhibit from 'How to Choose Leadership Patterns' by Robert Tannenbaum & Warren Schmidt, May–June 1973. © 1973 by the Harvard Business School Publishing Corporation. All rights reserved.

4 David Gunzareth, "Murdoch, Rupert K.," The Museum of Broadcast Communications (May 27, 2008), at http://www.museum.tv/archives/etv/M/htmlM/murdochrupe/murdochrupe.htm; Johnnie L. Roberts, "Murdoch, Ink.," Newsweek, April 28, 2008 (May 27, 2008), at http://www.newsweek.com/id/132852; BBC News, "Murdoch: I Decide Sun's politics," November 24, 2007 (May 27, 2008), at http://news.bbc.co.uk/2/hi/uk_news/7110532.stm; Mark Jurkowitz, "How Different Is Murdoch's New Wall Street Journal?" April 23, 2008 (May 27, 2008), at http://journalism.org/node/10769; Richard Siklos and Andrew Ross Sorkin, "Murdoch on Owning the Wall Street Journal," The New York Times, May 4, 2007 (May 27, 2008), at http://www.nytimes.com/2007/05/04/business/media/04murdoch.html?pagewanted=print.

5 David A. Waldman and Francis J. Yammarino, "CEO Charismatic Leadership: Levels-of-Management and Levels-of-Analysis Effects," Academy of Management Review, 1999, vol. 24, no. 2, 266–285.

6 Jane Howell and Boas Shamir, "The Role of Followers in the Charismatic Leadership Process: Relationships and Their Consequences," Academy of Management Review, January 2005, 96–112.

7 Clive Thompson, "The See-Through CEO," Wired, March 2007 (July 2, 2008), at http://www.wired.com/wired/archive/15.04/wired40_ceo.html.

8 J. Richard Hackman and Ruth Wageman, "A Theory of Team Coaching," Academy of Management Review, April 2005, 269–287.

9 "How Women Lead," Newsweek, October 24, 2005, 46–70.

10 Steven Berglas, "What You Can Learn from Steve Jobs," http://www.inc.com; "Apple's Bold Swim Downstream," BusinessWeek, January 24, 2006, 32–35; "The Seed of Apple's Innovation," BusinessWeek, October 12, 2005, 86–87; Alan Deutschman, The Second Coming of Steve Jobs (New York: Broadway Publishing, 2001); Brent Schlender, "How Big Can Apple Get?" Fortune, February 21, 2005, 122–128; "Steve Jobs' Magic Kingdom," BusinessWeek, February 6, 2006, 62–69 (source of quote); Lev Grossman, "Invention Of the Year: The iPhone," Time, October 31, 2007 (May 27, 2008), at http://www.time.com/time/business/article/0,8599,1678581,00.html.

11 Jerry Useem, "Boeing vs. Boeing," Fortune, October 2, 2000, 148–160; "Airbus Prepares to 'Bet the Company' As It Builds a Huge New Jet," Wall Street Journal, November 3, 1999, A1, A10.

12 Ricky W. Griffin, Management, 8th ed. (Boston: Houghton Mifflin Company, 2005), 282. Used with permission.

13 "Accommodating the A380," Wall Street Journal, November 29, 2005, B1; "Boeing Roars Ahead," BusinessWeek, November 7, 2005, 44–45; "Boeing's New Tailwind," Newsweek, December 5, 2005, 45; Judith Crown, "Even More Boeing 787 Delays?" BusinessWeek, April 4, 2008 (May 27, 2008), at http://www.businessweek.com/bwdaily/dnflash/content/apr2008/db2008043_948354.htm?campaign_id=rss_daily; Aaron Karp, ATW Daily News, April 9, 2008 (May 27, 2008), at http://www.atwonline.com/news/story.html?storyID=12338; "Airbus: New Delays for A380 Deliveries," CNNMoney.com, May 13, 2008 (May 27, 2008), at http://money.cnn.com/2008/05/13/news/international/airbus_delay.ap/index.htm?postversion=2008051304; "Airbus A380 Delays Not Disclosed for Months," MSNBC.com, May 29, 2007 (May 27, 2008), at http://www.msnbc.msn.com/id/18918869/.

14 "Making Decisions in Real Time," Fortune, June 26, 2000, 332–334; see also Malcolm Gladwell, Blink (New York: Little, Brown, 2005).

15 Charles P. Wallace, "Adidas—Back in the Game," Fortune, August 18, 1997, 176–182.

16 Barry M. Staw and Jerry Ross, "Good Money After Bad," Psychology Today, February 1988, 30–33; D. Ramona Bobocel and John Meyer, "Escalating Commitment to a Failing Course of Action: Separating the Roles of Choice and Justification," Journal of Applied Psychology, vol. 79, 1994, 360–363.

17 Gerry McNamara and Philip Bromiley, "Risk and Return in Organizational Decision Making," Academy of Management Journal, vol. 42, 1999, 330–339.

18 See Brian O'Reilly, "What It Takes to Start a Startup," Fortune, June 7, 1999, 135–140, for an example.

Chapter 10

1 "NetFlix Takes Off," BusinessWeek, April 25, 2009, p. 47.

2 Lathryn Tyler, "Taking E-Learning to the Next Level," HRMagazine, February 2005, 56–61.

3 "Some Employers Offer ID Theft Coverage," USA Today, September 12, 2005, 1B.

4 "FedEx, Goodyear Make Big Pension Plan Changes," Workforce Management (March 1, 2007), at http://www.workforce.com/section/00/article/24/77/95.html.

5 Henry R. Cheeseman, Business Law: Ethical, International, and E-Commerce Environment, 5th ed. (Upper Saddle River, NJ: Prentice Hall, 2004), Chapter 41.

6 Gary Dessler, Human Resource Management, 9th ed. (Upper Saddle River, NJ: Prentice Hall, 2003), 31–32.

7 Henry R. Cheeseman, Business Law: Ethical, International, and E-Commerce Environment, 5th ed. (Upper Saddle River, NJ: Prentice Hall, 2004), 806–810; Gary Dessler, Human Resource Management, 9th ed. (Upper Saddle River, NJ: Prentice Hall, 2003), 94–99.

8 Texas Tech University: Health Sciences Center, at http://www.ttuhsc.edu/hr/Employment/FAQs.aspx#usapa, accessed June 6, 2008; Richard S. Dunham, "The Patriot Act: Business Balks," BusinessWeek, (November 10, 2005), at http://www.businessweek.com/bwdaily/dnflash/nov2005/nf20051110_9709_db016.htm.

9 U.S. Department of Labor, Bureau of Labor Statistics, at http://www.bls.gov/news.release/union2.nr0.htm, accessed June 6, 2008.

10 U.S. Department of Labor, Bureau of Labor Statistics, at http://www.bls.gov/news.release/pdf/wkstp.pdf, accessed June 6, 2008.

Chapter 11

1 Janet Adamy, "At Starbucks, a Tall Order for New Cuts, Store Closures," Wall Street Journal, January 29, 2009, pp. B1, B4; Associated Press, "Want Fries with That?" Columbia Daily Tribune, February 3, 2009, p. 6B; Rick Wartzman, "A Marketing Spill on Starbucks' Hands," BusinessWeek, February 20, 2009, at http://www.businessweek.com/managing/content/feb2009/ca20090220_819348.htm; Michael Arndt, "McDonald's Specialty Coffee Kick," May 14, 2008, at http://www.businessweek.com/bwdaily/dnflash/content/may2008/db20080514_138620.htm; Associated Press, "Starbucks to Sell Value-Meal Pairings for $3.95," MSNBC. com, February 9, 2009, at http://www.msnbc.msn.com/id/29099087.

[2] American Marketing Association, "Marketing Definitions" (March 9, 2009), at http://www.marketingpower.com.

[3] Philip Kotler and Gary Armstrong, *Principles of Marketing*, 12th ed. (Upper Saddle River, NJ: Prentice Hall, 2008), 7.

[4] Shawn McCarthy and Greg Keenan, "Ottawa Demands Lower Auto Worker Costs," *The Globe and Mail*, January 19, 2009, at http://v1business.theglobe andmail.com/servlet/story/RTGAM.20 090119.wrautos19/BNStory/Business; Gail Edmondson, Ian Rowley, Nandini Lakshman, David Welch, and Dexter Roberts, "The Race to Build Really Cheap Cars," *BusinessWeek*, April 23, 2007, at http://www.businessweek.com/ magazine/content/07_17/b4031064 .htm; McClatchy Newspapers (Las Vegas), "Downsizing to 'Right-Sizing,'" *Columbia Daily Tribune: Saturday Business*, January 31, 2009, page 10; Jim Henry, "Prius Hybrid Aimed Small, Stood Tall," *Automotive News*, October 29, 2007, page 150 (3 pages) at http://www.autonews .com/apps/pbcs.dll/article?AID=/2007 1029/ANA06/710290326/1078&Profile =1078#; Burrelles Luce, "Hitting the Right Note: Best Practices for Corporate Social Responsibility (CSR) Marketing," *E-Newsletter*, July 2007, at http://luceonline .us/newsletter/default_july07.php.

[5] Shawn McCarthy and Greg Keenan, "Ottawa Demands Lower Auto Worker Costs," *The Globe and Mail*, January 19, 2009, at http://v1business. theglobeandmail.com/servlet/story/ RTGAM.20090119.wrautos19/BNStory/ Business; McClatchy Newspapers, "Lemons Into Lemonade," *Columbia Daily Tribune*, February 2, 2009, page 7B.

[6] McClatchy Newspapers, "Airbus to Be Allowed to Bid to Replace Air Force One," *Columbia Daily Tribune*, January 25, 2009, page 4D.

[7] Steve Schifferes, "The Triumph of Lean Production," *BBC News*, February 27, 2007, at http://news.bbc.co.uk/2/hi/ business/6346315stm.

[8] "Financial Cards in Poland," Euromonitor International, (May 2008), at http://www. euromonitor.com/Consumer_Finance_ in_Poland.

[9] "2008 Brand Keys Customer Loyalty Engagement Index," (March 18, 2008), at http://www.brandkeys.com/ awards/cli08.cfm.

[10] *U.S. Department of Commerce, Statistical Abstract of the United States: 2009* (Washington, DC: Bureau of the Census, 2008), Tables No. 413, 1006, and 1016; *National Income and Products Account Table*, Table 1.1.5 Gross Domestic Product, February 27, 2009 at http://www.bea.gov/ national/index.htm.

[11] Ibid.

[12] "Packaged Goods See Record Number of New Products in 2006," Convenience Store News, (January 24, 2007), at http://www.allbusiness.com/retail-trade/food-stores/4490789-1.html.

[13] Adapted from Jay Heizer and Barry Render, *Operations Management*, 7th ed. (Upper Saddle River, NJ: Prentice Hall, 2004), 157.

[14] "Best Global Brands 2008," *BusinessWeek*, accessed March 13, 2009 at http://bwnt .businessweek.com/interactive_reports/ global_brand_2008/.

[15] Judy Strauss, Adel El-Ansary, and Raymond Frost, *E-Marketing*, 5th ed. (Upper Saddle River, NJ: Prentice Hall, 2007); "Ten Corporate Blogs Worth Reading," February 19, 2009, at http://www.blogtrepreneuer .com/2009/02/19/ten-corporate-blogs-worth-reading/.

[16] McClatchy Newspapers (Minneapolis), "Social Networking Sites Make Powerful Job-Hunting Tools," *Columbia Daily Tribune*, January 21, 2009, 7B; Press Release, "LinkedIn Launches New Tools to Boost HR Professionals' Efficiency as Responses to Job Postings Double in Challenging Economy," February 2, 2009, at http://press.linkedin.com/linkedin-new-hr-tools.

Chapter 12

[1] Apple Inc. Form 10–Q (March 29, 2008), at http://media.corporate-ir.net/ media_files/irol/10/107357/AAPL_ 10Q_Q2FY08.pdf; Jim Dalrymple, Jonathan Seff, and Philip Michaels, "Apple Reports Record Profit for First Quarter," *Macworld*, January 21, 2009, at http://www.macworld.com/article/ 138362/2009/01/earnings.html

[2] See "DoJ Probes Digital Music Pricing," *Techtree* (March 6, 2006), at http://www. techtree.com/techtree/jsp/article.jsp? article_id=71743&cat_id=643; Jim Dalrymple, "Apple Now Number 2 Music Retailer in the U.S.," *Network World* (February 26, 2008), at http://www. networkworld.com/news/2008/ 022608-apple-now-number-2-music. html; "iTunes Increasing Its Dominance," Telecom (April 30, 2008), at http:// web20.telecomtv.com/pages/?newsid= 43081&id=e9381817-0593-417a-8639- c4c53e2a2a10&view=news; "iTunes Store Top Music Retailer in the U.S." (April 3, 2008), at http://www.apple. com/pr/library/2008/04/03itunes. html; Chris Maxcer, "iTunes Tops Music Vendor Charts," *E-Commerce Times* (April 4, 2008), at http://www. ecommercetimes.com/story/ iTunes-Tops-Music-Vendor-Charts-62458.html; Mark Guarino, "Vinyl Records Gain New Life on South and West Sides of Chicago," *chicagotribune.com*, January 22, 2009, accessed at http://archives .chicagotribune.com/2009/jan/22/ local/chi-vinyl_city_zonejan22

[3] Edward F. Moltzen, "HP Passes Dell as Top PC Maker Worldwide," *Information Week* (October 19, 2006), at http://www.informationweek.com/ news/personal_tech/showArticle .jhtml?articleID=193400624.

[4] "About Carbonite," at http://www .carbonite.com/about/.

[5] Lee S. Crane, "Seven Questions to Ask Before Running Your Next Reverse Auction," *Purchasing* (March 13, 2008), at http://www.purchasing.com/article/ CA6537987.html; "MediaBids.com Adds Over 325 Newspapers & Magazines to *Print* Advertising Marketplace," MediaBids.com (March 4, 2008), at http://express-press-release.net/47/MediaBids.com AddsOver325Newspapers& MagazinestoPrintAdvertisingMarket place.php.

[6] "Wowowow.com Gives a Voice to Mature Women," TimesOnline, April 6, 2008, at http://technology.timesonline.co.uk/to l/news/tech_and_web/the_web/article 3662890.ece; Stephanie Rosenbloom, "Boldface in Cyberspace: It's a Woman's Domain," The New York Times, March 6, 2008, at http://www.nytimes.com/2008/ 03/06/fashion/06WOW.html; Geraldine Baum, "It's Web 101 for This Experienced Intern," Los Angeles Times, March 6, 2009, at http://articles.latimes.com/2009/ mar/06/nation/na-senior-intern6; "Think Up at wowOwow: The Executive Intern Program," at http://wowowow. com/think/think-executive-intern-program-244863.

7 Plunkett Research, Ltd., *Retail Industry Statistics: U.S. Retail Industry Overview (2004)* (June 23, 2005), at http://www.plunkettresearch.com/retail.

8 *The Avon Opportunity: Annual Report 2008*, at www.avoncompany.com/investor/annualreport/index.html.

9 "Over 875 Million Consumers Have Shopped Online—the Number of Internet Shoppers Up 40% in Two Years," *Reuters* (January 27, 2008), at http://www.reuters.com/article/press Release/idUS16394+28-Jan-2008+PRN20080128; *Yahoo! Finance*, at http://finance.yahoo.com, accessed March 12, 2009.

10 Melissa Dowling, "Online Sales Continue to Climb," Multichannel Merchant (March 1, 2008), at http://www.multichannelmerchant.com/webchannel/marketing/online_sales_continue.

11 "Highlight Free Shipping Offers in Online Marketing Campaigns," *ClickThrough Search Engine Marketing Services*, February 16, 2009, at http://www.clickthrough-marketing.com/Highlight-free-shipping-offers-in-online-marketing-campaigns/19027764/; "Free Shipping Strategies Gain Retailers Loyal Customers," *ManageSmarter*, March 30, 2009, at http://www.salesandmarketing.com/msg/content_display/sales/e3i1a3d96e3863d2d6c87ae575ab65dca5e.

12 Kimberly S. Johnson, "Ford, GM to Cover Car Payments if Buyer Loses Job," *The Seattle Times*, March 31, 2009, at http://abcnews.go.com/Business/IndustryInfo/wireStory?Id=7215.

13 Amy Gunderson, "Using Stock to Pay for a Vacation," *HalogenLife*, December 8, 2008, at http://www.halogenlife.com/articles/1618-using-stock-to-pay-for-a-vacation; Robert Curley, "Party Like It's July '08 with Elite Island Resorts," *About.com*, December 11, 2008, at http://gocaribbean.about.com/b/2008/12/11/party-like-its-july-08-with-elite-island-resorts-htm.

14 "Univision's Audience Growth Continues While English-Language Networks Decline," (press release) *Yahoo! Finance*, April 1, 2009, at http://finance.yahoo.com/news/. "Univision Announces 2007 Fourth Quarter and Full Year Results" (March 5, 2008), at http://u.univision.com/contentroot/uol/

10portada/sp/pdf/corp_releases/2008/NOMETA_03-05-2008-2en.pdf; David Dodson, "Minority Groups' Share of $10 Trillion U.S. Consumer Market Is Growing Steadily, According to Annual Buying Power Study from Terry College's Selig Center for Economic Growth," (July 31, 2007), at http://www.terry.uga.edu/news/releases/2007/minority_buying_power_report.html.

15 "TNS Media Intelligence Reports U.S. Advertising Expenditures Grew 0.2 Percent in 2007," *TNS Media Intelligence*, March 25, 2008, at http://www.tns-mi.com/news/03252008.htm; "2007 U.S. Advertising Expenditures Wrap-up: Spend Up Just 0.2%," at http://www.marketingcharts.com/television/tns-issues-2007-us-advertising-expenditures-wrap-up-spend-up-just-02-3952/.

16 "TNS Media Intelligence Reports U.S. Advertising Expenditures Grew 0.2 Percent in 2007," *TNS Media Intelligence*, March 25, 2008, at http://www.tns-mi.com/news/03252008.htm; "2007 U.S. Advertising Expenditures Wrap-up: Spend Up Just 0.2%," at http://www.marketingcharts.com/television/tns-issues-2007-us-advertising-expenditures-wrap-up-spend-up-just-02-3952/.

17 Nat Ives, "Consumers Are Bugged By Many Ads," *Advertising Age*, December 1, 2008, 6.

18 "Ads Now Watching Shoppers," *Columbia Daily Tribune* (Associated Press), February 3, 2009, 7B.

19 Estimated from "TNS Media Intelligence Reports U.S. Advertising Expenditure Grew 0.2% in 2007," *TNS Media Intelligence*, March 25, 2008 at http://www.tns-mi.com/news/03252008.htm; "2007 US Advertising Expenditures Wrap-up: Spend Up Just 0.2%," at www.marketingcharts.com/television/tns-issues-2007-us-advertising-expenditures-wrap-up-spend-up-just-02-3952/; "Ad Spending Totals By Media and Domestic Ad Spending By Category," *Advertising Age* (June 20, 2007), at http://adage.com/datacenter/article?article_id=118652.

20 Associated Press, "New Arrest in Wendy's Finger Case," MSNBC.com (May 19, 2005), at http://www.msnbc.msn.com/id/7844274.

21 Ron Insana, "Wendy's Knew from Start Story Was a Hoax," *USA Today* (June 5, 2005), at http://www.usatoday.com/

money/companies/management/2005-06-05-insana-wendys_x.htm.

Chapter 13

1 M.P. McQueen, "Cyber-Scams On the Uptick In Downturn," *The Wall Street Journal*, January 29, 2009, D1, D4; Joseph De Avila, "Beware of Facebook 'Friends' Who May Trash Your Laptop," *The Wall Street Journal*, January 29, 2009, D1, D4; Byron Acohido and Jon Swartz, "Data Scams Have Kicked into High Gear as Markets Tumble," *USAToday*, January 28, 2009, at http://www.usatoday.com/tech/news/computersecurity/2009-01-28-hackers-data-scams_N.htm; Chris Wragge, "FBI Warns of High-Tech Cyber ID Theft," wcbstv.com, April 8, 2009, at http://wcbstv.com/local/cyber.criminals.fbi.2.980245.html; Jordan Robertson, "Bad Economy Helps Web Scammers Recruit 'Mules'," *abc News*, December 9, 2008, at http://abcnews.go.com/print?id=6422327.

2 "RIM Adds 2.6 Million Subscribers on BlackBerry Bold/Storm Release," *Telecommunications Industry News*, February 15, 2009, at http://www.teleclick.ca/2009/02/rim-adds-26-million-subscribers-on-blackberry-boldstorm-release/.

3 See http://www.xmnavtraffic.com.

4 "Lockheed Martin Aeronautics: Siemen's PLM Software," *Siemens*, at http://www.p/m.automation.siemans.com/en_us/about-us/success/case_s, accessed June 16, 2009.

5 Laura Northrup, "Timbuk2 Really, Really Wants You to Be Happy with Their Bags," *The Consumerist*, June 5, 2009, at http://www.consumerist.com/5280357/timbuk2_really-really-wants-you-to-be.

6 David LaGesse, "How to Turn Social Networking into a Job Offer," *U.S. News & World Report*, May 11, 2009, at http://www.usnews.com/money/careers/articles/2009/05/11/how-to-turn-social-networking-into-a-job-offer.html.

7 3D Systems, "3D Systems Helps Walter Reed Army Medical Center Rebuild Lives," at http://www.3dsystems.com/appsolutions/casestudies/walter_reed.asp, accessed 6/15/2009; "Hannah Hickey, "Camera in a Pill Offers Cheaper, Easier Window on Your Insides," UWNews.org (January 24, 2008), at http://uwnews.org/article.asp?articleid=39292.

8 See http://www.internetworldstats.com/stats.htm.

9 See University of Birmingham, "Internet Map as of 16th January 2006," at http://www.eee.bham.ac.uk/com_test/dsnl.aspx.

10 "ABN AMRO Mortgage Group Offers OneFee to Ford Motor Company Employees," Mortgage Mag, February 14, 2005, at http://www.mortgagemag.com/n/502_003.htm; An Intranet's Life Cycle," morebusiness.com (June 16, 1999), at http://www.morebusiness.com/getting_started/website/d928247851.brc

11 Major modifications of diagrams at the BlackBerry Web site, modified from Research in Motion, Limited, technical images, at http://www.blackberry.com/images/technical/bes_exchange_architecture.gif.

12 Emily Bazar, "Bartering Booms During Economic Tough Times," USA Today, February 25, 2009, at http://usatoday.com/tech/webguide/internetlife/2009-02-25-barter_N.htm; Joseph Anthony, "Bartering Can Boost Your Budget and Business," at http://microsoft.com/smallbusiness/resources/startups/budgeting-expenses/bartering-can-boost-your-budget-and-business.aspx#Barteringcanboostyourbudgetandbusiness, accessed June 8, 2009; Donna Wright, "Hard Times Create Boom of Local Bartering," BradentonHerald.com, March 8, 2009, at http://www.bradenton.com/874/v-print/story/1277848.html; "The Advantages of Business Bartering," acat http://www.u-exchange.com/advantages-business-bartering, accessed June 8, 2009.

13 "What Do Bartering Websites Do?" at http://www.peopletradingservices.com, accessed June 8, 2009.

14 "Kroger Tailors Ads to Its Customers," Columbia Daily Tribune, January 12, 2009, 7B.

15 "Data Mining Examples & Testimonials," at http://www.data-mining-software.com/data_mining_examples.htm, accessed 6/11/2008.

16 "LaidOffCamp Events," LaidOffCamp, at http://laidoffcamp.com/laidoffcamp-events/.

17 Rupa Dev, "Laid-Off Gen Yers Use Social Networking for Jobs," The Loop21.com, June 10, 2009, at http://www.theloop21.com/news/laid-gen-yers-use-social-networking-for-jobs; "LaidOffCamp Events," LaidOffCamp, at http://laidoffcamp.com/

laidoffcamp-events/; Rich Whittle, "On the Rebound: Chris Hutchins," March 19, 2009, Chris Hutchins—Google Profile, at http://www.google.com/profiles/Christopher-Hutchins; Dave Ramel, "Job Hunting? Use Social Networks to Make Crucial Connections," ComputerWorld.com, May 7, 2009 at http://www.computerworld.com/s/article/9132611/Job_hunting_Use_social_networks_to_make_crucial_connections.

18 Rupa Dev, "Laid-Off Gen Yers Use Social Networking for Jobs," The Loop21.com, June 10, 2009, http://www.theloop21.com/news/laid-gen-yers-use-social-networking-for-jobs.

19 Jo Marchant, "Virtual Fossils Reveal How Ancient Creatures Lived," NewScientist, May 27, 2009, at http://www.newscientist.com/article/mg20227103.500-virtual-fossils-reveal-how-ancient-creatures-lived.html.

20 Phuong Tram, "Facebook and Privacy Invasions," Imprint Online, June 15, 2008 at http://imprint.uwaterloo.ca/index.php?option=com_content&task=view&id=2570&Itemid=57; Jacqui Cheng, "Canadian Group: Facebook 'A Minefield of Privacy Invasion," May 30, 2008, at http://arstechnica.com/tech-policy/news/2008/05/canadian-group-files-complaint-over-facebook-privacy.ars; "Cell Phones a Much Bigger Privacy Risk Than Facebook," Fox News, February 20, 2009, at http://www.foxnews.com/printer_friendly_story/0,3566,497544,00.html.

21 Alex Leary, "Wi-Fi Cloaks a New Breed of Intruder," St. Petersburg Times (July 4, 2005), at http://www.sptimes.com/2005/07/04/State/Wi_Fi_cloaks_a_new_br.shtml.

22 Eliot Van Buskirk, "iTunes Store May Capture One-Quarter of Worldwide Music by 2012," Wired (April 27, 2008), at http://www.wired.com/entertainment/music/news/2008/04/itunes_birthday; Christopher Burgess and Richard Power, "How to Avoid Intellectual Property Theft," CIO (July 10, 2006), at http://www.cio.com/article/22837; Hiawatha Bray, "Music Industry Aims to Send in Radio Cops," Boston Globe (November 15, 2004), at http://www.boston.com/business/articles/2004/11/15/music_industry_aims_to_send_in_radio_cops/; Ethan Smith and Yukari Iwatani Kane, "Apple

Changes Tune on Music Pricing," The Wall Street Journal, Jan. 7, 2009, at http://online.wsj.com/article/SB123126062001057765.

23 See http://www.webopedia.com/TERM/S/spyware.html.

24 "Ferris Research and Abaca Technology Corporation Hold Anti-Spam Webinar," NewswireToday, April 9, 2008, at http://www.newswiretoday.com/news/32531/.

25 Brad Carlson, "Organizations Face New Records-Destruction Rule," Idaho Business Review (July 25, 2005), at http://www.idahobusiness.net/archive.htm/2005/07/25/Organizations-face-new-recordsdestruction-rule.

Chapter 14

1 Adam Piore, "Fraud Scene Investigator," Portfolio, (March 10, 2008), at http://www.portfolio.com/careers/job-of-the-week/2008/03/10/Forensic-Accountant-Al-Vondra; Kartik Goyal and Subramanian Sharma, "India Orders Fraud Office Probe Into Satyam Computer Accounts, Bloomberg.com, January 13, 2009, at http://www.bloomberg.com/apps/news?pid=20601091&refer=india&sid=ayhBmRJs7nh0.

2 Adam Smith, "The Reasons Fraud Spikes in a Recession," Time, May 20, 2009, at http://www.time.com/time/printout/0,8816,1899798,00.html; "Recession-Proof Career: Forensic Accounting and IT Auditing Financial Fraud Increases in Economic Recessions," UAB Media Relations, November 6, 2008, at http://main.uab.edu/Sites/MediaRelations/articles/54133/; Will Kenyon, "Five Tips for Combating Fraud in the Recession," Finance Week, March 23, 2009, at http://www.financeweek.co.uk/print/30570.

3 See Marshall B. Romney and Paul John Steinbart, Accounting Information Systems, 11th ed. (Upper Saddle River, NJ: Prentice Hall, 2009), Chapter 1.

4 See Anthony A. Atkinson, Robert S. Kaplan, Ella Mae Matsumura, and S. Mark Young, Management Accounting, 5th ed. (Upper Saddle River, NJ: Prentice Hall, 2007), Chapter 1.

5 See Walter T. Harrison and Charles T. Horngren, Financial Accounting and Financial Tips, 7th ed. (Upper Saddle River, NJ: Prentice Hall, 2007), Chapter 1.

[6] See Alvin A. Arens, Mark S. Beasley, and Randal J. Elder, *Auditing and Assurance Services and ACL Software*, 12th ed. (Upper Saddle River, NJ: Prentice Hall, 2008), Chapter 1.

[7] See Meg Pollard et al., *Financial and Managerial Accounting* Ch. 1–14 (Upper Saddle River, NJ: Prentice Hall, 2008), Chapter 1.

[8] Myra A. Thomas, "It's Not About Balance—It's About Reality," *Jobs in the Money* (November 30, 2007), at http://www.jobsinthemoney.com/news.php?articleID=513.

[9] "CPA Vision Project," American Institute of Certified Public Accountants, at http://www.aicpa.org/vision/index.htm on July 1, 2009.

[10] D. Larry Crumbley, Lester E. Heitger, and G. Stevenson Smith, *Forensic and Investigative Accounting*, 4th ed. (Chicago: CCH Incorporated, 2009), Chapter 1.

[11] "Executive Summary of the Sarbanes-Oxley Act of 2002 P.L. 107–204," Conference of State Bank Supervisors, at http://www.csbs.org/Content/NavigationMenu/LegislativeAffairs/Summaries/Executive_Summary_of.htm; "Summary of the Provisions of the Sarbanes-Oxley Act of 2002," AICPA, at http://thecaq.aicpa.org/Resources/Sarbanes+Oxley/Summary+of+the+Provisions+of+the+Sarbanes-Oxley+Act+of+2002.htm.

[12] *Annual Report for Fiscal Year Ended December 31, 2008, FORM 10-K, Google, Inc.* (U.S. Securities and Exchange Commission, 2009), 64–67.

[13] Ibid.

[14] Ibid.

[15] Ibid.

[16] Iain MacWhirter, "Mortgage Madness Will End in Inflation, Inflation, Inflation OPINION," *The Sunday Herald*, September 16, 2007, at http://findarticles.com/p/articles/mi_qn4156/is_20070916/ai_n20503579/.

[17] Louis R. Woodhill, "One Way to Deal With Toxic Assets," *Real Clear Markets*, January 23, 2009, at http://www.realclearmarkets.com/articles/2009/01/one_way_to_deal_with_toxic_ass.html; Patrick F. Gannon, "Demystifying Mark-To-Market," *Forbes.com*, April 21, 2009, at http://www.forbes.com/2009/04/21/mark-to-market-personal-finance-guru-insights-accounting-standards.html.

[18] Steven L. Henning, "Controlling the Real-World Risks of Mark-to-Market Valuation,"

WebCPA, June 1, 2009, at http://www.webcpa.com/ato_issues/2009_9/-50466-1.html?pg=3; John Berlau, "The Mark-to-Market Relief Rally," *OpenMarket.org*, April 2, 2009, at http://www.openmarket.org/2009/04/02/the-mark-to-market-relief-rally/.

[19] "Instant View: U.S. Eases Mark-to-Market Accounting, April 2, 2009, *Reuters*, at http://www.reuters.com; John Berlau, "The Mark-to-Market Relief Rally," *OpenMarket.org*, April 2, 2009, at http://www.openmarket.org/2009/04/02/the-mark-to-market-relief-rally/; Kara Scannell, "FASB Eases Mark-to-Market Rules," *WSJ.com*, April 2, 2009, at http://online.wsj.com/article.SB12386773956082309.html.

[20] Rafe Needleman, "Twitter CEO: The Revenue's Coming Soon, But I Won't Tell You How," *CNet.com*, December 2, 2008 at http://news.cnet.com/8301-17939_109-10112037-2html; "What's Twitter Worth?" *KnowledgeToday*, May 7, 2009 at http://knowledgetoday.wharton.upenn.edu/2009/05/whats-twittwr-worth.html; Chris Snyder, "Twitter Could 'Go for Years' without Earning a Dime, Investor Says," *Epicenter: The Business of Tech*, February 13, 2009, at http://www.wired.com/epicenter/2009/02/twitter-still-l/.

[21] "Twitter Raises $35 Million from Venture Investors," *The Wall Street Journal*, February 15, 2009 at http://online.wsj.com/article/SB123457085701286361.html; Tricia Duryee, "Twitter Buys Start-up's Assets; Hires Founder Rael Dornfest," *mocoNews.net*, November 24, 2008, at http://moconews.net/article/419-twitter-buys-start-ups-assets-hires; Brian Deagon, "Twitter Truly Making Money—for Some Application Developers," *Investor's Business Daily*, May 27, 2009, at http://www.investors.com//NewsAndAnalysis/Article.aspx?id=477977.

[22] "Code of Professional Conduct," AICPA, at http://infotech.aicpa.org/Resources/Privacy/Federal+State+and+Other+Professional+Regulations/AICPA+Code+of+Professional+Conduct/.

[23] "The Corporate Scandal Sheet," Citizen Works (August 2004), at http://www.citizenworks.org/enron/corp-scandal.php; "Largest Health Care Fraud Case in U.S. History Settled," Department of Justice (June 26, 2003), at http://www.usdoj.gov/opa/pr/2003/June/03_civ_386.htm; "Waste Management, Inc. Founder and Three Other Former Top

Officers Settle SEC Fraud Action for $30.8 Million," U.S. Securities and Exchange Commission, Litigation Release No. 19351 (August 29, 2005), at http://www.sec.gov/litigation/litreleases/lr19351.htm; "Kozlowski Is Found Guilty," TheStreet.com (June 17, 2005), at http://www.thestreet.com/story/10228619/1/kozlowski-is-found-guilty.html; "SEC Charges Time Warner with Fraud . . . ," U.S. Securities and Exchange Commission, Release 2005–38 (March 21, 2005), at http://www.sec.gov/news/press/2005-38.htm.

Chapter 15

[1] Manav Tanneeru, "How a 'Perfect Storm' Led to the Economic Crisis," *CNN.com*, January 29, 2009, at http://www.cnn.com/economic.crisis.explainer/index.html; Associated Press, "IMF: U.S. Banks May Lose $2.7 Trillion, *CBS News*, April 21, 2009, at http://www.cbsnews.com/stories/2009/04/21/business/main4959108.shtml; Mark Landler, "The U.S. Financial Crisis is Spreading to Europe," *The New York Times*, October 1, 2008, at http://www.nytimes.com/2008/10/01/business/worldbusiness/01global.html; Ben Rooney, "Bank Failure List Tops 45," *CNNMoney.com*, June 26, 2009, at http://money.cnn.com/2009/06/26/news/companies/bank_failure/index.htm; Sudeep Reddy and Geoffrey T. Smith, "Fed Reserved as Slump Eases," *The Wall Street Journal*, June 25, 2009, page A1; Maurice Tamman and David Enrich, "Local Banks Face Big Losses," *The Wall Street Journal*, May 19, 2009, page A1; "Failed Bank List," U.S. Federal Deposit Insurance Corporation, July 7, 2009, accessed at http://www.fdic.gov/bank/individual/failed/banklist.html; Geoffrey T. Smith, "ECB Lends Record $622 Billion in Bid to Ease Crisis," *The Wall Street Journal*, June 25, 2009, page A9.

[2] "Money Stock Measures," Federal Reserve, at http://www.federalreserve.gov/releases/h6/hist/h6hist1.txt, accessed 7/9/2009.

[3] Ibid.

[4] Ibid.

[5] Watson Wyatt, "2009 Global Pension Assets Study," *IWS Documented News Daily Postings*, January 26, 2009, at http://iwsdocumentednewsdaily.blogspot.com/2009/01/iws-watson-wyatt-2009-global-pension.html; Joshua

Brockman, "Stocks Weigh Down U.S. Pension Funds," *NPR*, July 15, 2009, at http://www.npr.org/templates/story/story.php?storyId=100818937; David Evans, "Hidden Pension Fiasco May Foment Another $1 Trillion Bailout," *Bloomberg.com*, March 3, 2009, at http://www.bloomberg.com/apps/news?pid=20670001&sid=alwTE0.

[6] Federal Reserve Board, at http://www.federalreserve.gov/releases/h15/data/Annual/H15_PRIME_NA.txt, accessed 7/15/2009.

[7] Shane M. Sherland, "The Past, Present, and Future of Subprime Mortgages," *Finance and Economics Discussion Series, Divisions of Research and Statistics and Monetary Affairs: Federal Reserve Board* (Washington, DC; November 2008).

[8] Richard Bitner, "Confessions of a Subprime Lender," *Newsweek* (March 12, 2008), at http://www.newsweek.com/id/121512/page/1; Tyler Cowen, "So We Thought. But Then Again . . ." New York Times (January 13, 2008), at http://www.nytimes.com/2008/01/13/business/13view.html?_r=2&scp=1&sq=Tyler+Cowen&oref=login&oref=slogin; Robert H. Frank, "Don't Blame All Borrowers," *Washington Post* (April 27, 2008), at http://www.washingtonpost.com/wp-dyn/content/article/2008/04/25/AR2008042502783.html.

[9] Bert Ely, "Don't Push Banks to Make Bad Loans," *The Wall Street Journal*, February 2, 2009, page A17; Aldo Svaldi, "Bank, Taxpayer Tug of War Over Use of Bailout," *The Denver Post*, December 28, 2008, at http://www.denverpost.com/fdcp?1235147271234; James Sterngold, "MidSouth Loses Would-Be Borrowers as TARP Fails with Louisianans," *Bloomberg.com*, February 12, 2009, at http://www.bloomberg.com/apps/news?pid=2067011098&sid=anccctVJnemE; Jeannine Aversa, "Banks Aren't Budging on Tight Lending Standards," *HuffingtonPost.com*, February 2, 2009, at http://www.huffingtonpost.com/2009/02/02/banks-arent-budging-on-ti_n_163325.html; Jeremy M. Simon, "Lending Standards Keep Tightening, Fed Says," *CreditCards.com*, May 4, 2009, at http://www.creditcards.com/credit-card-news/2009-q1-senior-loan-officers-survey-lending-standards-tighten-1276.php; Stan Liebowitz,

"House of Cards," *New York Post*, September 24, 2008, at http://www.nypost.com/seven/09242008/postopinion/opedcolumnists/item_S6MsT275m3Ybbsm3TdxIxN.

[10] "Electronic Funds transfer," (July 15, 2009), at http://fms.treas.gov/eft/index.html.

[11] Ross Kerber, "Withdrawing from the ATM Habit," *boston.com*, February 19, 2008, at http://www.boston.com/business/personal finance/articles/2008/02/19/withdrawing_from_the_atm_habit/; "Global ATM Market to Pass 2.5 Million by 2013," *the-infoshop.com (press release)*, September 10, 2008, at http://www.the-infoshop.com/press/rbr71603_en.shtml.

[12] "Troubled Banks and Failed Banks: Opportunities for Investment," *Client Alert, Latham & Watkins LLP*, at http://www.lw.com/resources.aspx?page=ClientAlertdetail&publication=2196, accessed January 28, 2009; Ralph F. MacDonald III, Christopher M. Kelly, Brett P. Barragate, Kevyn D. Orr, and James C. Olson, "United States: Bank Failures in 2008 and a Look Ahead to 2009," *Jones Day*, January 28, 2009, at http://www.mondaq.com/article.asp?articleid=72796; "2008United States Bank Failures," *Wikipedia*, at http://www.wikipedia.org/wiki/2008_United_States_bank_failures, accessed January 28, 2009; Rob Williams, "How Secure Is the FDIC Deposit Insurance Fund?" *Charles Schwab*, June 8, 2009, at http://www.schwab.com/public/schwab/research_strategies/market_1nsight/investing_strategies/other_choices/how_secure_is_the_fdic_deposit_insurance_fund.html.

[13] From http://www.federalreserve.gov/otherfrb.htm.

[14] "Supporting the Nation's Payment System," The Federal Reserve Bank of Philadelphia, July 9, 2009, at http://www.philadelphiafed.org/about-the-fed/who-we-are/payment-system.cfm; "Check Restructuring Initiative at the Reserve Banks," *Board of Governors of the Federal Reserve System*, July 8, 2009, at http://www.federalreserve.gov/paymentssystems/checkrestruct/default.htm.

[15] "Historical Changes of the Target Federal Funds and Discount Rates," *Federal Reserve Bank of New York*, at http://www.newyorkfed.org/markets/

statistics/dlyrates/fedrate.html, accessed 7/16/2009.

[16] See http://www.treasurydirect.gov; http://www.investopedia.com/university/moneymarket.

[17] Jon Hilsenrath and Liz Rappaport, "Fed Inches Toward Plan to Purchase U.S. Bonds," *The Wall Street Journal*, January 29, 2009, page A4; Neil Irwin, "Fed to Pump $1.2 Trillion into Markets," *The Washington Post*, March 19, 2009, at http://www.washingtonpost.com/wp-dyn/content/article/2009/03/18/AR2009031802283.html; Rita Nazareth, "Most U.S. Stocks Rise on Durable Goods, Pare Gains on Fed," *Bloomberg.com*, June 24, 2009, at http://www.bloomberg.com/apps/news?pid=20670001&sid=a_dIjb; Jon Hilsenrath, "Fed to Keep Lid on Bond Buys," *The Wall Street Journal*, June 12, 2009, at http://www.online.wsj.com/article/SB124477575898508951.html.

[18] David Goldman, "CNNMoney.com's Bailout Tracker," *CNNMoney.com*, July 17, 2009, at http://money.cnn.com/news/storysupplement/economy/bailouttracker/; The Associated Press, "Treasury: 10 Big Banks Can Repay Bailout," *MSNBC.com*, June 9, 2009, at http://www.msnbc.msn.com/id/31183784/.

[19] Michael R. Crittenden, "Regulators See Risk in U.S. Bank Stakes, *The Wall Street Journal*, April 23, 2009, at http://online.wsj.com/article/SB124051525463449225.html; Rebecca Christie, "Treasury May Keep U.S. Bank Stakes After Buyback (Update 3)," *Bloomberg.com*, April 17, 2009, at http://www.bloomberg.com/apps/news?pid=newsarchive&sid=a9F3N8vvrHgY; David Goldman, "CNNMoney.com's Bailout Tracker," *CNNMoney.com*, July 17, 2009, at http://money.cnn.com/news/storysupplement/economy/bailouttracker/; Mark Jickling, Fannie Mae and Freddie Mac in Conservatorship," *CRS Report for* Congress, September 15, 2008, at http://fpc.state.gov/documents/organization/110097.pdf.

[20] "U.S. Authorities Fine Arab Bank," *Al Bawaba* (August 18, 2005), 1; Paul R. Osborne, "BSA/AML Compliance Provides Opportunity to Improve Security and Enhance Customer Experience," *ABA Bank Compliance*, July/August 2005, 4.

[21] Jason Webb, "American Express Bank Forfeits $55 Million for Bank Secrecy Act Violations," *Associated Content*, August 8,

2007, at http://www.associatedcontent.com/article/339208/american_express_bank_forfeits_55_million.html?cat=17; "Banco Popular de Puerto Rico Enters into Deferred Prosecution Agreement with U.S. Department of Justice," *U.S. Department of Justice*, January 16, 2006, at http://www.usdoj.gov/opa/pr/2003/January/03_crm_024.htm; Union Bank of California Enters into Deferred Prosecution Agreement and Forfeits $21.6 Million to Resolve Bank Secrecy Act Violations," *U.S. Department of Justice*, September 17, 2007, at http://www.usdoj.gov/opa/pr/2007/September/07_crm_726.html.

22 F. Kaid Benfield, "Philadelphia's New Green Bank, Ready for Business," *HuffingtonPost.com*, April 23, 2009, at http://www.huffingtonpost.com/f-kaid-benfield/philadelphias-new-green-ba_b_190490.html; Nathanial Gronewold, "'Green Banks' Sprout from Ruins of Economic Crisis," *The New York Times*, April 6, 2009, at http://www.nytimes.com/gwire/2009/04/06/greenwire-green-banks-sprout-from-ruins-of-economic-crisis-10437.html; Jeff Yeager, "Meet the Bank We Don't Hate," thedailygreen, accessed July 8, 2009 at http://www.thedailygreen.com/living-green/blogs/save-money/e3bank-green-banks-460409; "e3bank's Guiding Principles," *e3bank.com*, accessed July 8, 2009 at http://e3bank.com/Guiding-Principles.php.

23 "Supporting the Nation's Payment System," *The Federal Reserve Bank of Philadelphia*, July 9, 2009, at http://www.philadelphiafed.org/about-the-fed/who-we-are/payment.system.cfm; "What Is ACH?" *NACHA: The Electronic Payments Association*, July 8, 2009, at http://nacha.org/About/what_is_ach_.htm; "NACHA Reports More Than 18.2 Billion ACH Payments in 2008," *NACHA*, April 6, 2009, at http://www.nacha.org/news/news/pressreleases/2009/2008 ACH Stats (Final).pdf; "International ACH Transactions," *First National Bank of Omaha*, July 8, 2009, at http://www.firstnational.com/001/html/en/commercial/comm_products_serv/cash_manage_treas_serv/receivable_processing/nacha_iat_resource.html.

24 "New Fed Pricing Expected to Spur Further Moves to Electronic Processing,"

Digital Transactions, November 6, 2007, at http://www.digitaltransactions.net/newsstory.cfm?newsid=1572.

25 Jeremy Simon, "Paper to Plastic: Checks and Cash Losing to Debit and Credit," CreditCards.com (October 3, 2007), at http://www.creditcards.com/credit-card-news/debit-credit-card-preferred-payment-1271.php.

26 Estimated from "Statistics for Smart Cards," *ePaynews.com* (July 3, 2008), at http://www.epaynews.com/statistics/scardstats.html.

Chapter 16

1 Andrew T. Gillies, "Carbon Emissions: The Next Sarbox," *Forbes.com*, December 12, 2007, at http://www.forbes.com/2007/12/06/greenhouse-carbon-inslee-biz-beltway-cz_atg_1206carbon.html; Europa.eu, "Questions and Answers on the Commission's Proposal to Revise the EU Emissions Trading System," January 23, 2008, at http://europa.eu/rapid/pressReleasesAction.do?reference=MEMO/08/35&format=HTML&aged=0&language=EN&guiLanguage=en; "Who Pays for Cap and Trade?" *The Wall Street Journal*, March 9, 2009, at http://online.wsj.com/article/SB123655590609066021.html.

2 "Advantages and Disadvantages of Mutual Funds," *The Motley Fool*, at http://www.fool.com, accessed February 11, 2008; "Who Pays for Cap and Trade?" *The Wall Street Journal*, March 9, 2009, at http://online.wsj.com/article/SB123655590609066021.html.

3 "Why Exchange-Traded Funds?," *Yahoo!* Finance Exchange-Traded Funds Center, at http://finance.yahoo.com/etf/education/02, on January 16 2008.

4 Katie Benner, "ETFs: A User's Guide," *Fortune*, February 19, 2007, page 112.

5 Walter Updegrave, "ETFs for the Long Run," February 8, 2007, *CNNMoney.com*, at http://cnnmoney.com/2007/02/05/pf/expert/expert2.moneymag/index.htm.

6 "U.S. Investment Banking Era Ends," *UPI.com*, September 22, 2008, at http://www.upi.com/Business_News/2008/09/22/US-Investment-banking-era-ends/UPI-96221222086983/.

7 New York Stock Exchange, July 22, 2009, at http://www.nyse.com.

8 "The State of Qatar Launches 'Qatar Exchange' as It Signs Today Formal Terms

of Strategic Partnership with NYSE Euronext," *NYSE News Release*, June 19, 2009, at http://www.nyse.com/press/1245406656784.html.

9 "List of Stock Exchanges," *Wikipedia*, the free encyclopedia, accessed July 22, 2009, at http://en.wikipedia.org/wiki/List_of_stock_exchanges.

10 "Chronology—Recent Consolidation Moves by Exchanges," *Reuters*, February 13, 2008, at http://www.reuters.com/article/idUSB27064320070223; Randy Grossman, "The Inevitable Stock Exchange Consolidation," *Advanced Trading*, June 16, 2006, at http://www.advancedtrading.com/showArticle.jhtml?articleID=196900426.

11 "Electronic Communication Networks (ECNs)," *U.S. Securities and Exchange Commission*, at http://www.sec.gov/answers/ecn.htm, accessed July 3, 2008; "Electronic Communication Network," *InvestorWords.com*, at http://www.investorwords.com/1679/Electronic_Communication_Network.html, accessed July 3, 2008.

12 "Electronic Communication Networks (ECNs)," *U.S. Securities and Exchange Commission*, at http://www.sec.gov/answers/ecn.htm, accessed July 3, 2008; "Island ECN—How Island Works," at http://ecommerce.hostip.info/pages/636/Island-Ecn-HOW-ISLAND-WORKS.html, accessed January 16, 2008.

13 Steven E. Norwitz (editor), "A Bear Market of Historic Proportions," *T. Rowe Price Report*, Spring 2009, page 1.

14 Alex Altman, "A Brief History of: Ponzi Schemes," *Time*, January 8, 2009, at http://www.time.com/time/magazine/article/0,9171,1870510,00.html; "How Much Did Madoff Scheme Cost?" *CNNMoney.com*, January 5, 2009, at http://money.cnn.com/2009/01/02/news/companies/madoff/index.htm; "The Man Who Figured Out Madoff's Scheme," *CBS News*, June 14, 2009, at http://www.cbsnews.com/stories/2009/02/27/60minutes/main4833667.shtml; Associated Press, "Investors Named in Madoff List," Columbia Daily Tribune, February 5, 2009, page 7B; Nicholas Varchaver, "Who Isn't a Madoff Victim? The List Is Telling," *CNNMoney.com*, December 17, 2008, at http://money.cnn.com/2008/12/16/news/madoff.hedges.fortune/index.htm?postversion=2008121710; John Slattery, "Madoff Investors May Be

Protected by Government," *WCBSTV.com*, December 16, 2008, at http://wcbstv .com/business/madoff.ponzi.scheme .2.888036.html.

[15] "Dow Jones to Change Composition of the Dow Jones Industrial Average," *Dow Jones (Press Release)*, June1, 2009, at http://www.djindexes.com/mdsidx/ html/pressrelease/press-release-archive.html#20090601.

[16] Carl Beidelman, *The Handbook of International Investing* (Chicago, 1987), p. 133.

[17] Ajay Kumar, "Can We Trust Moody's, Fitch, Standard & Poor?" *CommodityOnline*, at http://www.commodityonline .com/printnews.php?news_id=15888, accessed July 22, 2009; David Evans and Caroline Salas, "Flawed Credit Ratings Reap Profits as Regulators Fail (Update 1)," *Bloomberg.com*, April 29, 2009, at http://www.bloomberg.com/ apps/news?pid=20670001&sid=au4oIx. judz4; Leslie Wayne, "Calpers Sues over Ratings of Securities," *The New York Times*, July 15, 2009, at http://www.nytimes .com/2009/07/15/business/15calpers .html.

[18] "Mortgage-Backed Securities," *U.S. Securities and Exchange Commission*, June 25, 2007, at http://www.sec.gov/ answers/mortgagesecurities.htm; "Mortgage-Backed Security," *riskglossary .com*, at http://www.riskglossary.com/ link/mortgage_backed_security.htm, accessed July 24, 2009.

[19] David Goldman, "Fannie, Freddie Ignored Warning Signs," *CNNMoney.com*, December 9, 2008, at http://money.cnn .com/2008/12/09/news/economy/ fannie_freddie_hearing/index.htm? postversion=2008120910.

[20] Glenn Somerville, "U.S. Seizes Fannie, Freddie, Aims to Calm Markets," Reuters, September 7, 2008, at http://www. reuters.com/article/newsOne/idUSN05 27106320080907.

[21] Tara Kaprowy, "Root Causes of Financial Crisis Complicated," *The Sentinel Echo*, September 30, 2008, at http://www.sentinel-echo.com/local/ local_story_274154552.html; Neil Irwin, "Fed to Pump $1.2 Trillion into Markets," *The Washington Post*, March 19, 2009, at http://www.washingtonpost .com/wp-dyn/content/article/2009/ 03/18/AR2009031802283.html; David Goldman, "Fannie, Freddie Ignored Warning Signs," *CNNMoney.com*,

December 9, 2008, at http://money .cnn.com/2008/12/09/news/economy/ fannie_freddie_hearing/index.htm? postversion=2008120910; Joe Reeser, "The Real Cause of the Current Financial Crisis," OpEdNews.com, September 27, 2008, at http://www.opednews .com/articles/The-Real-Cause-of-the-Curr-by-Joe-Reeser-080926-83.html.

[22] New York Stock Exchange at http://www.nyse.com/about/listed/lcd data.html?ticker=GOOG; http://www. nyse.com/about/listed/lcddata.html?tic ker=GE; http://www.nyse.com/ about/listed/lcddata.html?ticker=DAL; http://www.nyse.com/about/listed/ lcddata.html?ticker=BRKA, accessed June 16, 2008.

[23] *CNN Money.com*, 12 February 2008.

SOURCES

Chapter 1

Figure 1.1: Adapted from Karl E. Case and Ray C. Fair, *Principles of Economics*, 8th ed., updated (Upper Saddle River, NJ: Prentice Hall, 2007). **Figure 1.2:** Data obtained from U.S. Department of Commerce Bureau of Economic Analysis, http://www.bea.gov/ bea/dn/gdplev.xls; U.S. Census Bureau, www.census.gov/popest/states/tables/ NST-EST2005–01.xls; www.census.gov/ popest/archives/1990s/; National Economic Accounts, at http://www.bea. gov/national/nipaweb/TableView. asp#Mid; From World Bank Development Indicators 2007–Feb 2008: International Comparison Program (May 29, 2008), at http://www.finfacts.com/biz10/ globalworldincomepercapita.htm. **Figure 1.3:** Data obtained from Big Mac Index Review 2007 (May 29, 2008), at http://www.woopidoo.com/reviews/ news/big-mac-index.htm. **Figure 1.4:** Source: Data obtained from U.S. Census Bureau (June 19, 2008), at http://www. census.gov/foreign-trade/balance/ c0004.html#2005.

Chapter 2

Figure 2.1: Based on Gerald S. Cavanaugh, *American Business Values: With International Perspectives*, 4th ed. (Upper Saddle River, NJ: Prentice Hall, 1998) 71, 84. **Figure 2.2:** Based on Andrew C. Revkin, "Who Cares About a

Few Degrees?" *New York Times*, December 12, 1997, F1.

Chapter 3

Figure 3.1: Data from http://www.sba. gov, accessed 3/6/2006, and U.S. Census Bureau, "Statistics About Business Size (including Small Business) from the U.S. Census Bureau," at http://www.census. gov/epcd/www/smallbus.html, accessed 4/25/2007. **Figure 3.2:** U.S. Census Bureau, "Statistical Abstract of the United States," at http://www.census.gov/prod/www/ statistical-abstract.html.

Chapter 4

Figure 4.1: Europe, at http://europa.eu/ abc/maps/index_en.htm, accessed June 4, 2008. **Figure 4.2:** Association of Southeast Asian Nations, at http://www. aseansec.org/74.htm, accessed June 4, 2008. **Figure 4.3:** U.S. Census Bureau: Foreign Trade Statistics, at http://www. census.gov/foreign-trade/statistics/ highlights/annual.html, accessed May 14, 2008. **Figure 4.4:** Source: U.S. Census Bureau: Foreign Trade Statistics, at http://www.census.gov/foreign-trade/ statistics/highlights/annual.html, accessed May 14, 2008.

Chapter 5

Figure 5.2: Adapted from Stephen P. Robbins and Mary Coulter, *Management*, 9th ed. (Upper Saddle River, NJ: Prentice Hall, 2007), 199.

Chapter 8

Figure 8.2: A. H. Maslow, *Motivation and Personality*, 2nd ed. (Upper Saddle River, NJ: Prentice Hall, 1970). Reprinted by permission of Prentice Hall Inc.

Chapter 9

Figure 9.1: Reprinted by permission of *Harvard Business Review*. Exhibit from 'How to Choose Leadership Patterns' by Robert Tannenbaum & Warren Schmidt, May–June 1973. © 1973 by the Harvard Business School Publishing Corporation. All rights reserved. **Figure 9.2:** From GRIFFIN. Management 8e. © 2005 South-Western, a part of Cengage Learning, Inc. Reproduced by permission. www.cengage.com/permissions.

Chapter 10

Figure 10.3a: http://www.dol.gov/asp/media/reports/workforce2007/ADW2007_Full_Text.pdf(p. 38).
Figure 10.3b: U.S. Department of Labor, "America's Dynamic Workforce," (August 2007), p. 38, at http://www.dol.gov/asp/media/reports/workforce2007/ADW2007_Full_Text.pdf.

Chapter 11

Figure 11.2: Adapted from Jay Heizer and Barry Render, *Operations Management*, 7th ed. (Upper Saddle River, NJ: Prentice Hall, 2004), 157.

Chapter 12

Table 12.1: "Favorite 50: The Online Retailers Shoppers Like Most," *Stores*, October 2008 © STORES Magazine. Used with permission.

Chapter 13

Figure 13.2: Major modifications of diagrams at the BlackBerry Web site, modified from Research in Motion, Limited, technical images, at http://www.blackberry.com/images/technical/bes_exchange_architecture.gif.

Chapter 14

Figure 14.1: Yahoo! Finance, at http://finance.yahoo.com/q/bs?s=goog&annual, accessed 12/11/2009.
Figure 14.2: Yahoo! Finance, at http://finance.yahoo.com/q/is?s=GOOG&annual, accessed 12/11/2009.
Figure 14.3: Yahoo! Finance, at http://finance.yahoo.com/q/cf?s=GOOG&annual, accessed 12/11/2009.

Chapter 15

Figure 15.2: http://www.federalreserve.gov/releases/h15/data/annual/h15_prime_na.txt.

Chapter 16

Figure 16.2: Dow Jones Industrial Average," *MSN.com*, at http://moneycentral.msn.com/investor/charts/chartdl.aspx?PT=7&compsyms=&D4=1&DD=1&D5=0&DCS=2&MA0=0&MA1=0&CP=1&C5=1&*Yahoo! Finance*, at http://finance.yahoo.com.

Figure 16.3: Carl Beidelman, *The Handbook of International Investing* (Chicago, 1987), p. 133.

Photo Credits

Chapter 1

Page 2/3: © Louis DeLuca/Dallas Morning News/CORBIS-NY. Page 6: © Mario Tama/Getty Images. Page 7: © Lilli Day/iStockphoto. Page 8: © FREDERIC J. BROWN/Getty Images, Inc.—Agence France Presse. Page 12: © Joe Raedle/Getty Images, Inc.—Getty News. Page 16: Corbis/Bettmann. Page 17: © Justin Sullivan/Getty Images, Inc.—Getty News.

Chapter 2

Page 20/21: © Chris Mueller/Redux Pictures. Page 22: © Michael Appleton, The New York Times/Redux Pictures. Page 23: © David Grossman/Photo Researchers, Inc. Page 23 (bottom): The Cartoon Bank. Page 26 (bottom): © Showcasepix/Newscom. Page 26 (top): © zumaphotos/Newscom. Page 27: © Tony Karumba/Getty Images. Page 30: © AFP/Getty Images, Inc.—Agence France Presse. Page 31: © Food and Drug Administration/Photo Researchers, Inc. Page 32: © Gregory Heisler/Getty Images/Time Life Pictures.

Chapter 3

Page 36/37: © Dan Kitwood/Getty Images, Inc.—Getty News. Page 39: © Thomas Nord/Shutterstock. Page 40: © Baris Simsek/iStockphoto. Page 42 (left): The Cartoon Bank. Page 42 (right): © Gary Walts, Syracue Newspapers/The Image Works. Page 45: © Tom Grundy/Shutterstock. Page 50: © Mark Richards/PhotoEdit Inc.

Chapter 4

Page 52/53: © Markel Redondo/Getty Images—Entertainment. Page 54: © Vincent Yu/AP Wide World Photos. Page 55: © Index Open/Photolibrary.com. Page 60: © Age fotostock/SuperStock, Inc. Page 62: © TOSHIFUMI KITAMURA/Getty Images, Inc.—Agence France Presse. Page 63: © KAZUHIRO NOGI/Getty Images, Inc.—Agence France

Presse. Page 64: © Alexandr Tovstenko/iStockphoto.

Chapter 5

Page 68/69: © Magunia,Joker, SV-Bilderdienst/The Image Works. Page 70: © ADRIAN DENNIS/Getty Images, Inc.—Agence France Presse. Page 70: © Mario Tama/Getty Images, Inc.—Getty News. Page 70: © Fred R. Conrad, Peter Yates/The New York Times/Redux Pictures. Page 71: © Jessica Brandi Lifland/Redux Pictures. Page 74: © G Newman Lowrance/Getty Images, Inc.—Allsport Photography. Page 75: The Cartoon Bank. Page 76: Kistone Photography. Page 77: © Peter Kramer/Getty Images. Page 80: © Justin Sullivan/Getty Images, Inc.—Getty News. Page 81: © Bob Daemmrich/PhotoEdit Inc. Page 83: © TONY AVELAR/Getty Images, Inc.—Agence France Presse.

Chapter 6

Page 84/85: © Jerome Chatin/Redux Pictures. Page 87 (right): © Damien Meyer/Getty Images, Inc.—Agence France Presse. Page 87 (left): © Getty Images Inc.—Hulton Archive Photos. Page 88: Steve Jones Photography. Page 89: © Justin Sullivan/Getty Images. Page 91: Vincent Prado. Page 95: © Justin Sullivan/Getty Images.

Chapter 7

Page 100/101: © Kevin Dyer/iStockphoto. Page 102 (left): © Andy Kropa/Redux. Page 102 (right): © Charles Eshelman/Getty Images—WireImage.com. Page 104: © Steve Prezant/Masterfile Stock Image Library. Page 106: © MMcMahon/Zefa/CORBIS- NY. Page 111: TOSHIFUMI KITAMURA Getty Images, Inc.—Agence France Presse. Page 112: © Chung Sung-Jun/Getty Images. Page 113: © Justin Sullivan/Getty Images, Inc.—Getty News.

Chapter 8

Page 118/119: © Jacob Wackerhausen/iStockphoto. Page 120: © Lester Lefkowitz/CORBIS- NY. Page 121: © Eric Hood/iStockphoto. Page 128: © Fernando Llano/AP Wide World Photos. Page 129 (top): The Cartoon Bank. Page 129 (bottom): CORBIS- NY. Page 130: © Justin Sullivan/Getty Images.

Chapter 9

Page 132/133: © Jerome Favre/Redux Pictures. Page 136: CORBIS- NY. Page 137: © Mark Wilson/Getty Images, Inc.—Getty News. Page 138: © NFL/ Wire Image/ Newscom. Page 140: © Chuck Savage/ CORBIS- NY. Page 141 (left): © Brad Barket/Getty Images—Entertainment. Page 141 (right): © JOHN MACDOUGALL/Getty Images, Inc.—Agence France Presse. 142: © Tony Avelar/Getty Images. Page 145: © Oliver Fantitsch/AP Wide World Photos.

Chapter 10

Page 148/149: © Yellow Dog Productions/ Getty Images, Inc. / Riser. Page 152: © Marine LAOUCHEZ/Getty Images, Inc.— Agence France Presse. Page 153: Getty Images. Page 155: © David Zalubowski/ AP Wide World Photos. Page 156: The Cartoon Bank. Page 157: © Samuel Zuder/Redux Pictures. Page 161: © Joyce Dopkeen/Redux Pictures.

Chapter 11

Page 164/165: © PAUL J. RICHARDS/Getty Images, Inc.—Agence France Presse. Page 167: Ting Shi. Page 168: © iStockphoto. Page 169: © CHESTER HIGGINS JR.,The New York Times/Redux Pictures. Page 170: © David M. Grossman/The Image Works. Page 171: The Cartoon Bank. Page 175: Jill Connelly. Page 177: Heidi Cody.

Page 179: © Todd Gipstein/CORBIS- NY. Page 180: © UPPA/Photoshot Holdings Ltd./Bruce Coleman.

Chapter 12

Page 182/183: © Justin Sullivan/Getty Images, Inc.—Getty News. Page 184: © Ed Kashi/CORBIS- NY. Page 187: © Guillermo Granja/CORBIS- NY. Page 188: © Jim West/Jim West. Page 190: © Joe Fornabaio/ The New York Times/Redux Pictures. Page 191: QVC, Inc. Page 192: © Tova R. Baruch/Tova R. Baruch. Page 193: © Laura Gangi Pond/Shutterstock.

Chapter 13

Page 198/199: © Dave Pilibosian/ iStockphoto. Page 200: © Ron Sachs-Pool/Getty Images, Inc.—Getty News. Page 202: © Alex Slobodkin/iStockphoto. Page 203 (top): CORBIS- NY. Page 203 (bottom): Getty Images. Page 205: © Justin Sullivan/Getty Images, Inc.—Getty News. Page 206: © Yuri Arcurs/Shutterstock. Page 207: © Porter Gifford/CORBIS- NY. Page 208: © Jeff Greenberg/The Image Works. Page 209: Photo Researchers, Inc. Page 210: © Elizabeth Dalziel/AP Wide World Photos.

Chapter 14

Page 214/215: © Johnny Lye/Shutterstock. Page 217: © F. Carter Smith/Polaris

Images. Page 220: © carroteater/ Shutterstock. Page 225: © iStockphoto. Page 226: The Cartoon Bank. Page 227: © Peter Macdiarmid/Getty Images, Inc.— Getty News.

Chapter 15

Page 230/231: © Norman Chan/ Shutterstock. Page 232: Photos.com. Page 233: © Vincent Laforet/Redux Pictures. Page 236 (top): © The New Yorker Collection 1997 J. B. Handelsman from cartoonbank.com. All Rights Reserved. Page 236 (bottom): © iStockphoto. Page 238: © Nikolai Ignatiev/arabianEye FZ LLC. Page 239: Jupiter Images. Page 242: © iStockphoto. Page 243: © Chris Hondros/Getty Images.

Chapter 16

Page 246/247: © Image 100/CORBIS- NY. Page 250: © CHANG W. LEE, The New York Times/Redux Pictures. Page 254: © TIMOTHY A. CLARY/Getty Images, Inc.—Agence France Presse. Page 259: © ANDREW COUNCILL, The New York Times/Redux Pictures. Page 260: Shaul Schwarz/CORBIS- NY. Page 261: © The New Yorker Collection 2000 P.C. Vey from cartoonbank.com. All Rights Reserved. Page 262: © FREDERIC J. BROWN/Getty Images, Inc.—Agence France Presse.

Glindex

A

Abercrombie & Fitch, 12, 27

Absenteeism an employee's not showing up for work, [121]

Absolute advantage ability to produce something more efficiently than any other country, [60–61]

Accommodative stance approach to social responsibility by which a company, if asked to do so, exceeds legal minimums in its commitments to groups and individuals in its social environment, [33]

Accountability obligation employees have to the manager for the successful completion of an assigned task, [92]

Accountants
    forensic, 218–219
    management, 218
    private, 218

Accounting comprehensive system for collecting, analyzing, and communicating financial information, [216]
    core competencies for, 218
    fair value, 225
    financial, 216
    forensic, 215
    managerial, 216
    reporting standards and practices, 224–225

Accounting equation Assets = Liabilities + Owners' Equity; used by accountants to balance data for the firm's financial transactions at various points in the year, [219–220]
    ethics and, 228–229

Accounting information system (AIS) organized procedure for identifying, measuring, recording, and retaining financial information for use in accounting statements and management reports, [216]

Accounts payable (payables) current liability consisting of bills owed to suppliers, plus wages and taxes due within the coming year, [222]

Acquisition purchase of one company by another, [50]

Activity ratio financial ratio for evaluating management's efficiency in using a firm's assets, [226]

Activity ratios, 228

Advertising media variety of communication devices for carrying a seller's message to potential customers, [195]

Advertising promotional tool consisting of paid, nonpersonal communication used by an identified sponsor to inform an audience about a product, [195]

AES Corporation, 128

Affirmative action plan written statement of how the organization intends to actively recruit, hire, and develop members of relevant protect classes, [157]

Agency law, 270

Agent individual or organization acting for an in the name of another party, [270]

Aggregate output total quantity of goods and services produced by an economic system during a given period, [13]

Aggressive growth funds, 250

AIDS, in workplace, 158

Airbus, 145, 169

Albania, 55

Amazon.com, 177

American Airlines, 86, 153

American Eagle Outfitters, 170

American Federation of Labor and Congress of Industrial Organizations (AFL-CIO), 160–161

American Marketing Association, 166

American Red Cross, 23, 86

American Society for Quality, 108

American Stock Exchange (AMEX), 251–252

Americans with Disabilities Act (1990), 153, 156

AmEx, 78

Anderson, Brad, 80

Angel investors outside investors who provide new capital for firms in return for a share of equity ownership, [257]

Anheuser-Busch, 27, 156

Ann Taylor, 80

Annual percentage rate (APR) one-year rate that is charged for borrowing, expressed as a percentage of the borrowed principal, [257]

Anti-virus software product that protects systems by searching incoming e-mails and data files for "signatures" of known viruses and virus-like characteristics, [212]

Apparelus.com, 193

Apparent authority agent's authority, based on the principals compliance, to bind a principal to a certain course of action, [270]

Appellate court court that reviews case records of trials whose findings have been appealed, [268]

Apple Computer, 12, 26, 43, 83, 142, 157, 183

Application forms, 152

Application servers, 204

Arbitration method of resolving a labor dispute in which both parties agree to submit to the judgment of a neutral party, [162]

Arthur Andersen, 139

Ash, Mary Kay, 138

Assembly line a same-steps layout in which a product moves step by step through a plant on conveyor belts or other equipment until it is complete, [108]

Asset allocation relative amount of funds invested in (or allocated to) each of several investment alternatives, [256]

Asset any economic resource expected to benefit a firm or an individual who owns it, [220]
    current, 221
    fixed, 222
    intangible, 221–222

Association of Certified Fraud Examiners (ACFE), 215

Association of Southeast Asian Nations (ASEAN) organization for economic, political, social, and cultural cooperation among Southeast Asian nations, [56], 57

Atlantic Richfield, 131

Attitudes person's beliefs and feelings about specific ideas, situations, or people, [122–123]

Audit systematic examination of a company's accounting system to determine whether its financial reports reliably represent its operations, [217]
    social, 34

Australia, 55

Authority power to make the decisions necessary to complete a task, [91]
    forms of, 92–93

Automated Clearing House (ACH) Network, 242–243

Automated teller machine (ATM) electronic machine that allows bank customers to conduct account-related activities 24 hours a day, 7 days a week, [237]

Avon Products, 141, 187, 191

B

Bakke, Dennis, 128

Balanced funds, 250

Balance of payments flow of all money into or out of a country, [58–59]

Balance of trade economic value of all the products that a country exports minus the economic value of all the products it imports, [15–16], [57]
    negative, 57
    positive, 57

Balance sheet financial statement that supplies detailed information about a firm's assets, liabilities, and owners' equity, [221–222]

Baldassarre, Frank, Jr., 242

Banana Republic, 12

Banker's acceptance bank promise, issued for a buyer, to pay a designated firm a specified amount at a future date, [236]

Banking crisis, U.S., 231

Bank of America, 178

Bankruptcy court-granted permission for a company to not pay some or all debts, [258]

Bankruptcy law, 271

Bank Secrecy Act (BSA), 241

Barbato, Mark, 175

Bargain retailer retailer carrying a wide range of products at bargain prices, [189]

Barnes, Brooks, 53

Bartering, Internet, 206

Bay Area Rapid Transit (BART), 104

B2B buying behavior, 173

Bear market period of falling stock prices marked by negative investor sentiments with motivation to sell ahead of anticipated losses, [253]

Bear Stearns, 241, 251

Behavioral approach to leadership approach focused on determining what behaviors are employed by leaders, [135]

Benefits compensation other than wages and salaries, [155–156]

Bengtson, Phil, 138

Ben & Jerry's, 65

Bergen, Candice, 190

Bernanke, Ben, 16

Best Buy, 80

Big business, crossover from, 43

"Big Five" personality traits five fundamental personality traits especially relevant to organizations, 122

Blackberry messaging device, 200, 204–205

Black & Decker, 174

Blink credit card, 243–244

Blockbuster, 42

Bloom, Diana, 149

Blue Bell, 81

Board of directors governing body of a corporation that reports to its shareholders and delegates power to run its day-to-day operations while remaining responsible for sustaining its assets, [49]

Boeing, 25, 134, 145, 169, 201

Bond, corporate, 258

Bondholders' claim request for court enforcement of a bond's terms of payment, [258]

Bond indenture legal document containing complete details of a bond issue, [258]

Bonds, 16

Bonus individual performance incentive in the form of a special payment made over and above the employee's salary, [154]

Book-entry ownership procedure that holds investors' shares in book-entry form, rather than issuing a physical paper certificate of ownership, [253]

Bookkeeping recording of accounting transactions, [216]

Book value value of a common stock expressed as the firm's owners' equity divided by the number of common shares, [249]

Boster, Adam, 106

Boston Beer, 77

Bowersox, Bob, 191

Boycott labor action in which workers refuse to buy the products of a targeted employer, [162]

BP, 21, 61

Brackett, Robert, 101

Branch office foreign office set up by an international or multinational firm, [64]

Brand awareness extent to which a brand name comes to mind when a consumer considers a particular product category, [177]

Brand competition competitive marketing that appeals to consumer perceptions of benefits of products offered by particular companies, [169]

Branding process of using symbols to communicate the qualities of a product made by a particular producer, [177–178]

Brand loyalty pattern of regular consumer purchasing based on satisfaction with a product's performance, [172]

Brazil, 14

Breakeven analysis for a particular selling price, assessment of the seller's costs versus revenues at various sales volumes, [185]

Breakeven point sales volume at which the seller's total revenue from sales equals total costs (variable and fixed) with neither profit nor loss, [185]

Bribery, 23

Brin, Sergey, 69, 74–75

British Airways, 29

Broker independent intermediary who matches numerous sellers and buyers as needed, often without knowing in advance who they will be, [188]

Budget detailed statement of estimated receipts and expenditures for a future period of time, [224]

Bulgaria, 55

Bull market period of rising stock prices, lasting 12 months or longer, featuring investor confidence for future gains and motivation to buy, [253]

Business continuation agreement special form of business insurance whereby owners arrange to buy the interests of deceased associates from their heirs, [266]

Business cycle short-term pattern of economic expansions and contractions, [13]

Business ethics ethical or unethical behaviors by employees in the context of their jobs, [22]
    company practices and, 25

Business financing, 248–249, 259–261

Business forms
    cooperatives, 47
    corporations, 47–50
    partnerships, 46–47
    sole proprietorships, 46

Business interruption insurance insurance covering income lost during times when a company is unable to conduct business, [264–265]

Business law, 268–271
  agency law, 270
  bankruptcy law, 271
  commercial law, 270–271
  contract law, 268
  international framework of, 271
  property law, 269–270
  tort law, 269

Business marketing, 173

Business (or competitive) strategy strategy, at the business-unit or product-line level, focusing on improving a firm's competitive position, [78]
  as driver of operations, 104–106

Business organization that provides goods or services to earn profits, [4]. See also **Small Business Administration (SBA)** government agency charged with assisting small businesses
  benefits of, 4
  external environments of, 4–5

Business ownership
  corporate, 47–50
  noncorporate, 45–47

Business plan document in which an entrepreneur summarizes her or his business strategy for a proposed new venture and how that strategy will be implemented, [41–42]

Business practice law law or regulation governing business practices in given countries, [66]

Business process reengineering rethinking and radical redesign of business processes to improve performance, quality, and productivity, [115]

Businesss forms
  cooperatives, 47
  corporations, 47–50
  partnerships, 46–47

Buzz marketing promotional method that relies on word of mouth to create buzz about products and ideas, [177]

C

Cabot Creamery, 47

Cafeteria benefits plan benefit plan that sets limits on benefits per employee, each of whom may choose from a variety of alternative benefits, [156]

California Public Employees Retirement Fund (Calpers), 258

Canada, 55

CAN-SPAM Act (2003), 213

Capacity amount of a product that a company can produce under normal conditions, [107]

Capacity competence required of individuals entering into a binding contract, [268]

Capital funds needed to create and operate a business enterprise, [6]

Capital gain profit realized from the increased value of an investment, [256]

Capitalism system that sanctions the private ownership of the factors of production and encourages entrepreneurship by offering profits as an incentive, [8]

Capital item expensive, long-lasting, infrequently purchased industrial good, such as a building, or industrial service, such as building maintenance, [174]

Carbonite, Inc., 186

Carbon trading, 247

CareerBuilder.com, 154

Carrefour, 189

Cartel association of producers whose purpose is to control supply and prices, [66]

Cash-value insurance, 280

Catalog showroom bargain retailer in which customers place orders for catalog items to be picked up at on-premises warehouses, [189]

"Catch Me If You Can (forensic accounting game), 218

Cell phone "gas station" kiosks, 167

Cellular One, 204

Centralized organization organization in which most decision-making authority is held by upper-level management, [90]

Certified Development Company (504) program, 43

Certified Fraud Examiner (CFE) professional designation administered by the Association of Certified Fraud Examiners in recognition of qualifications for a specialty area within forensic accounting, [219]

Certified management accountant (CMA) professional designation awarded by the Institute of Management Accountants in recognition of management accounting qualifications, [218]

Certified public accountant (CPA) accountant licensed by the state and offering services to the public, [216–217]

Chain of command reporting relationships within a company, [86]

Chambers, John, 44

Chamitoff, Ken, 106

Change, managing, 82–83

Chaparral Steel, 203–204

Charismatic leadership type of influence based on a leader's personal charisma, [137–139]

Charitable giving, 23

Check clearing, 239

Check demand deposit order instructing a bank to pay a given sum to a specified payee, [233]

Checking account (demand deposit) bank account funds, owned by the depositor, that may be withdrawn at any time by check or cash, [233]

Check 21, 243

Chenault, Kenneth, 70, 78

Chief executive officer (CEO) top manager who is responsible for the overall performance of a corporation, [49]

Chief financial offer (CFO), 74

Chief information officer (CIO), 73

China, 3, 7, 55

Chipolte Mexican Grill, 79

Chiquita, 66

Chrysler, 113, 161

Circle K, 189

Circuit City, 18, 80

Cisco, 44, 178

Citigroup, 157, 258

Clark Equipment, 92

Classical theory of motivation theory holding that workers are motivated solely by money, [124]

Clayton Act (1914), 13

Clean Harbors, 45

Clean Water Act, 21

Clients, 204

Client-server network common business network in which clients make requests for information or resources and servers provide the services, [204]

Closely held (or private) corporation corporation whose stock is held by only a few people and is not available for sale to the general public, [47–48]

Coalition informal alliance of individuals or groups formed to achieve a common goal, [146]

Coca-Cola, 63, 73, 78, 177, 261

Code of Professional Conduct code of ethics for CPAs as maintained and enforced by the AICPA, [228–229]

Codes of conduct
  adopting written, 25
  Google's, 24

Cold Stone Creamery, 63

Collateral asset pledged for the fulfillment of repaying a loan, [257]

Collective bargaining process by which labor and management negotiate conditions of employment and draft a labor contract for union-represented workers, [161–163]

Collusion illegal agreement between two or more companies to commit a wrongful act, [29]

Commercial bank company that accepts deposits that it uses to make loans, earn profits, pay interest to depositors, and pay dividends to owners, [234]

Commercial finance companies, 235

Commercial law, 270–271

Committee and team authority authority granted to committees or teams involved in a firm's daily operations, [93]

Common law body of decisions handed down by courts ruling on individual cases, [267]

Common stock most basic form of ownership, including voting rights on major issues, in a company, [248–249]

Communism political system in which the government owns and operates all factors of production, [7]

Comparative advantage ability to produce some products more efficiently than others, [61]

Compensation system total package of rewards that organizations provide to individuals in return for their labor, [154]

Compensatory damages monetary payments intended to redress injury actually suffered because of a tort, [269]

Competition vying among businesses for the same resources or customers, [11]
  brand, 169
  degrees of, 11–12
  international, 168–169
  in market economy, 10–12
  monopolistic, 11–12
  perfect, 11

Competitive advantage ability to produce some products more efficiently than others, [61]
  forms of, 60–61
  with lean operations, 113

Competitive product analysis process by which a company analyzes a competitor's products to identify desirable improvements, [114]

Compound growth compounding of interest over time–with each additional time period, interest returns accumulate, [248]

Computer-aided design (CAD) IS with software that helps knowledge workers design products by simulating them and displaying them in three-dimensional graphics, [209]

Computer-based scheduling, 109–110

Computer network group of two or more computers linked together by some form of cabling or by wireless technology to share data or resources, such as a printer, [204]

Computer viruses, 211

Conceptual skills abilities to think in the abstract, diagnose and analyze different situations, and see beyond the present situation, [74–75]

Conflict of interest, 23

Conlin, Michelle, 152

Conscientiousness, 122

Consideration item of value exchanged between parties to create a valid contract, [268]

Consistency dimension of quality that refers to sameness of product quality from unit to unit, [108]

Consumer behavior study of the decision process by which people buy and consume products, [171–172]
  influences on, 172
  process of, 172–173

Consumer Bill of Rights, 29, 30

Consumer finance companies, 235

Consumer goods physical products purchased by consumers for personal use, [166]

Consumerism form of social activism dedicated to protecting the rights of consumers in their dealings with businesses, [29]

Consumer price index (CPI) measure of the prices of typical products purchased by consumers living in urban areas, [17], 161

The Container Store, 27

Contemporary Landscape Services, 86

Contests, 196

Continental Airlines, 27, 72, 130

Contingency planning identification of aspects of a business or its environment that might entail changes in strategy, [82]

Contingent workers employee hired on something other than full-time basis to supplement an organization's permanent workforce, [159–160]

Contract agreement between two or more parties enforceable in court, [268]

Contract law, 268

Contributions, 123

Controller person who managers all of a firm's accounting activities (chief accounting officer), [216]

Controlling management process of monitoring an organization's performance to ensure that it is meeting its goals, [72–73]

Convenience good/convenience service inexpensive good or service purchased and consumed rapidly and regularly, [174]

Convenience store retail store offering easy accessibility, extended hours, and fast service, [189]

Cooper, Roy, 187

Cooperative form of ownership in which a group of sole proprietorships and/or partnerships agree to work together for common benefits, [47]

Copyright exclusive ownership right belonging to the creator of a book, article, design, illustration, photo, film, or musical work, [270]

Core competencies for accounting the combination of skills, technology, and knowledge that will be necessary for the future CPA, [218]

Corporate blogs comments and opinions published on the web by or for an organization to promote its activities, [178]

Corporate bond formal pledge obligating the issuer (the company) to pay interest periodically and repay the principal at maturity, [258]

Corporate culture the shared experiences, stories, beliefs, and norms that characterize an organization, [82–83]

Corporate foundations, 33

Corporate governance roles of shareholders, directors, and other managers in corporate decision making and accountability, [49]

Corporate raider investor conducting a type of hostile corporate takeover against the wishes of the company, [260]

Corporate strategy strategy for determining a firm's overall attitude toward growth and the way it will manage its business or product lines, [78]

Corporation business that is legally considered an entity separate from its owners and is liable for its own debts; owners' liabilities extend to the limits of their investments, [48]

  advantages, 48
  disadvantages, 48
  going public, 259–260
  special issues, 50
  types of, 49

Costco, 189

Cost of goods sold costs of obtaining materials for making the products sold by a firm during the year, [223]

Cost-of-living adjustment (COLA) labor contract clause tying future raises to changes in consumer purchasing power, [161]

Cost of revenues costs that a company incurs to obtain revenues from other companies, [223]

Cost-oriented pricing pricing that considers the firm's desire to make a profit and its need to cover production costs, [184]

Counterproductive behaviors behaviors that detract from organization performance, [120–121]

Coupon sales-promotion technique in which a certificate is issued entitling the buyer to a reduced price, [196]

Courtyard by Marriott, 108

Craigslist, 149

Crate & Barrel, 190

Creative selling personal-selling task in which sales people try to persuade buyers to purchase products by providing information about their benefits, [195–196]

Credit cards, 275–276

Credit checks, 153

Credit union nonprofit, cooperative financial institution owned and run by its members, usually employees of a particular organization, [234–235]

Crisis management organization's methods for dealing with emergencies, [81–82]

Cross-cultural leadership, 141–142

Cuba, 66

Currency (cash) government-issued paper money and coins, [233]

Current asset asset that can or will be converted into cash within a year, [221]

Current dividend/interest yield yearly dollar amount of income divided by the investment's current market value, expressed as a percentage, [256]

Current liability debt that must be paid within one year, [222]

Current ratio financial ratio for measuring a company's ability to pay current debts out of current assets, [226]

Customer departmentalization dividing of an organization to offer products and meet needs for identifiable customer groups, [89]

Custom-products layout physical arrangement of production activities that groups equipment and people according to function, [107–108]

Cybermall collection of virtual storefronts (business Web sites) representing a variety of products and product lines on the Internet, [192]

Cyclical unemployment, 18

D

Daewoo, 117

Daiei, 189

Daimler AG, 49

D'Amore, Massimo F., 89

Data mining the application of electronic technologies for searching, sifting, and reorganizing pools of data to uncover useful information, [208]

Data raw facts and figures that, by themselves, may not have much meaning, [207]

Data warehousing the collection, storage, and retrieval of data in electronic files, [207–208]

Davis, James, 121

Debit card plastic card that allows an individual to transfer money between accounts, [244]

Debt company's total liabilities, [226]
  national, 16

Debt financing longterm borrowing from sources outside a company, [262]

Decentralized organization organization in which a great deal of decision-making authority is delegated to levels of management at points below the top, [90]

Decision making choosing one alternative from among several options, [143]
  behavioral aspects of, 146–147
  rational, 143–145

Decision-making hierarchy, 90–93

Decision-making skills skills in defining problems and selecting the best courses of action, [75]

Decision support system (DSS) interactive system that creates virtual business models for a particular kind of decision and tests them with different data to see how they respond, [210]

Default failure of a borrower to make payment when due to a lender, [258]

Defensive stance approach to social responsibility by which a company meets only minimum legal requirements in its commitments to groups and individuals in its social environment, [33]

Deflation, 240

Delegation process through which a manager allocates work to subordinates, [91–92]

Dell, Michael, 38, 40, 116

Dell Computer, 38, 42, 48, 65, 116, 184, 191

Delphi Automotive Systems, 188

Delta Air Lines, 50

Demand and supply schedule assessment of the relationships among different levels of demand and supply at different price levels, [9]

Demand curve graph showing how many units of a product will be demanded (bought) at different prices, [9]

Demand willingness and ability of buyers to purchase a good or service, [9]

Demographic segmentation, 171

Demographic Variables characteristics of populations that may be considered in developing a segmentation strategy, [171]

Denial of service (DoS) attacks, 210

Departmentalization process of grouping jobs into logical units, [88–90]
  multiple forms of, 89–90

Department store large product-line retailer characterized by organization into specialized departments, [189]

Depreciation accounting method for distributing the cost of an asset over its useful life, [221]

Depression prolonged and deep recession, [18]

Deregulation elimination of rules that restrict business activity, [267]

Detailed schedule schedule showing daily work assignments with start and stop times for assigned jobs, [109]

Direct Channel distribution channel in which a product travels from producer to consumer without intermediaries, [187]

Direct-response retailing form of nonstore retailing in which firms directly interact with customers to inform them of products and to receive sales orders, [190]

Direct selling form of nonstore retailing typified by door-to-door sales, [190–191]

Discount brokers, 253

Discount house bargain retailer that generates large sales volume by offering goods at substantial price reductions, [189]

Discount price reduction offered as an incentive to purchase, [186]

Discount rate interest rate at which member banks can borrow money from the Fed, [240]

Discover Financial Services, 51

Discriminatory harassment, 121

Disney, Roy, 87–88

Disney, Walt, 72, 87–88

Distribution channel network of interdependent companies through which a product passes from producer to end user, [187–189]

Distribution mix combination of distribution channels by which a firm gets its products to end users, [187–189]

Distribution (place) part of the marketing mix concerned with getting products from producers to consumers, [170]

Diversification purchase of several different kinds of investments rather than just one, [256]

Diversity, workforce, 159

Divestiture strategy whereby a firm sells one or more of its business units, [50]

Dividend payment to shareholders, on a per-shared basis, out of the company's earnings, [249]

Dividends, 49

Divisional structure organizational structure in which corporate divisions operate as autonomous businesses under the larger corporate umbrella, [94–95]

Division department that resembles a separate business in that it produces and markets its own products, [94–95]

Dole, 66

Domestic business environment environment in which a firm conducts its operations and derives its revenues, [4]

Domino Sugar, 157

Donald, Jim, 134

Double Click, 70

Double taxation situation in which taxes may be payable both by a corporation on its profits and by shareholders on dividend incomes, [48]

Dow Jones Industrial Average (DJIA) oldest and most widely cited market index based on the prices of 30 blue-chip, large-cap industrial firms on the NYSE, [254]

DreamWorks, 50

Drug tests, 153

Duke Energy, 82

Dumping selling a product abroad for less than the cost of production at home, [66–67]

Duncan, David, 26

Dunkin' Donuts, 165

Dynamic pricing, 186

Dynegy, 217

E

Earnings cycle, 225

Earnings per share profitability ratio measuring the net profit that the company earns for each share of outstanding stock, [227–228]

Eastern Europe, 55

eBay, 177, 178

E-catalog nonstore retailing in which the Internet is used to display products, [191]

E-commerce use of the Internet and other electronic means for retailing and business-to-business transactions, 44, [200]

Economic environment relevant conditions that exist in the economic system in which a company operates, [5]

Economic indicator statistic that helps assess the performance of an economy, [13]

Economic system nation's system for allocating its resources among its citizens, [5]

types of, 6–9

Edmunds, Gladys, 45

Edmunds Travel Consultants, 45

Electronic Arts, 91, 119

Electronic communication network (ECN) electronic trading system that brings buyers and sellers together outside traditional stock exchanges, [252]

Electronic conferencing IT that allows groups of people to communicate simultaneously from various locations via e-mail, phone, or video, [204]

Electronic funds transfer (EFT) communication of fund-transfer information over wire, cable, or microwave, [237]

Electronic retailing nonstore retailing in which information about the seller's products and services is connected to consumers' computers, allowing consumers to receive the information and purchase the products in the home, [191]

Electronic storefront commercial Web site at which customers gather information about products and buying opportunities,

place orders, and pay for purchases, [191–192]

Elite Island Resorts, 193

Ells, Steve, 79

E-mail, 75

E-mail servers, 204

Embargo government order banning exportation and/or importation of a particular product or all products from a particular company, [65–67]

Eminent domain principle that the government may claim private land for public use by buying it at a fair price, [270]

Emissions trading (ET), 247

Emissions Trading Scheme (ETS), 247

Emotional intelligence (emotional quotient, EQ), [122]

Emotionality, 122

Emotional motives reasons for purchasing a product that are based on nonobjective factors, [173]

Empathy, 122

Employee behavior pattern of actions by the members of an organization that directly or indirectly influences the organization's effectiveness, [120]

Employee-focused leader behavior leader behavior focusing on satisfaction, motivation, and well-being of employees, [136]

Employee information system (skills inventories) computerized system containing information on each employee's education, skills, work experiences, and career aspirations, [151]

Employee Retirement Income Security Act (1974), 158

Employment at will principle, increasingly modified by legislation and judicial decision, that organizations should be able to retain or dismiss employees at will, [158]

Encryption system software that assigns an e-mail message to a unique code number (digital fingerprint) for each computer so only that computer, not others, can open and read the message, [212]

England. See United Kingdom

Enron, 139

Entergy, 157

Enterprise Rent-a-Car, 157

Enterprise resource planning, 201

Entrepreneur individual who accepts the risks and opportunities involved in creating and operating a new business venture, [6]

Entrepreneurs

characteristics of, 40–41

Entrepreneurs business persons who accept both the risks and the opportunities involved in creating and operating a new business venture, [40]

Entrepreneurship process of seeking business opportunities under conditions of risk, [40]

Environmental analysis process of scanning the business environment for threats and opportunities, [79]

Environmental management system, 115

Environmental Protection Agency (EPA), 267

E-partnering, 78

Equal Employment Opportunity Commission (EEOC), 267

Equal Employment Opportunity Commission (EEOC) federal agency enforcing several discrimination-related laws, [156–157]

Equal employment opportunity legally mandated nondiscrimination in employment on the basis of race, creed, sex, or national origin, [156]

Equity financing using the owners' funds from inside the company as the source for long-term funding, [262–263]

Equity Marketing, 175

Equity theory theory of motivation holding that people evaluate their treatment by the organization relative to the treatment of others, [127]

Escalation of commitment condition which a decision maker becomes so committed to a course of action that she or he stays with it even when it appears to have been wrong, [146]

Ethical behavior behavior conforming to generally accepted norms concerning beneficial and harmful actions

decision making steps for, 24

Ethical behavior behavior conforming to generally accepted social norms concerning beneficial and harmful actions, [22]

Ethical leadership leader behaviors that reflect high ethical standards, [143]

Ethics beliefs about what is right or wrong and good or bad in actions that affect others, [22]

accounting and, 228–229
in advertising, 29–30
business, 22
individual, 22
managerial, 22

Ethics programs, instituting, 25

e3bank, 242

Euro common currency shared among most of the members of the European Union (excluding Denmark, Sweden, and the United Kingdom), [60]

Europe, 55

European Union, 55, 271

European Union (EU) organization for economic, social, and security cooperation among European nations, [56]

Everex Systems, 180

Exchange rate rate at which the currency of one nation can be exchanged for the currency of another nation, [59–60]

Exchange-traded fund (EFT) bundle of stocks or bonds that are in an index that tracks the overall movement of a market but, unlike a mutual fund, can be traded like a stock, [250]

Expectancy theory theory of motivation holding that people are motivated to work toward rewards that they want and that they believe they have a reasonable chance of obtaining, [126–127]

Expense item industrial product purchased and consumed rapidly and regularly for daily operations, [174]

Exporter firm that distributes and sells products to one or more foreign countries, [62–63]

Export product make or grown domestically but shipped and sold abroad, [54]

Express authority agent's authority, derived from written agreement, to bind a principal to a certain course of action, [270]

Express warranty warranty whose terms are specifically stated by the seller, [271]

External environment everything outside an organization's boundaries that might affect it, [4–5]

External recruiting process of attracting persons outside the organization to apply for jobs, [151]

Extranet system that allows outsiders limited access to a firm's internal information network, [203–204]

Extraversion, 122

ExxonMobil, 25, 63, 91

F

Facebook, 37

Face value (par value) amount of money that the bond buyer (lender) lent the issuer and that the lender will receive upon repayment, [258]

Factors of production resources used in the production of goods and services–labor, capital, entrepreneurs, physical resources, and information resources, [5]

capital, 6
competitive advantage and, 60–61
entrepreneur, 6
information resources, 6
physical resources, 6

Factory outlet bargain retailer owned by the manufacturer whose product it sells, [189]

Fair Labor Standards Act (1938), 158

Fair value accounting, 225

False Claims Act (1863), 31

Fannie Mae, 241, 259

Favoritism, 23

Federal Deposit Insurance Corporation (FDIC) federal agency that guarantees the safety of deposits up to $100,000 in the financial institutions that it insures, [237–238]

Federal Emergency Management Agency (FEMA), 72

Federal funds rate (key rate) interest rate at which commercial banks lend reserves to each other, usually overnight, [240]

Federal Housing Finance Agency (FHFA), 241

Federal Open Market Committee, 239

Federal Reserve Act (1913), 238

Federal Reserve System (the Fed) central bank of the United States, which acts as the government's bank, serves member commercial banks, and controls the nation's money supply, 17, [238–241]

functions of, 239–240
structure of, 238–239
tools of, 240–241

Federal Trade Commission (FTC), 28, 267

FedEx, 43, 95, 105, 106, 108, 155, 194

Ferguson, Mark, 86

Film industry, 53

Finance company nondeposit institution that specializes in making loans to businesses and consumers, [235]

Financial accounting field of accounting concerned with external users of a company's financial information, [216]

Financial managers, 74

Financial planning, 41–42

Financial planning process of looking at one's current financial condition, identifying one's goals, and anticipating requirements for meeting those goals, [272–276]

Financial services, growth of, 235–237

Financial statement any of several types of reports summarizing a company's financial status to stakeholders and to aid managerial decision making, [220–224]
    analyzing, 226–228
    balance sheet, 221–222
    budgets, 224
    income statements, 222–223
    statements of cash flows, 223–224

Fiorina, Carly, 98

Firewall security system with special software or hardware devices designed to keep computers safe from hackers, 205, [212]

First-line manager manager responsible for supervising the work of employees, [73]

Fiscal policies policies that a government uses to direct how it collects and spends revenue, [17–18]

Fixed asset asset with long-term use or value, such as land, buildings, and equipment, [221]

Fixed cost cost that is incurred regardless of the quantity of a product produced and sold, [185]

Fixed pricing, 186

Flat organizational structure characteristic of decentralized companies with relatively few layers of management, [90–91], 92

Flextime programs method of increasing job satisfaction by allowing workers to adjust work schedules on a daily or weekly basis, [130]

Florida Citrus Growers, 47

FM2, 259

Follow-up operations control activity for ensuring that production decisions are being implemented, [111]

Food and Drug Administration (FDA), 267

Ford Motor Company, 29, 63, 65, 86–87, 113, 161

Foreign direct investment (FDI) arrangement in which a firm buys or established tangible assets in another, [65]

Forensic accounting, 215

Forensic accounting the practice of accounting for legal purposes, [218–219]

Form utility, 102, 166

"Four Ps" of marketing mix, 169–170

France, 9, 55

Franchise arrangement in which a buyer (franchisee) purchases the right to sell

the good or service of the seller (franchiser), [42]

Franchisees, 42

Franchisers, 42

Freddie Mac, 241, 259

Freedom of choice, 10–11

Freelancers Union, 161

Full disclosure guideline that financial statements should not include just numbers but should also furnish management's interpretations and explanations of those numbers, [225]

Full-service brokers, 253

Functional departmentalization dividing of an organization according to groups functions or activities, [88–89]

Functional strategy strategy by which managers in specific areas decide how best to achieve corporate goals through productivity, [78–79]

Functional structure organization structure in which authority is determined by the relationships between group functions and activities, [94]

G

Gainsharing plan incentive plan that rewards groups for productivity improvements, [155]

Gamesa Corporation, 167

GameStop, 27

Gandhi, Mohandas, 136

Gantt chart production schedule that breaks down large projects into steps to be performed and specifies the time required to perform each stop, [110]

Gap, 48, 157

Gates, Bill, 134

Geek Squad, 80

GEICO, 187

Gender, leadership and, 141

General Agreement on Tariffs and Trade (GATT) international trade agreement to encourage the multilateral reduction or elimination of trade barriers, [56]

General Electric (GE), 27, 29, 97, 102

Generally accepted accounting principles (GAAP) accounting guidelines that govern the content and form of financial reports, [217]

General Motors (GM), 17, 113, 161, 170, 258

General (or active) partner who actively manages a firm and who has unlimited liability for its debts, [46]

General partnership business with two or more owners who share in both the operation of the firm and the financial responsibility for its debts, [46]
    advantages of, 46
    alternatives to, 46–47
    disadvantages of, 46

Geographic departmentalization dividing of an organization according to the areas of the country or the world served by a business, [89]

Geographic segmentation, 171

Geographic variables geographic units that may be considered in developing a segmentation strategy, [171]

Germany, 55

Ghosn, Carlos, 133

Ghriskey, Timothy M., 95

Global business environment international forces that affect a business, [4]

Globalization process by which the world economy is becoming a single interdependent system, [54]
    ups and downs of, 64

Global management skills, 75

Global supply chains, 116–117

Goal objective that a business hopes and plans to achieve, [76]
    strategic, 79
    types of, 78

Goals
    setting, 41

Goal setting, 76–77

Godiva, 108

Goldberg, Whoopi, 190

Goldman Sachs, 251, 258

Goods operations (goods production) activities producing tangible products, such as radios, newspapers, buses, and textbooks, [102]

Goodwill amount paid for an existing business above the value of its other assets, [222]

Goodyear, 155

Google, 41, 69–70, 177, 220, 222, 224, 260
    code of conduct of, 25

Gordon, Gil, 131

Great Britain. See United Kingdom

Green companies, 247

Green marketing marketing of environmentally friendly goods, [29]

Greenwashing using advertising to project a green image without adopting substantive environmentally friendly changes, [28]

Gross domestic product (GDP) total value of all goods and services produced within a given period by a national economy through domestic factors of production, [14]
    nominal, 14
    per capita, 14
    real, 14

Gross national product (GNP) total value of all goods and services produced by a national economy within a given period regardless of where the factors of production are located, [14]

Gross profit preliminary, quick-to-calculate profit figure calculated from the firm's revenues minus its cost of revenues (the direct costs of getting the revenues), [223]

Groupware, 206

Grubman, Jack, 26

H

Hacker cybercriminal who gains unauthorized access to a computer network, either to steal information, money, or property or to tamper with data, [210–211]

Halliburton, 64, 151, 154–155

Harassment
    hostile work environment, 158
    quid pro quo, 158
    sexual, 158

Hardware physical components of a computer network, such as keyboards, monitors, system units, and printers, [205]

Hastings, Reed, 71, 152

Hawthorne effect tendency for productivity to increase when workers believe they are receiving special attention from management, [124–125]

Helton, Todd, 155

Henderson, Jill, 123

Hendrickson, Lisa, 180

Hershey, 63

Herzberg, Frederick, 126

Hewlett-Packard (HP), 27, 72, 86, 98, 154, 194

Hierarchy of human needs model theory of motivation describing five levels of human needs and arguing that basic needs must be fulfilled before people work to satisfy higher-level needs, [125]

High-contact system level of customer contact in which the customer is part of the system during service delivery, [104]

Hitler, Adolf, 138

Hoffman, Reid, 180

Home country, 5

Home Depot, 189

Home ownership, financial commitments of, 276–278

Home Shopping Network, 204

Honda, 28

Horizon Software International, 45

Hostile work environment form of sexual harassment deriving from off-color jobs, lewd comments, and so fort, [158]

Human relations skills skills in understanding and getting along with people, [74]

Human resource (HR) planning, 150–151

Human resource management (HRM) set of organizational activities directed at attracting, developing, and maintaining an effective workforce, [150]
    contemporary legal issues in, 158–159

Human resource managers, 73

Human resources (HR) physical and mental capabilities of people as they contribute to economic production, [6]
    developing, 153–156
    selecting, 151–153

Hurricane Katrina, 22, 157

Hutchins, Chris, 208

Hypertext transfer protocol (HTTP) communications protocol used for the World Wide Web, in which related pieces of information on separate Web pages are connected using hyperlinks, [203]

I

IBM, 63, 194

IBP, 33

Ideas, marketers and, 166–167

Identity theft unauthorized use of personal information (such as Social Security number and address) to get loans, credit cards, or other monetary benefits by impersonating the victim, [211]
    preventing, 212

Implied authority agent's authority, derived from business custom, to bind a principal to a certain course of action, [270]

Implied warranty warranty, dictated by law, based on the principle that products should fulfill advertised promises and serve the purposes for which they are manufactured and sold, [271]

Importer firm that buys products in foreign markets and then imports them for resale in its home country, [62–63]

Import product made or grown abroad but sold domestically, [54]

Incentive program special compensation program designed to motivate high performance, [154]

Income statement (profit-and-loss statement) financial statement listing a firm's annual revenues and expenses so that a bottom line shows annual profit or loss, [222–223]

Independent agent foreign individual or organization that agrees to represent an exporter's interests, [63–64]

Index-matching EFTs, 255

Individual differences personal attributes that vary from one person to another, [122]

Individual retirement account (IRA) tax-deferred pension fund that wage earners set up to supplement retirement funds, [236]

Indonesia, 55

Inducements, 123

Industrial goods physical products purchased by companies to produce other products, [166]

Industrial market organizational market consisting of firms that buy goods that are either converted into products or used during production, [173]

Inflation, 240

Inflation situation that occurs when widespread price increases occur throughout an economic system, [17]

Informal organization network, unrelated to the firm's formal authority structure, of everyday social interactions among company employees, [98–99]

Information managers, 73

Information meaningful, useful interpretation of data, [207]

Information resources data and other information that businesses use, [6]

Information system (IS) system that uses IT resources to convert data into information and to collect, process, and transmit that information for use in decision making, [207]
    types of, 209–210

Information systems managers managers who operate the systems used for gathering, organizing, and distributing information, [207]

Information technology (IT) various appliances and devices for creating, storing, exchanging, and using information in diverse modes, including visual images, voice, multimedia, and business data, [200]
building blocks, 202–206
impacts of, [200–202]

Initial public offering (IPO) first sale of a company's stock to the general public, [259–260]

Insider trading illegal practice of using special knowledge about a firm for profit or gain, [31–32]

Institutional market organizational market consisting of such nongovernmental buyers of goods and services as hospitals, churches, museums, and charitable organizations, [173]

Insurance company nondeposit institution that invests funds collected as premiums charged for insurance coverage, [235]

Insurance policy a formal agreement to pay the policyholder a specified amount in the event of certain losses, [265]

Insurance premium fee paid to an insurance company by an policyholder for insurance coverage, [265]

Intangibility, 103

Intangible asset nonphysical asset, such as patent or trademark, that has economic value in the form of expected benefit, [221–222]

Intangible personal property property that cannot be seen but that exists by virtue of written documentation, [269]

Integrated marketing strategy strategy that blends together the Four Ps of marketing to ensure their compatibility with one another and with the company's nonmarketing activities as well, [170]

Intel, 43

Intellectual property something produced by the intellect or mind that has commercial value, [211], [269]

Intentional tort tort resulting from the deliberation actions of a party, [269]

Interactive marketing nonstore retailing that uses a Web site to provide real-time sales and customer service, [192]

Interest fee paid to a lender for the use of borrowed funds; like a rental fee, [257]

Intermediary individual or firm that helps to distribute a product, [187]

Intermediate goal goal set for a period of one to five years into the future, [78]

International competition competitive marketing of domestic products against foreign products, [169]

Internal recruiting process of considering present employees as candidates for openings, [151]

International bank structure, 244–245

International business management, 61–65

International firm firm that conducts a significant portion of its business in foreign countries, [63]

International law general set of cooperative agreements and guidelines established by countries to govern the actions of individual, businesses, and nations, [271]

International marketing mix, 178–179

International marketplaces, 54–56

International Monetary Fund (IMF) UN agency consisting of about 150 nations that have combined resources to promote stable exchange rates, provide temporary short-term loans, and serve other purposes, [244–245]

International Organization for Standardization, 115

International organizational structures approaches to organizational structure developed in response to the need to manufacture, purchase, and sell in global markets, [97]

International payment process, 244

International trade, barriers to, 65–67

Internet gigantic system of interconnected computers–more than 100 million computers in over 100 countries, [203]

Interviews, 152–153

Intraday trading, 250

Intranet organization's private network of internally linked Web sites accessible only to employees, [203]

Intrapreneuring process of creating and maintaining the innovation and flexibility of small-business environment within the confines of a large organization, [98–99]

Intuition innate belief about something, often without conscious consideration, [146]

Inventory control process of receiving, storing, handling, and counting of all raw materials, partly finished goods, and finished goods, [112]

Investment bank financial institution that specializes in issuing and reselling new securities, [251]

Involuntary bankruptcy bankruptcy proceedings initiated by the creditors of an indebted individual or organization, [271]

Ireland, 55

ISO 1400 certification program attesting to the fact that a factory, laboratory, or office has improved its environmental performance, [115]

ISO 9000 program certifying that a factory, laboratory, or office has met the quality management standards set by the International Organization for Standardization, [115]

iTunes, 12, 79, 183, 186

J

Jackson, Phil, 139

Japan, 3, 55

JetBlue, 12

Job analysis systematic analysis of jobs within an organization, [150]

Job description description of the duties and responsibilities of a job, its working conditions, and the tools, materials, equipment, and information used to perform it, [150]

Job enrichment method of increasing job satisfaction by adding one or more motivating factors to job activities, [129–130]

Job redesign programs, [130]

Job rotation programs, 129–130

Jobs, Steve, 83, 138, 142, 183

Job satisfaction degree of enjoyment that people derive from performing their jobs, [123]

Job shops, 107–108

Job specialization process of identifying the specific jobs that need to be done and designing the people who will perform them, [87]

Job specification description of the skills, abilities, and other credentials and qualifications required by a job, [150]

John Paul II (pope), 138

Johnson, Kelly, 99

Johnson & Johnson, 25, 94–95

Joint venture strategic alliance in which the collaboration involves joint ownership of the new venture, [50]

JPMorgan Chase, 251

Jung, Andrea, 141

Junk bonds, 258

Just-in-time (JIT) production type of lean production system that brings together all materials at the precise time they are required at each production stage, [111]

K

Karlgaard, Richard, 119

Karoshi, 119

Kautzman, Frank, 175

Kelleher, Herb, 72

Kelman, Glenn, 140

Kennedy, John F., 29

Key person insurance special form of business insurance designed to offset expenses entailed by the loss of key employees, [266]

KFC, 78

King, Martin Luther, Jr., 138

Kinko's Copy Centers, 108

Knowledge information system information system that supports knowledge workers by providing resources to create, store, use, and transmit new knowledge for useful applications, [209]

Knowledge workers employees who are of value because of the knowledge they possess, [159], 161

information systems for, 209

Koch, James, 77

Kodak, 18

Korean Air Lines, 29

Kozlowski, Dennis, 27

Kraft Foods, 88

Kroc, Ray, 42

Kroger, 27

Kroger Co., 207–208

Kyoto Protocol on Climate Change, 247

L

Labor (human resources) physical and mental capabilities of people as they contribute to economic production, [6]

Labor relations process of dealing with employees who are represented by a union, [160]

Labor union group of individuals working together to achieve shared job-related goals, such as higher pay, shorter working hours, more job security, greater benefits or better working conditions, [160–161]

contemporary, 160

future of, 160–161

LaidOffCamp, 208

Law of demand principle that buyers will purchase (demand) more of a product as its price drops and less as its price increases, [9]

Law of supply principle that producers will offer (supply) more of a product for

sale as its price rises and less as its price drops, [9]

Laws codified rules of behavior enforced by a society, [267]

types of, 267–268

Lay, Kenneth, 32

Layout planning, 107–108

Leadership neutralizers factors that may render leader behaviors ineffective, [139–140]

Leadership substitutes individual, task, and organizational characteristics that tend to outweigh the need for a leader to initiate or direct employee performance, [139]

Leadership the processes and behaviors used by someone, such as a manager, to motivate, inspire, and influence the behaviors of other

emerging issues in, 142–143

ethical, 143

strategic, 142–143

virtual, 143

Leadership the processes and behaviors used by someone, such as a manager, to motivate, inspire, and influence the behaviors of others, [134]

behavioral approaches to, 135–136

changing nature of, 140–142

charismatic, 138–139

continuum, 137

cross-cultural, 141–142

decision making and, 143–147

emerging issues in, 142–143

ethical, 143

gender and, 141

issues in, 139–140

nature of, 134

neutralizers, 139–140

situational approach to, 136–137

strategic, 142

substitutes, 139

through eyes of followers, 137–139

trait approach to, 135

transformational, 137–138

virtual, 143

Leading management process of guiding and motivating employees to meet an organization's objectives, [72]

Leaner operations, 113

Lean production system production system designed for smooth production flows that avoid inefficiencies, eliminate unnecessary inventories, and continuously improve production processes, [111]

Learning organization, 97–98

Lehman Brothers, 241, 251, 258

Leonard, Wayne, 157

Lesar, David, 154–155

Letter of credit bank promise, issued for a buyer, to pay a designated firm a certain amount of money if specified conditions are met, [236]

Leverage ability to finance an investment through borrowed funds, [226]

Leveraged buyouts, 226

Levi Strauss, 73, 89

Lexus, 26

Liability debt owed by a firm to an outside organization or individual, [220]

Liability insurance insurance covering losses resulting from damage to people or property when the insured party is judged liable, [265]

Licensed brand brand-name product for whose name the seller has purchased the right from an organization or individual, [178]

Licensing agreements, 64

Licensing arrangement arrangement in which firms choose foreign individuals or organizations to manufacture or market their products in another country, [64]

Lids, 189

Life insurance, 279–280

Limited liability corporation (LLC) hybrid of a publicly held corporation and a partnership in which owners are taxed as partners but enjoy the benefits of limited liability, [48]

Limited liability legal principle holding investors liable for a firm's debts only to the limits of their personal investments in it, [48]

Limited partner partner who does not share in a firm's management and is liable for its debts only to the limits of said partner's investment, [46–47]

Limited partnership type of partnership consisting of limited partners and a general (or active) partner, [46–47]

Lincoln, Abraham, 136

Line authority organization structure in which authority flows in a direct chain of command from the top of the company to the bottom, [92]

Line department department directly linked to the production and sales of a specific product, [92]

Linens-N-Things, 80

LinkedIn, 180

Liquidity ease with which an asset can be converted into cash, [221]

Loan principal amount of money that is loaned and must be repaid, [257]

Local area network (LAN) computers that are linked in a small area, such as all of a firm's computers within a single building, [204]

Local content law law requiring that products sold in a particular country be at least partly made there, [66]

Lockout management tactic whereby workers are denied access to the employer's workplace, [162]

Long-term goal goal set for an extended time, typically five years or more into the future, [78]

Long-term liability debt that is not due for at least one year, [222]

Low-contact system level of customer contact in which the customer need not be part of the system to receive the service, [104]

M

Mail order (catalog marketing) form of nonstore retailing in which customers place orders for catalog merchandise received through the mail, [190]

Make-to-order operations activities for one-of-a-kind or custom-made production, [104]

Make-to-stock operations activities for producing standardized products for mass consumption, [104]

Management accountant private accountant who provides financial services to support managers in various business activities within a firm, [218]

Management advisory services assistance provided by CPA firms in areas such as financial planning, information systems design, and other areas of concern for client firms, [217–218]

Management by objectives (MBO) set of procedures involving both managers and subordinates insetting goals and evaluating processes, [128–129]

Management information system (MIS) computer system that supports managers by providing information–reports, schedules, plans, and budgets–that can used for making decisions, [209]

Management process of planning, organizing, leading, and controlling an organization's resources to achieve its goals, [71]

Managerial ethics standards of behavior that guide individual managers in their work, [22]

Managerial (management) accounting field of accounting that serves internal users of a company's financial information, [216]

Market capitalization (market cap) total dollar value of all the company's outstanding shares, [261]

Market economy

Market economy economy in which individuals control production and allocation decisions through supply and demand, [7–8]

Market index statistical indicator designed to measure the performance of a large group of stocks or track the price changes of a stock market, [253]

Marketing activity, set of institutions and processes for creating, communicating, delivering, and enhancing offerings that have value for customers, clients, partners, and society at large, [166]

Marketing manager manager who plans and implements the marketing activities that result in the transfer of products from producer to consumer, [169]

Marketing mix combination of product, pricing, promotion, and distribution strategies used to market products, [169]

Marketing plan detailed strategy for focusing marketing efforts on consumers' needs and wants, [169]

Market mechanism for exchange between buyers and sellers of a particular good or service, [8]

Market price (equilibrium price) profit-maximizing price at which the quantity of goods demanded and the quantity of goods supplied are equal, [9]

Market segmentation process of dividing a market into categories of customer types, or "segments," [170–171]

Market share company's percentage of the total industry sales for a specific product type, [184]

Market value current price of a share of stock in the stock market, [249]

Markup amount added to an item's purchase cost to sell it at a profit, [184–185]

Mass-customization principle in which companies produce in large volumes, but each unit features the unique options the customer prefers, [201]

Master limited partnership form of ownership that sells shares to investors who receive profits and that pays taxes on income from profits, [47]

Master production schedule schedule showing which products will be produced and when, in upcoming time periods, [109]

Materials management process of planning, organizing, and controlling the flow of materials from sources of supply through distribution of finished goods, [111–112]

Matrix structure organizational structure created by superimposing one form of structure onto another, [95–96]

Maturity date (due date) future date when repayment of a bond is due from the bond issuer (borrower), [258]

Matz, Jack, 40

Mayer, Marissa, 133

Maytag, 117

McCain, John, 133, 259

McDonald's Corporation, 34, 42, 62, 64, 90, 107, 177, 178

McGregor, Douglas, 125

McKim, Alan, 45

McNerney, Jim, 134

Mead, Margaret, 190

MediaBids.com, 186

Media mix combination of advertising media chosen to carry a message about a product, [195]

Mediation method of resolving a labor dispute in which a third party suggests, but does not impose, a settlement, [162]

Meetings, 75

Mellinger, Doug, 44

Merchandise inventory, 221

Merck, 29

Merger union of two corporations to form a new corporation, [50]

Merit salary individual incentive linking compensation to performance in nonsales jobs, [154–155]

Merkel, Angela, 141

Methods improvement, 108

Methods planning, 108–109

Metro, 189

Metropolitan Life, 131

Mexico, 55

Microsoft, 43

Middle manager manager responsible for implementing the strategies and working toward the goals set by top managers, [73]

Middlemen. See **Intermediary**

Miller, William, 254

Minority enterprise small-business investment companies (MESBICs), 43

Missionary selling personal-selling task in which salespeople promote their firms and products rather than try to close sales, [196]

Mission statement organization's statement of how it will achieve its purpose in the environment in which it conducts it business, [77–78]

Mixed market economy economic system featuring characteristics of both planned and market economies, [8]

M-1 measure of the money supply that includes only the most liquid (spendable) forms of money, [233–234]

Monetary policies policies that a government uses to control the size of its money supply, [18–19]

Monetary policy management of the nation's economic growth by managing money supply and interest rates, [240]

Money market funds, 249–250

Money market mutual fund fund of short-term, low-risk financial securities purchased with the pooled assets of investor-owners, [233]

Money object that is portable, divisible, durable, and stable and that serves as medium of exchange, a store of value, and a measure of worth, [232]

    characteristics of, 232

    functions of, 232

    M-1 measure of, 233

    M-2 measure of, 233–234

Monopolistic competition market or industry characterized by numerous buyers and relatively numerous sellers trying to differentiate their products from their competitors, [11–12]

Monopoly market or industry in which there is only one producer that can therefore set the prices of its products, [13]

Morgan, J.P., 27

Morgan Stanley, 50, 251

Mortgage-backed security (MBS) mortgages pooled together to form a debt obligation–a bond–that entitles the holder

(investor) to cash that flows in from the bundled mortgages, [259]

Mortgage loan loan secured by property (the home) being purchased, [277]

Motivation set of forces that cause people to behave in certain way, [124]

    classical theory of, 124

    contemporary theory, 126–127

    early behavioral theory, 124–126

    strategies and techniques for enhancing, 127–131

M-2 measure of the money supply that includes all the components of M-1 plus the forms of money that can be easily converted into spendable forms, [233–234]

Mulally, Alan, 87

Multinational firm firm that designs, produces, and markets products in many nations, [63]

Multinational (or transnational) corporation form of corporation spanning national boundaries, [49]

Murdoch, Rupert, 137, 138

Mutual fund company that pools cash investments from individuals and organizations to purchase a portfolio of stocks, bonds, and other securities, [249–250]

Mutual savings bank financial institution whose depositors are owners sharing in its profits, [234]

N

NASDAQ Composite Index market index that includes all NASDAQ-listed companies, both domestic and foreign, with a high proportion of technology companies and small-cap stocks, [255]

National Association of Securities Dealers Automated Quotation (NASDAQ) System world's oldest electronic stock market consisting of dealers who buy and sell securities over a network of electronic communications, [252]

National brand brand-name product produced by, widely distributed by, and carrying the name of a manufacturer, [178]

National competitive advantage international competitive advantage stemming from a combination of factor conditions, demand conditions, related and supporting industries and firm strategies, structures, and rivalries, [61]

Outsourcing practice of paying suppliers and distributors to perform certain business processes or to provide needed materials or services, [62]
    global supply chains and, 116–117

Owners' equity amount of money that owners would receive if they sold all of a firm's assets and paid all of its liabilities, [220]

Ownership utility, 166

P

Pacific Asia, 55–56

Packaging physical container in which a product is sold, advertised, or protected, [178]

Page, Larry, 69–70, 74–75

Paid-in capital money that is invested in a company by its owners, [222]

Paperwork, 75

Participative management and empowerment method of increasing job satisfaction by giving employees a voice in the management of their jobs and the company, [129]

Partnerships
    general, 46
    limited, 46–47
    master limited, 47

Patent exclusive legal right to use and license a manufactured item or substance, manufacturing process, or object design, [270]

Patriot Act. See USA PATRIOT Act (2002)

Pay-for-knowledge plan incentive plan to encourage employees to learn new skills or become proficient at different jobs, [155]

Pay for performance (variable pay) individual incentive that rewards a manager for especially productive output, [155]

Peanut butter salmonella outbreak of 2008, 101

Peanut Corporation of America, 33

Pearson PLC, 78

Penetration pricing setting an initially low rice to establish a new product in the market, [186]

Pension fund nondeposit pool of funds managed to provide retirement income for its members, [235]

PeopleTradingServices.com, 206

PepsiCo, 78, 85, 89, 90, 261

Perfect competition market or industry characterized by numerous small firms producing an identical product, [11]

Performance appraisal evaluation of an employee's job performance in order to determine the degree to which the employee is performing effectively, [153–154]

Performance behaviors total set of work-related behaviors that the organization expects employees to display, [120]

Performance dimension of quality that refers to how well a product does what it is supposed to do, [108]

Personality relatively stable set of psychological attributes that distinguish one person from another, [122]

Personal net worth value of one's total assets minus one's total liabilities (debts), [272]

Personal selling promotional tool in which a salesperson communicates one-on-one with potential customers, [195–196]

Person-job fit extent to which person's contributions and the organization's inducements match one another, [124]

Personnel. See **Human resources (HR)** physical and mental capabilities of people as they contribute to economic production

Philippines, 55

Photo-Kicks, 106

Physical distribution activities needed to move a product efficiently from manufacturer to consumer, [192–194]

Physical exams, 153

Physical resources, [6]

Picketing labor action in which workers publicize their grievances at the entrance to an employer's facility, [162]

Pizza Hut, 64, 78

Place utility, 103, 166

Planned economy economy that relies on a centralized government to control all or most factors of production and to make all or most production and allocation desires, [7]

Planning management process of determining what an organization needs to do and how best to get it done, [71]
    human resource, 150–151
    operations, 106–109

Plans, levels of, 81

Poilâne bakery, 60

Point-of-sale (POS) display sales-promotion technique in which product displays are located in certain areas to stimulate purchase or to provide information on a product, [196]

Point-of-sale (POS) terminal electronic device that transfers funds from the customer's bank account to pay for retail purchases, [244]

Political-legal environment relationship between business and government, [5], 167

Polygraph tests, 153

Ponoko.com, 201

Ponzi, Charles, 254

Portfolio combined holdings of all the financial investments of any company or individual, [256]

Positioning process of establishing an identifiable product image in the minds of consumers, [194]

Positive reinforcement reward that follows desired behaviors, [128]

Postini, 70

Post office protocol (POP) one of the basic communications protocols used to receive e-mail, [203]

Premium sales-promotion technique in which offers of free or reduced-price items are used to stimulate purchases, [196]

Price appreciation increase in the dollar value of an investment at two points in time (the amount by which the price of a security increases), [256]

Price gouging, 29

Priceline.com, 186

Price lining setting a limited number of prices for certain categories of products, [186]

Prices, determining, 184–185

Price skimming setting an initially high price to cover new product costs and generate a profit, [186]

Pricing

strategies, 186
    tactics, 186

Pricing objectives the goals that sellers hope to achieve in pricing products for sale, [184]

Pricing process of determining the best price at which to sell a product, [170], [184]
    dynamic, 186
    fixed, 186
    odd-even, 186
    penetration, 186
    psychological, 186

Primary agents of interest, 24

Primary securities market market in which new stocks and bonds are bought and sold by firms and governments, [251]

Prime rate interest rte available to a bank's most creditworthy customers, [235]

Prince, Jessica V., 188

Principal individual or organization authorizing an agent to act on its behalf, [270]

The Principles of Scientific Management (Taylor), 124

Print servers, 204

Private accountant salaried accountant hired by a business to carry out its day-to-day financial activities, [218]

Private brand (private label) brand name product that a wholesaler or retailer has commissioned from a manufacturer, [178]

Private enterprise economic system that allows individuals to pursue their own interests without undue government restriction, [11]

Private pension funds, 235

Private placements, 251

Private property rights, 11

Private warehouse warehouse owned by and providing storage for a single company, [192]

Privatization process of converting government enterprises into privately owned companies, [8]

Proactive stance approach to social responsibility by which a company actively seeks opportunities to contribute to the well-being of groups and individuals in its social responsibility, [34]

Process departmentalization dividing of an organization according to production processes used to create a good or service, [88]

Process flowchart, 108

Procter & Gamble, 73

Product departmentalization dividing of an organization according to specific products or services being created, [88]

Product differentiation creation of a product feature or product image that differs enough from existing produces to attract customers, [170]

Product features tangible and intangible qualities that a company builds into its products, [174]

Production, just-in-time, 111

Product good, service, or idea that is marketed to fill consumers' needs and wants, [169]

Productivity measure of economic growth that compares how much a system produces with the resources needed to produce it, [15]

Product liability tort in which a company is responsible for injuries caused by its products, [269]

Product life cycle (PLC) series of stages in a product's commercial life, [176]

Product line group of products that are closely related because they function in a similar manner or are sold to the same customer group who will use them in similar ways, [174]

Product mix group of products that a firm makes available for sale, [174–175]

Product mortality rates, 175

Product placement a promotional tactic for brand exposure in which characters in television, film, music, magazines, or video games use a real product with its brand visible to viewers, [177]

Product positioning process of fixing, adapting and communicating the nature of a product, [171]

Products

    branding, 177–178
    defined, 174–175
    developing new, 175–176
    identifying, 176–178

Professional corporation form of ownership allowing professionals to take advantage of corporate benefits while granting them limited business liability and unlimited professional liability, [48]

Profitability ratio financial ratio for measuring a firm's potential earnings, [226], 227–228

Profit center separate company unit responsible for its own costs and profits, [88]

Profit difference between a business's revenues and its expenses, [4], 11

Profit-maximizing objectives, 184

Profit-sharing plan incentive plan for distributing bonuses to employees when company profits rise above a certain level, [155]

Project scheduling, 110

Promotional mix combination of tools used to promote a product, [194]

Promotion aspect of the marketing mix concerned with the most effective techniques for communicating information about products, [170], [194–197]

Property anything of value to which a person or business has sole right of ownership, [269]

Property insurance insurance covering losses resulting from physical damage to

or loss of the insured's real estate or personal property, [265]

Property law, 269–270

Prospectus registration statement filed with the SEC, containing information for prospective investors about a security to be offered and the issuing company, [249]

Protected class set of individuals who by nature of one or more common characteristics is protected under the law from discrimination on the basis of that characteristic, [156]

Protectionism practice of protecting domestic business against foreign competition, [66]

Protectionist tariffs, 66

PRT Group, 44

Psychographic variables consumer characteristics, such as lifestyles, opinions, interests, and attitudes that may be considered in developing a segmentation strategy, [171]

Psychological contract set of expectations held by an employee concerning what he or she will contribute to an organization (contributions) and what the organization will in return provided the employee (inducements), [123–124]

Psychological pricing pricing tactic that takes advantage of the fact that consumers do not always respond rationally to stated prices, [186]

Publicity promotional tool in which information about a company, a product, or an event is transmitted by the general mass media to attract public attention, [197]

Publicly held (or private) corporation corporation whose stock is widely held and available for sale to the general public, [48]

Public pension funds, 235

Public relations company-influenced information directed at building goodwill with the public or dealing with unfavorable events, [197]

Public warehouse independently owned and operated warehouse that stores goods for many firms, [192]

Punishment unpleasant consequences of an undesirable behavior, [128]

Punitive damages fines imposed over and above any actual losses suffered by a plaintiff, [269]

Purchasing acquisition of the materials and services that a firm needs to produce its products, [111]

Purchasing power parity principle that exchange rates are set so that the prices of similar products in different countries are about the same, [14]

Q

Quality combination of characteristics of a product or service that bear on its ability to satisfy stated or implied needs, [108]

Quality control action of ensuring that operations produce products that meet specific quality standards, [112]

Quality improvement team TQM tool in which collaborative groups of employees from various work areas work together to improve quality by solving common shared production problems, [114]

Quality ownership principle of total quality management that holds that quality belongs to each person who creates it while performing a job, [114]

Quest Diagnostics, 167

Quid pro quo harassment form of sexual harassment in which sexual favors are requested in return for job-related benefits, [158]

Quinlan, Mary Lou, 119

Quinn, Ann, 161

Quota restriction on the number of products of a certain type that can be imported into a country, [65]

QVC, 191, 192

R

Raju, Ramalinga, 215

Ralph Lauren, 12

Rational decision making, 143–145

Rational motives reasons for purchasing a product that are based on logical evaluation of product attributes, [173]

Real GDP gross domestic product (GDP) adjusted to account for changes in currency values and price changes, [14–15]

Real growth rate, 13–14

Recession period during which aggregate output, as measured by GDP, declines, [18]

Recruiting process of attracting qualified persons to apply for jobs an organization is seeking to fill, [151]
    external, 151
    internal, 151

Reengineering, 115

Reference checks, 153

Register of Known Spam Operators (ROKSO), 213

Regulatory (administrative) law law made by the authority of administrative agencies, [267]

Related diversification, 78

Relationship marketing marketing strategy that emphasizes lasting relationships with customers and suppliers, [167]

Reliant Energy, 82

RE/MAX, 42

Renault, 133

Replacement chart list of each management position, who occupies it, how long that person will likely stay in the job, and who is qualified as a replacement, [151]

Reporting relationships, 86

Research in Motion (RIM), 204

Reseller market organizational market consisting of intermediaries that buy and resell finished goods, [173]

Reserve requirement percentage of its deposits that a bank must hold in cash or on deposit with the Fed, [240]

Responsibility duty to perform an assigned task, [92]

Retailer intermediary who sells products directly to consumers, [187]

Retailing, 189–192
    nonstore, 190–192

Retail outlets, types of, 189–192

Retained earnings earnings retained by a firm for its use rather than paid out as dividends, [222], 263

Retirement planning, 273–274

Retirement plans, 155–156

Revenue recognition formal recording and reporting of revenues at the appropriate time, [225]

Revenues funds that flow into a business from the sale of goods or services, [222]

Revenue tariffs, 66

Reverse advertising auctions, 186

Revised Uniform Limited Partnership Act, 46

Risk avoidance the practice of avoiding risk by declining or ceasing to participate in an activity, [264]

Risk control the practice of minimizing the frequency or severity of losses from risky activities, [264]

Risk management the process of conserving the firm's earning power and assets by reducing the threat of losses due to uncontrollable events, [264–266]

Risk propensity extent to which a decision maker is willing to gamble when making a decision, [146–147]

Risk retention the practice of covering a firm's losses with its own funds, [264]

Risk-return (risk-reward) relationship principle that safe investments tend to offer lower returns whereas riskier investments tend to offer higher returns (rewards), [255–256]

Risk transfer the practice of transferring a firm's risk to another firm, [264]

Risk uncertainty about future events, [264]

Rockefeller, John D., 27

Romania, 55

Ronald McDonald House program, 34

Roosevelt, Eleanor, 136

Roth IRA provision allowing individual retirement savings with tax-free accumulated earnings, [279]

Routers, 212

Rubbermaid, 98

Rule of 72, 248

Russell 2000 Index specialty index that uses 2000 stocks to measure the performance of the smallest U.S. companies, [255]

Russia, 55

S

Sabotage, 121

Saks, 156

Salary compensation in the form of money paid for discharging the responsibilities of a job, [154]

Sales Agent independent intermediary who generally deals in the related product lines of a few producers and forms long-term relationships to represent those producers and meet the needs of many customers, [188]

Sales forecasting, 41

Sales promotion short-term promotional activity designed to encourage consumer buying, industrial sales, or cooperation from distributors, [196–197]

Salvation Army, 23

Same-steps layout physical arrangement of production steps designed to make one type of product in a fixed sequence of activities according to its production requirements, [108]

Samsung Electronics, 117

Samuel Adams beer, 77

Sant, Roger, 128

Sarbanes-Oxley Act of 2002 (Sarbox) enactment of federal regulations to restore public trust in accounting practices by imposing new requirements on financial activities in publicly traded corporations, 32, [219]

Satyam Computer Services, Ltd., 215

Save-A-Lot, 105

Savings and loan association (S&L) financial institution accepting deposits and making loans primarily for home mortgages, [234]

S.C. Johnson, 29

Scardino, Marjorie, 70

Schedules
  detailed, 109
  master production, 109
  project, 110
  staff, 109–110

Schuessler, Jack, 197

Schultz, Howard, 6

Scientific management, 124

S corporation hybrid of a closely held corporation and a partnership, organized and operated like a corporation but treated as partnership for tax purposes, [48]

Sears, 80, 88, 178

Secondary securities market market in which existing (not new) stocks and bonds are sold to the public, [251]

Secured loan (asset-backed loan) loan to finance an asset, backed by the borrower pledging the asset as collateral to the lender, [257]

Securities and Exchange Commission (SEC) government agency that regulates U.S. securities markets, 31, [251]

Securities investment dealer (broker) financial institution that buys and sells stocks and bonds both for investors and for its own accounts, [235]

Securities markets markets in which stocks and bonds are sold, [250–251]

Securities stocks, bonds, and mutual funds representing secured, or asset-based, claims by investors against issuers, [250–251]

Security policies, 212

Seither, Mickey, 157

Self-awareness, 122

Servers, 204

Service Corps of Retired Executives (SCORE), 43

Service operations (service production) activities producing intangible and tangible products, such as entertainment, transportation, and education, [102]

Services products having nonphysical features, such as information, expertise, or an activity that can be purchased, [166]

7-Eleven, 42, 189

72, Rule of, 248

Sexual harassment unwelcome sexual advances in the workplace, [158]

Sharper Image, 190

Shell Oil, 98

Sherman Antitrust Act (1890), 13

Shinohara, Yoshiko, 41

Shopping agent (e-agent) e-intermediary (middleman) in the Internet distribution channel that assists users in finding products and prices but does not take possession of products, [191]

Shopping good/shopping service moderately expensive, infrequently purchased good or service, [174]

Shortage situation in which quantity demanded exceeds quantity supplied, [10]

Short-term goal goal set for the very near future, [78]

Silent partner, 46

Short-term solvency ratio financial ratio for measuring a company's ability to pay immediate debts, [226]

Simple message transfer protocol (SMTP) basic communications protocol used to send e-mail, [203]

Singapore, 55

Sinegal, James, 70

Singleton, Tommie, 215

Situational approach to leadership approach that assumes that appropriate leader behavior varies from one situation to another, [136–137]

Skills inventories, 151

SlimFast, 65

Slovakia, 107

Small Business Administration (SBA) government agency charged with assisting small businesses, [38]

Small Business Administration (SBA) loan programs, 43

Small Business Development Center (SBDC) SBA program designed to consolidate information from various disciplines and make available to small businesses, [43]

Small business independently owned business that has relatively little influence in its market, [38]
  contributions to big business by, 39
  factors contributing to failures of, 44–45
  factors contributing to success of, 45
  financing, 42–43

importance of, in U.S. economy, 38–39
innovation and, 38–39
job creation and, 38
marketing mix and, 179–181
popular areas of enterprise, 39–40
social responsibility and, 34
starting, 42
start-ups by minorities and women, 43–44
start-up trends in, 43–44

Small-business investment companies (SBICs) government regulated investment company that borrows money from the SBA to invest in or lend to a small business, [43]

Smart card credit-card-sized plastic card with an embedded computer chip that can be programmed with electronic money, [244]

Smith, Fred, 95

Smith, Liz, 190

Sneed, Simone, 149

So, Peter, 64

Social audits systematic analysis of firm's success in using funds earmarked for meeting its social responsibility goals, [34]

Social consciousness, contemporary, 27

Socialism planned economic system in which the government owns and operates only selected major sources of production, [7–8]

Social networking, 177–178, 180, 190, 202

Social responsibility attempt of a business to balance its commitments to groups and individuals in its environment, including customers, other businesses, employees, investors, and local communities, [26]
  approaches to, 32–33
  managing programs for, 34
  small business and, 34
  toward customers, 28–30
  toward employees, 30–31
  toward environment, 28

Social skills, 122

Sociocultural environment customs, mores, values, and demographic characteristics of the society in which an organization functions, [5], 167

Software programs that tell the computer's hardware what resources to use and how to use them, [206]

Sole proprietorships business owned and usually operated by one person who is responsible for all of its debts, [46]
  advantages of, [46]
  disadvantages of, [46]

Solvency ratio financial ratio, either short- or long-term, for estimating the borrower's ability to repay debt, [226]

Sony, 30, 116

Southern Company, 90

South Korea, 55

Southwest Airlines, 43

Spain, 55

The Spamhaus Project, 213

Spam junk e-mail sent to a mailing list or a newsgroup, [211–212]
    avoiding, 212–213

Span of control number of people supervised by one manager, [91], 92

Specialty good/specialty service expensive, rarely purchased good or service, [174]

Specialty store retail store carrying one product line or category of related products, [189]

Speculative risk risk involving the possibility of gain or loss, [264]

Speed to market strategy of introducing new products to respond quickly to customer or market changes, [175]

Spiders, 255

Spin-off strategy of setting up one or more corporate units as new, independent corporations, [50]

S&P 500 market index of U.S. equities based on the performance of 500 large-cap stocks representing various sectors of the overall equities market, [254–255]

Spyware program unknowingly downloaded by users that monitors their computer activities, gathering e-mail addresses, credit card numbers, and other information that it transmits to someone outside the host system, [211]
    avoiding, 212–213

Sreekanti, Kumar, 26

Stability condition in which the amount of money available in an economic system and the quantity of goods and services produced in it are growing at about the same rate, [17]

Stabilization policy government economic policy intended to smooth out fluctuations in output and unemployment and to stabilize prices, [18]

Staff authority authority based on expertise that usually involves counseling and advising line managers, 93

Staff members advisers and counselors who help line departments in making decisions, but do not have the authority to make final decisions, [93]

Staff schedule assigned working times in upcoming days for each employee on each work shift, [109–110]

Stakeholder model of responsibility, 26–27

Standard of living total quantity and quality of goods and services people can purchase with the currency used in their economic system, [13]

Standard & Poor's Depository Receipts (SPDRS), 255

Starbucks, 6, 27, 29, 48, 78, 134, 165

State Farm Insurance, 39

Statement of cash flows financial statement describing a firm's yearly cash receipts and cash payments, [223–224]

Statements of financial position, 221–222

Statutory law law created by constitution(s) or by federal, state, or local legislative acts, [267]

Stewart, Martha, 32

Stock, 49

Stock broker individual or organization that receives and executes buy and sell orders on behalf of outside customers in return for commission, [252–253]

Stock exchange an organization of individuals to provide an institutional auction setting in which stocks can be bought and sold, [251–252]
    global, 252

Stockholder (or **shareholder**) owner of shares of stock in a corporation, [49]

Stock portion of ownership of a corporation, [248]

Stock split stock dividend paid in additional shares to shareholders, thus increasing the number of outstanding shares, [260]

Strategic alliance arrangement (also called **joint venture**) in which a company finds a foreign partner to contribute approximately half of the resources need to establish and operate a new business in the partner's country, [64–65]

Strategic alliance strategy in which two or more organizations collaborate on a project for mutual gain, [50]

Strategic goal goal derived directly from a firm's mission statement, [79]

Strategic leadership leader's ability to understand the complexities of both the organization and the environment and to lead change in the organization so as to enhance its competitiveness, [142]

Strategic management process of helping an organization maintain an effective alignment with its environments, [76–80]

Strategic plans plan reflecting decisions about resource allocations, company priorities, and steps needed to meet strategic goals, [81]

Strategy, 78–79

Strategy broad set of organizational plans for implementing the decisions made for achieving organizational goals, [76]
    as driver of operations, 104–106
    formulating, 78–80
    types of, 78

Strategy formulation creation of a broad program for defining and meeting an organization's goals, [79]

Strict product liability principle that liability can result not from a producer's negligence but from a defect in the product itself, [269]

Strikebreaker worker hired as a permanent or temporary replacement for a striking employee, [162]

Strike labor action in which employees temporarily walk off the job and refuse to work, [162]

Subprime loans, 236

Subsidy government payment to help a domestic business compete with foreign firms, [66]

Substitute product product that is dissimilar from those of competitors but that can fulfill the same need, [169]

Subway, 42

Sumalindo Lestari Jaya, 30

Supermarket large product-line retailer offering a variety of food and food-related items in specialized departments, [189]

Supplier selection process of finding and choosing suppliers from whom to buy, [111]

Supply chain management (SCM) principle of looking at the supply chain as a whole to improve the overall flow through the system, [115–117]

Supply chain (value chain) flow of information, materials, and services that starts with raw-material suppliers and continues adding value through other stages in the network of firms until the product reaches the end customer, [115]

Supply curve graph showing how many units of a product will be supplied (offered for sale) at different prices, [9]

Supply willingness and ability of producers to offer a good or service for sale, [9]

Surplus situation in which quantity supplied exceeds quantity demanded, [10]

Suzlon Energy Limited, 167

Sweat equity, 46

SWOT analysis identification and analysis of organizational strengths and weaknesses and environmental opportunities and threats as part of strategy formulation, [79]

T

Taco Bell, 78, 107

Tactical plans are shorter-term plans for implementing specific aspects of the company's strategic plans. They typically involve upper and middle management, [81]

Taiwan, 55

Tall organizational structures characteristic of centralized companies with multiple layers of management, [91], 92

Tangible personal property any movable item that can be owned, bought, sold, or leased, [269]

Tangible real property land and anything attached to it, [269]

Target, 27, 167, 205–206

Target market group of people that have similar wants and needs and can be expected to show interest in the same products, [170–171]

Tariff tax levied on imported products, [66]

Tasked-focused leader behavior leader behavior focusing on how task should be performed in order to meet certain goals and to achieve certain performance, [135–136]

Tax services assistance provided by CPAs for tax preparation and tax planning, [217]

Taylor, Frederick, 124

Team organization, 97

Teamsters, 160–161

Technical environment, 167

Technical skills skills needed to perform specialized task, [74]

Technological environment all the ways by which firms create value for their constituents, [4–5]

Technology skills
 management and, 75–76

Telecommuting form of flextime that allows people to perform some or all of a job away from the standard office setting, [130–131]

Telemarketing form of nonstore retailing in which the telephone is used to sell directly to consumers, [190]

Telephone calls, 75

Tempstaff, 41, 159–160

Temp work (temping), 149–150

Tender offer offer to buy shares made by a prospective buyer directly to a target corporation's shareholders, who then

make individual decisions about whether to sell, [48]

Term insurance, 280

Thailand, 55

Theft, 121

Theory X theory of motivation holding that people are naturally lazy and uncooperative, [125]

Theory Y theory of motivation holding that people are naturally energetic, growth-oriented, self-motivated, and interested in being productive, [125]

3M, 27, 98, 105

Timbuk2, 201

Time deposit ban funds that have a fixed term of time to maturity and cannot be withdrawn earlier or transferred by check, [233]

Time management skills skills associated with the productive use of time, [75]

Time utility, 102, 166

Time value of money principle that invested money grows, over time, by earning interest or some other form of return, [248]

Tindell, Kip, 134

T-Mobile, 204

TNT Post Group N.V., 8

Tomlin, Lily, 190

Top manager manager responsible for a firm's overall performance and effectiveness, [73]

Tort civil injury to people, property, or reputation for which compensation must be paid, [269]

Tort law, 269

Toshiba, 194

Total quality management (TQM) sum of all activities involved in getting high-quality goods and services into the marketplace, [112–115]

Toyota, 27, 67, 105, 106, 111

Trade deficit situation in which a country's imports exceed its exports, creating a negative balance of trade, [57–58]

Trademark exclusive legal right to use a brand name or symbol, [270]

Trade show sales-promotion technique in which various members of an industry gather to display, demonstrate, and sell products, [196–197]

Trade surplus situation in which a country's exports exceed its imports, creating a positive balance of trade, [58]

Trading floor, 251

Traditional individual retirement account (IRA) provision allowing individual tax-deferred retirement savings, [278–280]

Trait approach to leadership approach focused on identifying the essential traits that distinguished leaders, [135]

Transactional leadership comparable to management, leadership that involves routine, regimented activities, [138]

Transformational leadership set of abilities that allows a leader to recognize the need for change, to create a vision to guide that change, and to execute the change effectively, [137–138]

Transportation activities in transporting resources to the producer and finished goods to customers, [112]

Treaty, defined, 56

Trial court general court that hears cases not specifically assigned another court, [268]

Trojan horses, 211, 213

Troubled Asset Relief Program (TARP), 231, 241

Trust services management by a bank of an estate, investments, or other assets on behalf of an individual, [236]

Tupperware, 187

Turner, Ted, 138

Turnover annual percentage of organization's workforce that leaves and must be replaced, [121]

Twitter, 227

Two-factor theory theory of motivation holding that job satisfaction depends on two factors, hygiene and motivation, [126]

Tyco, 22, 27

U

Underwrite, 251

Unemployment level of joblessness among people actively seeking work in an economic system, [16–17]

Unethical behavior behavior that does not conform to generally accepted social norms concerning beneficial and harmful actions, [22]

Unfair pricing, 29

Uniform Commercial Code (UCC) body of standardized laws governing the rights of buyers and sellers in transactions, [270]

Unilever, 65

Union Butterfield, 121

Union Carbide, 86

United Auto Workers (UAW), 161

United Kingdom, 5, 55

United States, 55
anti-crime and anti-terrorism regulations, 241–242
film industry of, 53
financial system of, 234–238
government intervention for stabilizing, 241
impact of electronic technologies on, 242–244
imports and exports of, 58–59
judicial system of, 268

United Way, 23

University of Minnesota, 86

Unlimited liability legal principle that holds owners responsible for paying off all debts of a business, [46]

Unsecured loan loan for which collateral is not required, [257]

Unstorability, 103

UPS, 26, 108, 111

Urban Outfitters, 91

U.S. legal system, 267–268

U.S. Supreme Court, 268

U.S. Xpress Enterprises, 192

USA PATRIOT Act (2002), 158–159, 242

Utility ability of a product to satisfy a human want or need, [102–103], [166]

Utility norms, 24–25

V

Value-added analysis process of evaluating all work activities, materials flows, and paperwork to determine the value that they add for customers, [114]

Value package product marketed as a bundle of value-adding attributes, including reasonable cost, [174]

Value relative comparison of a product's benefits versus its cost, [166]

Vanderbilt, Cornelius, 27

Variable cost cost that changes with the quantity of a product produced and sold, [185]

Venture capital company group of small investors who invest money in companies with rapid growth potential, [43]

Venture capital private funds from wealthy individuals seeking investment opportunities in new growth companies, [257–258]

Vestibule training, off-the-job training conducted in a simulated environment [153]

Video marketing nonstore retailing to consumers via home television, [192]

Vietnam, 7

Viral marketing type of buzz marketing that relies on the Internet to spread information like a "virus" from person to person about products and ideas, [177–178]

Virgin Airlines, 29

Virtual leadership leadership in settings where leaders and followers interact electronically rather than in face-to-face settings, [143]

Virtual organization, 97

Vodafone, 204

Volkswagen, 29, 65

Voluntary bankruptcy bankruptcy proceedings initiated by an indebted individual or organization, [271]

Volvo, 65

Vondra, Al, 215

VSAT satellite communications network of geographically dispersed transmitter-receivers (transceivers) that send signals to and receive signals from a satellite, exchanging voice, video, and data transmissions, [204]

W

Wage reopener clause clause allowing wage rates to be renegotiated during the life of a labor contract, [161]

Wages compensation in for form of money paid for time worked, [154]

Waksal, Sam, 32

Wal-Mart, 12, 27, 43, 66, 97, 107, 157, 183, 188, 189, 204, 207, 208

Walsworth Publishing Company, 209–210

Walt Disney Company, 50, 81–82

Walton, Sam, 72

Wang, Vera, 133

Warehousing physical distribution operation concerned with the storage of goods, [192]

Warehousing storage of incoming materials for production and finished goods for distribution to customers, [112]

Warranty seller's promise to stand by its products or services if a problem occurs after the sale, [270–271]

Washington Post, 208

Watkins, Sherron, 32

Waxman, Henry, 259

Wegmans Food Markets, 26

Weill, Sandy, 26

Wells Fargo, 156

Wendy's, 197

Wenner, Jann, 169

Wenner Media, 169

Whistle-blower employee who detects and tries to put an end to a company's unethical, illegal, or socially irresponsible actions by publicizing them, [30–31]

Whole Foods Market, 27, 29, 91, 167

Whole-life insurance, 280

Wholesale club bargain retailer offering large discounts on brand-name merchandise to customers who have paid annual membership fees, [189]

Wholesaler intermediary who sells products to other businesses for resale to final consumers, [187]

Wholesaling, 189

Wide area network (WAN) computers that are linked over long distances through telephone lines, microwave signals, or satellite communications, [204]

Wi-Fi technology using wireless local area network, [205]

Wiggins, Sandy, 242

Williams, Evan, 227

Williamson, Bob, 45

WiMAX, 205

Wireless local area network (WLAN) local area network with wireless access points for PC users, [205]

Wireless mooching, 210–211

Wireless wide area network (WWAN) network that uses airborne electronic signals instead of wires to link computers and electronic devices over long distances, [204–205]

Workers' compensation coverage coverage provided by a firm to employees for medical expenses, loss of wages, and rehabilitation costs resulting from job-related injuries or disease, [265]

Workers' compensation insurance legally required insurance for compensating workers injured on the job, [155]

Workforce diversity the range of workers' attitudes, values, beliefs, and behaviors that differ by gender, race, age, ethnicity, physical ability, and other relevant characteristics, [159]

Workplace aggression/violence, 121

Work sharing (job sharing) method of increasing job satisfaction by allowing two or more people to share a single full-time job, [130]

Work slowdown labor action in which workers perform jobs at a slower than normal pace, [162]

Work teams groups of operating employees who are empowered to plan and organize their own work and to perform that work with a minimum of supervision, [93]

World Bank UN agency that provides a limited scope of financial services, such as funding improvements in underdeveloped countries, [244]

World Trade Organization (WTO) organization through which member nations negotiate trading agreements and resolve disputes about trade policies and practices, [56–57], 271

World Wide Web branch of the Internet consisting of interlinked hypertext documents, or Web pages, [203]

Worms, 211, 213

WowOwow.com, 190

X

Xanga, 29

Xerox, 98

XM Radio, 12, 200

Y

Yahoo!, 177

YouTube, 70

Yum!, 78

Z

Zero response time, 181

Zombori, Sandor, 119

Zuckerberg, Mark, 37